Managing Sino-American Crises:
Case Studies and Analysis

Managing Sino-American Crises: Case Studies and Analysis

Michael D. Swaine
Zhang Tuosheng
Editors

with Danielle F. S. Cohen

CARNEGIE ENDOWMENT FOR INTERNATIONAL PEACE
Washington, D.C.

Carnegie Endowment for International Peace
1779 Massachusetts Avenue, N.W., Washington, D.C. 20036
202-483-7600, Fax 202-483-1840
www.CarnegieEndowment.org

The Carnegie Endowment for International Peace normally does not take institutional positions on public policy issues; the views and recommendations presented in this publication do not necessarily represent the views of the Carnegie Endowment, its officers, staff, or trustees.

To order, contact:
Hopkins Fulfillment Service
P.O. Box 50370, Baltimore, MD 21211-4370
1-800-537-5487 or 1-410-516-6956
Fax 1-410-516-6998

Typesetting by Stephen McDougal
Printed by United Book Press

Library of Congress Cataloging-in-Publication data

Managing Sino-American crises : case studies and analysis / Michael D. Swaine and Zhang Tuosheng, editors; with Danielle F. S. Cohen.
   p. cm.
   Some chapters originated as papers delivered at a Sino-American conference on crisis management held in Beijing in 2004 and sponsored jointly by China Program of the Carnegie Endowment for International Peace and China Foundation for International and Strategic Studies.
   Summary: "Sensitivities and suspicions between Washington and Beijing have heightened as China's global power and influence have grown. Chinese and American officials and participants in past confrontations, and scholars from both countries explore the changing features of crisis behavior and their implications for defusing future encounters"—Provided by publisher.
Includes bibliographical references and index.
   ISBN-13: 978-0-87003-228-8 (pbk.)
   ISBN-10: 0-87003-228-3 (pbk.)
   ISBN-13: 978-0-87003-229-5 (cloth)
   ISBN-10: 0-87003-229-1 (cloth)
   1. United States—Foreign relations—China—Case studies. 2. China—Foreign relations—United States—Case studies. 3. Crisis management in government—United States—Case studies. 4. Crisis management in government—China—Case studies. 5. United States—Foreign relations—1945-1989—Case studies. 6. United States—Foreign relations—1989—Case studies. I. Swaine, Michael D. II. Zhang, Tuosheng. III. Cohen, Danielle F. S. IV. Title.

E183.8.C5M3185 2006
327.7305109'045—dc22
   2006018186

11 10 09 08 07 06   1 2 3 4 5   1st Printing 2006

Contents

Contents v

Acknowledgments vii

Acronyms ix

Foreword xi
        Jessica T. Mathews and Chen Zhiya

1   Understanding the Historical Record 1
        Michael D. Swaine

2   Concepts and Methods in the Study of International
     Crisis Management 103
        Jonathan Wilkenfeld

3   Pattern of Sino-American Crises: A Chinese Perspective . . . 133
        Wang Jisi and Xu Hui

4   Crisis Management in China and in the United States:
     A Comparative Study 149
        Xia Liping

5   "Resist America": China's Role in the Korean and
     Vietnam Wars 179
        Zhang Baijia

6   U.S. Crisis Management Vis-à-vis China: Korea
     and Vietnam 215
        Allen S. Whiting

7   U.S. "Management" of Three Taiwan Strait "Crises" 251
    Robert L. Suettinger

8   Chinese Decision Making in Three Military Actions
    Across the Taiwan Strait 293
    Niu Jun

9   The Chinese Embassy Bombing: Evidence of Crisis
    Management? 327
    Kurt M. Campbell and Richard Weitz

10 Chinese Crisis Management During the 1999 Embassy
    Bombing Incident 351
    Wu Baiyi

11 The April 2001 EP-3 Incident: The U.S. Point of View . . . 377
    Dennis C. Blair and David V. Bonfili

12 The Sino-American Aircraft Collision: Lessons for Crisis
    Management 391
    Zhang Tuosheng

13 Conclusion: Implications, Questions, and
    Recommendations 423
    Michael D. Swaine

Bibliography 453

Index 495

Contributors 515

Carnegie Endowment for International Peace 519

Acknowledgments

THIS VOLUME WOULD NOT HAVE APPEARED without the selfless dedication and talents of several individuals. First and foremost, we owe a major debt of gratitude to Danielle F. S. Cohen, the junior fellow of the Carnegie China Program in 2005–2006. With her many skills as translator, editor, researcher, and writer, Danielle played a major role in turning a collection of papers into a polished and organic whole. This book would not exist without her efforts. We also greatly appreciate the time and effort expended by Fu Xiao of the China Foundation for International and Strategic Studies. She assisted us immensely in this genuinely collaborative undertaking by coordinating a range of tasks, from paper revision and translation to fact checking. Doris Grage, assistant in the China Program, also provided indispensable support along the way. Carrie Mullen, Phyllis Jask, and Ilonka Oszvald were immensely helpful through the production process. Mary Marik provided excellent copy-editing. George Perkovich and Alan Romberg provided us with many insightful comments, which have greatly improved the quality of this manuscript. We are also grateful to Alastair Iain Johnston for his thoughtful comments on earlier versions of this manuscript. These have been incorporated into the final draft. We also wish to thank Huang Jing for his invaluable advice and support throughout the production of this book. Finally, we deeply appreciate the time, effort, and expertise contributed by the Chinese and American authors and the other participants in the 2004 Beijing conference. They made this a truly unprecedented undertaking.

Acronyms

ACS	Army Chief of Staff
APNSA	Assistant to the President for National Security Affairs
ASEAN	Association of Southeast Asian Nations
C4ISR	Command, control, communications, computers, intelligence, surveillance, and reconnaissance
CCP	Chinese Communist Party
CIA	Central Intelligence Agency
CINCPAC	Commander in Chief of the Pacific
CMC	Central Military Commission
CNN	Cable News Network
DRV	Democratic Republic of Vietnam
EP-3	Electronic Patrol (aircraft)
FDSP	Federal Directorate for Supply and Procurement
GVN	Government of the Republic of Vietnam (South Vietnam)
ICB	International Crisis Behavior
INR	Bureau of Intelligence and Research (U.S. State Department)
JCS	Joint Chiefs of Staff
JDAM	Joint Direct Attack Munitions
KMT	Kuomintang
LOC	Lines of communication
MFA	Ministry of Foreign Affairs
MFN	Most-favored nation

MiG	Soviet airplane (designed by the Mikoyan-Gurevich design bureau)
NATO	North Atlantic Treaty Organization
NFLV	National Front for the Liberation of Vietnam
NIE	National Intelligence Estimate
NSC	National Security Council
OAS	Organization of American States
OSD	Office of the Secretary of Defense
PLA	People's Liberation Army
PRC	People's Republic of China
ROC	Republic of China (Taiwan)
ROE	Rules of engagement
ROK	Republic of Korea (South Korea)
SAM	Surface-to-air (missiles)
SNIE	Special National Intelligence Estimate
U.S.	United States
UN	United Nations
USSR	Soviet Union

Foreword

DURING THE LAST DECADE ALONE, the United States and China have experienced three tense standoffs: the 1995–1996 confrontation over Taiwan; the 1999 bombing of the Chinese embassy in Belgrade; and the 2001 collision between U.S. and Chinese military aircraft off the coast of China. Together with earlier Sino-American crises or near crises, including the Korean War, the Taiwan Strait crises of the 1950s, and the prospect of large-scale Chinese intervention during the Vietnam War, these incidents and the processes leading to their eventual resolution reveal not only the propensity for serious confrontation in Sino-U.S. relations but also—in some instances—the shortcomings of each country's crisis management.

Sino-American relations have been remarkably stable. The two countries have avoided major rifts and increased their cooperation on a range of economic, security, and global issues. Overall, they have made significant progress toward a more constructive relationship. However, the United States, a superpower, and China, a rising power, are still far from establishing a high level of mutual strategic trust and mutually beneficial relations, and the road ahead presents more than a few dangerous obstacles. As Chinese and American power and influence grow, mutual sensitivities and suspicions between Washington and Beijing are also likely to intensify. Thus, the possibility of political-military crises and perhaps even conflict cannot be eliminated. If such a confrontation were to occur, its consequences would be extremely damaging, not only for the two powers involved but also for the larger Asian and global environments.

This potentially dangerous situation points to the need to deepen mutual understanding of how both governments perceive and handle political-military crises. The aim of such an undertaking should be to provide both sides with the means to more effectively anticipate, avoid, or successfully manage future crises, and thereby to strengthen overall cooperation, control and lessen differences, and reduce misperceptions. Such an effort requires both a more thorough and comparative examination of past crisis interactions between Washington and Beijing and the application of insights developed by broader conceptual studies of crisis management.

This volume contributes significantly to such an effort. It contains an unprecedented collection of studies by Chinese and American scholars, as well as former government officials who served during past Sino-American crises or near crises. The book combines insightful analyses of Sino-U.S. crisis management, including four sets of paired case studies that examine the seven crises or near crises that have occurred between the two countries since the PRC's founding in 1949. Many of the chapters make use of data that have never before been published.

Most of the chapters in this volume originated as papers delivered at a 2004 conference on crisis management that was held in Beijing and sponsored jointly by the China Program of the Carnegie Endowment for International Peace (CEIP) and the China Foundation for International and Strategic Studies (CFISS). The conference was organized by Michael D. Swaine of the Carnegie Endowment and Chen Zhiya of CFISS, with support from Zhang Tuosheng of CFISS, Alastair I. Johnston of Harvard University, and Huang Jing of the Brookings Institution. It brought together leading Chinese and American scholars on Sino-American security relations and former senior U.S. officials directly involved in several of the crises examined herein. The meeting provided an unprecedented forum for these individuals to engage in frank discussions of the scholarly papers presented, as well as additional crisis-related perceptions and actions in both countries.

To complement these chapters, in the English version,[1] Michael D. Swaine has added a rigorous framework for evaluating the dynamics of Chinese and American crisis behavior. He presents eight major principles for effective crisis management, drawn from the work of Chinese and American scholars, and six key sets of variables that influence the ability of states to manage crises effectively. Based on this framework, he identifies several implications for the management of future bilateral crises.[2]

This study suggests that the United States and China will likely confront significant challenges in managing any future major political-military crisis. On the positive side, both countries possess some characteristics that would help them avoid or manage future crises, such as a strong desire to avoid armed conflict, a respect for the other side's resolve in a serious crisis, and an approval, at least in theory, of many of the rules of prudent crisis management. Moreover, some negative features of past Sino-American crisis behavior have disappeared over time. Examples include the intense hostility of the Cold War era and the absence of direct communication between the two sides. Unfortunately, many other negative features persist—especially regarding crisis-related perceptions and images—while some troubling new features have also emerged. Perhaps most disturbing, these tentative conclusions suggest that a serious Sino-American crisis over Taiwan in particular would probably be extremely difficult—albeit not impossible—to manage.

We believe that success in strengthening Sino-U.S. crisis management requires not only a real desire to do so, but also earnest methods of approach. The two countries could significantly improve the prevention and handling of future crises by undertaking recommendations in several areas outlined in the conclusion of this volume. We hope that this volume will mark a good first step toward an improvement in crisis management techniques.

—Jessica T. Mathews
President, Carnegie Endowment
for International Peace

—Chen Zhiya
Secretary General, China Foundation
for International and Strategic Studies

NOTES

1. CFISS will publish a Chinese-language edition of this volume for use in China. The Chinese and American versions of this book share a common spirit, but they are not identical. The Chinese version contains some changes in structure and content that were agreed upon by both sides. These reflect differences in viewpoint and interpretation on a relatively small number of issues. On most issues, the two sides hold very similar views.

2. The Chinese co-editor, Zhang Tuosheng, and CFISS do not necessarily endorse all of the views conveyed by Michael D. Swaine in the introduction and conclusion of this volume.

1

Understanding the Historical Record

Michael D. Swaine

ANY ATTEMPT TO EXAMINE CRISIS BEHAVIOR and assess the prospect for effective crisis management between the United States and China must begin by defining the term "crisis" and the attributes of crisis management.

KEY TERMS

What Is a Political-Military Crisis?

In most American analyses, a political-military crisis is defined by three factors:

- Key or core interests of the actors are involved,
- Time element or sense of urgency exists, and
- Great advances or threats (or both) to the interests of all sides are possible, including the threat of military conflict and, in the case of major powers, a potential threat to the structure of the international system.[1]

An international crisis begins with a disruptive action or event that activates these conditions for one or more states. Such a precipitating factor could occur accidentally or deliberately; it could be entirely unexpected or emerge unsurprisingly (or seemingly unavoidably) from a long-standing, tense confrontation. It might also be caused by the actions of a third party or parties. In a full-blown political-military crisis, the parties involved are aware (or believe) that a threat of significant military conflict exists. In a near crisis, there is no realistic probability of such military conflict despite the existence of a conflict of interest and time pressures. Nonetheless, even near crises can significantly damage the political, diplomatic, and economic relationships of the states concerned and, in some cases, increase the probability of a future full-blown crisis.[2] Hence, crises and near crises are viewed as significant events meriting careful management. Of the incidents investigated in this volume, the Taiwan Strait crises of 1954–1955, 1958, and 1995–1996 are regarded as full-blown political-military crises (although many U.S. officials apparently viewed the latter as something less than a crisis[3]); and the 1999 bombing of the Chinese embassy and the 2001 EP-3 aircraft incident are viewed as near crises.[4] The Korean and Vietnam Wars contained both elements of full-blown crisis behavior and large-scale military conflict.[5]

A crisis (or near-crisis) situation usually presents an apparent threat or an opportunity, or both, for one or more of the states involved. A crisis emerges when neither side is willing to back down in the face of such a perceived threat and/or opportunity. As Alexander George argues, some crises emerge in ways that leave one actor no choice but to counter its adversary. Other crises emerge only because one actor decides to accept a challenge from the other and to oppose it. Still other crises are deliberately initiated by one side in an effort to take advantage of an apparent opportunity and thereby cause a favorable change in the status quo.[6] Many scholars believe that international crises are unusual situations, largely triggered by abrupt changes in the behavior of a foreign nation (or nations) or an external political event. These observers hold that crises cause the disturbance of otherwise stable international relations and usually last for a short period of time.[7]

Many Chinese analysts generally agree with the above definition of a political-military crisis. However, some American (and perhaps a few Chinese) observers mistakenly believe that the Chinese are particularly inclined to view crises as opportunities for gain. To support this claim, they erroneously assert that the word crisis (*weiji*) in Chinese combines the words "danger" (*wei*) and "opportunity" (*ji*). In fact, *ji* does not mean "opportunity" in this context, but rather "a critical or incipient moment." Hence, for most Chinese, a crisis denotes ". . . a perilous situation when one should be especially wary . . . [and] *not* a juncture when one goes looking for advantages . . ." A crisis is first and foremost a dangerous event that has the potential to produce a range of outcomes, good and bad. In other words, although Chinese analysts recognize that a crisis can—under some circumstances—present both a threat and an opportunity, their basic understanding of the word and the concept is similar to the American understanding.[8] On the other hand, some differences of emphasis and interpretation do seem to exist between American and Chinese analysts regarding certain characteristics of a crisis or near crisis.

For example, some Chinese analysts argue that crises are not qualitatively distinctive or relatively uncommon events. They believe that crises reflect the inherently competitive and unstable nature of international relations and differ from other situations only in the level and intensity of actions and signals. Also, in the view of some Chinese analysts, crises often arise primarily from domestic, not foreign, factors, at least initially. They can also persist over a long period of time.[9] Still, it is unclear that such differences are widely held in China today, or exert a major impact on how Sino-American crises are handled.[10] Both Chinese and American scholars today emphasize that the most critical element of a crisis is the existence of a threat to core interests that can present both a danger of military conflict (or significant diplomatic-political damage) and (in some arguably fewer instances) an opportunity for gain. Moreover, although many Chinese scholars do not necessarily view crises as always distinctive and urgent events, they recognize that such features can occur in certain contexts. Indeed, the historical circumstances of the Sino-American crises examined in this volume suggest that both sides often recognized a sense of urgency throughout each crisis, and viewed each crisis or near crisis as a distinctive event.

What Is Crisis Management?

Attempts at crisis management do not seek to resolve the basic issue that created the crisis. If successful, crisis management merely defuses the crisis and decreases the risks of escalation.[11] Crises differ substantially in their structure and dynamics, in the importance of what is at stake for each actor, and in the level of risks and opportunities confronting each actor. Crises also differ in the larger diplomatic and military environment and in the domestic and international constraints on (and ultimate motivations of) key decision makers. However, the acute policy challenge posed by every political-military crisis emerges from the inherent tension between the desire to protect or advance key interests and the need to avoid provoking unwanted escalation and conflict. In more specific operational terms, every policy maker in a political-military crisis faces a dilemma: on the one hand the need or desire to signal commitment and resolve in advancing or protecting one's interests without provoking unwanted escalation or conflict; on the other hand the need or desire to signal accommodation or conciliation without conveying weakness or capitulation and, thus, inviting aggression and undesired escalation.[12]

Decision makers, whether deliberately or unconsciously, usually apply one or more specific political-military crisis management bargaining strategies to deal with this policy challenge and to attain other objectives during a crisis.[13] These include both offensive strategies, that is, those that are compellence oriented and intended to alter the situation at the expense of the adversary, and defensive strategies, that is, those that are deterrence oriented and intended merely to prevent or reverse gains.[14] Moreover, such strategies are usually combined or used in sequence during crises. Successful crisis management occurs when the parties involved are eventually able to avoid the worst case and to defuse one or more elements of the crisis—particularly the possibility of military conflict—while also protecting or advancing their core interests.[15]

As Alexander George asserts, such success is highly dependent on the strength of the decision makers' incentives for avoiding war, the opportunities available to decision makers for managing crises, and the level of skill they bring to bear in any crisis management effort.[16] Nonetheless, scholars of political-military crises identify several so-called rules of prudence or requirements for crisis management that can increase the likelihood of a successful outcome.[17] Alastair Iain Johnston has reduced these requirements to eight basic principles, which are adapted below.[18]

1. Maintain direct channels of communication and send signals that are clear, specific, and detailed. Direct communication can reduce confusion during a crisis and lower the probability of sending unclear signals. This requires trusted, authoritative communication links and a clear understanding by all sides of what constitutes a signal. In addition, many experts believe that crisis communications should contain several specific demands. This allows an adversary to accept some demands and reject others, leading to the possibility of a perceived compromise. In contrast, a small number of vague demands can reduce and narrow the adversary's choices, thus lowering the likelihood of compromise. To send clear and specific signals, political leaders must send unified messages and exercise firm control over communication channels. Moreover, proper signaling requires some understanding of the adversary's policy-making process and history of crisis communication. Crisis decision makers must be able to answer several questions: Who speaks authoritatively in a crisis? What is the specific target and purpose of a given signal? What actions or events constitute signals and what do not? What is meant by specific words and phrases used in crisis signaling? Proper signaling also requires a predictable decision-making apparatus that is reasonably transparent and obedient to the senior leadership.

2. **Focus on limited objectives and employ means on behalf of such objectives; sacrifice unlimited goals.** In a political-military crisis, both sides should seek to limit the speed of escalation and avoid unwanted escalation. This allows for more careful and effective diplomacy and bargaining and reduces the chance of inadvertent confrontation or conflict. The adoption of limited goals and means helps to control the speed of escalation by lowering the stakes and reducing the risks confronting decision makers. Decision makers find it very difficult to discard unlimited goals if one or both sides believe the crisis presents a solid opportunity to make major gains or regard the stakes involved as high.

3. **Preserve military flexibility and civilian control, escalate slowly, and respond symmetrically (in a "tit-for-tat" manner).** This very important point is closely related to the previous point. To maximize the chances for success in the bargaining that is central to effective crisis management, each side needs time to analyze the signals from the other side and develop the most appropriate, rational responses. The decision-making process will become overly simplified and destabilizing responses will become more likely if the time between moves is extremely short and the adversary escalates dramatically. To minimize such dan-

gerous consequences, crisis decision makers should escalate slowly, allowing the other side to respond to each move, and eschew major escalatory leaps in favor of incremental, symmetrical, tit-for-tat responses.[19] This principle is very difficult to implement if one or more participants strongly emphasize the need to seize the initiative through sudden, decisive (perhaps preemptive) actions in order to show resolve.

In addition, the movement of military forces and any threats of force must be consistent with one's diplomatic objectives, and the chance of accidental, provocative military moves must be minimized. Moreover, diplomatic-military moves should signal a desire to negotiate a resolution of the crisis rather than to seek a military solution. This requires strict, informed leadership control over military options and the selection, timing, and coordination of military movements and responses.[20] Such a requirement is extremely difficult if the military possesses an offensive operational doctrine; operates under fixed, preexisting plans; and adheres to an overall decision-making process that is somewhat unresponsive or unpredictable.

4. Avoid ideological or principled lock-in positions that encourage zero-sum approaches to a crisis and limit options or bargaining room; do not confuse moral or principled positions with conflicts of interest. To avoid adverse outcomes in a crisis such as war or a major loss of political status within the international system, participants must be willing to negotiate, make trade-offs, and compromise to some degree. These actions are extremely difficult if one or both sides adopt extreme, ideological, or absolutist positions, especially in public. Such a hardline approach tends to view conflict as zero-sum. Moreover, the public display of a hardline approach can turn an issue into a matter of principle in the minds of the public and the leadership alike and, thus, potentially threaten the integrity, and even the legitimacy, of the government. Such situations will inevitably constrain bargaining choices and make it extremely difficult to compromise or back down in a crisis. This can lead to the so-called commitment trap, in which leaders feel compelled to act on commitments or threats, once publicly stated, out of fear that the public will view accommodation or compromise as a sign of weakness and perhaps even betrayal.[21] The public invocation of principles associated with absolutist positions can also encourage the impression that conflict is virtually unavoidable and that efforts to prevent it are therefore almost futile. This kind of fatalistic thinking shortens the time frame for diplomacy and negotiation, reduces the acceptability of dissenting views within each society, and creates an almost self-fulfilling outcome.

5. Exercise self-restraint, and do not respond to all provocative moves. Sometimes the best way to limit the speed of escalation in a crisis is by not responding to the adversary's provocation. Refraining from a response allows decision makers to observe the evolution of their opponent's strategy. When the senior leadership is highly risk acceptant or prone to the commitment trap, such self-restraint is difficult. This kind of an adverse decision-making style is more likely to appear when hard-liners or leaders who do not accept opposing views dominate the decision-making process. An adverse decision-making style also appears when leaders believe the crisis presents a closing window of opportunity.

6. Avoid extreme pressure, ultimatums, or threats to the adversary's core values; and preserve the adversary's option to back down in a "face-saving" manner. In a tense political-military crisis, the use of ultimatums, intense pressure, and dire threats can be extremely dangerous. These tactics are especially risky if the adversary believes it is unable to retreat without suffering even greater damage or humiliation and if the threats and ultimatums are designed to compel (rather than deter) behavior. Such measures can lead the adversary to feel desperate and become more risk acceptant. This, in turn, may cause the adversary to employ preemptive military or diplomatic actions designed to convey resolve or to deny the opponent the capacity to make good on its threats. The dangers of such a situation are especially acute if the adversary has adopted unlimited objectives or a principled stance, or both, and believes that one or both have come under threat. Alexander George notes that the player with superior military power in a crisis often overlooks the potentially compensatory effects of the weaker party's motivation to overcome such aggressive behavior.[22] Thus, the stronger power is often tempted to apply these inadvisable measures in the mistaken belief that its power will ensure compliance.

7. Divide large, integrated, hard-to-resolve disputes into smaller, more manageable issues, thereby building trust and facilitating trade-offs. A successfully negotiated crisis usually requires the prior creation of a certain level of mutual trust. Such trust often emerges on the basis of a history of a successful resolution of disputes through direct negotiations. These successes create a habit of cooperation that can lead both sides to believe the other is at least a potential long-term bargaining partner. Such an outcome is more likely if adversaries first attempt to reach agreement on smaller issues of contention. Thus, in a crisis, both sides should attempt to divide difficult, integrated issues into smaller, more manageable parts. Such a strategy would be particularly difficult if crisis behavior were subject to the kinds of conditions that weaken observance of many of the preceding principles. In particular, the invocation of ideological lock-in positions, the existence of extremely high stakes, and threats to the core values of one or both sides would create challenges for this divide-and-conquer strategy.

8. Think ahead about the unintended consequences of one's actions. Effective crisis management requires careful strategic thought. In particular, decision makers must consider how the adversary will likely act and react over several moves. The pressure-laden atmosphere of a political-military crisis makes it extremely difficult for leaders to think through all the possible unintended, negative consequences of a move or countermove, especially over several iterations. This problem is compounded by the tendency of crisis decision makers to underestimate the negative effects of their actions on the adversary and overestimate the positive effects. This is particularly true of more tough-minded, aggressive, or antagonistic leaders (so-called hard-liners). Such individuals often suffer from a variant of the so-called "fundamental attribution error." This refers to the tendency of an actor to attribute another actor's bad behavior to that actor's disposition and that actor's good behavior to pressure from the first actor, while also attributing its own good behavior to its disposition and its bad behavior to the situation the other actor has created. In other words, hard-liners tend to downplay or ignore the interactive, feedback relationship between their tough behavior and the tough behavior of the other side, and overemphasize the role of personality and a leader's "preexisting subjective disposition" in explaining crisis behavior.[23] This produces a tendency toward wishful thinking and generally weakens the effort to accurately think through moves and counter moves in a crisis.

These eight principles suggest that certain types of crisis bargaining behaviors or strategies are less risky than others. For example, as Alexander George points out, attempts at limited probes and the controlled, gradual application of pressure give a challenger a good opportunity to monitor and control risks. In contrast, efforts at blackmail or moves to establish faits accomplis are based on the assumption that the adversary will be too intimidated or insufficiently motivated to resist, or that the adversary will not respond with military action because it has made no prior commitment to do so or lacks the capacity to react. Because these strategies allow little opportunity to monitor and control risks, war might rapidly follow if such assumptions are incorrect. A strategy of slow attrition might initially entail low risks but could force the adversary to escalate greatly as it is damaged to the point where it is prompted to undertake a major provocation.[24] Strategies of coercive diplomacy and limited escalation are also significantly risky. The latter strategy works only when accompanied by effective deterrence of counterescalation by the opponent—a difficult undertaking.[25] George adds, "Coercive diplomacy is a particularly beguiling strategy for strong powers that suffer an encroachment from a weaker state because it seems to promise success without bloodshed or much expenditure of resources." Proponents of this strategy, however, "often fail to consider whether a weaker opponent's strong motivation will compensate for its inferior capabilities" by leading it to counter vigorously attempts at coercion. This strategy is also "highly problematic" if it is combined with "stringent demands that strengthen the opponent's motivation to resist."[26]

Although the eight crisis management principles (and the most closely associated low-risk strategies for crisis bargaining) clearly offer some benefits by reducing the possibility of conflict, they might also produce serious disadvantages in a crisis. Alexander L. George suggests, for example, that an exclusive commitment to accommodationist, low-risk strategies might ultimately fail by preserving peace at the expense of core state interests. Moreover, such strategies might prove to be entirely ineffective or, worse yet, convey an image of weakness to the adversary that emboldens it to apply coercion or force. This suggests that success in crisis management is extremely context dependent and reliant on subjective assessments of the overall costs and benefits presented by a particular situation. Even under the most optimal conditions, crisis management can still produce adverse outcomes.

Finally, most if not all of the above eight principles might be entirely inappropriate if the objective of a leadership is to "win" a crisis (that is, to get the other side to back down unilaterally). In other words, the above principles and associated strategies might actually weaken a leadership's bargaining power if one sees the crisis as essentially a win/lose situation. Therefore, the principles of crisis management are not always consistent with some of the core principles of the application of military power. Moreover, as suggested in the above discussion of the third crisis management principle, it is important for civilian leaders to be aware that the operational impulses and standard operating procedures of militaries might not be consistent with crisis management.[27]

VARIABLES AND ISSUES INFLUENCING CRISIS BEHAVIOR

A wide range of cognitive, structural, and procedural variables influences how states will behave in a crisis and, in particular, their ability and willingness to apply the above eight principles of effective crisis management. One can identify at least six basic sets of variables that influence crisis behavior:

- Elite perceptions and beliefs,
- Domestic politics and public opinion,
- Decision-making structure and process,
- Information and intelligence receipt and processing,
- International environment, and
- Idiosyncratic or special features.

The following section examines each of these areas in some detail, beginning with a summary of the general relevance of each area to crisis behavior on the basis of the scholarly literature. This is followed by a detailed assessment of the specific crisis-relevant features of each variable in the Chinese and U.S. cases, based largely on past Sino-American crises. The latter undertaking places particular emphasis on the observations by the authors of the chapters contained in this volume as well as the remarks of participants at the 2004 Beijing conference.

Elite Perceptions and Beliefs

The scholarly literature relating to crises and crisis management tends to focus to a very large extent on elite perceptions and beliefs as critical

variables that influence the cause, evolution, and consequences of political-military crises. Elite views precede a crisis and provide the framework within which diplomatic and military interaction occurs. Elite
views color the expectation of compromise, confrontation, or conflict
that is likely to emerge during a crisis. Elite views also largely determine
the level of trust to be anticipated in crisis negotiations.[28] The literature
on this subject focuses on four major sets of issues:

- Basic elite images of one's own country and one's adversary that
  influence the motives and objectives employed in a crisis, along with
  general elite beliefs regarding the nature of political-military crises
  (including crises between China and the United States);
- Elite views on the value or use of coercion or force, accommodation,
  and persuasion, including efforts to explain and justify a position
  and communicate appropriate assurances of one's limited objectives
  during a crisis[29];
- Elite views toward risk taking, the requirements of crisis stability,
  and the best means of controlling escalation and maintaining deterrence in a crisis;
- Elite views toward crisis signaling, especially the best way to signal
  resolve without provoking dangerous responses or to signal accommodation without conveying weakness.[30]

Elite images, views, and beliefs of relevance to these four sets of issues
can vary greatly, at least in theory. On one extreme are those hypothetical individuals who tend to view crises in largely zero-sum terms and
assume that the adversary is aggressive, while they are fundamentally
peace-loving though highly determined to defend their vital interests.
This viewpoint also believes that escalation is highly controllable and
inadvertent war is highly unlikely or impossible. These ideal types of
leaders favor either faits accomplis or strong, decisive, coercive actions
over incremental strategies. They believe that war results from insufficient resolve or excessive efforts at accommodation or persuasion and
that some types of conflict might produce major benefits (or be better
than the alternative) under certain circumstances.

On the other theoretical extreme are those individuals who tend to
assume that crises can be positive-sum events. Such leaders may assume

that they and their adversary operate from largely or exclusively defensive motives. This viewpoint believes that escalation control is extremely problematic if one puts even a modest stress on coercion. It favors incremental strategies and shuns war at virtually all costs. Hence, such leaders generally assume that conflict results from the escalatory spiral that is triggered by coercive moves instead of from a failure to show resolve. This approach stresses accommodation and crisis prevention over management or give-and-take bargaining.[31] In reality, of course, most if not all political-military leaders fall somewhere between these idealized extremes, and in some cases combine both hardline and accommodationist views.

Studies of Chinese and U.S. leadership attitudes and Sino-American crisis interactions have produced a wide range of findings relevant to the above issues.

SELF-IMAGE AND MOTIVES. Much of the American and Chinese literature suggests that the leadership of the People's Republic of China (PRC) views their nation as an aspiring yet nonaggressive great power, increasingly confident yet also acutely sensitive to domestic and external challenges to its stability and status. China's leaders, and many ordinary Chinese citizens, possess a strong memory of the nation's supposed historical victimization and manipulation at the hands of stronger powers.[32] There is also a prevalent belief among China's citizens and leaders that stronger foreign powers are especially inclined to prey upon China when the country is facing internal weakness or disarray.[33] Thus, in past crises, Chinese leaders have been prepared to go to significant lengths to avoid the appearance of being weak and giving in to great-power pressures or of engaging in overtly predatory or manipulative behavior themselves.

Chinese leaders have also at times evinced a very strong commitment to specific basic principles and core interests. They have been especially concerned with those issues associated with the defense of China's territorial integrity and sovereignty, both of which are closely related to national dignity and recovery from past humiliations.[34] In particular, Chinese observers have generally viewed PRC behavior during most post-1949 territorial crises as a totally justifiable kind of preventive deterrence action designed to prevent the erosion of the territorial status quo accepted by China's leaders in 1949. Chinese observers believe that such crisis behavior was designed to either ward off imminent or existing threats to critical border areas or to defend against more ambiguous attempts to intimidate China, "test" its resolve, or ascertain the stability of its leadership.[35]

China has also displayed a strong impulse to view the triggering issue in past crises as a clear matter of principle or basic values, such as right and wrong or fairness and unfairness. These principles or values are often associated with permanent beliefs regarding sovereignty, interstate relations, and behavior that is in general deemed just or moral.[36] For some observers, this has at times led to a tendency by Chinese leaders to view crisis confrontations in zero-sum terms, involving the defense of moral principles against unjust acts.[37] This tendency has been augmented by a sense of vulnerability when confronting a superior power. Thus, in past crises, China has often believed it was compelled to act because the other side would not heed warnings and recognize its unjust behavior or because the other side bullied China or carried out an unjustifiable use of force that required a counter.[38]

Many current Chinese observers of Beijing's crisis behavior—including many authors of the case studies in this volume—insist that under the influence of the "opening up" policy to the outside world and with the emergence of the post–Deng Xiaoping leadership, China's leaders are becoming less "absolutist" and increasingly attentive to international law and international mechanisms when they evaluate crises (or near crises) and assess their responses.[39] In other words, as one Chinese participant at the February 2004 Beijing conference stated, "While moral principles and values still matter greatly, they neither exist in isolation nor automatically outweigh other considerations."[40] The extent to which principles or basic values might dominate elite thinking can vary greatly, depending on the specific features of the crisis in question.

As suggested above, many analysts of Chinese crisis behavior argue that early PRC leaders such as Mao Zedong often viewed crises as opportunities to achieve foreign policy objectives. In particular, crises arguably were used to consolidate support from potential friends and allies during periods of potential threat, to probe an adversary's intentions, and to cause difficulties between an adversary and its allies. Crises have also been used to weaken an adversary's resolve and internal support for its policies or simply to deter or compel an adversary, hopefully leading to a beneficial change in the political-military situation.[41] As with the role of moral principles in crises, many of today's Chinese scholars emphasize that this Chinese approach toward crises has changed significantly under the reforms and particularly since the end of the Cold War. These scholars believe that, in a fundamental sense, China's leaders now perceive crises as primarily disruptive events that interfere with their domestic and international agendas and thus contain very few if any opportunities for gain. Consequently, China now attaches more importance to avoiding or resolving crises early on. These observers argue (correctly, in my view) that China's behavior during political-military crises in the 1990s was generally reactive and contingent, involving limited and for the most part flexible demands.[42]

Finally, Chinese leaders have often been very attentive to the larger international environment—and not merely bilateral interactions—when confronting a crisis. During the Sino-Indian border crisis of 1962, for example, Beijing became extremely sensitive to Indian attacks along the border in part because of fears of possible Soviet collusion. Chinese officials were also concerned that a weak Chinese response to India might embolden the United States to support Nationalist Chinese attacks on the mainland during a period of domestic economic decline and social turmoil. Mao feared the creation of a Moscow–New Delhi–Washington alliance of sorts against China.[43] During the lead-up to Chinese intervention in the Korean War, Mao and other Chinese leaders were concerned that U.S. military intervention reflected a broader effort by the United States to pressure China in other areas, such as Taiwan (Republic of China, or ROC) and Southeast Asia.[44]

Most American scholars agree that the U.S. leadership views the United States as the sole global superpower, with critical regional and global interests and responsibilities involving the maintenance of the security of key friends and allies, the preservation of peace and stability, and the advancement of prosperity in key regions of the world. U.S. leaders also view the United States as a crucial force for democratic change and a protector of political freedoms and human rights worldwide. In the western Pacific, the United States sees itself as an indispensable security partner and broker. This position requires the United States to maintain access and freedom in the economic, technological, and military realms and to prevent the emergence of any hostile power in the region. As a result of these responsibilities, U.S. leaders have a strong stake in maintaining the credibility and authority of Washington's words and actions as well as its superior military and economic capabilities and its political relationships in Asia and beyond.[45]

The United States has viewed its behavior during past political-military crises (and particularly those occurring in Asia) as a response to clear threats to these key interests and responsibilities. In each instance, U.S. leaders have tended to view themselves as seeking to manage a crisis with caution and restraint while showing enormous resolve when necessary. In particular, U.S. leaders have often viewed crises as exceptional and usually negative events largely thrust upon them by circumstances or the aggressive designs of other powers and almost always threatening peace and stability or other U.S. interests.[46] U.S. leaders believe that crises usually require management through negotiation and, in many instances, compromise. Ideally, the two sides will reach an explicit agreement or understanding on each side's responsibilities, rights, and interests under the postcrisis situation. During this process, the United States views itself as naturally seeking to protect its most vital interests as well as generally avoiding adoption of an absolutist approach if compromise is seen as a possible and useful means of resolving the crisis. In other words, the objective in a crisis is often to attain an optimal—sometimes positive-sum—resolution under the existing circumstances while key U.S. interests are preserved. Moreover, U.S. leaders have generally viewed themselves as attempting to resolve a crisis on the basis of international law and in accordance with accepted international norms.[47]

Many scholars at the same time note that Washington has not shied from leveling coercive threats or employing armed force to communicate resolve and protect its vital interests during a crisis. Indeed, as discussed in greater detail below, U.S. leaders have often viewed U.S. coercion and even a limited use of force as indispensable means to the successful resolution of a crisis, especially when confronting a non-nuclear power. They have even at times leveled nuclear threats of various types against non-nuclear adversaries in a conflict or crisis. Such confidence derives to a great extent from the belief that the United States since World War II has enjoyed escalation dominance in such confrontations as a result of its superior military power. In addition, U.S. leaders have at times invoked absolutist principles such as the defense of justice, freedom from oppression, and democracy to justify their crisis behavior, thus qualifying to some extent their commitment to optimal, positive-sum resolutions.[48]

Finally, it is certainly the case that past U.S. leaders, like most leaders, have also at times viewed political-military crises as opportunities to achieve specific foreign policy objectives. Thomas J. Christensen, for example, argues that Harry Truman, in order to generate greater public support for his grand strategy of the late 1940s, attempted to use the Korean War to strengthen his larger effort to advance a public crusade against communism.[49] On the other hand, one can argue that U.S. leaders have confronted greater domestic problems than their Chinese counterparts in manipulating crises in this manner, given the obstacles presented by the legal system and popular and congressional opinion.[50] Moreover, there is little evidence to indicate that U.S. decision makers have deliberately *created* serious political-military crises in order to attain political or strategic objectives.

These beliefs suggest that U.S. leaders might assume the United States would enjoy a distinct advantage in a crisis with a weaker—albeit nuclear-armed—power such as China. The U.S. commitment to preserving its credibility and its dominant position in the western Pacific, along with its superior conventional and overwhelming nuclear capabilities, indicate to some observers that Washington could communicate resolve and deter undesired behavior more effectively than Beijing in a situation such as a confrontation over Taiwan.[51]

IMAGE OF THE ADVERSARY. Most of the literature on Chinese views toward the United States in areas relevant to crises presents a consistent picture. China views the United States as constantly striving to maintain its system of global and regional dominance, usually through a reliance on superior economic and military power. In recent years, Chinese observers have stressed the view that the United States has often acted without international (that is, United Nations) approval. In particular, Chinese scholarly sources and Chinese participants at the 2004 Beijing conference suggest that Washington is willing to violate unilaterally what China regards as vital international principles—such as the territorial integrity and sovereignty of other states—in order to achieve its national objectives. Many Chinese detect an excessive sense of self-importance among U.S. leaders.[52] Moreover, many Chinese believe that the United States is a hegemonic and antisocialist power and, consequently, views China as a significant and growing strategic threat to its dominant global position. Hence, the United States is often seen as offensively oriented, seeking in many ways to constrain China's increasing power and limit its options internationally. In the past, these efforts have allegedly included attempts to use other powers such as Nationalist China, South Korea, and Japan as proxies. Today, the United States is often viewed as seeking to constrain China's rise by preventing the reunification of Taiwan with the mainland or by encouraging Taiwan independence.[53] Moreover, the Chinese perceive the United States to be a hypocritical power that claims to promote democracy and human rights, while actually pursuing its own national interests. This image is particularly important because it adds a strong emotional element to anti-American images in China and throughout the world.[54]

Despite all this, most Chinese analysts also view the United States today as desiring, for largely economic and political reasons, at least workable (if not fully cooperative and amicable) relations with China. This U.S. interest has deepened considerably since the advent of the global war on terrorism and the worsening of the slow-motion nuclear crisis on the Korean peninsula. Many Chinese analysts believe that these two events have forced Washington not only to divert its attention, at least temporarily, from the long-term strategic challenge posed by China's rise but also to collaborate more closely with and depend on Beijing to address these and other more pressing concerns.[55] Many in China believe that U.S. leaders could easily adopt a more hostile stance toward China if the strategic environment were to shift again, allowing U.S. suspicions and animosity toward Beijing to return to the forefront.[56]

Given these basic views, many Chinese analysts believe the United States has at times precipitated or manipulated political-military crises to reaffirm or preserve its dominance. The United States may also want to test the resolve of potential adversaries, especially major powers.[57] Xia Liping argues in this volume that U.S. leaders often regard crisis management involving a small or medium-sized nation as a process by which the United States can win by forcing its adversary to concede and thereby can advance its own interests. In such instances, the objective of crisis management is to force the enemy to make the greatest concession possible while itself making the smallest concession possible. When the United States deals with a more powerful state, however—such as a nuclear power—the Chinese see Washington as defining crisis management as "the process of 'winning' a crisis while at the same time keeping it within more tolerable limits of danger and risk to both sides."[58] In this case, the goal is to resolve the crisis on U.S. terms without the use of force.[59]

This general image of the United States as aggressive and potentially threatening in political-military crises is to some extent qualified by yet another perception: some Chinese analysts view the United States as vulnerable or deterrable in specific types of crises, such as a confrontation with China over Taiwan. Chinese observers clearly recognize that the United States has superior power and a large variety of means it can call on to manage a crisis, including economic sanctions, diplomatic isolation, military encirclement, and the mobilization of allies and perhaps the United Nations (UN). However, many in China also view the United States as constrained in a political-military crisis by a fear of casualties, prolonged conflict, and economic cost. In contrast, many in China—and some Western scholars—view Beijing as less deterred by such factors, especially in crises involving vital interests such as territorial integrity.[60] Moreover, many Chinese firmly believe that the United States will most likely have less at stake in a crisis with China over Taiwan, given the critical importance of the island to Beijing as a territorial and sovereignty issue.[61] Indeed, many think the loss of Taiwan could result in the collapse of the Chinese government.

For all these reasons, many Chinese observers believe the United States can in most instances more easily choose to avoid a territorial crisis with China that involves the use of force. Many Chinese think the United States would view armed conflict, particularly prolonged armed conflict, as unnecessary and too costly. This suggests to some in China that the United States would be more easily deterrable in such a crisis than would China or, at least, that a military clash could be avoided. That is, China could forcefully deter Taiwan independence without risking a war with the United States.[62] The Chinese are not sanguine on this point, however. Many also assert that the United States would not easily concede positions in a crisis with China over Taiwan, given what they believe is the arrogance of American power.

Another factor that can influence China's basic image of the United States is the level of hostility ascribed to Washington at a particular point in time. Beijing often designates other powers as friendly, hostile, or neutral toward China.[63] Such a designation is apparently a quasi-formal label (*dingwei*) that can heavily influence assessments and recommendations produced by Chinese elites and advisers and, thus, can significantly shape Beijing's crisis behavior. A power is more likely to be treated as an adversary in a crisis if overall bilateral relations are in a state of hostility or obvious tension, or simply if friendly relations are not predominant in the relationship (that is, a condition of "neither friend nor foe" [*feidi feiyou*] prevails).[64]

Until at least the early 1970s, China's leaders clearly regarded the United States as a hostile power and, hence, as an archenemy of "New China." Since the opening up period in the late 1970s and early 1980s and the subsequent collapse of the Soviet Union, the Chinese government has relabeled the United States as neither friend nor foe but has generally sought to avoid characterizing Washington as an adversary or enemy.[65] Indeed, participants at the 2004 Beijing conference insisted that China's leaders sincerely hope to develop a long-term, stable partnership of constructive cooperation with the United States by expanding areas of mutual interest between the two countries. These areas include economic cooperation, regional stability, prevention of the proliferation of weapons of mass destruction, antiterrorism, and environmental protection.

U.S. images of China that are of relevance to crisis interactions have changed significantly since the height of the Cold War. For most of the period from the late 1940s to the late 1960s, many U.S. national security elites viewed Maoist China as a militant, fanatical, and aggressive regime despite its power limitations. They also saw China as a surrogate for (and servant of) Soviet expansionism. Hence, U.S. leaders perceived China to be a dangerous security threat to areas along its periphery, including many U.S. allies and friends.[66] At the same time, before Chinese intervention in the Korean War in late 1950, U.S. leaders viewed their Chinese counterparts as heavily distracted by the need to restore domestic stability and rebuild the economy after World War II and the Chinese civil war and, hence, unwilling to undertake an armed conflict with the vastly superior U.S. military. As Allen Whiting notes in this volume, these faulty assumptions led U.S. leaders to believe that China should not have any concerns about U.S. military involvement in the Korean conflict. U.S. decision makers reached this incorrect conclusion because they believed the Soviets did not seem interested in intervening on the peninsula unless China was attacked directly, and Washington had publicly reassured Beijing that it had no intention of undertaking such an attack.

The massive Chinese intervention in the Korean War and the large loss of life accompanying forced collectivization and the Great Leap Forward during the late 1950s confirmed to many U.S. leaders that China's Communist Party leadership was extremely cruel and aggressive. U.S. leaders concluded that Chinese leaders were often willing to sacrifice large numbers of soldiers and citizens to achieve their domestic and foreign objectives.[67] U.S. leaders believed the basic objective of China's foreign policies during the 1950s–1960s was the establishment of Chinese hegemony in the Far East (and perhaps beyond) as part of a larger effort to overthrow the advanced capitalist states and eject the United States from Asia. They characterized China's approach to international politics as a kind of guerrilla warfare. U.S. leaders primarily conceived of Chinese foreign and security policies in terms of conflict rather than negotiation. They believed China's policies were marked by a zero-sum approach to allies and enemies.[68] U.S. intelligence analysts attributed Chinese perceptions and postures to communist ideology and the leadership's experience during the struggle for power. U.S. intelligence analysts also attributed Chinese behavior to traditional Chinese feelings of arrogance and superiority over other peoples and to modern-day nationalist and hegemonic beliefs.[69]

As a result of their supposed arrogant self-confidence, revolutionary fervor, and distorted view of the world, China's leaders were perceived by U.S. observers to be prone to seriously miscalculating risks in a crisis. In an apparent contradiction, however, most National Intelligence Estimates (NIEs) of the 1950s–1960s also generally recognized that China's actual foreign policy behavior was quite cautious and calculative, not highly irrational or risk acceptant. Since the conclusion of the Korean War, China had emphasized indirection, political maneuver, and subversion and had avoided any direct confrontation or clash with the United States. Overall, Washington saw Beijing as unlikely to employ military conquest to gain its objectives, although it believed Beijing was quite willing to use limited amounts of force to defend its borders. The NIEs explained this gap between words and actions almost solely in terms of China's relative inferiority in terms of power. In particular, China was largely restrained by U.S. military dominance across Asia. Thus, some NIEs of the late 1950s and early 1960s asserted that nuclear weapons, once acquired, would increase China's willingness to engage in provocative or high-risk behavior, especially along its periphery.

Such an assessment of China's security views left little room for the possibility that the Chinese leadership might be motivated more by insecurity than by confidence, and more by a desire to protect and preserve a somewhat precarious domestic order than to expand its revolutionary power and influence at every available opportunity. There was little indication that beliefs associated with Chinese nationalism and a sense of victimization might predominate over communist fanaticism.[70]

By the early 1970s to the middle of that decade, NIEs finally dropped much of the Cold War imagery and language regarding PRC perceptions and motives. Although the NIEs noted that China continued to display verbal hostility and latent aggressiveness, they saw no Chinese desire to use military force to threaten or attack other states, and they found no indications that Beijing was moving toward a policy of expansionism or even higher risk taking. The NIEs described China's policy regarding the use of force as "generally cautious" and limited to defense against real and imminent threats to Chinese territory or vital interests. In general, NIEs of this period saw China as having moved from its previous intransigence to a "more flexible approach" involving attempts to play on Soviet fears of a Sino-American rapprochement. These NIEs saw China as acting primarily to deter external threats from a position of weakness.

U.S. intelligence analysts also by this time accepted the view that nuclear weapons would likely produce greater caution in the Chinese leadership, especially regarding a possible direct confrontation with the United States or the Soviet Union, because Chinese leaders would be aware that their possession of a small nuclear weapons arsenal made a preemptive nuclear strike against them more likely.[71] At the same time, the U.S. leadership clearly recognized the obvious willingness of China's government to employ low levels of conventional force against a superior nuclear-armed power, as illustrated by the Sino-Soviet border clash of 1969. In contrast with earlier assessments of Chinese restraint in the face of superior power, U.S. analysts explained China's aggressiveness toward the Soviet Union as deriving from a desire not to show weakness when confronted with Soviet intimidation. They also cited a parallel Chinese desire to control risk by not positioning large People's Liberation Army (PLA) forces close to the Soviet border or engaging in any massive buildup.[72]

The U.S. image of China shifted markedly during the 1980s, largely as a result of Beijing's abandonment of Maoist values in favor of an opening up policy driven by market-led economic development and the emergence of a Sino-American coalition aimed at countering Soviet power. U.S. leaders saw their Chinese counterparts as pragmatic, cautious, and largely conflict averse. By the period of the late 1980s and early 1990s, however, a growing minority of U.S. observers began to express serious concern over the implications for the U.S. position in Asia of a rapidly growing, reform-oriented China with interests expanding beyond its borders. They regarded China as an emerging great power that would eventually translate its growing economic and technological prowess into military capabilities and influence and thereby possibly challenge U.S. predominance in the Asia Pacific region. Yet, until at least the mid-1990s, most U.S. defense observers and elites still viewed the Chinese military as backward. It lacked any significant power projection capabilities in maritime Asia and still possessed only a very small, retaliatory, counter-value-oriented nuclear force. Beijing was also highly focused on domestic stability and development.

By 2000–2001, however, a significant number of U.S. observers came to identify China as America's major post–Cold War strategic threat. These observers saw China as a rising power potentially hostile to U.S. interests over the medium to long term and a possible initiator of armed aggression against Taiwan over the near to medium term.[73] This viewpoint emerged largely in response to indications in the late 1990s that Beijing was succeeding in resolving a range of deficiencies in the defense arena and acquiring new (largely naval and air) capabilities of concern to the United States, especially in the context of a potential military crisis over Taiwan.

Despite this possibility, the long-term strategic attention of the United States since September 11, 2001, has no longer focused on how to deal with a rising China, but rather on how to work with the major powers—including China—to combat terrorism. This outlook has quieted voices of alarm regarding China in the U.S. government and defense circles. It has led to a greater stress by defense officials on the enhancement of dialogue and cooperation with China and the basic need to avoid a confrontation over Taiwan. At the same time, U.S. observers view China as increasingly determined to acquire the military capability to defend or advance its interests regarding Taiwan and increase its overall influence in Asia. As a result, although they still perceive China as cautious and constrained by its outward-oriented, market-centered reform agenda, some U.S. analysts nonetheless see China as capable of miscalculating its political, military, and economic leverage and interests in a possible crisis with the United States over Taiwan or other issues. For some U.S. observers, this means that China's increasing power—combined with a belief in China's superior level of commitment to the issue—might eventually lead Beijing to precipitate a major crisis over Taiwan by using military force to communicate its unshakeable resolve or to compel a resolution of the issue on its own terms.[74]

VIEWS ABOUT COERCION, ACCOMMODATION, AND PERSUASION. Several Chinese scholars argue in this volume that Chinese leaders have seemed overall to follow the maxim "on just grounds, to our advantage, and with restraint" (*youli, youli, youjie*) in assessing how and when to use coercion or force, accommodation, and persuasion in a crisis. This principle, used often by Mao Zedong during China's struggle against Japan during World War II, comprises three points:

- Do not attack unless attacked. Never attack others without provocation, but, once attacked, do not fail to return the blow. This is the defensive nature of the principle.
- Do not fight decisive actions unless sure of victory. Never fight without certainty of success, unless failing to fight would likely present a worse outcome. Utilize contradictions among the enemy. Apply your strong point(s) and reduce the enemy's strong point(s). Be prag-

matic and aware of the limited nature of objectives and strength. With a strong power, set appropriate war objectives; do not exceed capabilities. Know when to stop, when to counter, and when to bring the fight to a close. Stop when the goals are attained; rethink if you cannot obtain your objectives. This is the limited nature of struggle.

- Do not be carried away with success. This is the temporary or contingent nature of each struggle.[75]

China adhered to this *youli, youli, youjie* maxim during the Korean War, the Sino-Vietnam Border War of 1979, and the Sino-Indian clash of 1962. Each crisis exhibited four phases. First was an initial diplomatic response to a sudden incident or development. Second, China conducted further analysis of the situation and decided on its bottom line for military action. Third, China sent early-warning signals to the opponent and undertook military preparations. Finally, if its opponent did not heed the warnings, China took military action, usually according to its original plan.[76] According to some Chinese observers, during the Korean and Vietnam Wars, the most crucial step in the Chinese strategy was to establish a red line for military intervention. From the Chinese perspective, preserving defensive lines at the 38th parallel in Korea and at the 17th parallel in Vietnam determined a secure distance for avoiding direct conflict between Chinese and U.S. armed forces.[77] China sent warning signals when U.S. forces approached these lines.

The *youli, youli, youjie* maxim suggests that Chinese leaders have usually used force only in response to force and have leveled coercive threats in response to threats. Many American scholars argue, however, that China has often *initiated* coercive threats or the use of force in a crisis as an effective political and psychological tool. In fact, some data, such as explored by Alastair Iain Johnston, show that during the Cold War China was more inclined than most of the other major powers to use limited levels of force, especially as an integral element of crisis bargaining.[78]

Several observers suggest that China has displayed a greater inclination to actually employ force as a political tool in a crisis than merely to threaten the use of force (as a form of deterrence), as is often the case in the West.[79] Specifically, in past political-military crises, such as those involving Taiwan, China's use of force was often intended to shape, deter, blunt, or reverse a crisis situation; probe or test intentions; and prevent escalation.[80] China has often used force to show resolve, a commitment to principle, and a corresponding refusal to submit to coercion or intimidation. China has also used force to produce psychological shock and uncertainty. This has sometimes occurred as part of a larger strategy designed to seize the political and military initiative via deception and surprise. At other times, China has used force to intimidate an opponent and, thus, to elicit caution and possibly concessions from the other side.[81] Moreover, as Thomas Christensen argues, the Chinese have "on several occasions . . . used force to affect and shape long-term political and security trends in the region and at home, not to resolve security problems permanently."[82] In this manner, from the Chinese perspective, a limited use of coercion or force under certain circumstances can prevent a much larger conflict, strengthen the foundations of peace, or achieve narrower Chinese objectives.[83]

According to many analysts, the amount and frequency of force applied by China, once initiated, is often calibrated to support the existing political situation and objectives and to accord with the prevailing balance of power. One U.S. analyst has observed, on the basis of a review of the existing (largely American) literature on China's use of force, that in past crises, Chinese leaders have often followed an initial overwhelming—albeit often limited—application of force with a pause. Chinese leaders may initiate this pause to lull an adversary into thinking China is backing down before China eliminates the threat through a subsequent strike. Chinese leaders may also initiate a pause to present an opportunity for the adversary to reconsider and back down or to avoid a serious escalation of the situation. At the same time, Beijing seeks to convey the impression that significant escalation is possible and acceptable, even though its focus remains on political objectives.[84] As this suggests, in some instances, a self-perception by China of overall weakness, not strength, can motivate the use of force as a deterrent. That is, China seeks to convey resolve and shock a stronger adversary into more cautious behavior.[85] Such a use of force usually demands sensitivity to the balance of power in the geographic area of the crisis and to problems of escalation and control. In line with this approach, the Chinese use of force in past crises was often followed by signs of accommodation or efforts at persuasion, at least privately, to avoid escalation, and to secure at least minimum gains.

Much of the above scholarly analysis of Chinese leadership perceptions regarding the use of coercion or force, accommodation, and persuasion in a crisis derives from the Mao Zedong and Deng Xiaoping eras. During those periods, Chinese leaders displayed a low threshold for the use of limited amounts of force, sometimes seemingly regardless of the human or economic cost involved and in some cases against a clearly superior adversary such as the Soviet Union. This tendency apparently derived primarily from a high level of confidence on the part of Mao and Deng in their ability to control escalation and their strong belief that a limited application of force was necessary to avoid a larger conflict or to defend core principles.[86] On the other hand, some American scholars argue that Chinese leaders have held offensive military approaches to crises during both modern and premodern periods of Chinese history (as part of an overall "hard" realpolitik approach to politics); these scholars emphasize China's need to show resolve and seize the initiative, often through preemptive attack.[87]

Post-Mao leaders continue to stress the need to show resolve and seize the initiative in a crisis. It is likely, however, that their willingness to use force in a crisis (especially high levels of force at an early stage of a crisis) has declined significantly. Indeed, many Chinese analysts, including many participants at the February 2004 Beijing conference, insist that China's approach to the use of force has changed markedly since the Mao and Deng eras. These observers believe that China's leaders no longer regard force as an effective tool for achieving limited political gains in a crisis. Hence, Chinese leaders have displayed an exceptional degree of caution in international confrontations since at least the end of the Cold War. These analysts assert that China has ruled out the use of force as an option in dealing with neighboring countries on territorial or border disputes and now proposes instead that such disputes be solved through negotiation on the basis of international law or shelved until the time is ripe for ultimate resolution.[88] In general, this viewpoint asserts that the Chinese leadership today regards the use of force in a foreign policy crisis as a last resort, to be considered only if core national interests are at stake, other (increasingly available) alternative approaches are exhausted, or China is faced with extreme provocation.[89] As a broad statement, this is probably accurate. The challenge, of course, is to determine when such conditions prevail.

According to Chinese participants at the 2004 Beijing conference, this viewpoint also applies to the Taiwan problem despite its status in Chinese thinking as a domestic issue.[90] The high stakes involved in the Taiwan issue and the accompanying Chinese need to convey a strong level of resolve have obviously resulted in decisions to engage in coercive military displays or threats, as during the Taiwan Strait crisis of 1995–1996. The Niu Jun chapter in this volume indicates that during that crisis China's leaders were determined to use military means to make a "powerful response" to what they viewed as "diplomatic provocations" by Washington in order to force the United States to "really realize the seriousness of the issue" and deter Taiwan separatists. Beijing hoped to contain the scope of the crisis by not attacking Taiwan directly and by avoiding any conflict with the United States.[91]

According to many analysts, the United States has used coercive threats of force or actual military force quite frequently since the end of World War II. Many such instances were attempts to influence the course of an existing political-military crisis or conflict in order to advance or protect what the United States sees as its great-power responsibilities and interests. In general, the use of force (as opposed to coercive threats) has been most closely associated with efforts to alter the material situation on the ground as a means of resolving a conflict or crisis on favorable terms. The United States has most often used actual military force in crises against considerably weaker powers. It has, however, leveled coercive threats or signaled a willingness to use force for both deterrence and compellence purposes against both weak and strong nations, including nuclear-armed powers or large conventional powers. Indeed, in general, the United States has employed or threatened the use of force in political-military crises more often than any other power, including China.[92] Equally significant, the United States has also leveled nuclear threats on several occasions during past crises, especially against China. In addition, the United States has also used its armed forces for political objectives (such as to maintain the authority of a foreign regime).[93]

To a large degree, the frequent use of force or coercion by U.S. decision makers reflects a high level of confidence in the efficacy of force and the ability to control escalation. Presumably, this confidence stems from the superior military capabilities of the United States, an assumption that military forces are tightly controlled by the civilian leadership, and the apparent belief that most adversaries in a political-military crisis are best deterred or compelled by such means.[94] Most U.S. uses of force have emphasized speed, power, precision, minimal casualties, and maximum disruption. Similar to China, the amount and frequency of force applied by the United States have usually been calibrated to support the existing political situation and objectives, and in consideration of the prevailing balance of power. U.S. constraints on or caution toward the actual use of force can be considerable if the opponent has significant capabilities.[95]

In general, U.S. leaders regard the military as only one of several possible coercive instruments. Other coercive instruments include economic, political, and diplomatic sanctions and pressure. Moreover, U.S. leaders often seem to assume that they can finely calibrate the level of military coercion via alerts and deployments and that the adversary can detect such signals. During the 1995–1996 Taiwan Strait crisis, for example, although the United States deployed two carrier battle groups to the vicinity to convey resolve, the second group never approached Taiwan apparently because the United States did not want to severely damage Sino-American relations. It is unclear whether the Chinese government understood this distinction.

Several of the Chinese participants in the 2004 Beijing conference argued that the use of force has occupied a more salient position in U.S. foreign policy overall than in the Chinese case. They remarked that Washington has resorted to the use of force very frequently since the end of the Cold War, thus confirming its importance to the U.S. national security strategy. Finally, they stated that, although concerns with casualties have at times constrained the scale of the use of force, the United States has been willing to pay a high price in terms of casualties if its fundamental interests were at stake. Clearly, the Chinese participants viewed the United States as far more likely than China to use force in an international political-military crisis today.

VIEWS ABOUT RISK TAKING, CRISIS STABILITY, AND ESCALATION CONTROL. These Chinese views toward crises and the use of force and coercion suggest that Chinese leaders believed—at least during past crises—that once a crisis began they could minimize risks and control unwanted escalation as long as they observed certain requirements largely associated with the *youli, youli, youjie* maxim. In particular, coercive threats or the use of force in past crises usually required the prior attainment of local superiority, strong control over one's armed forces (marked by very clear rules of engagement [ROE] and the coordination of military with political-diplomatic moves), and efforts to seize and maintain the initiative, often using tactical surprise and deception. The successful use of force or coercion also required a sense of knowing when to stop the political and military actions, and it required the use of pauses and tit-for-tat moves. Furthermore, successful use of force or coercion required clear and appropriate signals, including demonstrations of a low intent to escalate in a major way through the absence of obvious alerts or large-scale mobilizations. In most instances, providing a way out for both sides was emphasized. Many of these features are illustrated in the case studies presented in this volume as well as in past studies of Chinese crisis behavior.[96]

Several of these notions are broadly similar to the rules of prudence contained in the general literature on crisis management[97] and summarized in the eight principles presented above. However, for Chinese leaders (as for U.S. leaders), conveying firm resolve through words and actions is also a major requirement of crisis bargaining and escalation control. In political-military crises during the Mao Zedong and Deng Xiaoping eras, Chinese leaders frequently communicated resolve by showing a clear willingness to sustain significant military costs or economic costs, or both. From an American viewpoint, this often involved the risk of significant escalation and excessive damage for what were usually limited objectives. From the Chinese perspective, the willingness to put major assets at risk in a crisis was (and probably remains) essential in order to prevent an even larger conflict and to attain or uphold core objectives or principles. Equally important, Chinese leaders tended to believe that a strong show of resolve was necessary in part to compensate for relative weakness.[98]

When combined with attempts to maximize constraining influences on the adversary (such as via attempts to influence elite and public opinion in other countries), Mao and Deng apparently believed that observance of the conditions associated with the *youli, youli, youjie* concept would decrease the risks involved in showing strong resolve and make deterrence more effective. This would limit escalation, largely by minimizing the likelihood of miscalculation or of a preemptive attack by the adversary. This would be especially true for those crises involving the use of military force to attain limited, primarily political objectives.[99] Such a risk acceptant viewpoint toward the use of force and escalation control apparently also held against a superior (including a nuclear-armed) foe, particularly if vital interests were at stake for China and if delay was seen as more dangerous than action.

According to Chinese observers, many of these requirements for effective crisis management remain relevant today. Moreover, these observers strongly insist that the Chinese commitment to absolute principles does not necessarily lead to uncompromising, zero-sum behavior or excessive risk taking in crises. In fact, according to the chapter by Wang Jisi in this volume, the Chinese government has employed elements of the *youli, youli, youjie* maxim in recent Sino-American crises or near crises as a rationale for compromise.[100]

On the other hand, adherence to the *youli, youli, youjie* maxim does not guarantee success in a crisis. As Allen Whiting notes in this volume, China's attempts at deterrence failed totally during the Korean War, in part because of faulty or ambiguous signaling and the distorted images held by each side toward the other. According to many American scholars, Beijing's attempt at compellence largely failed during the Sino-Vietnam Border War of 1979 as well, again in part because of ambiguous signaling and the use of pauses. During this crisis, there were also clear limits on the ability of China to level credible escalatory threats, primarily because of Soviet pressure. Beijing's experience during the border war with Vietnam illustrates the difficulties created by the effort to prevent unwanted escalation while conveying strong resolve in a crisis.[101]

In addition, excessive confidence in the *youli, youli, youjie* maxim arguably resulted in dangerous risk taking in the past. Many American scholars believe, for example, that in 1969 Mao Zedong took enormous risks when he initiated military conflict against the Soviet Union along the Ussuri (Wusuli) River. Mao apparently instigated and manipulated this crisis in order to distract from the failures of the Cultural Revolution and to convey resolve or defiance against what he saw as a superior bullying power.[102] He apparently believed that China's observance of the above maxim, and hence of many of the eight requirements for crisis management would limit escalation. However, the Soviet Union considered launching a major (possibly nuclear) strike on China after the Chinese attacks. Some American scholars believe that the Soviet Union ultimately escalated its pressure to the point that Mao was eventually compelled to negotiate against his will to avoid any further escalation.[103] In contrast, some Chinese scholars, including some participants at the 2004 Beijing conference, believe that further escalation of the crisis (presumably to all-out war) was avoided largely because of Mao's uncontested supremacy over the Chinese Communist Party (CCP) and the military. In any event, it is unlikely that the current and future Chinese leadership will be so bold as to initiate crises or use force against an overwhelmingly superior power in an effort to attain the above objectives, and with full confidence in the controlling effects of the *youli, youli, youjie* maxim.

U.S. leaders have clearly recognized that control can become problematic in a tense political-military crisis, especially one between two large nuclear powers such as Beijing and Washington. Since the Korean War, the United States has strongly emphasized avoiding direct military conflict with Beijing.[104] Like the Chinese, U.S. leaders seem to recognize the importance of many of the same prudent approaches to crisis management, yet they also believe firmly in the need to display resolve in unmistakable terms. U.S. leaders apparently believe that undesired conflict often results from the failure to demonstrate such resolve early in a major crisis. U.S. decision makers minimize the inherent tension between these two sets of requirements (and hence the danger of undesired escalation in a crisis) by placing great confidence in accurate intelligence and clear communication, close control over military forces (involving strict ROE), and the deterrent effect of the overwhelming superiority of U.S. military power, both conventional and nuclear.

As indicated above, however, such confidence—when combined with an image of the opponent as a "crisis-mongering" aggressor—has at times led U.S. decision makers to downplay prudence in favor of conveying resolve through extremely strong coercive (including nuclear) threats and military alerts or displays. U.S. decision makers have engaged in dramatic escalations over incremental, tit-for-tat exchanges, thus arguably increasing the potential for instability.[105] As the chapter by Robert Suettinger in this volume indicates, Secretary of State John Foster Dulles and President Dwight D. Eisenhower threatened China with the use of tactical nuclear weapons during the 1954–1955 Taiwan Strait crisis. Dulles also threatened the use of high levels of force (perhaps including nuclear weapons) during the second Taiwan Strait crisis in September 1958.[106] In a threat of a much lesser order, the United States also sent two aircraft carrier battle groups to Taiwan to show its resolve during the 1995–1996 Taiwan Strait crisis and thus engaged in significant vertical escalation.[107] Such a calculus has probably not changed significantly since then and suggests that U.S. leaders may be inclined to act preemptively or escalate dramatically in certain kinds of future crises.

Two distinctive viewpoints are apparent in U.S. decision-making circles regarding the type of dramatic escalation Washington should bring to bear in a crisis. One viewpoint favors the use of military bluffs and even nuclear threats over the avoidance of bluffs or conventional threats. This position reflects confidence in U.S. nuclear superiority (and hence escalation dominance) and a fear of loss of direct civilian control over specific actions if conventional (as opposed to nuclear) forces are used to signal in a crisis. Another viewpoint favors the opposite approach and seeks to avoid bluffs and nuclear escalation threats. This stance stresses the use of conventional force, in some cases to establish a "non-nuclear *fait accompli*."[108]

Some U.S. analysts such as Abram Shulsky argue that, regardless of their form, dramatic U.S. military escalations are particularly necessary in Sino-American crises because China is not deterred by lower-level threats or deployments, given the positive view Chinese leaders hold toward such actions as tools in crisis management.[109] Chinese scholars completely reject this argument. They point to the greater restraint that is evident in Chinese thinking toward crises and the use of force today.[110]

Although U.S. decision makers are arguably more inclined than other leaders to level strong coercive threats, they have displayed considerable caution toward the actual use of force against capable opponents. Indeed, some U.S. participants at the 2004 Beijing conference remarked that context is extremely important in assessing risk in a crisis. One participant insisted that Washington would not automatically assume that Beijing must be the weaker and more vulnerable party in a crisis. China's relative capabilities and the level of risks confronting the United States would depend on the circumstances of the particular crisis. Under some circumstances, one U.S. observer remarked, China might have capabilities equal or even superior to those the United States could apply to the situation. This suggests that a significant gap between U.S. words and actions might emerge in a crisis. Whether true or not, this could reinforce the view, held by some Chinese, that the United States could be somewhat easily deterred in a crisis over Taiwan.

VIEWS ABOUT AND FEATURES OF CRISIS SIGNALING. The form, type, timing, and context of signals have greatly influenced the course of past political-military crises between China and the United States. The application of preexisting interpretations or images to crisis signals has also been particularly important.

Several of the case studies in this volume indicate that the absence of credible, private, and consistent lines of communication has produced significant problems during Sino-American crises. During the Korean War, China's warnings to the United States not to cross the 38th parallel were dismissed in part because they were indirect, oral, and conveyed by an individual—Ambassador K. M. Panikkar of India—whom U.S. decision makers such as Secretary of State Dean Acheson and Assistant Secretary of State Dean Rusk did not regard as credible.[111] During the Taiwan Strait crises of 1954–1955 and 1958, Beijing and Washington communicated largely through press conferences, radio and TV speeches, and public media. This situation impaired each side from understanding the other's goals, actions, and domestic politics.[112] Likewise, during the Vietnam War, Beijing sent messages to the United States through Edgar Snow (an American writer), President Muhammad Ayub Khan of Pakistan, and the British chargé d'affaires stating that China would not provoke a war but would fight back if the United States attacked China or threatened the existence of North Vietnam.[113] The lack of a trusted, direct channel of communication meant that neither side could clarify the meaning of a signal with a high degree of reliability.[114]

Even after full diplomatic contacts were established between Washington and Beijing, the two sides continued to lack a trusted channel of communication. Suettinger points out that during the Taiwan Strait crisis of 1995–1996 Washington felt that, despite direct contacts, China was not candid about its goals and intentions, largely because of the extensive PRC use of "standard memorized talking points."[115] According to at least one participant at the 2004 Beijing conference, U.S. decision makers also did not know for sure whether their messages and signals were being accurately received by the top Chinese leadership because their primary direct channel of communication was via a subordinate official who served as the head of the State Council Foreign Affairs Office. Moreover, during the subsequent EP-3 incident of 2001, China and the United States were unable to establish contact quickly. Washington became extremely frustrated by Beijing's initial lack of response despite repeated U.S. calls to Chinese officials.[116] Much of the delay was apparently due to the fact that many senior leaders were in the countryside planting trees as part of a holiday observance when the incident occurred. According to Zhang Tuosheng, this problem reflected the fact that the two sides lacked adequate channels of communication during emergencies.[117]

Finally, Chinese misreadings of U.S. gestures or signals have occurred because of a lack of complete information, presumably resulting in part from an absence of direct contact. Participants at the 2004 Beijing conference noted, for example, that the Chinese side misinterpreted Secretary of State Madeleine K. Albright's letter of apology to China following the accidental bombing of the Chinese embassy in Belgrade in 1999 as the final, official word on the subject. In fact, it was not.

Some participants at the 2004 Beijing conference remarked that Chinese signals can also be misinterpreted today because the Chinese system is less monolithic than in the past. Hence, somewhat different messages can emerge from different individuals and organizations. During the Maoist era, strong centralized control usually guaranteed a single message. Today, a much more complex and amorphous process—which involves much more internal consultation and the possibility that different messages exist—can slow down reaction time and distort signaling. Chinese participants at the 2004 Beijing conference noted, however, that the United States is arguably even less monolithic than China and thus faces more problems in this respect. The Chinese participants contended that the nature of the U.S. system often gives rise to mixed messages that alternate between clarity and vagueness. They argued that in many cases China's messages have been much clearer than those of the United States.

Many signaling problems also occur regardless of the presence or absence of a reliable and speedy communications channel. The political and cultural context has heavily influenced the sending and the reading of specific signals. Chinese participants at the February 2004 Beijing conference noted that the Chinese leadership tended to believe the worst about U.S. signals during the 1995–1996 Taiwan Strait crisis because bilateral relations had worsened considerably beforehand. This negative environment led Chinese leaders to conclude, incorrectly, that Washington was probing China's bottom line when it *inter alia* reversed its stance and granted a visa to the then-president of Taiwan, Lee Teng-hui, allegedly refused to work with Beijing to lessen the consequences of the decision, and then deployed what Beijing viewed as an excessive amount of force (that is, two carrier battle groups) to the Taiwan area.[118] Similarly, according to Wu Baiyi, during the 1999 embassy bombing crisis, the two sides did not talk for several days primarily because of a lack of political trust. At one point, moreover, Chinese officials delayed a direct dialogue between the two sides because of the fear that it would produce a "negative conversation" between President Bill Clinton and President Jiang Zemin, thus resulting in an impasse. According to Wu, the United States incorrectly saw this refusal to hold a direct conversation as a hostile signal.[119] In addition, Chinese crisis signals have often lacked specificity or have been cloaked in ideological phrases, thus potentially creating misunderstanding.[120]

Some American observers believe that misunderstandings have occurred in past crises because of mirror imaging. In particular, China's adversaries have interpreted certain signals or moves by Beijing as they themselves would have intended them. Shulsky, for example, argues that China's use of restrained rhetoric, absence of military deployments, and pauses in military attacks during crises have at times led adversaries to conclude incorrectly that their own resolute rhetoric and actions were deterring Chinese behavior. Often Beijing was instead attempting to regroup, infiltrate, draw the adversary in deeper, or simply communicate restraint and prudence on its own initiative.[121]

Sometimes Beijing's apparent preference for less convincing verbal warnings over what might arguably be seen as more credible overt military deployments or alerts reflected the tactics of an inferior power in a crisis. During the Korean War and the Sino-Soviet border clash, for example, China's leaders apparently avoided the use of overt military signals in order to maintain the element of surprise. They also hoped to permit the concentration of a superior force at the enemy's point of weakness, in preparation for the possible failure of deterrence or compellence.[122] Such behavior often prompted the adversary to assume, incorrectly, that China was irresolute.[123] Of course, at times, military signaling is entirely inappropriate. According to Wu Baiyi, during the EP-3 incident, the Chinese government intentionally increased the diplomatic rank of those sending messages to Washington—from Wang Yingfan to Tang Jiaxuan to Hu Jintao—in order to show the United States the seriousness of the situation.[124]

Finally, some American analysts have argued that China's crisis signaling is an expression of a more offensively oriented crisis bargaining approach as opposed to a more prudent crisis management signaling of the type outlined above. These analysts argue that Chinese crisis signals are primarily designed to convey warnings and to prepare the ground for decisive moves and eventual military conflict if the adversary does not comply. They believe that Chinese crisis signals are not primarily designed to negotiate the resolution of a crisis or to avoid a conflict via prolonged diplomatic signaling and negotiation.[125]

Chinese participants at the 2004 Beijing conference strongly rejected this argument, however, even for the Mao and Deng eras. They insisted that even though China's leaders might have already relinquished much hope that the crisis could be resolved when they issued their signals, in most cases, Chinese signals were nonetheless intended to de-escalate the situation.[126] In fact, neither argument is correct as a general proposition although both contain elements of truth. On the one hand, Chinese signaling has often consisted of deterrence-oriented warnings that, when ignored, often resulted in escalation. On the other hand, the ultimate purpose of such warnings was usually to de-escalate the crisis, if possible. Whether such behavior is more or less offensively oriented depends on whether Chinese warnings were intended as serious ultimatums. The record is unclear on this point.

The United States, like China, has used a wide variety of signals during political-military crises. These signals have been public and private, diplomatic and military, clear and ambiguous, and highly threatening and restrained.[127] Although the type and timing of signals has often depended on the nature of the crisis, the larger political context, and the preferences of the president, the United States has generally strongly emphasized the use of military alerts or deployments to convey resolve in a major crisis. U.S. leaders have usually also seemed to prefer clear, decisive signals and direct, timely communication with the other side over more ambiguous, incremental moves and indirect or delayed communication. This approach to signaling derives to a significant extent from a confidence in U.S. military superiority and the belief that clarity, directness, and timeliness in signaling are important components of successful crisis management.[128]

Exceptions to this general rule have occurred at times. Suettinger, for example, argues in his chapter that Eisenhower intentionally used ambiguity to his advantage during the Taiwan Strait crisis. Moreover, some of the Chinese participants at the 2004 Beijing conference argued that the United States has employed vague and inconsistent signals to an even greater degree than China. This is sometimes connected with alleged inconsistencies or contradictions in U.S. diplomacy. For example, the United States claims to be indifferent toward the outcome of the Taipei-Beijing imbroglio as long as it is peacefully resolved. On the other hand, it arms Taipei and supports Taiwan's democratic development in ways that, for many Chinese, encourage greater movement toward independence, thus suggesting a U.S. preference for that outcome.

Domestic Politics and Public Opinion

The domestic political and social environment within which crisis decision makers operate can significantly condition crisis behavior and leadership attempts to manage a crisis successfully. The domestic political and social environment, for example, can limit or shape options, increase rigidity, slow response times, and distort signals in a crisis. The literature on such domestic factors focuses primarily on two areas: (1) the impact of leadership politics (including the specific distribution of power and personal relationships among the senior national security elite as well as their individual political objectives) and (2) the influence of the media, public opinion, and other forms of popular pressure on the government.[129]

In most states, crisis decisions that affect national security and potentially involve the use of military force, whether indirect or direct, are highly controlled by a small number of senior political and military leaders. The concentration of power among the senior elite and the way they interact to determine, implement, and revise key crisis decisions can vary significantly, however. In some cases, there is a relatively high concentration of power among sharply competitive elites who operate through largely informal processes. In other cases, there is a relatively diffused level of power among less competitive elites who operate on the basis of primarily formal institutions and procedures.

Crisis behavior within authoritarian regimes often reflects the views, personalities, and interests of the paramount leader and, to a lesser extent, the most senior military and civilian colleagues of that leader. In the case of tightly controlled totalitarian states dominated by a single, often charismatic autocrat, the supreme ruler often makes critical crisis decisions alone, with little if any meaningful input from other senior leaders.[130] Moreover, within such highly centralized regimes, the opinion of ordinary citizens rarely, if ever, exerts a significant, independent influence upon such decisions. The paramount leader or the leader's subordinates generally manipulate the views of the public and the media, when relevant.

Some analysts believe that authoritarian leaders at times create or exacerbate crises to distract public attention from internal problems, to bolster their prestige and authority among the masses, to mobilize popular support for specific policies, or to combat challenges by other senior figures.[131] Dominant authoritarian leaders may also be more able and willing to take risks during a crisis than their less powerful counterparts because of the absence of any meaningful internal checks on their authority and the high possibility that such individuals possess an inflated sense of their own power and intelligence. Dominant leaders of authoritarian states can arguably also make decisions more quickly and perhaps more efficiently in a crisis, which can be an advantage under certain conditions.

In more mature, less tightly controlled authoritarian regimes, crisis decisions can involve a greater degree of genuine consultation among senior leaders, advisers, and implementers. In some instances, genuine collective decision making can occur in which the senior leader must obtain the tacit or explicit consent of colleagues on all key crisis decisions. In addition, within authoritarian regimes the dynamics of power competition among the senior leadership can have a great influence on crisis behavior because of the highly personalized nature of power within such states and the absence or scarcity of clear procedures and institutions for mediating conflict and resolving political succession. In other words, to an even greater degree than might occur in a regime dominated by a single extremely powerful leader, one or more leaders can manipulate a crisis to generate support among the public or to attack rivals for power. Such looser authoritarian regimes are at the same time more open to outside contact and permit greater freedom of movement and social, economic, and cultural activity among the populace. Under such circumstances, individuals or groups outside the senior elite can possess the motivation and the means to express attitudes or even to pressure the government on various national security–related issues and, therefore, to influence the course of a crisis.[132]

Crisis behavior within nonauthoritarian, liberal democratic regimes is also largely dominated by a small number of senior political and military leaders. In fact, within the senior elite, it is arguably the case that a president or prime minister exerts more power over key crisis decisions than does a counterpart within a loose authoritarian system. A president or prime minister possesses formal authority as commander in chief, head of the executive branch, or creator of the governmental cabinet. In contrast, an authoritarian leader, as the first among equals, holds a relatively weaker political and institutional position within a less formal and often highly competitive leadership structure. In a democracy, the media and public opinion can exert a significant, ongoing influence over senior elected leaders during a crisis, particularly a prolonged crisis. Remarks by highly-respected news commentators and media coverage in general can significantly influence the level of public support for the president or prime minister and the administration during a lengthy crisis. Such support can in turn influence legislative positions toward both the crisis and other policy actions taken by the government and can affect the political fortunes of the chief executive and the chief executive's party in future elections.[133]

These political and social factors can significantly influence decisions made by a nonauthoritarian government during key stages of a crisis. At the same time, the type of influence they exert can vary widely, depending in part on the subjective views of senior decision makers regarding the acceptability and importance of public opinion.[134] Under some circumstances, political concerns can intensify the so-called commitment trap discussed above, locking leaders into aggressive courses of action. Therefore, some analysts argue the commitment trap strengthens the credibility of coercive threats by democratic leaders, given the potentially high cost involved in retreating from a stated position.[135] However, similar threats by leaders of totalitarian regimes might be viewed as equally credible, given these leaders' ability to ignore popular or elite counterpressures. Some scholarly studies also argue that leaders of democratic systems at times use crises for domestic political ends, such as to gain support for a grand strategy.[136]

Domestic factors are often critically important for both China and the United States in a political-military crisis. In some instances, they may be more important than external factors. In fact, some observers of Chinese crisis behavior, including some of the Chinese participants at the 2004 Beijing conference, believe that domestic interests always trump foreign policy interests in a crisis. Still, little is known about the critical details regarding the specific manner, degree, and conditionality of such influence, especially in the Chinese case. In addition, each government displays a woefully inadequate understanding of how domestic factors influence the other side's crisis behavior.

The Chinese experience largely confirms the above theories concerning the behavior of both tight and loose authoritarian regimes. Crisis decisions in China have been undertaken by a small, leading nucleus of civilian and military figures led—or, in some instances, entirely dominated—by the paramount leader. The paramount leader has often performed a unique role as initiator, shaper, guider, and implementer of crisis decisions. The views, authority, prestige, specific institutional power, personal contacts, and decision-making style of the paramount leader have thus likely exerted decisive influence over Chinese crisis decision making. The specific pattern of control and level of influence over the decision-making process exercised by the paramount leader has varied significantly over time, however. This variation is largely due to differences in the personality and power of the paramount leader and the broader evolution of the Chinese political-military leadership structure from a charismatic-revolutionary regime to a more mature, institutionalized authoritarian system.[137]

Mao Zedong was clearly the dominant decision maker in all major crises or near crises from the 1950s until the early 1970s. Although the senior party leadership as a whole (usually consisting of the Politburo Standing Committee) often debated and analyzed crisis situations, in every instance Mao shaped or determined the leadership's basic assessment of the precipitating crisis and influenced the formulation and evaluation of possible crisis options. He either directly made the decision to use force or guaranteed that a formal organization over which he presided would make the decision. Mao also played a major role in supervising the implementation of crisis decisions and led the effort to evaluate and adjust crisis behavior over time. Often, Mao's superior authority allowed him to strike compromises in a crisis that less powerful leaders might have been unwilling or unable to make for fear of being attacked by their rivals.[138] In carrying out these activities, Mao was assisted by one or two senior colleagues responsible for critical diplomatic-political or military activities.[139] Together, these leaders constituted a type of informal leadership nucleus in charge of all key crisis decisions in the area of national security crisis management. In many crises, lower-level officials were almost completely left in the dark regarding a particular decision. Nonetheless, they would implement the decision according to established policies provided from above. As a result, the Mao era crisis decision-making process usually produced a single decision with a single message.

The basic leadership dynamics of the crisis decision-making process remained essentially the same during the Dengist era from the late 1970s to the early 1990s. Deng Xiaoping dominated decision making before and during crises such as the Sino-Vietnam Border War of 1979.[140] Deng, however, was arguably more compelled than Mao to consult during crises and compromise with his senior colleagues, especially those retired or semiretired cadres of the revolutionary generation.[141]

The role of the paramount leader in political-military crises has changed in more significant ways since Mao and Deng. Although Jiang Zemin and Hu Jintao have apparently exercised considerable power over major crises or near crises, their ability to shape or influence, much less control, crisis decision making has been considerably less than that of Deng and certainly of Mao.[142] This is largely because individual leaders of the post-Mao–post-Deng era command far less authority and prestige than their predecessors and have fewer personal contacts among a narrower range of institutions.[143] Thus, to govern effectively, the paramount leader must seriously consider the views and actions of senior colleagues within the Politburo Standing Committee. These views and actions may, at times, constrain the paramount leader. Moreover, in crises that potentially involve the use of force, the paramount leader must also no doubt pay particularly close attention to the views of senior military leaders.[144] In short, the decision-making process has to some significant degree become more collective in nature since the Deng era.[145] As a result, the bureaucratic and political interests and views of civilian and senior leaders (including differences between hard-liners and soft-liners) can exert a significant influence over Beijing's behavior in a political-military crisis. For example, according to some Chinese observers, China's top leaders especially need to explain and justify themselves to those internal forces that advocate a tougher line against Taiwan.[146]

The limited evidence available suggests that the 1995–1996 Taiwan Strait crisis reflected the more complex leadership dynamic in place in China today.[147] Overall, Jiang Zemin apparently played a central role in each major crisis decision because of his authority as party general secretary and chairman of the CCP Central Military Commission (CMC) and because of his position as director of the CCP's Taiwan Affairs Leading Small Group, a critical policy coordination body for China's Taiwan policy.[148] As CMC chairman and CCP general secretary, Jiang approved all the military exercises and missile "tests" undertaken during the crisis, although it is highly unlikely that he supervised, much less directed, military operations as Mao and Deng had done.[149] Like Mao and Deng, Jiang also had to consult with his colleagues during each stage of the crisis. At one stage, Jiang had to present arguments against a direct confrontation with the United States.[150] In carrying out this leadership role, Jiang acted as first among equals, directing a largely collaborative—albeit at times contentious—policy process.[151]

As predicted by the theoretical literature, some scholarly studies have also shown that Chinese leaders such as Mao have attempted to use crises to bolster internal authority or support for their political positions through distraction or mobilization. In general, the effort to use external crises to mobilize populations for political purposes or to velop national power has been more evident in China than attempts to use crises as a means of diverting domestic dissent during periods of internal unrest.[152]

Little concrete evidence is available on the extent to which the media and public sentiment have influenced the Chinese decision-making process during specific political-military crises. The paramount leader and senior colleagues have primarily used the Chinese media to build domestic and foreign support for their actions and policies, to control public reactions to unfolding crises, and to convey specific messages to foreign governments as part of Beijing's overall efforts to influence adversaries during a crisis. In recent years, the government has also used the media to both stimulate and dampen nationalist public reactions to the actions of adversaries.[153]

In general, during the post-Deng era, the propaganda apparatus and the media have become less subservient to the views and decisions of the senior leadership. The propaganda apparatus tends to be more conservative than other institutions (and perhaps some leaders) and is primarily oriented toward domestic audiences. The broader media are more diverse in their viewpoints and are often dominated by younger individuals. The broader media sometimes both direct and reflect public sentiment, thus creating an avenue for more independent pressure on the leadership during a crisis.[154] However, one Chinese participant at the 2004 Beijing conference stated that, since the embassy bombing of 1999, the Chinese government has greatly strengthened its control over the media, especially the mainstream media.

Public views and actions did not play a significant independent role during the major political-military crises of the Maoist and Dengist eras. Moreover, although some public anger toward President Lee Teng-hui and the United States was evident during the 1995–1996 Taiwan Strait crisis, there is no solid evidence that such sentiments directly influenced the perceptions or specific actions taken by the leadership at that time. During these crises, Chinese leaders generally did not need to worry about or play to specific public views or pressure.[155] This situation has changed notably since the late 1990s, however, as nationalist sentiments have become more openly and stridently expressed among the populace and criticism of the U.S. government has grown by leaps and bounds.

The internet and cell phones in particular have become particularly important—in Chinese cities—for the rapid receipt and dissemination of news and information and the expression of public views, and for the organization of demonstrations, with and without government permission or encouragement. Nationalist, anti-U.S. sentiments and protests were very evident in the Chinese response to the Belgrade embassy bombing and the EP-3 incident.[156] More recently, large numbers of Chinese protestors conducted angry, anti-Japanese protests in several Chinese cities, fueled by internet and cell phone communications.[157] Some Chinese participants at the 2004 Beijing conference stated that public pressure in crises with the United States has become a far more serious issue for Chinese leaders than for U.S. leaders.[158]

More evident nationalist feelings among the public and the growing complexity of some issues that are confronted during a crisis require much greater levels of coordination within the government and, at times, a much greater level of solicitation of views from nongovernmental experts than has occurred in the past.[159] The public expression of (sometimes extreme) nationalist views and sentiments challenges the ability of the Chinese government to maintain a balanced and prudent course of action in a crisis, rather than to be led by more extremist viewpoints. Such public expressions can greatly reinforce the desire of China's leaders to avoid appearing weak, irresolute, intimidated, or not fully in control of events during a confrontation with a foreign power, especially the United States. The Chinese leadership apparently fears that efforts to suppress ultra-nationalist demonstrations might provoke a severe public backlash that could undermine the legitimacy of the regime. That said, it is difficult to assess exactly how nationalist sentiments among the populace influence the crisis behavior of the Chinese government. Such public views could prompt senior leaders to become either more risk acceptant or more risk averse, depending on the circumstances. Leaders might create or aggravate popular nationalist sentiments for their own political purposes. Alternatively, strong public sentiments could pressure leaders to resolve a crisis quickly without further escalation, perhaps because of the fear that angry protests might eventually turn against the government. This probably means that Chinese leaders will attempt to use nationalist sentiments to their advantage in a crisis. This could prolong or intensify the event in many instances. On the other hand, Chinese leaders will also endeavor to maintain strong control over public behavior and resolve the incident before nationalist pressures become excessive. The timing and form of this delicate balance will depend greatly on the nature of the crisis and the apparent success of the Chinese government in handling it to the satisfaction of the public.

The Chinese government obviously sought to channel, control, and perhaps manipulate popular views and behavior during recent crises such as the Belgrade embassy bombing and the EP-3 incident.[160] Kurt Campbell argues that, following the embassy bombing, Chinese authorities—for reasons that are not entirely clear—initially permitted large public protests outside U.S. diplomatic facilities. Beijing may have sought to use the public protests to strengthen its hand in negotiations with Washington by showing that the crisis was extremely volatile and required careful handling (and perhaps U.S. concessions) to avoid a major deterioration in relations.[161] Beijing may have also sought to use the protests to strengthen its domestic legitimacy by showing publicly that it sympathized with the Chinese people's righteous indignation.[162] In any event, according to Wu Baiyi, the Chinese government soon attempted to manage—and then dampen—these protests. Both Kurt Campbell and Wu Baiyi suggest that Beijing eventually decided to suppress the protests in large part because of concerns that they might seriously damage relations with the United States. Beijing was also concerned that public sentiment might turn against the Chinese government if the demonstrations were allowed to continue, thus confirming, in this instance, the above hypothesis.[163]

Overall, the Chinese participants in the 2004 Beijing conference insisted that Chinese leaders no longer need to use crises to build popular and elite support for the government because China's top priority today is no longer Maoist "class struggles at home and abroad." Instead, Chinese leaders seek economic development, which requires a peaceful and benevolent international environment. Chinese participants pointed out that the Chinese leadership sees popular nationalism as a double-edged sword that provides no reliable foundation for political legitimacy in the long run. In addition, some Chinese participants recognized that the voices of both the general public and the news media in China will become increasingly independent over the long run. They also stressed that the Chinese government adamantly believes that on some subjects the Chinese public has extremely strong views that the government cannot ignore. Perhaps the most notable example of this, in their view, is the public's opposition to Taiwan independence.

Domestic factors have often played a critical role in how the U.S. government has handled crises with China. The U.S. president today probably possesses more power in a political-military crisis than does the president's Chinese counterpart. On the other hand, it is also undeniably true that the media and public opinion can shape the perceptions and actions of a U.S. president in an intense political-military crisis, even when the president is inclined to downplay such factors. This is especially the case if the crisis is prolonged.[164] Such domestic factors can exert both negative and positive influences, intensifying the so-called commitment trap while also increasing the credibility of U.S. signals of resolve.

Broader domestic political considerations can also influence presidential calculations in a crisis. The preexisting balance of political forces in Congress is particularly important, as is the overall public mood toward the adversary in a crisis. Several of the chapters in this volume suggest that pressures created at the time by the U.S. Congress and the public have played more of a role than concerns over how the handling of a crisis might affect a leader's future reelection chances. Allen Whiting, for example, argues that Congress and the public complicated the calculations of President Harry S. Truman and Secretary of State Dean Acheson during the lead-up to the Chinese intervention in the Korean War, especially regarding whether to attack China or withdraw from Korea. In particular, the two leaders faced considerable pressure from the Republican right and Senator Joseph R. McCarthy (R-Wis.) as well as from the public via the media.[165]

Suettinger remarks that President Eisenhower's perceptions and actions during the 1954–1955 and 1958 Taiwan Strait crises were most likely influenced by congressional sentiment and public opinion, albeit in different ways. In the earlier crisis, Eisenhower had a freer hand in confronting China because of strong anticommunist views among the public and members of Congress. Congress in particular was heavily influenced by the China lobby, which supported Chiang Kai-shek and his government on Taiwan. This gave Eisenhower considerable freedom of action despite the stark division of the Republican Party between ultraconservatives and moderates. In contrast, Eisenhower faced far more opposition in 1958 from the Congress, which by then had a Democratic Party majority, and a public that was deeply concerned with the administration's nuclear threats.[166]

Domestic politics also played a particularly important role in influencing presidential decisions during the subsequent 1995–1996 Taiwan Strait crisis. Suettinger argues that President Bill Clinton faced a hostile Republican Congress that opposed many elements of his Taiwan policy and supported Lee Teng-hui's visit to Cornell University. Public opinion had not fully recovered from the 1989 Tiananmen incident. Moreover, in the mid-1990s there were fewer strategic reasons to maintain positive relations with China. In contrast, public support for Taiwan, which was democratizing, was high. Taiwanese lobbying was particularly effective in gaining congressional support.[167] Ultimately, Clinton was forced to grant Lee Teng-hui a visa to visit Cornell—despite a clear awareness among many senior officials of the dangers involved for Sino-U.S. relations—to avoid having Congress pass a binding resolution that could diminish the president's control over foreign policy. Moreover, subsequent U.S. actions during the crisis, including the deployment of two U.S. carriers to the Taiwan area, were taken in part to mollify congressional pressure for more hard-line actions.[168]

Concerns about public opinion were also important to U.S. crisis management during the EP-3 incident. Former commander in chief of the U.S. Pacific Command, Dennis Blair, indicates in this volume that U.S. officials felt pressure to quickly release a statement regarding the incident in order to avoid press reports based on leaks and rumors and to avoid charges of a "cover-up."[169] U.S. government officials did not want the Chinese decision to hold the EP-3 crew on Hainan Island to be portrayed as a hostage crisis that bore similarities to the Iranian hostage crisis. They feared that a public perception of a hostage crisis could greatly damage both Sino-American relations and the power of President George W. Bush.[170] Analyst Paul Godwin argues that throughout the crisis the Bush administration faced pressure from right-wing Republicans and conservative media commentators such as William Kristol to take a hard-line stance toward China.[171]

Finally, one major factor to consider regarding the role of domestic pressure on both U.S. and Chinese leaders during a crisis is the effect of such pressure on the other side. Does the presence of strong domestic public pressure on a crisis decision maker increase his or her leverage vis-à-vis the adversary by increasing, for example, the credibility of appeals by the former for caution or restraint by the latter? Alternatively, does it undermine such leverage, because the adversary does not understand the role of domestic pressure on the other side, for example, or because such domestic pressure complicates signaling? This issue will require further research.[172]

Decision-Making Structure and Process

The American literature on political-military crises places a great emphasis on the impact of the formal and informal structure and processes of the decision-making system upon leadership perceptions and behavior. The mechanism for making decisions shapes the ultimate content of those decisions. The literature suggests that the most important issues include the influence of intragroup dynamics (especially between the senior leader and the leader's top advisers); the effect of interbureaucratic competition (the so-called "bureaucratic politics" model), and the excessive reliance by decision makers on limited sources of intelligence or information provided by the bureaucracy.[173] Another particularly important issue is the fact of time constraints and the resulting reliance on preexisting organizational perspectives and processes (including standard operating procedures or preexisting military plans).[174]

These factors can directly influence critical components of crisis behavior such as threat perception, the speed and efficiency of decisions, the availability of options, the quality and type of intelligence received, and the level of central control over aspects of implementation. These potential problems may be more present within well-established regimes with highly institutionalized patterns of governance. Such regimes rely on more complex, deeply ingrained patterns of decision making than less institutionalized, more personalized systems of rule. It is not surprising, therefore, that the literature on this subject largely focuses on crisis decision making within the U.S. political system.

In China, the importance of organizational structures and processes in crisis decision making has apparently increased as the Chinese political system has become more bureaucratic and functionally specialized.

The increasing dependence of China's senior leaders upon complex structures to collect and process critical information, implement policies, and generate support for specific decisions has also raised the importance of organizational structures and processes. That said, not enough information is available in the historical record to draw reasonably reliable conclusions about how organizations and related bureaucratic and policy-making procedures have specifically shaped, constrained, or even perhaps undermined the perceptions and actions of China's paramount leader and his senior associates during a political-military crisis. Nonetheless, some general observations can be made on the basis of existing literature and new information and insights contained in the case studies presented in this volume.

During the Mao Zedong era, political and military organizations served largely to facilitate and strengthen Mao's exercise of decision-making power vis-à-vis his senior colleagues and over the system as a whole. Specifically, upper-level policy organs such as the CCP Central Committee, Politburo, Politburo Standing Committee, CCP Central Military Commission, central work conferences, party plenums, and the government council (the precursor to the State Council) were used by Mao to

- Discuss a crisis situation and assess the pros and cons of various possible policy actions;
- Identify those who supported or opposed a particular policy action (especially actions favored by Mao);
- Persuade or co-opt the majority of the senior leadership into ultimately supporting Mao's preferred course of action, which presumably made it more difficult to level blame against Mao and his closest associates in the event of policy failure while it also strengthened the paramount leader's overall authority within the system;
- Approve formally the implementation of decisions and recommendations taken by subordinate organs; and
- Legitimate actions and decisions taken by Mao and his senior associates in the eyes of the larger political and military elite.

Lower-level bureaucratic organizations served primarily as instruments for intelligence and information collection and processing and for policy coordination and implementation, sometimes under the direct command of Mao or Premier Zhou Enlai. Participants at these meetings sometimes formulated and presented specific action recommendations to Mao and the senior leadership during a crisis. Special organizations—sometimes regional in orientation—were at times formed to facilitate the use of military force during crises involving armed conflict.[175]

Very little solid information is available on the types and purposes of specific organizations used during crises that took place during the Deng Xiaoping and Jiang Zemin eras. Yet organizational and procedural factors undoubtedly grew in complexity and importance during these periods. As the absolute power of individual leaders has declined in China, the level of bureaucratic and technical specialization of the elite has increased and become more compartmentalized. The potential use-of-force situations leaders face during crises have arguably become more complex and technically demanding. As a result, the leadership's dependence on more sophisticated organizations and formal procedures has grown. These organizations may also be more independent or assertive. In particular, Chinese leaders during political-military crises have almost certainly become more reliant on specialized expertise held by members of organizations such as the military and the Ministry of Foreign Affairs (MFA) and by experts attached to a wide (and growing) range of government institutes.

The dearth of information regarding the increasingly important organizational and procedural context of the post-Mao era is perhaps best explained by two simple facts: First, crises during the Deng and Jiang eras have been less momentous than crises (such as the Korean War) during the Maoist era and hence have been examined in less detail. Second, the Chinese government regards more recent crises as highly sensitive events that cannot be openly examined. Nonetheless, some partial and tentative observations on the role of organizations and the procedures in the decision-making process can be made from the limited information obtained by the author, including information provided in this volume.

Although the same type of high-level organizations apparently served much the same function during crises in the Deng era as they did in the Mao era, there were some differences. During the Sino-Vietnam Border War of 1979, for example, regular and enlarged meetings of the Politburo, the Politburo Standing Committee, central work conferences, and a party plenum deliberated over and formally adopted key decisions regarding the use of force against Vietnam. In partial contrast with the Mao era, these organs (or at least the Politburo Standing Committee) probably served more as foci for genuine deliberation and decision making than as mechanisms to facilitate or legitimate the paramount leader's positions and strengthen his authority. Still, Deng's role in shaping (and hence dominating) the actions taken by the bureaucracy remained critical.[176]

Little information is available on the role played by lower-level organizations during crisis decisions in the Deng era, but it appears that their role was similar to what it was during the Maoist period. The CMC, for example, was critical in assessing the military situation. Deng was apparently more directly involved in these deliberations than Mao, who usually assigned Zhou Enlai to supervise such meetings on his behalf. Moreover, in 1979 Deng created a northern front under the command of Li Desheng to defend against a possible Soviet attack and a southern front under the command of Xu Shiyou to organize the attack on Vietnam. Beijing later created the Eastern Xinjiang Military Region to strengthen the defense against the Soviet Union.[177]

During the Jiang era (and probably during the Hu Jintao era as well), many of these same upper-level and lower-level organs were involved in the crisis decision-making process.[178] The chapter by Wu Baiyi suggests that the MFA was the most important ministry-level organization during the embassy bombing crisis of 1999. It provided critical advice to the senior party leadership and took the lead in implementing leaders' decisions while it shaped and coordinated the activities of other organizations.[179] At the same time, there is no question that the number and sophistication of the bureaucratic actors and specialist advisers involved in all aspects of Chinese policy making have grown significantly since at least the early 1990s.[180] According to well-informed Chinese observers, senior leaders are increasingly dependent upon subordinate functional bureaucracies (and in some cases outside experts) for the receipt of important information and analyses and the formulation of proposals during a political-military crisis or foreign policy incident. Thus, it is virtually certain that state and party organs and related policy-making procedures—as well as government-related scholars—have increasingly influenced the crisis perceptions and actions of Jiang Zemin, Hu Jintao, and other members of the post-Deng senior leadership. The more complex and institutionalized nature of the decision-making process suggests that the senior leadership, particularly the paramount leader, is less able to dominate some aspects of decision making such as intelligence and policy implementation. Moreover, despite efforts to place operational control in the hands of the MFA, more diverse messages almost certainly emerge from the Chinese government during a crisis today. This reflects the involvement in various aspects of the decision making or implementation process of a larger number of more relatively autonomous actors and perhaps the lack of clear procedures for managing crises. This more complex and diverse process could slow reaction time and distort signaling.[181] Thus, overall, the Chinese system today is no doubt increasingly prone to the organizational influences on crisis behavior that are evident in more institutionalized political systems.[182]

The Chinese military deserves particular attention for its role in the crisis decision-making process. During the Maoist era, senior military leaders enjoyed considerable prestige and were well known by their colleagues within the civilian apparatus, many of whom were former military leaders themselves. Hence, individual military leaders could, and sometimes did, vigorously advocate their views. They even questioned Mao's viewpoint at times. If the decision in question involved military deployments, Mao would have to listen carefully to their views. Yet, the military did not in any sense check Mao's decision-making power. Moreover, even though military commanders had considerable freedom in implementing the orders given to units in the field, Mao usually issued such orders, was informed of the movement of all major units, and at times personally directed their movements. He also ensured the observance of strict ROE in political-military crises.[183]

Today, military leaders do not have such close personal ties to civilian leaders. The relationship between civilian and military heads is largely professional and is shaped by the functions of their respective institutions. Some personal links do form at senior levels as a result of the personnel promotion process and frequent contact during policy meetings. However, the high level of personal familiarity, close interaction between senior civilian and military leaders, and significant authority of senior military leaders within upper decision-making circles evident during the Maoist era no longer exist. Senior civilian leaders today have little knowledge of military affairs and must carefully consider the views of military leaders during a crisis if relevant. In some instances, this means that civilian leaders must essentially depend upon the professional views and judgment of their military colleagues regarding technical military issues. However, as in the Maoist era, military leaders cannot veto or dictate decisions of civilian leaders.[184] Indeed, according to several Chinese participants at the 2004 Beijing conference, the party leadership continues to exercise total control over the military, especially during crises.

That said, as in other political systems, the information supplied to the senior Chinese leadership by military sources and the operational plans and procedures of the military can significantly shape the perceptions and options of senior civilian decision makers in a crisis. For example, some U.S. observers believe that military reports on the aircraft collision during the EP-3 incident were the sole source of information provided to the senior leadership and could not be independently confirmed by the leaders. Some of the U.S. participants at the 2004 Beijing conference related that, as the 1995–1996 Taiwan Strait crisis evolved, China's senior leadership apparently never reexamined an already approved operational plan for exercises and missile firings that had been drawn up by the military.[185]

Several Chinese participants at the 2004 Beijing conference stated that, since the embassy bombing incident, task forces or coordinating mechanisms have been established at both the decision-making and working levels to improve the handling of domestic and foreign crises. The senior leadership has established the National Security Leading Group to handle national security issues. However, the detailed functions and responsibilities of these groups and their relationships with one another and with the top leadership are unclear. In particular, the relationship of the National Security Leading Group to supreme decision-making bodies such as the Politburo Standing Committee cannot be determined.

The United States has been the focus of most of the general Western literature on the influence of the decision-making system upon crisis behavior. This literature indicates that the U.S. crisis decision-making apparatus has also evolved over time—although probably not as much as in the Chinese case—as part of the broader evolution of the national security decision-making process. Relatively well-defined structures and procedures for national security decision making were first established in response to the outbreak of the Cold War and the emergence of the so-called national security state in the late 1940s and early 1950s. Organizationally, this system centered on the National Security Council (NSC), created in 1947 under President Harry S. Truman to address domestic, foreign, and military policies in the context of U.S. national security. The NSC originally comprised the president, the vice president, the secretaries of state and defense, and other officials from the executive and military branches who were included at the president's discretion, such as the director of the Central Intelligence Agency and the chairman of the Joint Chiefs of Staff (JCS). The NSC also had a staff headed by an executive secretary, who was appointed by the president.[186] The function of the NSC and associated groups and their importance to the president in the overall national security policy process has differed somewhat in each administration.[187] The power of the NSC as a whole and the influence of the NSC adviser and the adviser's staff have also evolved over time.[188]

In general, the U.S. decision-making system during political-military crises has centered on the president (sometimes assisted by unofficial close personal advisers), the president's national security team (which includes many of those posts that originally constituted the NSC as well as the now powerful national security adviser, who is supported by the NSC staff), and several relevant implementing civilian and military bureaucracies. Although fairly formal in structure and function from the outset, this system became increasingly institutionalized over time in tandem with the evolution of the NSC structure according to the preferences and foibles of each president. Most bureaucratic participants eventually acquired very well-defined lines of authority and responsibility during the crisis decision-making process that were focused primarily upon the production of intelligence, information, and analysis and the provision of options and recommendations for the president. The military in particular has played a critical role in many U.S. political-military crises through its implementation of the senior leadership's decisions, provision of critical intelligence, or the direct involvement of its top officers in decisions.

Even in its early post–World War II years, the U.S. crisis decision-making system was probably relatively more formalized, predictable, and transparent than its Chinese counterpart. In the implementation phase, it was perhaps less subject than in the Chinese case to the direct control and intervention of the paramount leader, the president. Over time, the U.S. crisis decision-making system has most likely become more efficient and systematic than has the Chinese system, eventually adapting procedures established for the standard interagency process that governs day-to-day policy deliberations.[189] Although the U.S. crisis decision-making process undoubtedly remains prone to the potential problems or features mentioned at the beginning of this section, some U.S. participants at the 2004 Beijing conference stressed the increasing role that area specialists have played in the U.S. crisis decision-making process.[190] Even more than in the Chinese case, in the United States a wide variety of individual and bureaucratic actors can influence high-level decisions at various stages of the process.

Several of these factors influenced U.S. behavior during Sino-American crises. Allen Whiting's analysis of the Korean conflict indicates that divisions among senior officials who advised President Truman about military actions such as military retaliation against Chinese territory, the use of Nationalist Chinese troops, and the imposition of a naval blockade resulted in deferred decisions and calls for further study at critical points in the escalating conflict. These divisions distracted Truman from "the problem of managing MacArthur."[191] Similarly, Suettinger argues that the crisis decisions of President Eisenhower and Secretary of State Dulles during the 1954–1955 Taiwan Strait crisis "occasionally came as a result of focused efforts to resolve internal U.S. government bureaucratic problems, rather than as well thought-out efforts to resolve the foreign affairs issue."[192]

Suettinger also shows how differences between Eisenhower and the U.S. military influenced both Taiwan Strait crises of the 1950s. Even though Eisenhower needed the support of the military to implement his policies during the crises, for example, he resisted giving them independent control over decisions to use tactical nuclear weapons, and he often disregarded their specific policy recommendations "either because they represented the fractured and parochial interests of the different services, or because he disagreed with their aggressive advocacy of the use of American military power."[193] Overall, Suettinger criticizes the crisis management process used by Eisenhower during both crises despite the president's strong use of the recently strengthened NSC system.[194]

Whiting argues that President Lyndon B. Johnson relied far less on any formal, regularized procedures and structures to make critical crisis-related decisions during the Vietnam War. Johnson rarely convened the NSC as a body to address the escalation of war in Vietnam and the resultant possibility of Chinese ground force intervention. The most critical decisions involved an informal Tuesday Lunch Group of varied membership. As a result of Johnson's reliance on unofficial, informal procedures and groups, it is difficult to determine when and under whose advice Johnson made his key decisions.[195] This also makes it extremely difficult to assess how the decision-making process itself might have influenced behavior. Whiting does offer one example of such influence: apparent inattention to specific ROE for U.S. aircraft flying over or near North Vietnam in early 1965 arguably resulted in an unintended air clash with PLA fighters over Hainan Island. This could have precipitated unwanted escalation, and it led to a belated stress on aspects of the ROE that precluded hot pursuit over the territorial sea or airspace of the PRC.[196]

Suettinger's analysis of the 1995–1996 Taiwan Strait crisis suggests that crisis decision making under President Clinton had become more inclusive, institutionalized, and systematic.[197] Yet, as in the past, the entire process was under the control of the president, who made all major decisions.[198] At the same time, many participants at the 2004 Beijing conference stressed that time management and policy distractions posed problems during this crisis. According to one knowledgeable participant, every member of the senior national security apparatus, except for Secretary of Defense William Perry, was completely preoccupied with other policy issues at the time. It is unclear exactly how this problem affected specific decisions.

The same features of the Clinton decision-making process were evident during the subsequent embassy bombing and EP-3 incidents. These near crises arguably involved in important decisions an even wider range of individuals and agencies as part of the intergovernmental negotiating process. According to Campbell, decision making during the embassy bombing incident was centered at the NSC. An interagency group comprising representatives from the White House, the State Department, and the Defense Department advised Clinton and other NSC members, but China experts played a very limited role in the decision-making process.[199] During this incident, bureaucratic actors produced significant complications for crisis management as did time constraints on senior decision makers. Campbell notes, for example, that the U.S. response was sluggish because of other preoccupations of senior U.S. decision makers and the reluctance of Defense Department officials to share information at high-level interagency meetings. Furthermore, North Atlantic Treaty Organization (NATO) guidelines limited the speedy release of information regarding the details of the incident. The Defense Department evinced a "distinct lack of enthusiasm" for the State Department's effort to convince the Chinese leaders that the bombing was accidental. The resulting problems of coordination and communication impeded the U.S. response and might have caused suspicious Chinese officials to attribute the debilitating tensions in Washington to more malicious factors.[200]

The EP-3 incident also involved a wide range of actors, including the U.S. embassy in Beijing, the Pacific Command, the Defense Department, the State Department, the White House, and intelligence agencies.[201] An interagency group headed by the State Department initially conducted negotiations for the release of the crew and airplane although the White House and the Defense Department remained involved. U.S. Ambassador Joseph Prueher and Chinese Assistant Foreign Minister Zhou Wenzhong met approximately twice daily for several days. They agreed on the framework for resolving the overall crisis and ultimately produced the letter to Foreign Minister Tang Jiaxuan that procured the U.S. crew's release.[202] After the release of the crew, the Defense Department headed the negotiations for the return of the aircraft.[203]

. The fact that the State Department and the Defense Department each managed different stages of negotiations with China perhaps increased the complexity of the interactions with the Chinese. This may also explain the abrupt change toward a more hard-line negotiating approach after the release of the crew. Zhang Tuosheng suggests that the U.S. decision-making process was not as highly centralized as China's.[204]

Information and Intelligence Receipt and Processing

Effective crisis management requires the receipt of a wide range of accurate, timely intelligence and information.[205] These data often incorporate, when necessary, a variety of perspectives and interpretations. They can provide pre-crisis warnings and information relevant to the situation, offer a running narrative of the development of the crisis, and identify possible contingencies that may occur as a result of the crisis.[206] In addition, intelligence and information can also influence the basic images of the adversary and other assumptions that decision makers bring to a crisis and thus shape all aspects of perception and behavior.

Scholarly analysis of this critical element of crisis decision making suggests that leaders often do not receive high-quality information and intelligence. Stan A. Taylor and Theodore J. Ralston identify four sets of problems:

- Communication problems occur when decision makers do not receive information in a timely and unbiased manner. This may arise because information is overcompartmentalized and thus not shared with teams that brief senior policy makers. At other times, information overload prevents analysts and decision-makers from examining and conveying all key reports.
- Bureaucratic problems occur when research on a particular topic of great relevance is not given high priority and consequently not granted funding or when intelligence agencies must compete for the opportunity to share their findings with the proper decision makers. On other occasions, routine bureaucratic procedures can delay the reporting of information to policy makers in a time-sensitive situation.
- Psychological impediments can include biases in interpreting new information owing to existing beliefs or pressure to adhere to policy assumptions. The need to incorporate piecemeal intelligence under tight time constraints and the stress caused by a crisis can also create obstacles.
- Ideological and political obstacles occur when intelligence analysts change, exclude, or present without analysis their intelligence in order to satisfy the views of the policy makers who receive it or to

further the interests of those who report it. At other times, policy makers may signal that they are receptive to only certain kinds of information.[207]

In addition, adversaries can deliberately manipulate intelligence and information through information warfare.[208] Such activities can disrupt crisis management by distorting the signals sent by each side and disrupting the communication channels between military and policy officials. Information warfare may also reduce the search for alternative actions to a few, desperate measures and distort views of each other's intentions and capabilities. Adversaries presumably employ information warfare to gain advantages in a crisis, but it can provoke unwanted escalation. Information warfare is particularly dangerous if the adversaries possess nuclear weapons, as would be the case in a Sino-American crisis.[209]

Many of the problems associated with intelligence and information are no doubt evident in Chinese decision making. Very few solid examples exist, however, of how such data have influenced specific crisis decisions made by the Chinese leadership. This dearth of examples is largely because the Chinese government regards intelligence and its use in the decision-making process as highly sensitive and, consequently, does not allow scholars to conduct research or publish on these topics. Almost none of the chapters by Chinese scholars appearing in this volume refer to specific items of intelligence or other forms of information received by Chinese leaders during the crisis decision-making process. Nonetheless, this section offers some general observations and hypotheses based on research and interviews conducted over many years as well as the few observations contained in this volume.

The amount and quality of intelligence and information provided to senior leaders during a crisis seem to have improved significantly since the early decades of the PRC. The Chinese government today has access to satellite surveillance on a real-time or near-real-time basis. The government utilizes a state-of-the-art, fiber-optic communications system within the country. A growing number of Chinese government agencies and their affiliates are active overseas, and they provide a wide range of intelligence and analysis to the central leadership. Moreover, every day the senior leadership also receives both Chinese and foreign news reports along with intelligence briefings. The Chinese system remains inferior to the U.S. system technically, however, and still exhibits some important deficiencies.

In China, as in other countries, unanticipated events can reduce information flows. According to Wu Baiyi, the Chinese government lacked critical information during the embassy bombing incident largely because the bombing had destroyed communications between Beijing and the Chinese embassy in Belgrade. As a result, intelligence agencies were not able to provide a comprehensive report by the time the senior leadership convened in Beijing to discuss the crisis. This forced the leaders to make decisions with inadequate information. Wu suggests that this situation prevented the rapid formulation of a clear-cut policy.[210]

Even in the absence of such unexpected disruptions, the lack of crisis-oriented structures and processes apparently hampers China's intelligence and information systems. Wu notes that China's government does not possess a structure equivalent to the NSC that could coordinate policy among the various diplomatic, defense, and security agencies during a crisis. As a result, China's processing of intelligence, coordination of simultaneous institutional negotiations, and creation of a consistent response during the embassy bombing incident were deficient.[211]

The stovepipe nature of the Chinese bureaucracy extends into the intelligence system and affects crisis decision making. In particular, the civilian and military intelligence systems are largely separate and self-contained. Although this is to varying degrees the case in other countries as well, many foreign observers believe that China's military intelligence apparatus is particularly insular and secretive, and this even affects the information flow to some senior civilian leaders, which can arguably limit or distort the information provided to such individuals during a crisis. Although some foreign experts believe such distortion occurred during the EP-3 incident, the Chinese participants at the 2004 Beijing conference completely rejected these assertions as well as this paragraph's general point regarding military intelligence. On the other hand, one direct U.S. participant in the negotiations with China, and at least one recent Chinese study, suggest that military control over the intelligence provided to the senior Chinese leadership played a significant—and probably adverse—role in the EP-3 incident.[212]

The United States has a well-developed bureaucratic process designed to bring a wide variety of intelligence and relevant information (such as news broadcasts) to the immediate attention of senior leaders during a crisis. Most of the theoretical literature on the problems associated with intelligence and information in relation to crisis decision making is based on the U.S. example. Moreover, past Sino-American political-military crises provide examples of several of these problems.

The lack of critical information during several Sino-American crises likely contributed to misperception and prompted decisions that greatly aggravated the unfolding situation. As the Whiting chapter suggests, during the Korean War, the absence of crucial intelligence on Chinese intentions and the size of Chinese forces deployed along and across the North Korean border in October–November 1950 contributed to the very high level of risk taking exhibited by General Douglas MacArthur and other U.S. leaders. In the absence of accurate intelligence, incorrect assumptions regarding Chinese views and actions prevailed. These inaccurate views led to a major military blunder.[213] According to Robert Suettinger, the United States lacked reliable knowledge of ROC and PRC intentions during the 1954–1955 Taiwan Strait crisis despite the existence of National Intelligence Estimates (NIEs) and Special National Intelligence Estimates (SNIEs).[214] Unlike during the Korean War, however, neither the lack of such critical intelligence nor the presence of inaccurate intelligence resulted in large-scale military conflict. Although Dulles and Eisenhower made public statements about using tactical nuclear weapons to defend Taiwan, intelligence reports apparently convinced Eisenhower to stop publicly equating nuclear weapons with conventional weapons. In this way, the use of intelligence contributed to the cessation of nuclear threats.[215]

During the Vietnam War, senior leaders continued to make crisis decisions in the absence of critical intelligence regarding Chinese motives or, more notably, in the midst of considerable intelligence debates. Lacking an intelligence consensus on the likely reaction of China to different types of possible U.S. attacks on North Vietnam during the critical escalatory period of 1964–1965, senior decision makers leaned toward analyses that downgraded the likelihood of massive intervention. This situation increased the attractiveness of options for gradual escalation short of ground force operations into North Vietnam that could test China's reaction. By the end of 1965, however, both intelligence estimates and the senior U.S. leadership had reached a consensus that U.S. intervention on the ground into North Vietnam would very likely produce a significant Chinese escalation. This assessment reinforced the prohibition against hot pursuit over Chinese territory and essentially precluded the option of attacking North Vietnam on the ground during the entire conflict.[216] Allen S. Whiting also suggests, however, that such cautionary intelligence estimates derived primarily from the experience of the Korean War, rather than any contemporary data. Whiting speculates, "Without the Korean precedent, the same factors that prompted miscalculation regarding Korea could very easily have led the United States to invade the North and resulted in a wider war."[217]

According to Suettinger, by the time of the Taiwan Strait crisis of 1995–1996, the provision of intelligence and other forms of relevant information to senior decision makers had become highly systematic, much more rapid, and far more thorough than in past crises. During the 1995–1996 crisis, the intelligence community "established a twenty-four-hour task force that monitored all-source information, prepared daily situation reports for select policy and intelligence officials, and brought information of special significance directly to the attention of senior policy makers."[218] Suettinger is quick to add that, although the presence of far more (presumably accurate) intelligence on a real-time basis and overall improvements in communication have improved the process of crisis management within the U.S. government, such developments do not guarantee that data will be used effectively. This is largely because senior U.S. officials never have enough time to comprehensively examine intelligence and other information.[219] Moreover, decision making remains a "very human, interactive process, dependent on interpersonal relationships among the president's principal foreign policy advisers."[220] Decision making is also subject to the ideological predispositions and personalities of the players. As a result, the small circle of decision makers involved in crisis decision making can distort the meaning of the intelligence and information they receive.

The bureaucracy can also limit or distort the kind of intelligence senior U.S. decision makers receive. According to the chapter by Kurt Campbell and Richard Weitz, the Pentagon leadership during high-level crisis management meetings did not share much information about the embassy bombing incident. This lack of information impeded efforts by an interagency working group to convince China that the bombing was accidental.[221] Most U.S. participants in this near crisis subsequently acknowledged feeling they were making hasty decisions with incomplete information. Campbell, who served as deputy assistant secretary of defense for Asia and the Pacific, quotes a participant: "I do not recall many other times during my tenure in government feeling so frustrated by secrecy and bureaucratic incompetence as during the Chinese bombing incident. It was just a disaster."[222]

International Environment

The international environment within which crisis participants operate strongly influences their crisis behavior. Important factors include:

- **State of relations among relevant powers at the time of the crisis.** Obviously, the general level of hostility and suspicion (or calm) that exists between any major powers with interests at stake in the crisis—regardless of whether such powers are directly involved—influences the calculations of leaders. Contending great powers can attempt to manipulate or even threaten lesser powers involved in political-military crises, especially if such powers are friends or allies of their adversary.
- **General response of the larger international community to the crisis.** The level of opposition of the international community to a specific crisis or to the position taken by one or more of the participants in a crisis can also greatly affect decision makers' perceptions and actions. Leaders might become more hesitant to escalate a crisis or take certain risks that they might otherwise take if the bulk of the international community is opposed to the crisis and favors its speedy and peaceful resolution.
- **Presence of other international crises.** The simultaneous unfolding of several crises can obviously influence behavior in any one crisis, especially if the actors involved are the same or are related in some significant manner.[223]

Past Sino-American crises have provided many examples of the impact of the larger international environment. This impact was most often expressed in the assumptions and beliefs held by senior decision makers as they entered a crisis or attempted to manage it. As several of the chapters in this volume indicate, during important periods in the crises over Chinese intervention in the Korean and Vietnam Wars and the Taiwan Strait crises of the 1950s, the larger environment of the Cold War clearly influenced crisis perceptions and behavior in Beijing and Washington. Particularly important factors included the antagonism between the Soviet Union and the United States, the level of cooperation between the Soviet Union and China, and the relationship of each power with key allies.

Whiting indicates that, during the Korean War, U.S. leaders wanted to show their determination to oppose the perceived Soviet-inspired aggression, build credibility with U.S. allies in Europe and Asia, and strengthen the UN as a platform for peace. Moscow's outlook and behavior were critical to U.S. calculations of risk because both China and North Korea were allied communist states. Americans assumed that the Soviet Union controlled Chinese behavior.[224] Variations of these factors also played a role in crisis decision making by U.S. leaders during the subsequent Vietnam War despite the emergence by that time of the Sino-Soviet rift. Whiting shows that U.S. leaders considered likely Soviet reactions when they assessed the consequences of escalation at critical periods.[225] As the chapters on the embassy bombing incident by Wu Baiyi and Kurt Campbell indicate, the larger involvement of the United States and NATO in the Kosovo crisis influenced both Chinese and U.S. attitudes toward the incident.[226] Finally, participants in the 2004 Beijing conference remarked that the U.S. government was greatly distracted by the Balkan crisis during the 1995–1996 Taiwan Strait crisis. It is also likely that the Chinese leadership's desire to avoid provoking Asian concerns over an increasingly powerful and aggressive China played some role in Beijing's calculations during that crisis. While this argument is not confirmed by the relevant chapters in this volume, Suettinger does state that some Asian governments advised the U.S. leadership not to let the crisis devolve into an armed conflict.[227]

Idiosyncratic or Special Features

A final set of variables that influences crisis behavior does not fit into any of the above categories. These variables include a range of irregular or largely unpredictable phenomena, including leadership personality, the impact of stress, weather conditions, the effect of third parties, and unanticipated technical issues.

In all political systems, leadership judgments regarding virtually all of the factors influencing crisis decision making are inevitably filtered through the personalities of the leaders involved. The type and level of influence exerted by leadership personality can traverse a wide gamut, depending on both the nature of the political system and the type of personality possessed by the paramount leader and the leader's senior associates. In particular, tight authoritarian systems can magnify the impact of personality features of supreme rulers to a greater degree than other kinds of political regimes. Personality type can vary widely, from the cool-headed, rational individual to the emotional, compulsive individual. At the extreme are psychotic or near-psychotic individuals who might exhibit paranoia, aggression, or major delusions in perception. Many researchers have studied the role of personality in foreign policy decision making (and thus presumably also in crisis decision making).[228] Additional research has examined the impact of personality on the establishment of decision-making paradigms.[229]

Political-military crises often generate intense psychological stress that can significantly distort perceptions and alter behavior in dangerous ways by causing the decision maker to make poor foreign policy decisions.[230] Researchers such as Robert Jervis argue that crisis decision makers can inadvertently analyze situations in ways that agree with their established beliefs.[231] Others, such as Irving Janis, find that crisis decision makers interpret events in ways that agree with how they wish to see them.[232] The range of poor crisis decision making that can result from stress thus varies widely, from oversimplification to the neglect of critical information.

The influence of third parties during a conflict or crisis can be significant. Unfortunately, most of this literature focuses on third-party intervention in international conflicts or crises by supposedly neutral outside major powers or international bodies, such as the United Nations, and is probably not very applicable to this analysis. Such intervention has rarely occurred in past Sino-American crises and is unlikely to occur in the future.[233]

Of greater relevance to Sino-American crises is the literature on multiactor crises. The literature on activities of smaller powers in relation to larger allied powers is particularly important. Much of this literature has focused on the involvement of the United States and the Soviet Union during the crises between their respective Middle East allies, Israel and Egypt. During these crises, the two superpowers "experienced a tension between the desire—at times, the necessity—to lend meaningful support to its regional ally and a determination not to allow itself to be drawn into a dangerous, war-threatening confrontation."[234]

The challenges of Middle East crises are not unlike those that might confront the United States in a crisis with China over Taiwan. Phil Williams analyzes the problems that superpowers confront in dealing with smaller allied powers. In particular, he analyzes the danger of a superpower being drawn into a conflict with other superpowers. Williams observes, "States closely allied to the superpowers and conscious primarily of their own needs, interests and objectives could demand a level of support that the superpowers find intolerable." States might also present dangers to the superpower if their leaders are "devious as well as headstrong, and attempt to embroil the superpowers in their conflicts to an unwarranted extent." As a result of such concerns, superpowers must avoid giving "blank cheques" to their allies and "scrupulously try to prevent any moves by the latter entangling them in a position from which it is impossible to extricate themselves."[235] This observation could potentially apply to U.S.-Taiwan relations in a future crisis with China over the island.[236]

Finally, technical issues, such as the failure of weapons or other machines at critical times, and other idiosyncratic factors, such as weather conditions, are poorly defined and relatively unpredictable. Hence, they have not been studied in any systematic manner and can only be cited as factors for crisis decision makers to keep in mind.

One of the most important factors influencing the management of certain Sino-American crises has been the personality of senior leaders. Many studies have found that the outlooks and dominant personalities of individuals such as Mao Zedong and Douglas MacArthur significantly influenced crises such as the Korean War, the Taiwan Strait crises of the 1950s, and the 1969 Sino-Soviet border conflict.[237] Whiting's analysis suggests that MacArthur's aggressive and self-confident personality created potential instabilities during the crisis over Chinese intervention in the Korean War. Suettinger states that Truman and

Eisenhower, in contrast, were both pragmatic and cautious individuals.[238] These personality traits arguably inclined both men to resist or reject outright the provocative recommendations presented to them by MacArthur (in the case of Truman) and the JCS (in the case of Eisenhower). Although Suettinger also discusses some of the general personality traits of Clinton and his senior foreign policy officials, he does not identify whether and how these traits influenced their decisions during the 1995–1996 Taiwan Strait crisis.[239]

The relative lack of emphasis in this volume's case studies on the impact of leadership personalities on crisis decision making probably reflects the absence of reliable data connecting specific personality traits to crisis perceptions or decisions, and, in the Chinese case, the fact that such analysis is still very sensitive, even for crises of the 1950s–1960s.

The role of stress is underexamined in the general literature on Sino-American crisis decision making and in the case studies contained in this volume. This area deserves further study, given its extensive treatment in the theoretical literature.

In contrast, many scholarly works and several of the chapters in this volume examine, either directly or in passing, the role of third parties in Sino-American crisis decision making. These studies have focused their attention primarily on Taiwan's influence during crises over the island. Taiwan has obviously served as a catalyst of political-military confrontations between China and the United States. During the Taiwan Strait crises of the 1950s and the 1990s, however, Taiwan played a far more active and direct role in decision making in two major ways.

First, through a very effective lobbying effort in Washington, Taiwan arguably raised the political stakes confronting senior U.S. leaders. Taiwan's lobbyists greatly reinforced, and perhaps created, an image in the minds of many U.S. politicians and a significant portion of the U.S. public of the island as a bulwark of resistance to communism that required determined U.S. backing.[240] In the context of the escalating Cold War of the 1950s, such an image may have increased pressure on Eisenhower and his associates to take a tough stance in the 1954–1955 and 1958 crises. This image was strengthened even further after Taiwan began to democratize in the late 1980s and Beijing reconfirmed its anti-democratic, repressive features during the 1989 Tiananmen Square incident.

Second, during all three Taiwan Strait crises, potential or actual moves and statements by Taipei raised the stakes involved. At times, Taipei's positions threatened to escalate the confrontation beyond levels acceptable to Washington (and perhaps Beijing). As Suettinger's chapter suggests, before and during the 1950s crises, the growing presence and possible employment by Taipei of Nationalist forces on or near the offshore islands arguably compelled Washington to deepen its commitment to defending the islands. At the same time, this had the potential to provoke a dangerous Chinese reaction. Thus, during these crises, Eisenhower had to deter China from launching a major attack on the islands and restrain Chiang Kai-shek from dragging the United States into a deeper confrontation.[241] During the 1995–1996 crisis, Lee Teng-hui directly precipitated, and then arguably escalated, the confrontation. Lee pressed the Clinton administration for permission to visit the United States by eliciting congressional support for such a visit. After arriving in the United States, Lee made provocative public statements.[242] As in the 1950s, Taiwan's behavior increased the risks involved in Washington's ongoing effort to deter Beijing while restraining Taipei.[243]

Another example of third-party involvement is the role of North and South Korea in the crises over Chinese involvement in the Korean and Vietnam Wars. North Korea's military assault on the South precipitated the Korean War. Pyongyang's subsequent successes and failures on the battlefield influenced U.S. and Chinese crisis calculations before, during, and (to a lesser extent) following China's massive intervention in the conflict. Beyond such military factors, Kim Il-sung's urgings in favor of Chinese intervention and the Chinese leadership's commitment to North Korea as a socialist ally undoubtedly reinforced Mao's resolve to intervene in the conflict. Such influence was largely contextual, however, and did not play a decisive or direct role in the crisis interactions between Beijing and Washington.[244] The same can generally be said regarding South Korea.[245] This assessment is reinforced by the fact that the chapters by Allen Whiting and Zhang Baijia in this volume do not present North and South Korea as important actors in Chinese and U.S. crisis decision making.

The UN and U.S. allies such as the United Kingdom did exert influence over specific U.S. decisions of relevance to Chinese intervention and escalation. Opposition by the United Kingdom and other powers to hot-pursuit air actions over Chinese territory by UN forces at critical junctures resulted in the prohibition of such engagement despite the fact that General MacArthur, President Truman, and Truman's senior advisers all favored them. More broadly, as Whiting states, "U.S. allies and UN members worked assiduously in Washington and New York to restrain what was seen as highly risky behavior by MacArthur and his hawkish supporters in Congress."[246]

North and South Vietnam also played an indirect, contextual role in the decision making between Beijing and Washington regarding the possibility of Chinese intervention during the Vietnam War. Hanoi's successful conduct of the war and Saigon's military failures obviously exerted a significant influence on U.S. decisions to intervene in and escalate the conflict, thereby presenting the danger of Chinese intervention. However, neither North nor South Vietnam determined or decisively influenced specific actions taken by Beijing or Washington regarding Chinese intervention.[247]

CASE STUDIES AND ANALYSIS

The following chapters provide detailed case studies on past Sino-American crises and broader conceptual observations relevant to Sino-American crisis management. This information, along with the general observations presented in this chapter, provides the basis for the conclusions discussed at the end of this volume.

NOTES

1. See Jonathan Wilkenfeld's discussion of crisis in chapter 2 of this volume. See also Michael Brecher and Jonathan Wilkenfeld, *A Study of Crisis* (Ann Arbor: University of Michigan Press, 2000). For a slightly different definition that stresses the element of surprise in the emergence of a crisis, see Charles F. Hermann, "International Crisis as a Situational Variable," in J. N. Rosenau, ed., *International Politics and Foreign Policy* (New York: Free Press, 1969), p. 414. See also Xia Liping's summary in chapter 4 of this volume of U.S. definitions of crisis.

2. See Jonathan Wilkenfeld's analysis of crises and near crises in chapter 2 of this volume.

3. According to some U.S. participants in the 2004 Beijing conference and interviews conducted by Iain Johnston with U.S. participants in the 1995–96 event.

4. One can argue that the embassy bombing and EP-3 incident did not demonstrate the heightened probability of military conflict that defines a true political-military crisis. They do, however, fit the other criteria of a crisis.

5. The crisis aspects of the Korean and Vietnam Wars centered on the dangerous interaction between escalating U.S. actions and possible Chinese military responses. This included massive Chinese intervention during the Korean War. The ongoing confrontation between Washington and Beijing during the Vietnam War might not constitute a true crisis to some observers because it did not involve a strong sense of urgency. It is nonetheless included in our case studies largely because the situation replicated some of the aspects of the Korean War and certainly could have escalated into a major crisis. As Zhang Baijia states in chapter 5 of this volume, Beijing viewed the situation in Vietnam as a crisis after the U.S. government escalated its military involvement in 1965. This introduction's categorization of the case studies examined in this volume as either "crises" or "near crises" does not in every instance accord with the definitions used by some of the chapter authors. Wang Jisi, for example, characterizes all the case studies in this volume as crises, while Robert Suettinger suggests that the Taiwan Strait crises were somehow "less significant" than other full-blown crises. Nonetheless, these arguably slight variations in definition do not alter the utility of the analysis presented in each chapter for our overall understanding of the features of U.S. and Chinese crisis behavior and crisis management.

6. Alexander L. George, "A Provisional Theory of Crisis Management," in Alexander L. George, ed., *Avoiding War: Problems of Crisis Management* (Boulder, Colo.: Westview Press, 1991), pp. 22–23.

7. Davis B. Bobrow, Steven Chan, and John A. Kringen, *Understanding Foreign Policy Decisions: The Chinese Case* (New York: Free Press, 1979).

8. For a thorough discussion of the definition of *weiji* and its common misunderstanding among non-Chinese, see Victor H. Mair, "How a misunderstanding about Chinese characters has led many astray," at: http://www.pinyin.info/chinese/crisis.html. I am indebted to Iain Johnston for drawing this issue to my attention.

9. Ibid.; also see Xia Liping's discussion in chapter 4 of this volume.

10. According to some Chinese observers, these types of views were arguably more prevalent during the Mao and Deng eras, when crises were viewed as an element of "capitalist" society and not part of socialism or socialist society.

11. In chapter 2 of this volume, Jonathan Wilkenfeld, citing Graham Evans and Jeffrey Newnham, *The Penguin Dictionary of International Relations* (London: Penguin Books, 1998), argues, "Crisis management is most often thought of as the 'attempt to control events during a crisis to prevent significant and systematic violence from occurring.'" In the bibliography, see also works by J. W. Burton, H. C. Kelman, M. Kleiboer, D. M. Kolb and E. F. Babbitt, K. Rupesinghe, and I. W. Zartman.

12. As Xia Liping's chapter in this volume indicates, this dual purpose of crisis management is clearly recognized by Chinese scholars. Xia states that Chinese scholars believe "crisis management provides the means to avoid the danger of conflicts and to seek and obtain a favorable turn of events." That is, crisis management provides the means to take advantage of the opportunity posed by the crisis.

13. It is essential to note that not all behavior by nation-states during a political-military crisis qualifies as deliberate crisis management. Some leaders, for example, might be focused almost exclusively on achieving certain objectives—e.g., winning by altering the status quo to better reflect their interests—rather than addressing the threat of unwanted escalation or conflict posed by the crisis. Such an objective can make crisis management much more difficult, if not impossible. On the other hand, in some (probably more likely) cases, behavior during a crisis that appears to be unrelated to crisis management per se is actually part of an overall effort to balance opportunity and threat and is thus a component of crisis management. Niu Jun and Zhang Baijia, for example, argue that Chinese behavior during the crises they examine did not always constitute "international crisis management" behavior. In chapter 8 of this volume, Niu characterizes Chinese behavior during those incidents as a form of "military confrontation decision making" that involved the use of military means to reach specific objectives (such as deterrence). These objectives can include, but are not limited to, the management of international crises. In chapter 5 of this volume, Zhang Baijia states that China's calculations and decision making during the Korean and Vietnam wars were generally based on long-term strategic thinking, and not on the desire to manage the crises in question. In fact, based on our definitions, it is clear that such seemingly separate Chinese considerations can be understood as important elements of China's overall

crisis management approach. This is especially true given China's obvious desire to address such considerations while it avoids a full-blown conflict with the United States.

14. Alexander George, "Strategies for Crisis Management," in George, ed., *Avoiding War*, pp. 379–393.

15. Glenn H. Snyder and Paul Diesing, *Conflict Among Nations: Bargaining, Decision-Making, and System Structure in International Crises* (Princeton, N.J.: Princeton University Press, 1977).

16. Alexander George, "Introduction to Part Two," in George, ed., *Avoiding War*, p. 32.

17. In "Findings and Recommendations," pp. 560–561, George remarks that the political and operational requirements of any crisis management approach or theory are not requirements in the strict sense of "constituting necessary or sufficient conditions for successful management of war-threatening confrontations." However, whether these conditions are adequately met can affect the outcome of a crisis, and a failure to adhere to these conditions can increase the likelihood of war.

18. Alastair Iain Johnston, "Eight Principles of Crisis Management," lecture to the Strategic Studies Institute, Communist Party of China Party School (Beijing, November 2000). Johnston relied heavily on the work of Hu Ping to develop these principles. See in particular Hu Ping, *Guoji Chongtu Fenxi yu Weiji Guanli Yanjiu* [Analysis of International Conflict and Research on Crisis Management] (Beijing: Junshi Yiwen Chubanshe, 1993), pp. 167–173. Hu Ping, a Chinese military scholar, systematized a set of general requirements for successful crisis management that is based primarily on the major American studies on the subject. See also Snyder and Diesing, *Conflict Among Nations,* and works (listed in the bibliography) by D. Frei, M. Brecher, and J. Wilkenfeld.

19. Robert Axelrod, *The Evolution of Cooperation* (New York: Basic Books, 1984). In Axelrod's formation, "tit for tat" means also de-escalating when the other side de-escalates, and even possibly de-escalating more in response to the other side than the other side's initial de-escalation.

20. See George, "A Provisional Theory of Crisis Management," in George, ed., *Avoiding War*, pp. 23–25. George also makes many of these points.

21. Scott Sagan, "The Commitment Trap: Why the United States Should Not Use Nuclear Threats to Deter Biological and Chemical Weapons Attacks," *International Security* 24, no. 4 (Spring 2000), pp. 85–115, discusses the notion of a "commitment trap." James D. Fearon, "Domestic Political Audiences and the Escalation of International Disputes," *American Political Science Review* 88, no. 3 (September 1994), pp. 577–592.

22. George, "Findings and Recommendations," in George, ed., *Avoiding War*, p. 554.

23. I am indebted to Iain Johnston for this insight.

24. George, "Strategies for Crisis Management," and "Findings and Recommendations," in George, ed., *Avoiding War*, pp. 379, and 553–554, respectively.

25. George, "Findings and Recommendations," in George, ed., *Avoiding War*, pp. 553–554.

26. Ibid., p. 554.

27. I am indebted to Iain Johnston for this insight.

28. We are indebted to Professor Allen Whiting for these observations.

29. When an all-out war erupts, crisis management ceases and efforts at achieving military victory or ending hostilities begin. These processes employ far less limited means and objectives and are thus markedly different in nature from crisis management.

30. For a particularly interesting discussion of many of these factors, see Alexander George, "The Operational Code: A Neglected Approach to the Study of Political Leaders and Decision-Making," *International Studies Quarterly* 132, no. 2 (June 1969), pp. 197–198. George notes that these images, attitudes, and beliefs are all influenced by the most basic views one holds concerning the relationship between ends and means in political behavior as well as elite (and public) assumptions and premises about the nature of politics, the nature of political conflict, and the role of the individual in history. See also George A. Miller, Eugene Galanter, and Karl H. Pribram, *Plans and the Structure of Behavior* (New York: Holt, 1960); and Ole R. Holsti, "Cognitive Dynamics and Images of the Enemy," in John C. Farrell and Asa P. Smith, eds., *Image and Reality in World Politics* (New York: Columbia University Press, 1967). Holsti examines the relationship between people's or organizations' belief systems or images and their perceptions and actions. On the basis of his analysis of Secretary of State John Foster Dulles's views toward the Soviet enemy, Holsti, on page 39, argues, "Every decision-maker is in part a prisoner of beliefs and expectations that inevitably shape his definition of reality." Consequently, Holsti suggests, "When decision-makers for both parties to a conflict adhere to rigid images of each other, there is little likelihood that even genuine attempts to resolve the issues will have the desired effect."

31. See J. Philip Rogers, "Crisis Bargaining Codes and Crisis Management," in George, ed., *Avoiding War*, pp. 413–442. Rogers has combined and categorized the full range of elite perceptions and beliefs regarding crises into a typology of four idealized approaches, termed crisis bargaining "codes" or

cognitive schema. Rogers stresses that such codes often take the form of unarticulated assumptions. These codes often operate on decision making in a less conscious, more context-dependent, and often more insidious fashion than is commonly understood. Rogers also notes that decision makers within the same national leadership can prefer different codes.

32. Michael D. Swaine and Ashley J. Tellis, *Interpreting China's Grand Strategy: Past, Present, and Future* (Santa Monica, Calif.: RAND, 2000), pp. 15–17.

33. Ibid., p. 17; Allen Whiting, *The Chinese Calculus of Deterrence: India and Indochina* (Ann Arbor: University of Michigan, Center for Chinese Studies, 2001), p. 202.

34. Most of China's past political-military crises have involved issues of territorial integrity and sovereignty in the form of (1) small-scale border conflicts, (2) contention for territorial seas and islands, (3) limited hostile intrusions into Chinese territory, (4) punitive attacks or counterattacks against alleged invaders or aggressors, and (5) the increased military presence of potential adversaries near China's borders.

35. See, for example, Zhang Baijia's analysis of the Korean and Vietnam Wars in chapter 5 of this volume and Niu Jun's analysis of the Taiwan Strait crises in chapter 8 of this volume. See also Paul H. B. Godwin, "Decision-Making Under Stress: The Unintentional Bombing of China's Belgrade Embassy and the EP-3 Collision," paper presented at the American Enterprise Institute, Heritage Foundation, and U.S. Army War College People's Liberation Army Conference (Carlisle Barracks, Penn., October 1–3, 2004, revised November 26, 2004), p. 29. Chinese sensitivity to sovereignty issues has also influenced the details of negotiations to resolve a crisis. During negotiations with Washington over the return of the damaged U.S. EP-3 aircraft, for example, Chinese officials insisted that the airplane could not be flown back to the United States because this would require it to reenter Chinese airspace, thus infringing upon Chinese sovereignty.

36. As Xia Liping points out in chapter 4 of this volume, for example, China has relied during past crises on what it holds to be self-evident and permanent principles, such as the "five principles of peaceful coexistence" and the one-China principle regarding Taiwan. Xia also quotes Jiang Zemin as stating that People's Republic of China (PRC) foreign policy should be based on principles, and he includes among Chinese values honesty, harmony, and good faith. Zhang Baijia argues that one reason China intervened in the Korean War was its principled support for morality and justice in international relations.

37. For more on Chinese moral posturing, see Swaine and Tellis, *Interpreting China's Grand Strategy*, pp. 76–77. See also Wang Jisi's description of the role of principles in Chinese decision making in chapter 3 of this volume.

38. See Swaine and Tellis, *Interpreting China's Grand Strategy*, pp. 76–77. See, for example, Zhang Baijia's analysis of the Korean War in chapter 5 of this volume.

39. See Xia Liping's discussion in chapter 4 of this volume. In analyzing Chinese behavior during the EP-3 incident, for example, Zhang Tuosheng argues in chapter 12 of this volume that Beijing placed considerable stress on the UN Convention on the Law of the Sea in addition to the concept of safeguarding sovereignty and the prevention of major damage to Sino-U.S. relations.

40. That said, there is no doubt that the principles of sovereignty and national honor continue to exert a significant influence on crisis perceptions in China. As Dennis C. Blair and David V. Bonfili state in chapter 11 of this volume, during the near crisis of the EP-3 incident in 2001, China's leaders insisted that the United States could not fly the repaired surveillance aircraft out of China because such an act would "further slight [Chinese] sovereignty."

41. Mark Burles and Abram N. Shulsky, *Patterns in China's Use of Force: Evidence From History and Doctrinal Writings* (Santa Monica, Calif.: RAND, 2000), pp. 16–20. This view has been especially prevalent among students of PRC crisis behavior during the 1950s and 1960s. See, for example, Melvin Gurtov and Byong-moo Hwang, *China Under Threat: The Politics of Strategy and Diplomacy* (Baltimore: Johns Hopkins University Press, 1980). Thomas J. Christensen, *Useful Adversaries: Grand Strategy, Domestic Mobilization, and Sino-American Conflict, 1947–1958* (Princeton, N.J.: Princeton University Press, 1996). Moreover, Christensen argues that during the late 1940s and 1950s, Chinese leaders manipulated international crises in order to obtain public support for specific security policies.

42. See Wilkenfeld's analysis in chapter 2 of this volume; Xia Liping's description of the "new security concepts," which emphasize "resolv[ing] disputes through the means of peaceful negotiations," in chapter 4 of this volume; and Niu Jun's analysis of the "limited" and "flexible" nature of Chinese crisis decision-making objectives in chapter 8 of this volume.

43. See Whiting, *Chinese Calculus of Deterrence*, p. 204.

44. Christensen, *Useful Adversaries*, p. 160; see Zhang Baijia's analysis in chapter 5 of this volume.

45. For recent official views that support such generalizations, see George W. Bush, "State of the Union Address by the President," speech (Washington,

D.C., January 31, 2006), www.whitehouse.gov/stateoftheunion/2006/; and Michael Michalak, "U.S. Views on Asia Regional Integration," remarks, International Institute of Monetary Affairs (Tokyo, January 25, 2006), www.state.gov/p/eap/rls/rm/60355.htm.

46. Shu Guang Zhang, *Deterrence and Strategic Culture: Chinese-American Confrontations, 1949–1958* (Ithaca, N.Y.: Cornell University Press, 1993), pp. 279–280; Bobrow, Chan, and Kringen, *Understanding Foreign Policy Decisions.*

47. See Xia Liping's analysis in chapter 4 of this volume.

48. For more on U.S. exceptionalism, see Seymour Martin Lipset, *American Exceptionalism: A Double-Edged Sword* (New York: W. W. Norton & Company, 1995).

49. Christensen, *Useful Adversaries,* p. 243.

50. See, for example, Ibid., p. 246.

51. This point is discussed in greater detail in the conclusion.

52. In chapter 4 of this volume, Xia Liping states that a notion of manifest destiny influences U.S. foreign policy, that the United States views itself as the "savior to the world," and that the United States is arrogantly determined to export democracy and to resolve specific problems without addressing broader underlying causes.

53. Many in China believe that U.S. policy toward Taiwan strives to maintain a constant situation of tension between Beijing and Taipei, marked by "neither war nor peace, neither unity nor independence" (*buzhan, buhe, butong, budu*).

54. I thank Alastair Iain Johnston for providing this insight.

55. Michael D. Swaine, "Exploiting a Strategic Opening," in Ashley J. Tellis and Michael Wills, eds., *Strategic Asia 2004–05: Confronting Terrorism in the Pursuit of Power* (Seattle: National Bureau of Asian Research, 2004), p. 76; Wang Jisi, "China's Changing Role in Asia," occasional paper, Atlantic Council of the United States, January 2004, p. 16, www.acus.org/docs/0401-China_Changing_Role_Asia.pdf.

56. Swaine, "Exploiting a Strategic Opening," p. 90. For more on the Chinese perception of a strategic opportunity, see Liu Jianfei, "Zhanlüe Jiyuqi yu ZhongMei Guanxi" [Period of Strategic Opportunity and Sino-U.S. Ties], *Liaowang,* January 20, 2003.

57. See Niu Jun's analysis in chapter 8 of this volume. Some in China believe that the United States sought to test China's resolve during the Taiwan Strait crisis of 1995–1996.

58. See Xia Liping, chapter 4 of this volume, quoting William R. Kintner and David C. Schwarz, *A Study on Crisis Management* (Philadelphia: Univer-

sity of Pennsylvania Foreign Policy Research Institute, 1965), appendix B, p. 21.

59. See Xia Liping, chapter 4 of this volume, quoting Leslie Lipson, from "Crisis Management or Crisis Prevention," *NATO Letter* (August–September 1966), p. 14.

60. See Burles and Shulsky, *Patterns in China's Use of Force,* p. 31, for an analysis on the Chinese willingness to suffer high casualties and approve the large-scale use of force.

61. One Chinese participant in the 2004 Beijing conference said, "The Taiwan problem concerns precisely China's core interests, while it concerns merely the United States' vital interests."

62. See Wang Jisi's analysis in chapter 3 of this volume. Wang also cites Brecher and Wilkenfeld's "positive power discrepancy" concept to bolster his point. Wang argues that past Sino-American Taiwan Strait crises avoided direct conflict because the United States (the more powerful state) did not need to use force to attain its objectives, while China (the weaker triggering state) did not desire direct military hostilities because of its weakness. Wang adds that a clear asymmetry of interest has existed in most Sino-American crises because of their location (Taiwan, near Hainan Island, Korea, and Vietnam), their connection with China's territorial integrity (Taiwan), or their link to the sovereignty principle (Taiwan and the Chinese embassy bombing incident of 1999). As a result, Wang argues that Chinese people tend to be self-righteous about such crises. They do not believe the United States has any moral right to become involved in Asian security, and they interpret U.S. actions in the context of power politics.

63. Such labeling is also used to describe China's status, position, or posture toward other states.

64. Ibid.

65. Ibid. However, Wang Jisi argues that, during recent crises such as the 1999 embassy bombing and the 2001 EP-3 crisis, Chinese opinion makers have occasionally lapsed into characterizations of the United States as an enemy.

66. Allen S. Whiting, in chapter 6 of this volume, states that during the 1950s, the U.S. leadership believed that the Soviet Union determined China's policies and that China would enter a conflict only if Moscow told it to do so.

67. See the recently declassified National Intelligence Estimates (NIEs) on China, analyzed in Michael D. Swaine, "China's Nuclear Weapons and Grand Strategy: A Detailed Outline," paper presented at the conference, "Tracking the Dragon: National Intelligence Estimates on China During the Era of Mao, 1948–1976," organized by the National Intelli-

gence Council; Woodrow Wilson International Center for Scholars; and U.S. Department of State, Bureau of Intelligence and Research (Washington, D.C., October 18, 2004). See also the product of this conference: *Tracking the Dragon: National Intelligence Estimates on China During the Era of Mao, 1948–1976*, ed. John K. Allen, Jr., John Carver, and Tom Elmore (Washington, D.C.: National Intelligence Council, 2004). With few exceptions, the U.S. NIEs of the 1950s and most of the 1960s argued that China's strategic outlook and posture was aggressive, assertive, arrogant, patronizing, and uncompromising.

68. The NIEs of this period asserted that the Chinese leadership (largely viewed as unified under Mao Zedong) would employ virtually any means to advance its objectives. These means included political pressure, intimidation, diplomatic maneuver, support for insurgent movements, coercion, and armed force. In particular, the Chinese communists were seen as strong proponents of the efficacy of and necessity for violence whenever possible.

69. As the NIEs suggest, many U.S. observers viewed the Vietnam War as critical to Chinese regional objectives. U.S. observers viewed China as seeking a decisive and humiliating defeat for the United States in Vietnam, even though most observers also recognized that China probably sought to avoid a direct clash with U.S. forces. Moreover, NIEs argued that a U.S. defeat in Vietnam would increase Beijing's alleged arrogance and aggressiveness, while the defeat of Chinese goals in Vietnam would check China's momentum in world affairs. Proponents of the NIE position thus argued that, for the Chinese, the stakes in Vietnam were high.

70. The distorted thinking produced by the largely monolithic imagery of Cold War hostility was reflected by the occasional mention in the NIEs of China's use of force against nearby border threats to validate the notion of a broadly militant and aggressive regime.

71. By 1974–1976, NIEs conveyed a somewhat detailed understanding of the likely purpose and structure of China's developing nuclear arsenal. They stated convincingly that China's modest nuclear arsenal was intended to prevent nuclear blackmail and deter an invasion or nuclear strike and that it might increase U.S. and Soviet hesitancy to intervene in local crises along China's periphery that involved China's interests. They also argued, somewhat obviously, that the deterrent value of China's nuclear weapons would increase as China acquired a long-range intercontinental ballistic missile. At the same time, the NIEs argued that China would continue to see the value of not initiating nuclear use at either the strategic or tactical level.

72. Swaine, "China's Nuclear Weapons and Grand Strategy."

73. See, for example, Evan A. Feigenbaum, "China's Challenge to *Pax Americana*," *Washington Quarterly* 24, no. 3 (July 2001), pp. 31–43; and Swaine and Tellis, *Interpreting China's Grand Strategy*, pp. 1–4.

74. Swaine, "Exploiting a Strategic Opening," pp. 76–80, 88; Wang Jisi, "China's Changing Role in Asia," p. 16; Thomas J. Christensen and Michael A. Glosny, "China: Sources of Stability in U.S.-China Security Relations," in Richard Ellings and Aaron Friedberg, eds., *Strategic Asia 2003–04: Fragility and Crisis* (Seattle: National Bureau of Asian Research, 2003), p. 57.

75. Mao Zedong, "Current Problems of Tactics in the Anti-Japanese United Front," in *Selected Works of Mao Tse-tung*, vol. 2 (Beijing: Foreign Languages Press, 1975), pp. 426–427. See Wang Jisi's analysis in chapter 3 of this volume. This set of guidelines is reflected by Mao's statement: "Despise the enemy strategically and take it seriously tactically." Wang notes that Mao used this strategy vis-à-vis the United States during the wars in Korea and Vietnam and in the first two Taiwan Strait crises. That is, in general, he issued strong rhetoric but took cautious actions. In chapter 4 of this volume, Xia Liping also invokes this maxim to explain Chinese views toward the use of force, persuasion, and accommodation. Xia argues that China advocates responding to force with force and to negotiation with negotiation while the United States uses a combined carrot-and-stick approach.

76. See Zhang Baijia's analysis in chapter 5 of this volume and Allen S. Whiting's analysis in chapter 6 of this volume. Also see Whiting, *Chinese Calculus of Deterrence*, for the definitive version of this description of the Chinese approach.

77. See, for example, Zhang Baijia's analysis in chapter 5 of this volume.

78. Alastair Iain Johnston, "China's Militarized Interstate Dispute Behavior 1949–1992: A First Cut at the Data," *China Quarterly*, no. 153 (March 1998). Johnston concludes that, during the Cold War, China was more prone to disputes than were most other major powers, except the United States, and tended to resort to higher levels of violence in disputes. The largest portion of Chinese dispute behavior involved territorial issues and the consolidation of long-standing territorial claims. He speculates that, if China does not face challenges to its territorial integrity and has sufficient international status, it may actually be less likely to become involved in disputes. However, once it becomes involved in a dispute, China will tend to escalate to a relatively high level of force. International Crisis Behavior Project, "Primary Data Collections: Version 6.0," University of Maryland, January 2006, http://www.cidcm.umd.edu/icb/Data/index.html. Data from

the International Crisis Behavior Project find that the PRC reacted more coercively than the initial action by the adversary that triggered the crisis in 6 of 14 crises (43 percent) through 2003. The United States' record is almost identical: the United States exhibited this behavior in 28 of 61 cases (46 percent).

79. Burles and Shulsky, *Patterns in China's Use of Force,* p. 31; Shu Guang Zhang, *Deterrence and Strategic Culture,* pp. 279–280. Shu Guang Zhang agrees that China has often in the past viewed the use (and not merely the demonstration) of force as an important means of crisis management, often taking preemptive military action to attain strategic advantage.

80. Some Chinese participants at the February 2004 Beijing conference argued that one primary purpose behind the use of force in past Taiwan Strait crises was to test how far the United States was willing to go to protect the island. That is, China wanted to determine whether the United States would help the Kuomintang (KMT) attack China and whether the United States supported Taiwan's independence.

81. Burles and Shulsky, *Patterns in China's Use of Force.* Burles and Shulsky observe that the strong need to show resolve has led Chinese leaders to discount the military and economic costs involved in using force, unless such costs clearly threaten regime stability.

82. Thomas J. Christensen, "Windows and War: Trend Analysis and Beijing's Use of Force," in *New Approaches to the Study of Chinese Foreign Policy,* ed. Alastair Iain Johnston and Robert S. Ross (Stanford: Stanford University Press, 2006), 51.

83. As Zhang Baijia remarks in chapter 5 of this volume, advocating force does not mean that one wants to launch a war. One can avoid major frictions through minor frictions or by "using a war to control a war." Whiting, in *Chinese Calculus of Deterrence,* p. 205, discusses the Chinese use of military force to deter and prepare for possible action. Examples include Chinese actions preceding the Korean War intervention, regarding India in 1962, and in Vietnam in 1965–1968.

84. Whiting, *Chinese Calculus of Deterrence;* Burles and Shulsky, *Patterns in China's Use of Force,* pp. 31, 41–42; Johnston, "China's Militarized Interstate Dispute Behavior 1949–1992," pp. 19–20. Shulsky states that during crises of the 1950s–1960s, China at times sought to establish a *fait accompli* through quick and decisive action and to force the adversary to risk significant escalation to reinstate the status quo ante. One should also note, however, that scholarly literature like the work by Johnston suggests that China is not more likely to undertake such risky international behavior during times of international crisis.

85. Burles and Shulsky, *Patterns in China's Use of Force,* 41. Shulsky argues that China's past use of force against a stronger power or the client of a stronger power suggests several tactics: "[First,] use of surprise to create psychological shock; [second,] inflicting casualties to create political pressure on the opponent; [third,] creation of tension to divide the opposing alliance or to create political problems for an opponent; [fourth,] creation of a *fait accompli,* presenting the opponent with a choice between acquiescence and escalation."

86. Moreover, as reiterated by Chinese participants at the 2004 Beijing conference, this willingness to use force when facing a superior power derived, in turn, partly from a sense of vulnerability and weakness. It also derived from the absence of other credible means of communicating resolve and exerting leverage in a crisis.

87. See Alastair Iain Johnston, *Cultural Realism: Strategic Culture and Grand Strategy in Chinese History* (Princeton, N.J.: Princeton University Press, 1995); and Alastair Iain Johnston, "Cultural Realism and Strategy in Maoist China," in Peter J. Katzenstein, ed., *The Culture of National Security: Norms and Identity in World Politics* (New York: Columbia University Press, 1996), pp. 216–270.

88. One recent study that confirms this restrained Chinese stance toward territorial or border disputes is Taylor Fravel, "Regime Insecurity and International Cooperation: Explaining China's Compromises in Territorial Disputes," *International Security* 30, no. 2 (Fall 2005).

89. According to several Chinese participants at the 2004 Beijing conference, several factors caused this change in approach. These factors include the passing of the revolutionary generation of Chinese leaders (who were arguably more militant in their outlook toward foreign policy issues and less constrained by domestic factors), the existence of a greater number of non-military levers of influence in crisis management, and the emergence of a new generation of leaders committed to the pursuit of stable and cooperative relations with other powers as an essential precondition for continued economic growth and domestic stability.

90. Discussions at the February 2004 conference; Wang Jisi, chapter 3 of this volume. In chapter 8 of this volume, Niu Jun states that Chinese leaders originally viewed the use of force as a way of achieving reunification with Taiwan, but they now see it as a way of maintaining strategic deterrence against Taiwan's de jure independence.

91. See Niu Jun's analysis in chapter 8 of this volume.

92. Johnston, "China's Militarized Interstate Dispute Behavior 1949–1992."

93. See Barry M. Blechman and Stephen S. Kaplan, *Force Without War: U.S. Armed Forces as a Political Instrument* (Washington, D.C.: Brookings Institution, 1978).

94. See, for example, George W. Bush, "The National Security Strategy of the United States of America," September 2002, www.whitehouse.gov/nsc/nss.pdf.

95. The United States, for example, did not use force directly against the Soviet Union during the Cold War because of the risk of mutually assured destruction. Michelle Maiese, "Limiting Escalation/De-escalation," Beyond Intractibility.org, January 2004, www.beyondintractability.org/essay/limiting_escalation/?nid=1089. According to Michelle Maiese, "George argues that three factors contributed to Kennedy's success in preventing escalation. First, he limited his demands to removal of the Soviet missiles from Cuba. Further demands would have only provoked greater Soviet resistance. Second, Kennedy began with a blockade, which did not involve the immediate use of force and bought him time to attempt to persuade the Soviets. Finally, both Khrushchev and Kennedy followed important operational principles of crisis management." This analysis is drawn from Alexander L. George, "The Cuban Missile Crisis," in Alexander L. George, *Forceful Persuasion: Coercive Diplomacy as an Alternative to War* (Washington, D.C.: United States Institute of Peace Press, 1991), pp. 31–37.

96. In chapter 5 of this volume, for example, Zhang Baijia states that, during the Vietnam War, China took a reciprocal or step-by-step approach to U.S. behavior. If the United States did not escalate the war, China would not escalate the war. Wu Baiyi remarks in chapter 10 of this volume that China has prevented crisis escalation in the past by initially increasing pressure. China may increase pressure through diplomatic negotiations, domestic and international public opinion, or elite declarations. China then deliberately de-escalates the crisis. In chapter 8 of this volume, Niu Jun argues that the deliberate adoption by China's leaders of limited policy objectives during the Taiwan Strait crises allowed them to be very flexible in their choice of policy responses.

97. See Whiting, *Chinese Calculus of Deterrence,* p. 217. Allen Whiting explicitly makes this point in his analysis of Chinese crisis behavior during the Maoist era.

98. Ibid., p. 202. Whiting argues that for Mao Zedong the best form of deterrence was belligerence. To be credible, words alone would not suffice; military actions were also necessary.

99. From the Chinese perspective, successful applications of this approach include the Taiwan Strait crises of 1954 and 1958 and the 1962 Sino-Indian border clash. See Niu Jun's analysis in chapter 8 of this volume.

100. In chapter 3 of this volume, Wang Jisi states that Beijing followed the basic pattern of *youli, youli, youjie* during the 1995–1996 Taiwan Strait crisis, the embassy bombing incident, and the EP-3 incident. In each case, Beijing initially protested strongly ("on just grounds"). Once the United States had partially compromised, Beijing declared a partial victory ("to our advantage"). Finally, China cooperated ("with restraint") to resolve the incident. According to Wang, this was possible because Beijing recognized that a stable relationship with Washington was in China's national interest, that the compromise they had reached did not sacrifice Chinese principles, and that China had attained the best possible outcome given its limited ability to exert pressure on the United States. See also Zhang Tuosheng's discussion of the EP-3 incident in chapter 12 of this volume.

101. James Mulvenon, "The Limits of Coercive Diplomacy: The 1979 Sino-Vietnamese Border War," *Journal of Northeast Asian Studies* 14, no. 3 (Fall 1995), pp. 68–88.

102. See Lyle J. Goldstein, "Return to Zhenbao Island: Who Started Shooting and Why It Matters," *The China Quarterly* 168 (2001): 985–997; and Xu Yan, "Chinese Leaders' Management of the Crises of Border Conflicts," unpublished paper presented at the 2004 Beijing conference.

103. For information on the Sino-Soviet crisis, see Thomas W. Robinson, "China Confronts the Soviet Union," in Roderick MacFarquhar and John K. Fairbanks, ed., *The Cambridge History of China,* vol. 15 (Cambridge: Cambridge University Press, 1991).

104. As Whiting indicates in chapter 6 of this volume, concerns over possible large-scale Chinese intervention significantly influenced U.S. leadership calculations regarding military action against Hanoi during the Vietnam War.

105. See John Lewis Gaddis, *Strategies of Containment* (New York: Oxford University Press, 1982), p. 214. Walt W. Rostow, an aide and Department of State official during the Kennedy and Johnson administrations and a developer of U.S. national security doctrine, used this phrase. Rostow nonetheless criticized the enormous instabilities that resulted from a disproportionate emphasis on massive retaliation via nuclear arms in a crisis or conflict. He favored a more symmetrical approach that stressed a more diversified response, albeit one designed to show very strong resolve.

106. According to Suettinger's analysis in chapter 7 of this volume, Eisenhower began to back away from these threats only after the U.S. public objected.

107. See Suettinger's analysis in chapter 7 of this volume. In chapter 4 of this volume, Xia Liping cites the U.S. carrier deployment in 1995–1996 as a clear example of limited brinkmanship or controlled escalation.

108. Rogers, "Crisis Bargaining Codes and Crisis Management," p. 418.

109. Burles and Shulsky, *Patterns in China's Use of Force,* p. 39. Shulsky cites not only the U.S. nuclear threats against China but also similar Soviet threats during the Sino-Soviet tensions of 1969–1970. Moreover, Shulsky does not limit his assessment to past Chinese behavior. He believes a strong U.S. approach would be particularly necessary in a future Taiwan crisis, given the high stakes involved for China.

110. At the same time, many U.S. and Chinese scholars agree that the risk for both sides of military alerts or other means to convey resolve is much lower in the case of a Sino-American crisis than it was for a U.S.-Soviet crisis. In the U.S.-Soviet case, the situation involved two tightly coupled nuclear forces wedded to war-fighting strategies. This view was expressed by both U.S. and Chinese participants at the Beijing 2004 conference.

111. See Whiting's analysis in chapter 6 of this volume. In chapter 4 of this volume, Xia Liping attributes such disbelief to the "arrogance and prejudice" of certain U.S. leaders. See also Zhang Baijia's analysis in chapter 5 of this volume. U.S. leaders were already inclined to believe that China would not intervene militarily because they assumed Moscow controlled Beijing's policy. The United States also believed China's focus was on restoring domestic stability. Moreover, the United States believed China would not intervene militarily because the United States had provided public reassurances that it would not attack China or threaten the regime. Some leaders in Washington also believed that public warnings by Zhou Enlai were attempts to influence UN deliberations rather than actual reflections of Chinese intent.

112. See Suettinger's analysis in chapter 7 of this volume. During the 1954–1955 crisis, for example, the United States did not understand the significance of the mutual defense treaty with Taiwan to the ROC-PRC civil war. Furthermore, according to Suettinger, the lack of communication during the first Taiwan Strait crisis meant that the underlying issues were never really resolved. This paved the way for the second crisis.

113. In chapter 5 of this volume, Zhang Baijia notes that China also indirectly communicated its resolve by deploying significant numbers of military support personnel to North Vietnam.

114. Zhang Baijia in chapter 5 notes, however, that signals during the Taiwan Strait crises and the Vietnam War were less misunderstood by both sides in large part because of lessons learned during the Korean War experience. Zhang states that during the Vietnam War, for example, the United States realized that it needed to keep a "safe distance" from China. Consequently, U.S. forces did not cross the 17th parallel. In chapter 7 of this volume, Suettinger also provides specific examples of improvements in interpretations of signals during the 1954–1955 and 1958 Taiwan Strait crises.

115. According to Suettinger's analysis in chapter 7 of this volume, full diplomatic contacts were maintained throughout the crisis and meetings were held at all levels. He does not discuss why the PRC preferred talking points to candid discussion.

116. Before the incident, Washington was also frustrated by the absence of any Chinese response to U.S. attempts to resolve the reconnaissance flights issue. See the analysis of Blair and Bonfili in chapter 11 of this volume.

117. See Zhang Tuosheng's analysis in chapter 12 of this volume. In chapter 11 of this volume, Blair and Bonfili are particularly critical of what they saw as a sluggish and grudging Chinese response during the early stages of the crisis.

118. In reality, domestic political considerations played a far more important role in these U.S. decisions, as discussed in greater detail below.

119. See Wu Baiyi's analysis in chapter 10 of this volume. The chapter 9 analysis by Kurt M. Campbell and Richard Weitz of U.S. behavior during the embassy incident does not confirm this. It merely states that Jiang Zemin initially refused to answer repeated phone calls from the White House via the Sino-American hotline. The implication is that China was being stubborn and was apparently holding out for a better apology.

120. Whiting, *Chinese Calculus of Deterrence,* pp. 211–212. One such phrase is, "China will not stand idly by," which can mean anything from a diplomatic to a full military response, or perhaps nothing at all. Xia Liping argues in chapter 4 of this volume that China's crisis signals have been "more reserved" than U.S. signals and that this is due to the reserved, indirect nature of Eastern cultures.

121. Burles and Shulsky, *Patterns in China's Use of Force.* This argument is also made to some degree in Whiting, *Chinese Calculus of Deterrence.* Whiting argues, based on his analysis of Chinese crisis behavior during the 1950s–1960s, that Chinese leaders have been very aware of the need to provide early-warning signals in a crisis and of the need to pace signals in ways that allow the enemy to respond.

122. This was confirmed by Chinese participants at the 2004 Beijing conference.

123. Christensen, *Useful Adversaries*. Christensen argues that the failure of Chinese leaders to use clear military deployments or alerts to signal resolve and the overall lack of military coordination in the communist camp before the Korean War and in the early phases of the war sent false signals of weakness or irresoluteness.

124. Wu Baiyi, chapter 10 of this volume.

125. Michael D. Swaine, "Chinese Crisis Management: Framework for Analysis, Tentative Observations, and Questions for the Future," in Andrew Scobell and Larry M. Wortzel, eds., *Chinese National Security Decisionmaking Under Stress* (Carlisle, Pa.: U.S. Army War College, 2005), pp. 21–22.

126. Indeed, during the Sino-Soviet military clash and subsequent crisis of 1969–1970, China usually moved incrementally, in a seemingly tit-for-tat fashion. Moreover, one might also conclude that, even if true, China's taking the offensive in its crisis signaling might not be that different from the U.S. approach.

127. In chapter 7 of this volume, for example, Suettinger points out that the United States alternated between "megaphone diplomacy" (loud, public threats) and "strategic ambiguity" during the Taiwan Strait crisis of 1954–1955.

128. Scott D. Sagan, "Nuclear Alerts and Crisis Management," *International Security* 9, no. 4 (Spring 1985): 99–139. Also, as Sagan argues in his analysis of U.S. nuclear signaling during past crises, military "standard operating procedures" (SOP) have at times influenced the profile of the signal sent, thus creating a potential discrepancy between the message intended by the civilian decision maker and the actual signal.

129. An example of the literature on leadership politics is Arjen Boin, Paul 't Hart, Eric Stern, and Bengt Sundelius, *The Politics of Crisis Management: Public Leadership Under Pressure* (Cambridge: Cambridge University Press, 2005). Examples of the role of leadership politics in the United States include Robert E. Hunter, *Organizing for National Security* (Washington, D.C.: Center for Strategic and International Studies, 1988); and William W. Newmann, *Managing National Security Policy: The President and the Process* (Pittsburgh, Pa.: University of Pittsburgh Press, 2003). One example of the influence of popular pressure is P. Stuart Robinson, *The Politics of International Crisis Escalation: Decision-Making Under Pressure* (London: Tauris Academic Studies, 1996).

Chinese participants at the 2004 Beijing conference also noted that such factors as the overall strength of governmental leadership, the nature of the crisis, and the appropriateness of governmental strategies in crisis interactions heavily influence the specific role played by domestic considerations.

130. Of course, in some cases, a supreme ruler might feel compelled to consider very seriously the views of his most senior associates, for political reasons or because of their superior expertise and judgment. This was apparently the case for Mao Zedong at times, as suggested in this volume and by other studies of his decision-making style.

131. Christensen, *Useful Adversaries,* pp. 9, 20–22, 245–246. Christensen, for example, argues that Mao manufactured the 1958 Taiwan Strait crisis as part of an effort to create and manipulate tensions with the United States in order to mobilize the Chinese peasantry to contribute more capital for heavy industrial and nuclear projects. See also Christensen, "Windows and War."

132. See Paul Booker, *Non-Democratic Regimes: Theory, Government and Politics* (New York: St. Martin's Press, 2000) for more on authoritarian regimes.

133. See Robert M. Entman, *Projections of Power: Framing News, Public Opinion, and U.S. Foreign Policy* (Chicago: University of Chicago Press, 2003), for more on the interaction between the executive branch and the media.

134. See Richard Sobel, *The Impact of Public Opinion on U.S. Foreign Policy Since Vietnam: Constraining the Colossus* (New York: Oxford University Press, 2001) and Douglas C. Foyle, "Public Opinion and Foreign Policy: Elite Beliefs as a Mediating Variable," *International Studies Quarterly* 41, no. 1 (March 1997): 141–170.

135. Sagan, "The Commitment Trap," pp. 85–115; Fearon, "Domestic Political Audiences and the Escalation of International Disputes."

136. See Christensen, *Useful Adversaries,* pp. 7–8.

137. Lyman Miller, "Leadership Analysis in an Era of Institutionalized Party Politics," paper presented at conference, "Behind the Bamboo Curtain: Chinese Leadership, Politics, and Policy," hosted by Carnegie Endowment for International Peace (Washington, D.C., 2005), www.carnegieendowment.org/files/Miller_Revised.pdf.

138. Swaine, "Chinese Crisis Management," pp. 24–25.

139. Mao's main adviser was Zhou Enlai. Mao was also advised by senior PLA leaders like Peng Dehuai and, during the late 1960s and early 1970s, Lin

Biao. See Wang Jisi's analysis in chapter 3 of this volume and Zhang Baijia's analysis in chapter 5 of this volume.

140. King C. Chen, *China's War With Vietnam, 1979: Issues, Decisions, and Implications* (Stanford, Calif.: Hoover Institution Press, 1987), p. 83. Specifically, Deng apparently performed many of the same activities in the border war as Mao Zedong had performed during the Korean War.

141. Michael D. Swaine, "Chinese Decision-Making Regarding Taiwan, 1979–2000," in David Lampton, ed., *The Making of Chinese Foreign and Security Policy in the Era of Reform, 1978–2000* (Stanford, Calif.: Stanford University Press, 2001), pp. 290, 293.

142. Ibid., p. 293; Swaine, "Chinese Crisis Management," pp. 25–26.

143. Lu Ning, *The Dynamics of Foreign-Policy Decisionmaking in China* (Boulder, Colo.: Westview Press, 1997); Lu Ning, "The Central Leadership, Supraministry Coordinating Bodies, State Council Ministries, and Party Departments," in Lampton, ed., *The Making of Chinese Foreign and Security Policy in the Era of Reform, 1978–2000,* pp. 39–60. As Wang Jisi states in chapter 3 of this volume, crisis management now requires more coordination within the government owing to better informed political elites, increasingly nationalistic sentiments, increasing freedom of expression, democratization, and the more complicated decision-making process. See also Suisheng Zhao, ed., *Across the Taiwan Strait: Mainland China, Taiwan, and the 1995–1996 Crisis* (New York: Routledge, 1999), p. 235.

144. See Ellis Joffe, "The People's Liberation Army and Politics: After the Fifteenth Party Congress," in *China Under Jiang Zemin,* ed. Hung-mao Tien and Yun-han Chu (Boulder, Colo.: Lynne Rienner, 2000), p. 103. Post-Deng leaders do not possess close, long-standing, personal ties with PLA leaders. They do not have direct military experience or particularly deep knowledge of military issues.

145. Ibid. As Joffe states, in reference to the Jiang Zemin era, the paramount leader "does not tower over his colleagues, and his standing does not endow him with the privilege of claiming final wisdom on all affairs of state. As a result, the policymaking process under his chairmanship is undoubtedly more open and dispersed among his senior colleagues."

146. Chinese participants in the 2004 Beijing conference remarked that the military signals Beijing employed in fall 1995 and spring 1996 were at least partly determined by the desire to mollify internal hard-liners.

147. Unfortunately, even less is known at this point about internal Chinese elite decision making during more recent near crises such as the embassy

bombing and the EP-3 incident. The chapters in this volume do not provide much information on this *specific* subject.

148. See Swaine, "Chinese Decision-Making Regarding Taiwan, 1979–2000," 293.

149. Although, as commander in chief and head of the CMC, Jiang probably held the formal authority to direct such operations, he is not a military expert and would likely have aggravated relations with the military leadership if he had attempted to do so. In chapter 7 of this volume, Suettinger merely states that Jiang, as chairman of the CMC, observed the November 1995 exercise at Dongshan.

150. See Robert G. Sutter, "The Taiwan Crisis of 1995–96 and U.S. Domestic Politics," in Greg Austin, ed., *Missile Diplomacy and Taiwan's Future: Innovations in Politics and Military Power* (Canberra, Australian National University, 1997), p. 68. According to Sutter, Jiang reportedly strongly defended a moderate stance toward the United States during a series of leadership meetings held in August–September 1995. Jiang "was successful in achieving a consensus behind such a stance, despite deeply felt skepticism and criticism from other leaders urging a harder line toward the United States."

151. See works on the 1995–1996 Taiwan Strait crisis by S. Zhao, A. Scobell, A. S. Whiting, R. S. Ross, and M. D. Swaine. A number of works by these authors are listed in the bibliography for this volume.

152. See Christensen, *Useful Adversaries,* 9, for examples of the former. See also Chen Jian, *China's Road to the Korean War: The Making of the Sino-American Confrontation* (New York: Columbia University Press, 1994); Lyle J. Goldstein, "Return to Zhenbao Island: Who Started Shooting and Why It Matters," *China Quarterly* 168 (December 2001), pp. 985–997; and Thomas W. Robinson, "China Confronts the Soviet Union." Robinson argues that Mao or Lin Biao might have manipulated the 1969 clash for several reasons: to undermine more moderate rivals, to strengthen Lin's and the military's claim to power, to divert popular attention from domestic chaos or justify a crackdown, or to spur the radical "revolutionary consciousness" of students. See Taylor Fravel, "Regime Insecurity and International Cooperation: Explaining China's Compromises in Territorial Disputes," *International Security* 30, no. 2 (Fall 2005), for a recent study that challenges the "diversionary war" hypothesis regarding China's past border crises. Fravel argues that Chinese leaders have usually attempted to cooperate, not escalate, the handling of contentious border disputes during periods of internal unrest. Johnston, "China's

Militarized Interstate Dispute Behavior 1949–1992" validates this point more broadly. Johnston argues that China was less likely to become involved in militarized interstate disputes during periods of domestic unrest. Moreover, historically, Chinese leaders have rarely initiated a political-military crisis for domestic political goals although they have pursued domestic political objectives during crises they did not initiate.

153. In his analysis of the embassy bombing incident in chapter 10 of this volume, Wu Baiyi provides numerous examples of Beijing's attempts to use the media to "guide the public toward solidarity and stability by supporting government decisions" and to avoid "confusing signals." The Chinese government also kept some information secret (such as a visit by the U.S. special envoy) to avoid inflaming the public. See also Wang Jisi's analysis in chapter 3 of this volume.

154. Swaine, "Chinese Crisis Management: Framework for Analysis, Tentative Observations, and Questions for the Future," p. 24.

155. On the other hand, the leadership was almost certainly sensitive to the view that a major humiliation or other adverse outcome could exert a major, negative impact on public opinion.

156. See Wu Baiyi's analysis of the embassy bombing in chapter 10 of this volume and Zhang Tuosheng's analysis of the EP-3 incident in chapter 12 of this volume.

157. Danielle F. S. Cohen, *Retracing the Triangle: China's Strategic Perceptions of Japan in the Post–Cold War Era,* Maryland Series in Contemporary Asian Studies, no. 181 (Baltimore: University of Maryland School of Law, 2005), pp. 57–61.

158. More broadly, Chinese participants remarked that the largest complicating factor in crisis signaling between China and the United States is the need to pacify internal objections or criticisms.

159. Wang Jisi makes this point in chapter 3 of this volume.

160. See Wu Baiyi's analysis of the embassy bombing in chapter 10 of this volume and Zhang Tuosheng's analysis of the EP-3 bombing in chapter 12.

161. According to the analysis of Campbell and Weitz in chapter 9 of this volume, some Americans indeed believed that Chinese opinion makers were manipulating popular feelings to spur anti-U.S. protests and force U.S. concessions. In chapter 10 of this volume, Wu Baiyi suggests that Beijing claimed that public pressure required it to be tougher on the United States in order to look like it was representing its domestic public, even as it sought to end the crisis. As Campbell and Weitz note, China's Ministry

of Foreign Affairs (MFA) sent a list of demands to the United States. The MFA requested that "U.S.-led NATO" apologize to the Chinese government, the Chinese people, and the victims' families. China also demanded that the United States investigate the incident, publicize its findings, punish those responsible, cease its military actions against Yugoslavia, and seek a political solution to the Kosovo crisis. According to the analysis of Dennis Blair and David Bonfili in chapter 11 of this volume, the Chinese leadership also claimed during the EP-3 incident that it was under intense public pressure to issue a tough response. Yet many U.S. officials wondered whether such pressure was real or induced because China's public obtains most of its news from the official, state-controlled media.

162. Another possibility is that Chinese policy makers allowed the protests to continue because they accepted the view (propounded by some Chinese scholars and observers) that the embassy bombing was a conspiracy against China. Also, the public opposition to the bombing fed into and supported the larger, preexisting Beijing position of opposition to the U.S. role as a "world policeman." This prompted the public to urge the government to make a strong response. See Wu Baiyi's analysis in chapter 10 of this volume. One must also consider the possibility that in many instances protests were permitted and allowed to continue beyond prudent limits as a result of decisions made by local authorities.

163. See the analysis of Campbell and Weitz in chapter 9 of this volume; Wu Baiyi's analysis in chapter 10; and Xia Liping's analysis in chapter 4. Both Wu Baiyi and Xia Liping remark that the Chinese government feels particularly pressured by public sentiment during a crisis, given the speed and depth of expression of nationalist views (expressed via public demonstrations; the Internet; and the less mainstream, market-oriented press) and the presence of "radical arguments and irrational assumptions." Xia Liping adds that the Chinese Internet commentators responded more quickly to events during the EP-3 incident than did the Chinese official media.

164. A former senior U.S. official in attendance at a follow-up event connected to the 2004 Beijing conference insisted that a U.S. president is relatively free from pressure or control by Congress and the public during the early stages of a crisis or during a short-lived crisis. This participant argued that the sense of urgency and threat that exists under such circumstances prompts such outside forces to defer to the authority and judgment of senior executive and military leaders, at least for a short period. As time passes, however, both the public and the legislature can exert a

growing influence over crisis behavior, especially if the president appears to be mismanaging the crisis or if differing opinions emerge regarding its origins and objectives. This point is arguably illustrated by the evolution of the current prolonged Iraqi crisis confronting the United States.

165. See Allen Whiting's analysis in chapter 6 of this volume.

166. See Robert Suettinger's analysis in chapter 7 of this volume.

167. Ibid.

168. These points were made at the 2004 Beijing conference by former senior U.S. officials directly involved in the Clinton decisions.

169. See Dennis Blair's analysis in chapter 11 of this volume.

170. Ibid.; David Bachman, "The United States and China: Rhetoric and Reality," *Current History* (September 2001), p. 261. As Bachman argues, Beijing and Washington resolved the crisis "just before Congress and the American public concluded that China was holding the crew hostage. Had that view taken hold earlier, United States-China relations would have gone into the deep freeze."

171. Godwin, "Decision-Making Under Stress," p. 24. Zhang Tuosheng argues in chapter 12 of this volume that Bush's need to appease right-wing Republicans during the EP-3 incident was a constraint on U.S. policy.

172. We are indebted to Alastair Iain Johnston for raising this question.

173. Many analysts have refined and criticized the bureaucratic politics model, arguing, for example, that although U.S. officials may be aware that their own government does not act with a unitary purpose—as would be predicted by the rational-actor model—they may still mistakenly ascribe such rational-actor behavior to other states. See J. Gary Clifford, "Bureaucratic Politics," *Journal of American History* 77 (June 1990), p. 163.

174. See works (listed in the bibliography) by O. R. Holsti, I. Janis, G. Herek, R. T. Johnson, A. L. George, T. J. McKeown, M. G. Hermann, P. Williams, R. C. Snyder, R. Hilsman, P. Y. Hammond, I. M. Destler, T. E. Cornin, S. Kernell, G. T. Allison, M. H. Halperin, B. Ripley, J. C. Thomson, and E. Rhodes.

175. Chen Jian, *China's Road to the Korean War;* Swaine, "Chinese Crisis Management: Framework for Analysis, Tentative Observations, and Questions for the Future," p. 25; Michael D. Swaine, "Chinese Decision-Making in Crisis Situations Involving the Use of Force" (unpublished manuscript). In chapter 5 of this volume, Zhang Baijia confirms some of these observations.

176. King C. Chen, *China's War With Vietnam, 1979,* p. 93. Chen states that Deng's leadership was apparently "an indispensable element to the accomplishment of the decisionmaking process."

177. Ibid., pp. 90, 92–93, 102.
178. In chapter 4 of this volume, Xia Liping confirms that, with the exception of the newly established Leading Group of National Security of the CCP Central Committee, many of the same high-level organs have been involved in crisis decision making. He states that the Politburo of the CCP Central Committee and its Standing Committee make major decisions. The Secretariat of the CCP Central Committee handles day-to-day work. The State Council, the CMC of the CCP, the Leading Group of National Security of the CCP Central Committee, the Leading Group of Foreign Affairs of the CCP Central Committee, the MFA, and the Ministry of National Security are all involved in crisis management.
179. See Wu Baiyi's analysis in chapter 10 of this volume.
180. Swaine, "Chinese Decision-Making Regarding Taiwan, 1979–2000," see especially pages 298–309.
181. Several Chinese participants at the 2004 Beijing conference stated that the Chinese government initially responded slowly to the embassy bombing incident of 1999 in part because the existing decision-making structure had no experience and no contingency plans for handling such a crisis.
182. This is probably the case, despite the indication that leadership control over the bureaucracy in recent crises such as the EP-3 incident was relatively effective, according to Chinese scholars. Zhang Tuosheng states in chapter 12 of this volume that the Chinese leadership determined the nature of the incident, decided on a policy of quick settlement, and kept a sharp focus on the dual objectives of maintaining state sovereignty and protecting the bilateral relationship. At the same time, China allowed for flexibility in the formulation, implementation, and readjustment of specific policies. Zhang also states, however, that negotiations over the aircraft were led by officials from both the MFA and the Ministry of National Defense. Unfortunately, Zhang provided no details on how officials from these two ministries interacted. "EP-3 Shijian Kaoyan Bushi Zhengfu Weiji Chuli Nengli" (The EP-3 Incident Tests the Bush Administration's Ability to Handle Crises), in *Guoji Weiji Guanli Kailun* (Introduction to International Crisis Management), ed. Yang Mingjie (Beijing: Shishi Chubanshe, n.d.), 256–257. Moreover, as discussed below, the leadership's handling of this incident might have been adversely influenced by its reliance on a separate and apparently autonomous intelligence channel controlled by the military.
183. Joffe, "The People's Liberation Army and Politics: After the Fifteenth Party Congress," p. 103; King C. Chen, *China's War With Vietnam, 1979;* Chen Jian, *China's Road to the Korean War.*

184. Joffe, "The People's Liberation Army and Politics: After the Fifteenth Party Congress," p. 103.

185. Chinese participants at the 2004 Beijing conference could not confirm or deny such comments. However, some participants suggested that the United States is probably equally prone to such potential problems in civil-military interactions during a crisis.

186. Karl F. Inderfurth and Loch Johnson, "National Security Advisers: Roles: Editors' Introduction," in Karl F. Inderfurth and Loch Johnson, eds., *Fateful Decisions: Inside the National Security Council* (New York: Oxford University Press, 2004), p. 133; David Rothkopf, *Running the World: The Inside Story of the National Security Council and the Architects of American Power* (New York: PublicAffairs, 2005), pp. 4–8. The coordinator of the NSC was originally called the "executive secretary." During the Eisenhower administration, the position was renamed "special assistant to the president for national security affairs." Under Nixon, the title was shortened to "the assistant for national security affairs," and the position became commonly known as "the national security adviser."

187. U.S. Department of State, Office of the Historian, "History of the National Security Council 1947–1997," August 1997, www.whitehouse.gov/nsc/history.html; and "The Modern NSC: Editors' Introduction," in Karl F. Inderfurth and Loch Johnson, eds., *Fateful Decisions: Inside the National Security Council*, pp. 97–106, provide overviews of how each president, while working within the overall structure stipulated by the National Security Act, structured his NSC. Truman's NSC emphasized the role of the Department of State. Eisenhower's NSC coordinated policy implementation in a highly organized fashion. Kennedy relied on the national security adviser and his staff rather than on the official NSC structure. Johnson made use of the national security adviser but also relied on his Tuesday Lunch Group. Under Nixon, the role of national security adviser rose to great prominence as Henry Kissinger and his NSC staff became powerful advisers. Henry Kissinger continued to hold such influence into the Ford administration. During Carter's administration, the national security adviser and his NSC staff developed ideas for foreign policy while the Department of State coordinated actual operations. Reagan attempted to create a more collegial, cooperative environment by decreasing the influence of the NSC and asking the chief of staff to coordinate White House policy. George H. W. Bush established the Principals Committee and the Deputies Committee of the NSC, two structures that persist. Clinton increased the number of people included in the NSC

by adding the secretary of the treasury, the U.S. representative to the UN, the assistants to the president for national security affairs and economic policy, and the White House chief of staff. Bush has maintained this system almost entirely, although his NSC does not include the U.S. representative to the UN.

188. See "The Modern NSC," p. 106. The national security adviser has become a powerful adviser to the president, not only the administrative coordinator of the NSC. Henry Kissinger under President Richard Nixon was the first national security adviser to rise to such prominence. With the increased prominence of the national security adviser, the NSC staff has also become increasingly powerful. Presidents have come to rely far more on the national security adviser, the NSC staff, and NSC subgroups such as the Principals (cabinet members) Committee and the Deputies (subcabinet members who serve as assistants to the principals) Committee rather than on formal meetings of the NSC. In particular, the establishment of the Principals Committee and the Deputies Committee marks a recent formalization of the NSC structure.

189. See "The Modern NSC," p. 106. The Chinese system has become increasingly consensus driven, complex, and fragmented (especially between civilian and military components). Hence, the Chinese system is increasingly subject to significant delays and distortions, although some Chinese observers would probably challenge such an assertion.

190. During the 1950s, specialists had almost no access to senior decision makers. This changed notably during the Vietnam War.

191. See Whiting's analysis in chapter 6 of this volume.

192. See Suettinger's analysis in chapter 7 of this volume.

193. Ibid. According to Suettinger, during the first Taiwan Strait crisis, Eisenhower was also having "a sharp disagreement with his military chiefs about the defense budget."

194. Ibid. Suettinger's description of the U.S. government's response to the 1954–1955 crisis as "reactive, ill-planned, and poorly communicated" can also be applied to the 1958 crisis.

195. See Whiting's analysis in chapter 6 of this volume.

196. Ibid.

197. See Suettinger's analysis in chapter 7 of this volume. During the crisis, the Department of State created a special task force to monitor information. The JCS, Pacific Command, and Department of Defense instituted a review of contingency plans and briefed the president. The intelligence community established a twenty-four-hour task force to monitor infor-

mation and inform policy makers. The NSC coordinated policy planning through meetings of principals and deputies committees and consulted with both Chinese and Taiwan officials. During the crisis, Defense Secretary William Perry made final recommendations on the deployment of U.S. forces in consultation with General John Shalikashvili and other senior defense officials, NSC advisers Anthony Lake and Samuel Berger, and Department of State officials Warren Christopher and Winston Lord. Lake and Berger conveyed the recommendations to Clinton, who approved them. The decisions were implemented through the military chain of command. Clear ROE guidelines were conveyed to U.S. ships and aircraft operating in the region.

198. See Suettinger's analysis in chapter 7 of this volume.

199. See Campbell and Weitz's analysis in chapter 9 of this volume.

200. Ibid.

201. See Blair and Bonfili's analysis in chapter 11 of this volume.

202. Godwin, "Decision-Making Under Stress," pp. 23–25.

203. See Blair and Bonfili's analysis in chapter 11 of this volume.

204. See Zhang Tuosheng's analysis in chapter 12 of this volume.

205. This subset of the decision-making process is examined as a separate subject because of its complexity and importance. This has become especially true during the information age. Intelligence generally includes closed-source (and often classified) data provided to decision makers by subordinate government agencies. Information includes the wide range of open-source, largely nongovernmental data available to decision makers, such as media reports.

206. Shaun P. McCarthy, *The Function of Intelligence in Crisis Management* (Aldershot, England: Ashgate, 1998), p. 43.

207. Stan A. Taylor and Theodore J. Ralston, "The Role of Intelligence in Crisis Management," in George, ed., *Avoiding War*, pp. 395–412; also McCarthy, *Function of Intelligence in Crisis Management*, especially the notes to chapter 2, for further sources on intelligence. See Charles C. Cogan, "Intelligence and Crisis Management: The Importance of Pre-Crisis," *Intelligence and National Security* 9, no. 4 (October 1994), pp. 633–650. A related problem, noted by Cogan, is that intelligence officers are often unable to persuade policy makers to consider their intelligence until a crisis actually occurs because policy makers are preoccupied with day-to-day matters and cannot focus on possible longer-term developments. See also Richard K. Betts, "Intelligence for Policymaking," in Gerald W. Hopple, Stephen J. Andriole, and Amos Freedy, eds., *Na-*

tional Security Crisis Forecasting and Management (Boulder, Colo.: Westview Press, 1984), pp. 19–32.

208. Stephen J. Cimbala, "Nuclear Crisis Management and Information Warfare," *Parameters* (Summer 1999), pp. 117–128. Cimbala defines information warfare as "activities by a state or non-state actor to exploit the content or process of information to its advantage in times of peace, crisis, or war, and to deny potential or actual foes the ability to exploit the same means against itself."

209. Ibid.

210. See Wu Baiyi's analysis in chapter 10 of this volume.

211. Ibid.

212. At least one knowledgeable U.S. participant in the crisis informed the author in a confidential interview that the Chinese Navy probably served as the sole source of information on the accident to the senior Chinese civilian and military leadership. The Navy command arguably had a vested interest in defending the reputation of their pilot who, in the view of U.S. officials, accidentally struck the U.S. EP-3 and caused the accident. Many observers suspect that the senior Chinese leadership could not independently substantiate the intelligence provided by the Navy about the collision. Presumably, the Chinese leadership would not want to refute directly such intelligence in the absence of information to the contrary. Hence, a situation might have emerged that essentially compelled the civilian leadership to accept the Navy's version of the accident (that is, that the U.S. aircraft deliberately caused the collision). This situation virtually ensured a hard-line approach to negotiations with Washington. In chapter 11 of this volume, Dennis Blair and David Bonfili refer to the possibility that the Chinese leadership was given faulty information by Navy authorities in Hainan. See also James Mulvenon, "Civil-Military Relations and the EP-3 Crisis: A Content Analysis," *China Leadership Monitor*, no. 1 (Winter 2002). "EP-3 Shijian Kaoyan Bushi Zhengfu Weiji Chuli Nengli" (The EP-3 Incident Tests the Bush Administration's Ability to Handle Crises), in *Guoji Weiji Guanli Kailun* (Introduction to International Crisis Management), pp. 256–57 indirectly suggests that the PRC response to the EP-3 collision too heavily relied on information from the PLA. While these critical comments are framed as statements about the U.S. military's role, the author clearly intends the reader to apply these lessons to the PLA as well. We are grateful to Alastair Iain Johnston for this comment.

213. See Allen Whiting's analysis in chapter 6 of this volume.

214. See Robert Suettinger's analysis in chapter 7 of this volume. Partly as a result of this, and despite the development of a "potentially effective crisis management system in the NSC," Eisenhower and Dulles at times sought their own intelligence assessments rather than relying on official channels.

215. Robert Suettinger, in chapter 7 of this volume, argues that such threats were made not as a result of any specific intelligence but because "Dulles and Eisenhower became worried about eroding morale in Taiwan and felt pressure from the JCS to authorize the use of nuclear weapons against PRC targets. . . ." Robert Suettinger's analysis in chapter 7 cites Robert Accinelli, *Crisis and Commitment: United States Policy Toward Taiwan, 1950–1955* (Chapel Hill: University of North Carolina Press, 1996), p. 214; Timothy J. Botti, *Ace in the Hole: Why the United States Did Not Use Nuclear Weapons in the Cold War, 1945 to 1965* (Westport, Conn.: Greenwood Press, 1996), p. 75. Suettinger states that Eisenhower stopped making the comparison after intelligence reports suggested that even tactical nuclear weapons might cause twelve to fourteen million casualties in China.

216. See Allen Whiting's analysis in chapter 6 of this volume.

217. Ibid.

218. See Robert Suettinger's analysis in chapter 7 of this volume.

219. This point was also made by U.S. participants in the 2004 Beijing conference.

220. See Robert Suettinger's analysis in chapter 7 of this volume.

221. See the analysis by Campbell and Weitz in chapter 9 of this volume. The authors add that the reasons such information was not provided probably included "a determination to remain focused on ongoing military operations, a recognition that the Air Force would be protective about its stealthy and expensive bomber, and their likely collective confusion over just what actually had occurred to cause such a disaster." They do not explain, however, why the president did not order the Pentagon to provide the necessary information.

222. See the analysis by Campbell and Weitz in chapter 9 of this volume.

223. Authors who have researched the impact of the international environment on the emergence of crises include K. Waltz, J. Mearsheimer, R. Gilpin, and S. D. Krasner (see bibliography for relevant titles).

224. See Allen Whiting's analysis in chapter 6 of this volume.

225. For an example, see ibid.

226. See Wu Baiyi's analysis in chapter 10 of this volume; see the analysis by Kurt Campbell and Richard Weitz in chapter 9 of this volume.

227. See Robert Suettinger's analysis in chapter 7 of this volume.

228. See the bibliography for works by authors such as L. S. Etheredge, M. G. Hermann, W. J. Crow, M. J. Driver, L. Falkowski, and D. G. Winter.

229. See the bibliography for works by authors such as R. M. Hogarth, D. Mefford, J. A. Rosati, A. Shlaim, G. H. Snyder, M. W. Reder (with Hogarth), and D. A. Sylvan.

230. This list of authors who research the role of stress in crisis decision-making is largely drawn from P. Stuart Robinson, *The Politics of International Crisis Escalation: Decision-Making Under Pressure,* pp. 1–13. Examples of this literature include works by: M. D. Wallace, K. Guttieri, S. G. Walker, T. M. Ostrum, C.-P. David, T. V. Paul, C. F. Hermann, O. R. Holsti, A. L. George, I. L. Janis, R. Marston, and R. Jervis.

231. Robert Jervis, *Perception and Misperception in International Politics* (Princeton, N.J.: Princeton University Press, 1976). Many authors elaborate on this theoretical argument, including John D. Steinbruner, *The Cybernetic Theory of Decision* (Princeton, N.J.: Princeton University Press, 1974); Snyder and Diesing, *Conflict Among Nations;* and Richard Ned Lebow, *Between Peace and War: The Nature of International Crisis* (Baltimore: Johns Hopkins University Press, 1990), p. 111. Others have applied this argument to empirical cases; for example, Alan Dowty, *Middle East Crisis: U.S. Decision-Making in 1958, 1970, and 1973* (Berkeley: University of California Press, 1984); and Michael Brecher, *Decisions in Crisis: Israel, 1967 and 1973* (Berkeley: University of California Press, 1980).

232. Irving L. Janis and Leon Mann, *Decision Making* (New York: Free Press, 1977); Irving L. Janis, *Victims of Groupthink* (Boston: Houghton Mifflin, 1972); Irving L. Janis, *Groupthink: Psychological Studies of Policy Decisions and Fiascos* (Boston: Houghton Mifflin, 1982). Lebow, *Between Peace and War,* p. 111, compares the views of Jervis and Janis.

233. The one partial example of such intervention among the crisis studies in this volume occurred during the Korean War and involved the UN. Although the UN definitely influenced U.S. crisis decision making during that crisis, it did not constitute an example of the type of separate, third-party intervention discussed in most of the literature because the United States intervened in the Korean War under UN auspices.

234. George, "Findings and Recommendations," in George, ed., *Avoiding War,* p. 563.

235. See Xia Liping's analysis in chapter 4 of this volume, citing Phil Williams, *Crisis Management: Confrontation and Diplomacy in the Nuclear Age* (London: Martin Robertson & Co. Ltd., 1976), pp. 100, 130–132.

236. Obviously this is a problem that is inherently more of an American one than a Chinese one, given the U.S. alliance relationships. A few exceptions may include crises involving Pakistan, North Korea, and as the Shanghai Cooperation Organization evolves, some Central Asian states. In these cases, the Chinese might view alliance credibility as an important interest. We are indebted to Alastair Iain Johnston for this observation.

237. See Whiting's analysis in chapter 6 of this volume; see Robert Suettinger's analysis in chapter 7 of this volume. For more on the Sino-Soviet border conflict, see Thomas W. Robinson, "China Confronts the Soviet Union."

238. See Robert Suettinger's analysis in chapter 7 of this volume.

239. Ibid. Suettinger, for example, describes Clinton as extraordinarily intelligent, informal, consultative, and impersonal. Secretary of State Warren Christopher was aloof, self-effacing, and careful, and he preferred calm deliberation to quick action.

240. Suettinger discusses the so-called China lobby (now the Taiwan lobby) in chapter 7 of this volume.

241. See Robert Suettinger's analysis in chapter 7 of this volume. Suettinger states: "[Chiang's] strong push for a mutual defense treaty, in the view of some analysts, may have been one of the reasons for the initial PRC attack on Quemoy in September 1954." He adds, more generally, that Chiang's behavior during the 1954–1955 crisis "restricted Eisenhower's policy options and set the stage for future crises." Suettinger also emphasizes Chiang's provocative and delimiting behavior during the 1958 crisis. He also makes the point, however, that Chiang's influence among U.S. leaders had declined considerably by that time, partly as a result of a sharp decline in the power of conservative Republicans in Congress.

242. See Robert Suettinger's analysis in chapter 7 of this volume.

243. See Robert Suettinger's analysis in chapter 7 of this volume. Suettinger states, "As in 1954 and 1958, Taiwan's pursuit of its own domestic political interests involved the United States in a crisis with the PRC, and its miscalculations about the PRC's response had important consequences for Washington." We should note that chapter 8 by Niu Jun does not generally confirm this assessment of Chiang's impact on U.S. crisis decision making. Like other Chinese scholars, Niu tends to view Chiang Kai-shek and Lee Teng-hui as acting in accordance with the U.S. desire to challenge, "test," or contain Beijing.

244. See Whiting's analysis in chapter 6 of this volume.

245. One might also include Taiwan. Chiang Kai-shek apparently attempted to use the conflict on the Korean peninsula to generate Western support

for a Nationalist counterattack on the mainland. However, his machinations were unsuccessful, and, in contrast with the situation during the Taiwan Strait crises, did not exert a major direct influence on crisis decision making regarding Chinese intervention in Korea. Taiwan played a role in the Korea crisis primarily in a contextual sense by reinforcing preexisting images and resolve in both Washington and Beijing. In 1950, Taiwan feared that the island might also become a target of acquisition by China, and Korea feared that it might become a staging ground for an assault by the United States.

246. See Whiting's analysis in chapter 6 of this volume.
247. Ibid.

2

Concepts and Methods in the Study of International Crisis Management

Jonathan Wilkenfeld

INTERSTATE MILITARY-SECURITY CRISES have been the most frequent type of hostile interaction in international politics during the past century. Although some evidence shows that the frequency of these crises is gradually declining in the post–Cold War system, the recent wars in Iraq and Afghanistan, the tension between India and Pakistan over Kashmir, and the nuclear standoffs with North Korea and Iran indicate that dangerous crises remain a potential disrupting force for the international system and regional subsystems. Crises can present overwhelming challenges to established institutions and belief systems and can change forever the distribution of power within the international system or in a regional subsystem.[1]

Systematic investigation makes it possible to better understand the causes, evolution, actor behaviors, outcomes, and consequences of crises. This knowledge, in turn, can facilitate efforts by scholars and policy makers to develop better mechanisms for crisis prevention, management, and resolution. In East Asia in general, and for the Taiwan Strait in particular, we must be ever mindful of the continuing tensions that can spawn serious international crises.

This chapter will review standard definitions of international and foreign policy crises and present some of the major findings of research by the International Crisis Behavior (ICB) Project on crises in the twentieth and the twenty-first centuries.[2] It will also raise conceptual issues that are vital to attempts to bring the academic and policy communities closer together in their approaches to crisis management. An extensive literature review concludes this chapter.[3] It is our intent that the framework for analysis and the summary of aggregate findings on crises presented in this chapter serve as useful reference points for more in-depth case study and comparative analysis.

DEFINITIONS

A *foreign policy crisis,* that is, a crisis for an individual state, is a situation with three necessary and sufficient conditions deriving from a change in the state's internal or external environment: (1) a threat to one or more basic values, (2) an awareness of finite time for response to the value threat, and (3) a heightened probability of involvement in military hostilities. All three must be perceived by the highest-level decision makers of the state actor concerned. There were 970 foreign policy crises for the period 1918–2002.

Two conditions define an *international crisis:* (1) a change in type or an increase in the intensity (or both) of disruptive (hostile verbal or physical) interactions between two or more states, with a heightened probability of military hostilities that, in turn, (2) destabilizes their relationship and challenges the structure of an international system—global, dominant, or subsystem. An international crisis begins with a disruptive action or event that creates a foreign policy crisis for one or more states. It ends with an act or event that denotes a qualitative reduction in conflictual activity.[4] There were 440 international crises during the period 1918–2002.

The Brecher-Wilkenfeld definitions of foreign policy and international crises differ from earlier standard definitions in several important respects. Charles Hermann, for example, proposed the following definition of crisis: "A crisis is a situation that (1) threatens high-priority goals of the decision-making unit, (2) restricts the amount of time available for response before the decision is transformed, and (3) surprises the members of the decision-making unit by its occurrence."[5] The clear differentiation between a crisis at the system level of analysis and a crisis as perceived by the leadership of a state at the actor level is a fundamental characteristic of the ICB Project crisis definitions. With regard to the Hermann definition, the ICB Project relaxes the requirement of surprise, arguing that, although many significant crises were not unanticipated, they nevertheless moved the decision makers into the high-stress mode of crisis management once they occurred. The Soviet imposition of a blockade on Berlin in 1948 was not unexpected by the United States, Britain, and France; yet it catalyzed a crisis when it occurred.

Similarly, we have relaxed the requirement for short response time. We posit, for example, that while the United States perceived a crisis on November 4, 1979, when Iranian students took over the U.S. embassy in Tehran, its major response did not come until April 24, 1980, when it attempted a rescue of the hostages. The ICB Project also allows for the possibility that the internal or domestic environment can trigger an international crisis, just as the military coup in Cyprus in July 1974 that ousted President Makarios triggered crises for Cyprus, Greece, and Turkey.

Finally, the ICB Project requires that each of the parties perceives a heightened probability of involvement in military hostilities. The December 13, 2001, attack on the Indian Parliament by Pakistani nationals immediately raised the probability of military hostilities between India and Pakistan higher than its normal high state. It will be particularly important to keep these definitional distinctions in mind as we examine evidence from twentieth-century crises.

Another key ICB Project concept is *protracted conflict*—also referred to in the literature as enduring rivalry.[6] Protracted conflicts are "hostile interactions which extend over long periods of time with sporadic outbreaks of open warfare fluctuating in frequency and intensity . . . [T]he stakes are very high. . . . [T]hey linger on in time . . . [and] are not specific events or even clusters of events at one point in time; they are processes."[7] Overall, 59 percent of all international crises in the twentieth century occurred as part of protracted conflicts, with the rate for Asia a staggering 75 percent. These Asian protracted conflicts include Afghanistan-Pakistan, China-Japan, China-Vietnam, India-Pakistan, Indochina, Indonesia, and Korea.

SCOPE OF ICB PROJECT

The ICB Project aggregate study is cross-national in scope and quantitative in form. Two types of analyses characterize the cross-national data

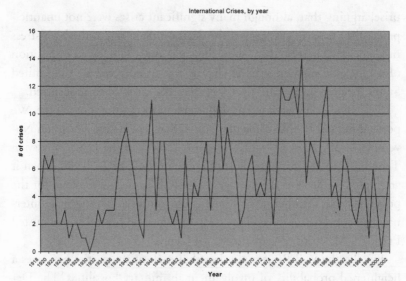

Figure 2-1: Distribution of International Crises, 1918–2002

set. One explores the distribution of crisis attributes over time, such as triggers and breakpoints, the gravity of value threat, crisis management techniques, the severity and centrality of violence, and crisis outcomes. The other focuses on the polarity of the international system at the time of a crisis, the extent of major-power activity, international and regional organization involvement, and similar systemic variables. The data set encompasses the twentieth century and the beginning of the twenty-first century and covers five different international systems: multipolar (1918–1939), World War II (1939–1945), bipolar (1945–1962), poly-centric (1963–1989), and unipolar (1990–2002). It incorporates the 135 new states that emerged at the end of the European imperial era. Figure 2-1 presents the distribution of crises for the period 1918–2002.[8]

The distribution of the 440 crises on a yearly basis provides a unique perspective on the ebb and flow of crises across this eighty-five-year period. Note that the number of states in the international system has increased almost fourfold during this period; thus, some of the more recent downward trends are even stronger than they appear in the graph. The clear decline in the yearly rate of international crises, particularly in the post-Cold War period, is noteworthy.

Number of Crises

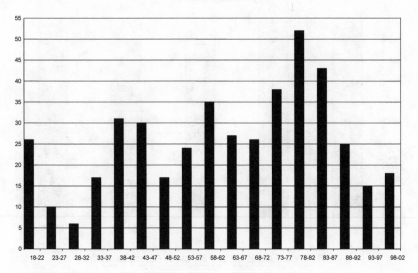

Figure 2-2: Number of Crises, in Five-Year Periods

TRENDS IN CRISES IN THE TWENTIETH CENTURY

The number of international crises per year increased steadily from 1918 to the late 1980s; this can be seen in the four-year aggregates in figure 2-2. There was a 46 percent increase in crises per year from the interwar era of multipolarity (1918–1939) to bipolarity (1945–1962), a further 39 percent increase from bipolarity to polycentrism (1963–1989), followed by a dramatic 50 percent *decline* from polycentrism to post–Cold War unipolarity. The decline in power of the Soviet Union in the late 1980s, culminating in its disintegration into fifteen independent states, coupled with the emergence of the United States as the dominant military power in the system, can partly explain this recent sharp reduction in the number of international crises per year. These events profoundly affected the nature and frequency of international crises.

Although the global system remains dangerous, the defining characteristics of international crises are less often present in the conflict situations that typify the post–Cold War unipolar era. Instead, there has been a proliferation of conflicts based on ethnicity, nationality, and religion, most of which—Al Qaeda aside—do not threaten the structure

Percentage of Crises

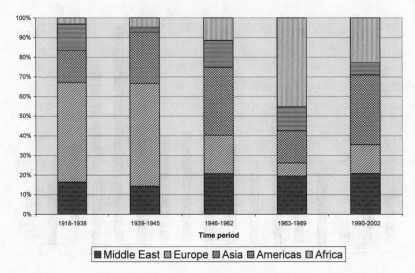

Figure 2-3: Location of International Crises in Time and Space

of the international system. It is helpful to more closely examine the crises that began in the immediate post–Cold War international system.

Figure 2-3 shows a significant shift in the locus of crises across the century, with particularly sharp increases for Africa and Asia and a sharp decline for Europe. Africa saw its largest increase from 1963 to 1989, when the continent accounted for 45 percent of all international crises for that era. After the Cold War ended, Africa accounted for only 24 percent. Asian crises were 34 percent of the total in the 1945–1962 bipolar period; this dropped to 16 percent in the 1963–1989 era and jumped again to 32 percent in the post–Cold War era. Meanwhile, crises in Europe dropped from 53 percent of all international crises from 1918 to 1945 to just 7 percent during polycentrism, and then rose to 13 percent in the post–Cold War era. The Middle East holds steady at about 20 percent during the entire post–World War II period.

ICB Project data show a shift in the states most responsible for triggering international crises since the end of World War II. The stars of the unipolar system since 1990 have been Iraq, which triggered five crises in this era, and Pakistan, which triggered two.[9] In the immediately previous polycentric era, from 1963 to 1989, the leading triggering states were South Africa, Libya, Israel, Pakistan, and Rhodesia-Zimbabwe.

International crises of the post–Cold War era are markedly different from those of the previous four decades. Threat, as perceived by the crisis actors, increased in gravity from high threat levels of 17 percent for the earlier eras to 32 percent for the post–Cold War era. Violent crisis management techniques were somewhat more prevalent among post–Cold War crises (63 percent) than those that preceded them (55 percent). Decisive outcomes are less common—perceptions of victory or defeat on the part of the actors characterized 47 percent of the earlier crises but only 34 percent of the post–Cold War crises.

It is interesting that the role of ethnicity has held steady for the entire period from 1945 to 2002—it has been a significant factor in about 30 percent of all crises in each successive era. This latter finding on ethnicity and crisis is particularly interesting because of the common perception that a rise in subnational and particularly ethnic conflict has accompanied the decline in international conflict and crisis in the post–Cold War era. Not only was that not the case, but we also find no evidence of an increase in the role of ethnicity in international crises.[10] In addition, protracted conflicts characterized about 55 percent of all crises across the entire eighty-five-year period, with the post–Cold War period showing particular activity in the India-Pakistan, Arab-Israel, Taiwan Strait, Korea, and Iraq regime protracted conflicts.

One of the more intriguing trends is the increasing use of mediation by the international community in attempts to resolve crises: the mediation rate was 22 percent during multipolarity (1918–1939), 27 percent during bipolarity (1945–1962), 35 percent during polycentrism (1963–1989), and 47 percent during post–Cold War unipolarity (1990–2001). This parallels other evidence we have found on the general shift in recent years toward mediated management of social conflicts.[11] Mediation appears to be less prevalent when one or more of the following conditions are absent: territorial issues are in contention, crises are characterized by multiple issues, ethnicity is involved, crisis actors are geographically contiguous, crises occur at the subsystem instead of at the dominant system level, and if extreme violence, often at the level of full-scale war, has occurred.

Thus, from the perspective of international politics, the system has become less dangerous. There is less potential for the conflict to spill over into the international system through hostility among nation-states; the crises that do arise are less likely to be embedded in ongoing protracted conflicts; and post–Cold War crises have been far more amenable to mediation on the part of the international community and its various organs. Nevertheless, a number of actors still exist whose propensity to become involved in crises continues unabated, and the seriousness of many of the crises they generate—in terms of levels of threat, the employment of violence in crisis management, and the tendency of some of these crises to involve large numbers of actors—continues to be a concern to the international community well into the first decade of the twenty-first century.[12] Finally, some of the most serious protracted conflicts, including Korea, Taiwan Strait, Arab-Israel, Greece-Turkey, and India-Pakistan, have carried over into the post–Cold War era while two new protracted conflicts, in Yugoslavia and Iraq, have emerged.

While the data examined above cover only the period through 2002, we now know that both the Al Qaeda-Afghanistan situation and the Iraq-U.S. crisis over weapons of mass destruction and the Iraqi regime have resulted in full-scale wars. This type of extremely violent conflict appears as an aberration to the trends we have noted in international crises of the post–Cold War era. As with all trends, we will have to wait for more data points before we will be able to posit the existence of a new pattern of behavior for the international system.

CRITICAL CONCEPTUAL AND DEFINITIONAL ISSUES

Several conceptual and definitional issues promise to be of particular importance for the international community in general and for potential crises involving China and the United States in particular.

Near Crises

Patrick James has introduced the concept of "near crisis" as a way to obtain greater understanding of why some international conflicts escalate to the level of a full-fledged crisis while others do not.[13] This is a critical point, because when we analyze three often-cited examples of recent "crises" involving the United States and China, we consider the

Taiwan Strait crisis of 1995–1996 to be a full international crisis behavior case but consider the Belgrade embassy bombing and the EP-3 incidents to be near crises.

James defines a near crisis as a conflict that approaches the intensity of an international crisis in the following way: each involved actor perceives a threat to basic values and a finite time for response but not an increased probability of military hostilities (that is, two of the three defining conditions for a foreign policy crisis exist, but not all three). In formal terms, possible escalation from near crisis to international crisis would be explained by the following factors:

$$c = b_0 + b_1 g1 + b_2 g2 + b_3 r1 + b_4 e1 + b_5 T1 + b_6 t2 + b_7 I1 + b_8 i2 + e$$
where

$c =$ likelihood of a near crisis escalating to an international crisis;

$g1 =$ proximity between states;

$g2 =$ contiguity between states;

$r1 =$ rivalry between states;

$e1 =$ ethnic dimension to the conflict;

$T1 =$ proportion of nondemocratic states in system;

$t2 =$ authoritarian or mixed dyad;

$I1 =$ nonintervention by international organizations;

$i2 =$ nonintervention by great powers and superpowers.[14]

Although it may sound simplistic, it is important for policy makers on both sides to make sure that crises are not treated as near crises, and that near crises are not treated as crises. A related issue is whether each side sees the crisis in the same way. Thus, it is extremely dangerous if one party sees the situation as only a near crisis because it does not perceive for itself the critical element of heightened probability of involvement in military hostilities, while the other party perceives the existence of all three defining characteristics of a crisis. This can lead to classic misperceptions and may ultimately lead to a full-scale crisis where one might have been avoided.

Table 2-1 lists the sixteen international crises in which China has been involved since the end of World War II, as identified by the ICB

Table 2-1. China's International Crises Since 1945

Crisis	Year of crisis trigger	U.S. involvement
China Civil War	1948	Yes
Korea War I	1950[1]	Yes
Korea War II	1950	Yes
Korea War III	1953	Yes
Taiwan Strait I	1954	Yes
Taiwan Strait II	1958	Yes
China-India Border I	1959	No
Taiwan Strait III	1962	No
China-India Border II	1962	No
Ussuri River	1969	No
Sino-Vietnam War	1978	No
Sino-Vietnam Clashes	1984	No
Sino-Vietnam Border	1987	No
Spratley Islands	1988	No
Taiwan Strait IV	1995	No
North Korea Nuclear II	2002	Yes

Source: International Crisis Behavior Project, University of Maryland.

Note: This table classifies crises according to criteria of the International Crisis Behavior Project at the University of Maryland. The names of crises in this table are similar to, but not identical with, terminology used in this volume.

[1] The International Crisis Behavior Project codes the Korean War of 1950–1953 as three separate crises, with the second and third crises being intrawar crises: Korea War I: June 25 to September 30, 1950; Korea War II: September 30, 1950 to July 10, 1951; Korea War III: April 16 to July 27, 1953. Conceptually, an intrawar crisis begins during an ongoing war and is characterized by an increase in the intensity of disruptive interaction and incipient change within the structure of an international system. It differs from all other international crises only in the setting in which it occurs, that is, during an ongoing war. An international crisis is identified as an intrawar crisis when three conditions obtain: (1) the crisis is an integral part of an ongoing war; (2) at least one of the principal adversaries is a continuing actor in that war; and (3) it is an interstate war, not a civil or a purely guerrilla war. The International Crisis Behavior Project classifies 18 percent of all crises as intrawar crises.

Project. Table 2-1 also indicates whether the United States was an actor in each crisis, that is, whether it too experienced high threat, finite time for response, and heightened probability of involvement in military hostilities. Two factors are important. First, although the involvement of the United States as a crisis actor characterized all Chinese crises through 1958, only one Chinese crisis since then has involved the United States directly as an actor.[15] Despite this one exception, this is a stunning finding. While observers might quibble over certain definitional rigidities that make this finding stark, it is nevertheless quite obvious that a shift occurred quite early in the dynamic of interaction between these two powers.

Second, table 2-1 shows that, although many observers consider the Vietnam War, the Taiwan Strait crisis of 1995–1996, the bombing of the Chinese embassy in 1999, and the EP-3 aircraft incident of 2001 as instances of crisis involving the United States and China, the ICB Project considers only the Taiwan Strait crisis as a U.S.-China international crisis and holds that the case did not involve the United States as a crisis actor. The other three cases did not demonstrate the necessary perception of a heightened probability of military hostilities, even for China. In this sense, these cases are strong candidates for what James has termed near crisis.

Differing Perceptions of Crises

Even when both parties recognize they are locked in a crisis, it does not necessarily mean they will view the dangers in the same way. Therefore, their coping mechanisms may be starkly different. According to Bobrow, Chan, and Kringen, national elites differ in their recognition, interpretation, and application of precedents as historical lessons.[16] In such a situation, there is again room for misperception, unintended escalation, and an inability to find mutually satisfying outcome strategies.

Perhaps the most interesting case is the contrast between Western and Chinese perspectives and tendencies. Bobrow, Chan, and Kringen in 1979 wrote that most Western observers believe that an international crisis:

- Is an unusual situation that triggers exceptional coping mechanisms by political institutions and individual decision makers;
- Creates stress for the units under analysis, which may include the international system, alliances, policy bureaucracies, or individual officials;
- Presents anomalous, irregular, deviant, and low-probability problems for policy treatment because a crisis is triggered by abrupt or acute changes in the behavior of foreign nations or external political movements;
- Portends the widespread disturbance of what would otherwise be an ongoing, stable set of international relationships;

- Involves threats posed to one's own interests by some foreign party;
- Evinces acts of conflict and violence in general and military-political threats and activities in particular; and
- Lasts for only a short length of time.[17]

The Chinese doctrinal conception of critical international incidents or crises differs substantially from the mainstream Western discussion. Thus, using the above seven-point classification, Bobrow, Chan, and Kringen propose that, to the Chinese, an international crisis:

- Differs from other situations only in the level and intensity of actions and signals;
- Provides opportunities to advance one's interests as well as causing stresses and dangers;
- Results from long-term economic processes and predictably reflects the normally competitive and antagonistic nature of international relations;
- Evinces the inherently unstable, fragile, turbulent, and perpetually changing nature of international relations;
- Stems primarily from domestic, not foreign, phenomena (at least in the initial stage);
- Entails the controlled use of confrontation and compromise, and centrally involves economic problems and solutions (military-political matters are only their concomitants or consequences); and
- Extends over a long time (dealing with such protracted phenomena requires persistent struggle, perseverance, and patience).[18]

The critical question is whether the contrasts in these conceptions of crisis endure today, given the enormous changes that have taken place in the international system. Does the West in general and the United States in particular still view crisis as an unusual occurrence that triggers exceptional coping mechanisms? Where does the George W. Bush doctrine of preemption fit into this Western conception? Do Chinese officials still view crisis as an opportunity to advance their international agenda? Or has China's emergence as a major player on the international political-diplomatic scene forced it more toward the Western conception of crisis, which associates crisis with stress and threat instead of opportunity? How might differences in what some call strategic culture help explain differences in policy options?[19] In the words of Johnston and Ross, "[W]ill China's growing stake in the global and regional capitalist economies and security institutions promote a profoundly status quo mentality among its leaders, who are desperate for the legitimacy that economic growth and international status can buy them[?]"[20]

Threat Crises and Opportunity Crises

Closely related to the notion of differing perceptions of crisis is the dichotomy between threat crises and opportunity crises. Zeev Maoz proposes that opportunity crises emerge as a result of a deliberate, conscious, and calculated initiative.[21] As Hemda Ben-Yehuda notes, stress is the key element differentiating these two situations. In the threat situation, all actors experience stress; but in the opportunity situation, there is an asymmetrical situation or stress gap between the adversaries. Ben-Yehuda argues: "The initiator of an opportunity crisis always anticipates gain as a result of the crisis it triggers. . . . If it perceives threat at all, it will be substantially lower than that perceived by the target state(s)."[22]

Focusing only on crises initiated by single states, Ben-Yehuda finds 187 threat crises and 106 opportunity crises among ICB Project cases for the period 1918–1994.[23] In many instances the opportunity actor will itself become a crisis actor because of the actions of the initial threat actor, but it is clear that stress levels will be lower, primarily because of the absence of the element of surprise. It should be quite clear that asymmetric crises, which mix opportunity and threat crisis actors, must be watched closely because of the heightened possibility that the parties will misperceive each other's intentions.

Crisis Management and Conflict Resolution

Just as crises are a specific type of conflict, crisis management differs from conflict resolution. An examination of the literature reveals that there exists neither a single definition of crisis management or conflict resolution nor any agreement regarding what constitutes the successful achievement of either of these outcomes.[24] Many scholars, in fact, either dispense with clear definitions of these terms or fail to specify distinctions between them, opting instead to speak of them as one and the same.[25] It is useful, however, to make such distinctions between the two because they are often separate, though sometimes interrelated, pursuits.

Crisis management is most often thought of as the "attempt to control events during a crisis to prevent significant and systematic violence from occurring."[26] The majority of the literature on crisis management looks at this concept from the perspective of a state in crisis.[27] From this viewpoint, crisis management is usually thought of as a problem faced by top-tier decision makers wherein they must discover the optimal combination of coercion and accommodation because their goal is to avoid war while still maximizing gains or minimizing losses.[28] Another way to think of this problem is to frame it as the attempt to balance coercive diplomacy and strategic military moves with risk control in the form of moves aimed at avoiding war.[29]

The primary and distinct mission of crisis intervention aimed at managing a crisis is to terminate the immediate crisis before it escalates or spreads. Several scholars frame this type of intervention as any effort aimed at settlement of the conflict, which entails simply a political agreement regarding the immediate issues under dispute or the violent interactions manifested between the parties, as distinct from resolution of the conflict.[30] As I. William Zartman puts it, management involves "eliminating the violent and violence-related means of pursuing the conflict, leaving it to be worked out on the purely political level."[31] Management implies a "temporary respite in an otherwise ongoing conflict," a neutralization of the destructive consequences of a conflict.[32] Thought of in this way, crisis management can include any of the following activities: deterrence moves and reactions to them, arbitration, repression of the conflict, containment of the conflict, arms reductions, or any solution that involves the disputants simply arriving at a consensus based on compromise, with or without the assistance of a mediator.[33] Management nearly always involves the division of power and commonly takes place in a power-bargaining situation.[34] Third parties acting as crisis managers often seek to slow the pace of events occurring between the conflicting parties, communicate constantly with these parties, and encourage the parties to be more flexible regarding their thoughts and actions.[35]

Conflict resolution differs from crisis management most fundamentally in the scope of objectives exhibited by mediators or negotiators.

Those engaging in conflict resolution are not simply concerned with controlling the negative, violent expressions and side effects of a conflictual relationship.[36] Their goal is to move beyond temporary settlements and toward eliminating the roots of the conflict between the parties, which is often an extremely difficult and labor- and time-intensive pursuit.[37] The challenge is to get the parties to redefine or restructure their relations in such a way that their goals no longer conflict or that they realize that they each can achieve their goals without conflict with each other.[38] If the elimination of conflict is not possible, conflict resolution initiatives may attempt to encourage parties to view conflict in a constructive, rather than a zero-sum, manner.[39]

Many of those arguing that conflict resolution is or should be the ultimate goal of conflict termination view conflict as a social construct—one that is not only most often the result of misperception or miscommunication, but one that is also malleable.[40] This perspective holds that conflict is deeply subjective and based on interests and values that are prone to change over time. Thus, the mediator pursuing conflict resolution seeks to alter the biases and misperceptions that are part of the disputants' decision-making processes.[41] Conflict resolution is aimed at "discovering possibilities for change, identifying conditions for change, and overcoming resistances to change."[42] This process often involves improving the diplomatic relations between the conflicting parties to the extent that they begin to cease viewing each other as adversaries. It also often entails altering the conditions of the disputants' relationship so that societal dialogue becomes more consensual.[43] Conflict resolution is advisable especially for conflicts where human needs such as identity, security, and other existential concerns are at stake and must be satisfied.[44]

Scholarly work on conflict resolution has described at length the structural conditions that must be present in the disputants' relationship for such resolution to be actualized, usually in terms of directives to the disputants or third parties. Temporary settlements should be only intermediate stages en route to an eradication of the roots of the conflict.[45] Jacob Bercovitch, in fact, argues that cease-fires and other temporary settlements are indicators of only partial mediation success.[46] Alternatively, the mediation processes that result in formal outcomes that resolve most of the issues in dispute allow for stable interactions between parties, and they generate opportunities for more positive future interactions between the parties. One may also define success in terms of the implementability and permanence of an outcome or of the degree of satisfaction of the parties with the results of the mediation effort—factors often associated with resolution instead of management.[47]

Analysts have duly noted that judging the success of conflict management and resolution on the basis of objective criteria is often futile because mediators and negotiators have different goals in mind when they engage in such processes.[48] As we have argued, conflict resolution and crisis management are, of course, related, but they are distinct goals and pursuits. If the goal is simply crisis management, success may be defined as "any written or unwritten mutually agreeable arrangements between parties that at least temporarily resolve or remove from contention one or more, but not necessarily all, of the issues underlying the dispute."[49] Marieke Kleiboer argues that mediators for whom settlement is the ultimate goal often see conflict as intrinsic to the relations between states and that it will hence never be fully eliminated.[50] Keeping the destructive manifestations of conflict in check is therefore the extent of what is possible.

Regardless of mediator or negotiator goals, it is often the case that crisis management is a necessary step that must be taken before trying to find a more deep-seated solution to the conflict that resolves all of the issues underlying the conflict within which the crisis occurs.[51] Keashly and Fisher argue for an approach to mediation contingent with the level of conflict intensity at any given point.[52] This allows for the combination of crisis management and conflict resolution objectives, depending on the stage of the conflict. Keashly and Fisher found conflict resolution in the form of consultation or problem solving to be especially useful as a precursor or follow-up to more intrusive forms of mediation aimed at management and settlement that are based on compromise.[53]

Joint Crises

In dealing with the general topic of crisis management, it is important to distinguish clearly among cases based on the interests of the parties concerned. For any dyad of states, including the United States and China, we propose three classes of situations based on interests:

- Diametrically opposed situations. Interests of the two parties diverge completely. The six crisis cases between 1948 and 1958 listed in table 2-1 constituted instances where, for the most part, the interests of the United States and China diverged completely. Both parties were crisis actors, and they were in crisis because core values of each were threatened by the other.

- Quasi-opposed situations. One party is a crisis actor—that is, one party perceives threat, finite time for response, and heightened probability of military hostilities—while the other party is an involved actor but not a crisis actor. During the Taiwan Strait crises of 1962 and 1995–1996, while China was clearly a crisis actor, the United States, although vitally interested and involved, was not an actor in the crisis.

- Jointly opposed situations. A situation in which the United States and China find themselves for the most part on the same side during the crisis. Most likely, they will both be involved actors, as was the case during the crises of India-Pakistan in 1999; Kashmir-Kargil in 1999; and the attack on India's Parliament in 2001. Or they may both be crisis actors, as in the North Korea nuclear crisis of 2002–2003, but they find themselves on roughly the same side of the issue.

These three situations obviously call for different modes of behavior, reflecting the complex relations between the two parties. Perception matters. Each party must be aware of the other side's interests in order to determine whether the two sets of interests are diametrically or quasi-opposed. Jointly opposed situations obviously offer the greatest opportunity for cooperative strategies, while those situations characterized as diametrically opposed are the most dangerous because they would appear to offer little opportunity for management or resolution. Indeed, diametrically opposed situations are largely zero-sum, while quasi-opposed situations are mixed-sum, allowing for the possibility of win-win strategies and outcomes.

CONCLUSION

After reviewing the state of the academic field of international crisis and crisis management and examining some trends in international crises during the past century, this chapter posed five conceptual and definitional issues that could help policy makers and analysts improve Sino-American crisis management. These comprised the concept of a near crisis, differing perceptions of crisis, threat crises versus opportunity crises, crisis management versus conflict resolution, and joint crises. Although crisis managers of great powers will always be constrained by a variety of domestic and international contextual variables and will bring to the table different traditions, practices, and historical records, they will increasingly need to be aware of each other's approach and background in order to reach more effective and stable outcomes. This chapter has sought to outline some of the key issues for attaining a better crisis management environment for the United States and China.

THE LITERATURE ON CRISIS

In Michael Brecher, *Crises in World Politics* (Oxford: Pergamon Press, 1993), Brecher separates the literature on crisis into works that deal with substance, models of crisis decision making, and methodology. In terms of crisis, the literature covers four topics: crisis anticipation, decision-making processes, crisis management and third-party intervention, and bargaining in crisis. Some of the earliest contemporary work by Charles A. McClelland on international crisis focused on crisis anticipation, most notably using event data to track changes in the patterns of interactions among contentious dyads as a way of enhancing early-warning capabilities. Examples include Charles A. McClelland, "The Acute International Crisis," in K. Knorr, ed., *The International System: Theoretical Essays* (Princeton, N.J.: Princeton University Press, 1961); Charles A. McClelland, "Action Structures and Communications in Two International Crises: Quemoy and Berlin," *Background* 7 (1964), pp. 201–215; Charles A. McClelland, "Access to Berlin: The Quantity and Variety of Events, 1948–1963," in J. D. Singer, *Quantitative International Politics* (New York: Free Press, 1968); and Charles A. McClelland, "The Beginning, Duration, and Abatement of International Crises: Comparisons in Two Conflict Arenas," in C. F. Hermann, ed., *International Crises: Insights and Evidence* (New York: Free Press, 1972).

Sophisticated early-warning analyses of conflict interactions in works by several scholars followed early work on the World Events Interaction

Survey (WEIS). Such works include Deborah J. Gerner and Philip Schrodt, "The Effects of Media Coverage on Crisis Assessment and Early Warning in the Middle East," in S. Schmeidl and H. Adelman, eds., *Early Warning and Early Response* (New York: Columbia University Press Online, 1998); Philip A. Schrodt and Deborah J. Gerner, "Empirical Indicators of Crisis Phase in the Arab-Israeli Conflict, 1979–1995," *Journal of Conflict Resolution* 41, no. 4 (1997), pp. 529–552; Philip A. Schrodt and Deborah J. Gerner, "Cluster Analysis as an Early Warning Technique for the Middle East, 1979–1996," in J. Davies and T. R. Gurr, eds., *Risk Assessment and Crisis Early Warning Systems* (New York: Rowman & Littlefield, 1998), pp. 95–107; Philip A. Schrodt and Deborah J. Gerner, "Cluster-Based Early Warning Indicators for Political Change in the Contemporary Levant," *American Political Science Review* 94, no. 4 (2000), pp. 803–817; John L. Davies and Ted Robert Gurr, *Preventive Measures: Building Risk Assessment and Crisis Early Warning Systems* (Lanham, Md.: Rowman & Littlefield, 1998); Monty G. Marshall and T. R. Gurr, *Peace and Conflict 2003* (College Park: University of Maryland, Center for International Development and Conflict Management, 2003); and Monty G. Marshall and T. R. Gurr, *Peace and Conflict 2005* (College Park, Md.: University of Maryland, Center for International Development and Conflict Management, 2005). There is, of course, a large literature on factors contributing to the failure of states to anticipate crisis and war.

Perhaps the most influential work on decision-making processes is Richard C. Snyder, H. W. Bruck, and B. Sapin, "Decision-Making as an Approach to the Study of International Politics," in R. Snyder, H. Bruck, and B. Sapin, eds., *Foreign Policy Decision-Making: An Approach to the Study of International Politics* (New York: Free Press, 1962), which presents a complex framework for analyzing foreign policy decision making. Peter F. Trumbore and Mark A. Boyer, "Two-Level Negotiations in International Crisis: Testing the Impact of Regime Type and Issue Area," *Journal of Peace Research* 37, no. 6 (2000), pp. 679–698 provides a game theoretic approach to decision-making processes.

Much of this work focused on the decision-making processes of specific states, usually major actors in the international system. Thus, for example, several experts wrote extensively on U.S. decision making during the Cuban missile crisis. These experts include Graham Allison, *The*

Essence of Decision: Explaining the Cuban Missile Crisis (Boston: Little Brown, 1971); Graham Allison and Philip Zelikow, *The Essence of Decision: Explaining the Cuban Missile Crisis,* 2nd ed. (New York: Longman, 1999); and Gregory Herek, Irving L. Janis, and Paul Huth, "Decisionmaking During International Crises: Is Quality of Process Related to Outcome?" *Journal of Conflict Resolution* 31, no. 3 (1987), pp. 203–226. Similarly, analysts have examined decision making by the Soviet Union during key Cold War crises. Hannes Adomeit, *Soviet Risk-Taking and Crisis Behavior* (London: Allen and Unwin, 1982), examines the 1948–1949 and 1961 Berlin crises. Galia Golan, *Yom Kippur and After: The Soviet Union and the Middle East Crisis* (Cambridge: Cambridge University Press, 1977); Galia Golan, "Soviet Decisionmaking in the Yom Kippur War, 1973," in J. Valenta and W. C. Potter, eds., *Soviet Decisionmaking for National Security* (Boston: Allen and Unwin, 1984); and Alvin Z. Rubinstein, *Red Star on the Nile: Soviet-Egyptian Influence Relationship Since the June War* (Princeton, N.J.: Princeton University Press, 1977) examine the 1973 Yom Kippur crisis-war. Karen Dawisha, *The Kremlin and the Prague Spring* (Berkeley: University of California Press, 1984), examines the 1968 Prague Spring crisis.

Other topics that have occupied scholars who have focused on the decision-making process in individual states include system structure, groupthink, group setting, use of force, operational codes, leadership performance, and historical lessons.

Crisis management and third-party intervention constitutes a third theme. Works that focus on this topic include Oran Young, *The Intermediaries: Third Parties in International Crises* (Princeton, N.J.: Princeton University Press, 1967); Ernst B. Haas, "Regime Decay: Conflict Management and International Organizations, 1945–1981," *International Organization* 37, no. 2 (1983), pp. 189–256; Ernst B. Haas, "Why We Still Need the United Nations," University of California Policy Papers in International Affairs no. 26 (Berkeley: University of California, Institute for International Studies), 1986; Michael Brecher and Jonathan Wilkenfeld, *Conflict, Crisis, and War* (Oxford: Pergamon, 1989); Jonathan Wilkenfeld et al., "Mediating International Crises: Cross-National and Experimental Perspectives," *Journal of Conflict Resolution* 47, no. 3 (2003), pp. 279–301; and Jonathan Wilkenfeld et al., *Mediating International Crises* (Oxford: Routledge, 2005).

Researchers have also explored coping mechanisms; see such works as Alexander L. George, "Case Studies and Theory Development," in P. G. Lauren, ed., *Diplomacy: New Approaches in History, Theory, and Policy* (New York: Free Press, 1979); Alexander A. George, "Crisis Management: The Interaction of Political and Military Considerations," *Survival* 26, no. 5 (1984), pp. 223–234; Alexander George, *Avoiding War: Problems of Crisis Management* (Boulder, Colo.: Westview Press, 1991); Alexander L. George and Richard Smoke, *Deterrence in American Foreign Policy* (New York: Columbia University Press, 1974); and Brecher and Wilkenfeld, *Conflict, Crisis, and War.*

A fourth theme is bargaining during crisis. Perhaps the most influential works are the following: Russell J. Leng, "When Will They Ever Learn: Coercive Bargaining in Recurrent Crises," *Journal of Conflict Resolution* 27 (1983), pp. 379–419; Russell J. Leng, "Structure and Action in Militarized Disputes," in C. F. Hermann, C. W. Kegley Jr., and J. N. Rosenau, eds., *New Directions in the Study of Foreign Policy* (Boston: Allen & Unwin, 1987); Russell J. Leng, *Interstate Crisis Behavior, 1816–1980: Realism Versus Reciprocity* (Cambridge: Cambridge University Press, 1993); Russell J. Leng, *Bargaining and Learning in Recurring Crises: The Soviet-American, Egyptian-Israeli, and Indo-Pakistani Rivalries* (Ann Arbor: University of Michigan Press, 2000); Russell J. Leng and J. David Singer, "Militarized Interstate Crises: The BCOW Typology and Its Applications," *International Studies Quarterly* 32 (1988), pp. 155–173; T. Clifton Morgan, *Untying the Knot of War: A Bargaining Theory of International Crises* (Ann Arbor: University of Michigan Press, 1994); Robert Powell, *In the Shadow of Power: States and Strategies in International Politics* (Princeton, N.J.: Princeton University Press, 1999); and James D. Fearon, "Rationalist Explanations for War," *International Organization* 49, no. 3 (1995).

Ole R. Holsti, "Crisis Decision Making," in P. E. Tetlock et al., eds., *Behavior, Society and Nuclear War* (New York: Oxford University Press, 1989), addresses models of decision making, Brecher's second category of crisis management decision-making literature. Early work on hostile interactions among parties to crises includes work by Ole R. Holsti such as "The 1914 Case," *American Political Science Review* 59, no. 2 (1965), pp. 365–378; and *Crisis, Escalation, War* (Montreal: McGill-Queen's University Press, 1972).

A focus on the conflict-begets-conflict model followed, in works such as Jonathan Wilkenfeld, Virginia Lussier, and Dale Tahtinen, "Conflict Interactions in the Middle East, 1949–1967," in *Journal of Conflict Resolution* (1972); Jonathan Wilkenfeld, "A Time-Series Perspective on Conflict in the Middle East," in P. McGowan, ed., *Sage International Yearbook of Foreign Policy Studies* (Los Angeles: Sage Publications, 1975); Jonathan Wilkenfeld, "Trigger-Response Transitions in Foreign Policy Crises, 1929–1985," in *Journal of Conflict Resolution* 35, no. 1 (1991), pp. 143–169; and Dina A. Zinnes and Jonathan Wilkenfeld, "An Analysis of Foreign Conflict Behavior of Nations," in W. F. Hanrieder, ed., *Comparative Foreign Policy: Theoretical Essays* (New York: McKay, 1971).

Many models of crisis decision making focused on psychological factors, including the notion of individual stress and how decision makers coped with stress under varying circumstances. The impact of stress on the search for information and policy options and on the ability of decision makers under stress to properly assess possible consequences of actions and to choose among options rationally became central concerns of scholars. Cognitive models of crisis decision making made significant inroads. Useful works on these topics include Robert Axelrod, *Structure of Decision: The Cognitive Maps of Political Elites* (Princeton, N.J.: Princeton University Press, 1976); Robert Jervis, *Perception and Misperception in International Politics* (Princeton, N.J.: Princeton University Press, 1976); Yaakov Y. I. Vertzberger, *The World in Their Minds: Information Processing, Cognition, and Perception in Foreign Policy Decision Making* (Stanford, Calif.: Stanford University Press, 1990); and Yaakov Y. I. Vertzberger, "Foreign Policy Decision Makers as Practical Intuitive Historian: Applied History and Its Shortcomings," *International Studies Quarterly* 30, no. 2 (1986), pp. 223–247.

One of the central issues for those who develop models of crisis decision making is the level of analysis. In "Crisis Decision Making," Ole R. Holsti proposes four levels: state, bureaucratic organization, decision-making group, and individual. Holsti then compares these levels in terms of conceptualization of decision making: sources of theory, insight, and evidence; premises; constraints on rational decision making; and prognosis—crisis versus noncrisis decisions. In crisis, failure to properly detect the level at which decision makers are making crisis decisions can lead to serious misperceptions on the part of the crisis participants.

Brecher's final category is those works that address methodology. Several authors address methodology in the qualitative sense. Harry Eckstein, "Case Study and Theory in Political Science," in F. I. Greenstein and N. W. Polsby, eds., *Handbook of Political Science* (Reading, Mass.: Addison, Wesley, 1975) covers the crucial case study. For the comparative case study using structured focused comparison, see Alexander L. George, "Case Studies and Theory Development"; and George and Smoke, *Deterrence in American Foreign Policy*. Michael Brecher, *The Foreign Policy System of Israel: Setting, Images, Process* (New Haven: Yale University Press, 1972); R. Ned Lebow, *Between Peace and War: The Nature of International Crisis* (Baltimore: Johns Hopkins University Press, 1981); and the numerous ICB Project case studies address structured empiricism.

Quantitative analysis of international crisis is divisible into roughly two main types. Aggregate cross-national studies share the belief that the systematic, social scientific study of the causes, evolution, actor behavior, outcomes, and consequences of crisis is possible, and that such knowledge will facilitate the effective management of crises so as to minimize their adverse effects on world order. This chapter examines one such sustained effort, the International Crisis Behavior Project. Other works include McClelland, "The Beginning, Duration, and Abatement of International Crises"; McClelland, "Access to Berlin"; McClelland, "Action Structures and Communications in Two International Crises"; Charles S. Gochman and Zeev Maoz, "Militarized Interstate Disputes, 1816–1976: Procedures, Patterns, Insights," *Journal of Conflict Resolution* 28, no. 4 (1984), pp. 585–615; Leng and Singer, "Militarized Interstate Crises"; Brecher and Wilkenfeld, *Conflict, Crisis, and War;* Michael Brecher and Jonathan Wilkenfeld, *Crises in the Twentieth Century: Handbook of International Crises* (Oxford: Pergamon, 1988); Michael Brecher and Jonathan Wilkenfeld, *A Study of Crisis* (Ann Arbor: University of Michigan Press, 2000); Jonathan Wilkenfeld and Michael Brecher, *Crises in the Twentieth Century: Handbook of Foreign Policy Crises* (Oxford: Pergamon, 1988); and David Rousseau et al., "Assessing the Dyadic Nature of the Democratic Peace, 1918–1988," *American Political Science Review* (1996).

The second quantitative approach to international crisis is based on game theory and experimental techniques. Game theoretic approaches include the investigation of the dynamics of crisis bargaining in Steven J. Brams and D. Marc Kilgour, *Game Theory and National Security* (New York: Basil Blackwell, 1988); the use of game theory to analyze the 1967 Middle East crisis in Benjamin D. Mor, *Decision and Interaction in Crisis: A Model of International Crisis Behavior* (Westport, Conn.: Praeger, 1993); the theory of international crisis in T. Clifton Morgan, *Untying the Knot of War;* and the theory of moves by crisis actors proposed in Steven Brams, *Theory of Moves* (New York: Cambridge University Press, 1994).

Jonathan Wilkenfeld and the Crisis and Negotiation (CAN) research team have used experimental simulation approaches to study a number of factors in international crisis. Tara E. Santmire et al., "The Impact of Cognitive Diversity on Crisis Negotiations," *Political Psychology* 19, no. 4 (1998), pp. 721–748, addresses cognitive complexity among crisis negotiators. Jonathan Wilkenfeld et al., "Mediating International Crises: Cross-National and Experimental Perspectives," focuses on the role of mediation in crisis management and conflict resolution. Mintz, Geva, and Sylvan are conducting related experimental work, available in such works as: Alex Mintz and Nehemia Geva, "Why Don't Democracies Fight Each Other?" *Journal of Conflict Resolution* 37, no. 3 (1993), pp. 484–503; Alex Mintz et al., "The Effect of Dynamic and Static Choice Sets on Political Decision Making: An Analysis Using the Decision Board Platform," *American Political Science Review* 91, no. 3 (1997); and D. A. Sylvan and D. M. Haddad, "Reasoning and Problem Representation in Foreign Policy: Groups, Individuals, and Stories," in D. A. Sylvan and J. F. Voss, eds., *Problem Representation in Foreign Policy Decision Making* (Cambridge: Cambridge University Press, 1998).

NOTES

1. Examples include Munich in 1938, the partition of Palestine in 1947, Dien Bien Phu in 1954, and the United Nations Special Commission (UNSCOM) inspections of 1997–1998.

2. Michael Brecher, Jonathan Wilkenfeld, and Sheila Moser, *Crises in the Twentieth Century: Handbook of International Crises* (Oxford: Pergamon, 1988); Michael Brecher and Jonathan Wilkenfeld, *A Study of Crisis* (Ann

Arbor: University of Michigan Press, 2000); Jonathan Wilkenfeld, Michael Brecher, and Sheila Moser, *Crises in the Twentieth Century: Handbook of Foreign Policy Crises* (Oxford: Pergamon, 1988). The disconnect between the important theoretical and conceptual work on crisis and the lack of hard empirical data with which to evaluate alternative theories of crisis behavior led in 1975 to the initiation of the International Crisis Behavior (ICB) Project. At the time, there was little systematic knowledge about:

- Crisis perceptions and the decision-making styles of such key actors as the Soviet Union and China;
- Myriad twentieth-century crises in regions other than Europe;
- Crises experienced by weak states;
- Role of alliance partners in crisis management;
- Immediate triggers of crises;
- Crisis outcomes;
- Consequences of crises for the power, status, behavior, and subsequent perceptions of particular states;
- Protracted conflicts (enduring rivalries); and
- A widely shared theory of crisis.

3. Michael Brecher, *Crises in World Politics* (Oxford: Pergamon Press, 1993). Michael Brecher has provided an excellent review of the literature on crisis in world politics. In terms of *substance,* the contemporary literature on international crisis focuses on crisis anticipation, decision-making processes, crisis management and third-party intervention, and bargaining in crisis. A second mode of crisis literature focuses on *models of crisis decision making.* The third focus of crisis literature is *methodology.*

4. Brecher and Wilkenfeld, *A Study of Crisis,* p. 5.

5. Charles F. Hermann, "International Crisis as a Situational Variable," in J. N. Rosenau, ed., *International Politics and Foreign Policy* (New York: Free Press, 1969), p. 414.

6. Gary Goertz and Paul Diehl, "(Enduring) Rivalries," in M. Midlarsky, ed., *Handbook of War Studies,* 2nd ed. (Ann Arbor: University of Michigan Press, 2000), pp. 222–267; Paul F. Diehl and Gary Goertz, *War and Peace in International Rivalry* (Ann Arbor: University of Michigan Press, 2000); Paul Hensel, "Interstate Rivalry and the Study of Militarized Conflict," in Frank P. Harvey and Ben D. Mor, eds., *Conflict in World Politics: Advances in the Study of Crisis, War and Peace* (New York: St. Martin's Press, 1998), pp. 162–204.

7. Edward Azar, "Protracted Social Conflicts and Second Track Diplomacy," in J. Davies and E. Kaufman, eds., *Second Track Citizens' Diplomacy: Con-*

cepts and Techniques for Conflict Transformation (Lanham, Md.: Rowman & Littlefield, 2002), pp. 15–30.

8. For additional information on the ICB Project data set and accompanying case summaries, see "International Crisis Behavior (ICB) Online," University of Maryland and McGill University, 2005, www.cidcm.umd.edu/icb/

9. The five crises Iraq triggered were the Gulf War, 1990–1991; Bubiyan, 1991; Iraq deployment in Kuwait, 1994; UNSCOM I, 1997–1998; and UNSCOM II, 1998. The two crises Pakistan triggered were Kargil, 1999; and the India Parliament attack, 2001.

10. Monty G. Marshall and T. R. Gurr, *Peace and Conflict 2003* (College Park: University of Maryland, Center for International Development and Conflict Management, 2003); Monty G. Marshall and T. R. Gurr, *Peace and Conflict 2005* (College Park: University of Maryland, Center for International Development and Conflict Management, 2005).

11. Jonathan Wilkenfeld et al., "Mediating International Crises: Cross-National and Experimental Perspectives," *Journal of Conflict Resolution* 47, no. 3 (September 2003): 279–301; Jonathan Wilkenfeld et al., *Mediating International Crises* (Oxford: Routledge, 2005).

12. Examples include the Gulf War, Kosovo, Democratic Republic of Congo, and the Iraq War.

13. E-mail conversation between the author and Patrick James, 2003.

14. Ibid.

15. This latter case, North Korea Nuclear II 2002–2003, is an example of a "jointly opposed" crisis, in which the United States and China found themselves for the most part on the same side in the crisis.

16. Davis B. Bobrow, Steven Chan, and John A. Kringen, *Understanding Foreign Policy Decisions: The Chinese Case* (New York: Free Press, 1979).

17. Ibid., pp. 47–52.

18. Ibid., p. 58.

19. Alastair Iain Johnston, *Cultural Realism: Strategic Culture and Grand Strategy in Chinese History* (Princeton, N.J.: Princeton University Press, 1995).

20. Alastair Iain Johnston and Robert S. Ross, "Conclusion," in Alastair Iain Johnston and Robert S. Ross, eds., *Engaging China: The Management of an Emerging Power* (London: Routledge, 1999), p. 280.

21. Zeev Maoz, "Crisis Initiation: A Theoretical Exploration of a Neglected Topic in International Crisis Theory," *Review of International Studies* 8, no. 4 (1982), pp. 215–232.

22. Hemda Ben-Yehuda, "Opportunity Crises: Framework and Findings, 1918–1994," *Conflict Management and Peace Science* 17, no. 1 (1999), p. 72.

23. Ibid., p. 84.

24. Glenn H. Snyder and Paul Diesing, *Conflict Among Nations: Bargaining, Decision-Making, and System Structure in International Crises* (Princeton, N.J.: Princeton University Press, 1977); Paul C. Stern and Daniel Druckman, "Evaluating Interventions in History: The Case of International Conflict Resolution," *International Studies Review* 2, no. 1 (2000), pp. 33–63.

25. Marieke Kleiboer, *The Multiple Realities of International Mediation* (Boulder, Colo.: Lynne Rienner, 1998). John A. Vasquez speaks of the need for a unified theory of conflict and conflict resolution, including management, precisely because of this widespread conceptual ambiguity; John A. Vasquez, "The Learning of Peace: Lessons From a Multidisciplinary Inquiry," in John A. Vasquez et al., eds., *Beyond Confrontation: Learning Conflict Resolution in the Post–Cold War Era* (Ann Arbor: University of Michigan Press, 1995), pp. 211–228.

26. Graham Evans and Jeffrey Newnham, *The Penguin Dictionary of International Relations* (London: Penguin Books, 1998), p. 104.

27. Benjamin Miller, "Explaining Great Power Cooperation in Conflict Management," *World Politics* 45, no. 1 (1992), pp. 1–46. Miller attempts to explain great-power cooperation in both crisis management and conflict resolution, regardless of third-party intervention. He concludes that cooperation in crisis management is most often the result of the structure of the international system, and cooperation in conflict resolution is most often the result of state-level and cognitive factors.

28. Snyder and Diesing, *Conflict Among Nations.*

29. Alexander L. George, "Crisis Management: The Interaction of Political and Military Considerations," *Survival* 26, no. 5 (September/October 1984), pp. 223–234; Alexander L. George, ed., *Avoiding War: Problems of Crisis Management* (Boulder, Colo.: Westview Press, 1991).

30. John W. Burton, *Resolving Deep-Rooted Conflict: A Handbook* (Lanham, Md.: University Press of America, 1987); John W. Burton, *Conflict: Resolution and Prevention* (New York: St. Martin's Press, 1990); Herbert C. Kelman, "Informal Mediation by the Scholar/Practitioner," in Jacob Bercovitch and Jeffrey Z. Rubin, eds., *Mediation in International Relations: Multiple Approaches to Conflict Management* (New York: St. Martin's Press, 1992); Deborah M. Kolb and Eileen F. Babbitt, "Mediation Practice on the Home Front: Implications for Global Conflict Resolution," in John A. Vasquez et al., eds., *Beyond Confrontation;* Kumar Rupesinghe, "Mediation in Internal Conflicts: Lessons from Sri Lanka," in Jacob Bercovitch,

ed., *Resolving International Conflicts: The Theory and Practice of Mediation* (Boulder, Colo.: Lynne Rienner, 1996); Kleiboer, *Multiple Realities of International Mediation;* Marieke Kleiboer, "Great Power Mediation: Using Leverage to Make Peace?" in Jacob Bercovitch, ed., *Studies in International Mediation: Essays in Honour of Jeffrey Z. Rubin* (Houndsmills, Basingstoke, Hampshire: Palgrave MacMillan, 2002).

31. I. William Zartman, "Toward the Resolution of International Conflicts," in I. William Zartman and J. Lewis Rasmussen, eds., *Peacemaking in International Conflict: Methods and Techniques* (Washington, D.C.: United States Institute of Peace Press, 1997), p. 11.

32. Kolb and Babbitt, "Mediation Practice on the Home Front"; Kleiboer, *Multiple Realities of International Mediation;* Oran R. Young, *The Intermediaries: Third Parties in International Crises* (Princeton, N.J.: Princeton University Press, 1967), p. 209. Young terms such pursuits as crisis control, which is "undertaken during serious crises to reduce the chances of . . . undesired warfare of major proportions getting out of control."

33. Burton, *Conflict.*

34. Kleiboer, *Multiple Realities of International Mediation.*

35. Ibid.; Christopher R. Mitchell, *Peacemaking and the Consultant's Role* (New York: Nichols Publishing, 1981).

36. Burton, *Conflict.*

37. Ibid.; John W. Burton, "The Resolution of Conflict," *International Studies Quarterly* 16, no. 2 (1972), pp. 5–29; Burton, *Resolving Deep-Rooted Conflict;* I. William Zartman, "Alternative Attempts at Crisis Management: Concepts and Processes," in Gilbert R. Winham, ed., *New Issues in International Crisis Management* (Boulder, Colo.: Westview Press, 1988), pp. 199–223; Zartman, "Toward the Resolution of International Conflicts"; Kolb and Babbitt, "Mediation Practice on the Home Front"; Rupesinghe, "Mediation in Internal Conflicts"; Kleiboer, *Multiple Realities of International Mediation.*

38. Lawrence Susskind and Eileen Babbitt, "Overcoming the Obstacles to Effective Mediation of International Disputes," in Bercovitch and Rubin, eds., *Mediation in International Relations,* pp. 30–51; Kleiboer, *Multiple Realities of International Mediation.*

39. Kleiboer, *Multiple Realities of International Mediation.*

40. Ibid.; Roger Fisher, *The Social Psychology of Intergroup and International Conflict Resolution* (New York: Springer-Verlag, 1990).

41. Loraleigh Keashly and Ronald J. Fisher, "A Contingency Perspective on Conflict Interventions: Theoretical and Practical Considerations," in

Bercovitch, ed., *Resolving International Conflicts,* pp. 235–261; Kleiboer, *Multiple Realities of International Mediation.*

42. Kelman, "Informal Mediation by the Scholar/Practitioner"; Herbert C. Kelman, "Interactive Problem-Solving: Informal Mediation by the Scholar-Practitioner," in Bercovitch, ed., *Studies in International Mediation,* p. 186.

43. Kleiboer, *Multiple Realities of International Mediation.*

44. Kelman, "Informal Mediation by the Scholar/Practitioner."

45. Kleiboer, *Multiple Realities of International Mediation.*

46. Jacob Bercovitch, "The Structure and Diversity of Mediation in International Relations," in Bercovitch and Rubin, eds., *Mediation in International Relations,* pp. 1–29. Others arguing that cease-fires are not indicators of conflict resolution success include John W. Burton, *Conflict and Communication: The Use of Controlled Communication in International Relations* (New York: Free Press, 1969); Burton, "Resolution of Conflict"; Burton, *Resolving Deep-Rooted Conflict;* Burton, *Conflict: Resolution and Prevention;* Ronald J. Fisher, "Third Party Consultation: A Method for the Study and Resolution of Conflict," *Journal of Conflict Resolution* 16, no. 1 (1972): pp. 67–94; Kelman, "Informal Mediation by the Scholar/Practitioner"; Vivienne Jabri, *Discourse on Violence: Conflict Analysis Reconsidered* (Manchester, England: Manchester University Press, 1996); Jacob Bercovitch and Patrick M. Regan, "Managing Risks in International Relations: The Mediation of Enduring Rivalries," in Gerald Schneider and Patricia A. Weitsman, eds., *Enforcing Cooperation* (New York: St. Martin's Press, 1997), pp. 185–201; Deiniol Lloyd Jones, "Mediation, Conflict Resolution and Critical Theory," *Review of International Studies* 26, no. 4 (2000), pp. 647–662.

47. Bercovitch, "Structure and Diversity of Mediation in International Relations"; Deborah Shmueli and Ariella Vranesky, "Environmental Mediation in International Relations," in Bercovitch, ed., *Resolving International Conflicts,* pp. 191–215.

48. Arthur N. Gilbert and Paul Gordon Lauren, "Crisis Management: An Assessment and Critique," *Journal of Conflict Resolution* 24, no. 4 (1980): pp. 641–664; Bercovitch, "Structure and Diversity of Mediation in International Relations."

49. William J. Dixon, "Third-Party Techniques for Preventing Conflict Escalation and Promoting Peaceful Settlement," *International Organization* 50, no. 4 (1996), p. 656.

50. Kleiboer, *Multiple Realities of International Mediation.*

51. Ibid.

52. Keashly and Fisher, "A Contingency Perspective."
53. Ibid.; Ronald J. Fisher and Loraleigh Keashly, "Distinguishing Third Party Interventions in Intergroup Conflict: Consultation Is *Not* Mediation," *Negotiation Journal* 4, no. 4 (1988), pp. 381–393; Daniel Druckman and Benjamin J. Broome, "Value Differences and Conflict Resolution: Familiarity or Liking?" *Journal of Conflict Resolution* 35, no. 4 (1991), pp. 571–593.

3

Pattern of Sino-American Crises:
A Chinese Perspective

Wang Jisi and Xu Hui

THE RELATIONSHIP BETWEEN THE UNITED STATES and the People's Republic of China (PRC) since 1949 has been characterized by conflicts and crises. In the post–World War II world, no other major power relationship, with the arguable exception of the U.S.-Soviet relationship, has experienced so many crises with so much intensity. Why have the two countries engaged in such frequent crises? Will the United States and China be able to avoid major political and military crises in the future, and how?

U.S. and Chinese scholars have conducted a great number of individual case studies of Sino-American crises. Rather than focusing on any of these crises, this chapter aims to (1) identify some common features in U.S.-China crises, (2) analyze the major factors that have determined China's crisis behavior, and (3) provide recommendations for preventing Sino-American crises in the future and, if they do occur, for better managing them.

CHARACTERISTICS OF SINO-AMERICAN CRISES

The Sino-American crises under discussion in this chapter refer to those that were related to military affairs, not to such situations as the political tensions following the Tiananmen incident in 1989. These crises include mainly the crisis that precipitated the two nations' involvement in

133

the Korean War, the two Taiwan Strait crises in the 1950s, the military confrontation during the Vietnam War, the tensions in the Taiwan Strait in March 1996, the NATO bombing of the Chinese embassy in Belgrade, and the air collision near Hainan Island in April 2001.

One distinctive feature of these crises is that they all occurred at a time when Sino-American relations were antagonistic or in a state of "non-foe, non-friend," as described by some analysts in the post–Cold War era. In the twenty-five years between 1971 and 1996, despite all the ideological and political disparities between the two countries, and despite the insolvability of the Taiwan issue, there were few omens of military confrontation. The passing of the Taiwan Relations Act by the U.S. Congress in 1979 as well as the continued U.S. arms sales to Taiwan resulted in strong Chinese rhetorical attacks on the United States, but the two countries were able to maintain a quasi alliance against Soviet expansionism. In fact, quiet yet significant military cooperation and intelligence sharing occurred between the two powers over regional security issues.[1]

The absence of any major crisis during this lengthy interval shows that, when both Beijing and Washington saw a common threat and did not view each other as actual or potential adversaries, they could reach a tacit understanding to prevent crisis even though the two sides did not undertake any visible and technical crisis management measures. Even after the Tiananmen turbulence in 1989, when the political atmosphere between Beijing and Washington soured and the Chinese leadership perceived the United States as the most hostile force threatening its very legitimacy, few observers anticipated any serious military crisis between the two countries until the events over Taiwan in 1995–1996.

The constantly invoked enemy image is another characteristic of the Sino-American crises. Both sides shaped this enemy image of the other before the Korean War in 1950. Both countries' leaders and the political elites largely shared this image. In the United States, the grand strategy, as designed in the important NSC-68 policy paper of April 1950, aimed at not only containing the Soviet Union but also opposing the spread of "communist tyranny," which was stereotyped by the image of "Red China." The political mobilization by the Truman administration at home was effective, especially against the background of McCarthyism.[2]

Likewise, but with much larger scope and much more effectiveness, the Chinese Communist Party (CCP) mobilized the whole nation to view the United States as the most ferocious and predatory imperialist power and the archenemy of New China. The direct military conflict between China and the United States during the Korean War only served to dramatize to each country the enemy image of the other. In all the later crises, the enemy image remained alive and made it difficult for both countries to manage the issue with more reconciliatory, down-to-earth approaches.

Political education in China since the Korean War has referred to the United States in distinctively negative terms, often as a political enemy and a security threat. In October 2000, for example, the Chinese leadership held widely reported activities to commemorate the fiftieth anniversary of China's participation in the Korean War, known in China as the "War to Resist U.S. Aggression and Aid Korea" (*kangMei yuanChao*). On this occasion, which was widely reported, Chinese leaders reemphasized that the war was a just, necessary, and victorious war that smashed the attempt by U.S. imperialism to occupy Korea and invade China. According to the official justification, not only did the war safeguard Chinese sovereignty and international security, but it also greatly ignited patriotic enthusiasm among the Chinese people and sped the development of the national economy. The highlighted commemoration of the Korean War was partly a response to "some people" (definitely referring to some Chinese political thinkers) who had "distorted the cause of sending Chinese troops and denied the historic significance of the war."[3] The enemy image was particularly vivid in China during the Belgrade bombing crisis in 1999 and was relevant in both China and the United States during the EP-3 crisis in 2001.

Despite the recurrent problem of the enemy image, both Beijing and Washington made strenuous efforts to prevent a direct military conflict with each other in all of these crises, and both based their decisions on rationality. This is the third characteristic of Sino-American crises. Zhou Enlai, with the endorsement of Mao Zedong, sent numerous public and private messages to the United States that China could not and would not "stand idly by" if U.S. forces tried to destroy North Korea totally. Unfortunately, General Douglas MacArthur missed and dismissed these messages. But there was no evidence that President Harry S. Truman,

Secretary of State Dean Acheson, or other decision makers in Washington would have supported MacArthur leading the U.S. Army right to the Korean-Chinese border if they had known that large numbers of Chinese troops had already been positioned to fight an all-out war and roll back the thrust of U.S. forces toward the Chinese border.

In later Sino-American crises, both sides applied remarkable restraint to avoid turning the tensions into a direct military engagement with each other. In each of the Taiwan Strait crises, the Chinese objective was more political than military and served to remind Taiwan and the United States of its seriousness in the struggle for reunification. The 1954–1955 Taiwan Strait crisis ensued when Mao Zedong planned to break up Washington's defense commitment to Taipei and wanted to remind the outside world of Beijing's commitment to the liberation of Taiwan.[4] The People's Liberation Army (PLA) attacked offshore islands held by the Kuomintang (KMT) to protest the possible signing of a defense pact between Washington and Taipei, which was nonetheless signed in December 1954. Leading U.S. politicians, especially those in Congress, were more concerned about communist expansion than about the strategic value of Taiwan, not to mention the offshore islands, to the United States. It was definitely not in their interest to provoke China.

Mao's motivation in ordering the shelling of the offshore islands during the 1958 Taiwan Strait crisis was related to the U.S. invasion of Lebanon in July 1958 and the international tensions thereafter. He explained in an internal meeting: "Honestly, this is an action we have been taking to aid the Arab people. This is meant to make the United States suffer. The United States has been bullying us for many years. When we have an opportunity, why don't we make them suffer a bit?"[5] Mao also wanted to use these tensions to boost Chinese morale and popular fervor in the Great Leap Forward, the radical movement he was launching. Despite the militant rhetoric typical of that time, Mao was extremely cautious and did not engage in an actual battle with U.S. forces. In August 1958, China discovered that U.S. naval ships were escorting the KMT fleet in providing logistical supplies for Quemoy, the largest of the offshore islands. When the field PLA commander asked whether they should attack the fleet, Mao's instruction was to "attack the KMT ships only. Don't attack the U.S. ships. If the U.S. ships open fire, don't return fire without an order."[6]

In the Belgrade bombing and EP-3 crises, neither side openly threat-ened to use force.[7] This pattern of behavior contrasts sharply with some of the other crises the two countries experienced, such as the Sino-Viet-nam Border War of 1979, the U.S. military showdowns with Iraq in 1991 and 2003, and the Kosovo crisis in 1999. In all these events, there was the readiness to use military forces if the political objective was not achieved.

The fourth characteristic is the involvement of a third party in all of the crises except for the EP-3 crisis. North Korea, Taiwan, Vietnam, and Yugoslavia were alternately the third parties. In the Korean, Taiwan Strait, and Vietnam crises, China and the United States engaged in cri-sis or military confrontation in order to assist an ally or their respective allies. In the embassy bombing crisis, Beijing had taken Belgrade's side in the Kosovo conflict and perceived "U.S.-led NATO" as an aggressor, which gave China every reason to believe that the missile attack was intentionally targeted at the Chinese embassy. In retrospect, neither China nor the United States gained a great deal strategically from the crises in which they aided a third party, despite the official rhetoric to justify their respective decisions.

ASYMMETRIES OF INTEREST, MEANS, AND SCOPE OF CHOICE

Compared with some other events the United States has experienced, such as Pearl Harbor, the Berlin crises in the 1950s, the Cuban missile crisis, and September 11, 2001, the Sino-American crises did not, at least from the Chinese perspective, happen in places where core security interests of the United States were in danger. Before the outbreak of the Korean War, the Truman administration had not defined the Korean peninsula as a key strategic area to defend with U.S. forces. Neither were Taiwan and South Vietnam of such strategic importance to the United States that the country should necessarily sacrifice the lives of U.S. soldiers to fight for them. In contrast, all the crises took place within or near China's national boundaries (Taiwan, Hainan, Korea, and Viet-nam), were related to China's territorial integrity (Taiwan) and sover-eignty (Taiwan and the Chinese embassy), and therefore affected the core interests and national dignity of China.

This asymmetry of interests gives rise to Chinese self-righteousness in viewing and reviewing these crises and conflicts. The Chinese tend to discredit any moral ground on the part of the United States to engage itself in Asian security affairs, particularly those affairs that may challenge China's core interests. The Chinese interpretations of U.S. behavior in all these events are based on their understanding of power politics as conducted by hegemonic and imperialist powers.

Meanwhile, Chinese officials also realize the asymmetry of national power and military capabilities between themselves and the Americans. In other words, the United States could apply more policy instruments— economic sanctions, diplomatic isolation, military encirclement, and the mobilization of its allies and even the United Nations—in managing crises with China. In comparison, China's capabilities and means have been rather limited. It either had to resort to force (or the threat of using force) from an inferior military position or had to resign itself to America's limited compromises. As the weaker adversary, however, China could cause immeasurable losses of U.S. lives and assets in a military confrontation with the United States, as shown in the Korean War. Therefore, determination, resolve, and limited nuclear deterrence would partly compensate for the inadequate material resources.

The asymmetry of power between China and the United States can partly explain why none of the Sino-American crises after the Korean War resulted in direct armed conflict. As Michael Brecher and Jonathan Wilkenfeld point out while discussing crises between adversaries:

> In the case of positive power discrepancy (a target state more powerful than a triggering entity), the target state need not necessarily employ violence in order to achieve its crisis objectives. In the case of negative power discrepancy (a target state weaker than a triggering entity), the target state would be ill-advised to employ violence in the face of a non-violent trigger emanating from a more powerful adversary.[8]

The three Taiwan Strait crises fit in well with the case of positive power discrepancy. The United States, the more powerful state, did not need to resort to force; and the triggering state, China, did not want to enter into a military conflict with a more powerful adversary.

The inadequacy of core U.S. interests and the relative adequacy of U.S. means should allow the United States to obtain a wide range of choices in coping with a crisis with China and with many other countries. Washington, for example, could choose to participate in the Korean War in 1950 but also choose to disengage itself from the Vietnam War in 1973. It could first choose not to engage in the Bosnia conflict but then change its mind and get involved. The Iraq War in 2003 was not a war of necessity but a war of choice.

On the basis of these observations, many Chinese analysts conclude that the United States may well refrain from confronting China militarily in a future cross-strait conflict. A representative analysis is that Taiwan is a core Chinese interest and is of only marginal importance to U.S. security. According to this reasoning, China should not be afraid of running the risk of taking forceful measures to deter Taiwan independence because the United States could choose not to involve itself in military terms. Washington might well consider a war with China unnecessary and too costly if it makes careful strategic calculations.

GUIDING PRINCIPLES

Since the founding of the CCP in 1921, the CCP has faced constant threats and challenges to its survival. Even today, when the CCP has more than sixty million members with an exceptionally solid political power base in China, its leadership still maintains strong crisis awareness as reflected in the continuous emphasis on fighting "infiltrative, subversive, and splittist activities" staged or supported by hostile forces abroad, particularly by the United States, against Beijing. This crisis awareness is reinforced by a deeply internalized consciousness shared among Chinese elites of the "one hundred years of humiliation," during which China was invaded, bullied, and divided by imperialist powers. Although crisis management (*weiji guanli*) is an imported concept, there have been rich experiences and literature in CCP history regarding how to cope with crisis. The Chinese followed the same steps in managing a crisis: identify the interests and objectives pursued, collect and analyze information, provide scenarios and predict their possible outcomes, choose the preferred scenario, and implement it.

Among the pertinent ideas in contemporary China about confronting a strategic rival, two guidelines are probably best known, most applicable, and most frequently cited. Both originated during the 1930s–1940s when the CCP faced more powerful enemies in the form of Japan and the KMT. The first guideline—"despise the enemy strategically and take it seriously tactically"—means to be politically and strategically principled but remain tactically flexible.[9]

In despising the United States strategically, Mao Zedong called it a "paper tiger," but this did not prevent him from taking it seriously during the crises in Korea, Vietnam, and the Taiwan Strait. Mao defended his paper-tiger theory by explaining that it was necessary to boost the morale and strengthen the moral conviction of the communists against a militarily formidable enemy. During all the crises in point, official statements always cited moral grounds (concepts included national sovereignty and territorial integrity, proletarian internationalism, and international equality) and righteousness and often made principled demands that might be seen by the United States as impractical or unreasonable. As Alastair Iain Johnston points out, "The symbolic set, for the most part, is disconnected from the programmatic decision rules governing strategy, and appears mostly in a habitual discourse designed, in part, to justify behavior in culturally acceptable terms."[10] This pattern of crisis behavior—strong rhetoric combined with cautious action—may not be peculiar to China. What is striking in the Chinese case is that the "habitual discourse" is ingrained in a more sophisticated political tradition, a longer history, and a prouder civilization. When this pattern of behavior meets an equally, if not more, self-righteous and definitely more powerful nation such as the United States, the contrast is interestingly sharp.

The other guideline, which contains three principles, also originated as a stipulation of Mao Zedong when the hard-line KMT-led forces were frequently attacking the communist forces during the War of Resistance Against Japan. Mao stated, "The three principles are to fight 'on just grounds,' 'to our advantage,' and 'with restraint.'" He further explained:

First, the principle of self-defence. We will not attack unless we are attacked; if we are attacked, we will certainly counterattack. That is to say, we must never attack others without provocation, but once attacked we must never fail to return the blow. Herein lies the defensive nature of our principle. The military attacks of the die-hards must be smashed—resolutely, thoroughly, wholly and completely. Second, the principle of victory. We will not fight unless we are sure of victory; we must never fight without a plan, without preparation, and without certainty of success. . . . Herein lies the limited nature of the struggle. Third, the principle of a truce. After repulsing one die-hard attack, we should know when to stop and bring that particular fight to a close before another attack is made on us. . . . On no account should we fight on day after day without cease, or be carried away by success. Herein lies the temporary nature of each struggle.[11]

"On just grounds, to our advantage, and with restraint" (*youli, youli, youjie*) is consistent with the principle of "despising the enemy strategically but taking the enemy seriously tactically" but is more applicable in political and operational terms. To justify the tactically offensive action, China called the border war with India in 1962 and the one with Vietnam in 1979 "defensive counterattacks." Probably basing its statements on the same reasoning, China during the EP-3 incident insisted from the beginning that "all responsibilities lie on the U.S. side," and China therefore presented a moral case in which the PLA was making a defensive move near Chinese coastal lines where the U.S. aircraft was on a mission of spying on China. Thus the technical and tactical complexities were of secondary importance in managing the crisis.

In practice, *youli, youli, youjie* as a principle is often invoked to provide the rationale for compromises when China has obtained limited objectives. In dealing with the crisis following Lee Teng-hui's visit to the United States in June 1995, for example, Beijing froze its ties with Washington by canceling a few high-level official visits and recalling its ambassador. The Clinton administration signaled with a few conciliatory gestures, such as President Bill Clinton himself reassuring Chinese officials of the one-China policy. U.S. Secretary of State Warren Christopher suggested a meeting with Chinese Foreign Minister Qian Qichen in Brunei, where both were scheduled to join Association of Southeast Asian Nations (ASEAN) foreign ministers for the ASEAN Regional Forum. Before his trip, Christopher sent a message to Qian, saying he would be carrying a letter from President Clinton to deliver to President Jiang Zemin. Christopher also made a speech in which he recognized the importance of China and reiterated the one-China policy. According to Qian Qichen's memoirs, when he considered these U.S. gestures, he agreed to meet with his U.S. counterpart on this international occasion as an action to "embody our diplomatic tactics of 'on just grounds, to our advantage, and with restraint' in contending with the United States."[12]

The pattern of Sino-American negotiations over their bilateral crises is discernable against their respective cultural backgrounds. While the Americans were accustomed to seeking a legal solution to a given diplomatic problem, Chinese officials tended to go back to their own political tradition for reference. A veteran U.S. participant in U.S.-China affairs observes:

> [I]n general . . . for Americans the term [negotiation] implied emphasis on compromise or a quid pro quo to resolve conflict, along with an emphasis on law and judicial systems as bases for determining what is just and for ensuring compliance. The Chinese tended to emphasize the permanence and self-evident truth of their principles, the use of conditional and non-permanent agreements to constrain conflict until these truths or principles prevail, and moral suasion as a basis for achieving conformity and thus harmony.[13]

Indeed, as China's negotiating behavior during the 1995–1996 Taiwan Strait crisis, the Belgrade bombing crisis, and the EP-3 crisis exemplifies, China followed the same pattern. The first step was that Beijing made strong protests "on just grounds," which in all these cases were pointed to the U.S. violation of China's national sovereignty and territorial integrity and placed the United States in a defensive and "unjust" position. The next step demanded that Washington admit its mistakes (if not its ill intentions) and make apologies for what it had done. In all these cases, the U.S. side had to compromise, though not to Beijing's total satisfaction. After the Chinese leadership was able to declare—generally to its domestic audiences—a limited success ("to our advantage"), it would react "with restraint." Chinese officials would explain internally that the Chinese government had achieved the maximum of success in negotiation given its limited capabilities in exerting pressure on the United States. After all, Beijing would declare, a stable relationship with the United States would be in China's national interest, and the compromise had not sacrificed China's principles.

What remained missing in this pattern were formal or legal solutions to the disputes. It looked as if the Chinese restraint was unilateral and temporary and that Beijing reserved the right to make further demands and take further actions. The U.S. wrongdoings thus were not to be forgotten and left behind but were instead recorded in history, and the United States owed new debts to the Chinese people. The Chinese government did not formally accept any of the U.S. official explanations of its behavior during these incidents. After the Belgrade bombing incident, the most disastrous of those crises in terms of Chinese psychological wounds, few people in China received any details of Washington's interpretation of what had happened during that tragedy.

LEARNING CURVE

U.S. scholars and analysts often wonder how and what Chinese leaders, officials, strategists, and analysts have learned from the experiences of the Sino-American crises. If one looks at the formal statements and written literature, one finds few reevaluations that contradict the previous justifications and accounts given by the Chinese government at the time of the crisis or conflict. Many Chinese writings, for example, continue to cite a well-known statement during the Korean War made by Omar Bradley, chairman of the U.S. Joint Chiefs of Staff, out of its context. What Bradley actually said in May 1951 testimony was that to expand the war beyond Korea to China, as General MacArthur had proposed, would be wrong: "Red China is not the powerful nation seeking to dominate the world. Frankly, in the opinion of the joint chiefs, this strategy [fighting for a united Korea and beyond] would involve us in the wrong war, at the wrong place, at the wrong time, with the wrong enemy."[14] However, official Chinese publications have always interpreted this statement as an authorized U.S. admission that the war with China in Korea was a wrong war and a defeat for the United States.

Still, in reviewing Chinese behavior since the 1950s, one does see a learning curve based on accumulated experiences, including negative lessons. Beijing made painstaking efforts during the Vietnam War not to encounter U.S. forces directly. Although the Belgrade bombing crisis has not been formally reexamined, it can be said that the EP-3 crisis was, from the Chinese perspective, better managed in some respects. Beijing's principled but nuanced response to the Iraq War in March 2003 also contrasted remarkably from its harsh political reaction to the war in Kosovo in 1999 that triggered the embassy bombing incident.

A more decisive learning curve is discernable in the fundamental differences between China's security strategy and conceptualization in the reform era since 1978 and its general outlook during the Mao years. Before China's reform and opening, Chinese leaders identified war and revolution as the tide of the day. The organizing principle in China's foreign policy was officially "proletarian internationalism," and Beijing supported a number of violent revolutions overseas. The official doctrine at that time was that a large-scale war with the United States (and later with the Soviet Union) could be postponed but was almost inevitable. Chinese leaders justified waging a tit-for-tat struggle against the United States in a given crisis despite its cautious deeds. The Chinese understanding of the outside world, and of the United States in particular, was superficial and ideologically oriented, making a rational choice in crisis management all the more difficult. All these were consistent with the domestic priority of carrying out the "continuous revolution under proletarian dictatorship" and based on "class struggle as the key link."

In comparison, during the reform years, especially since the mid-1990s, "peace and development" are seen as the main features in world affairs. China's national interests have officially guided its foreign policy. Chinese leaders advocate peaceful coexistence and noninterference in other countries' domestic affairs as guiding principles in international relations. Chinese officials see no possibility of an imminent world war. They refer to military means as the last resort in settling the Taiwan issue because peaceful reunification with Taiwan is desirable and possible. Information collection in foreign relations is tremendously improved. In Sino-American relations, Chinese leaders since Deng Xiaoping have advocated increasing trust, reducing troubles, developing cooperation, and refraining from confrontation. China's security and foreign policies must safeguard and serve the central task of economic modernization. At various levels of policy making and implementation, Beijing has established a number of confidence-building mechanisms with Washington to reduce the possibility of conflict.

During recent years, particularly since the outbreak of severe acute respiratory syndrome (SARS) in the spring of 2003, the Chinese government has paid special attention to the techniques of crisis management. A number of publications, including both translated works and Chinese-language writings, are available to Chinese officials and general readers. The Central Communist Party School and leading universities are offering new courses and lectures on crisis management. The establishment of research centers of crisis management further supports this trend. Although only in a beginning stage, they bode well for better understanding of crisis management and better management of future crises.

ACTIONS TO BE TAKEN

"Good is not good enough." To attempt to prevent as well as better manage any future Sino-American crises, we need concrete and operational channels and confidence-building measures between Beijing and Washington. However, past experiences and lessons tell us that the removal of the enemy image is more fundamental. We have heard too many official pronouncements about strategic partnership and constructive and cooperative relationships without enough incremental and measurable enhancement of mutual trust between the two bodies politic. One sobering reminder is the unhealed scar on the Chinese body politic left by the Belgrade bombing; the vast majority of Chinese political elites remain convinced that the missile attack intentionally targeted the Chinese embassy.

In spite of the learning curve discussed above, many of China's political elites today are impressed with Mao's "despising the enemy strategically" and do not possess adequate information about what the Chinese leadership under Mao did in "tactically taking the enemy seriously." A popular expectation in present-day China is that the national interests and national dignity should be enhanced more effectively by a combination of Deng's domestic policies and Mao's foreign and defense policies.

The deficiencies in the decision-making process during the pre-reform period should not allow us to neglect one point: Mao Zedong, with the assistance of Zhou Enlai and other leaders but without much bureaucratic encumbrance, was able to make the most authoritative decisions, both strategically and tactically. The general public and lower-level officials were almost completely in the dark when the masses were mobilized, but they voluntarily followed all the policies. In many cases, Mao's charisma, prestige, and political skills obscured Beijing's compromises. Today, as political elites are much better informed of state affairs, as nationalistic sentiments are rising, as freedom of expression and democratization are taking root in Chinese society, and as decision-making processes are increasingly complicated, crisis management requires greater coordination and cooperation within the government. With regard to the prevention of Sino-American crises, greater coordination and cooperation between the two sides are all the more necessary under these changing circumstances.

NOTES

1. See Robert S. Ross, *Negotiating Cooperation: The United States and China 1969–1989* (Stanford, Calif.: Stanford University Press, 1995), pp. 144–150, 236–239, for an account of U.S.-PRC military relations during the Carter and Reagan administrations. In the Reagan years, there were four categories of military technology that the United States would not sell to China: technology that would improve Chinese capability regarding strategic missiles, nuclear weapons, intelligence, and antisubmarine warfare. Within these constraints, Washington would sell China only defensive equipment that would not threaten U.S. allies in the region or alter the mainland-Taiwan military balance, thereby invoking the Taiwan Relations Act.

2. See Thomas J. Christensen, *Useful Adversaries: Grand Strategy, Domestic Mobilization, and Sino-American Conflict, 1947–1958* (Princeton, N.J.: Princeton University Press, 1996), pp. 122–133 for a detailed discussion of such political mobilization in America.

3. "Canjian Jinian Chaoxian Zhanzheng" [Commemoration of the Fiftieth Anniversary of the Korean War], *Dangdai Zhongguo Shi Yanjiu* [Contemporary China History Studies], no. 6 (2000), pp. 6–83, a collection of articles, provides relevant examples.

4. Gong Li, "Liangci Taiwan Haixia Weiji.de Chengyin yu Zhong Mei Zhijian.de Jiaoliang" [Causes of the Two Taiwan Strait Crises and the Struggle Between China and the United States], in Jiang Changbin and Robert Ross, eds., *Cong Duizhi Zouxiang Huanhe: Lengzhan Shiqi Zhong Mei Guanxi Zai Tantao* [From Confrontation to Détente: Sino-U.S. Relations During the Cold War Revisited] (Beijing: Shijie Zhishi Chubanshe, 2000), pp. 41–48, illustrates well Mao's motivations for triggering a crisis at that time.

5. Ibid., p. 56.

6. Ye Fei, "Mao Zhuxi Zhihui Paoji Jinmen" [Chairman Mao in Command of Shelling Jinmen], *People's Daily*, December 24, 1993, quoted in Su Ge, *Meiguo Duihua Zhengce yu Taiwan Wenti* [U.S. Policy Toward China and the Taiwan Question] (Beijing: Shijie Zhishi Chubanshe, 1998), p. 303.

7. The authors' assumption regarding the Belgrade bombing is that the Clinton administration did not intend it to trigger a crisis with China. Of all the Chinese interpretations of the incident we have heard, no one argues that the Americans deliberately staged it to provoke a military response from China.

8. Michael Brecher and Jonathan Wilkenfeld, *A Study of Crisis* (Ann Arbor: University of Michigan Press, 2000), p. 177.

9. Mao Zedong elaborated on this principle in 1957: "We have developed a concept over a long period for the struggle against the enemy, namely, strategically we should despise all our enemies, but tactically we should take them all seriously. In other words, with regard to the whole we must despise the enemy, but with regard to each specific problem we must take him seriously. If we do not despise him with regard to the whole, we shall commit opportunist errors. . . . But with regard to specific problems and specific enemies, if we do not take them seriously, we shall commit adventurist errors." *Selected Works of Mao Tse-tung*, vol. 5 (Beijing: Foreign Languages Press, 1977), pp. 517–518.

10. Alastair Iain Johnston argues: "There is evidence of two Chinese strategic cultures, one a symbolic or idealized set of assumptions and ranked preferences, and one an operational set that had a nontrivial effect on strategic choice in the Ming period. The symbolic set, for the most part, is disconnected from the programmatic decision rules governing strategy, and appears mostly in a habitual discourse designed, in part, to justify behavior in culturally acceptable terms. The operational set reflects what I call a *parabellum* or hard realpolitik strategic culture that, in essence, argues that the best way of dealing with security threats is to eliminate them through

the use of force. This preference is tempered by an explicit sensitivity to one's relative capability to do this." Alastair Iain Johnston, *Cultural Realism: Strategic Culture and Grand Strategy in Chinese History* (Princeton, N.J.: Princeton University Press, 1995), p. x.

11. Mao Zedong, "Current Problems of Tactics in the Anti-Japanese United Front," in *Selected Works of Mao Tse-tung*, vol. 2 (Beijing: Foreign Languages Press, 1975), pp. 426–427.

12. Qian Qichen, *Waijiao Shi Ji* [Ten Stories of a Diplomat] (Beijing: Shijie Zhishi Chubanshe, 2003), p. 311.

13. Alfred D. Wilhelm Jr., *The Chinese at the Negotiating Table* (Washington, D.C.: National Defense University Press, 1994), p. 5.

14. Cited in Akira Iriye, *Across the Pacific: An Inner History of American-East Asian Relations* (New York: Harcourt Brace Jovanovich, 1967), p. 289.

4

Crisis Management in China and in the United States: A Comparative Study

Xia Liping

SINCE THE ESTABLISHMENT OF THE People's Republic of China (PRC), China and the United States have gone through several security-military crises. At present, the two countries share broad and important common economic and security interests that are the basis for establishing constructive cooperative relations between them. The stability and development of Sino-American relations are beneficial not only for the people of the two countries but also for the security and peace of the Asia-Pacific region as well as the world. However, some people in the United States are still concerned that China may become an adversary, so they try to contain China and even try to make use of Taiwan to restrict China. A small number of separatists on Taiwan are waiting for an opportunity to split Taiwan from China. Under these circumstances, the potential exists for a crisis between China and the United States. Comparative studies of crisis management between China and the United States may help prevent and resolve crises that may occur in the future.

GUIDELINES AND THEORIES OF CRISIS MANAGEMENT

The guidelines and theories of crisis management in China and the United States show some similarities, but they also show some important differences. These differences have an important influence on the two countries' practice of crisis management.

Views of Crisis

Although both sides think both dangers and opportunities exist in crises of international politics, they have differing understandings about the objectives of crisis management. Chinese culture defines crisis as "a potential disaster or danger."[1] At the same time, Chinese culture, given its tradition of dialectics, also regards the *ji* in crisis (*weiji*) as expressing the presence of an "opportunity." This means that a crisis can become "a favorable turn" if policy makers deal with it properly. Crisis management provides the means to avoid the danger of conflicts and to seek and obtain a favorable turn of events. Some Chinese scholars hold:

> [International] military crisis is a particular societal state of affairs. This is a vicious state of affairs, which is caused by the intensification of some contradictions and would undermine normal international relationships. This is also a state of affairs that would change or undermine the current balance of the international system. Crisis is neither peace nor war, but a chaos between war and peace. . . . [I]t may lead to either new instability and confusion or the resolution of some contradictions; it may also be the last step leading to war, or the last mountain to overcome to realize long-term peace.[2]

During the era of war and revolution, from the 1950s to the second half of the 1960s, Chinese leaders used "the theory of the noose" to deal with crises with the United States in international politics. Mao Zedong said, "These intense situations produced by the United States have gone to the opposite of what Americans hope, and have had the effect of mobilizing the people of the world to oppose the American invaders."[3]

During the present era of what is called peace and development, the Chinese government has put forward the New Security Concept, which hold mutual trust, mutual benefit, equality, and coordination as their core. The goals of improving mutual trust through dialogue and improving common security through cooperation are important components of the New Security Concept, which have become an important part of China's foreign policy. The New Security Concept also aims to "resolve disputes through the means of peaceful negotiations and to have broad and deep cooperation to deal with security problems of common concern, so as to eliminate hidden dangers and to prevent wars and armed conflicts."[4] China thinks that, at present, common security interests between countries have increased greatly, mutual interdependence has been deepening, and the model of the security system has been changing from the zero-sum game to the pursuit of win-win situations.[5] These new theories have become important guidelines of current Chinese attempts to deal with international crises. The U.S. scholar, Oran R. Young, argues:

> A crisis in international politics is a process of interaction occurring at higher levels of perceived intensity than the ordinary flow of events and characterized by: a sharp break from the ordinary flow of politics; shortness of duration; a rise in the perceived prospects that violence will break out; and significant implications for the stability of some system or subsystem (or pattern of relationships) in international politics.[6]

Another scholar, Phil Williams, argues, "An international crisis is a confrontation of two or more states, usually occupying a short time period, in which the probability of an outbreak of war between the participants is perceived to increase significantly."[7]

In the United States, three academic schools provide explanations of crisis management. The first school regards crisis management as the peaceful resolution of conflicts and thinks that the success of crisis management depends totally on whether a war is avoided. It stresses that crisis itself is the real enemy. It holds that, because nuclear weapons have the capability of mass destruction, nuclear powers must avoid taking high risks. Before any actor takes a new action, it must first measure whether it is highly likely to lead to war; if so, it should choose a less dangerous action. Proponents of this school believe that all parties have common interests in eliminating the danger of war and normalizing the situation, so in fact they are partners.

The second school regards crisis management as a process of striving to achieve a certain objective. The objective of crisis management is to force the adversary to concede and, thus, further advance one's own interests in international politics. This school thinks that crisis is an opportunity to enhance its own interests, and that the adversary country, not the crisis itself, is the enemy. The second school holds that before one actor takes a new action, it must first measure whether the action can force the adversary to concede; if it must take riskier action to realize its expectation, it should take this action. The role of crisis management for each side is figuring out how to force the adversary to make the bigger concession while itself making the smallest concession possible.

The third school takes the middle road; it defines crisis management as "the process of 'winning' a crisis while at the same time keeping it within tolerable limits of danger and risk to both sides."[8] It holds that the goal of crisis management is "reaching a solution acceptable to both sides without resorting to force."[9] This school of thought emphasizes that, during a crisis, the two sides want not only to achieve their own objectives but also prioritize lessening the crisis and avoiding misfortune. The essence of crisis management is to attempt to balance and reconcile these goals. The reason is that the common interest of the nuclear powers is to prevent crises between them from escalating into a nuclear conflict. Moreover, even if a problem between them causes a crisis, they still have common interests in other areas.

In practice, the United States usually pursues the policy supported by the second school when it deals with a crisis with middle or small countries. When it goes through a crisis with a nuclear power, especially when the crisis does not threaten the key interests of the United States, the United States usually pursues the policy advocated by the third school.

Since September 11, 2001, the United States has also recognized the importance of cooperation with major powers. In a June 2002 commencement speech at West Point, President George W. Bush said: "We have our best chance since the rise of the nation state in the seventeenth century to build a world where the great powers compete in peace instead of prepare for war."[10] In a September 11, 2002, *New York Times* op-ed, President Bush wrote: "Competition between great nations is inevitable, but armed conflict in our world is not." He stated, "America's greatest opportunity is to create a balance of world power that favors human freedom."[11] The September 2002 *National Security Strategy of the United States of America* holds, "Today, the world's great powers find ourselves on the same side—united by common dangers of terrorist violence and chaos." Quoting President Bush's speech at West Point, the national security strategy states, "We will preserve the peace by building good relations among the great powers."[12] China's New Security Concept and the framework the Bush administration is willing to build for cooperation among the great powers to maintain peace will be beneficial for enhancing the establishment of a crisis management mechanism between China and the United States.

Crisis Decision Making

China usually follows realist precepts in crisis management decision making. However, some U.S. officials sometimes exaggerate the threat from China, overestimate the U.S. capability, and underestimate the determination of China to defend its key national interests.

The factors that influence U.S. policy makers include motives, purposes, the international strategic situation, comparison of power, U.S. national interests, U.S. internal politics, and the personalities of U.S. policy makers. Chinese leaders usually make reactive decisions according to their analyses of these factors as well as China's national interests and the common interests of the people of the world.

Phil Williams argues that decision making by the government of a country in crisis "tends to be a mixture of rational, logical inferences on the one hand, and non-rational pressures and influences on the other."[13] Theoretically, the ideal crisis policy is guided by "strategic rationality" or "comprehensive rationality."[14] "Strategic rationality" has the following criteria:

> First . . . foreign policy is guided by a "controlling intelligence" . . . there exists a unitary or monolithic decision-making body, capable of making explicit its major values and objectives and pursuing them in a diligent and systematic manner. . . . Second . . . the constituent members of this decision-making body are statesmen and officials endowed with a strong sense of responsibility and concerned predominantly with protecting and advancing the interests of their state in a competitive and highly dangerous environment. . . . Third . . . before embarking upon a particular strategy in this "chess game," policy makers consider very carefully the probable responses of other

states . . . the choice is made "on the basis of a sober calculation of potential gains and losses, and probabilities of enemy actions. . . ." Fourth [is] the primacy of foreign policy over domestic politics . . . statesmen act in accord with reasoned and logical calculation rather than non-rational domestic pressures.[15]

In reality, however, various political factors influence and restrict strategic rationality and limit the ability to obtain comprehensive rationality. The level of rationality depends on the particulars of the situation.[16]

During the process of decision making, U.S. leaders sometimes make mistakes caused by prejudice and arrogance. During the Korean War, for example, President Harry S. Truman and Secretary of State Dean Acheson "had evidently convinced themselves that legitimate Chinese national interests were not importantly threatened or affected by the U.S. occupation of North Korea or by plans for unifying it with South Korea."[17] They underestimated China's serious concerns about the U.S. occupation of Korea. Consequently, they sent U.S. troops to cross the 38th parallel near the China-Korea border, ignoring the serious warning from the Chinese government. General Douglas MacArthur, commander in chief of the U.S. Far East Command, was more prejudiced and arrogant. On October 15, 1950, President Truman met General MacArthur and other high-ranking military officials at Wake Island. In a briefing about the Korea situation, General MacArthur acknowledged the more than 400,000 Chinese Communist Party (CCP) troops massed in Manchuria, but he predicted that, given the air supremacy of UN forces, the CCP would not dispatch a large number of regular troops to the front lines in Korea because the UN air forces would attack and annihilate them before they reached Pyongyang.[18] No one present objected. General MacArthur guaranteed to President Truman that the war in Korea would be over by Thanksgiving, and he would then be able to withdraw the Eighth Army to Japan before Christmas. MacArthur believed that an election to formally achieve Korean reunification might be possible as soon as January 1951.[19] When President Truman asked about the possibility of "Chinese or Soviet interference," General MacArthur said the chances were "very little."[20]

By comparison, at that time, the United States was more careful in dealing with the Soviet Union. After the outbreak of the Korean War, when the United States began military aid to South Korea, the aid was limited to air and naval support. At the same time, the U.S. government sent letters to the Soviet government, requesting the Soviets to guarantee that they were not responsible for this unprovoked and unauthorized attack and to use their influence over North Korean authorities to persuade them to withdraw their troops immediately. After the Soviet government replied that the Soviet Union had withdrawn its troops from Korea earlier than the United States had, reiterated its traditional principle of noninterference in the internal affairs of other countries, and commented it was sticking to its principle of not permitting other outside forces to interfere in the internal affairs of Korea, the U.S. government concluded that the Soviet Union was not willing to be directly involved in the Korean War. The United States therefore decided to send a large number of conventional forces to Korea to fight.[21]

Force and Negotiation

China advocates the use of the dual tactics of force and negotiation in order to handle its opponents' use of these two tactics, while the United States pursues a policy of "carrots and sticks." This situation has two levels of meaning. First, it means that China must use negotiations to deal with the negotiations of its adversary, and it must use military methods to deal with military methods of its adversary. Second, it means that China should use cooperation to deal with cooperation from the other side, and use fighting to deal with fighting from the other side. Crisis management in international politics is the comprehensive use of political, military, diplomatic, and economic means, but other means are mainly effective by supporting diplomacy. Zhou Enlai said, "Diplomatic work has two sides: one side is unity, another side is struggle."[22] Both sides are "manifested through diplomacy. . . . Diplomacy is the same as military affairs; it is no more than a 'soft attack.'"[23]

The United States has pursued the policy of carrots and sticks for a long time. This policy holds that the United States should not only intimidate its adversaries through force and strong diplomatic pressure, but it should also provide some benefits in order to lure its adversary into making concessions. There are many examples of this approach in international political crises involving the United States. During the

Cuban missile crisis in 1962, for example, the United States dispatched naval and air forces to blockade Cuba; but it also used its commitment not to invade Cuba as a bargaining condition and agreed to withdraw its missiles in Turkey aimed at the Soviet Union. In another example, during the North Korean nuclear crisis in 1993–1994, the United States on one hand threatened North Korea with sanctions and even threatened to launch an attack against nuclear facilities in North Korea; on the other hand, the United States during bargaining expressed its willingness to replace North Korean graphite reactors with light-water reactors, provide North Korea with 500,000 tons of heavy oil annually until the light-water reactors were established, and establish diplomatic relations with North Korea.

Moderation vs. Brinkmanship

The concept of acting "on just grounds, to our advantage, and with restraint" (*youli, youli, youjie*) is one of the main strategic tactics the PRC uses during its diplomatic and military struggles. It is also one of the important guidelines China uses when it deals with international crises. According to this concept, one must dare to fight and be adept at fighting. While acting in a just and reasonable manner (and abiding by international law), one must strive to obtain some objective benefit for China. One must also know when and where to stop and how to determine a reasonable and suitable goal.

The tactic of *youli, youli, youjie* is also relevant to the national defense policy of defensiveness and the military strategy of active defense, two strategies that the PRC has pursued since its establishment and that have heavily influenced its thinking on crisis management. The essence of these strategies is as follows: First, maintain a position of self-defense by not being the first to fire a gun and gain mastery by counterattacking. The main strategy is: "If others leave me alone, I will leave them alone. If a person attacks me, I must attack them."[24] Second, the important objectives are containing war and maintaining peace. Third, when an enemy invades or launches attacks, the country's leaders should mobilize every citizen to fight in the war. Mobilized people with inferior equipment can defeat an enemy with superior equipment.

In sum, China has tried its best to show its sincerity to resolve disputes through peaceful means when it becomes involved in crises with its neighbors. However, when crises between China and the superpowers occur, especially when a crisis relates to China's fundamental national interests such as the Taiwan issue, China also will dare to engage in the necessary struggle and engage in a trial of strength.

During crises in international politics, the United States often acts according to the theory of controlled escalation and the strategy of limited brinkmanship. U.S. scholars argue that the concept of escalation is the core of sound crisis management, and escalation may be the only method to effectively resolve a conflict. As Kintner and Schwarz argue, "The aim of crisis management is to escalate to the most favorable position but at the same time to the least possible extent."[25] Phil Williams argues:

> [D]eliberate escalation contains elements of the "rationality-of-irrationality" tactic as it is intended to convince the opponent that one is innately reckless. . . . Escalation tactics depend in large part for their success on shock value, on the impressions of doubt, confusion and fear they are able to create in the opponent's mind.[26]

Williams argues that, during a crisis, an actor can escalate through a "straightforward increase in either the actual or the potential level of violence" or through an "escalation of issues." An actor can pursue an "escalation of issues" through either "vertical escalation" or "horizontal escalation," respectively. Vertical escalation is to raise the level of the crisis. During the Taiwan Strait crisis in 1996, for example, the United States sent two aircraft carriers to an area near the Taiwan Strait. Horizontal escalation is the expansion of the scope of a crisis. If one side has inferior conventional forces in the region of the crisis, for example, it may bring pressure to bear on its adversary in other regions, where it has superiority in its forces.[27]

Crisis escalation tactics are in fact "coercive bargaining operations" intended to use coercive action and pressure to force the adversary to make concessions or to be willing to reconcile. Among the tactics of coercion, the most famous is "deterrent threat," the objective of which is to convince the adversary that, if the adversary ignores threats regarding its behavior, it will certainly receive the declared punishment.[28] However, coercive bargaining is also a policy of "limited risk." The more one side escalates, the more its interests become involved in the crisis and, consequently, the more risk it endures. This can "diminish or destroy the policy makers' control over events" and lead the two sides to confront each other.[29]

During international crises, the United States also sometimes used the strategy of brinkmanship. That is, the United States stood at the threshold between coercive bargaining and the brink of war, and it even passed over the threshold in order to compel the adversary to make concessions. During the 1955 Taiwan Strait crisis, for example, President Dwight D. Eisenhower declared that the United States would use tactical nuclear weapons in the event of an all-out war in Asia.[30] Secretary of State John Foster Dulles said, "The ability to get to the verge without getting into the war is the necessary art. If you try to run away from it, if you are scared to go to the brink, you are lost."[31] Phil Williams argues, however, that "brinkmanship may be a necessary art, it is certainly not an easy art to master, and the penalties for mistakes or miscalculations are stark. Although brinkmanship and escalation are vital to crisis management, they make the equally central task of 'disaster avoidance' both more formidable and more urgent."[32] Hence, Williams argues that both sides should be conciliatory but firm, emphasize their common interests while they relegate the core conflict to a position of less importance, and focus on maintaining common interests while peacefully resolving the crisis.

MECHANISMS FOR SINO-AMERICAN CRISIS MANAGEMENT DECISION MAKING

Since the end of the Cold War, several security-military crises have occurred between China and the United States, including Lee Teng-hui's visit to the United States in 1995, the Taiwan Strait crisis in 1995–1996, the NATO bombing of the Chinese embassy in Belgrade in 1999, and the EP-3 collision in 2001. Both countries have accumulated some experience with crisis management through the resolution of these crises and have begun to establish some mechanisms of crisis management.

Because of different political systems, cultures, and traditions, the gap between the mechanisms of crisis management of the two countries is relatively large, and China and the United States will need a long period to adapt to each other.

China's leadership system reflects the CCP as the core of the leadership as well as the principle of democratic centralism. When China is involved in international political crises, usually the Political Bureau of the Central Committee of the CCP and its Standing Committee make major decisions. The Secretariat of the CCP Central Committee is responsible for handling the Central Committee's day-to-day work, including dealing with crisis management.[33] The State Council, the Central Military Commission of the CCP, the Leading Group of National Security of the Central Committee of the CCP, the Leading Group of Foreign Affairs of the Central Committee of the CCP, the Ministry of Foreign Affairs, and the Ministry of State Security participate and handle affairs related to crisis management.[34]

The mechanism of decision making in the crisis management of the United States operates with the U.S. president as the core. Usually the U.S. president makes decisions about crisis management after consulting with senior advisers or working groups. The U.S. president can convene conferences of the National Security Council to discuss crisis situations or form a high-level working group to help the president to make the most suitable decisions. High-level working groups for crisis management usually include the vice president, the secretary of state, the national security adviser, the secretary of defense, the chairman of the Joint Chiefs of Staff, the director of the Central Intelligence Agency (CIA), and the secretary of the treasury, among others.

Williams argues that the optimum number of people in a crisis management decision-making group is twelve to seventeen people because this number of people is sufficient to ensure the participation of representatives of all the major related government organizations, and it allows for candid discussions with few opportunities to divulge secrets about the policy decision.[35] During the 1962 Cuban missile crisis, President John F. Kennedy established a seventeen-person high-level working group. The average number of people participating in these crisis decision-making discussions was fourteen to fifteen people. In June 1950, before President Harry Truman made the decision to send U.S. ground forces to fight on the Korean peninsula, he convened six important meetings attended by twelve to fifteen persons.

Daniel Frei argues that it is important for U.S. government officials to consult with experts of international law because many crises involve problems of international law. Measures to cope with crisis should be in accordance with international law because any violation of international law will damage the United States in terms of international politics. During the Cuban missile crisis, the legal advisers of the U.S. Department of State proposed the use of the new phrase, "defensive quarantine," to describe the U.S. blockade of Cuba because the new phrase would indicate that action taken by the United States was defensive in terms of politics. They also suggested that the United States should use the Organization of American States (OAS) to invoke a legal provision of the Rio de Janeiro Treaty of Mutual Assistance to authorize the defensive quarantine against Cuba rather than invoke only the right to self-defense found in Article 51 of the Charter of the United Nations. Because it would be very difficult for a country to get an authorization from a regional organization like the OAS under Article 8 of the Charter of the United Nations, other countries would be unable to use this issue as a precedent in the future.[36]

PATTERNS OF SINO-AMERICAN CRISIS MANAGEMENT DECISION MAKING

China and the United States share common as well as divergent patterns of crisis management decision making. Their biggest commonality in the patterns of decision making for crisis management is that when crises occur, both make great efforts to seek broad sympathy and support from the international community and other countries. This is also a manifestation of a universal rule of diplomacy. The two countries display several differences in patterns of decision making for crisis management.

Laws vs. Principles and Morality

The United States places great importance on laws; China stresses principles and morality and places much more importance on agreements to restrict confrontation.

When managing international political crisis, the United States attaches great importance to international law as the legal foundation of its actions and to indicate its impartiality. The United States also makes use of international mechanisms to organize coalitions and to call on the international community. During the Korean War, for example, the United States used the United Nations Security Council to pass a resolution to organize the United Nations to interfere in Korean internal affairs. In situations in which it is impossible for the United States to invoke provisions of international laws, the United States even uses its internal laws and unilateral commitments to justify interfering in other countries' internal affairs. During the 1995–1996 Taiwan Strait crisis, for example, the United States used the Taiwan Relations Act passed by the U.S. Congress as the basis for sending two aircraft carriers near the Taiwan Strait to interfere in China's internal affairs.

As Alfred Wilhelm argues, "The Chinese tended to emphasize the permanence and self-evident truth of their principles," such as the one-China principle and the Five Principles of Peaceful Coexistence.[37] Wilhelm argues that one can divide China's principles into three categories: "The first are principles that the Chinese publicly announce must be met prior to any formal negotiations. The second are principles that are objective for the conference. The third are general principles."[38] Chinese leaders are also skilled at using "moral suasion as a basis for achieving conformity and thus harmony."[39]

Former assistant secretary of state for East Asian and Pacific Affairs Richard H. Solomon argues that Chinese officials have a partiality for reaching political agreements by ambiguously stating their principles and intentions, and they prefer to publicize these political agreements through press releases, communiqués, and joint statements rather than through formal treaties or contracts.[40] During recent years, however, China has gradually attached more importance to using already existing and newly formed agreements to prevent conflicts. China and the United States have signed agreements on the creation of a secure, direct hotline, for example, and also an agreement on a military security consultation mechanism for the high seas. Those agreements indicated the efforts of both countries to prevent unexpected conflicts and to reduce the possibilities of crisis between the two sides. In recent years, with China gradually integrating itself deeply into the international community, Beijing has been placing increasing importance on using international law and international mechanisms to safeguard its national interests and the common interests of people around the world.

Lives and Freedom vs. Saving Face

The United States has attached great importance to the value of people's lives and freedom; China has given more importance to saving face.

When an international political crisis erupts, the U.S. government is most concerned about the safety and freedom of its personnel. Solving this problem often makes the crisis turn into a matter of solving some issues that do not touch upon basic U.S. interests. In August 1955, for example, when Sino-American talks at the ambassadorial level began, the Chinese government declared that China would release eleven U.S. spies. This not only improved the atmosphere of the talks and gained the initiative for China but also gained for China the sympathy and support of the international community. Likewise, in April 2001, after a U.S. espionage aircraft collided with China's fighter aircraft and landed on the airport on Hainan Island, the U.S. side was most concerned about the safety and return of its flight crew, and it sent officials from its embassy in Beijing to visit them. President George W. Bush openly asked Chinese authorities several times to release members of the flight crew so that they could return home as soon as possible. To persuade the Chinese side to let the crew go home, the United States had to send a letter of apology about the collision to China in the name of the U.S. ambassador. When the U.S. flight crew arrived back in the United States, the crisis was basically resolved.

Because of the characteristics of East Asian culture, at the same time that China values human lives, it attaches special importance to the concept of face. After both the U.S.-led NATO bombing of the Chinese embassy in Belgrade in 1999 and the espionage aircraft collision in 2001, for example, the Chinese government asked the U.S. government to apologize to the Chinese people and regarded this as one of China's main requests.

Compromise vs. Retaining a Well-Considered Initial Position

The United States usually looks for a compromise that is beneficial for itself, while China sometimes first finds a basic position that is beneficial for both sides and sticks to it to the end.

During negotiations, the U.S. government has been good at coercive bargaining, trying to find a way of resolving crises that would be beneficial to U.S. interests through mutual compromise and mutual exchanges. Kenneth T. Young argues, "Without both diplomacy and power, negotiation with Peking is unlikely or impossible."[41] During international crises, the United States has sometimes used the so-called Trollope ploy, in which it accepted one of the two mutually contradictory proposals from its opponent, or even accepted a proposal that had not been put forward by its opponent, so as to spur its opponent to accept what the United States had accepted.[42] During the Cuban missile crisis, for example, Soviet leader Nikita Khrushchev sent two letters to President John F. Kennedy: one suggested that the Soviet Union would take a tough line toward the U.S. blockade of Cuba and the other indicated a moderate and even yielding attitude. At the time, the U.S. government did not know which letter was sent to the U.S. government first. Under this situation, U.S. decision makers decided to regard the second letter as the real position of the Soviet government and to intentionally ignore the information in the first letter. Coral Bell argues: "It was this creative use of ambiguity which enabled the settlement to be reached."[43]

Reflecting on his experiences in China, former secretary of state Henry Kissinger expressed admiration for the Chinese method of negotiating. Whereas negotiators from other countries use the so-called salami approach, by which they try to "slice their concessions as thinly as possible over as long a period of time as possible," Chinese negotiators were far more consistent, Kissinger wrote. Kissinger argued that Chinese negotiators tended to "determine as well as possible the nature of a reasonable solution, get there in one jump, and then stick to that position." Although some criticized this tactic as one of "preemptive concession," Kissinger believed the use of this tactic made negotiators more able to defend their position by avoiding "the cumulative impact over a long period of a series of marginal moves in which process always threatens to dominate substance."[44]

Richard H. Solomon, former U.S. assistant secretary of state for East Asia and Pacific Affairs, describing the consistent characteristics of Chinese negotiating behavior, argued that Chinese officials have clear objectives and careful plans for their negotiations but are sometimes unable to sufficiently control the process. Consequently they "often 'feel their way' in situations they do not fully understand."[45] Solomon argues that the concluding stages of Chinese negotiations, while differing according to the circumstances, are highly consistent:

> The negotiator will quickly conclude an agreement after a protracted assessment of his counterpart's position. The end-game phase of a negotiation is usually brief, businesslike, and conducted at a high level of authority as the negotiators give concrete expression in some formal document to the principles and objectives that have been discussed at length by lower-level officials in the assessment phase.[46]

IMPORTANT FACTORS AFFECTING SINO-AMERICAN CRISIS MANAGEMENT

Six factors are important to both China and the United States as they formulate their crisis management relationship.

Balance of Strength and National Interests

Strength includes power and the determination and ability to use it. Strength in this context refers to national power, including both hard power and soft power. In the United States, there is a dispute about whether the balance of strength or the magnitude of national interests at stake plays the main role in the management of international political crises. One school holds that balance of strength played a major role in crisis management between the two superpowers. Zbigniew Brzezinski, former national security adviser to President Jimmy Carter, said that, if there had been a balance of strategic forces between the United States and Soviet Union during the Cuban missile crisis, "it might have proven much more difficult for the United States to achieve its principal objective in Cuba (the removal of hostile missiles) through the exercise of its conventional superiority (naval blockade)."[47]

Another school holds that the imbalance of the superpower's national interests might be the most important factor determining the results of crisis between them. McGeorge Bundy said: "A decision that would bring even one hydrogen bomb on one city of one's own country would be recognized in advance as a catastrophic blunder, ten bombs on ten cities would be a disaster beyond history, and a hundred bombs on a hundred cities are unthinkable."[48] Under this situation, "nuclear holocaust will hardly be an attractive option even to the side that has the capacity to 'win.'"[49] Therefore, "so long as neither superpower regards nuclear war with equanimity . . . the strategic balance is unlikely to be the major determinant of either side's resolve."[50] Williams further argues, "The asymmetry of interest may well have been the most important factor in determining the outcome of the Cuban Missile Crisis."[51] Because the missiles deployed in Cuba by the Soviet Union threatened the key national interests of the United States, and the withdrawal of the missiles from Cuba by the Soviet Union would not harm the key national interests of the Soviet Union, the Soviet Union made concessions under strong pressure from the United States and in response to the local conventional military superiority of the United States in the Caribbean Sea area.

The balance of strength and the balance of national interests between China and the United States will become two basic variables for determining the results of a crisis. The main determinant of the results of Sino-American crisis will be the interaction between the two countries' balance of national interests and balance of strength. But the balance of interests between the two sides will become the most important factor determining the results of crisis between China and the United States. China is not a superpower and has only a very small number of nuclear weapons. The models of action of the United States and the Soviet Union during the Cold War are not suitable for Sino-American relations. The fact that China has some nuclear retaliation capabilities is an important factor: as long as the United States cannot be sure it can destroy all of China's strategic nuclear forces after its first strike or that it can prevent

China from responding to a nuclear first strike from the United States, the strategic imbalance between the United States and China will not become the major factor determining the results of a crisis between the two countries.

Balance of national interests is often more important than balance of strength. One can use a cost-benefit analysis to evaluate the results of the interactions between the two sides. The Taiwan issue is a key national interest of China, for example, but it is only one of many important national interests of the United States. In terms of the balance of interests, this is beneficial for China. The Taiwan issue will also be influenced by other variables. Both China and the United States have strong points and weak points in East Asia. If there is a crisis between China and the United States over Taiwan, the interaction of the balance of national interests and the balance of strength of the two countries will determine the result.

Structure of a Crisis

The structure of a crisis refers to what causes or constitutes a crisis. Crises between China and the United States can be classified into five types on the basis of the causes of the crisis:

- Conflicts in China's peripheral areas, as in the Korean War;
- Issue of Taiwan, as in the 1955 and 1958 Taiwan Strait crises;
- Accidental violence, as in the 1999 NATO bombing of the Chinese embassy in Belgrade and the 2001 EP-3 collision;
- China's internal issues, such as the 1989 Tiananmen Square incident; and
- Disputes between the two sides over nonproliferation issues, such as the Yinhe incident.

The first and second types of crises involved the two countries' national interests to a far greater extent than the three other types of crises; one type even caused the two countries to fight during the Korean War. The latter three types of crises involved the two countries' national interests to a far lesser extent, so the difficulties of crisis management were relatively smaller.

Foreign Strategies

The two countries' foreign strategies are the basis for the formation and determination of their guidelines for crisis management. On August 3, 2002, for example, President Chen Shui-bian of Taiwan, probing the red line of both mainland China and the United States, openly advocated "a state on either side." President Chen also wanted to provoke a crisis in the Taiwan Strait so as to cause deterioration in cross-strait relations and incite anti-mainland sentiment. At the time, the Bush administration regarded antiterrorism as the highest priority of its global strategy and was preparing to launch a war against Iraq, so Washington openly expressed its dissatisfaction with Chen's moves, which had the potential to throw the strategic plans of the United States into disarray. Moreover, the fact that Chen had rashly suggested "a state on either side" without prior consultation angered the Bush administration. At the same time, the United States continued to use Taiwan to contain China. Under these circumstances, the Bush administration readjusted its policy toward Taiwan, which had been leaning too heavily toward the Taiwanese side, and declared that the United States did not support Taiwan's independence. But the United States also stressed that China and Taiwan must resolve the issue through peaceful means. The United States continued to develop U.S.-Taiwan military cooperation.

China's foreign strategy is determined by its national development strategy. To achieve its goal to become a middle-level developed country by the middle of the twenty-first century, China needs the international security environment to be peaceful for a long time. China would like to develop constructive cooperative relations with the United States. However, China will insist on its one-China position and will never permit Taiwan to separate from China because Taiwan is related to the important sovereignty issue of China.

Domestic Political Factors

Although foreign policy has some independent and special characteristics, inevitably it is influenced by domestic politics. Domestic politics also influence countries' decision making during international political crises. However, one should not exaggerate the influence. Phil Williams argues, "Although domestic politics should not be overlooked in any worthwhile analysis of crisis decision making, it is misleading to attribute to them the dominant influence that some recent observers have claimed."[52] The U.S. Congress, media, and interest groups all influence U.S. decision-making processes to some extent. When a Sino-American crisis erupted in the past, some members of the U.S. Congress adopted extreme attitudes because they wanted to attract voters and media attention. Alfred Wilhelm states that, during the Taiwan Strait crisis in 1958, "the mood of much of the Congress was bellicose. Senator William Knowland's call for a naval blockade was representative of some of the more extreme feelings."[53]

During recent years, the U.S. news media have continued to become more commercialized. To attract the public's attention, the U.S. media sometimes create a hubbub about some issues. After the 2001 EP-3 collision, for example, some in the U.S. media accused China of inhumanely detaining the U.S. crew, which hurt the friendly feelings between the Chinese and the American people and spurred the Bush administration to pursue a tough policy regarding the incident. U.S. interest groups usually lobby members of Congress and officials and make use of the media to influence the crisis management decision-making process. In 1995, for example, the lobby of interest groups representing Taiwan influenced the Clinton administration to agree to then-Taiwan president Lee Teng-hui's visit to the United States, which led to a Sino-American crisis.

Public opinion also sometimes influences China's crisis management decision making. The Internet has some influence over the methods of crisis management the Chinese government uses and its attitudes toward a crisis. According to Li Xiwang, the reaction of the Chinese media to the 2001 EP-3 collision was relatively slow. Furthermore, after President George W. Bush made a tough speech about the incident, Chinese official media did not report it, but some Chinese media on the Internet translated and published Bush's speech. Chinese citizens then expressed on the Internet their anger toward the United States. Under these circumstances, the attitude and approach of the Chinese government toward the incident changed to some extent, and the voices of Chinese officials and the public converged.

Relations with Allies and Friends

Relations with allies and friendly countries sometimes cause crises in international politics and heavily influence crisis decision making. Since the end of World War II, the United States has had NATO in Europe and five bilateral military allies in the Asia-Pacific region. In addition, although the United States abrogated the U.S.-Taiwan Mutual Defense Treaty when China and the United States established diplomatic ties in 1979, it has still sold weapons to Taiwan in accordance with the Taiwan Relations Act. Since George W. Bush took office in 2001, the United States has strengthened its military cooperation with Taiwan, making Taiwan a de facto ally. The United States has made use of its allies and friends in order to maintain its leadership in the world.

The United States may be drawn into crises by its allies and friends. Phil Williams holds: "Equally intractable problems could arise in relations with allies. States closely allied to the superpowers and conscious primarily of their own needs, interests and objectives could demand a level of support that the superpowers find intolerable."[54] Williams charges, "Other dangers arise where the clients or allies are devious as well as headstrong, and attempt to embroil the superpowers in their conflicts to an unwarranted extent.[55] Therefore, Williams says, superpowers avoid giving "blank cheques" to their allies and "scrupulously try to prevent any moves by the latter entangling them in a position from which it is impossible to extricate themselves."[56] Even in a unipolar world, this assertion matters because a major power with nuclear weapons and strong conventional armed forces has capabilities to deter the United States from involving itself in an armed conflict with the major power.

Since the end of World War II, many of the instances in which the United States has been drawn into a crisis or a conflict have been when U.S. allies or friends drew them in. The Taiwan issue has involved Sino-American relations in crises several times. Taiwan authorities have wanted to make use of U.S. power to achieve their own objectives. In the 1950s and 1960s, the Chiang Kai-shek regime tried to rely on the United States to counterattack the mainland. Lee Teng-hui and Chen Shui-bian have tried to make use of the United States to realize Taiwan independence. During the 1996 Taiwan Strait crisis, Lee Teng-hui asked the prime minister of Japan, Ryutaro Hashimoto, to send a delegation to the United States to appeal for the United States to send troops to defend Taiwan. Under these circumstances, President Bill Clinton sent two aircraft carriers to the area near the Taiwan Strait.

An armed conflict between the United States and China because of the Taiwan issue is not in the national interest of the United States. Such an armed conflict would incur serious losses for both countries, although China's suffering might be much greater than that of the United States. Therefore, preventing Taiwan from declaring de jure independence will be beneficial for the common interest of both China and the United States.

Culture and Value Systems

China and the United States have different cultures and value systems, and their cultures and values have affected both countries' foreign policies, including decision making in crisis management. President Jiang Zemin described Chinese values in an October 2002 speech at the George Bush Presidential Library and Museum:

> The Chinese nation has inherited from ancient times a fine tradition of honesty, harmony and good faith—values that China consistently abides by in the conduct of relations with other countries. . . . Confucius said more than two thousand years ago, "In human relationships, a gentleman seeks harmony but not uniformity." That is to say, harmony but not sameness; reserving differences without coming into conflict. We believe that the world's civilizations, social systems and development models can come together for exchanges and emulation. They can learn from one another, benefit from their respective strengths in a peaceful competition and achieve common development by seeking common ground while putting aside differences.[57]

In U.S. culture, manifest destiny is a notion that argues that the United States should spread civilization to the wilderness; this is a belief that the United States must act as a savior to enlighten weak nations—an extremely arrogant way of thinking. Because of its faith in its manifest destiny, the United States requires other countries to accept its free-market and free-democracy systems as it exports democracy. The strategy of exporting democracy is obviously derived from the same origins. Wang Xiaode argues: "Those values that affect the United States' foreign policy decision making are deeply rooted in U.S. culture. When specific U.S. diplomatic policies reflect these values, they generally become an open and legal cover or plausible explanation for the United States' pursuit of its own interests."[58]

Chinese culture is used to seeing issues from a macroscopic perspective, so Chinese people usually put their principles forward first. It would be easier to resolve problems if principles were defined first. Western culture is accustomed to looking at issues from a microscopic perspective, so Western people usually want to resolve some urgent specific problems first. Through the process of resolving problems, they establish an overall framework. In the current world, the cultures and value systems of both China and the United States should coexist and learn from each other. During crisis management, we should prevent the cultural differences of the two countries from causing conflicts.

IMPORTANT ISSUES IN SINO-AMERICAN CRISIS MANAGEMENT

Crisis control and management is one of the important functions of diplomacy, and it is also an art of struggle. Excellent decision making in crisis management needs not only innovation and constructive wisdom but also resourceful, decisive, flexible, and painstaking diplomatic skill. Because China and the United States are different in cultures, values, foreign strategies, foreign policies, and mechanisms of decision making, the two countries need to go through a process of mutual adaptation to each other and mutual fitting in with each other. During the process, we should pay great attention to these issues.

Objectives Should Be Limited

During a crisis, if both sides want to realize their biggest political goals, it will unavoidably lead to armed conflict. Therefore, while both sides defend their key national interests, which are not negotiable, they should also recognize that in order to manage the crisis effectively both sides will likely not reach their grandest political goals in most situations. Both sides should get a clear understanding of their nonnegotiable national interests as well as the issues on which they can make concessions and compromise, so as to define their appropriate political goals in crisis management. The United States, for example, should recognize that the one-China principle is a key national interest of China and is non-negotiable. At the same time, China feels the greatest sincerity and will make the greatest efforts to realize peaceful unification. Phil Williams argues, "Leaving an adversary a way of retreating without humiliation, or framing one's aspirations and objectives to accommodate the vital interests of others, are central features of skilful diplomacy."[59] One can use this as a reference when the two sides are defining their crisis management objectives and conducting crisis diplomacy.

Signals Should Be Clear and Understandable

During a crisis, signals in communication between the two sides should be as clear as possible so that decision makers on each side can understand signals from the other side correctly. When signals are related to military action, decision makers should make great efforts to avoid misunderstanding and miscalculation that could lead to armed conflict. On June 25, 1950, for example, the Korean War erupted. After the Incheon landing on September 15, 1950, U.S. troops penetrated north, across the 38th parallel, and were pressing on toward the China–North Korea border. At this time, China sent several clear warnings to the United States. On September 30, 1950, Premier Zhou Enlai, on behalf of the Chinese government, spoke publicly in Beijing and pointed out, "The Chinese people cannot tolerate foreign imperialism and cannot take a laissez-faire attitude while imperialists wantonly invade its neighbors."[60]

On October 3, 1950, Premier Zhou Enlai met India's ambassador to the PRC and asked that the Indian government communicate to the United States that if the U.S. Army crossed the 38th parallel China could not sit by and watch; it would have to get involved. That was another Chinese warning to the United States through diplomatic channels to avoid the situation of China having to send its troops to North

Korea. Because of the arrogance and prejudice of some U.S. politicians at that time, the U.S. government ignored the warnings from China and sent its troops across the 38th parallel and onward to the Yalu River.

Phil Williams argues that before Beijing decided to dispatch troops to Korea, "Peking [had signaled] to Washington that it would not remain idle if North Korea was invaded." The United States, however, disregarded these warnings because of several factors:

> In the first place, the signals were probably neither sufficiently loud nor particularly clear. The lack of direct diplomatic contact between Peking and Washington hindered communication and meant that China had to rely primarily upon diplomatic intermediaries and public announcements. One such intermediary was the Indian ambassador in Peking, who apparently conveyed Chinese anxieties and threat of intervention to the United States. These were not taken very seriously, partly because the channel itself was suspect: the ambassador was regarded as pro-Chinese and therefore unreliable. Firm public statements and warnings by Chou En-lai were also dismissed as crude attempts to influence United Nations deliberations, rather than given credence as serious evidence of Chinese intent.[61]

Michael Pillsbury, a U.S. expert on China who has experience in academia as well as government, argues that if the Chinese government had declared that China would send a half million troops to Korea to fight if U.S. troops went across the 38th parallel, U.S. troops would not have invaded North Korea.[62]

These comments indicate not only that both sides should send clear signals but also that decision makers on each side should abandon their prejudice and arrogance when they read signals from the other side. At the same time, both sides should consider the impacts of different cultural backgrounds on the communication of signals. Americans are used to sending direct and clear threats to others. Eastern culture is much more reserved. Accordingly, China's signals, including warnings, are usually reserved.

On one hand, the ambiguous signals concerning military action were probably disastrous. On the other hand, ambiguity in diplomacy is probably constructive. Sometimes one side wants to show that it is firm and determined not to compromise in the face of pressure. At the same time, it should also indicate its flexibility, which will be necessary for the final resolution of the problem. Both sides should also connect language signals and nonlanguage signals to control and resolve a crisis.

Rules and Mechanisms Should Be Set Up

To deal with and control crises well in international politics, especially crises between China and the United States, both sides should establish mechanisms for crisis management with strong leadership, proper policy, good coordination, and quick access to information. Moreover, China and the United States must establish smooth communication mechanisms and channels. During recent years, the two countries have made some progress in establishing a hotline between the two countries' leaders and multilevel strategic dialogue mechanisms. The 1990s offered many opportunities to practice crisis management, and both sides accumulated this kind of experience. Both sides formed some new conventions for crisis control and resolution that helped the two countries become accustomed to each other's crisis management style.

Channels of Communication Should Be Diversified

To prevent and resolve future crises, China and the United States should also attach importance to diversified channels of communication, including both official and unofficial. When a crisis erupts, personal communications between the leaders of the two countries are also very important. Thus, the two countries should establish a mechanism of regular exchanges of visits between their leaders in order to increase mutual understanding and mutual trust.

Historic experiences also show that during a crisis unofficial channels can become important for communicating information and seeking ways to resolve the crisis. Phil Williams highlights that, during the Cuban missile crisis, the United States and the Soviet Union used "all the 'basic channels of communication,'" but, Williams argued, "Probably most important were unofficial channels, which can sometimes appear very attractive in crises. . . . 'Trusted emissaries' can provide a valuable if 'extra-diplomatic' channel of communication." Alexander Fomin, a senior Soviet intelligence official in the United States, had "his own direct channels of communication to the Kremlin. . . . [His talks with] John Scali, diplomatic correspondent of the American Broadcasting Company, . . . broke the deadlock and first 'suggested a formula for negotiations.'"[63]

NOTES

1. Luo Zhufeng, *Hanyu Dacidian* [A Chinese Dictionary], 2nd ed. (Hong Kong: Sanlian Shudian [Xianggang] Youxian Gonsi/Hanyu Dacidian Chubanshe, 1988), p. 527.
2. *Dangdai Guoji Weiji* [Current International Crisis] (Beijing: Junshi Kexue Chubanshe, 1988), p. 258.
3. Xie Yixian, *Zhongguo Dangdai Waijiaoshi 1949–1955* [The History of Contemporary Diplomatic Relations of China: 1949–1995] (Beijing: Zhongguo Qingnian Chubanshe, 1997), pp. 138–139. During Mao Zedong's speech at the Supreme State Council on September 8, 1958, Mao Zedong said that U.S. involvement in Taiwan, establishment of hundreds of military bases around the world, and creation of tension in the world are nooses around the neck of the United States.
4. Chinese Delegation to the ASEAN Security Forum, "Document About China's Position on New Concept of Security," *People's Daily*, August 2, 2002.
5. Ibid.
6. Oran R. Young, *The Politics of Force: Bargaining During International Crises* (Princeton, N.J.: Princeton University Press, 1968), p. 15.
7. Phil Williams, *Crisis Management: Confrontation and Diplomacy in the Nuclear Age* (London: Martin Robertson & Co. Ltd., 1976), p. 25.
8. William R. Kintner and David C. Schwarz, *A Study on Crisis Management* (Philadelphia, Pa.: University of Pennsylvania Foreign Policy Research Institute, 1965), appendix B, p. 21.
9. Leslie Lipson quoted in "Crisis Management or Crisis Prevention," NATO Letter (August–September 1966), p. 14.
10. "President Bush Delivers Graduation Speech at West Point," White House, Office of the Press Secretary, Washington, D.C., June 1, 2002, www.whitehouse.gov/news/releases/2002/06/20020601-3.html.

11. George W. Bush, "Securing Freedom's Triumph," *New York Times*, September 11, 2002, p. A33.

12. *National Security Strategy of the United States of America,* White House, National Security Council, Washington, D.C., September 17, 2002, www.whitehouse.gov/nsc/nss.pdf.

13. Williams, *Crisis Management*, p. 65.

14. Ibid., pp. 60–63.

15. Ibid., p. 63.

16. Ibid.

17. Alexander George and Richard Smoke, *Deterrence in American Foreign Policy: Theory and Practice* (New York: Columbia University Press, 1974), p. 215, quoted in Williams, *Crisis Management*, p. 187.

18. South Korean Ministry of Defense War History Compilation Committee, *Chaoxian Zhanzheng* [Korean War], vol. 1 (Heilongjiang: Heilongjiang Ethnicity Publishing House, 1988), p. 4. This is a Chinese translation of the original Korean text.

19. Harry S. Truman, *Memoirs by Harry S. Truman: Years of Trial and Hope*, vol. 2 (New York: Doubleday & Co., 1956), pp. 365–366.

20. Ibid., p. 366.

21. Truman, *Memoirs by Harry S. Truman.*

22. Ministry of Foreign Affairs of the People's Republic of China and the CCP Central Committee Literature Research Division, eds., *Zhou Enlai Waijiao Wenxuan* [Selected Works of Zhou Enlai on Diplomacy] (Beijing: Zhongyang Wenxian Chubanshe, 1990), p. 2.

23. Ibid.

24. *Selections from Mao Zedong* (Beijing: Renmin Chubanshe, 1964), p. 580.

25. Kintner and Schwarz, *A Study on Crisis Management,* appendix B, p. 3.

26. Williams, *Crisis Management*, p. 147.

27. Ibid.

28. Ibid., pp. 137–138.

29. Ibid., p. 174.

30. Dwight D. Eisenhower, "(56) President's Press Conference March 16, 1955," in "1955 Addresses of President Dwight D. Eisenhower," Eisenhower Presidential Library and Museum, Audiovisual Department, Abilene, Kans., p. 76, www.eisenhower.archives.gov/avwebsite/PDF/55text.pdf.

31. Quoted by Paul H. Nitze, in "A Shaky Balance of Brinkmanship," in Ivo D. Duchacek, ed., *Conflict and Cooperation Among Nations* (New York: Holt, Rinehart and Winston, 1960), p. 394.

32. Williams, *Crisis Management,* p. 136.

33. *Zhongguo Gongchandang Zhangcheng* [Constitution of the Chinese Communist Party] (Beijing: Renmin Chubanshe, 2002), p. 18. The Constitution was revised and adopted at the 16th National Congress of the CCP on November 14, 2002. According to the Constitution, when the Central Committee plenary conference ends, the Politburo and its Standing Committee exercise the Central Committee's official powers. The Secretariat of the Central Committee is the working body for the Politburo and its Standing Committee.

34. Yang Jiemian, *Houlengzhan Shiqi.de ZhongMei Guanxi: Waijiao Zhengce Bijiao Yanjiu* [Sino-U.S. Relations During the Post–Cold War Period: A Foreign Policy Comparison] (Shanghai: Shanghai Renmin Chubanshe, 2000), pp. 104–122. This book recounts the functions of the State Council, Military Commission of the CCP Central Committee, Central Committee of the CCP Foreign Affairs Working Leadership Group, Ministry of Foreign Affairs, and the National Security Office regarding China's policy toward the United States.

35. Williams, *Crisis Management*, p. 71.

36. Daniel Frei, ed., *International Crises and Crisis Management: An East-West Symposium* (Farnborough, England: Saxon House, 1978), p. 14.

37. Alfred D. Wilhelm Jr., "Sino-American Negotiations: The Chinese Approach" (UMI Dissertation Service, 1987), p. 15.

38. Ibid., 77.

39. Ibid., 15.

40. Richard H. Solomon, *Chinese Negotiating Behavior: Pursuing Interests Through "Old Friends"* (Washington, D.C.: United States Institute of Peace, 1999).

41. Kenneth T. Young, *Negotiating with the Chinese Communists: The United States Experience, 1953–1967* (New York: McGraw-Hill Book Co., 1968), p. 371.

42. Coral Bell, *The Conventions of Crisis: A Study in Diplomatic Management* (London: Oxford University of International Affairs, 1971), p. 74.

43. Ibid., p. 75.

44. Henry Kissinger, *White House Years* (Boston: Little Brown, 1979), p. 752.

45. Richard H. Solomon, *Chinese Negotiating Behavior*, p. 17.

46. Ibid., p. 147.

47. Zbigniew Brzezinski, "USA/USSR: The Power Relationship," in Subcommittee on National Security and International Operations of the Committee on Government Operations, United States Senate, *International Negotiation: The Impact of the Changing Power Balance: Selected Comments* (Washington, D.C.: U.S. Government Printing Office, 1971), p. 9.

48. Quoted in Williams, *Crisis Management*, p. 158.
49. Ibid.
50. Ibid.
51. Ibid., p. 160.
52. Ibid., p. 89.
53. Wilhelm, "Sino-American Negotiations," pp. 210–211.
54. Williams, *Crisis Management*, p. 100.
55. Ibid., p. 132.
56. Ibid., pp. 130–131.
57. "Speech by President Jiang Zemin at George Bush Presidential Library," Beijing: Ministry of Foreign Affairs (October 24, 2002), www.fmprc.gov.cn/eng/topics/3719/3721/t19082.htm.
58. Wang Xiaode, *Meiguo Wenhua yu Waijiao* [U.S. Culture and Foreign Policy] (Beijing: Shijie Zhishi Chubanshe, 2000), p. 11.
59. Williams, *Crisis Management*, p. 200.
60. Xie Yixian, *Zhongguo Dangdai Waijiaoshi 1949–1955* [History of Contemporary Diplomatic Relations of China: 1949–1995], p. 45.
61. Williams, *Crisis Management*, p. 185.
62. Michael Pillsbury, discussion with author, Washington, D.C., February 1995.
63. Williams, *Crisis Management*, p. 190.

5

"Resist America": China's Role in the Korean and Vietnam Wars

Zhang Baijia

THE KOREAN WAR AND THE VIETNAM WAR were two regional wars that occurred in Asia after the end of the Second World War. They were fought on a large scale; both lasted for several years, and both had far-reaching repercussions. In China, people generally refer to the Korean War as "Resist America, Support Korea" (*kangmeiyuanchao*) and to the Vietnam War as "Support Vietnam, Resist America" (*yuanyuekangmei*). Compared with the "Korean War" and the "Vietnam War," the Chinese phrasing is more accurate in terms of the role of China in the two wars and the two different forms of Sino-American confrontation. For China, the outbreak and escalation of the two wars were not entirely unexpected. As it dealt with the two wars, China's considerations and its decision making were generally strategic. Crisis management was present only during certain stages of the decision-making process. This article will focus on two aspects: the background of the wars and China's crisis management during the wars.

CHINA'S CRISIS MANAGEMENT DURING THE KOREAN WAR

It was exactly four months from the outbreak of the Korean War on June 25, 1950, to the first gunshot by the China People's Volunteer Army on October 25 of the same year. Faced with a serious external

179

threat to national security, the Chinese Communist Party (CCP) Central Committee decided to send troops to resist U.S. aggression and aid Korea. The decision-making process involved can be regarded as the first major crisis management situation after the founding of the People's Republic of China (PRC).

Security Situation During the Early Days of the PRC

From October 1, 1949, when the PRC was founded, to June 25, 1950, when the Korean War broke out, China's security situation was tense and unstable in both the domestic and the international contexts.

At the end of World War II, two major features of the international arena were the coming of the Cold War between the United States and the Soviet Union and the fact that many Asian countries had won national liberation and independence. Against this background, a civil war swept across China and ended with the CCP in victory. The founding of the PRC upset the strategic balance in the Far East envisioned in Yalta by the United States and the Soviet Union and increased the complexities in Asia and, in particular, in China's neighboring areas. The success of the CCP set an example for and greatly heightened the morale of the communist parties in other Asian countries. The United States, opposed to the spread of communism, started to build a new line of defense around China to contain the expansion of communism.

In the early days of the PRC, the CCP leaders faced three tasks: consolidating the newly born nation; building the national economy devastated by many years of war; and unifying China by wiping out the remnants of Kuomintang (KMT) military forces, preparing to march into Tibet, and preparing to liberate Taiwan. China took a significant diplomatic step by signing the Sino-Soviet Treaty of Friendship, Alliance, and Mutual Assistance. The treaty improved Sino-Soviet relations, provided a security guarantee and economic assistance for China, and made it easier for China to fulfill its domestic tasks. At the same time, however, it aggravated the tension between China and the United States.

The United States was China's major external threat during this period. The revolution in China led by the CCP was distinctively anti-imperialist in nature, which explained the antagonism between the PRC and the United States from the very beginning. The Cold War had no doubt intensified such antagonism. During China's civil war, the U.S. government carried out the policy of supporting Chiang Kai-shek in his fight against communism. After the revolution succeeded, Washington was reluctant to admit the failure of its China policy or to recognize the PRC. From the point of view of CCP leaders, the United States threatened both the revolution and the security of the newly founded nation.

Although CCP leaders heightened their vigilance toward U.S. armed intervention, they had come to believe that the United States was less and less likely to intervene directly in China's revolution because the KMT had failed and the PRC had been founded. At that time, Sino-American relations were strained, but they were not in outright confrontation. The Truman administration was still hesitating, watching, and fluctuating in its China policy considerations. Without the Korean War, or if the United States had not intervened when the Liberation Army tried to cross the Taiwan Strait, the tension between the two countries might have eased in two or three years and the United States and China might have established a normal, though perhaps not really a friendly, relationship. At least there had been such opportunities.

Issue of Korean Unification

Korea is a close neighbor of China. Modern history shows that the two countries' security concerns are closely related. Japan first invaded the Korean peninsula and, from there, expanded to mainland China. Chinese and Korean people supported each other and fought together against Japanese colonial rule and aggressive expansion. During the War of Resistance Against Japan, troops led by Kim Il-sung were in fact a division of China's allied forces against Japan and mainly fought within Chinese boundaries. Only after the Soviet Union became engaged in war against Japan did Kim Il-sung return to North Korea with the Soviet Army. To a great extent, China's attitude toward Korea and its reaction to the outbreak of the war can explain such special relationships.

After the end of World War II, Korea eliminated the colonial rule of Japan and won national independence. However, the issue of national unification emerged. The Cold War and the development of internal conflicts made the temporary military demarcation line separating the areas in which the United States and the Soviet Union accepted surrender on the Korean peninsula at the end of World War II evolve into a line dividing North and South Korea as well as defining the Cold War front in Northeast Asia. At that time, neither North nor South Korea recognized the legal standing of the 38th parallel set by the United States and the Soviet Union. The Korean War was unavoidable because the outbreak of the Cold War created a situation in which national liberation and independence in Asia conflicted with national unification.

China and Korea are close neighbors and have always been on good terms. Right before and after the founding of the PRC, however, China was preoccupied with its internal affairs and played a very limited role in the Korea issue. U.S. and Soviet policies toward Korea and Korea's internal situations were the main determinants of the development of the Korea situation. In Russian archival material released in recent years, one can find the following three important facts: First, North Korea started consultations with China on the war in April–May 1949. At that time, Mao Zedong agreed to provide troops and arms in assistance, but this ran counter to North Korea's intention to launch military attacks on South Korea in the near term.[1] Second, in January 1950, Kim Il-sung proposed to the Soviet Union a plan to unify Korea by force, which won the approval of Stalin.[2] China was kept in the dark as North Korea and the Soviet Union worked out this plan. Third, Kim Il-sung visited Beijing on May 13, 1950, and informed Chinese leaders of the decision made by North Korea and Soviet Union. Kim stated that North Korea did not need China's assistance and asked for only the consent of Chinese comrades to the decision. Because Mao Zedong and Zhou Enlai were surprised about the common decision by the Soviet Union and North Korea, they checked with Stalin immediately—on the same day, in fact.[3]

Mao Zedong later recollected that, in the early 1950s when he visited Moscow, he told Stalin that the key to the North Korea issue was preventing the South from attacking the North; he had warned Korean comrades on four occasions that the imperialists would interfere if the war broke out.[4] Later Kim Il-sung came to Beijing for China's support. Although Mao was skeptical about the rash plan made by North Korea, he found it difficult to argue against it for several reasons. First, Kim Il-sung's plan won Stalin's approval and the Soviet Union's assistance. Second, since China had just unified the mainland through the liberation war, Mao could not simply tell Kim not to follow the same path. Third, on the basis of the communist doctrine of internationalism, nations that had already achieved revolutionary victory were obligated to support other people's fight for liberation.

After the outbreak of the Korean War, the already tense security situation for the PRC immediately became extremely grave. Sino-American relations went from antagonism to confrontation. The United States seized the outbreak of the war as an opportunity to send the U.S. Seventh Fleet to the Taiwan Strait in addition to the country's armed intervention in Korea. Afterward, the U.S. Army crossed the 38th parallel and carried the flames of war to the Yalu River, where China borders Korea. At the same time, there was an upsurge of domestic threats to the newly founded nation. The precarious KMT regime in Taiwan felt sudden relief and sensed an opportunity to counterattack the mainland. The remnants of reactionary forces on the mainland were once again on the move.

China believed that the United States had infringed upon its sovereignty and territorial integrity, threatened the security of the newly founded nation, and interrupted the unification process. Thus, the Chinese government had no choice but to respond quickly to such a serious provocation and crisis.

Decision to Send Troops to Resist U.S. Aggression and Aid Korea

The Korean War broke out on June 25, 1950. On June 27, President Truman declared the implementation of armed intervention against Korea, and the U.S. Seventh Fleet sailed into the Taiwan Strait. Zhou Enlai, as China's foreign minister, made a statement on June 28 protesting the U.S. armed invasion of Taiwan's territorial waters, a part of Chinese territories.[5] The overall situation and its impact on China remained unclear at that time. On June 30, Mao and Zhou decided to postpone Taiwan's liberation and sent representatives to Korea so as to keep in touch with Kim Il-sung, but they still jointly signed the 1950 decision on the demobilization of People's Liberation Army (PLA) as originally scheduled.[6] Although China's initial response focused on protesting the U.S. invasion of Taiwan's territorial waters, the Chinese leaders really worried that the United States would use the opportunity to implement a series of plans to intervene in Asian affairs. According to Zhou Enlai, after the war broke out in Korea, the Truman administration worked out the comprehensive plan to invade Asia in addition to its plans for armed intervention in Korea and Taiwan. Zhou charged that the Truman administration linked the Korean issue with the issue of Taiwan and the Far East.[7]

In the early days of the war, the North Korean troops had the upper hand. However, Chinese leaders were not optimistic about the future. In early July, Zhou Enlai observed that the Korean War would not end very quickly and that it would become more complicated and last for one to three years or even longer, depending on various factors.[8] In response to this situation, Chinese leaders started to consider countermeasures and made preparations accordingly. Mao Zedong and Zhou Enlai thought that it was necessary to immediately build up nine divisions of Chinese forces along the China-Korea border in order to enter North Korea for operations when United Nations (UN) forces crossed the 38th parallel. They informed Stalin of their belief. On July 5, 1950, Stalin replied and agreed with them and also mentioned that the Soviet Union would provide air cover.[9] Zhou Enlai presided over two national defense meetings on July 7 and July 10 that addressed national defense matters and various issues concerning the establishment of the Northeast Frontier Defense Army. On July 13, the Central Military Commission officially made the decision to defend the northeast frontier.[10] On August 4, the Politburo convened to discuss what China should do. Mao said that if the United States won, it would threaten China. Therefore, China must support Korea, using the volunteer army, and must be prepared to intervene at an opportune time.[11]

After this, Chinese leaders became increasingly worried. As early as the beginning of July, Mao suspected that the U.S. Army might land in Incheon to launch a counterattack.[12] On August 23, the Combat Bureau under the General Staff of the CMC drew the same conclusion after an analysis of the Korean War situation and observed that the U.S. Army was going to land very soon. Mao and Zhou agreed that this was critical and immediately made the following decisions. First, the Northeast Frontier Defense Army must be ready for war at any time by the end of September. Second, Chinese officials should immediately inform the North Korean government and the Soviet government of the possibilities of the enemy landing in places like Incheon and that North Korea must be prepared for the worst. Third, the General Staff and the Ministry of Foreign Affairs should keep a close watch on the latest developments of the Korean War.[13] In the following days, Mao and Zhou repeatedly emphasized the growing possibility of a prolonged war in Korea. On September 15, before dawn, the U.S. Army landed in Incheon and captured the city. Later, U.S. and South Korean troops launched a counterattack on all fronts, and the war situation in Korea completely turned around. The worst-case scenario Mao had warned about had become reality.

China made a series of diplomatic moves after the outbreak of the Korean War. In late August, Zhou Enlai called several times for the UN Security Council and UN secretary-general to denounce the U.S. aggression, support the Soviet proposal on peaceful mediation of the Korean issue, and call for the termination of military action and the withdrawal of all foreign troops from Korea. At the same time, Zhou raised protests about the U.S. invasion of the Chinese territory of Taiwan and the fact that the U.S. Air Force had been trespassing into China's airspace. These diplomatic moves had limited impact and could not relieve the crisis or prevent the war from escalating.[14]

In late September, China sent warning signals. During a September 21, 1950, meeting with K. M. Panikkar, India's ambassador to China, Zhou Enlai clearly stated that, because the UN did not recognize the legitimate status of the PRC representative, China would not bear any responsibilities of the UN. A few days later, the acting chief of the General Staff, Nie Rongzhen, pointed out to Panikkar that China definitely could not tolerate the bombing of Northeast China by the U.S. Air Force and would need to respond. Panikkar observed that a tough reaction would push China into a war with the United States and cost China eight to ten years of development. Nie Rongzhen immediately answered, "We have thought about everything; they might even throw an atomic bomb and kill millions; but a nation cannot defend its independence without making any sacrifices."[15] Immediately following Panikkar's report of this to his government, the Indian government conveyed the message to the United Kingdom and the United States.

On September 29, 1950, after learning of the U.S. assertion that the United States would advance north of the 38th parallel, the CCP Central Committee decided to warn against U.S. attempts to expand the Korean War. The following day, in a speech at the national conference of the CCP Central Committee commemorating the first anniversary of the founding of the PRC, Zhou Enlai stated, "The Chinese people love peace. But we are not and never will be afraid of fighting against invasion in order to safeguard peace. The Chinese people will never put up with foreign aggression, nor will we ignore imperialists' barbaric invasion upon our neighbors."[16]

China received Kim Il-sung's request for military assistance on October 1. In the meantime, China also received a telegram from Stalin that expressed his hope that China would send troops to aid North Korea.[17] Later, China learned that the South Korean troops had crossed the 38th parallel and the U.S. Army was fully prepared. On October 3, Zhou Enlai summoned Panikkar to an emergency meeting and warned again that China would "intervene and will not just sit by and watch" the U.S. troops attempting to cross the 38th parallel and expand the war.[18] In so doing, Zhou declared the bottom line where China would have to take military action. The same day, the Indian government shared information about the situation with the British and stated that the decision made by the Chinese people was final. If U.S. troops crossed the 38th parallel, it would mean the escalation of the Korean conflict.[19] The U.S. government received the message from the British shortly afterward.

During the first half of October, the CCP Central Committee had to make its final decision. The Politburo of the CCP Central Committee held several meetings, Mao Zedong presiding, and discussed whether to send troops to assist Korea. Mao drafted a telegram to Stalin on October 2 about the decision to send volunteers to Korea. However, because the Politburo failed to reach a consensus at its meeting that afternoon, the well-known telegram was probably never sent.[20] After the meeting, Mao summoned the Soviet ambassador, Nikolai Vasilievich Roshchin, and asked him to tell Stalin that sending volunteers to assist Korea now "might have very serious consequences" and "many comrades on the CCP Central Committee believe that being cautious is necessary." For the present, Mao argued, China had better "not dispatch troops and make proactive preparations instead." Mao made it clear: "We have not reached the final decision on this issue and this is a tentative telegram."[21] At the same time, Mao also proposed to send Zhou Enlai and Lin Biao to the Soviet Union to consult with Stalin in person.

On October 4–5, the enlarged meeting of the Politburo was held in the Zhongnanhai compound, and participants further discussed whether to send troops to Korea. It was a turning point in China's decision making. Mao suggested that, in order to listen to all the different opinions, there should be no minutes of this conference. All that today's historians know for certain is that, at the beginning of the conference, although Mao Zedong clearly favored sending troops, participants had different opinions. At the end of the conference, supported by Peng Dehuai, who would become the military commander of China's forces during the Korean War, Mao and his opinion achieved the upper hand. The result of this meeting was the strategic decision to "resist America, support Korea, guard the homeland" (kangmeiyuanchao, baojiaweiguo).

In the process of deciding to dispatch troops, Peng Dehuai played an important role. In his recollection later, he concisely mentioned his support to Mao Zedong, but he gave no further explanation of his reasons. Wang Yazhi, Peng's secretary at the time, recalled that at the beginning Peng did not advocate sending troops because he disapproved of the fact that the Soviet Union was not willing to act in its own capacity, but had China send troops instead. Chinese troops were sure of winning if they fought against South Korean forces; but if they fought against U.S. forces, they would have great difficulties.

To win Peng Dehuai's support, Mao Zedong talked with him privately and listed three reasons: first, the Soviet Union had agreed to provide China with military equipment; second, the strategic focus of the United States was in Europe, and it was impossible for the United States to deploy all its forces in Asia; and, third, if U.S. forces defeated Chinese forces—even if the United States invaded Northeast China—it was not serious because that would mean that the United States owed China. Thus, China could get even with the United States later. If China did not fight with the United States this time, there would be no opportunity. Therefore, Peng decided to support Mao's opinion.[22] At a meeting on the afternoon of October 5, Peng said, "It is necessary to send troops to aid Korea. Even if we were defeated, that would mean the Liberation War was postponed for several years. If the United States forces were deployed along the Yalu river and Taiwan and if it wants to launch a war, it is easy for it to find an excuse."[23]

On October 6, entrusted by Mao, Zhou Enlai presided over a meeting of senior leaders of the CCP, the State Council, and the military to discuss the deployment of volunteers in Korea. Zhou emphasized that the question was not whether China wanted to fight because the enemy had left it with no choice but to fight. How could China stand by when the Korean government was repeatedly requesting its military assistance? The party Central Committee and Chairman Mao had made up their minds. The current issue thus was how to reach a victory after sending troops, not whether to send troops at all.[24] On October 7, 1950, U.S. forces crossed the 38th parallel. On October 8, Mao Zedong issued the official order to organize the Chinese People's volunteers and informed Kim Il-sung: "Based on the current situation, we have decided to send volunteers to Korea and help you to resist the invaders."[25]

Before the volunteers were dispatched, one issue of vital importance was a discussion with the Soviet Union of issues of Soviet military assistance and of the Soviet Air Force covering the ground volunteer forces. On October 8, Zhou Enlai and Lin Biao flew to the Soviet Union for a meeting with Stalin. Because it was a matter of great importance and urgency, the time for Sino-Soviet consultations was limited. This chapter will not go into great detail about the talks with Stalin, but two things show the up-and-down nature of the talks.

First, a delay occurred in the deployment of the Chinese volunteers because of Stalin's reluctance to provide air cover immediately. But China's determination to send troops did not waver. Second, this process was actually the final bargaining between China and the Soviet Union. Because China needed as much assistance and as strong a commitment as it could secure from the Soviet Union, Zhou Enlai emphasized China's difficulties in sending troops. But Stalin, cautious and skeptical, was not going to promise anything before he made sure of China's determination to go to war.

Five days after the volunteers went into battle, the Soviet Air Force appeared for the first time over the Yalu River, much earlier than the two and a half months Stalin promised at the end of the negotiation.

During the Korean War, the Soviet Air Force at first was intended only to protect the airspace over the Chinese frontiers. Later, the Soviets extended the coverage to the communication lines north of Korea. The Air Force, however, never assumed the task of covering the Chinese volunteer ground forces.

On October 19, Peng Dehuai quietly led the volunteers across the Yalu River. Gunshots of the first battle occurred on October 25, marking the end of the decision-making process on whether to send troops.

ISSUES IN CHINA'S DECISION MAKING LEADING UP TO THE KOREAN WAR

The outbreak of the Korean War was unexpected for the United States. But after war broke out, U.S. reaction was swift. In comparison, China acted much more cautiously in responding to the U.S. involvement in the Korean War and took a much longer time to make decisions. Chinese leaders faced three basic difficulties in the decision-making process.

First, China became involved in the problem of liberating Korea through various factors beyond its control; moreover, the situation was extremely urgent. After war broke out, the United States immediately intervened with armed forces and linked the war with the Taiwan issue, while Stalin quickly decided to avoid direct confrontation with the United States in the face of the unexpected reaction from the United States. The Korean People's Army suffered great military frustrations, and the war reached the Yalu River. Thus, China was pushed to the forefront of the Korean War and forced to decide to send troops.

Second, during the decision-making process, the United States, an obvious adversary, was much more powerful than China in terms of its military and economic strengths and its availability of crisis management tools and the number of policy alternatives. In addition to calling on its military forces, the United States could also resort to economic sanctions, impose diplomatic pressure, and mobilize support from allies. China, in contrast, had very limited resources, and its only choice that might be effective was to send troops and enter the war.

Third, China made its decision in an extremely volatile situation both at home and abroad, with many variables and great risks. One must consider all factors involved. A decision could cause a chain reaction and different consequences. A decision about war was, however, a matter of vital importance and great urgency. Error or delay was unacceptable. The Chinese leaders had to bear the consequences of the decisions they made. Everyone was under great pressure.

These difficulties led the Chinese leaders to focus on three questions in the decision-making process.

Red Line of Military Action

Mao Zedong considered the 38th parallel to be the "red line." He recalled, "If American imperialism interferes, but they don't cross the 38th parallel, we will not do anything; if they cross the parallel, we will fight with them."[26] From the perspectives of principles and reaching common understanding, this was a relatively easy question to deal with. The decision to resist U.S. aggression and aid Korea reflects two essential factors China must consider in dealing with issues concerning neighboring countries. One is national security needs and the other is the practice of morality and justice in international relations. The two factors are interrelated. Even without the Cold War, China could not afford to allow a big power to invade its neighboring countries and extend military influence to Chinese frontiers. If China let big powers have their way, China would then have no sense of security, no national prestige, and no dignity at all. That's why Mao Zedong said, "When other nations are in great danger and we just stand there without doing anything, we will feel bad whatever excuses there are."[27] Zhou Enlai said, "We cannot shut our eyes to the imperialists invading our neighbors without any resistance."

The crossing of the 38th parallel by the U.S. Army was the precondition for China to enter the war. Whether the United States crossed the 38th parallel depended on judgments about the situation at the highest level of U.S. authority. The United States entirely ignored the repeated warning signals from China because the U.S. decision makers believed, first, that China was not in the position to confront the United States; second, the existence of the Sino-Soviet alliance would make China decide not to get involved because it would follow what the Soviet Union did; and, third, in its warning signals, China failed to send a clear message about whether it would enter the war.[28] Evidently, the United States judged wrongly about China. The United States underestimated China's determination and capability.

Also, a U.S. error in judgment is related to China adopting a tactic of concealing its dispatch of troops. China's military strength, especially its lack of air supremacy, dictated that at the same time that China issued warnings it had to also conceal its imminent plans to adopt military measures. In terms of crisis management, the negative side of China's concealing its dispatch of troops was to weaken the credibility of China's warning to the United States. If China had decided to publicly dispatch troops, and the United States did not abandon its plans to bring war to the Yalu River, China would have had no way to guarantee that its troops would not be severely attacked by the U.S. Air Force. Faced with two difficult scenarios, one should say that the advantages of China's choice were greater than its disadvantages.

Even though it is hard now to get a clear idea of the details of how the Chinese leaders reached a unified decision, one definite point is that it was the troops crossing the 38th parallel that helped Chinese leaders to reach a final consensus to send troops and enter the war. During the most crucial days, developments made Chinese policy makers more convinced that war between China and the United States was inevitable. Mao Zedong pointed out shortly afterwards:

> Everybody knows that if the U.S. troops had not invaded Taiwan and DPRK and reached our northeast frontiers, the Chinese people would not have entered the war with the United States. Since the American invaders have attacked us, we had to hold up the flag of resisting aggression. It is entirely necessary and justified.[29]

Pros and Cons of Sending Troops

When making a decision, one has to weigh the potential gains and losses. All decisions have costs. If the crisis has already arrived, decision makers are often in a situation of having to choose the better option from two bad options. Trying to seek a good outcome is not the first step in decision making; instead it is preventing the situation from deteriorating and trying to take the initiative. The decision-making process of sending troops to resist U.S. aggression and aid Korea is a typical example.

When China made the decision to send troops, a major concern was that the Army was inadequately equipped and trained and that a few divisions might not be of any significant help. Moreover, an even more important misgiving was that China faced many domestic difficulties. The new nation needed a peaceful environment in which to consolidate its political power and work for economic recovery and development.[30]

After careful analysis, however, Mao Zedong and Zhou Enlai concluded that China would pay dearly if it did not send troops to Korea. First, Northeast China, especially the southern part of this region, was China's most important heavy industrial center. China would have no peaceful environment for its domestic construction if U.S. troops were right at its frontier. Second, it would cost just as much in financial, material, and military resources to move factories and to build a defense line that ran hundreds of kilometers if China adopted passive defense measures and built a defense system. What is more, no one could tell when the situation would end. Third, if China failed to act against the United States, it would fall into a passive position. The enemy would become insatiable and covet more. Fourth, the Chinese people would feel threatened for a long period of time. Neighboring countries might follow suit and succumb to imperialist pressure. Thus, the cause of world peace and democracy would meet with great setbacks.

War was not in the interests of China, the camp of peace and democracy, and Asian nations fighting for liberation and independence,[31] but sending troops to the war might help China gain the initiative. Zhou Enlai said, "If we strike it [the United States] and make it become trapped in the mud in Korea, our enemy won't be able to attack China and there will be conflicts arising within the enemy camp."[32] At the same time, CCP leaders were confident in China's experienced armed forces. They believed that the People's Army had unique advantages over the U.S. troops. China had a chance of attaining a victory. After comparing the pros and cons, Mao Zedong concluded, "In short, we believe we should and must enter the war. Involvement has great benefits and non-involvement has great harm."[33]

Dispatch of Troops, Prospects for Involvement, and Resulting Goal

The purpose, prospects, and final goal of sending troops must be taken into consideration, and all of these must be clarified during the process of decision making and crisis management. As for the purpose, no further explanation was needed because the slogan of the war—"Resist U.S. aggression, aid Korea, and protect our homeland"—says it all. This section will elaborate more on the CCP leaders' estimates about the prospects of involvement and the goal to be reached.

In deciding to participate in the war, Mao considered various possibilities. The most optimistic was that Chinese forces would drive U.S. forces off the entire Korean peninsula; the worst was that U.S. forces would force Chinese forces back after the Chinese forces crossed the Yalu River. Among the various possibilities, the Chinese leaders believed two possible consequences of China's involvement were most likely.

The first was a stalemate between the armies of China and the United States. In this case, the United States would publicly declare war against China and extend the war to the mainland, with a consequence of destroying the development of China's economic plans and arousing complaints from the national bourgeois and other groups. China must prepare for the worst possibility rather than the situation that was most likely to occur.[34] In a telegram addressed to Stalin on October 2, 1950, Mao stressed this worst possible consequence. Chinese leaders believed the existence of the Sino-Soviet alliance would lead to the outbreak of a world war if the United States extended the war to China. This was not very likely to happen. Zhou Enlai pointed out, "We would call it risking danger in desperation if the United States went all reckless and started a world war because the United States, in reality, has not made the proper preparations. An army of less than 2 million is not up to a world war."[35]

The second possible consequence was that Chinese troops would be able to stop the United States, localize the war, and then seek a peaceful settlement. This was what China tried to achieve, and it was on that basis that China set up its goal of involvement. This fact is often overlooked by researchers. Afterward, people tended to exaggerate Mao's confidence, erroneously believing that, when he made the decision to dispatch troops, he held fast to the lofty aspiration of driving U.S. troops out of the entire Korean peninsula.

In fact, Zhou Enlai made China's main objective clear soon after the volunteers set out. He pointed out during a meeting of the China People's Political Consultative Conference national committee on October 24, 1950, that

> American imperialists want to oppress other peoples by force. We are going to frustrate them and make them fall back. And then we can seek to settle the problem. We are not inflexible. If the enemy beat a retreat in the face of difficulties, we can reach a settlement through negotiations within or outside the UN framework, because we prefer peace to war.[36]

Zhou stated on many occasions that China's purpose was to make the United States think rationally and retreat, localize the war, and force it to accept peace. This was a more realistic outcome and was the result China pursued. "To resist U.S. aggression, aid Korea and protect our homeland is what we want. We are confident that we have the ability to make it happen."[37]

At the first stage, the Chinese forces were deployed according to this purpose. From a series of telegrams sent by Mao Zedong beginning October 15, 1950, one can see that the tentative plan was to establish a defensive line in the northern area of North Korea that had not been occupied by the enemy and, at the same time, wait for chances to fight with the South Korean forces while trying to avoid fighting with the U.S. forces immediately.[38] Mao and Peng changed their plans temporarily and decided to strike the dispersed U.S. troops only because U.S. forces advanced northward so fast. Even so, Mao sent a telegram to Peng on October 23 and emphasized, "We should do something reliable, not do anything beyond our capability." After an analysis of advantages and disadvantages of the first battle, Mao asked Peng to win the first battle in order to make it possible to "force the United States to have diplomatic negotiation with us."[39]

In short, the process of deciding to send troops to resist U.S. aggression and aid Korea is a classic example of PRC crisis management. The process has three characteristics. First, in the state of emergency, the senior leaders of the CCP aired their opinions freely and made a thorough analysis of the pros and cons of all possibilities, laying a reliable foundation for their final decisions.[40] Second, the Chinese leaders showed foresight about developments in the Korean War, and they considered the worst possibilities. Thus, preparations for sending troops started ahead of time and continued uninterruptedly despite the twists and turns during the decision-making process. All this made it possible to implement the decision without delay once the decision was made. Third, the goal was based on the circumstances and in accordance with the principle of acting according to one's abilities (*lianglierxing*). But this objective did not remain absolutely firm during the war. After obtaining battle successes, Mao again wanted to drive the U.S. forces entirely out of Korea, but Peng quickly told him that China's military lacked sufficient strength. Peng's estimate was correct, and in the vicinity of the 38th parallel, the United States and China reached a balance of power. The way the war ended showed that China on the whole had achieved its original limited goal.

CHINA'S CRISIS MANAGEMENT DURING THE VIETNAM WAR

Unlike the Korean War, the Vietnam War escalated beyond its origins. On the basis of the fighting style of U.S. troops, the Vietnam War can be divided into three stages: special warfare (May 1961–February 1965), local warfare (February 1965–January 1969), and the "Vietnamization" of the war (January 1969–February 1975). Before the United States became directly involved in the Vietnam War, China had already set up its guidelines for aiding Vietnam in its resistance against the United States. During the entire period of the Vietnam War, China developed its policies step by step, according to the actual situation. It was only when China was responding to the U.S. escalation as the United States moved from special warfare to local warfare that the Chinese decision-making process could be called crisis management.

Change from "Support Vietnam, Resist France" (*yuanyuekangfa*) to "Support Vietnam, Resist America" (*yuanyuekangmei*)

Like Korea, Vietnam is a close neighbor of China. In the past, the Chinese and Vietnamese people stood side by side in battles against foreign invasions. During the time of the founding of the People's Republic of China, the Indochina Communist Party led by Ho Chi Minh was fighting an arduous war against the French. The Indochina Communist Party had limited contacts with the CCP before 1949 in spite of their long historical relationship.

In January 1950, Ho Chi Minh met with Stalin and Mao Zedong in Moscow, when Mao was visiting the Soviet Union. Ho asked for assistance from the two countries. Considering the world political pattern after World War II, the impact of the Soviet-French relationship on Europe, and the fact that Vietnam was far from the Soviet Union, Stalin decided to let China assist Vietnam. Mao discussed the situation with Liu Shaoqi who was at that time responsible for day-to-day policy in Beijing.

Mao and Liu decided that China should support Vietnam in its resistance against France even if that would mean sacrificing the possibility of establishing diplomatic relations with France. They also decided that support should be given to Vietnam through the sharing of experiences, giving advice, sending groups of advisers, and providing military and economic assistance. China's support had two distinct features: openness and limitation. Although the scope of aid was large, no troops were sent directly. It was different from the decisions made later to resist U.S. aggression and aid Korea.

On January 18, 1950, China recognized the Democratic Republic of Vietnam, thus becoming the first country to do so. After that, China provided assistance to Vietnam as agreed. The aid from China caused the state of war in Indochina to undergo tremendous changes. After the Viet Minh (Vietnamese Independence League) with support from China won a significant victory in the war against France, Chinese leaders promptly decided to strive for a cease-fire through the Geneva Conference held in the summer of 1954. The successful implementation of this decision played an important role in safeguarding China's security and avoiding another local war like the one in Korea.

After the 1954 Geneva Conference, France gradually withdrew its troops from South Vietnam, and the United States stepped into its place. On the Vietnam issue, conflicts among China, North Vietnam, and the United States were inevitable because, fundamentally, each had entirely different goals. China and Vietnam agreed to a cease-fire in Geneva with a view to facilitating the unification of Vietnam. The United States, however, wanted to build South Vietnam into an anticommunist stronghold and maintain a divided Vietnam. In 1955, Ngo Dinh Diem established the government of the Republic of Vietnam with the support of the United States. Beginning in 1959, armed fighting against the United States and Ngo took place in South Vietnam. Because the situation had changed, the Central Committee of the Vietnam Communist Party decided to initiate an armed struggle in the South with a view to liberation.

North Vietnamese leaders set forth new guidelines for the conflict in South Vietnam during a meeting with Chinese leaders in May 1960. The CCP Central Committee agreed with the decision of Vietnamese comrades.[41] The National Front for the Liberation of Vietnam (NFLV) was set up in December 1960. China took the lead in recognizing the organization; this recognition marked the establishment of China's policy of aiding Vietnam in its resistance against the United States.

Reaction of China to U.S. Escalation

To stabilize the situation in South Vietnam, President John F. Kennedy dispatched 400 troops—called special technical units—and sent 100 military advisers to South Vietnam on May 14, 1961.

The direct involvement of the United States immediately drew the attention of the leaders of Vietnam and China. Vietnam decided at once to enlarge the establishment of its army units in both the South and the North. China responded as well. In the early 1960s, China was having great difficulties both at home and abroad, and its frontier security was threatened from many directions, but the southeast front was clearly defined as the place China was going to focus its strategic defense. In the summer of 1962, Ho Chi Minh, chairman of the Democratic Republic of Vietnam (DRV), and Nguyen Chi Thanh, head of the South Vietnam Labor Party, visited Beijing. The leaders of the two countries analyzed together the new situation as the United States had reinforced its aggression in Vietnam. Upon Vietnam's request, the Chinese leaders decided then and there to provide Vietnam without charge enough weapons to equip 230 battalions.[42] After that, China's assistance to the NFLV grew continuously.

In 1963, Vietnam started to worry about a U.S. invasion of North Vietnam. Under these circumstances, the Vietnamese leaders requested that, in addition to weaponry assistance, China join the Vietnamese Army in combat if the United States expanded the war to the North. Luo Ruiqing led a military delegation to visit Vietnam in March to begin discussions on military combat cooperation between China and Vietnam. Van Tien Dung, chief of the General Staff of the Vietnam People's Army, led a military delegation to visit China in July. The two sides exchanged views on the ways to cooperate in combat and signed related documents and an agreement on providing military assistance to Vietnam. In September 1963, China, Vietnam, Laos, and Indonesia Communist Party leaders met in Conghua, Guangdong Province, to discuss the situation in Southeast Asia. During the meeting, Zhou Enlai promised the leaders of the other three parties that "China is the rear for the revolutionary causes in Southeast Asia. There will be no shirking the responsibility. We will do our best to support the anti-imperialist struggles in Southeast Asia."[43]

In July 1964, China, Vietnam, and Laos held a Communist Party meeting in Hanoi. Participants from China included Zhou Enlai, Chen Yi, Wu Xiuquan, and Yang Chengwu. Delegates from Vietnam were Ho Chi Minh, Le Duan, Truong Chinh, Pham Van Dong, Vo Nguyen Giap, Van Tien Dung, and Nguyen Chi Thanh. Souphanouvong and Kaysone Phomvihane from Laos also attended. This was the most important summit meeting of the three parties before the escalation of the Vietnam War. The meeting set out the guidelines and principles for China, Vietnam, and Laos to send troops to fight against U.S. aggression. Moreover, the meeting also set out guidelines and principles for China as it dealt with the escalation of the war. Zhou Enlai posited that the war might play out in one of two ways: either the United States would intensify special warfare, or the United States would escalate what was special warfare into a new local warfare, which meant directly sending troops to South Vietnam and Laos and bombing or attacking North Vietnam. China would definitely openly support the struggles of the Southeast Asian peoples no matter what policy the United States adopted. Zhou stressed, "Our guideline is to try as much as possible to prevent the war from escalating and at the same time, make proactive preparations for the second possibility." If the war escalated, China's guideline would be, "If the United States moves, China moves; if the United States dispatches troops, China dispatches troops."[44]

Around the time of the three-party meeting in Hanoi, the PLA conducted a series of preparations to support Vietnam and resist America; they were based on the policies as determined by the Central Committee of the CCP. The land, marine, and air forces all made necessary readjustments in their deployment. The troops dispatched for Vietnam operations, having finished combat readiness training and all other preparations, were ready to go into war at any time.

On August 2, 1964, the torpedo boat units of the DRV exchanged shots with a U.S. warship patrolling provocatively in the Beibu Gulf (the United States calls it the Gulf of Tonkin). The U.S. government, waiting for this for a long time, seized the opportunity immediately and started to escalate the war step by step. On August 5, U.S. aircraft bombed targets in North Vietnam for the first time. The U.S. Congress, giving a green light to expanding the operations in Vietnam, adopted the Gulf of Tonkin Resolution the same day.

Because China and Vietnam had accurately estimated the U.S. intention to escalate the war and had made proper preparations, both were able to respond quickly. On August 5, the General Staff of the PLA ordered the relevant military areas and arms into combat readiness and requested them to keep close watch on the movements of U.S. troops and get ready for any sudden attacks.[45] On the same day, Zhou Enlai and Luo Ruiqing cabled Ho Chi Minh, Pham Van Dong, and Van Tien Dung; this message showed China's great concern over the incident and suggested Vietnam "make investigations and work out countermeasures for a better response."[46] Soon after, China made clear its bottom line—when it would have to take direct military action.

On August 6, the Chinese government stated that the premeditated armed U.S. aggression against the DRV was the first step in moving to "the brink of war" and also the first step in the U.S. escalation of the warfare in Indochina. At the same time the Chinese government solemnly declared, "The DRV and China are as mutually dependent as close neighbors. The Vietnamese people and the Chinese people are like brothers. U.S. attack on DRV means attack on China. The Chinese people will never stand by and watch."[47] In the following days, assemblies and demonstrations occurred across China; they involved a total of 20 million people who expressed support for the Vietnamese people.

In March 1965, President Lyndon B. Johnson endorsed the strategic bombing campaign, "Operation Rolling Thunder," on the pretense that the NFLV had attacked U.S. troops at the air base at Pleiku. Later, Johnson endorsed dispatching ground troops to South Vietnam, which signaled that special warfare had escalated into local warfare in which U.S. troops played the leading role, fighting in the South and bombing the North. The United States made thinly veiled threats of war against China to dissuade China from supporting Vietnam. The U.S. media were busy claiming that in the Vietnam War there would be no so-called sanctuary, as there had been during the Korean War. U.S. airplanes, in the meantime, went on frequent reconnaissance and harassment missions in China's airspace over Vietnam's border with China.

The Chinese government responded most strongly to U.S. war threats and promptly took four measures:

First, China announced it would send troops to fight the U.S. armed forces when the Vietnamese people made such a request. A March 25 *People's Daily* editorial said the Chinese people would offer all necessary material support to the South Vietnamese people, including armaments and other combat materials, and that "we are ready to send our own soldiers at any time to join the South Vietnamese people in combat and eliminate the U.S. invaders when necessary." Later, Foreign Minister Chen Yi reiterated this in his letter to Xuan Thuy, the foreign minister of the DRV.

Second, China decided to attack U.S. airplanes trespassing in its airspace. On April 8–9, an intruding U.S. airplane over Hainan Island launched a missile at a patrolling Chinese marine aircraft on guard. In response, the military of China immediately decided to change the practice of only monitoring, but not attacking, U.S. airplane intrusions. Instead, China would strike resolutely all intruding U.S. military aircraft. Yang Chengwu, deputy chief of the General Staff of the PLA, formally raised this proposal in a report submitted to the CCP Central Committee and Zhou Enlai on April 8. They sent the report to Mao Zedong after Zhou reviewed it. On April 9, Mao commented, "We should and must determinedly strike U.S. airplanes trespassing upon Hainan Island . . . the U.S. planes have been probing around for quite

some time. Now they are really defying us! We absolutely must resolutely strike them."[48] Afterward, the PLA's Naval Air Force and Air Force
went into combat to guard China's airspace and shot down many U.S.
airplanes in places like Hainan Island and Guangxi.

Third, the whole country went into combat readiness. On April 14,
the CCP Central Committee ordered that the Chinese people should
strengthen preparations for war. The order said that the United States
was making moves in Vietnam to expand the war and directly invade
the DRV, posing a serious threat to Chinese security. China could not
afford to ignore U.S. aggression and was expected to be ready to join the
Vietnamese people in combat at any time. Under these circumstances,
China had to reinforce its preparations for war. Because the enemy might
take chances, China ought to prepare for the worst in both its mind and
its work. It was possible that the United States would bomb China's
military facilities, industrial bases, communication hubs, and major cities and even fight on Chinese land. China should be prepared for war,
be it big or small.[49]

Finally, China conveyed messages through various channels to the
United States. These messages expressed China's wishes to avoid war
with the United States on one hand and showed China's readiness for
war on the other. On January 9, 1965, Mao Zedong, in a meeting with
the American writer, Edgar Snow, said, "We are not going to start the
war from our side; only when the United States attacks shall we fight
back. History will be our witness." Mao also said, "The United States
may decide by itself whether to send troops to China. But I don't think
it will gain anything from fighting with us. If the United States thinks
the same way, it probably won't come. As I've already said, please rest
assured that we won't attack the United States."[50]

During an April 2 meeting with Gohar Ayub Khan, president of
Pakistan, Zhou Enlai requested that Khan tell the United States the
following, "First, China will not provoke a war with the United States.
Second, what the Chinese people say counts. Third, China is prepared."
Zhou Enlai said, "If the United States imposes a war upon the Chinese
people, the Chinese people will fight back to the end. There is no other
way out." In response to rumors that, if the United States declared war
on China, the United States would only bomb and not send ground
forces, thus restricting the scale of war, Zhou said straightforwardly,

"Such a way of fighting won't do. If the United States just throws bombs from the sky, we may fight our own way on the ground. If the United States engages in comprehensive bombing of China, this means it is war, and there is no such thing as a restrained war, as every soldier knows."[51]

To make sure that the message was sent to the U.S. side, Chen Yi on May 31 requested an appointment with the British chargé d'affaires and asked him to forward Zhou Enlai's message to the United States. One week later, the British chargé d'affaires told officials of the West European Department of China's Ministry of Foreign Affairs that Britain had passed the message to U.S. Secretary of State Dean Rusk. U.S. analysts believed that Zhou Enlai's message was "extraordinarily moderate" and showed the "CCP did not want to have direct involvement in the war." Therefore, they "warned that the United States should avoid engaging in actions against China.[52]

Dispatch of Support Troops to Vietnam

After the United States escalated the Vietnam War, Vietnamese leaders estimated the United States aimed to make up its losses in the South by bombing the North. Only when the United States landed massively and launched attacks in North Vietnam would the war become a large-scale local war. Under the circumstances, leaders in Vietnam did not think it very likely that the U.S. ground forces would attack the North directly. They realized, however, that they should not underestimate that possibility. The guidelines of the Vietnamese Communist Party and the government were to reinforce the fighting in the South, step up the efforts to defend the airspace in North Vietnam, and try to restrict ground warfare to the South and U.S. attacks on the North to bombing only. China supported these guiding principles of Vietnam. To deal with the escalation of the war, China and Vietnam began to discuss issues of sending Chinese support troops to Vietnam.

In April 1965, First Secretary Le Duan of the Labor Party and Minister of National Defense Vo Nguyen Giap were entrusted by Ho Chi Minh to lead a delegation to visit China. During meetings in China, Vietnam formally requested the CCP and the Chinese government to send Chinese troops to Vietnam. Liu Shaoqi, on behalf of China, answered definitely that aiding Vietnam in its resistance against the United States was "the Chinese people's obligation and the CCP's obligation" and that "our guideline is that we will offer whatever you need and we have to assist you as much as possible." Because of historical contradictions between China and Vietnam, the entry of Chinese troops into Vietnam would be sensitive and could raise misgivings on the part of the Vietnamese people. For this reason, Liu Shaoqi particularly emphasized the Chinese principle: "If you do not invite us, we will not go. If you invite us to one area, we will go to that area. The right to take the initiative is entirely in your hands."[53] Through this meeting, the two communist parties reached an agreement that China would send support troops to Vietnam.

On May 16, Ho Chi Minh, who was recuperating in China, met with Chairman Mao Zedong in Changsha to exchange views on major issues, including the Vietnam War. Ho told Mao that the Vietnamese people knew that they could not have self-respect without defeating the United States and that they were prepared to fight for five, ten, or twenty years. Mao replied that the United States would not be able to defeat Vietnam and could not fight for twenty years and that Vietnam would win its war with the United States because the United States was afraid of Vietnam.[54] During this meeting, Ho also told Mao that the Vietnamese government had decided to transfer more troops from the rear to the battlefront, which might affect the work in the rear. Ho wondered whether China could take over some of the services in the rear of the battle in Vietnam so that Vietnam could transfer troops to the front line. Mao agreed immediately and joked that there was absolutely no problem because it was President Ho's order and China would follow all Vietnamese orders because the front line was in Vietnam. Mao added that actually both Vietnam and China had to follow the steps of the United States after all and fight wherever the United States forced them to.[55]

During this time, Vo Nguyen Giap and Van Tien Dung visited China one after another and agreed with Chinese military leaders during detailed discussions that China would send support troops to North Vietnam in accord with the spirit of the two-party meetings. Both sides agreed that the Chinese support troops, upon entrance into Vietnam, would be under the command of Vietnam People's Army headquarters and be assigned tasks by Vietnam. As for the title of the support troops, the two parties first agreed to call them "Volunteers Enlisted in Vietnam People's Army" for the antiaircraft artillery units and "China Volunteer Engineering Brigade" for the construction units. Later the two groups were unified and both were renamed "China Rear Service Units."

On June 9, 1965, the first group of Chinese volunteer forces, the second detachment of the China Volunteer Engineering Brigade, marched into Vietnam. Thus began the Chinese military operation in support of Vietnam. When the Vietnam War was at its fiercest, China sent the largest number of supporting troops and shouldered the heaviest tasks. The PLA sent aerial defense, engineering, railway, and rear service troops to North Vietnam. By the end of March 1969, China had sent a total of twenty-three detachments, ninety-five regiments, and eighty-three battalions to Vietnam, which amounted to 320,000 personnel. At the height of the support, China sent 170,000 people in a single year.[56]

Lessening of Tension Between China and the United States

After military contact occurs, it is often hard for parties to the conflict to control the level of violence. On the battlefield of the Vietnam War, both China and the United States seemed to have drawn lessons from the Korean War because neither wished to engage in face-to-face conflicts. Therefore, the Vietnam War did not become another war between China and the United States.

During their aid to Vietnam in its resistance against the United States, the toughest issue for Chinese decision makers would be satisfying Vietnam's continuing requests for support while avoiding large-scale direct confrontation with the United States. When faced with the U.S. escalation of the war, China made great efforts to let the United States know that China had no intention of fighting a war against the United States. China's response would be reciprocal to U.S. actions. If the United States restricted its military involvement in South Vietnam, China would not send troops to enter the war. If the United States restricted its intrusion upon North Vietnam to battles on the sea and in the air, Chinese troops would engage only in air defense, engineering, and rear services in the North. Obviously, the United States got the message and never sent ground forces to North Vietnam.

Except for several messages sent privately because China and the United States lacked direct relations at that time, the exchange between China and the United States was conducted by showing intentions through their military postures. Depending on whether they wanted to express these intentions, they revealed or concealed relevant information. Both sides had some experience with this, so they were able to have a tacit understanding. When fighting during the Vietnam War was fierce, support troops from China entered Vietnam quietly. China did not announce any missions, neither did Chinese troops fight on the front lines.

China wanted to warn the United States but still leave room. In fact, the United States soon learned the whereabouts of the Chinese troops aiding Vietnam. Starting in late August 1965, U.S. airplanes continuously attacked Chinese antiaircraft artillery forces, railway forces, and defense engineering troops. A Saigon radio station announced: "Volunteers from China have marched into the north of Vietnam." Captured U.S. pilots and South Vietnamese secret agents also confessed that U.S. pilots were ordered to bomb Chinese soldiers wearing "blue clothes."[57]

U.S. officials never publicly disclosed the fact that Chinese troops had entered North Vietnam. This made the Chinese leaders realize the United States did not intend to further escalate the war. In November 1968, Mao Zedong said to the Vietnamese prime minister:

> For many years, the U.S. Army has neither attacked North Vietnam, nor blockaded Hai Phong, nor bombed the center of Hanoi. It holds back a trick or two. Sometime it said to "vigorously pursue," but when your planes flew back and forth from our country, it did not do that. So it is empty talk. Another example, it knows that there are so many Chinese working in North Vietnam, but never mentions that.[58]

Owing to the restraint of China and the United States and to the countries' understanding of each other's restraint, the two countries were eventually able to control the escalation of the Vietnam War.

In 1968, under great pressure both at home and abroad, the U.S. government started to progressively lower the level of war and limit the bombing in North Vietnam to the area south of the 20th parallel. The United States started peace negotiations with DRV representatives in Paris on May 10, 1968. On October 31, President Johnson announced a cessation of bombing, gunfire, and maritime raids in North Vietnam. Later, upon agreement by China and Vietnam, all support troops from China withdrew from Vietnam and went back to China in July 1970 after fulfilling their set tasks.[59] When both China and the United States started to withdraw from the brink of war, the normalization of the relationship between the two countries was already secretly under way.

CHARACTERISTICS OF CHINA'S DECISION MAKING DURING CRISIS

The Korean War and the Vietnam War reflected the confrontations between China and the United States during the era of the Cold War. Both confrontations involved China's neighbors. We often say that usually a third party plays a role in Sino-American relations. As to the Korean War and the Vietnam War, the third parties had some special characteristics.

At that time, China, North Korea, and Vietnam faced the same historical task of seeking national independence and reunification. All three countries were led by communist parties and had similar ideologies. In addition, because of geographical and historical reasons, China maintained close relations with these two countries and regarded them as keys to China's national security. Thus, China on principle supported both North Korean and Vietnamese efforts to seek their national independence and reunification. However, there was another side in both Sino-North Korea and Sino-Vietnam relations: both countries were at least somewhat wary of China. They hoped to get support from China, but they worried that China's aid could influence their internal affairs. China therefore did not take the initiative to support and aid them. When they had some requirements, China always reacted positively. The specific means of the aid depended on the situation. Because of U.S. large-scale armed interference in both countries, which also threatened China's national security, confrontation between China and the United States became unavoidable.

When Chinese leaders dealt with these two crises, from the very beginning they considered the use of force. On one hand, they viewed the United States as a powerful antagonist that evidenced great hostility toward China; on the other hand, Chinese leaders such as Mao Zedong and Zhou Enlai were professional revolutionaries who had experienced countless crises and who had rich battle experiences. Therefore, when the two crises emerged, it was natural for Mao and Zhou to think of the use of force. One should emphasize that considering the use of force does not mean wanting to launch a war. When Chinese leaders face a crisis, their instinct is to seek the best while they also prepare for the worst. The experiences accumulated while dealing with relations between the CCP and the KMT showed that it was possible to avoid major frictions through minor frictions, and even to consider the concept of using a war to control a war (*yizhanzhizhan*) as a means of resolving a crisis.

From the two examples of the Korean War and the Vietnam War, one can see that Chinese decision making follows a rough procedure when a crisis occurs: first, make preliminary diplomatic responses to sudden incidents or the current situation; second, analyze the situation and define the red line that, if crossed, would trigger military action; third, send warning signals to the opponent and be ready to take military action; and, fourth, if the opponent ignores signals and crosses the red line, take actions based on the fixed plan. If the opponent accepts the warning, the crisis relaxes.

China's internal decision-making mechanism was quite simple when Chinese leaders dealt with these two crises. High-level officials within the CCP made the crucial decisions according to the principle of democratic centralism. High-level officials could exchange their opinions and seek unity of thinking in two ways: one was to hold high-level meetings such as Politburo meetings or extended meetings of the Politburo; the other was to have a talk with some individuals and seek common knowledge. After unifying the thinking of the various leaders, Mao Zedong made the final decision.

The decision to send troops to Korea was one of the best examples of the principle of democratic centralism. To China, the complicated problem of these two wars was that some decisions needed consultation and coordination with allied countries. At the early stage of the Korean War, it was difficult to coordinate among China, the Soviet Union, and North Korea; it was much easier to coordinate China and Vietnam during the escalation of the Vietnam War. The contradiction in Sino-Vietnam relations emerged after Vietnam and the United States had peace talks, and these conflicts expanded after China and the United States began to reconcile.

When China dealt with these two crises, China's basic principle and thinking remained the same: first, China did not intend to provoke a war with the United States, but China did not fear a war and prepared for the worst; second, as the United States took one step, China responded. The key to China's position was to define the red line of when to send troops. This line in the Korean War was the 38th parallel; the line in the Vietnam War was the 17th parallel. China sent strong warning signals when U.S. forces approached these two lines. In China's view, the two lines determined a safe distance for avoiding direct confrontation between China and the United States. China's use of these two red lines as triggers to send troops to participate in the war also shows that China's attitude was defensive, not offensive.

At the early stages of the Korean War, the United States did not realize the significance of the 38th parallel. The United States mistakenly thought that, if the war was not expanded to Chinese territory, there would be no confrontation between the United States and China. When the Vietnam War escalated, the United States cautiously kept a safe distance from China, and U.S. ground forces never crossed the 17th parallel. In addition, because of experiences during the Korean War and in the process of the escalation of the Vietnam War, both sides exchanged information effectively by means of public declarations, private messages, and battlefield postures. Both sides learned to distinguish bluff from realistic threats, and each understood the range and limit of operations of the opponent. China knew to what extent the United States was involved in the war, and the United States also was aware of how much aid China would provide to Vietnam. One can say that the two sides established initial trust during the confrontation. The differences between the Korean War and Vietnam War made the type and the result of the two confrontations quite different: the first was direct confrontation that led to long-term estrangement between China and the United

States; the second was indirect confrontation and both sides were on the way to reconciliation even before the confrontation ended.

NOTES

1. Shen Zhihua, ed., *Chaoxian Zhanzheng: Eguo Dang'anguan.de Jiemi Wenjian* [Korean War: Released Files from Russian Archives], vol. 1, Institute of Modern History; Historical Materials Series no. 48 (Taipei: Academia Sinica, n.d.), pp. 187–190.
2. Ibid., pp. 305, 309.
3. Ibid., pp. 381–383.
4. Mao Zedong, speech to the central delegation of the Soviet Union, September 23, 1956.
5. CCP Central Committee Literature Research Division and the PLA Academy of Military Sciences, eds., *Zhou Enlai Junshi Wenxuan* [Selected Works of Zhou Enlai on Military Affairs], vol. 4 (Beijing: Renmin Chubanshe, 1997), p. 29.
6. Liu Wusheng and Du Hongqi, eds., *Zhou Enlai Junshi Huodong Jishi* [Chronicles of Zhou Enlai's Military Activities], vol. 2 (Beijing: Zhongyang Wenxian Chubanshe, 2000), pp. 128–129.
7. Ibid.
8. Jin Chongji, ed., *Zhou Enlai Zhuan* [Biography of Zhou Enlai] (Beijing: Zhongyang Wenxian Chubanshe, 1998), p. 1009.
9. Shen Zhihua, ed. *Chaoxian Zhanzheng: Eguo Dang'anguan.de Jiemi Wenjian* [Korean War: Released Files from Russian Archives], p. 431. Although no one has yet found the telegram to Stalin from Mao Zedong and Zhou Enlai, the reply from Stalin has been discovered.
10. CCP Central Committee Literature Research Division and the PLA Academy of Military Sciences, eds., *Zhou Enlai Junshi Wenxuan* [Selected Works of Zhou Enlai on Military Affairs], p. 34.
11. Pang Xianzhi and Jin Chongji, eds., *Mao Zedong Zhuan, 1949–1976* [Biography of Mao Zedong, 1949–1976], vol. 1 (Beijing: Zhongyang Wenxian Chubanshe, 2003), p. 109.
12. Sun Baosheng, "Mao Zedong Cengjing Yuyan Meijun Keneng zai Renchuan Denglu" [Mao Zedong Predicted That the U.S. Army Might Land in Incheon], *Junshi Shilin* [Military History Facts], no. 5 (1990).
13. Liu and Du, eds., *Zhou Enlai Junshi Huodong Jishi* [Chronicles of Zhou Enlai's Military Activities], p. 137.

14. Only in late October did the UN Security Council put China's accusations on its agenda and allow the Chinese government to send delegates to participate in its discussions. At that time, however, the Korean situation had changed significantly, as the U.S. troops had crossed the 38th parallel and the Chinese People's Volunteer Army had marched into Korea.

15. See Chai Zhiwen and Zhao Yongtian, *Banmendian Tanpan* [Panmunjeom Negotiations] (Beijing: Jiefangjun Chubanshe, 1989), p. 74, for Nie Rongzhen's speeches.

16. Ministry of Foreign Affairs of the People's Republic of China and the CCP Central Committee Literature Research Division, eds., *Zhou Enlai Waijiao Wenxuan* [Selected Works of Zhou Enlai on Diplomacy] (Beijing: Zhongyang Wenxian Chubanshe, 1990), pp. 23–24.

17. Pang and Jin, eds., *Mao Zedong Zhuan, 1949–1976* [Biography of Mao Zedong, 1949–1976], p. 113; Shen Zhihua, ed., *Chaoxian Zhanzheng: Eguo Dang'anguan.de Jiemi Wenjian* [Korean War: Released Files from Russian Archives], p. 571.

18. CCP Central Committee Literature Research Division and the PLA Academy of Military Sciences, eds., *Zhou Enlai Junshi Wenxuan* [Selected Works of Zhou Enlai on Military Affairs], pp. 66–68.

19. U.S. Department of State, *Foreign Relations of the United States, 1950*, vol. 7 (Korea) (Washington, D.C.: U.S. Government Printing Office, 1976), p. 850.

20. CCP Central Committee Literature Research Division, ed., *Mao Zedong Wenji* [Collected Works of Mao Zedong], vol. 6 (Beijing: Renmin Chubanshe, 1999), pp. 97–99. The notes specified that the telegram was never sent.

21. Shen Zhihua, ed., *Chaoxian Zhanzheng: Eguo Dang'anguan.de Jiemi Wenjian* [Korean War: Released Files from Russian Archives], pp. 576–577.

22. Wang Yazhi, secretary to Peng Dehuai, interview with the author, August 20, 2004.

23. Peng Dehuai, *Peng Dehuai Zishu* [Peng Dehuai on Himself] (Beijing, Renmin Chubanshe, 1981), pp. 257–258.

24. CCP Central Committee Literature Research Division, ed., *Zhou Enlai Nianpu 1949–1976* [Chronicle of the Life of Zhou Enlai, 1949—1976], vol. 1 (Beijing: Zhongyang Wenxian Chubanshe, 1997), p. 84.

25. CCP Central Committee Literature Research Division and the PLA Academy of Military Sciences, eds., *Mao Zedong Junshi Wenji* [Selected Works of Mao Zedong on Military Affairs], vol. 6 (Beijing: Renmin Chubanshe, 1993), p. 111.

26. On September 23, Mao Zedong talked with the Central Delegation of the Soviet Communist Party.

27. Peng Dehuai, *Peng Dehuai Zishu* [Peng Dehuai on Himself], p. 257.

28. See Lin Limin, *Ezhi Zhongguo: Chaoxian Zhanzheng yu ZhongMei Guanxi* [Containing China: The Korean War and Sino-U.S. Relations] (Beijing: Shijie Zhishi Chubanshe, 2000), pp. 176–182. Section 3 of chapter 4 explains how U.S. decision makers estimated China's response and whether China would send troops before the U.S. Army crossed the 38th parallel.

29. CCP Central Committee Literature Research Division, ed., *Mao Zedong Wenji* [Collected Works of Mao Zedong], vol. 6, p. 184.

30. See *Peng Dehuai Junshi Wenxuan* [Selected Works of Peng Dehuai on Military Affairs] (Beijing: Zhongyang Wenxian Chubanshe, 1988), pp. 320–321.

31. CCP Central Committee Literature Research Division and the PLA Academy of Military Sciences, eds., *Zhou Enlai Junshi Wenxuan* [Selected Works of Zhou Enlai on Military Affairs], pp. 73–75, 112–114.

32. Ibid., p. 75.

33. CCP Central Committee Literature Research Division, ed., *Mao Zedong Wenji* [Collected Works of Mao Zedong], vol. 6, p. 104.

34. Ibid., p. 98.

35. CCP Central Committee Literature Research Division and the PLA Academy of Military Sciences, eds., *Zhou Enlai Junshi Wenxuan* [Selected Works of Zhou Enlai on Military Affairs], pp. 92–93.

36. Ibid., pp. 75–76.

37. Ibid., pp. 92, 109.

38. CCP Central Committee Literature Research Division and the PLA Academy of Military Sciences, eds., *Ma Zedong Junshi Wenji* [Selected Works of Mao Zedong on Military Affairs], pp. 120–146. According to the recollection of Wang Yazhi, Lin Biao proposed the first stage of military deployment (when the Chinese volunteers entered Korea). In contrast with the usual thinking, Lin Biao was not against sending troops, and he actively put forward some proposals on this issue.

39. CCP Central Committee Literature Research Division, ed., *Mao Zedong Wenji* [Collected Works of Mao Zedong], vol. 6, pp. 140–141.

40. Actually, before the war, the existence of disputes among high-level CCP officials was not unusual. It was only after the Korean War that Mao gradually became unable to tolerate opinions that differed from his own.

41. Guo Ming, ed., *ZhongYue Guanxi Yanbian Sishinian* [Four Decades of Evolving Sino-Vietnam Relations] (Guilin, Guangxi: Guangxi Renmin Chubanshe, 1992), p. 67.

42. Xie Chengwen, Huang Zhengji, and Zhang Changyi, *San Da Tupo* [Three Major Breakthroughs] (Beijing: Jiefangjun Chubanshe, 1994), p. 230.

43. Tong Xiaopeng, *Fengyu Sishinian* [Four Decades: Trials and Hardships], vol. 2 (Beijing: Zhongyang Wenxian Chubanshe, 1996), p. 219.

44. See Ibid., pp. 220–221, for information on the Hanoi party meeting in July 1964.

45. Wang Dinglie, ed., *Dangdai Zhongguo Kongjun* [Modern China Air Force] (Beijing: Shehui Kexue Chubanshe, 1989), p. 384.

46. "Yuenan KangFa, KangMei Douzheng Shiqi.de ZhongYue Guanxi" [Sino-Vietnam Relations During Vietnam Resistance Against France and America], *People's Daily*, November 20, 1979.

47. *People's Daily*, August 6, 1964.

48. CCP Central Committee Literature Research Division and the PLA Academy of Military Sciences, eds., *Ma Zedong Junshi Wenji* [Selected Works of Mao Zedong on Military Affairs], p. 403.

49. CCP Central Committee Literature Research Division, ed., *Jianguo Yilai Mao Zedong Wengao* [Manuscripts by Mao Zedong Since the Founding of the PRC], vol. 11 (Beijing: Zhongyang Wenxian Chubanshe, 1996), pp. 359–360.

50. Ministry of Foreign Affairs of the People's Republic of China and the CCP Central Committee Literature Research Division, eds., *Mao Zedong Waijiao Wenxuan* [Selected Works of Mao Zedong on Diplomatic Affairs] (Beijing: Zhongyang Wenxian Chubanshe and Shijie Zhishi Chubanshe, 1994), p. 544.

51. Ministry of Foreign Affairs of the People's Republic of China and the CCP Central Committee Literature Research Division, eds., *Zhou Enlai Waijiao Wenxuan* [Selected Works of Zhou Enlai on Diplomatic Affairs], p. 443.

52. Li Danhui, "Sanbaxian yu Shiqiduxian—Chaoxian yu Yuezhan Qijian ZhongMei Xinxi Goutong Bijiao Yanjiu" [The 38th Parallel and the 17th Parallel—Comparative Studies on Exchange of Information Between China and the U.S. in the Korean War and in the Vietnam War], in *Zhonggong Dangshi Yanjiu* [Studies on History of the Communist Party of China], vol. 3, 2001.

53. "Yuenan KangFa, KangMei Douzheng Shiqi.de ZhongYue Guanxi" [Sino-Vietnam Relations During Vietnam Resistance Against France and America]; Qu Aiguo, Bao Mingrong, and Xiao Zuyue, eds., *YuanYue KangMei—Zhongguo Zhiyuanbudui zai Yuenan* [Aiding Vietnam in Its Resistance Against the United States—China Supporting Troops in Vietnam] (Beijing: Junshi Kexue Chubanshe, 1995), p. 11.

54. Hong Zuojun, "Fengyu Qianzaiqing" [A Millennium of Trials and Hard-ships], in *Lishi Shunjian.de Huisu* [Flashbacks of Historical Moments] (Beijing: Dangdai Shijie Chubanshe, 1997), p. 133.

55. Ibid., pp. 134–135.

56. Qu Aiguo, Bao Mingrong, and Xiao Zuyue, eds., *YuanYue KangMei—Zhongguo Zhiyuanbudui zai Yuenan* [Aiding Vietnam in Its Resistance Against the United States—China Supporting Troops in Vietnam], p. 12.

57. At that time, Chinese artillery forces in Vietnam wore the uniform of Viet-namese forces, while the Chinese corps of engineers wore blue.

58. Ministry of Foreign Affairs of the People's Republic of China and the CCP Central Committee Literature Research Division, eds., *Mao Zedong Waijiao Wenxuan* [Selected Works of Mao Zedong on Diplomacy], p. 582.

59. In May 1972, the Nixon administration resumed its massive bombing of North Vietnam, which ended in August 1973. Upon Vietnam's request, China once again sent support troops to North Vietnam to take on tasks like ground transportation and minesweeping in the sea.

6

U.S. Crisis Management Vis-à-vis China: Korea and Vietnam

Allen S. Whiting

IN CRISES, DECISION MAKERS FACE THREATS to their states' basic values, finite time for response, and heightened probability that military hostilities will erupt.[1] Under these conditions, decision makers are likely to be few, organizational involvement will be limited, and standard operating procedures will be compressed.[2] Such conditions are not conducive to the rational calculation of national interest or successful communication for conflict avoidance between antagonists. These circumstances exemplify U.S. crisis management vis-à-vis China in two Korean War cases: the initial Chinese intervention in mid-October 1950 and the subsequent massive engagement with United Nations (UN) forces following General Douglas MacArthur's home-by-Christmas offensive in late November. Both instances shocked Washington as wholly unanticipated and threatened dire consequences for the U.S. military intervention in the Korean War. Furthermore, both instances raised the specter of possible Soviet involvement and world war. The total absence of direct communication with Beijing further complicated U.S. responses.

The initial Chinese intervention triggered a flurry of meetings that reaffirmed the initial U.S. decision to take over North Korea after defeating its aggression in the South. The crisis between the United States and China eased within a week as Chinese "volunteers" broke contact and remained quiescent. The massive engagement by the Chinese, however, forced UN forces to abandon North Korea and stabilize defensive positions in the South. The United States made no retaliation against the Chinese mainland despite a range of military options recommended within the State Department and Defense Department. President Harry S. Truman and Secretary of State Dean Acheson opposed such a move, as did U.S. allies such as Great Britain. The crisis lasted several weeks and ended only after the UN abandoned Seoul for a second time and secured a line below the 38th parallel. Decision makers feared a worst-case Soviet intervention if they attacked China and consequently did not take any action.

The Vietnam War does not present a classic case of crisis decision making with respect to China. U.S. involvement began with the French defeat by Ho Chi Minh's forces in 1954. It expanded incrementally in 1962 with the large increase in U.S. advisers, and it culminated with the commitment of air and ground units in 1965. The question of serious Chinese involvement arose only after the bombing of North Vietnam and the subsequent deployment of U.S. ground forces in South Vietnam. Beijing responded with public statements that cautioned Washington, and Beijing secretly deployed up to 350,000 antiaircraft and logistics personnel to the North.[3] When U.S. and South Vietnamese forces faced rising losses, invasion of the North to cut Hanoi's supply of men and matériel offered a logical alternative to stalemate in the South. Both the geographic extent of the bombing and the proposed invasion required the United States to calculate the likelihood of Chinese intervention and, as such, created crises in decision making. Once again, the total absence of direct communication between Washington and Beijing further complicated the situation.

Both conflicts took place in the context of the Cold War, which centered on the U.S.-Soviet confrontation. Although China was involved as a secondary actor in Korea, its participation was sufficient to inflict one of the worst defeats in U.S. military history. China was a peripheral actor in Vietnam, but it posed a threat of major intervention sufficient to deter invasion of the North and, inter alia, impose a military stalemate on U.S. forces. The Cold War context and the lack of diplomatic relations between Beijing and Washington differentiate these situations from whatever may arise in the future. Nonetheless, they deserve review as case studies in U.S. crisis management regarding U.S.-Chinese interaction.

KOREAN WAR

The involvement of China and the United States during the early months of the Korean War can be divided in three phases.

Lead-Up to Chinese Intervention: June–October 1950

The first crisis of the Korean War arose when North Korean forces crossed the 38th parallel on June 25, 1950. Washington's military response restored the status quo ante and provided an auspicious precedent for meeting the Chinese intervention that fall. Secretary of Defense George C. Marshall and General Douglas MacArthur, commander of UN forces in Korea, agreed that it was unwise to fight the Chinese intervention in Korea because of the threat of a wider war.[4] Truman and Acheson moved quickly to take the situation to the United Nations. A small group of Department of State and Department of Defense officials agreed to strong military responses by MacArthur's forces in Japan. The foremost factors behind these decisions were the desires to show U.S. determination against perceived Soviet-inspired aggression, build credibility with U.S. allies in Europe and Asia, and strengthen the UN as a platform for peace. After North Korean forces had exhausted their initial push down the peninsula, leaving the United States only a toehold in the southern tip, strengthened U.S.-ROK (Republic of Korea) counterattacks and bombing turned the tide of battle. MacArthur's daring landing at Incheon in September threatened to cut across North Korean supply lines in the middle of the peninsula. Seoul quickly fell, and the United States virtually restored the status quo ante along the 38th parallel by October 1.

Moscow's behavior was critical to U.S. calculations of risk during this first crisis because of North Korea's status as a Soviet satellite. The Soviet boycott of the UN Security Council, ostensibly in protest against the refusal to shift recognition from the Republic of China (ROC; Taiwan) to the People's Republic of China (PRC; China) continued until August. The Soviets did not protest the bombing of a North Korean oil depot near the Soviet border, and their diplomatic response to the accidental strafing of a Soviet air base in early October seemed perfunctory. There was no evidence of Soviet military involvement in either the North

Korean advance or retreat. Instead, the Soviet representative at the UN proposed a cease-fire, and Russian diplomats in New York were socially amenable. The resulting consensus in Washington was that there was no threat of a wider war. The United States assumed that if the Soviets intended to become involved, the U.S. crossing of the 38th parallel would trigger their response. An advance U.S. estimate assumed that if the Soviets did not respond, "there would be some reason to believe that the Soviet Union had decided to follow a hands-off policy."[5] As had been expected, Moscow stood aside as the United States crossed the 38th parallel.

China also remained on the sidelines at first. On June 27, Truman ordered the U.S. Seventh Fleet to neutralize the Taiwan Strait, thereby deterring offensive action by either the United States or the PRC. On July 6, Zhou Enlai protested to the UN secretary-general over "armed aggression against the territory of China and in total violation of the United Nations Charter." Yet China did not take further action, suggesting Beijing sought to avoid involvement in the Korean War. However, as indicators emerged in August of a U.S. intention to cross the 38th parallel, Chinese warnings intensified. On September 25, Nie Rongzhen, PLA acting chief of staff, told the ambassador of India in Beijing, K. M. Panikkar, that China would not "sit back with folded hands and let the Americans come up to the border." He continued, "We know what we are in for, but at all costs American aggression must be stopped."[6] On September 30, Zhou Enlai publicly warned, "The Chinese people absolutely will not tolerate foreign aggression, nor will they supinely tolerate seeing their neighbors being savagely invaded by the imperialists."[7] On October 1, UN forces crossed the parallel. The following day, Zhou informed Panikkar "the South Koreans did not matter but American intrusion into North Korea would encounter Chinese resistance."[8]

Policy makers quickly dismissed this concatenation of unprecedentedly explicit warnings. Indeed, Washington soon shifted its attention. Decades later, Acheson stated, "Zhou's words were a warning, not to be disregarded, but on the other hand, not an authoritative statement of policy."[9] Acheson dismissed this warning at the time as "a bluff, pending more information" because China transmitted it orally to an Indian ambassador whose credibility fell short in Washington.[10] But O. Edmund Clubb, director of the Office of Chinese Affairs and the foremost foreign service specialist on China, disagreed.[11] He argued the warning meant the Sino-Soviet partners were "prepared to risk the danger of World War III." Both Livingston Merchant, deputy assistant secretary of state for Far Eastern affairs, and U. Alexis Johnson from Northeast Asian affairs supported Clubb's views. Their views did not sway Dean Rusk, at that time the assistant secretary of state for Far Eastern affairs. In a brief for the October 15 Truman-MacArthur meeting at Wake Island, Rusk took Acheson's position. MacArthur in turn assured Truman that there was little likelihood of Chinese intervention and that the United States would totally defeat China in the unlikely event they did intervene.

A set of prior assumptions framed the discussion of Chinese intervention by U.S. policy makers. First and foremost was the perception that Moscow determined Beijing's policy.[12] U.S. decision makers felt that China would intervene only at the behest of Moscow. They believed Moscow was unlikely to encourage China to intervene because, given the Sino-Soviet treaty, this would lead to general war, something to which Soviet behavior seemed clearly opposed. Second, U.S. decision makers believed China's primary interest was the restoration of domestic stability after nearly two decades of Japanese invasion and civil war. In this context, they felt China would perceive North Korea, a Soviet satellite, as literally peripheral. Following this logic, Chinese intervention seemed unlikely. Third, Washington provided public reassurances that it had no intention of attacking China or threatening the regime. While the United States intervened in the Taiwan Strait, U.S. officials explicitly rejected Chinese Nationalist action against the mainland. Consequently, U.S. decision makers felt Beijing should not have any defensive concerns. In sum, these assumptions led U.S. officials to believe the PRC would not open itself to U.S. retaliation by intervening in Korea because the PLA lacked the air and naval capabilities to withstand sustained blockade and bombardment.

U.S. policy makers did not engage in any serious, systematic studies of alternative strategies and tactics in the event that China did enter the war. A September 27 Joint Chiefs of Staff (JCS) directive to MacArthur did, however, address this possible contingency. The directive authorized MacArthur to pursue the destruction of the North Korean armed forces north of the 38th parallel,

... provided that at the time of such operations there has been no entry into North Korea by major Soviet or Chinese Communist Forces, no announcement of intended entry, nor a threat to counter our operations militarily in North Korea. Under no circumstances, however, will your forces cross the Manchurian or USSR borders and, as a matter of policy, no non-Korean Ground Forces will be used . . . in the area along the Manchurian border . . . [no] Air or Naval action against Manchuria or against USSR territory. . . . You will not discontinue Air and Naval operations north of the 38th parallel merely because the presence of Soviet or Chinese Communist troops is detected in a target area, but if the Soviet Union or Chinese Communists should announce in advance their intention to reoccupy North Korea and give warning, either explicitly or implicitly, that their forces should not be attacked you should refer the matter to Washington.[13]

On the same day, Marshall sent MacArthur an eyes-only telegram that implicitly softened the tone: "We want you to feel unhampered tactically and strategically to proceed north of the 38th parallel." MacArthur's reply foreshadowed his subsequent behavior: "Unless and until the enemy capitulates, I regard all Korea as open for our military operations."[14]

First Crisis: Initial Chinese Intervention, October 26–November 8, 1950

On October 26–27, major fighting broke out between Chinese communist "volunteers" (members of the People's Liberation Army, or PLA) and both ROK and U.S. forces. In four days, the PLA shattered the ROK II Corps and caused the 8th U.S. Cavalry to lose half of its equipment and strength before breaking contact. General Walton Walker informed MacArthur that "well organized and well trained units" had ambushed his units. On October 31, Soviet MIGs began appearing over North Korea.

These events triggered an intensive period of consultations among U.S. decision makers that specifically addressed the particulars of tactical operations but not the overall question of strategy. Central in this period was the position of General MacArthur as (1) commander in charge of UN as well as U.S. forces, (2) planner of the very risky Incheon landing (opposed by the JCS) that had ended North Korean occupation of the South in September 1950, and (3) political activist with a penchant for publicity. On November 4, MacArthur's initial cable cautioned against "hasty conclusions" and advised waiting for "a more complete accumulation of military facts." However, the next day he ordered, through General George E. Stratemeyer, air attacks on the Korean sides of all Yalu river bridges and the destruction of all means of communications, installations, factories, cities, and villages in North Korea, excepting the Yalu dams and hydroelectric plants.

Stratemeyer informed the Pentagon of this order three hours before U.S. forces were to attack the bridges. Deputy Secretary of Defense Robert Lovett told Acheson the attempt might fail and risked striking Antung. Rusk added that the United States had promised London that they would not attack Chinese targets without consulting with the British and, furthermore, the British cabinet was meeting that morning to review policy with Beijing. The UN Security Council responded to Washington's request for an urgent meeting to consider MacArthur's report of Chinese intervention. Acheson telephoned Marshall, who thought someone should ask the JCS to postpone MacArthur's actions until Truman could approve the plan. The president then approved any actions necessary for security of the troops, provided the facts be ascertained first. According to Acheson, MacArthur had not yet reported any Chinese troops crossing the bridges. On this basis, the JCS repeated the prohibition against bombing within five miles of the border and declared the United States was committed to refrain from attacking Manchuria without consulting London. Moreover, the JCS asked MacArthur to explain his desire to strike the bridges.

MacArthur responded:

> Men and material in large force are pouring across all bridges over the Yalu from Manchuria. This movement not only jeopardizes but threatens the ultimate destruction of the forces under my command. . . . Under the gravest protest that I can make, I am suspending the strike and carrying out your instructions. . . . I believe your instructions may well result in a calamity of major proportions.

Truman thereupon told the JCS to "give him the 'go ahead.'" Truman's approval is manifested in the JCS's reply to MacArthur:

> We agree that the destruction of the Yalu bridges will contribute materially to the security of the forces under your command unless this action resulted in increased Chinese Communist effort . . . in response to what they might well construe as an attack on Manchuria. . . . You are authorized to go ahead with your planned bombing in Korea near the frontier including targets at Sinuiju and Korean end of Yalu bridges provided at the time of this message you still find such action essential to safety of your forces.

On November 7, MacArthur protested the "present restrictions" against flights over Manchuria, which "provides a complete sanctuary for hostile air immediately upon their crossing the Manchuria–North Korean border."[15] The question of "hot pursuit" concerned U.S. allies, in particular the British, who believed it would increase the risk of greater Chinese intervention. All the top officials—Truman, Acheson, Marshall, and the JCS—agreed with MacArthur's request to lift the restrictions against flights over Manchuria, but all the other governments they consulted were opposed to such a policy shift. The United States consequently dropped the proposal to change this policy.

These tactical questions raised the larger issue of U.S.-UN objectives in Korea, with the JCS alerting MacArthur on November 8 that the present goal of destroying "North Korean armed forces" might be "reexamined." Replying before the National Security Council (NSC) meeting on November 9, MacArthur claimed that anything less than his proclaimed "end the war offensive" around November 15 "would condemn us to an indefinite retention of our military forces along difficult defense lines," so angering the ROK forces as to lead them to collapse "or even turn against us." He condemned as "wishful thinking at its very worst that the Chinese Communists after . . . establishing themselves within North Korea would abide by any limitations upon further expansion southward." In particular, MacArthur believed the British notion of leaving a buffer zone below the Yalu was comparable with the Munich appeasement of Hitler in 1938: "To give up any portion of North Korea to the aggression of the Chinese Communists would be the greatest defeat of the free world in recent times . . . bankrupt our leadership in Asia and render untenable our position both politically and militarily." He closed his remarks confidently with the plea "that we press on to complete victory which I believe can be achieved if our determination and indomitable will do not desert us."[16]

Meanwhile, Chinese communist forces virtually disappeared from combat, raising questions about their actual strength and ultimate intentions. At the NSC meeting, General Walter Bedell Smith, CIA director, estimated that PLA forces in Korea numbered 30,000–40,000, with perhaps 350,000 troops in Manchuria that could be added in two to three months, thereby halting further UN advance or forcing a UN retreat. General Omar Bradley questioned whether U.S. air attacks could prevent this reinforcement from occurring if they were not allowed to operate in Manchuria. The JCS saw three possible PRC goals: (1) protect the electric power base on the Yalu essential for Manchuria's electricity needs, (2) push back UN forces and cause a war of attrition, and (3) drive "us off the peninsula."[17] Participants at the meeting agreed that the State Department should try to contact Beijing to discern the PRC's intentions and any grounds for a possible settlement but also that MacArthur should continue his actions within Korea at his discretion.

U.S. officials accepted MacArthur's plan for a further advance despite the initial contact with Chinese forces because of two primary factors. First, the CIA estimate of the number of PLA troops at 40,000 maximum did not seem overwhelming given the 100,000 frontline UN troops. U.S. officials did not believe the presence of these PLA troops indicated PRC plans for a massive engagement. They believed the intelligence reports from Tokyo were at least approximate reflections of evidence collected by U.S. forces during the ten days of combat. Later, after the second round of fighting in November–December, Washington undertook an investigation to determine why the estimate of the Far East Command had been so wrong. It found that high-level staff had apparently withheld evidence from MacArthur and from the JCS that did not support MacArthur's planned offensive so as not to counter his Wake Island forecast that China would present no serious challenge.[18]

Second, the United States believed that China would have already intervened if it had any intention of doing so. On October 28, General Charles A. Willoughby, MacArthur's G-2, wrote, "The auspicious time for intervention has long since passed; it is difficult to believe that such a move, if planned, would have been postponed to a time when remnant North Korea forces have been reduced to a low point of effectiveness." On October 31, Bradley held China to be "halfway between" the marginal and total involvement expected by the military.[19] Given the widespread U.S. view that Moscow was directing Beijing, Smith's November 9 memorandum to the NSC strengthened the view that changes in the UN bombing strategy would not influence China's decision to intervene: "The probability is that the Soviet Government has not yet made a decision directly to launch a general war over the Korean-Chinese situation. There is a good chance that they will not in the immediate future take such a decision." Therefore, "action by U.N. forces to attack troop concentrations or airfields north of the Yalu River, or to pursue enemy aircraft into Chinese territory would not increase the already substantial risk. . . . The Kremlin's basic decision for or against war would hardly be influenced by this local provocation in this area."[20]

Acheson's effort to reach Beijing through Sweden failed. On November 10, Zhou Enlai announced his acceptance of the November 8 Security Council invitation to participate in a discussion of the Korean matter, with the PRC delegation set to arrive on November 16. This announcement seemed to promise direct communication between the United States and the PRC at the UN, but the PRC group did not arrive until November 24. On November 17, MacArthur told the JCS he would launch his offensive to secure the Yalu line on November 24, before the river froze and permitted massive PLA crossings. On November 21, at a State Department–Defense Department meeting, Acheson voiced concern among U.S. allies over an expanded war but would not interfere with MacArthur's directive. Marshall suggested preempting outsider initiatives by proposing a demilitarized area after the cessation of enemy resistance. On November 24, the JCS queried MacArthur about stopping his offensive on the heights 10 to 25 miles from the Yalu, with ROK troops occupying forward positions. On November 26, MacArthur dismissed this proposal as "utterly impossible" and declared, "Our forces are committed to seize the entire border area and in the east have already occupied a sector of the Yalu River with no noticeable political or military Soviet or Chinese reactions."[21]

The State Department intelligence estimate for the "most likely Soviet-Chinese course" of action foresaw:

a. continuation of Chinese-North Korea holding operations in North Korea until . . . preparations have been completed and until prospects of securing U.S. withdrawals from Korea through intimidation and diplomatic maneuvers have been exhausted; b. In case of the failure of these tactics, increasing unofficial Chinese intervention in Korea to, if necessary, the point of large scale military operations; c. Increasing Soviet support of the Chinese in equipment, planes, technical advisers, and of necessary "volunteers" to the extent required to prevent a Chinese defeat.[22]

Nonetheless, all top officials agreed that in the absence of clear evidence on Chinese intentions, the U.S.-UN forces should use a renewed offensive to determine Chinese intentions.

Nearly thirty years later, Acheson wrote:

As I look back, the critical period stands out as the three weeks from October 26 to November 17. Then, all the dangers from dispersal of our own forces and intervention by the Chinese were manifest. We were all deeply apprehensive. We were frank with one another, but not quite frank enough. I was unwilling to urge on the President a military course that his military advisers would not propose . . . because it ran counter to American tradition of the proper powers of the theater commander. . . . If General Marshall and the Chiefs had proposed withdrawal to the Pyongyang-Wonsan line . . . and if the President had backed them, as he undoubtedly would have—disaster would probably have been averted.[23]

Second Crisis: Full Chinese Intervention, November 24, 1950

MacArthur did not change the disposition of his forces after the first PLA contact, leaving the two forces 50 miles apart in the upper peninsula. Chinese troops countered his offensive massively, driving U.S. and ROK armies back down the peninsula in rapid retreat and inflicting more than 11,000 casualties in two days. The UN held 110,000 troops against an estimated 256,000 Chinese and 10,000 North Korean troops.[24] During the next several weeks, the administration and its allies considered a wide range of political and military responses. Advocates and opponents of military measures against China shifted their positions as the situation in Korea first worsened and then stabilized in mid-January.

The U.S. preoccupation with Soviet intent and readiness for a wider war, however, was consistent throughout. Successive developments indicated that there was no serious threat of Soviet military action elsewhere. Soviet military action would come, if at all, as a consequence of attacking China. As before, U.S. decision makers saw Beijing as the agent of Moscow and neglected to study China's own interests and motivations.

Washington never made any extraordinary effort to contact Beijing directly. In late December, owing to Washington's distrust of the Indian ambassador in Beijing, the United States chose Stockholm, not New Delhi, as the location through which to communicate its willingness to discuss a cease-fire and to examine wider issues in the western Pacific following the accomplishment of a cease-fire. Such efforts were unsuccessful. Multilateral efforts at the UN to broker a PRC-U.S. agreement on a cease-fire failed as both sides held fast to unacceptable demands.[25] China insisted on the withdrawal of all foreign troops from Korea, the removal of the U.S. Seventh Fleet from the Taiwan Strait, and the recognition of Beijing's claim to the UN seat. Washington insisted that China could not attach any political conditions to a cease-fire. The issue was resolved on the battlefield.

Three aspects deserve attention for their role in exacerbating decision making during the second Korean crisis. First, the UN military front disintegrated rapidly, intensifying requirements for assessment of the situation, as shown below by the chronology of Tokyo's cables and Washington responses. Second, in contrast with the earlier crisis, the administration faced increasing criticism from congressional and media opponents. Although official records make only passing reference to domestic pressures, these records understate the degree to which Truman and Acheson were apprehensive about reactions to their consideration of the contrasting policies—attacking China versus withdrawal from

Korea—advocated by opposing sources. The Republican right and Senator Joseph R. McCarthy (R-Wis.) had already heavily attacked their China policy. Now, responsible voices of public opinion questioned the ends as well as the means of pending decisions. Third, to a far greater degree than ever before, U.S. allies and UN members worked assiduously in Washington and New York to restrain what was seen as highly risky behavior by MacArthur and his hawkish supporters in Congress. Space precludes fuller treatment of these aspects of the crisis decision making, which occupy considerable space in the memoirs by Truman and Acheson as well as in subsequent histories.

On November 28, MacArthur reported, "We face an entirely new war," with China seeking the "complete destruction" of his forces. At an NSC meeting that day, Marshall and members of the JCS argued against a separate war with China because they believed the United States should act with the UN mandate to assure its continued support. Adhering to the UN mandate meant keeping the war limited, refraining from attacks on the mainland, and refraining from the use of Chinese Nationalist forces because such an action might cause the British to withdraw their more effective troops. The United States could not replace troop losses before January and could not provide new divisions before March.

In a series of statements to U.S., British, and Japanese media, MacArthur broadcast his dismay at the decision to deny him the ability to strike across the Yalu, thereby placing the UN forces under "an enormous handicap, without precedent in military history."[26] On December 3, MacArthur told the JCS he faced "the entire Chinese nation in an undeclared war and unless some positive and immediate action is taken . . . steady attrition leading to final destruction [of UN forces] can reasonably be contemplated."[27] On December 6, he estimated the number of PLA troops in Korea at 268,000, with 550,000 more across the Yalu and "about 4 million men under arms" in China. To verify MacArthur's views, Marshall sent General John Lawton Collins to Tokyo for an independent assessment.

Intelligence analyses saw Beijing's goal as ousting the UN forces from Korea, even if this raised the risk of a wider war. Such analyses argued that Moscow would provide the necessary men and matériel, including antiaircraft defense of Manchurian targets and much greater Soviet participation, should UN attacks go beyond the immediate area. Analysts believed the Soviet goal was the diversion of U.S. forces from elsewhere, especially Europe, where such a diversion of troops would disrupt the newly emergent North Atlantic Treaty Organization. Such analyses charged that, if the United States avoided war with China and withdrew from Korea, it could then more aggressively pursue communist targets in Southeast Asia and beyond.[28]

Given this combination of increasingly pessimistic reports from Tokyo and worst-case intelligence estimates, U.S. officials faced two unpalatable alternatives: retaliation against the mainland or withdrawal from the peninsula. On December 3, the Pentagon warned that the United States must evacuate the X Corps and that U.S. forces would sustain heavy casualties unless a cease-fire occurred. Marshall and Acheson opposed seeking a cease-fire because of the disarray of UN forces, and they argued that the United States could not abandon the South Koreans by evacuating U.S. troops. Acheson opposed the bombing of Manchurian airfields and bases except as a last-ditch resort necessary to save U.S. troops. He believed such a decision should be made by Truman and Marshall, not MacArthur. Rusk cited the British precedent during the two World Wars of hanging tough and argued for stiffening UN forces so they could damage Chinese troops more heavily.

On December 26, Truman summoned Marshall, Bradley, Acheson, and Secretary of the Treasury John Snyder to Blair House. Acheson proposed the revision and sharpening of MacArthur's directives. Acheson believed that withdrawal from Korea should occur only as a military necessity and that defense lines should be based on maximum threat to the enemy and safety for UN troops. Marshall and MacArthur believed the greater threat of wider war precluded fighting it in Korea. Marshall, Bradley, and Acheson rewrote the original directive on December 27 with Truman's authorization and dispatched it on December 29: "Your directive now is to defend in successive positions, subject to the safety of your troops as your primary consideration, inflicting as much damage to hostile forces in Korea as is possible."[29] MacArthur was also to determine "the last reasonable opportunity for an orderly evacuation" of the peninsula. MacArthur responded vigorously:

Should a policy determination be reached by our government to recognize the State of War which has been forced on us by the Chinese authorities and to take retaliatory measures within our capability we could: (1) Blockade the coast of China; (2) Destroy through naval gunfire and air bombardment China's industrial capacity to wage war; (3) Secure reinforcements from the Nationalist garrison on Formosa to strengthen our position in Korea . . . (4) Release existing restrictions upon the Formosa garrison for diversionary action (possibly leading to counter-invasion) against vulnerable areas of the Chinese mainland.[30]

MacArthur won support in the Pentagon for some, if not all, of his recommendations.

Bradley warned of a congressional response if evacuation was not accompanied by retaliation: "We used to say that an attack on a platoon of the United States troops meant war. Would anyone believe it now if we don't react to the Chinese attack?" He noted China was "actually sending military forces against us and did not call it war, and yet if we drop one bomb across the Yalu they say we are making war against them."[31] On December 27, in the Joint Strategic Plans Committee, Navy and Air Force members recommended holding certain bridgeheads during increased air attacks with extension to China "as necessary," using Chinese Nationalist troops in Korea, helping Taipei impose an undeclared naval blockade, and activating guerillas in China. The Army expressed reserve regarding the use of Taiwan's troops at the present, although it held open the option of possibly using Taiwanese troops later against Hainan and the mainland. The Army did, however, support a naval and air blockade. Admiral Forrest Sherman, chief of naval operations, endorsed a naval blockade with or without UN agreement because it was "time for unilateral action by the United States." The second PLA offensive of January 1 drove UN forces below the 38th parallel. This added strength to MacArthur's alarms. On January 12, the JCS endorsed most of these proposals, advancing them at the NSC on January 17.

Acheson countered by calling for an examination of the actual use of Chinese Nationalist troops in Korea and noted the impact their use might have on the Europe-first strategy. He also questioned the comparative impact of a naval blockade compared with tougher economic measures. He presented a State Department analysis that reemphasized the U.S. commitment to its allies to limit the war in Korea, the impossibility of securing UN endorsement for military action against China, and the negative effect such action would have more widely on confidence in U.S. assurances. This analysis raised an implicit challenge to the original argument for intervention in June, namely U.S. credibility. Finally, the paper questioned whether limited U.S. military action would deter China from further aggression or cause the communists to lose control.[32]

Marshall and Bradley pointed to rising domestic pressure for retaliation against China. In this way, Marshall placed U.S. interests before the interests of the UN or Britain. Robert Strong, head of the National Security Resources Board, claimed a naval blockade would wreck China's internal communications and heavily burden the Soviet Union. Given these split views between the Departments of State and Defense, Truman deferred a decision and called for further study of the recommended Chinese Nationalist role.

As the NSC discussions continued, the UN position stabilized. On December 23, General Walker, in command of the Eighth Army, died in a jeep accident. Two days later, he was replaced by General Matthew Ridgeway, who took charge of the combined Eighth Army–X Corps force. Ridgeway's forceful direction, air bombardment of the extended PLA logistics, and devastating attack on the massed PLA offensive units halted the enemy's advance. As the NSC meetings began, General Collins and General Hoyt Vandenberg, chief of staff of the U.S. Air Force, returned from Korea to testify that the military situation had again improved.

At the second meeting, on January 18, 1951, the JCS conceded that the prospect of UN forces being confined to a beachhead had influenced their initial paper. They now agreed that the United States should not attempt a blockade unless total withdrawal were necessary and even in that situation should not attempt a unilateral blockade. The JCS argued that aerial reconnaissance should not overfly Manchuria and that Chinese Nationalist forces were unnecessary. In sum, "[O]ur actions now are based on the premise that we should do nothing to spread the war outside Korea."[33] This statement resolved State-Pentagon differences and allowed Truman to focus on the problem of managing MacArthur. He eventually solved this problem by firing MacArthur.

This did not end the military challenge posed by Chinese intervention. Ridgeway repulsed a third Chinese offensive that spring with a counterattack that virtually restored the status quo ante for a second time, now somewhat more advantageous to the UN positions. The immediate diplomatic agenda of the United States was to win a UN resolution condemning Beijing as an aggressor, a necessary prelude to imposing a total economic embargo. More diplomatic and military challenges followed, notably the challenge of probing for communist interest in negotiations toward a cease-fire while coping with further PLA offensives. The two sides did not reach an armistice until July 1953. However, after January 1951, no Chinese actions occurred that required reconsideration of the decisions already in place. In May 1951, these decisions underwent intensive public reexamination through congressional hearings on the firing of MacArthur in April, but no changes to these decisions occurred then or under the next administration of President Dwight D. Eisenhower.

In sum, crisis decision making initially prompted the successful reversal of North Korean aggression in June 1950. However, in addressing the 38th parallel crossing in October, U.S. decision makers failed to anticipate the resultant Chinese intervention. Worse, crisis decision making in November after brief but bloody encounters with Chinese troops failed to forestall General MacArthur's November offensive. The collision of MacArthur's offensive with massive Chinese forces triggered better crisis decision making in December. The administration succeeded in managing a humiliating U.S. retreat from all of North Korea without expanding the war to China. In doing so, the administration avoided the worst-case outcome of a wider conflict but took a serious blow to U.S. prestige.

FROM KOREA TO VIETNAM

Two aspects of crisis decision making link Sino-American relations during the two wars. First, Washington did not have direct relations with Beijing in either case. Both times, China issued public threats of action in response to U.S. intervention, and the United States issued public reassurances, amplified through third parties, of its limited objectives.

Given the absence of direct diplomatic exchanges or back-channel communications, both parties were left to rely on their own perceptions of the other party's intentions. Second, the Chinese intervention in Korea affected U.S. behavior during the Vietnam War. Dean Rusk, secretary of state during the Vietnam War, later stated:

> Our conduct of the war and especially the bombing of North Vietnam were influenced by the possibility of Chinese intervention. . . . [W]ith our policy of gradual response, at no time did we present Beijing and Moscow with a major change in the war that forced them to decide whether or not to intervene. . . . We downplayed the importance of our own military actions for the benefit of the Chinese and Soviets, not wanting to provoke them into responding. . . . Our Chinese specialists stated almost unanimously that if we sent ground operations into North Vietnam, the chances of Chinese intervention were high and for that reason I strongly opposed U.S. ground operations versus North Vietnam . . . [that] would likely have triggered Hanoi's mutual security pact with China . . . We watched for potential mobilization of Chinese forces, avoided bombing territory adjacent to China, and tried to avoid threatening the Chinese or leaving our own intentions unclear as had been done by General MacArthur's advance to the Yalu.[34]

As Rusk acknowledged, "One military memo discussed American ground forces invading North Vietnam and opined that such an invasion . . . would not 'bring in the Chinese.'" The memo continued, "But if they do come in, that will mean nuclear war."

Other critical aspects differentiate Korea from Vietnam. Unlike in Korea, China's behavior did not cause a sense of crisis in Vietnam. Instead, it was the recurring instability in Saigon that drove U.S. decisions for escalation in terms of the number of troops to be deployed, the extent and nature of air attacks, and the response to Hanoi's infiltration routes in Laos and Vietnam. Nevertheless, at each step of escalation, the United States needed to calculate Chinese responses.

The manner of crisis decision making also differentiates the two cases. During the Korean War, Truman, Acheson, and a small circle of offi-

cials from the Departments of State and Defense—formally constituting the new NSC—met to address the problems posed by Chinese intervention. Records of these meetings exist and are available to researchers. President Lyndon B. Johnson, however, eschewed the bureaucratic
process and rarely convened the NSC as such. The more critical the
matter, as with the rapid increase of troops in 1965, the less he turned to
the NSC and the more he turned to the Tuesday Lunch Group.[35] The
members of the Tuesday Lunch Group varied, but the core consisted of
Rusk, Secretary of Defense Robert McNamara, and the chairman of the
JCS; later it included the CIA head. The only records of these meetings
are informal notes by the participants, especially Johnson's close aide,
Jack Valenti. The lack of official records makes it a challenge for historians to determine exactly who said what and why. Johnson rarely revealed his own decisions.[36]

Those close to Johnson provided a multiplicity of advice. Sometimes
Johnson's advisers lacked the clearance to see intelligence on Chinese
military activities pertinent to the likelihood of conflict.[37] On occasion,
Johnson met alone with someone such as Rusk, whose views were more
frequently given to the president in private than voiced in a group.
Johnson also initiated a personal discussion with George Ball about Ball's
strongly worded opposition to an escalation, which emphasized the risk
of a Chinese intervention. In February–March 1966, Johnson met at
length with the Vietnam Working Group in the Cabinet Room. Each
meeting included from eight to seventeen top officials who responded
to searching questions that Johnson asked them on an individual basis.[38] Johnson regularly asked officials such as McNamara, McGeorge
Bundy, William P. Bundy, and Ball to elaborate on their differing views.
The result is an abundance of telephone transcripts, personal notes,
memoirs, interviews, oral histories, and official records. Nevertheless,
the most careful writers with the best access to the available files agree
on the difficulty of determining exactly when Johnson arrived at his
critical decisions and under whose advice.[39]

Another difference between the management of the two crises is the
incremental nature of decision making during the Vietnam War. Following the Gulf of Tonkin Resolution in August 1964, Johnson made
no further presidential announcements or requests for congressional
approval. The escalation of the war continued gradually, however, and

included such steps as an increase in the number of "advisers" to Saigon and their expanded role, the increases in the number of military forces and the expansion of their missions, and the shift in bombing strategy from retaliation to attrition.

VIETNAM: THE CHINESE PUZZLE

A crucial difference between U.S. decision making in the Korean and Vietnam Wars was the level of attention and debate among U.S. decision makers on the risk of Chinese intervention.

Early Debates in the Johnson Administration

In February 1964, seven months before President Johnson first seriously considered escalation in Vietnam, Walt Rostow, head of policy planning at the State Department, proposed an attack on North Vietnam, arguing that there was no risk of a Chinese response. He argued that Vietnam would avoid "virtual vassalage" from China and that China would keep Vietnam from sending troops to South Vietnam in fear of escalation.[40] In March, a joint CIA–State Department intelligence study found that Hanoi was likely to persist if the United States attacked and that Beijing was likely to assist Hanoi if it faced defeat.[41] Rostow, charging the study lacked military input, rejected it and called for a special national intelligence estimate (SNIE), issued on May 25, 1964. The SNIE forecast there was "not a high risk of Chinese Communist intervention unless major U.S./GVN [Government of the Republic of Vietnam (South Vietnam)] ground units had moved well into the DRV [Democratic Republic of Vietnam (North Vietnam)] . . . or possibly, the Chinese had committed their air and subsequently suffered attack on CCAF [Chinese Communist Air Force] bases in China."[42] The same day, National Security Adviser McGeorge Bundy's memo to Johnson recommended "selected and carefully graduated military force against North Vietnam." He expressed the "hope and best estimate of most of your advisers" that this would be "without a major military reply from Red China."[43]

The language of the SNIE concealed several points of contention that persisted during the coming months. The prevailing definition of Chinese intervention posited a literal repeat of the Korean War: massive forces sweeping into North Vietnam and possibly further. U.S. analysts did not consider lower-level involvement by Beijing. Similarly, U.S. analysis saw air commitments by China to include fighter cover for North Vietnam and possibly bombers further south. They hypothesized that the provocation for such a Chinese response, still considered unlikely, would be the provision of a "major" force "moving well" into North Vietnam. In this context, they did not see the possibility of interdiction of the Laotian infiltration route by cutting across lower North Vietnam, as proposed later. Notably, this SNIE and its many successors did not focus primarily on the prospect of Chinese intervention; instead they were consistently titled, "Possible Consequences of Certain U.S. Actions with Respect to Vietnam and Laos." Under this rubric, U.S. analysis considered Hanoi as the central actor and Moscow and Beijing as secondary actors. The downgrading of the likelihood of Chinese intervention by U.S. analysts facilitated their acceptance of options for escalation, but the gradual increase in Chinese involvement affected the U.S. calculation of the risk of Chinese intervention. Such changing assessments were evident in the content of the intelligence estimates issued during this period.

On July 6, 1964, Foreign Minister Chen Yi warned that the Chinese people would not look on "with folded arms" while the United States attacked North Vietnam. A July 9 People's Daily editorial claimed the United States posed "a threat to China's peace and security." On August 2, North Vietnamese torpedo boats tried to hit U.S. intelligence destroyers in the Gulf of Tonkin. President Johnson responded by ordering strikes against North Vietnam's maritime bases. Beijing did not take any overt action but on August 6 declared, "Aggression against the Democratic Republic of Vietnam means aggression against China."[44] On October 9, the next SNIE noted that, given U.S.-GVN escalation, "Peiping might commit units of its air force to defensive action over North Vietnam at this point, but in view of the magnitude of U.S. air and naval superiority we doubt that Peiping would do so."[45]

The view expressed in this SNIE supported military proposals for U.S. escalation that emerged in the fall. On November 1, guerrillas attacked the U.S. base at Bien Hoa, knocking out thirteen B-57 bombers in addition to killing and wounding several U.S. troops. The JCS recommended immediate retaliation by thirty B-52 bombers from Guam that would strike the Phuc Yen airfield in the North, followed by the use of carrier planes to strike the petroleum, oil, and lubricants storage at Hanoi and Haiphong together with adjacent airfields. The JCS did not expect a Chinese reaction. But on November 14, the White House replied with "concern that proposed U.S. retaliatory/punitive actions would trigger NVN/Chicom [North Vietnamese and Chinese] air and ground retaliatory acts."[46] The next SNIE, issued on November 26, repeated the language of the previous document—that China "might" respond but that they "doubt[ed]" that would be the case. The State Department's director of the Bureau of Intelligence and Research (INR) dissented in a footnote, arguing that U.S.-GVN escalation "would probably evoke employment over North Vietnam of Chinese air from Chinese bases." He noted that the "new NingMing [sic] airstrip . . . ready in 1965 strongly suggests Chinese preparation to test U.S. adherence to the privileged sanctuary concept."[47] The mention of the privileged-sanctuary concept referred to the Korean War precedent in which the United States failed to attack the Chinese bases used by Russian and Chinese pilots who were engaging UN planes over North Korea. More recently, Washington had warned of "hot pursuit" if any such developments occurred again.

On February 7, 1965, Viet Cong troops attacked a U.S. helicopter base and barracks at Pleiku, killing 8 and wounding 126. McGeorge Bundy, in Saigon at the time, immediately called for retaliation and the continuation of the systematic bombing of the North.[48] A February 11 SNIE claimed China probably would not "put in ground forces" in response to the U.S. bombing, but if bombing hit the most northern part "China might react over North Vietnam with fighters from its own bases." Again, INR was more concerned about the possibility of Chinese intervention, arguing that China "would probably" do so.[49] U.S. photographic intelligence showed the existence of a new airfield and the expansion of an existing air base to include duplicate facilities, suggesting a second air force, presumably Vietnamese, would use the air base. In January, joint PRC-DRV air exercises covered an area 12 miles below the border, and later a joint radar grid linked both sides of the border down to the 17th parallel.[50]

These developments prompted closer U.S. attention to the Chinese puzzle as Beijing reacted more aggressively. On March 8, a joint State-Defense long-range China study explored several scenarios that focused on the entire range of Chinese responses through 1971. Unlike the standard national intelligence estimate (NIE), the study went to a board of directors that included McNamara; both Bundys; Ambassador Llewellyn Thompson; chairman of the JCS, General Earle Wheeler; and Deputy Secretary of Defense Cyrus Vance. The NIE concluded that China was likely to intervene if North Vietnam was in jeopardy, if the Chinese borders were endangered, or if large Kuomintang forces entered the war. If there was no Chinese ground involvement and if air defense of Vietnam came from Chinese bases, the United States would be at a disadvantage if it did not strike back. If Chinese ground forces entered the war, nuclear weapons might be necessary for the United States to destroy Chinese military or industrial centers although the nuclear strike would serve mainly as a psychological blow.[51]

On April 30, Rostow and Thompson initiated a short-range report on likely U.S.-China confrontation scenarios in 1965, such as the use of Chinese bases against U.S. bombing. The short-range report was also to assess the use of nuclear weapons against China.[52]

Meanwhile, some possibilities, previously only hypothetical, became reality. First, Chinese fighters crossed into North Vietnam, shadowing or attacking U.S. reconnaissance aircraft that had overflown China or were headed in that direction.[53] Second, on April 9, MIGs scrambled against U.S. fighters over Hainan Island. According to Washington, this incident resulted in the downing of a U.S. plane by the Chinese. Beijing immediately denied this account, claiming, "One U.S. plane was hit by a missile fired by another and crashed in the area of Hainan."[54] Whatever the facts, this engagement demonstrated China's willingness to risk escalation in its response to U.S. overflights. The Chinese denial of the incident was an attempt to forestall Washington's use of the incident as a reason for retaliation. This unprecedented event troubled top officials. Rusk reacted privately in frustration over the ambiguous situation: "When are the Chinese going to really come in?"[55]

The Defense Department informed President Johnson at midnight of the pilot of the downed plane being "just about over [Hainan]."

Johnson asked, "What was he doing over the island?"

General Cox replied, "We feel that probably in the business of fighting off the attacks, he strayed over the island."

Johnson queried further, "Where were the others engaged?"

Cox answered, . . . "off the coast."

The president continued, "Did they all wind up getting over the island?"

Cox responded, "It sounds like they did."[56]

This concern prompted the JCS on April 17 to emphasize to the Commander in Chief Pacific (CINCPAC) key portions of "Approved JCS Rules of Engagement, Southeast Asia" that sharply differentiated China from the rest of the area. The document stated China's claimed 12-mile territorial limit at sea "shall be observed," and "*no pursuit* is authorized into territorial sea or air space of Communist China," even though it sanctioned hot pursuit elsewhere.[57] These instructions aimed to avoid future Hainan engagements, inadvertent or not. On April 28, a SNIE addressed the possible consequences of U.S. retaliation should future engagements occur: "As U.S. strikes against fighter bases in South China continued . . . we think it somewhat more likely that they would make a major military response to the continuation or expansion of U.S. strikes against China."[58]

Intensified U.S. bombing of North Vietnam failed to halt the supply of men and munitions to the South. Given these developments, the next SNIE addressed the proposed expansion of raids above the 20th parallel and found it "likely China would provide additional support, e.g., ground equipment and personnel for air defense purposes or engineering help for constructing and repairing airfields . . . probably also supply fighter aircraft provided they could be based in North Vietnam. They would not wish to use bases in China because of risk of U.S. retaliation against them." INR dissented, arguing the expanded U.S. bombing "would probably evoke their employment over North Vietnam of Chinese air defense from bases in China."[59]

In mid-June, another coup d'état in Saigon moved General William Westmoreland to declare that the United States must supplement its 75,000 troops already in Vietnam with an additional 90,000 troops in order to strengthen its position in the ground war.[60] This represented a major change in strategy because, in effect, the United States would replace the GVN. A secondary part of Westmoreland's program was the greatly expanded bombing of North Vietnam. Concern about China's response hung over both aspects of the overall proposal. On July 1, the Defense Department's "Program of Expanded Military and Political Moves re Vietnam," addressed actions regarding China:

[First:] *Destroy rail and highway bridges leading from China to Hanoi.* There are fifteen highways, five railroads, and eight highway/railroad bridges north and east of Hanoi. The railroads now carry between 1600 and 1900 short tons per day. Roads to Hanoi from China can support considerable truck traffic. It would take approximately 1000 sorties to carry out strikes on the 28 bridge[s], with 85 percent probability of dropping one span in each case. . . . [Second:] *Conduct intensive armed reconnaissance of LOCs [lines of communication] from China* . . . so long as no U.S. or GVN troops attack Chinese territory, the Chinese probably will not send regular ground forces or aircraft into the war.[61]

Under Secretary of State George Ball vigorously countered Secretary of Defense McNamara's support of the Defense Department memo. Ball opposed another ground war in Asia and called for withdrawal at some point. As an added concern, he also focused on the indicators of increased involvement by Beijing. Assistant Secretary for East Asia William Bundy called for a middle-ground strategy that would very slowly test the limits of bombing, by selecting targets least likely to provoke China and remote from the border. President Johnson faced growing pressures from both supporters and opponents of dramatic escalation. On July 1, McGeorge Bundy advised Johnson on how to manage a key meeting:

Rusk and McNamara feel strongly the George Ball paper should not be argued with you in front of any audience larger than yourself, Rusk, McNamara, Ball and me. They feel it is exceedingly dangerous to have this possibility reported in a wider circle. Moreover both of them feel great reluctance about expressing their innermost thoughts to you in front of any larger group. . . . The disadvantage of this is that it cuts you off from a chance to talk freely with some other men who have expert opinion—like Thompson and General Wheeler.

Johnson agreed to keep the meeting small. Bundy then recommended, "My hunch is that you will want to listen hard to George Ball and then reject his proposal . . . then move to the narrow choice between my brother's course and McNamara's."[62] William Bundy's middle-ground approach won out. On July 28, Johnson announced, at the end of a press conference, that he would send an additional 50,000 troops to Vietnam.

Westmoreland's request for additional troops had prompted a sharp exchange between the president and the Army chief of staff (ACS) on July 22, during which Johnson declared, "There are millions of Chinese. I think they are going to put their stack in."

The ACS replied, "I don't think they will."

But Johnson countered, "MacArthur didn't think they would come in either."

The ACS argued, "Yes, but this is not comparable to Korea."

The president pressed further, "But China has plenty of divisions to move in, don't they?"

"Yes, they do."

"Then what would we do?"

The ACS answered, "If so we have another ball game. I would increase the buildup near North Vietnam."

Johnson persisted, "If they move in thirty-one divisions, what does it take on our part?"

McNamara interjected, "If the Thai contribute forces . . . [it would] take 300,000 plus what we needed to combat the Vietcong."[63]

The intelligence debate on bombing continued in a July 23 SNIE that addressed the LOCs issue: "In cutting the main roads and rail lines the chances are about even China would engage the U.S. over North Vietnam from bases in China." However, "if large numbers of U.S. aircraft operated close to the frontiers of China the likelihood of hostile encounter is high." INR dissented, charging that "the chances are *better* than even." Another dissent, signed by the Defense Intelligence Agency, the Army, the Air Force, and the National Security Agency, argued Chinese action was "unlikely."[64] The United States largely removed geographic limits on bombing the North, except for the immediate border area and the northeast.

China Ups the Ante

On September 15, 1965, the United States approved attacks on two railroad and highway bridges going to China northwest of Hanoi, while CINCPAC noted there were no longer any constraints on striking the northeast quadrant.[65] On September 20, Beijing claimed the first downing of an F-104 aircraft; Washington confirmed it. Two days later, a SNIE looked at simultaneous strikes at surface-to-air missile (SAM) sites, airfields, thermal plants, and LOCs to China and found no change from earlier sanguine estimates of Beijing's likely response. INR dissented from the entire text, arguing that Vietnamese planes would have safe haven on Chinese bases, the presence of more Chinese defensive patrols would increase accidental encounters, and more PLA antiaircraft and engineer units would enter Vietnam.[66] McNamara widened the buffer area for aircraft operations from 15 to 20 miles below the border. But on October 5, Beijing claimed to have shot down a second F-104; Washington did not confirm or deny this incident.

At the end of 1965, a major debate engaged top officials in Washington, at CINCPAC, and in Saigon over whether to try a longer pause in the bombing of the North than had been tried before; this would test Hanoi's willingness to stop the war in the South. These officials proposed that, should Hanoi fail to respond favorably, U.S. involvement could be escalated further by attacking all LOCs to China, mining Haiphong harbor, bombing all airfields, and interdicting infiltration routes in Laos with invasion above the demilitarized zone in addition to greatly increasing the number of U.S. forces in the South.

As before, Beijing was not pivotal to the debate, but arguments over China's possible responses to U.S. actions arose frequently. An examination of the mounting evidence of Chinese involvement appeared to foreshadow increased Chinese commitment to the war. Intelligence analysis showed an intermittent flow since June of regular PLA engineering and antiaircraft units that repaired LOCs under U.S. attack while presumably suffering casualties. China had initiated or activated five major airfields in southern China, where they had gathered half of Beijing's MIG-19s. China's only known SAM site covered a rail junction that was vital for Hanoi. In the area from Hainan through southern China, intensified civil defense measures included air raid drills, blood typing, and shelter programs. Meanwhile, strong anti-U.S. and pro-Vietnam propaganda attacks appeared on national radio and in print media in China, but they were not amplified in foreign transmissions.[67] This policy alerted domestic audiences to the Chinese position without alerting foreign audiences. A December 10 SNIE repeated the standard forecast: "We believe China would not comply" if Hanoi asked to use Chinese bases. However, this time the Army and National Security Agency joined the standard INR dissent. They argued the chances were 50-50 "if the U.S. hits near the border China would use its own planes."[68]

On December 15, 1965, the U.S. ambassador to Laos, William Sullivan, proposed that U.S. air and sea cover should be given to ground forces landing near the 20th parallel and should cut across North Vietnam to the Laotian border and the infiltration route. The United States would tell Hanoi it would hold this territory until Hanoi agreed to U.S. terms for a political settlement in the South. The United States would notify Beijing in advance that no further U.S. advance northward would occur, so as not to threaten Chinese interests. On December 27, William Bundy replied that study of a limited invasion had already determined:

> Once China decided the die was cast, it is hard to know what limits it would place on its actions. While it would presumably be in the Chinese hope to keep the war off its own territory, it nevertheless seems likely the Chinese would feel free to involve Laos and perhaps launch a diversionary threat toward or into Thailand. . . . In conclusion it would appear that U.S. action in southern North Viet-Nam [sic] should be avoided until we have reached the conclusion that infiltration of the south must absolutely be cut off and that we are prepared for a war with Communist China.[69]

This study finally invalidated one option that had long been advocated by Rostow, as acknowledged in his memoir.[70]

Hanoi did not respond favorably to the pause, and escalation expanded piecemeal. On April 12, 1966, Beijing announced the downing of another U.S. plane; Washington confirmed it. CINCPAC restrictions on U.S. air activities spelled out the China problem:

(a) no attacks are authorized thirty nautical miles below the border from Laos to 106 degrees East and twenty-five nautical miles onward to the Gulf of Tonkin; (b) no flight paths for conducting strikes will occur closer than twenty nautical miles of the border, and (c) aircraft in immediate pursuit can enter restricted target areas but must stop at the border.[71]

There were no further hostile encounters between the United States and China until September 1966, when Beijing reported China had damaged two U.S. fighters; Washington admitted this was "possible." Separate encounters in April, May, June, and August 1967 resulted in six U.S. losses according to Beijing; Washington did not confirm any of these losses.[72] The incremental pressing by U.S. forces against the Chinese border area marginally raised the risk of larger engagements, but the prohibition against hot pursuit by U.S. forces prevented the dangerous repercussions that could have resulted from a U.S. attack on Chinese bases, including the likelihood of a major expansion of the war.

IN RETROSPECT

Analysts can readily, if superficially, evaluate crisis management by the result: war or no war. By this measure, Korea proved disastrous for Sino-American relations, while U.S. decision making in Vietnam was successful. Decision makers of the Vietnam War learned from the mistakes of the Korean War. During the Korean War, Washington failed to correctly assess China's interests and its willingness to risk war. Dean Rusk, when he was assistant secretary of state, rejected the forecast of likely Chinese intervention given by his top foreign service officer specializing in China. Instead, Rusk held Chinese intervention would be illogical, given Beijing's dire state after more than a decade of Japanese invasion and civil war and the risk of U.S. reaction. In September 1950, Rusk had publicly argued strongly for a united Korea under UN auspices and warned against Beijing's attempts to promote further communist advances elsewhere. In this context, Rusk's desire for a U.S. victory in Korea overcame the doubts expressed by his subordinates. This combination of logical analysis and political predisposition prompted Rusk to join Acheson in sending MacArthur across the 38th parallel while warning MacArthur to watch for signs of a possible Chinese intervention. General George C. Marshall, in turn, affirmed MacArthur's prerogative as commander in the field to feel unlimited in his decisions "tactically and strategically." Giving such freedom to the field commander was standard in military tradition, but it counteracted Rusk's warning to stay alert for a Chinese intervention, with wholly unanticipated consequences.

In sum, the political predisposition of key actors, deep-rooted traditions of bureaucratic behavior, and the domestic context can drive or distort crisis decision making in ways that are contrary to intelligence analyses of the opponent's will and intentions. When comparing mutual military capabilities, analysts can project logical inferences of will and intention that are inconsistent with the opponent's political predisposition, traditions, and domestic context.

During the Vietnam War, President Johnson and his advisers wanted to pursue escalation against Hanoi without provoking Beijing to become involved. Without the Korean precedent, the same factors that prompted miscalculation regarding Korea could very easily have led the United States to invade the North and resulted in a wider war. The Cold War had led to assumptions of Sino-Soviet unity in promoting communist advances everywhere, especially in Southeast Asia. Beijing's willingness to back Hanoi reinforced this assumption. The political turmoil from the Cultural Revolution and Mao's apparent purge of his top leadership invited exploitation of seeming vulnerability. The comparative military advantage for a U.S. air attack argued for a strong response to Chinese intervention. Military and civilian advocates pressed for such a response. Fortunately, the background of Korea, especially for Dean Rusk, secretary of state during the Vietnam War, blocked such action. This time, the miscalculation was about the strength of Hanoi's will and not about Beijing's.

NOTES

1. Michael Brecher and Jonathan Wilkenfeld, *A Study of Crisis* (Ann Arbor: University of Michigan Press, 1997), p. 3.

2. For a systematic formulation of hypotheses empirically demonstrated see Glenn D. Paige, *The Korean Decision, June 14–30, 1950* (New York: Free Press, 1968), chap. 11.

3. See Chen Jian, "China's Involvement in the Vietnam War, 1964–69," *China Quarterly* 142 (June 1995), pp. 356–387; Allen S. Whiting, *The Chinese Calculus of Deterrence: India and Indochina* (Ann Arbor: University of Michigan, Center for Chinese Studies, 2001), chap. 6.

4. Paige, *The Korean Decision,* provides the most complete description and analysis of this case study.

5. Rosemary Foot, *The Wrong War: American Policy and the Dimensions of the Korean Conflict, 1950–1953* (Ithaca, N.Y.: Cornell University Press, 1985), p. 75, citing National Security Council directive 81/l. Foot's analysis of Washington's decisions during the initial stages of the Chinese intervention reflects thorough research in U.S. and British archives and provides a main basis for this chapter. She provides full citations throughout, which are not repeated here.

6. K. M. Panikkar, *In Two Chinas: Memoirs of a Diplomat* (London: Allen and Unwin, 1955), p. 108.

7. Zhou Enlai to the Central People's Government Council, *People's China,* vol. 2, no. 8, October 16, 1950, in Allen S. Whiting, *China Crosses The Yalu: The Decision to Enter the Korean War* (New York: Macmillan, 1960), p. 108. Zhou continued at length to demonstrate that "the U.S. government has displayed itself as the most dangerous foe to the PRC."

8. Panikkar, *In Two Chinas,* p. 110.

9. Dean Acheson, *Present at the Creation: My Years in the State Department* (New York: Norton and Co., 1969), p. 452.

10. Foot, *The Wrong War,* p. 79.

11. Clubb had been the last consul general in Beijing before the Korean War; he left in April 1950.

12. Foot, *The Wrong War,* pp. 74–87, traces this view in detail.

13. Acheson, *Present at the Creation,* pp. 452–453.

14. Ibid., p. 453.

15. Ibid., p. 465.

16. William Stueck, *The Korean War: An International History* (Princeton, N.J.: Princeton University Press, 1995), p. 114. The author draws extensively

on *Foreign Relations of the United States, 1950*, vol. 7 (Korea) (Washington: D.C., U.S. Government Printing Office, 1976) in addition to other sources. Full citations are not repeated here.

17. Ibid., p. 115.

18. In late December, a three-person team arriving in Tokyo found evidence showing much larger Chinese forces already in Korea by mid-November than had been reported. S. L. A. Marshall, a member of the team, recounted in a personal interview with the author that Major General Courtney Whitney, longtime aid to MacArthur, showed this file to the group and claimed Major General Charles Willoughby, an intelligence officer, had kept the evidence from MacArthur to remain in MacArthur's favor, ahead of Whitney. In his memoir, Whitney does not allude to the gross discrepancy between the Tokyo estimates and the later encounter with more than 200,000 Chinese. Courtney Whitney, *MacArthur: His Rendezvous With History* (New York: Alfred A. Knopf, 1956). In the third week of November, the Far East Command put Chinese forces between 70,051 and 44,851; James McGovern, *To The Yalu: From The Chinese Invasion of Korea to MacArthur's Dismissal* (New York: William Morrow and Company, 1972), p. 90.

19. Stueck, *The Korean War*, pp. 112–113. A G-2 is a U.S. Army intelligence officer who is assigned to a general's staff.

20. Foot, *The Wrong War*, p. 98.

21. Whitney, *MacArthur*, p. 419.

22. Ibid., p. 117.

23. Acheson, *Present at the Creation*, p. 468.

24. Foot, *The Wrong War*, p. 101.

25. Stueck, *The Korean War*, pp. 138–142.

26. Acheson, *Present at the Creation*, pp. 472.

27. Stueck, *The Korean War*, p. 134.

28. Acheson, *Present at the Creation*, p. 474.

29. Ibid., p. 514.

30. Foot, *The Wrong War*, p. 114.

31. Ibid., p. 117.

32. Ibid., p. 129.

33. Ibid., pp. 129–130.

34. Dean Rusk and Richard Rusk, *As I Saw It* (New York: Norton and Company, 1990), pp. 456–457.

35. David M. Barrett, *Uncertain Warriors: Lyndon Johnson and His Vietnam Advisers* (Lawrence: University of Kansas, 1993), presents the most carefully based study.

36. Jack Valenti, *A Very Human President* (New York: Norton and Company, 1975). Valenti's notes provide more information for the historian than his memoir.

37. Radio intercepts, in particular, identified PLA units in North Vietnam beginning in late 1965; analysis of the intercepts was limited to high officials.

38. Valenti, *A Very Human President*, pp. 84–85.

39. Kai Bird, *The Color of Truth: McGeorge Bundy and William Bundy: Brothers in Arms* (New York: Simon and Schuster, 1998), p. 337. After examining the sequence of debate and papers generated by the Bundy brothers and Ball in mid-1966, Bird concludes, "In retrospect, it seems clear that the president's mind was already made up," and "what followed in the ensuing weeks was not careful deliberation but a charade . . . [with] his Wise Men."

40. Harold P. Ford, *CIA and the Vietnam Policymakers: Three Episodes: 1962–1968* (Washington, D.C.: Center for the Study of Intelligence, 1998), p. 48.

41. Office of National Estimates, CIA; and Office for Research, Far East, Bureau of Intelligence and Research (INR), U.S. Department of State. I headed this INR office at the time.

42. SNIE 50-2-64, May 25, 1964, in *Pentagon Papers: The Defense Department History of United States Decisionmaking on Vietnam*, Senator Gravel Edition, vol. 3 (Boston: Beacon Press, 1971), pp. 378–380.

43. Ibid.

44. *Peking Review*, no. 32, August 7, 1964.

45. SNIE 10-3-64, a compendium of INR files on the Vietnam War, publication forthcoming; hereafter: INR Compendium.

46. *The Joint Chiefs of Staff and the War in Vietnam, 1960–1968, Part 1* (Washington, D.C.: Department of Defense, n.d.), chap. 13, pp. 10–12; hereafter: *JCS History*.

47. INR Compendium, RFE-64-257, November 28, 1964, emphasized that the airfield was only a few miles from the border and therefore more appropriate for forward defense of Vietnam than of China; in addition, recent deployment of jets to South China and evidence of Sino-Vietnamese air defense cooperation "strongly suggests" this "may be preparatory to providing air defense for the Hanoi-Haiphong area against U.S. air attacks."

48. For a graphic and detailed reconstruction of Bundy's reaction, see Bird, *Color of Truth*, pp. 306–308.

49. INR Compendium, SNIE 10-3-65 and SNIE 10.3/1-65.

50. Whiting, *Chinese Calculus of Deterrence*, pp. 176–177.

51. INR Compendium.

52. Ibid., SDG-65-0071.

53. Ibid.; also Allen S. Whiting, "Asian Communist Reaction to U.S. Escalation in Vietnam," March 26, 1965.

54. Details in Whiting, *Chinese Calculus of Deterrence,* pp. 178–179.

55. Personal query to the author while serving with INR, April 9, 1965.

56. Michael Beschloss, *Reaching for Glory: Lyndon Johnson's Secret White House Tapes, 1964–1965* (New York: Simon and Schuster, 2001), pp. 274–276.

57. JCS message to CINCPAC, 009294/170122Z April 1965, from Lyndon Baines Johnson Library and Museum, personal files of Robert McNamara on deposit with the National Security Archive, Washington, D.C. Italics in original.

58. INR Compendium, SNIE 10-5-65, April 28, 1965. INR footnoted that the Chinese ground response "will come . . . very soon after continuation of such retaliatory strikes."

59. Ibid., SNIE 10-6-65, June 2, 1965.

60. Bird, *Color of Truth*, pp. 332–328, gives a full description and analysis of exchanges among the highest participants and the outcome.

61. U.S. Department of Defense memorandum, July 1, 1965, from Lyndon Baines Johnson Library and Museum, personal files of Robert McNamara on deposit with the National Security Archive, Washington, D.C. Underline in original.

62. McGeorge Bundy memorandums, July 1, 1965; U.S. Department of Defense memorandum, July 1, 1965; from Lyndon Baines Johnson Library and Museum, personal files of Robert McNamara on deposit with the National Security Archive, Washington, D.C.

63. Valenti, *A Very Human President*, pp. 348–349.

64. INR Compendium, SNIE 10-9-65, July 23, 1965. Italics in original.

65. *JCS History.*

66. Ibid., SNIE 10-11-65, September 22, 1965.

67. INR Compendium, "China and the War in Vietnam," Radio Free Europe, December 5, 1965; this "did not yet foreshadow an immediate Chinese intervention, either in the air or with ground combat troops . . . but the indicators are converging."

68. INR Compendium, SNIE 10-12-65, December 10, 1965.

69. William Conrad Gibbons, *The U.S. Government and the Vietnam War: Executive and Legislative Relationships* (Princeton, N.J.: Princeton University Press, 1995), part 4, pp. 193–195.

70. Walt W. Rostow, *A Diffusion of Power* (New York: Macmillan, 1972), p. 286.

71. *JCS History,* "Operating Instructions Which Impose Operating Limitations in North Vietnam (From current CINCPAC Basic OP ORDER)."

72. Whiting, *Chinese Calculus of Deterrence,* p. 179.

7

U.S. "Management" of Three
Taiwan Strait "Crises"

Robert L. Suettinger

THIS CHAPTER WILL DISCUSS THREE so-called crises that affected relations between the People's Republic of China (PRC) and the United States over issues related to Taiwan, focusing in particular on how the executive branch of the U.S. government "managed" the complex issues involved. There may be some question about whether all three events actually constituted crises. Certainly in comparison with decision making during the Korean War, the Vietnam conflict, or the Iraq action, the Taiwan Strait disputes seem less significant. Nor would it necessarily be accurate to judge that the reason they did not escalate into open conflict was effective crisis management by one side or the other.

However, taking a generic definition of crisis as an unexpected situation that threatens high-value goals of decision makers and offers a short time for response, I examine how these events were handled by the Eisenhower and Clinton administrations as exercises in crisis management. My methodology is relatively straightforward: First, I describe key events and decisions in chronological order. Next, I evaluate the impact of a specific set of variables, namely (1) principal decision makers, including the president and the president's foreign policy advisers; (2) principal bureaucracies (especially Department of State, Department of Defense, the Joint Chiefs of Staff [JCS], and the National Security Council [NSC]) and procedures; (3) the general state of bilateral relations and communications between the United States and China; (4) domestic U.S. politics, including the roles of Congress, the media, and public opinion; and (5) the impact of other foreign policy issues, especially the actions of the government of the Republic of China (ROC, or Taiwan), and including the views of key U.S. allies. In the conclusions, I offer some judgments on the crisis management process of the U.S. government and the development of the process over time.

FIRST OFFSHORE ISLANDS CRISIS, AUGUST 1954–MAY 1955

The domestic political background strongly influenced how the administration of President Dwight D. Eisenhower handled the first offshore islands crisis in August 1954. Eisenhower became president during a period of intense anticommunism. Although Eisenhower himself was not an ideologue, strong voices within the Republican Party urged an offensive against what they called "world communism." Eisenhower's secretary of state, John Foster Dulles, spoke early and often of "rolling back" the Iron Curtain. Meanwhile, since the late 1940s, various members of Congress had charged that certain State Department China specialists were procommunist, and several specialists were suspended from duty. In October 1953, Senator Joseph R. McCarthy (R-Wis.) charged in open hearings that communists had infiltrated the military. Eisenhower was outraged but powerless to stop the public relations furor that surrounded McCarthy's sensational charges.

In March 1953, Eisenhower approved a reorganization of the NSC staff. Eisenhower wanted a more efficient, cohesive policy review staff responsible to the president, and he asked Robert Cutler, whom he appointed special assistant for national security affairs, to oversee this project. Eisenhower also wrestled with a military leadership that was the product of intense interservice rivalries and congressional political battles. Like the NSC, the JCS and the Department of Defense were created by the National Security Act of 1947. The act was amended in 1949 to strengthen the role of the secretary of defense and to establish a chairman of the JCS to preside over JCS deliberations, assist with policy-making recommendations, and notify the secretary and the president in case of major disagreements. The chairman did not have a vote, nor did he have command authority, but he was politically influential by virtue of having regular access to the president. On August 15, 1953, Admiral Arthur W. Radford, former commander of the U.S. Pacific Fleet, became chairman of the JCS.[1]

Final arrangements for the armistice ending the Korean War and attempts to prevent the collapse of French forces fighting against communist insurgents in Vietnam dominated Asia policy in the early years of Eisenhower's first term. Following the May defeat of French forces at Dien Bien Phu by Viet Minh guerrillas, an agreement at the Geneva Conference on Indochina divided Vietnam at the 17th parallel, pending free elections in 1955. The conference was perhaps most memorable for John Foster Dulles's refusal to shake hands with Premier Zhou Enlai.

In this context, the offshore islands crisis gathered momentum relatively quickly. In December 1953, the ROC, under informal U.S. protection since the Korean War, formally presented Washington with a draft of a mutual defense treaty. The U.S. State Department began redrafting it in order to avoid an obligation of U.S. forces to help defend the offshore islands.[2] At the same time, however, ROC and PRC air and naval forces began skirmishing near the Dachen (Tachen) Islands, off the coast of Zhejiang Province. These skirmishes effectively prevented further consideration of the treaty because Washington was wary of signing a defense agreement with a country already engaged in active combat. Once the fighting died down, negotiations resumed in early July 1954.

On July 16, *People's Daily*, the official newspaper of the Chinese Communist Party, accused Washington of seeking to sign a mutual defense treaty with the ROC that would link up with other treaty commitments in Asia. It warned of "protracted grave consequences" if it was signed. Eisenhower told reporters a few days later that a mutual defense treaty with Taiwan was "under consideration" but had not yet been decided. On July 24, a *People's Daily* editorial proclaimed, "The Chinese people once more declare to the whole world that Taiwan is China's territory and they are determined to liberate it."[3]

There is no indication that Washington fully understood the role that the mutual defense treaty played in the PRC-ROC civil war or that the treaty was about to become a casus belli. Eisenhower and Dulles evidently saw PRC pressure on Taiwan as just another instance of communist aggression that they must resist. In mid-August, the NSC began consideration of NSC 5429, a review of U.S. policy in the Far East. The draft contained several alternative approaches, ranging from treating China on the same footing as Russia, to seeking a reduction of Chinese power by means short of war, to using force to prevent any further communist expansion in Asia. Eisenhower postponed a decision, pending a report from Dulles after Dulles traveled to the region.[4]

In early August, the ROC president, Chiang Kai-shek, had moved 58,000 troops to Quemoy (also known as Chin-men, Kinmen, or Jinmen), an island two miles off the PRC port city of Xiamen (Hsiamen or Amoy), and 12,000 soldiers to the Matsu (also known as Mazu) Islands, off the Fujian coast near Fuzhou. Responding to further PRC threats, Eisenhower quipped publicly that any invasion of Taiwan "will have to run over the [U.S. Navy's] Seventh Fleet."[5] Eisenhower entertained serious doubts about the defensibility of the offshore islands, however, and he continued to temporize on signing the treaty out of concern that the United States could be drawn into a conflict it could not win.

On September 3, PRC artillery opened a massive barrage on Quemoy, firing perhaps as many as 5,000 shells. Two U.S. military officers were among those killed. The United States immediately ordered three carrier battle groups of the Seventh Fleet to the Taiwan region for training maneuvers.[6] The ROC military, with U.S. concurrence, began shelling Xiamen and attacking it with aircraft.

On September 9, Vice President Richard Nixon chaired an NSC meeting to discuss the Quemoy situation, but in the absence of Eisenhower (on vacation in Colorado) and Dulles (in Manila), no decisions were reached. That same day, Dulles conferred with Chiang Kai-shek in Taipei but made no formal commitments because of persistent concerns about the offshore islands' defensibility.[7]

Eisenhower convened a special NSC meeting on September 12 at Lowry Air Force Base, outside Denver, to discuss the situation. The joint chiefs were divided, with hawks advocating giving U.S. forces the option of attacking mainland targets, using nuclear weapons if necessary. General Matthew Ridgway and Secretary of Defense Charles Wilson dissented. Dulles and Eisenhower talked of the "horrible dilemma" posed by the situation because ROC morale and U.S. prestige would suffer if the islands were lost, but they questioned whether morale and prestige were worth a general war with China that could include nuclear weapons. Eisenhower proposed seeking congressional approval for action to support the ROC and agreed with Dulles's proposal to freeze the situation by obtaining a United Nations (UN) Security Council cease-fire resolution.[8]

In late September, with U.S. concurrence, ROC forces reduced military action against Xiamen; PRC forces reciprocated by reducing the shelling of Quemoy. The U.S. Navy ended its maneuvers in the area and ordered ROC air attacks on mainland targets to stop.[9] In October, conciliatory gestures by both sides led to a near cessation of hostilities. Negotiations on the mutual defense treaty continued. At an October 28 NSC meeting, Dulles recommended that the United States seek a restrictive U.S.-ROC defense treaty that would exclude the offshore islands. The JCS opposed the recommendation, preferring a unilateral (nontreaty) commitment that would include the offshore islands.[10] After Republicans lost control of Congress during midterm elections on November 2, Eisenhower approved Dulles's proposal for a limited defense treaty and his recommendation to seek a UN cease-fire resolution.

Dulles and the ambassador from the ROC, K. C. Yeh, initialed the agreed text of the U.S.-Taiwan Mutual Defense Treaty and an exchange of notes on November 23, 1954. The treaty applied specifically to Taiwan and the Penghu Islands (also known as the Pescadores) as well as to "such other territories as may be determined by mutual consent"; thus it dodged the question of the offshore islands. The notes became a binding commitment that ROC military forces would not initiate offensive actions against the PRC without U.S. consent.[11]

On the same day, PRC courts sentenced to long prison terms eleven U.S. airmen whose leaflet-dropping aircraft had been downed over northern China in January 1953. U.S. reaction was sharp and emotional, with some members of Congress calling for a naval blockade of China and seizure of Chinese ships.[12] The final treaty was signed on December 2 and was immediately denounced by PRC media as "open occupation of China's territory" by the United States. Zhou Enlai warned of "grave consequences" if the United States did not withdraw its military forces from Taiwan. PRC artillery recommended heavy shelling of the Quemoy garrisons.[13]

The NSC reviewed Eisenhower's overall policy toward East Asia in late December, resulting in a policy of continuing pressure toward the

PRC but with a more carefully calibrated approach to the use of military force. The United States would strive to disrupt the Sino-Soviet alliance, "reduce Communist Chinese power and prestige," and defend its Asian interests "if necessary at the risk but without being provocative of war." The revised U.S. policy even kept open the option of reaching negotiated settlements with the PRC government.[14]

The crisis escalated in early January 1955, when PRC airplanes attacked the Dachen Islands again. On January 18, PRC troops launched an amphibious assault on the island of Yikiangshan (Yijiangshan), in the Yuchen Islands north of the Dachens, capturing the island in two hours.[15] The following day, Eisenhower, Dulles, and Radford agreed on a new approach, which involved the U.S.-assisted evacuation of all the offshore islands except Quemoy; a strengthened commitment to the defense of Quemoy, at least until a UN cease-fire could be arranged; and a request for a broad congressional mandate for military action by U.S. forces. Dulles presented the plan—he included Matsu among the islands to defend—to the NSC, where it was heavily criticized by Cutler, Wilson, and Secretary of the Treasury George M. Humphrey. Eisenhower supported the plan, however, noting that both Nationalist Chinese morale and U.S. credibility depended on the safekeeping of the principal offshore garrisons.[16] Two days later, the NSC formally approved the U.S.-assisted evacuation of the Dachens and a strengthened U.S. commitment to the defense of Quemoy and Matsu.

On January 24, Eisenhower sent a message to Congress with a draft of what would become known as the Formosa Resolution. Portraying PRC military actions since September 1954 as a "serious danger to the security of our country and of the entire Pacific area and indeed to the peace of the world," the draft resolution authorized the use of U.S. armed forces for

> . . . securing and protecting Formosa and the Pescadores [Penghu Islands] against armed attack, this authority to include the securing and protecting of such related positions and territories of that area now in friendly hands and the taking of such other measures as he [the president] judges to be required or appropriate in assuring the defense of Formosa and the Pescadores.[17]

It passed quickly, giving Eisenhower blanket freedom of action in the Taiwan Strait.[18] Beijing denounced the resolution as a "bare-faced war cry."

Chiang Kai-shek, angry at the U.S. refusal to publicly state its determination to actively defend Matsu, at first declined to order the evacuation of the Dachen Islands. But after private reassurances from Eisenhower and the U.S. Senate's ratification of the U.S.-ROC Mutual Defense Treaty on February 9, Chiang formally requested U.S. evacuation assistance. Shortly afterward, the islands were occupied by PRC troops.[19]

En route to a meeting with Chiang Kai-shek in early March, Dulles was alarmed by briefings from the Pacific Fleet Command about PRC preparations to attack Quemoy and Matsu, and he warned Eisenhower that preemptive action by Nationalist forces might be necessary to prevent a situation that would involve U.S. forces in combat, perhaps requiring the use of nuclear weapons.[20] During a private meeting with Dulles, Eisenhower suggested that the secretary raise with the NSC the issue of using tactical nuclear weapons in defending Quemoy and Matsu. This Dulles did on March 10, suggesting that ROC forces might not hold out effectively against a concerted Chinese attack and that U.S. forces might need to use nuclear weapons to attack PRC rear support areas.[21]

Dulles made the threat public at a press conference on March 15, observing that the United States was "prepared to use tactical nuclear weapons in response to a major communist move in the Taiwan area." The next day, Eisenhower, at a press conference, confirmed he would use tactical atomic weapons if there were war in the Far East.[22] After a delay of several days, Beijing accused Washington of practicing "atomic diplomacy."

As war jitters grew in Washington, the chairman of the JCS, Admiral Radford, developed a proposal to give China a "bloody nose," beginning with a private threat to "take all necessary steps" to protect Taiwan, followed by an upgrade of U.S. forces in the region. Eisenhower, however, remained determined to keep the policy process under his own control. Promising his press secretary he would "just confuse" the U.S. press about the situation in the Taiwan Strait, Eisenhower dodged a question at his March 23 news conference on the potential use of nuclear weapons.[23]

But tensions continued to rise. On March 25, the chief of naval operations, Admiral Robert B. Carney, told reporters that the president was planning to "destroy Red China's military potential" and suggested war might begin by mid-April.[24] At an NSC meeting at the end of the month, Admiral Radford outlined a robust plan to use tactical nuclear weapons to bomb Chinese airfields while mining and blockading Chinese ports in case of an attack on ROC forward positions. Even Dulles registered alarm at the plan, while Eisenhower warned against "underestimating the sanity of the Chinese Communists." No decision was made about Radford's plans.[25]

In response to continuing public outcry, Eisenhower began to back away from threatening rhetoric.[26] On April 1, he met privately with Dulles; Radford; Wilson; Humphrey; his personal aide, Colonel Andrew Goodpaster; and several others to discuss an effort to persuade Chiang to withdraw voluntarily from the offshore islands, perhaps in exchange for stationing a division of U.S. Marines on Taiwan.[27] They decided to dispatch Radford and Assistant Secretary of State for Far Eastern Affairs Walter Robertson to Taipei to convince Chiang that neither U.S. nor ROC interests would be served by a "full out" defense of Quemoy and Matsu. Eisenhower wanted Chiang to consider withdrawing most civilians and reducing troop presence to a minimum and was even prepared to blockade southern China in return for such an evacuation.[28]

Zhou Enlai rendered moot the Radford-Robertson mission—unsuccessful, in any case—at the April 18–24 Asian-African Conference in Bandung, Indonesia. Zhou publicly stated:

> [T]he Chinese people do not want to have a war with the United States of America. The Chinese government is willing to sit down and enter into negotiations with the U.S. government to discuss the question of relaxing tension in the Far East, and especially the question of relaxing tension in the Taiwan area.[29]

U.S. observers were quick to recognize an easing of the PRC position and urged the U.S. government to respond positively.

Although the administration's response was slow and ambiguous, tensions in the region abated quickly, particularly as U.S. military officials refused to allow ROC aircraft to bomb mainland targets after mid-April. Artillery exchanges tapered off, and Dulles rejected Chiang's complaints about limiting his freedom of action. On July 31, 1955, just before representatives of the United States and PRC were to meet in Geneva to discuss "issues of mutual concern," Beijing released the eleven airmen sentenced to prison in 1954. Although begun with high hopes, the talks themselves were not very productive and were stalemated within six months.

U.S. Policymaking Considerations

PERSONALITIES. There is little doubt that President Eisenhower and Secretary of State John Foster Dulles played the key decision-making roles throughout this crisis. Although Dulles was long considered the more forceful, and therefore more influential, player in the foreign policy apparatus, careful studies based on documentary evidence make abundantly clear that the president was fully involved in the key decision points, such as the September 12, 1954, NSC meeting in Denver; the March NSC meetings that raised the possibility of using nuclear weapons against China; and the April efforts, though ineffectual, to defuse the crisis.

Eisenhower had enormous experience and interest in foreign affairs. Innately cautious, a consensus builder, and a believer in staff work and proper procedures, the former commander of Allied forces in Europe during World War II also understood the need to avoid recklessly pushing for war. In the face of often surprisingly confrontational policy recommendations from the JCS, Eisenhower maintained a measured approach, recognizing the damage to other national values that war would cause. Lacking good intelligence about the goals of Chinese (or Soviet) leaders, Eisenhower assumed they were more pragmatic and less prone to fanatical action than some U.S. ideologues argued. After careful efforts to restructure the NSC, Eisenhower was conscientious about attending its meetings, and he devoted more time to foreign affairs issues than any other.[30]

Eisenhower understood the value of maintaining U.S. policy initiative and of keeping U.S. adversaries guessing about how the United

States would react to various situations in the Taiwan Strait. He consciously sought to create doubt about U.S. intentions, so as to keep decision-making options open for as long as possible. Thus, he resisted putting on paper any solid commitment to use U.S. military forces for the defense of the offshore islands. He also wanted the PRC and its Russian allies to have doubts (and disagreements) about whether the United States would use nuclear weapons in the Far East. One biographer noted: "Throughout this crisis the president maintained his stance of strategic ambiguity and in so doing made indecision—or at least the appearance of indecision—his ally."[31] Revisionist biographer Robert A. Divine enthused, "The beauty of Eisenhower's policy is that to this day no one can be sure whether or not he would have responded militarily to an invasion of the offshore islands, and whether he would have used nuclear weapons."[32]

Less generous critics might argue, however, that Eisenhower had only a limited understanding of Asian affairs, still less of China, and subscribed readily to ideologically based assessments of the PRC as aggressive, fanatical, and totally hostile to the United States and its interests. Even his proposals for solutions to the crisis, though perhaps suitable from a purely military perspective, were politically naive. Moreover, there is little evidence to suggest that the confusion that might have been sown in Moscow, Beijing, or even Taipei actually worked to U.S. advantage.

John Foster Dulles was perhaps better schooled in Asian affairs, but his rigid anticommunist perspectives colored his policy approaches throughout his tenure as secretary of state. He was more attuned to the sentiments of extreme Republicans in Congress than to his own department. On those occasions when members of Congress attacked specific individuals in the State Department, Dulles seemed to side with the political critics against his own staff. A lawyer by profession, Dulles was intellectually sharper than Eisenhower; he was also less risk averse and more ideological, and he tended to make policy pronouncements in freewheeling press conferences with reporters. But he had a very close and loyal relationship with Eisenhower.

Dulles was an indefatigable maneuverer and negotiator, willing to go to extraordinary lengths to pursue U.S. goals and strengthen alliances. He was not a pragmatist; he was a man who pressed both allies and adversaries alike with a strong sense of moral commitment, particularly his resistance to communism. Dulles did not enjoy especially good personal relations with either his counterparts or his subordinates, who found him rigid, suspicious, and even cruel.[33]

Other individuals who significantly influenced Eisenhower's foreign policy inclinations included Admiral Arthur Radford, chairman of the JCS (and former commander of U.S. forces in the Pacific); Defense Secretary Charles E. Wilson; Treasury Secretary George M. Humphrey; and Robert Cutler, who was special assistant for national security affairs during Eisenhower's first term. Colonel Andrew Goodpaster, Eisenhower's strategic and policy staff secretary, undertook many private information-gathering missions for the president, and many believed him to have more influence on the president than Cutler did.

BUREAUCRACIES. Throughout much of this crisis, the State Department was under heavy criticism from the right wing of the Republican Party for being riddled with communist sympathizers. Many blamed the department, and particularly former secretary of state Dean Acheson, for "losing" China by not supporting the Nationalist Party (Kuomintang or KMT) sufficiently and for causing the Korean War through misunderstanding of the stakes involved.[34] The State Department suffered from low morale and wielded little influence bureaucratically, aside from that commanded by Dulles and some key aides. Certainly, many exceptional foreign service officers contributed to both Dulles's expertise and the NSC-run policy planning process, but there were few, if any, points during the management of this crisis where the State Department rather than the secretary played a meaningful role.

Likewise, the Department of Defense was not a key player in the crisis management process. Although Secretary Wilson was considered close to the president, he did not parlay that into influence in decision-making councils. His department, strengthened at the beginning of Eisenhower's first term, was still finding its bureaucratic feet, and the Office of the Secretary of Defense (OSD) was still rather small and inexperienced.[35] Wilson's attention was focused mainly on establishing principles of civilian control of the armed forces, managing the downsizing of U.S. military forces after the Korean War, and establishing a dependable budgeting process. He tended to defer policy issues to the JCS. On those occasions when his views did register, it is clear that Wilson was a sharp critic of Chiang Kai-shek, a deep skeptic about the advisability of defending the offshore islands, and very dubious of JCS aggressiveness.[36]

The JCS played a very prominent role in this crisis. Created in the image of the Joint Staff of World War II, the JCS reflected postwar interservice rivalries. National security planners and many military leaders themselves recognized the need for a centralized command structure for U.S. military forces and for centralized control of the military budget. But strong-willed military officers from various services—particularly the Navy—were unwilling to give up control of their particular resources and lobbied hard with conservative Republicans in Congress to block the establishment of a unified command structure.[37]

Eisenhower disliked the organizational structure of the JCS and tried unsuccessfully to change it. During the Taiwan crisis, he was also having a sharp disagreement with his military chiefs about the defense budget, particularly in getting them to reduce military expenditures so as to focus government efforts on developing the U.S. economy.[38] He often disregarded specific policy recommendations of the JCS, either because they represented the fractured and parochial interests of the different services or because he disagreed with their aggressive advocacy of the use of U.S. military power. Eisenhower was particularly wary of allowing the military to have independent control over decisions to use tactical nuclear weapons, a power he believed should remain presidential. Notwithstanding his disagreements with his military advisers, Eisenhower recognized he needed their support to carry out U.S. policy, and he believed—correctly—that he knew how to control them.

The NSC was clearly Eisenhower's preferred bureaucracy for the consideration and formulation of foreign policy decisions. Eisenhower's system was created by Robert Cutler in a series of exchanges and papers from December 1952 to March 1953. Cutler recommended a more structured organization and process because he knew that Eisenhower "had a penchant for careful staff work and believed that effective planning involved a creative process of debate among advisers compelled to work toward agreed recommendations."[39]

Cutler, who became the first assistant to the president for national security affairs (APNSA), replaced the former NSC senior staff with a policy planning board comprising individuals at the assistant secretary level nominated by the official members of the NSC.[40] Cutler saw the proper role of the APNSA as a facilitator. The planning board, chaired by the APNSA and meeting twice weekly, tasked and reviewed policy recommendation papers prepared by the Departments of State and Defense. The NSC itself, which Eisenhower personally chaired, met weekly. These meetings usually began with an intelligence briefing by the director of central intelligence, followed by a discussion of the planning board's policy papers. Decision proposals went to the president in the form of "NSC Actions," and, after approval, they went to the Operations Coordinating Board of the NSC for implementation. The Operations Coordinating Board met weekly at the State Department and was composed of the APNSA, the under secretary of state for political affairs, the deputy secretary of defense, and a number of other senior officials. It created interagency working groups for various policy areas.[41]

The prominence of the NSC is reflected in the fact that, during the 1954–1955 offshore islands crisis, the NSC discussed the issue at twenty-one separate weekly meetings.[42] It is important to note, however, that the Eisenhower NSC was not itself a decision-making or crisis management organization, nor did it involve itself directly in policy implementation. Eisenhower made all key decisions alone or in consultation with key advisers. NSC meetings were critical, however, for the circulation of information, the airing of departmental views and disagreements, and the education of key policy makers. Eisenhower later wrote: "To my mind, the secret of a sound, satisfactory decision made on an emergency basis has always been that the responsible official has been 'living with the problem' before it becomes acute." He advised John F. Kennedy that the NSC was "the most important weekly meeting of the government."[43]

Later critics of the Eisenhower NSC noted that it was a prisoner of rigidly bureaucratic processes, with formal agendas, weekly meetings, and coordinated policy papers. Critics also believed its composition—most staff were senior officials from various bureaucracies—discouraged innovation and squelched new policy approaches. The NSC was not designed to operate as an independent policy actor, and it did not do so during the Eisenhower administration. The more powerful, free-wheeling NSC was a product of later presidents.

Although several of the policy-relevant intelligence publications from this period are available through the *Foreign Relations of the United States* series, there are too many gaps in the public record to allow for a comprehensive evaluation of the role intelligence played in the development and resolution of this crisis. A few general observations may be pertinent, however. It is important to note that the director of central intelligence was Allen Dulles, younger brother of Secretary of State John Foster Dulles, and that the two maintained very close contact during their respective tenures. Allen Dulles also had good relations with Eisenhower, who accorded the Central Intelligence Agency (CIA) considerable leeway in operational matters.

At key points during the crisis, national intelligence estimates (NIEs) and special national intelligence estimates (SNIEs) played important roles in providing NSC policy makers with the facts, analysis, and predictions of future developments regarding Taiwan and the PRC. Issued by the Office of National Estimates of the CIA, they were the product of interagency drafting and coordination, based on the best intelligence information available at that time, and were specifically intended to address topics of current policy interest.[44]

COMMUNICATIONS WITH CHINA. The United States and the PRC had no form of direct communication during this first crisis period. Diplomatic relations had not been established, nor were there interests sections in the embassies of other nations. Diplomats from both sides studiously avoided each other in capitals where both had representation. Both travel and economic contacts were highly restricted. Speeches and papers by U.S. policy makers were filled with Cold War rhetoric and were hostile toward communists in general and to "Red China" in particular. PRC leaders displayed similarly ideological hostility.

Washington seemed to alternate between a form of megaphone diplomacy, issuing loud and very public threats, and strategic ambiguity, keeping both Beijing and Taipei in the dark about when and under what circumstances the United States would use military force in Taiwan's defense. Particularly in March 1955, when Dulles and Eisenhower became worried about eroding morale in Taiwan and felt pressure from the JCS to authorize the use of nuclear weapons against PRC targets, both men made very public statements about using tactical nuclear weapons to defend Taiwan. Eisenhower even compared tactical nuclear weapons with conventional weapons, at least until he received an intelligence estimate later that month suggesting even using tactical nuclear weapons might cause 12 to 14 million casualties on the mainland.[45] Some U.S. scholars believe the public threat to use nuclear weapons to defend Taiwan played a significant role in persuading Beijing to call off the crisis the following month although that judgment cannot be confirmed.[46]

DOMESTIC POLITICS. One of America's most effective "political generals" during World War II, Eisenhower as president continued to display sensitivity to partisan politics, public opinion, bureaucratic rivalries, and interpersonal relationships. As a member of a Republican Party badly divided between ultraconservatives and what might be called moderates in the political center, Eisenhower carefully placated the right while he simultaneously attempted to undermine the influence of ultraconservatives and maintain steady and moderate domestic and foreign policy courses.

Perhaps because of the Republican loss of Congress, Eisenhower submitted his proposal for military action in the Taiwan Strait to Congress for approval in January 1955, just after the new legislators were sworn in and before more concerted opposition to his foreign policy plans could coalesce. Despite some reservations within the Democratic Party leadership about the wisdom of staking U.S. prestige on defending the "indefensible" offshore islands, Eisenhower won easy approval for his flexible and noncommittal plans.

Congress at that time was heavily influenced by what became known as the China lobby, operating through the Committee of One Million. As Sadako Ogata writes:

The China lobby was a complex association of individuals and groups whose common purpose was to secure the backing and support of the United States for the Nationalist government of Chiang Kai-shek. At the "inner core" were those Chinese and Americans "whose personal interests were immediately dependent upon a continuation of U.S. aid to Chiang." The others consisted of "a kaleidoscopic array of affiliates who . . . included . . . anticommunists, those who had missionary interests in China, or those who seized on the issue to fight against the Roosevelt and Truman administrations."[47]

After Dulles and Eisenhower raised the stakes in the strait by threatening nuclear retaliation, public support for U.S. defense of the offshore islands—within both the media and Congress—diminished, perhaps reinforcing the president's own doubts about the wisdom of committing U.S. nuclear forces to a nonessential objective. Although the final phase of the crisis happened too quickly for public doubts to become part of Eisenhower's decision-making agenda, they would play a greater role in the second iteration of the crisis.

FOREIGN AND TAIWAN FACTORS. Some intermediaries tried to facilitate communications between Beijing and Washington. During visits to Beijing, India's prime minister, Jawaharlal Nehru, and the UN secretary-general, Dag Hammarskjöld, tried to ameliorate tensions. Dulles distrusted both, however, and largely ignored their efforts. England was the foreign government with the most influence on Washington's thinking. Prime Minister Winston Churchill and President Eisenhower kept up a lively correspondence during the early phases of the crisis. Likewise, Foreign Secretary Anthony Eden exerted considerable personal and policy influence on John Foster Dulles, although the two men were not personally close. England, taking particular exception to U.S. threats to use nuclear weapons, advised caution throughout the crisis.

ROC Generalissimo Chiang Kai-shek played a key role in the development of the 1954–1955 crisis. Although completely dependent on U.S. military support for his regime's survival, Chiang managed to shape U.S. policies and perceptions. Despite being openly disliked and distrusted by many influential Washington policy makers, Chiang maintained strong support within Congress through the actions and funding of the China lobby. Two key policy makers, Arthur Radford of the JCS and Walter Robertson, assistant secretary of state for Far Eastern affairs, were considered personally close to Chiang.

Chiang could be said, at least in part, to have precipitated the crisis by heavily manning the vulnerable garrisons in the Dachens, Matsu, and Quemoy offshore islands and using them to carry out espionage and subversion missions against coastal areas on the mainland. His strong push for a mutual defense treaty, in the view of some analysts, may have been one of the reasons for the initial PRC attack on Quemoy in September 1954. Chiang also wielded influence by refusing to go along with Eisenhower administration initiatives. His staunch refusal to abandon the offshore islands despite the ROC's admitted inability to defend them, his rejection of proposals for a UN-mandated cease-fire, and his rebuff of Eisenhower's proposal for a drawdown of ROC forces on Quemoy and Matsu in return for increased U.S. force deployments on Taiwan and a blockade of some mainland ports all restricted Eisenhower's policy options and set the stage for future crises.

Conclusions

One cannot credibly describe the Eisenhower administration's handling of the 1954 Taiwan Strait crisis as a masterpiece of crisis management. Seldom knowledgeable of what either Beijing or Taipei was planning, the U.S. government seemed sometimes to act almost without guidance or purpose. Its response to the crisis was reactive, ill-planned, and poorly communicated. Despite the development of a potentially effective crisis management system in the NSC, Eisenhower and Dulles often seemed to react personally to the crisis and occasionally sought their own intelligence assessments rather than rely on assessments coming through official channels. Neither had a particularly deep understanding of or interest in the situation in the Far East, and they seldom were able to consider China policy problems as distinct from their Cold War focus on the Soviet Union. Their decisions occasionally came as a result of focused efforts to resolve internal U.S. government bureaucratic problems instead of as well-thought-out efforts to resolve the foreign affairs issue. Robert Accinelli argues:

> [T]he final phase of the crisis witnessed an erratic fluctuation between restraint and risk taking and between flexibility and firmness in the administration's decisions, punctuated by a number of eye-catching turnabouts. In the end, Eisenhower and Dulles succeeded in extracting themselves from their painful predicament in the offshore islands only because of the timely offer of direct talks from Chou En-lai at Bandung.[48]

SECOND OFFSHORE ISLANDS CRISIS, AUGUST 1958–OCTOBER 1958

Given the failure to resolve the issues that precipitated the first offshore islands crisis, it is hardly surprising that the issue reappeared. Although the United States and the PRC had been holding direct talks in Geneva since August 1955, there was little real communication or negotiation. Compromise was difficult, with Beijing demanding the United States withdraw from Taiwan entirely and the United States pressing for a declaration forswearing the use of force in the Taiwan Strait. Eisenhower disagreed with the ROC's determination to hold onto the offshore islands and sought to avoid any agreements or actions that would bring the United States into a major conflict with China in their defense. Chiang Kai-shek, however, saw the islands as an important component of his efforts to recover the mainland, and he deployed an additional 100,000 troops—nearly one-third of the ROC Army—to Quemoy and Matsu in 1957. From these forward outposts, the ROC Army launched innumerable small forays into China to gather intelligence, disrupt communications, and sow discord.

New elements in the situation preceded the second crisis. In the United States, Eisenhower won reelection decisively, but his health declined early in his second term. Anticommunism declined in importance, and more of the administration's foreign affairs attention was focused on the Middle East, troubled relations with allies, and the growing threat of the Soviet Union. In China, domestic difficulties loomed as Mao Zedong sought the rapid communization of the countryside and launched more political campaigns against those he distrusted. Relations with the Soviet Union were growing more uneasy, particularly after Soviet leader Nikita Khrushchev denounced Stalin's "cult of personality" at the twentieth congress of the Communist Party of the Soviet Union in 1956. China sought Soviet assistance in developing a nuclear weapons capability but met with some reluctance on the part of the Soviet Union. Khrushchev's growing concerns about Mao were reinforced by Mao's 1957 dismissal of the United States and its nuclear weapons as "paper tigers."

Frustrated at the shrill ideological tone and lack of progress in U.S.-PRC bilateral talks in Geneva, Washington proposed reducing the rank of its representative to the talks to the subambassadorial level. China rejected the proposal, and talks were suspended in late 1957. In June 1958, the United States proposed the talks be moved from Geneva to Warsaw. China demanded they resume in Geneva within fifteen days.

In July, cross-strait tensions accelerated with reports of significant numbers of fighter aircraft being moved to airfields across from Taiwan and of dogfights between PRC and ROC aircraft. Chiang warned the United States that China was preparing an attack on Taiwan, and he requested more fighter aircraft and air defense equipment. U.S. naval forces, including several aircraft carriers, moved toward the region.

In early August, the NSC began to discuss the issue regularly. On August 14, the chairman of the JCS, General Nathan Twining, proposed that U.S. forces help Taiwan defend the offshore islands against PRC attack, using nuclear weapons as necessary against mainland targets. Eisenhower complained that Chiang's stationing of 100,000 troops there limited his options because a defeat would reduce the ability of the ROC Army to defend Taiwan itself.[49] On August 22, Eisenhower met with John Foster Dulles, Allen Dulles, Nathan Twining, Chief of Naval Operations Arleigh Burke, and others. They decided to send more artillery and antiaircraft equipment to Taiwan and to deploy a sixth aircraft carrier and five U.S. fighter squadrons to Taiwan.[50]

In a replay of the 1954 crisis, PRC artillery opened up a heavy barrage against ROC forces on the island of Quemoy on August 23, 1958. Two days later, Eisenhower approved augmenting the Seventh Fleet in the Taiwan Strait region to prepare for escorting ROC vessels resupplying Quemoy and Matsu. He refused to allow anyone other than himself to authorize the use of nuclear weapons, however.[51]

The crisis escalated step-by-step during the next two weeks, with Beijing threatening an invasion of Quemoy and the "liquidation" of Taiwan, Washington authorizing U.S. Navy escorts for ROC resupply vessels going into Quemoy, and China declaring a 12-mile territorial-water limit that pointedly included Quemoy.

On September 4, John Foster Dulles and Eisenhower met to craft a public statement to discuss the extent of U.S. support for the ROC. Dulles told Eisenhower he believed the Soviets were involved and would probably respond if the United States used nuclear weapons. Nonetheless, Dulles insisted the United States must be prepared to risk a general war.[52] After the meeting, Dulles made an on-the-record eight-point statement indicating the United States would "not hesitate" to use armed force "in insuring the defense of Taiwan." As for the offshore islands, he declared that the "naked use of force" by the PRC would "forecast a widespread use of force in the Far East which would endanger vital free world positions and the security of the United States." He concluded by expressing U.S. interest in a peaceful end to the crisis.[53]

On September 5, Foreign Minister Andrei Gromyko of the Soviet Union flew to Beijing for consultations and reportedly cautioned China not to challenge U.S. power.[54] The following day, Premier Zhou Enlai issued a statement saying the PRC was willing to resume ambassadorial talks with the United States. Eisenhower responded positively but cautiously. In another signal of caution, U.S. ships began escorting ROC resupply convoys to Quemoy on September 7, stopping just outside the 3-mile territorial-waters limit. Although there was some interference from PRC artillery, there were no air attacks, and resupply efforts succeeded.

Nonetheless, the rhetorical element of the crisis escalated with a September 7 letter from Khrushchev to Eisenhower warning that the Soviets would consider a U.S. attack on China to be an attack on the Soviet Union. In a September 11 televised speech, Eisenhower compared China's aggression with that of Adolf Hitler, vowed there would be no appeasement, and linked the defense of Quemoy and Matsu to the security of Taiwan. Nonetheless, he concluded his speech with the reassuring statement, "I believe there is not going to be any war."[55]

Talks resumed on September 15 in Warsaw between Ambassador Joseph Beam of the United States and Ambassador Wang Bingnan of the PRC. Beam proposed a cease-fire first, to be followed by other measures to reduce tension. Wang countered with a proposal for an agreed announcement, accompanied by separate U.S. and PRC statements. Two days later, Ambassador Beam offered a counterproposal, and the talks continued. Dulles concluded the talks would not reconcile the two countries' positions but that they offered good cover for public opinion and a possible means of reducing tensions.

Disseminated on September 16, SNIE 100-11-58, "Probable Chinese Communist and Soviet Intentions in the Taiwan Strait," noted that neither China nor Russia appeared to be making preparations for a serious attack on the offshore islands or a general war.[56] Nonetheless,

Khrushchev's September 19 letter to Eisenhower supported the PRC position on Taiwan, demanded that the United States withdraw its forces, and reminded Washington that the Soviet Union possessed nuclear weapons and would respond to a nuclear attack on China. Eisenhower and Dulles rejected the letter as filled with "false accusations, abusive and intemperate language, and inadmissible threats."[57]

Soviet bluster aside, Washington attempted to communicate with Beijing through intermediaries. On September 21, Eisenhower told the British foreign secretary, Selwyn Lloyd, that he was "against the use of even tactical atomic weapons in a limited operation" such as the off-shore islands.[58] Zhou Enlai signaled in late September that his main concern was the ROC use of the offshore islands to attack the mainland. Dulles responded that the United States would respond positively to a de facto truce.[59]

By late September, General Twining, chairman of the JCS, informed the White House that the resupply crisis for Quemoy had passed and recommended that the United States renew efforts to persuade Taiwan to evacuate Quemoy and Matsu if the PRC eased its pressure. The ROC Air Force, supplied with U.S. technology, had established air supremacy over the Taiwan Strait. U.S. advisers refused permission for ROC forces to attack PRC bases. In a press conference, Dulles stated that, if a formal or de facto cease-fire could be arranged in the region, it would "not be wise" for the ROC to maintain large forces on the offshore islands. He also posited that a KMT return to the mainland was "highly hypothetical."[60] Chiang Kai-shek was reportedly appalled at Dulles's remarks.

On October 6, the PRC defense minister, Peng Dehuai, broadcast a message to Taiwan, saying that the shelling of Quemoy would be suspended for seven days so resupply efforts could proceed unhindered, providing the United States did not escort the resupply ships. Washington responded positively, despite ROC objections. The cease-fire was extended for another two weeks on October 13.

Dulles visited Taipei from October 21 to 23 for consultations with Chiang Kai-shek. Dulles suggested the ROC renounce the use of force to recover the mainland, avoid commando raids and overflights, stop using the offshore islands for military action against the PRC, and reduce the Quemoy garrison. The joint communiqué, however, said only that the ROC would rely primarily on Sun Yat-sen's "Three People's

Principles" rather than military force to restore freedom to the main-land.[61] Two days later, Peng Dehuai announced that, so long as U.S. ships did not provide escort, shelling of Quemoy would be suspended on even-numbered days, effectively ending the crisis. On November 17, the United States and the ROC signed a memorandum of understand-ing, with Taipei agreeing to reduce the Quemoy garrison by 15,000 troops in exchange for more U.S. military equipment.

U.S. Policy Considerations

PERSONALITIES AND BUREAUCRACIES. Despite their health problems, Eisenhower remained the principal decision maker in foreign affairs and John Foster Dulles remained his key adviser. Some have speculated that Dulles became even more influential as Eisenhower weakened, but there was little evidence of that in 1958. Eisenhower's caution, his aversion to intentional provocation, his preference for guarded communication, and his determination to retain the policy initiative (as well as control of nuclear weapons) remained hallmarks of his policy management approach. Dulles—perhaps because of the diminution of political pressure from the conservative wing of the Republican Party—seemed less dogmatic and more attentive to the concerns of U.S. allies. He also appeared more will-ing to confront Chiang Kai-shek. Andrew Goodpaster, promoted to gen-eral, continued to be a key adviser to the president and was present at many crucial decision-making meetings in the White House.

Major personnel changes were made in the Pentagon, in both OSD and the JCS. Neil H. McElroy replaced Charles Wilson as secretary of defense in October 1957. Generally speaking, McElroy did not play a major role in policy planning issues outside the Department of Defense. In 1955, General Maxwell Taylor and Admiral Arleigh Burke replaced Army Chief of Staff Matthew Ridgway and Chief of Naval Operations Robert Carney, respectively. General Nathan Twining replaced Arthur Radford as JCS chairman in 1957. The changes in personnel did not fundamentally alter the joint chiefs' advocacy of an explicit commit-ment to use U.S. forces to defend Quemoy and Matsu and to permit theater commanders to authorize the use of tactical nuclear weapons against Chinese targets. Eisenhower and Dulles resisted both ideas.

In the NSC, Dillon Anderson initially replaced Robert Cutler as assistant to the president for national security affairs. Following Cutler's brief return to the position, Gordon Gray, formerly an assistant secretary of defense, became the APNSA.[62] After Dulles's death in 1959, Gray became Eisenhower's principal foreign policy adviser; his role somewhat resembled the role of later national security advisers.[63]

COMMUNICATIONS WITH CHINA. Although formal U.S.-PRC negotiations began in the wake of the 1954 crisis, they did not facilitate meaningful communications between the two countries either before or during the 1958 tensions. Because few other channels of communication were open, each side's understanding of the other's position was nearly as flawed as it had been in 1954. The ambassadorial talks were still effectively suspended when tensions began in the Taiwan Strait. The United States readily accepted Zhou Enlai's proposal for their resumption, considering it a sign that both sides wished to avoid hostilities and negotiate a solution to the conflict. However, the talks were used, as before, largely for laying out maximalist positions and propaganda posturing; they were never relevant to the solution of the crisis. When both sides understood their lack of common ground, the negotiations again became empty and symbolic.

As in 1954, both sides rejected the assistance of the UN and relied on intermediaries to convey privately their more serious messages about intentions. They continued to communicate through press conferences, speeches broadcast on radio and television, and other public media, knowing full well the other side was listening. Neither side had a very well-developed understanding of the domestic politics of the other, and both appeared to draw erroneous conclusions about the other's goals and intentions.

DOMESTIC POLITICS. The most conspicuous difference between the two crises of the offshore islands and Eisenhower's handling of them was the more skeptical role played by Congress and the media during the latter crisis. In 1955, the president won easy congressional approval for the Formosa Resolution. In 1958, with Democrats firmly in control of Congress and with the main anticommunist politicians much reduced in authority, challenges to Eisenhower's policies were more common.

The fundamental flaw of his handling of the crisis—namely his threat to use nuclear weapons and precipitate a general nuclear war involving both China and the Soviet Union to defend tiny islets of no strategic importance to the United States—was obvious to all. Washington pundits, including former secretary of state Dean Acheson, attacked this position. Joseph Alsop wrote on September 10 that "[t]he policy makers have painted the United States into a fantastic corner, in which we have to choose between joining in the defense of these wretched little offshore islands, or suffering incalculable further losses all over the world."[64]

Public opinion turned sharply against defending the offshore islands as the linkage to potential nuclear war became clearer. The State Department reported in late September that 80 percent of the mail received on the topic was opposed to U.S. policy, while a Gallup poll showed 90 percent in favor of a plan that would put the islands under UN trusteeship.[65] Congressional sentiment turned against Eisenhower as the crisis escalated. The Democratic Advisory Council declared in mid-October that the Eisenhower administration had "led us to the brink of isolation from our allies and to the brink of having to fight a nuclear war inadequately prepared and alone."[66] While it is impossible to document the impact of these factors on Eisenhower's decision making, they very likely played a role in his efforts to end the crisis quickly.

FOREIGN FACTORS, TAIWAN'S ROLE. The Soviet Union's role merits far more attention than it can receive in this chapter. In 1958, Soviet power was on the rise, and Khrushchev could threaten nuclear retaliation against the United States with impunity. At the same time, however, the Soviet Union was working hard to improve its overall relations with the United States while its ties with Beijing were deteriorating sharply over ideological, economic, and strategic differences. Although publicly supporting China's Taiwan gambit, Soviet leaders and diplomats alike were privately alarmed at the recklessness of Beijing's approach and advised caution in their meetings with Chinese counterparts. Eisenhower and Dulles, although concerned about the risk of the Taiwan conflict escalating into general war with the Soviet Union, seemed unfazed by Khrushchev's threats, which were inconsistent with intelligence reporting on actual Soviet military preparations. Nonetheless, the addition of the Soviet factor in an already complicated and potentially dangerous situation reinforced the view in Washington that the massive-retaliation strategy was failing.

From the earliest phases of the 1958 crisis, it was clear that Chiang Kai-shek's influence over Washington's decision making had decreased. In some ways, he was perceived as much a part of the problem as was the communist government on the mainland. With the sharp decline of conservative Republican power in Congress, Chiang's influence on the Eisenhower administration also declined. Most of the policy discussions involved questions of how to avoid a serious military setback in the offshore islands, followed by recommendations on how to persuade Chiang to reduce his military presence there after the tensions eased. Both Eisenhower and Dulles were careful to distance the United States publicly from ROC efforts to use Quemoy and Matsu for military harassment and subversion of the mainland. Dulles publicly criticized the ROC's heavy deployment of troops on Quemoy as "rather foolish" and made clear in late September that the United States would not support further military action to "recover the mainland." Still, there were no indications that the administration was prepared to discipline Chiang or punish the ROC for drawing the United States into a dangerous crisis.

Conclusions

A comparison of the handling of the 1954–1955 and 1958 Taiwan Strait crises shows little real change in the Eisenhower administration's *so-called* crisis management procedures. Eisenhower still made all decisions personally, acting cautiously, consulting widely through the NSC, patiently waiting for the right moment to act, then bringing considerable political authority and military strength to bear.[67] Secretary Dulles was Eisenhower's principal adviser and public spokesman. Arguments continue as to who was the more influential in directing U.S. policy. Andrew Goodpaster was Eisenhower's eyes and ears, occasionally acting outside formal channels to obtain information and cooperation. The NSC acted as a policy facilitator and coordinator, providing both necessary information and an arena in which policy differences could be aired freely before the president. The JCS was an important sounding board on policy considerations and essential in the effective implementation of decisions, but Eisenhower kept the chiefs under tight control, insisting on civilian control of the military and refusing to relinquish the authority to employ nuclear weapons to field commanders.

But again, it is hard to credit Eisenhower for deft handling of the crisis. Communications with friend and adversary alike were inadequate, and information flows within the policy community were slow and stovepiped. Consequently, in both crises, the administration missed important signals from the PRC and implemented decisions as the crises were easing that re-escalated tensions. In both cases, the United States failed to examine the underlying causes of the crisis or deal with them so as to avoid future problems. Moreover, decisions to threaten the use of nuclear weapons were highly risky, based on inaccurate perceptions of how such threats would be received, and occasionally insensitive to domestic and foreign concerns about the morality and efficacy of nuclear war.

TAIWAN STRAIT CRISIS, 1995–1996

Because the events of the 1995–1996 period are more familiar, I will avoid a lengthy chronology of the crisis.[68] In early May 1994, President Lee Teng-hui of Taiwan made a refueling stop at Hickham Air Force Base in Hawaii en route to Central America, but he refused to leave his airplane because of unsatisfactory protocol preparations on the ground. Members of Congress sharply criticized Lee's treatment by the Clinton administration. On September 7, the NSC and the State Department publicized the results of a review of U.S. policy toward Taiwan, easing some official travel and contact restrictions that had been in effect since the normalization of U.S.-PRC relations in 1979 but maintaining the de facto prohibition on private visits to the United States by senior Taiwan officials. Beijing immediately protested the changes.

In November's midterm congressional elections, the Democrats lost control of both houses of Congress, a stinging setback for President Bill Clinton and his foreign and domestic policies. Early in 1995, Republicans mounted a serious challenge to his Taiwan policy. Republican Speaker of the House of Representatives Newt Gingrich expressed public support for granting Lee Teng-hui a visa to visit his alma mater, Cornell University, to make a speech in June 1995.

In late January, PRC President Jiang Zemin made an eight-point proposal to ease tensions with Taiwan, but Lee ignored the opportunity to improve cross-strait ties, choosing instead to move ahead with his trip to Cornell. Following frequent complaints from PRC interlocutors and the Chinese media, Secretary of State Warren Christopher told Vice Premier Qian Qichen on April 17 that he believed the visit by Lee to Cornell was "inconsistent" with U.S. policy on maintaining only unofficial relations with Taiwan but that Congress was pressing hard. Proving Christopher's point, in early May, the House and Senate overwhelmingly passed nonbinding resolutions urging Clinton to allow Lee to visit Cornell. They submitted binding legislation for committee consideration pending the administration's decision.

On May 17, Secretary of State Christopher, Secretary of Defense William Perry, and APNSA Anthony Lake agreed to facilitate a Lee visit. Two days later, Clinton approved an NSC decision memo to allow an unofficial Lee visit to Cornell. On May 22, the White House officially announced the decision, and Beijing unsuccessfully demanded a reversal. At Cornell on June 9, Lee delivered a speech extolling the achievements of the "Republic of China on Taiwan."

Beijing's reaction was far-reaching. During the next month, Beijing broke off almost all dialogue with Washington, withdrew its ambassador, and began a media campaign to vilify Lee as a "splittist." In late June, the People's Liberation Army (PLA) began the first of several joint service exercises in the Taiwan Strait, about 75 miles from Quemoy. In late July, it conducted a test of surface-to-surface missiles in the Taiwan Strait, 80 to 90 miles north of Taiwan. Washington issued a relatively mild protest. Other exercises followed through the end of the year, often precipitating a corresponding exercise by ROC forces.

Seeking to patch up the long-troubled bilateral relationship, Christopher met Qian in Brunei in late July, conveying to him Clinton's letter to Jiang Zemin about U.S.-Taiwan relations. In late August, a State Department under secretary visiting Beijing brought along an invitation to Jiang to pay a visit to the United States for a summit meeting with Clinton. The October 25 meeting seemed to halt the deterioration of U.S.-China relations.

PRC military pressure on Taiwan continued, however, with a massive exercise in November at Dongshan, on the Fujian coast, observed by Jiang in his capacity as chairman of the Central Military Commission. Believing Beijing was ignoring Washington's interest in preserving stability in the Taiwan Strait, the NSC began, in late November, informal contingency planning for hostilities in the Taiwan Strait, in consultation with State and the JCS.[69]

At an NSC-sponsored policy breakfast in early January, Lake learned from a former Defense Department official that Chinese military officers had told the former official the previous October that they believed the United States would not come to Taiwan's aid because Washington "cared more about Los Angeles than about Taiwan"—an implied threat to employ nuclear weapons in case of conflict over Taiwan.[70] Lake subsequently ordered the Deputies Committee and the Principals Committee to review overall China policy. On February 19, the Principals Committee agreed to invite senior PRC diplomat Liu Huaqiu to meet with Lake and other senior U.S. officials for in-depth discussions of bilateral relations and the Taiwan situation. Meanwhile, the chairman of the JCS, General John Shalikashvili, briefed Clinton on contingency planning for a Taiwan Strait conflict.[71]

On March 5, Beijing declared a "closure area" for shipping and aircraft 25–30 miles off the coast of Taiwan for the purpose of clearing the area for surface-to-surface missile tests. Washington issued a strong protest. Two days later, PRC Second Artillery forces launched three M-9 missiles into the closure area, just as Liu Huaqiu was arriving in Washington for talks. Despite U.S. anger at the attempt to intimidate Taiwan voters before their late March presidential election, Lake held several hours of intensive talks with Liu on March 8.

The following day, Lake, Christopher, Perry, Shalikashvili, and several others agreed to dispatch two aircraft carrier battle groups to the Taiwan region. Lake presented the plan to Clinton, who approved it. Two days later, the U.S. aircraft carrier *Independence* deployed east of Taiwan, while the *Nimitz* left the Persian Gulf for deployment west of the Philippines. Deputy National Security Adviser Samuel Berger met with Ding Mou-shih, head of Taiwan's National Security Council, for an in-depth discussion of ongoing tensions.

Amid considerable Chinese anger over perceived U.S. interference in China's domestic affairs, the PLA began a large exercise on Pingtan Island, at the northern end of the Taiwan Strait, on March 18. These exercises concluded on March 23, the same day as Taiwan's presidential elections and the arrival of the *Nimitz* in the West Pacific. Lee won 54 percent of the vote. Subsequently, the ROC called off its corresponding military exercises, tensions diminished sharply, and U.S. naval forces departed the region quietly.

U.S. Policy Considerations

In a chapter of this nature, it is impossible to catalogue the changes that occurred in the U.S. policy-making community and its processes, the international environment, domestic considerations, and U.S.-China relations in the forty years between crises in the Taiwan Strait. The basic structures and bureaucracies have generally remained the same, but other changes are both enormous and analytically significant. The assumption is that readers are familiar with most of this; thus, the focus is on the crisis management performance of the Clinton administration during the 1995–1996 tensions.

PERSONALITIES. William Jefferson Clinton was not a foreign policy president. During the 1992 presidential election, he defeated George H. W. Bush—whom he accused of paying too much attention to international affairs—by stressing the domestic economy and basic American ideals. He had not served in the military, and he had spent most of his political career as governor of a largely rural southern state. Absent a crisis situation, he was content to leave foreign policy in the hands of experienced experts such as Secretary of State Warren Christopher; National Security Adviser Anthony Lake and his deputy, Samuel R. Berger; and Ambassador to the UN Madeleine K. Albright. Like his predecessors, Clinton had abandoned regular meetings of the formal NSC and delegated policy consideration authority to the Principals Committee; he expected Lake and Berger to keep him informed of relevant policy issues through NSC action and information memoranda as well as private briefings.

Clinton was extraordinarily intelligent and a "quick study" of complex issues, including foreign policy, but the dissolution of the Soviet Union and the Eastern bloc in 1990–1991 and the rapidly growing prosperity worldwide caused him to feel little pressure to be proactive in foreign policy. Instead, he supported a values-based approach. Clinton's relations with the uniformed military were strained from the outset. He tried to ease restrictions against homosexuals in the military but met strong resistance from the JCS and from public opinion. His first foreign policy crisis, Somalia, went badly in October, leaving him skeptical of both the use of military forces and the advice of the JCS.

Clinton's general view of China in 1995 was negative because of China's human rights practices, and his efforts to use China's most-favored-nation (MFN) trade status to pressure the Beijing government into improving its human rights policies in 1993–1994 had ended in failure. Clinton had visited Taiwan several times when he was governor of Arkansas, and he was impressed with its democratization. Like many of his predecessors, he often focused on the domestic political component of foreign policy issues, and his basic response to the Lee Teng-hui visa issue was related to his understanding of congressional opinion on the issue and his belief in freedom, including freedom of travel.[72] Although aware of the risks of a negative PRC reaction to his May 19 decision, he went ahead anyway in order to avoid dealing with veto-proof binding legislation from Congress.

Secretary of State Warren Christopher, a lawyer who had served as deputy secretary during the Carter administration, was aloof, self-effacing, and careful. Although very knowledgeable about foreign affairs, he was more skilled at patient negotiation than strategic thinking, and he preferred calm deliberation to quick action. Far more attentive to Bosnia and the Middle East, Christopher seemed uncomfortable with China issues. In his 1993 confirmation hearings, he spoke of hopes for the "peaceful evolution" of China away from communism, and he was a strong proponent of pressuring China on human rights issues. After his 1994 trip to China turned into a public relations nightmare, with the PRC government arresting dissidents and subjecting him to intense criticism of U.S. policy in face-to-face negotiating sessions, Christopher considered resigning as secretary. His relations with Clinton, while correct and frequent, could not be characterized as warm.

By the 1990s, the State Department had become a large, sprawling bureaucracy, with multiple disputes raging between regional bureaus seeking to maintain good relations with their client countries and with functional bureaus working on such issues as nonproliferation, democracy, and human rights and labor trying to satisfy domestic constituencies by pressing for sanctions or other punishment of countries that violated U.S. law or international norms. Christopher seemed to dislike adjudicating these disputes.

Winston Lord served as assistant secretary of state for East Asian and Pacific Affairs. Broadly experienced in Asian affairs, Lord had served on Henry Kissinger's NSC staff during the Nixon administration and was appointed ambassador to Beijing in 1985. In that capacity, Lord was a firsthand witness to the 1989 "democracy movement" in China and was appalled at the June 4, 1989, crackdown, which occurred just after he had left his post. Lord became a severe critic of the Bush administration's efforts to normalize relations after the Tiananmen events, and he advised the Clinton presidential campaign in 1992. As assistant secretary, he helped develop the 1993 plan to impose sanctions on China if it did not meet certain human rights criteria.

In 1994–1995, as congressional pressure to improve relations with Taiwan increased, Christopher appeared reluctant to change guidelines for contacts between U.S. and Taiwan officials, in part because he had helped develop the framework for unofficial relations in 1978–1979. He and Lord strongly resisted pressure to grant Lee Teng-hui a visa to visit Cornell. After the White House made the decision, however, both worked tirelessly to deal with the subsequent downturn in relations and to manage the crisis.

Anthony Lake and Samuel R. "Sandy" Berger, who served as assistant and principal deputy assistant to the president for national security affairs, were Clinton's two most influential foreign policy officials. Lake, a former foreign service officer who resigned in protest after the 1970 invasion of Cambodia, returned to head the State Department's Policy Planning Staff during the Carter administration and then turned to academia. At the urging of Berger, with whom he had served on the Policy Planning Staff, Lake joined the Clinton campaign in 1991 as senior foreign policy adviser.

Diffident and cerebral, Lake wanted to return the APNSA position to that of a policy facilitator and coordinator, and he worked sincerely to avoid the kind of power struggles between the State Department and the NSC that had become common in the Kennedy, Nixon, Carter, and Reagan administrations. Recognizing that even the more informal Principals and Deputies Committees still did not provide the kind of close communication that good policy making—and crisis management—required, he set up informal breakfasts and lunches with Christopher and Defense Secretary William Perry, as well as other officials, to talk through issues, pre-position decisions, and avert bureaucratic disagreements.[73] Nonetheless, policy disagreements did take place, and China issues became prominent among them. By 1995, friends and academics were encouraging Lake to take a more activist role, representing the president, in China policy. After the Lee Teng-hui visit and the sharp downturn in bilateral relations, he began to do so.

Berger, a successful trade lawyer and Democratic Party activist, probably had closer personal relations with Clinton than Lake did, but he worked well and loyally as deputy national security adviser. He paid careful attention to China policy, trying to avoid the rough patches brought about by domestic politics. He was the main force behind the 1994 effort to de-link China's MFN status from its human rights performance. Berger also opposed allowing Lee Teng-hui to visit the United States in 1995, but he was not in a position to prevent it.[74]

BUREAUCRACIES. As in any administration, bureaucratic competition and policy disputes within the Clinton administration were sharp and frequent. But its crisis management routines were reasonably well-developed, and, while the Taiwan Strait situation in 1995–1996 may not be a textbook crisis, elements of that system came into play in early 1996.

- The State Department created a special task force that monitored the information flow twenty-four hours a day, including frequent conversations with the U.S. embassy in Beijing. The task force encouraged embassy officers and military attachés to maintain contacts with Chinese officials and report back fully.
- The JCS, Commander in Chief Pacific, and the Defense Department instituted a review of contingency planning for the Taiwan Strait and prepared a briefing for the president on possible contingencies and his response options.
- The intelligence community established a twenty-four-hour task force that monitored all-source information, prepared daily situation re-

ports for select policy and intelligence officials, and brought information of special significance directly to the attention of senior policy makers.

- The NSC coordinated policy planning through a series of Principals and Deputies Committee meetings, held in the Situation Room of the White House, which has state-of-the-art communications capabilities to allow contact with any embassy, bureaucracy, or major military command. The NSC also consulted with a senior Chinese foreign affairs official and a Taiwanese foreign affairs principal to ensure all sides had a full understanding of U.S. policy, strategy, intentions, and preferences for a resolution of tensions.

Secretary of Defense Perry, in consultation with General Shalikashvili and other senior defense officials, Lake, Berger, Christopher, and Lord, made final recommendations on the deployment of U.S. forces. Lake and Berger conveyed the recommendations to Clinton, who approved them on March 9. They were implemented through the military chain of command. Clear rules of engagement were transmitted to U.S. ships and aircraft operating in the region, with specific instructions not to enter the Taiwan Strait itself, nor to interfere with PLA exercises in any way.[75]

As a result of these and equally careful preparations on the PRC side—with the exception of public rhetoric, which tended toward the extreme and somewhat counteracted official communication—there were no skirmishes, close calls, dogfights, or other encounters between the military forces of the PRC and either the United States or Taiwan. When the election and the PLA exercises were complete, U.S. naval forces quietly departed the region, and the situation returned to normal.

COMMUNICATIONS WITH CHINA. Despite the strain in bilateral relations and the lack of ambassadorial-level representation during part of the crisis, the nature of communications between Beijing and Washington was of a completely different order than during the earlier crises. Full diplomatic contacts were maintained throughout the period, despite the breaking off of key dialogues on specific topics. As can often be said of formal diplomatic discourse, frank and candid exchanges of views may not have occurred at all times, but there was no shortage of opportunities to engage. Meetings were held at all levels, including a presidential summit, a meeting between Jiang Zemin and Vice President Al Gore, and several meetings at the under secretary and assistant secretary levels. To ensure that the highest levels of the Chinese government were fully aware of U.S. policy toward Taiwan and other issues, Lake held extensive talks with his counterpart, which played a key role in soon ending the crisis and enabling an overall recovery afterward.

Lake's main goal was to eliminate any strategic ambiguity about how the United States intended to respond to the situation in the Taiwan Strait. He believed PRC officials were poorly informed about U.S. intentions, interests, and resolve, and he wanted to ensure they received a clear message from the highest levels of the administration. Although many found the concept of strategic ambiguity clever, Lake considered it unhelpful in these particular circumstances.

Clarity was less than complete within the U.S. government about the domestic politics of the PRC, its real intentions vis-à-vis Taiwan, or its military capabilities to attack Taiwan or one of the offshore islands. Despite both official and unofficial Chinese reassurances that the PLA exercises would not become an actual military attack on Taiwan's territory, the U.S. government maintained a wary readiness to respond to such an event. Communications with PRC officials, even those with Liu Huaqiu, did not impart a sense of confidence that the Chinese government was being as candid as the United States about its goals and intentions. Much of the PRC side of the conversation still consisted of standard memorized talking points. The continuing absence of a trusted channel of communication in U.S.-China relations is a problem that needs to be addressed in any consideration of improved crisis management techniques.

DOMESTIC POLITICS. Domestic politics played a significant role in the lead-up to the 1996 crisis, although it was not a major factor in its actual management. Although improvements in U.S.-China relations had lifted somewhat the overall U.S. public image of the PRC after the post-Tiananmen nadir, China was still not considered a friendly country. Moreover, the strategic rationale for the relationship had long since declined, and few Americans supported doing favors for Beijing on issues such as granting Lee Teng-hui a visa. Public support for Taiwan, on the other hand, was very high, mostly owing to growing admiration for its democratization and its high-profile involvement in trade development in many U.S. localities. In Congress, support for Taiwan was even more pronounced, in part because of the effective lobbying activities of the Taiwan government and its friends, although this was in no way comparable with the China lobby of the 1950s. Overwhelming congressional support for granting Lee Teng-hui a visa was a large factor in President Clinton's May 1995 decision, which precipitated the crisis.

Members of Congress kept up a steady stream of resolutions, hearings, and letters to the president about the Taiwan Strait crisis in 1996. Many demanded a firmer response to PRC threats, while some called for executive-congressional consultation on how to deal with the crisis, as called for by the Taiwan Relations Act.[76] This played a negligible role in the actions of the executive branch. Key members of congressional committees, of course, were kept informed of decisions on the deployment of U.S. forces, and all letters and inquiries were answered. Moreover, senior State Department and Defense Department officials testified at congressional hearings throughout February and March; and State, Defense, and White House press spokespersons kept the public (and the Chinese government) well-briefed on the U.S. government's view of the situation.

But crisis management remained a presidential prerogative, and decision making in crisis situations was generally restricted to a small number of Clinton's most trusted advisers. In those times when the decision involves national security and must be made in a short time, virtually every president has set aside partisan politics, bureaucratic disputes, and personal differences in order to most effectively make necessary decisions. Although congressional investigators are certain to second-guess the decision in the future, their views are seldom a major factor in real-time foreign policy decisions.

FOREIGN FACTORS, TAIWAN'S ROLE. Throughout the crisis, the U.S. government was besieged with requests from other Asian governments to avoid a degeneration of the Taiwan crisis into armed conflict, which would destabilize the region. Their requests and advice were fully a part of U.S. deliberations and were very much part of the presentations on the issue that were made to senior Taiwan and PRC officials. The United

States was careful to cast its interests, and its rationale for dispatching military forces, as related to the maintenance of regional stability rather than as favoritism toward either party.

Although the crisis probably enhanced the margin of Lee Teng-hui's victory in the March 23 presidential election, it definitely strained U.S.-Taiwan relations. Some U.S. officials felt betrayed and angered by Lee's speech at Cornell and by the cavalier disregard for U.S. interests shown throughout by Lee and other Taiwan officials. Winston Lord, for example, refused to meet again with Taiwan's unofficial representative in Washington, Benjamin Lu, who was replaced not long after the crisis ended.[77] As in 1954 and 1958, Taiwan's pursuit of its own domestic political interests involved the United States in a crisis with the PRC, and its miscalculations about the PRC's response had important consequences for Washington. Subsequent experiences with both Lee and his successor, Chen Shui-bian, have given many policy makers in Washington a great sense of skepticism about Taiwan's—as well as Beijing's—seeming eagerness to ignore or define for their own purposes what U.S. interests are.

Conclusions

In all three crisis management situations, the president was the principal actor who made the decisions about the conduct of U.S. diplomacy and the deployment of its military forces. Both Eisenhower and Clinton—and every president in between—developed a crisis management system suitable to his leadership and decision-making style. Eisenhower's was formal, bureaucratic, and hands-on; Clinton's was informal, consultative, and impersonal. Both operated within official bureaucratic structures, with the State Department, Defense Department, JCS, Central Intelligence Agency, and the NSC staff playing the key roles. Informal relationships among and between the principals of those organizations, and their various relationships with the president, heavily affected the recommendations they presented to the president and how he handled them. In all cases, the NSC played a critical role in organizing meetings, conveying the president's interests, adjudicating bureaucratic disputes, and clarifying the necessary decisions.

Improvements in communications and information processing have enhanced the speed of crisis management within the government but have not simplified the decision-making process, which is still a very human, interactive process, dependent on interpersonal relationships among the president's principal foreign policy advisers. Up-to-the-minute intelligence information is now available to all the players although their ability to absorb it usefully into the decision-making or crisis management process may be open to question. This facilitates responses to emergency situations, although none of the Taiwan Strait crises presented any emergencies requiring instantaneous response. Nonetheless, final decisions are still made on paper, even though records are kept electronically.

The improvement in communication between the United States and China has significantly improved the process of crisis management, if not the process of dispute resolution. Although much remains to be done in improving levels of candor and perhaps in discussing the true sources of tension in cross-strait relations, the quality of official, "track two," and nonofficial communication has markedly enhanced both governments' abilities to plan for, avert, and deal with crisis situations.

It is noteworthy that good sense prevailed in all three of the cross-strait crises under discussion. That is, the United States and China managed to avoid making decisions that would result in direct conflict over Taiwan-related issues. Despite occasionally poor or virtually nonexistent communications, missed signals, shrill rhetoric, domestic politics, uncertain intentions, confused or conflicting positions of different decision makers, and other impediments to clear-headed decision making, the United States and the PRC managed to rein in at the precipice. Both sides may recognize implicitly, if they perhaps cannot say so directly, that a conflict over Taiwan would be tragic and unnecessary. In no case would the gains for either side be worth the costs. There is no solution to the complicated issues involved that the use of military force could readily achieve. Crisis management is primarily a matter of containing frustrations by managing domestic pressures (antihegemonism or anticommunism) and maintaining patience with volatile Taiwan politics.

NOTES

1. Amy B. Zegart, *Flawed by Design: The Evolution of the CIA, JCS, and NSC* (Palo Alto, Calif.: Stanford University Press, 1999), chaps. 4 and 5; Gordon Nathaniel Lederman, *Reorganizing the Joint Chiefs of Staff: The Goldwater-Nichols Act of 1986* (Westport, Conn.: Greenwood Press, 1999), pp. 16–19.

2. Thomas E. Stolper, *China, Taiwan, and the Offshore Islands: Together With an Implication for Outer Mongolia and Sino-Soviet Relations* (Armonk, N.Y.: M. E. Sharpe, Inc., 1985), p. 23.

3. Ibid., p. 26.

4. NSC 5429, "Review of U.S. Policy in the Far East," August 4, 1954, in *Foreign Relations of the United States, 1952–1954,* vol. 12 (East Asia and the Pacific) (Washington, D.C.: U.S. Government Printing Office, 1984), pp. 696–703, cited in Robert Accinelli, *Crisis and Commitment: United States Policy Toward Taiwan, 1950–1955* (Chapel Hill: University of North Carolina Press, 1996), pp. 153–154.

5. Ibid., p. 154.

6. Stolper, *China, Taiwan, and the Offshore Islands,* p. 39.

7. Ibid., p. 40.

8. Accinelli, *Crisis and Commitment,* pp. 160–163.

9. Ibid., p. 164; Stolper, *China, Taiwan, and the Offshore Islands,* p. 42.

10. Accinelli, *Crisis and Commitment,* p. 172.

11. Ibid., p. 175; Stolper, *China, Taiwan, and the Offshore Islands,* p. 51.

12. Accinelli, *Crisis and Commitment,* p. 178.

13. Ibid., pp. 178–179; Stolper, *China, Taiwan, and the Offshore Islands,* pp. 50–51.

14. Accinelli, *Crisis and Commitment,* pp. 180–181. The policy document was known as NSC 5429/2.

15. Stolper, *China, Taiwan, and the Offshore Islands,* p. 66.

16. Ibid., pp. 67–68; Accinelli, *Crisis and Commitment,* pp. 187–189; see also Eisenhower Presidential Library and Museum, "NSC Summaries of Discussion: The Eisenhower Period," web site of Department of Political Science, University of California–Los Angeles, www.polisci.ucla.edu/faculty/trachtenberg/guide/nsc.html.

17. Quoted in Accinelli, *Crisis and Commitment,* pp. 191–192; Dwight D. Eisenhower, *Mandate for Change, 1953–1956* (Garden City, N.Y.: Doubleday & Co., 1963), p. 468.

18. Stolper, *China, Taiwan, and the Offshore Islands,* pp. 68–69.

19. Ibid., pp. 76–77.
20. Accinelli, *Crisis and Commitment*, p. 212.
21. Ibid.; Eisenhower, *Mandate for Change*, p. 476.
22. Accinelli, *Crisis and Commitment*, p. 214; Eisenhower, *Mandate for Change*, p. 477.
23. Accinelli, *Crisis and Commitment*, p. 216; Stolper, *China, Taiwan, and the Offshore Islands*, p. 90.
24. GlobalSecurity.org, "First Taiwan Strait Crisis: Quemoy and Matsu Islands," 2005, http://www.globalsecurity.org/military/ops/quemoy_matsu.htm; Accinelli, *Crisis and Commitment*, p. 217.
25. Accinelli, *Crisis and Commitment*, p. 217.
26. Eisenhower, *Mandate for Change*, pp. 479–480.
27. Accinelli, *Crisis and Commitment*, p. 220.
28. Stolper, *China, Taiwan, and the Offshore Islands*, p. 102; Accinelli, *Crisis and Commitment*, pp. 220–223.
29. Quoted in Stolper, *China, Taiwan, and the Offshore Islands*, p. 105.
30. U.S. Department of State, Office of the Historian, "History of the National Security Council, 1947–1997," August 1997, www.whitehouse.gov/nsc/history.html.
31. Martin J. Medhurst, *Dwight D. Eisenhower: Strategic Communicator* (Westport, Conn.: Greenwood Press, 1993), p. 78.
32. Robert A. Divine, *Eisenhower and the Cold War* (New York: Oxford University Press, 1981), p. 65.
33. Richard Goold-Adams, *John Foster Dulles: A Reappraisal* (New York, Appleton-Century-Crofts, 1962), chap. 16.
34. Among many works on this subject, see, in particular, Richard M. Fried, *Nightmare in Red: The McCarthy Era in Perspective* (New York: Oxford University Press, 1991); and Robert Griffith, *The Politics of Fear: Joseph R. McCarthy and the Senate* (Amherst: University of Massachusetts Press, 1987).
35. Gerard Clarfield, *Security With Solvency: Dwight D. Eisenhower and the Shaping of the American Military Establishment* (Westport, Conn.: Praeger, 1999), pp. 96–100.
36. Stolper, *China, Taiwan, and the Offshore Islands*, p. 58.
37. Amy B. Zegart, *Flawed by Design;* see especially chapter 4.
38. Clarfield, *Security With Solvency*, p. 139.
39. U.S. Department of State, Office of the Historian, "History of the National Security Council, 1947–1997"; see also Alfred Dick Sander, *Eisenhower's Executive Office* (Westport, Conn.: Greenwood Press, 1999), chap. 4.

40. Composition of the NSC has varied over time, but its core members are the president, the vice president, the secretary of state, and the secretary of defense; during the Eisenhower years, the secretary of the treasury, the chairman of the Joint Chiefs of Staff, and the director of the Central Intelligence Agency also regularly attended NSC meetings.

41. U.S. Department of State, Office of the Historian, "History of the National Security Council"; Sander, *Eisenhower's Executive Office*.

42. "NSC Summaries of Discussion: The Eisenhower Period."

43. Cited in Fred I. Greenstein and Richard H. Immerman, "Effective National Security Advising: Recovering the Eisenhower Legacy," in *Political Science Quarterly* 115 (2000), pp. 335*ff.*

44. Of particular importance were SNIE 100-4-54, "The Situation with Respect to Certain Islands off the Coast of Mainland China, 4 September 1954," in *Foreign Relations of the United States (FRUS), 1952–1954,* vol. 14 (China and Japan) (Washington, D.C.: U.S. Government Printing Office, 1985), pp. 563–571; SNIE 100-4/1-54, "The Situation with Respect to the Nationalist Occupied Islands off the Coast of Mainland China, 10 September 1954," in *FRUS, 1952–1954,* vol. 14, pp. 595–597; NIE 43-54, "Probable Developments in Taiwan Through Mid-1956, 14 September 1954," in *FRUS, 1952–1954,* vol. 14, pp. 628–645; SNIE 100-3-55, "Communist Reactions to Certain Possible U.S. Courses of Action with Respect to the Islands off the Coast of China, 25 January 1955," in *FRUS, 1955–1957,* vol. 2 (China) (Washington, D.C.: U.S. Government Printing Office, 1986), p. 127; NIE 100-4-55, "Communist Capabilities and Intentions with Respect to the Offshore Islands and Taiwan through 1955, and Communist and Non-Communist Reactions with Respect to the Defense of Taiwan, 16 March 1955," in *FRUS, 1955–1957,* vol. 2, pp. 376–380; and NIE 100-4/1-55, "Morale on Taiwan, 16 April 1955," in *FRUS, 1955–1957,* vol. 2, pp. 479–489.

45. Accinelli, *Crisis and Commitment,* p. 214; Timothy J. Botti, *Ace in the Hole: Why the United States Did Not Use Nuclear Weapons in the Cold War, 1945 to 1965* (Westport, Conn.: Greenwood Press, 1996), p. 75.

46. See, for example, Divine, *Eisenhower and the Cold War,* p. 64.

47. Sadako Ogata, *Normalization with China: A Comparative Study of U.S. and Japanese Processes* (Berkeley: University of California, Institute of East Asian Studies, 1988), p. 3. Quotation from Ross Y. Koen, *The China Lobby in American Politics* (New York: Harper and Row, 1974).

48. Accinelli, *Crisis and Commitment,* p. 232.

49. U.S. Department of State, Office of the Spokesman, "Foreign Relations of the United States: Summaries of FRUS Volumes: Foreign Relations of the

United States 1958–60, Volume 19, China, August 12, 1996," http://dosfan.lib.uic.edu/erc/frus/summaries/960812_FRUS_XIX_1958-60.html.

50. Botti, *Ace in the Hole,* p. 104.

51. U.S. Department of State, Office of the Spokesman, "Foreign Relations of the United States: Summaries of FRUS Volumes."

52. Botti, *Ace in the Hole,* p. 106.

53. U.S. Department of State, Office of the Spokesman, "Foreign Relations of the United States: Summaries of FRUS Volumes."

54. Botti, *Ace in the Hole,* p. 106.

55. Divine, *Eisenhower and the Cold War,* p. 68.

56. Botti, *Ace in the Hole,* pp. 107, 269.

57. U.S. Department of State, Office of the Spokesman, "Foreign Relations of the United States: Summaries of FRUS Volumes."

58. Ibid.; Divine, *Eisenhower and the Cold War,* p. 70; Botti, *Ace in the Hole,* p. 107.

59. U.S. Department of State, Office of the Spokesman, "Foreign Relations of the United States: Summaries of FRUS Volumes."

60. Ibid.; D. F. Fleming, *The Cold War and Its Origins, 1917–1960,* vol. 2 (Garden City, N.Y.: Doubleday & Co., 1961), p. 938.

61. U.S. Department of State, Office of the Spokesman, "Foreign Relations of the United States: Summaries of FRUS Volumes."

62. Sander, *Eisenhower's Executive Office,* p. 99.

63. Ibid., p. 101.

64. Joseph Alsop, *Washington Evening Bulletin,* September 10, 1958, in Fleming, *The Cold War,* pp. 934–935.

65. Fleming, *The Cold War,* pp. 937–938.

66. Ibid.

67. Eisenhower's crisis management style is discussed in Amos Kiewe, *The Modern Presidency and Crisis Rhetoric* (Westport, Conn.: Praeger, 1994), pp. 25–26.

68. Those who wish to examine the specific events of the period in detail should refer to Alan Romberg, *Rein In at the Brink of the Precipice: American Policy Toward Taiwan and U.S.-PRC Relations* (Washington, D.C.: Henry L. Stimson Center, 2003), chap. 7; Robert Suettinger, *Beyond Tiananmen: The Politics of U.S.-China Relations, 1989–2000* (Washington, D.C.: Brookings Institution Press, 2003), chap. 6; Patrick Tyler, *A Great Wall, Six Presidents and China—An Investigative History* (New York: Public Affairs, 1999); John W. Garver, *Face Off: China, the United States, and Taiwan's Democratization* (Seattle: University of Washington Press, 1997);

292 | ROBERT L. SUETTINGER

James Mann, *About Face: A History of America's Curious Relationship with China, from Nixon to Clinton* (New York: Alfred A. Knopf, 1999).

69. Suettinger, *Beyond Tiananmen*, pp. 247–248.

70. Ibid., 248. See also Patrick Tyler, "As China Threatens Taiwan, It Makes Sure U.S. Listens," *New York Times,* January 24, 1996, A3.

71. Suettinger, *Beyond Tiananmen*, p. 251.

72. Ibid., p. 215.

73. Ibid., pp. 158–159.

74. Ibid., p. 216.

75. Hong Kong and other Chinese media claims that U.S. forces stayed out of the Taiwan Strait out of fear of PRC submarines are far-fetched, at best. See, for example, "Fourth Wave of Military Exercises to Be Conducted at End of May," *Sing Tao Jih Pao,* April 29, 1996.

76. Section 3C of the Taiwan Relations Act stipulates: "The President is directed to inform the Congress promptly of any threat to the security or the social or economic system of the people on Taiwan and any danger to the interests of the United States arising therefrom. The President and the Congress shall determine, in accordance with constitutional processes, appropriate action by the United States in response to any such danger." *Taiwan Relations Act,* Public Law 96-8, 96th Cong. (April 10, 1979), http://usinfo.state.gov/eap/Archive_Index/Taiwan_Relations_Act.html.

77. Winston Lord, interview with author, April 5, 2000.

8

Chinese Decision Making in Three Military Actions Across the Taiwan Strait

Niu Jun

THIS CHAPTER EXPLORES THE BASIC FEATURES of the Chinese decision-making process during the three military confrontations across the Taiwan Strait in 1954–1955, 1958, and 1995–1996. Chinese scholars have extensively studied decision making during military confrontations in the 1950s. They have detailed the decision-making process and analyzed the complexity of the motives behind Chinese decisions. Recent publications demonstrate that major progress is being made in this research.[1] It should also be admitted that research in this area remains inadequate because archives are not available to the public. Up to now, Chinese academics have shed little light on the decision-making process in 1995–1996 mainly because of the lack of basic historical documents owing to how recent this crisis was. This situation changed slightly when the former vice premier and foreign minister, Qian Qichen, published his memoirs, *Ten Stories of a Diplomat,* in 2003. Exchanges with U.S. colleagues and limited historical literature available in the United States are helpful in conducting deeper research into the issue, but, generally speaking, the lessons U.S. scholars can provide are relatively limited.[2]

This chapter discusses three basic problems in the decision-making process during the three military confrontations across the Taiwan Strait. These three problems are very basic, but that does not mean that they are unimportant or that others have already completely examined and clearly explained them.

First, accomplishing national reunification is the first and foremost political pursuit of China. In practice, the Chinese leadership constantly implements policies for national reunification, including the preparation to use military means to either reunify Taiwan under some circumstances or prevent Taiwan from separating from China. The three military confrontations are all particular means taken by the Chinese government to pursue the aim of national reunification during those particular stages. As a result, they share the same nature. Analysts, recognizing this constant, overriding objective of Chinese decision making, should undertake further research on the specific roles and aims of the military confrontations across the Taiwan Strait.

Second, all three military confrontations took place when Sino-American relations were deteriorating or unstable, and all represent China's responses to U.S. policies to some extent. Several questions still require further research: To what extent were the military actions responses to U.S. policies? What factors made Chinese decision makers believe it necessary and possible to take military action?

Third, Chinese policy making during all three military confrontations shares some common characteristics. These include the nature of decision-making objectives, which are both diverse and limited, and the flexibility to adjust policy. It is precisely these characteristics that make the decision-making process much more complicated. Confined by inadequate archives, researchers cannot discover some aspects of Chinese decision making, so it is hard to say that the generalizations and discussions of the features of Chinese decision making have been adequate and complete.

This chapter speaks of "military confrontation decision making" rather than "Taiwan Strait crisis management" mainly to show that the nature of Chinese decision making is clearly different from that in the United States. For Chinese decision makers, military action is but one of the various means to resolve complicated problems or even to prevent a crisis. The military exercises in 1995–1996 are one typical example of preemptive military deterrence. Obviously, China's use of military operations in the Taiwan Strait is not necessarily the same as "international crisis management" as defined by U.S. decision-making theory. The term "military confrontation decision making" refers to decision makers' use of military action to reach objectives, which can include but is not limited to the management of international crises.

Of course, emphasizing the differences between Chinese and U.S. decision making does not mean the theory of international crisis management has no analytical power regarding China's policies toward military action in the Taiwan Strait. This Chinese decision making has two priorities. First, when preparing plans for military action, Chinese decision makers attempt to design effective measures for preventing the development of a military conflict with the United States. Second, in the event that U.S. military forces do intervene in a military conflict across the Taiwan Strait, China would try to control the crisis between the United States and China and prevent it from escalating to a military conflict between the two countries. Such considerations in essence are undoubtedly international crisis management. It is necessary to conduct specific research toward the management of the military tension across the Taiwan Strait, but what should be emphasized is that the U.S. concept of international crisis management does not fully explain Chinese decision-making behavior during cross-strait military confrontations.

ROLE OF MILITARY CONFRONTATION IN CHINA'S REUNIFICATION STRATEGY

To define the nature of Chinese decision making during the three military confrontations across the Taiwan Strait, one must first determine the status and role of military confrontations in China's national reunification process. Because the accomplishment of national reunification is an unswerving political pursuit and a constant process in China, military confrontations, including the bombardment of Quemoy, attacking and occupying coastal islands, and military exercises of various scales, are but means for national reunification rather than forms of international crisis management. Furthermore, each military confrontation from the very beginning included the intention and measures to prevent the occurrence of an international crisis, or, in other words, to avoid as far as possible international military conflicts caused by military confrontations in the Taiwan Strait.

As early as the spring of 1949, when victory was gained in the battle of the Yangtze River crossing, one of the focal points of the People's Liberation Army (PLA) gradually became to attack Taiwan and realize national reunification. When the People's Republic of China (PRC) was founded in October 1949, its leadership set as one of its strategic tasks the liberation of Taiwan, which had to be accomplished at an early stage.[3] According to the vision of the Chinese Communist Party (CCP) Central Committee, the liberation of Taiwan would be accomplished in three steps. The first was to establish modern naval and air forces in order to obtain naval and air supremacy in the Taiwan Strait. The second step was to gradually liberate the coastal islands of Zhejiang and Fujian Provinces, which the Kuomintang (KMT) Army still occupied, so as to ensure the safety of ports and navigation lines and to establish military bases for attacking Taiwan. The third step was to wage a cross-strait war in 1950–1951 and realize national reunification.[4] The three-step plan originally targeted the early 1950s as the deadline for its accomplishment. The Korean War transformed it into a two-step strategy: taking coastal islands first and then liberating Taiwan, with no clear time frame identified. Chinese leaders also considered nonmilitary means for national reunification but only as a vision or supplementary means that was not very important in the reunification strategy of the time.[5]

The Korean War broke out on June 25, 1950. Two days later, the Truman administration declared a blockade of the Taiwan Strait by the Seventh Fleet and stationed U.S. Air Force units in Taiwan. The blockade of the Taiwan Strait by the U.S. Navy and the development of the Korean War forced Chinese leaders to postpone the original combat plan, but the postponement was temporary. Actually the PLA had never stopped its war with the KMT Army in the coastal areas as these conflicts continued on a small scale. The PLA, for example, shelled Quemoy on a small scale as early as January 1953.[6] Up until 1952, the main combat actions of the PLA were to clear maritime bandits supported by the KMT Army and break through the KMT Army's maritime blockade by seizing some coastal islands. These were all defensive measures.[7]

As of summer 1953, the PLA Navy and the East China Army Command issued orders to project power along China's southeast coast and take the offense against the naval and air forces of the KMT.[8] The PLA stationed air defense troops in Shanghai, Guangzhou, Beijing, and

Qingdao, completing air defense deployment for major cities.[9] In March 1954, a naval air force joined the combat, and it gained air supremacy over the Zhejiang coast in July, opening the first military confrontation in the Taiwan Strait.[10] At approximately the same time, the Central Military Commission (CMC) formulated strategic guidelines for taking the coastal islands, that is, attacking on an island-by-island basis from north to south and taking small islands first and then big ones (*congxiaodaoda, youbeixiangnan, zhudaojingong*).[11]

Actions from the bombarding of Quemoy in September 1954 to the takeover of Yijiangshan Island in January 1955 were merely part of the PLA strategy to control coastal islands. These actions were the natural result of a military plan and were both offensive and defensive military operations. Their purpose was to directly coordinate the current CCP Central Committee's "call for the necessary liberation of Taiwan" as well as to break through Taiwan's blockade of mainland ports and prevent its military harassment in the coastal areas. Because the U.S. administration of President Dwight D. Eisenhower advocated a release-Chiang policy beginning in February 1953, the KMT military began to emphasize military harassment of the coastal areas.[12] On July 16–17, 1953, for example, among its other activities the KMT military concentrated 12,000 troops to attack Fujian Province's Dongshan Island.

The military actions aimed at taking hold of islands along the Zhejiang coast in 1955 did not extend to Quemoy and Matsu outside the Fujian coast. Available literature suggests that the PLA had not at that time completed necessary military preparations for taking over Quemoy and Matsu. The combat plan for attacking and taking over Quemoy formulated by the PLA general headquarters staff in October 1953 did not win support from leaders of the East China Military Command. Mao Zedong also thought the plan too costly and the victory uncertain, and he vetoed the plan in late December 1953.[13] One can therefore reasonably infer that the combat principle of attacking on an island-by-island basis from north to south and taking small islands first and then big ones did not have a fixed and unchangeable timeline.

Accordingly, when the situation across the Taiwan Strait relaxed between the spring and summer of 1955, China immediately intensified its preparations for war, targeting Quemoy and Matsu. On July 8, the CMC met and discussed the combat plan for Quemoy. On July 14,

Mao Zedong approved the decision taken at the meeting.[14] At a meeting in Xiamen on September 10, Peng Dehuai put forward a specific battle plan for taking over Xiamen, which the CMC approved.[15] To meet the needs of a war, the Nanjing Military Command conducted a major internal adjustment in the spring of 1956, and the government established the Fujian Military Command to take direct responsibility for an offensive against Quemoy and Matsu. In 1957, the railway linking Yingtan and Xiamen was completed. In spring 1958, the CMC discussed the most opportune moment to implement plans to station the PLA Air Force in Fujian and the possible outcomes, including the reaction of the United States. In July, the CMC decided that the Air Force would promptly enter frontier airports in Fujian as planned. According to the CMC plan, shelling of Quemoy began on August 23, 1958, and the PLA prepared to invade Quemoy at an opportune moment.[16]

Tension across the Taiwan Strait relaxed in October 1958 partly because Mao Zedong and other Chinese leaders began to reconsider the role of Quemoy and Matsu in reunifying with Taiwan. The whole process of bombarding Quemoy in the summer of 1958 showed that the PLA had not made a decision beforehand about the landing on Quemoy. In fact, in October the PLA terminated the process of taking over coastal islands. The plan to attack the coastal islands as part of the larger strategy of achieving reunification with Taiwan basically was aborted.

After October, no large-scale military conflicts took place between the mainland and Taiwan over coastal islands. China's reunification strategy entered into a new and more complicated stage. The PLA's continuation of intermittent shelling of Quemoy had a symbolic meaning. China's leaders, through this unique military action, showed the world that the civil war between the CCP and the KMT had not yet ended; moreover, China's leaders resisted the U.S. plan to maintain the separation between Taiwan and the mainland. The large-scale war preparations by the PLA along the southeast coast during the summer of 1962 were therefore defensive military deployments, and their purpose was to defeat Taiwanese authorities' attempts to use the mainland's temporary economic troubles to launch military attacks against the southeast coast.[17] The military antagonism between the two sides during this period objectively intensified the Taiwan Strait situation, and the civil war was certainly not yet complete.

Sino-American relations began to normalize after the visit to China by President Richard M. Nixon in 1972. In 1979, China and the United States established diplomatic ties. After that, the Chinese government gradually formed a strategy of "peaceful reunification" to resolve the question of Taiwan. On September 30, 1981, Ye Jianying, chairman of the Standing Committee of the National People's Congress, declared the "Nine Principles for Peaceful Reunification of the Motherland."[18] These principles marked a strategic transformation of China's reunification strategy from one that relied mainly on the use of force to one that focused more on political and peaceful means.

Adoption of the peaceful reunification policy led to a relative lowering of the role of military means in reunifying Taiwan. That is to say, the main method of liberating Taiwan moved away from using the military and moved toward maintaining strategic deterrence. Yet, regardless of whether military means are the main method or an auxiliary method, the use of the military as a means of deterrence must remain a part of the strategy of reunification with Taiwan. At the beginning, during the process of Sino-American normalization, China used deterrence to stress to the United States that the Taiwan question was China's internal affair, one in which the United States had no right to interfere, thereby emphasizing China's sovereignty over Taiwan.[19] The substance of military deterrence was gradually enriched and was fully expounded in 2000 in the white paper, "The One-China Principle and the Taiwan Issue." The paper opposed foreign interference, Taiwan independence, and the idea that negotiations to peacefully resolve the issue of reunification could extend indefinitely.[20] One can infer that, during different periods of peaceful reunification, the focus of military deterrence will vary. Generally speaking, military deterrence comprises three scenarios.

The first is to prevent meddling in the Taiwan question by foreign countries. The questions of how China defines "meddling" and which types of meddling would cause the Chinese side to use force or resume its use of force as a main method for achieving reunification are issues requiring further research. In brief, the bottom line should be to prevent the military and political relations between the foreign country and Taiwan from resulting in expansion of proindependence Taiwanese forces or obviously damaging China's reunification strategy in a certain period.[21]

The second scenario is that the forces of proindependence in Taiwan might grow to such an extent that Taiwan might declare independence, or independence might become a trend that is difficult to resist by other means. Acts along this line include attempts to gain international legitimacy for Taiwan independence through so-called pragmatic diplomacy.[22]

The third scenario is linked to the second one, that is, the process of negotiating for a peaceful reunification is characterized by "procrastination" and a "failure to resolve" the issue.[23] This has not become a big issue because the Chinese government has not put forward any explicit time schedule.

The military exercises in the Taiwan Strait by the PLA in 1995–1996 show that military means constitute an important method of preemptive deterrence in the strategy of peaceful reunification, and military means aim at preventing a serious deterioration of the situation in the complicated and long process toward peaceful reunification.

SINO-AMERICAN RELATIONS AND CHINESE DECISION MAKING

During the three military confrontations in the Taiwan Strait, China largely responded to U.S. policies. The two military actions in the 1950s occurred against the backdrop of military confrontations with the United States. The one in 1995–1996 was merely one more acute problem among many conflicts between China and the United States since their relations seriously deteriorated after 1989.

The Taiwan question has been directly related to Sino-American confrontation. Chinese leaders paid close attention to U.S. policy from the very beginning of mobilization for the liberation of Taiwan. Although stating that "Taiwan was the last stronghold of the U.S. imperialists' aggression against China," they thought that the United States was not likely to directly launch a military intervention.[24] This judgment, made in approximately 1950, went through a fundamental change caused by the blockade of the Taiwan Strait by the United States after the outbreak of the Korean War. Since then any military action taken by China in the Taiwan Strait has been directly related to U.S. policies.

In 1954–1955, Chinese leaders decided to conduct military action in the Taiwan Strait for two main reasons. The first was the sharp escalation of military conflicts between the mainland and Taiwan over coastal islands. The background for this included the Eisenhower administration's policy of "liberating" Chiang Kai-shek. The second was the beginning of consultations between the U.S. and Taiwanese authorities on the signing of a common defense treaty. Past research has basically revealed the role of these two factors but has failed to provide reasonable explanations for the relation between the two.

PLA leaders began in 1952 to plan to fight the KMT Army over islands along the Fujian and Zhejiang coasts. Military actions began roughly at the time of the conclusion of the Korean War, when PLA leaders also began to plan for the liberation of Quemoy.[25] Nonetheless, when the Korean armistice agreement was signed in the summer of 1953, a new feature in the Taiwan Strait situation was that the KMT Army, encouraged by the Eisenhower administration's policy, strengthened its military action along the Zhejiang coast. Against this background, the military actions taken by the PLA in the summer of 1953 were aimed at both implementing the set policy of reunification with Taiwan and disrupting the U.S. support of Chiang's offensive against the offshore islands. The influence of the latter might even have been more direct. Because Chinese leaders already linked Taiwanese military actions and U.S. exercises in the Taiwan Strait, they defined U.S. support of Chiang's offensive as a component of America's antagonistic policy toward China.[26] From the perspective of Sino-American relations, the PLA's military action in the southeast coastal areas was defensive.

Military action by the PLA actually began in the summer of 1953.[27] The combination of military action by the PLA in 1954 and the large-scale liberation-of-Taiwan publicity campaign in late July responded mainly to the consultation between the United States and Taiwan about the signing of a treaty for a military alliance. In early July 1954, Zhou Enlai came back to China during a recess in the Geneva Conference to report to the decision makers about the conference. At the Politburo meeting on July 6, Mao Zedong specifically talked about using publicity and diplomacy, including a condemnation of U.S. policy, to prevent the United States from signing a military treaty with Taiwan.[28] Participants at this meeting discussed U.S.-Taiwan relations and were obviously deeply worried about the development of U.S-Taiwan military relations.[29]

It is possible that because there were dissenting views about the UN deliberations on Taiwan's status, Chinese leaders found it necessary to take more explicit and firmer actions to demonstrate China's position on the question of Taiwan.[30] On July 23, 1954, the *People's Daily* issued an editorial entitled "We Must Liberate Taiwan," which was followed by large-scale publicity in the Chinese media. According to the CCP Central Committee's telegram to Zhou Enlai on July 27:

> After the end of the Korea War, we did not put this task forward to the people in a timely manner (it was late by about half a year), nor did we take necessary measures and carry out effective work in the military, diplomatic, and publicity areas in the light of this task in a timely manner, which was inappropriate. If we do not put forward the task and begin our preparations now, we will be making a serious political mistake.[31]

This reflects the fact that the CCP Central Committee at that time definitely felt a sense of urgency and worried that the Taiwan problem would become internationalized.

Many researchers believe that the publicity and military action taken by China were designed to prevent the signing of a mutual defense treaty between the United States and Taiwan and conclude that China did not realize its goal but, rather, accelerated the signing of the U.S.-Taiwan Mutual Defense Treaty.[32] Although this argument makes sense to some extent, it is obviously too simplistic. First, it can hardly be convincing to say that Mao Zedong and other Chinese leaders truly believed that statements in newspapers and limited military action along the coast would be adequate to prevent the signing of the U.S.-Taiwan treaty. After all, they had rich political and military experience. They had just completed a three-year negotiation with the United States about the armistice on the Korean peninsula and had not very long before pointed out very clearly that diplomatic contacts with the United States were necessary to prevent the signing of such a treaty.[33]

The key to the problem is likely the understanding by the Chinese leaders of the scope of the U.S-Taiwan treaty. In their view, the treaty would cover islands along the Zhejiang and Fujian coasts and might expand the scope of the blockade of the mainland to the "coast of Guangdong Province and Tokyo Bay."[34] As a result, it would not only cause a protracted separation of Taiwan from the mainland but also pose a more serious security threat to the mainland. Consequently, the PLA would not be able to fulfill its set plan of taking over coastal islands. In this sense, to take over islands held by the KMT Army was a strategic action with both offensive and defensive objectives, and it was designed to both create conditions for reunification and prevent coastal islands from being included in the U.S.-Taiwan Mutual Defense Treaty and becoming strongholds for a U.S. attack against the mainland.

Chinese leaders' intensified publicity about the liberation of Taiwan and their reactions to the U.S-Taiwan consultation for a military treaty actually had two purposes. One was to demonstrate, through publicity and military action, China's sovereignty over Taiwan, opposition to internationalization of the Taiwan question, and, most important, China's opposition to a military treaty between the United States and Taiwan. The second purpose was to intensify military operations to seize the coastal islands and take over the Dachen Islands along the Zhejiang coast before the signing of the U.S-Taiwan joint defense treaty. In his instructions to the Eastern China Military Command on November 11, 1954, Chief of Staff Su Yu instructed the troops to fight to prevent the U.S-Taiwan joint defense treaty from covering islands along the mainland coasts that were occupied by KMT Army.[35] The order for combat issued by the general headquarters staff on November 30 further demonstrated that the decision of the PLA to storm and capture the Zhejiang Province offshore islands was aimed mainly at preventing the islands from being covered by the U.S-Taiwan treaty.[36] The campaign to take over Yijiangshan Island reflected the serious worry on the part of the Chinese military about the situation under the shadow of the U.S-Taiwan treaty.[37]

The above analysis shows that in the decision-making process in 1954–1955, although political targets and military targets were coordinated, taking over the coastal islands occupied by the KMT Army was the substantive goal. Taking over the islands constituted the most important action to demonstrate China's sovereignty over Taiwan, to realize the plan to take over all coastal islands, to exclude islands along the Zhejiang coast from the scope of a prospective U.S.-Taiwan mutual defense treaty, and to eliminate security threats posed by U.S. or Taiwanese use of the coastal islands against the mainland.

Because taking over coastal islands was both a strategic step toward the liberation of Taiwan and an imperative security question, it is reasonable to infer that the Chinese leaders cared greatly about whether the U.S.-Taiwan treaty was to cover islands along the mainland coast. From this perspective, one should not simply conclude that the decisions made by the Chinese leaders in order to "prevent a U.S.-Taiwan treaty" failed. The problem is that Chinese leaders probably did not consider a situation in which the United States supported the defense of the island of Taiwan and at the same time encouraged or demanded that Chiang Kai-shek give up coastal islands so as to avoid military conflict with the mainland, the result of which would have created a further distance between the mainland and Taiwan.

Analysts in both China and the United States have already discussed the Chinese decisions in 1958 about the bombardment of Quemoy. Since the 1990s, research has sought a motive for decision making in Chinese domestic politics and has produced valuable results.[38] Results of this research exhibit obvious flaws, however, in failing to reveal the causal relationship between the 1954–1955 and 1958 military actions, particularly the role of Sino-American relations.

A problem left over from the military action in 1954–1955 was China's failure to take over all coastal islands occupied by Chiang's army as well as the failure to know exactly whether the U.S-Taiwan joint defense treaty would cover the islands Chiang occupied along the Fujian coast. Thus, decision makers considered it necessary to take further military action against islands along the Fujian coast following their capture and stabilize China's control over the coastal islands off Guangdong Province and Zhejiang Province. Military preparedness and Sino-American relations determined the opportune time for military action. Other factors, such as the demands of domestic politics (the Great Leap Forward, for example), the influence of Sino-Soviet relations, and Mao's ideological considerations, were not as important. Furthermore, it was very difficult to determine the influence of these factors in the decision-making process.

The PLA had barely completed its military preparations for war against Quemoy and Matsu in summer 1958; however, after the PLA Air Force entered Fujian in July, the PLA basically completed its air defense of the province in coordination with other troops and began battles for air supremacy. Although the PLA was still unable to attack and occupy Quemoy and Matsu, it had secured conditions after a limited offensive. The key factors that should be taken into account were the situation of Sino-American relations and Chinese leaders' judgments about the China policies of the United States.

The Sino-American summits at the ambassadorial level beginning in summer 1955 were interrupted in December 1957. Even during the negotiations, the United States did not stop helping the Taiwanese authorities strengthen their military forces, including the deployment of surface-to-surface tactical missiles in 1957. This forced the Chinese leaders to reconsider how to promote reunification. As early as March 1956, Chinese leaders realized that the United States might take the opportunity of Sino-American negotiations to freeze the Taiwan question and strengthen the U.S. military presence in Taiwan, Quemoy, and Matsu. In view of this, China could not allow the issue to drag on indefinitely.[39]

Shortly after the interruption of the Sino-American ambassadorial negotiations, in mid-June 1958, Mao made it clear to the Ministry of Foreign Affairs that he found it necessary to readjust policy toward the United States that had been in place since 1954. Mao stated that China should persist in its struggle with the United States rather than develop relations with the U.S. government.[40] On June 30, the Chinese government issued a public statement demanding the resumption of ambassadorial negotiations with a time limit and stressing the seriousness of the Taiwan question in Sino-U.S. relations and China's being "fully capable of liberating Taiwan."[41] In a memo, Mao explained the relationship between the bombardment of Quemoy and China's change of policy toward the United States, that is, the objective of the bombardment was directly against Chiang Kai-shek and indirectly against the United States. Mao stated: "The United States has bullied us for so many years. Why don't we take this opportunity to teach them a lesson?" He continued that the purpose was "to observe and test the determination of the United States."[42]

If China's pursuit of reunification is taken as a continuous and uninterrupted process and Sino-U.S. ambassadorial-level meetings are taken as a way to resolve the Taiwan question, it is logical to conclude that the bombardment of Quemoy in the summer of 1958 was merely a military choice made by Chinese leaders when they found Sino-U.S. negotiations at an impasse. There was simply no other better way to promote reunification with Taiwan, including the seizure of Quemoy and Matsu, and force the United States back to the negotiating table. Admittedly, one outcome of the bombardment was a change of Mao's plan to quickly seize Quemoy and Matsu.

The military confrontation in 1995–1996 also took place during a period in which Sino-American relations had been experiencing continued deterioration since summer 1989. Sino-U.S. relations were turbulent following the enormous changes in Eastern Europe and the disintegration of the former Soviet Union. If one wishes to understand the 1996 military confrontation between China and the United States in the Taiwan Strait from the perspective of Sino-U.S. relations, one must not neglect two fundamental premises.

First, the 1996 military confrontation was one of the serious conflicts and disputes between China and the United States during that period, when Sino-U.S. relations as a whole were in a very difficult situation. China and the United States found themselves in conflict with each other in almost all fields, including intellectual property rights, human rights, proliferation of weapons of mass destruction, most-favored-nation (MFN) status for China, and the U.S. sanctions against China. The two countries' bilateral relations on the whole were confrontational.

Second, the two countries settled almost all conflicts through confrontation or by means of a process that included elements of confrontation. The continuous confrontation in the human rights field, for example, led to a confrontation on MFN status beginning in 1993. Differences regarding weapons proliferation that first appeared in 1993 led to the Yinhe incident, in which the United States intercepted a Chinese ship that it believed to be transporting illegal chemicals to Iran. In 1994–1995, differences regarding intellectual property rights led Sino-U.S. relations to the brink of a trade war.[43]

Just as conflicts and contradictions took place in almost all fields and almost all conflicts moved from confrontation to relaxation, so did the Taiwan Strait question. During an atmosphere of strong mistrust and confrontation between China and the United States, Chinese decision makers defined certain acts of the U.S. government—including the granting of a visa to Lee Teng-hui to visit the United States—as "diplomatic provocations . . . to test China's bottom line on the Taiwan question . . . amid rising anti-China forces in the world."[44]

Of course, Chinese decision makers came to this judgment not only because of the tense general mood in bilateral relations. Two basic facts also played rather important roles in causing the tensions in the Taiwan Strait. First, one month before the U.S. government declared it would grant a visa for Lee Teng-hui's visit, Secretary of State Warren Christopher promised Foreign Minister Qian Qichen that the Clinton administration would not allow Lee to visit the United States.[45] In his memoirs, Qian mentioned that Chinese leaders felt "shocked and angry" about the lack of trustworthiness on the part of the United States.[46] Qian's comment shows that Chinese policy makers believed that, regarding the Taiwan problem, they already could not trust U.S. promises and must adopt actions to force the United States to restrain its words and actions.

Another important event was that the Chinese government tried time and again to negotiate through diplomatic means with the United States to eliminate the negative effects of Lee's visit to the United States and to repair the "political foundations of Sino-U.S. relations" that had been "seriously damaged." However, the Clinton administration did not wish to make an adequate effort to save the situation from deterioration. Thus, the Chinese leaders judged that the Clinton administration operated under the illusion that China would make concessions on the question of Lee's visit if the United States made only a few gestures. The Chinese government further decided that it had to make a powerful response to force the United States to "really realize the seriousness of the issue."[47] One can thus see the military exercises that began in the autumn of 1995 as a measure taken to stress the seriousness of the Taiwan question and to demonstrate China's determination and capability to the United States. Policy analysts in China understood the purpose of the PLA action in the Taiwan Strait as to "deter Taiwan independence and teach the United States a lesson" (zhensheTaidu, qiaodaMeiguo).

The above analysis roughly reveals the major influence of Sino-U.S. relations on Chinese decisions to take military action in the Taiwan Strait. Chinese military decisions were usually products of acute confrontation or serious deterioration of Sino-U.S. relations on the question of Taiwan. It is of course still necessary to carry out in-depth, detailed, and specialized research and analysis on how Sino-U.S. relations influence some specific decisions in China. In the various stages of military decision making in the three cases of cross-strait tensions, for example, how did Chinese leaders judge the intention of the United States, how did their judgment come into being, and what influence did the judgment produce on the decision making?

The aforementioned conclusion inevitably leads us to question the exact meaning and origin of the so-called cross-strait crisis as defined by U.S. academics specializing in China. In other words, is preventing the United States and China from engaging in a Taiwan crisis truly so complicated and difficult as imagined by many? In 1995–1996, the Americans themselves created the dangerous situation, which they could have avoided in the first place. Then they sought a solution through international crisis management. Such cases happen very often given the way the U.S. government deals with cross-strait relations. The U.S. government should not continue to act in such a strange manner.

BASIC CHARACTERISTICS OF CHINESE DECISION MAKING

According to Mao Zedong, even after one determines an objective, the channels and means to realize this objective are not fixed or unchangeable. At the strategic level, reunification is the objective while the paths, means, and the length of the process one undertakes to realize the objective will identify themselves in the process. Similarly, at the tactical level, the objective of each military action in the Taiwan Strait is also fixed, but the way in which it is implemented is not. One could say this is the key to understanding China's decision making regarding military action in the Taiwan Strait.

All three military confrontations in the Taiwan Strait share some common characteristics such as the diversity and limited nature of decision-making objectives and the flexibility in policy adjustments. It is precisely these characteristics that cause the decision-making process to be relatively complicated and, to some extent, confusing. Although other characteristics of Chinese decision making exist, this chapter will focus on these characteristics because of space constraints.

The diversity of decision-making targets refers to the fact that no decision making was designed to reach a single military objective. Instead, actions were taken for multiple diplomatic, political, and military purposes.

The limited nature of decision-making objectives in China can be seen in two aspects. First, the objectives of military action were limited. In particular, they strictly adhered to the strategic plan. When seizing the offshore islands, for example, Chinese troops carried out their strategic plans step-by-step. No attempt was made to rashly attack and occupy Quemoy and Matsu.

Second, during each instance of decision making, Chinese officials explicitly stressed that the PLA would not launch an offensive against U.S. troops and would make serious efforts to avoid a military conflict with the United States. During each occasion in which Chinese policy makers resorted to arms in the Taiwan Strait, regardless of the concrete reasons for that action, they always regarded avoiding conflict with the United States as a relatively important objective. In each situation in which the Chinese decision makers resorted to force in the Taiwan Strait, for example, they chose the time (the end of 1954 and the summer of 1958) at which the United States was least likely to intervene directly. Each time, the objective of the PLA's military action regarded not causing the United States to directly intervene as a limitation (for example, in 1954–1955 when China seized the Dachen archipelago and in 1958 when China shelled only Quemoy). The PLA also chose methods for its military action that were least likely to cause the United States to directly intervene (for example, the 1958 shelling of Quemoy and the 1995–1996 military exercises). Chinese strategic principles deeply influenced the decisions of China's leaders regarding military strategy, particularly regarding military battles.

The diversity and limited nature of decision-making targets led to flexibility in policy adjustment. Bearing the macroscopic objective in mind, Chinese leaders revised the scope and intensity of military action from time to time on the basis of target priorities and outcomes of military action. The purpose was to maintain flexibility and avoid escalation of military action to an extent difficult to control.

These characteristics were evident in all three military actions across the Taiwan Strait. The objectives of the 1954–1955 military action were threefold. The first objective was to rapidly gain control of the Dachen Islands off the Zhejiang coast.[48] The second was to prevent the United States from signing a defense treaty with Taiwan. Further analysis is necessary in this regard. Generally speaking, the objective was to prevent the United States from signing such a treaty, but in terms of military deployment and implementation, the bottom line was to prevent such a treaty from covering islands along the Zhejiang and Fujian coasts or even islands along the Guangdong coast that the PLA had already seized.[49] The third objective was to demonstrate China's sovereignty over Taiwan and its determination to liberate Taiwan and prevent the internationalization of the Taiwan question.[50]

While pursuing these three objectives, Chinese decision makers adopted rather prudent military action. From the very beginning, Chinese decision makers drew two clear boundaries for the military action in 1954–1955. The first was to concentrate on the coastal islands rather than conduct a direct offensive against the island of Taiwan. Chinese leaders were very cautious about whether they should seize Quemoy, Matsu, and other islands along the Fujian coast. Chinese leaders already realized that, given U.S. military intervention, reunification of Taiwan would be a long-term and complicated task that could not be accomplished in just one go.[51]

The second limitation they drew was to avoid military conflict with the United States as far as possible. Mao Zedong estimated that the taking over of the Dachen Islands outside of the Zhejiang coast would not cause large-scale U.S. military intervention.[52] This was certainly a very important reason for the PLA to choose the Dachen Islands as the first target of their offensive. Before the battle began, Mao Zedong stressed time and again that the PLA should avoid military conflict with U.S. troops. Mao even thought about revising the schedule for the battle for Yijiangshan Island.[53] Chinese leaders also took diplomatic measures to demonstrate that the PLA's actions would be limited to islands very near the mainland coast.[54]

Policy adjustments during this stage were manifested mainly through policies toward Quemoy, Matsu, and the other islands off the coast of Fujian. In summer 1954, when military action began, the PLA had not completed preparations for taking over Quemoy and Matsu and was not prepared to land on the island immediately to carry out this operation. After the KMT Army withdrew from the Dachen Islands in February 1955, Chinese decision makers were immediately faced with the issue of Quemoy and Matsu. Mao Zedong had considered the possibility of the KMT Army withdrawing on its own, under military pressure. In a March 14 directive to Peng Dehuai, Mao said that, when the enemy left Matsu or any other islands, the Chinese troops should let them go without attacking them or hindering their withdrawal.[55] Zhou Enlai also explained the Chinese position to the Indian representative to the UN as including the peaceful recovery of the islands.[56] At the same time, the PLA accelerated its deployment of the Air Force in Fujian province. On one hand, this deployment was coordinated with diplomatic efforts; on the other hand, it prepared for future military activities.[57] This was one reason the PLA did not immediately halt its military moves after taking over the Dachen Islands on February 28.

Because the PLA did not intend to land on Quemoy and Matsu at a time an international war could potentially break out in the Taiwan Strait, Chinese leaders immediately stopped large-scale military action and shifted their focus to negotiating with the United States.[58] On April 23, during the Bandung Conference, Zhou Enlai issued a public statement expressing hope for a relaxation of Sino-American tensions. The first round of military action across the Taiwan Strait came to an end.

In recent years many researchers have studied the motives of Chinese decision makers and their objectives when then bombarded Quemoy in summer 1958. Research has focused on Mao Zedong's extremely optimistic appraisal of the international situation, domestic political considerations, and the radicalization of diplomatic thought. This literature considers the encouragement of the Great Leap Forward and China's assistance to Arab national liberation movements in the Middle East as the main reasons for the PRC decision to shell Quemoy.[59] This point of view is undoubtedly very enlightened, but it does not fairly answer an obvious question: Why did Mao Zedong believe that the international situation was favorable enough for China to support national liberation movements in the Middle East at the same time that China could not push forward the reunification strategy with Taiwan at home, namely the seizure of the offshore islands? This question is hard to evade and indicates that current research about the importance and influence of the reunification strategy is insufficient.

A common problem of many analyses is that they neglect the relationship between the 1958 bombarding of Quemoy and the takeover of the coastal islands in 1954–1955. From the perspective of the two-step strategy for reunification with Taiwan, the final seizure of the Fujian coastal islands, including Quemoy and Matsu, was the last step in the strategy to completely seize the offshore islands. It was most possible that Mao decided to bombard Quemoy to promote the reunification strategy through military action. If one understands the PLA's strategic plan and the military preparations that continued unceasingly after the spring of 1955, one can also understand that the reason Mao did not mention the objective of reunification in many of his talks is likely that among the Chinese leadership this objective did not require emphasis. From 1955 to December 1957, for example, Mao clearly pointed out that before the PLA Air Force prepared to enter Fujian province in 1958, Peng Dehuai had already proposed the deployment of the Air Force into Fujian on five occasions.[60]

Shortly after Mao's proposal to deploy the Air Force into Fujian in 1958, leaders including Fujian provincial party secretary Ye Fei and Air Force commander in chief Liu Yalou told Mao Zedong and the CMC on January 19, 1958, about the various likely responses from the Americans and Taiwanese to the Chinese deployment of the Air Force to Fujian. The Chinese response they suggested included "seize Quemoy and Matsu, these two vulnerable points." Namely, these leaders advocated using airplanes, naval warships, and artillery to conduct a blockade, with the result being to "possibly force the enemies on the two islands to withdraw" or at the least force Chiang Kai-shek to "stop bombing Fujian."[61] They suggested commencing military activities as early as July or August. At a meeting of the CMC of the CCP Central Committee soon afterwards and in a report given to Mao Zedong, Peng Dehuai pointed out that the PLA already possessed the ability to shell Quemoy and Matsu to initiate a blockade and advocated beginning these activities in July or August.[62]

The PLA leadership's discussions and later published articles by Mao make it clear that the primary motive or objective of bombarding Quemoy was to force the KMT Army out of islands along the Fujian coast.[63] Mao's exhortation to "observe and test the determination of the Americans" was also an objective of the military action, but it mainly reveals that Mao at that time was not sure whether the bombardment would drive KMT troops out of Fujian islands. The key was still the U.S. policy, namely whether the United States was determined to intervene directly in a military conflict over the islands off the coast of Fujian province.[64] Some decision makers at that time thought that Chiang Kai-shek would not easily give up Quemoy and Matsu.[65]

In summary, China had two objectives in its bombardment of Quemoy in 1958. The top priority was to drive KMT forces out of Quemoy and Matsu, thus completing its plan for taking over all coastal islands. The other objective was to obtain an exact understanding of the bottom line of U.S. policy toward the Taiwan Strait, specifically, at what point would the United States engage in direct military intervention. As to the things Mao talked about—supporting people's revolutions in the Middle East, fueling the Great Leap Forward, or placing a noose around the United States—they were all secondary political objectives.

The bombardment of Quemoy in summer 1958 continued to have limitations placed on it. The first was not to attack the island of Taiwan. According to CMC instructions, the scope of activities of the PLA Air Force in Fujian was mainly above Quemoy and Matsu, with the purpose of obtaining air supremacy over Fujian Province. Air strikes would be launched on Taiwan only if the KMT Air Force bombed mainland cities such as Shanghai and Hangzhou.[66] When the bombardment of the island began, the CMC made it clear that the Navy and Air Force should not go into the open sea or attack the island of Taiwan.[67]

The second limitation was not to directly engage in conflict with the U.S. troops or conduct any military action that might lead to the direct involvement of U.S. troops. Other authors have already described this limitation.[68] One can infer that even though Mao used relatively positive words, such as "revolutionary forces are prevailing," to describe the international system as extremely favorable to China, one cannot say that Mao already could not rationally judge the international system. In his view the benefits of a positive international situation were actually relatively limited. Mao merely meant that the power of the United States was dispersed to such an extent that, if China adopted limited military measures in the Fujian coastal islands, the United States would find it difficult to conduct a direct military intervention.[69] As to where the limitations of military action lay, China's leaders were gradually testing this through their ongoing military activity.

One question worth considering is whether Mao urged Soviet leader Nikita Khrushchev to visit China before China shelled Quemoy because Mao wanted China to enjoy the deterrent factor of Soviet support vis-à-vis the United States. Speaking to Sino-Soviet issues such as the long-wave transceiver and the common nuclear-powered submarine fleet, Mao on July 22 condemned the Soviet Union's attempts to continue its policy of "controlling" China's "great power-ism." Mao also requested that Khrushchev visit China to clarify these issues.[70] This incident caused Khrushchev to visit China from July 31 to August 3.

Khrushchev and Mao released an official report of their meeting, which included a proclamation that the two countries had "reached a full agreement regarding the adoption of measures to oppose aggression and protect peace."[71] Mao sought to use Khrushchev's visit to produce a belief in the international community that the Soviet Union supported China's shelling of Quemoy. It is difficult to imagine that, at a time when the PLA was trying its hardest to prepare to shell Quemoy, Mao would risk the important Sino-Soviet alliance for a long-range receiver and a common fleet. In fact, that was not the case; high-level leaders of the Soviet Union and China were at that time meeting at talks that included the two countries' defense ministers, and one can anticipate that this put pressure on U.S. decision makers. In passing, one should point out that when the campaign to seize the offshore islands began in 1954, Khrushchev had already visited Beijing the preceding October.

Policy adjustment was obvious in the process of the 1958 bombardment of Quemoy. When the bombardment of Quemoy began to show results and the United States showed its unwillingness to be drawn into a military crisis over the Fujian Islands, Chinese decision makers finally decided not to take over Quemoy and Matsu for the time being and to pack them together with the Taiwan Island and Penghu Islands.[72] The decision actually marked an end to the attacks on the coastal islands. Many works have already discussed at length the process of policy adjustment.

There are three reasons for the important policy adjustment. To begin with, the scope of the U.S. military deployment exceeded the expectation of Chinese leaders and validated Mao's initial prudence.[73] Of course, from another perspective, Mao's estimation of whether the United

States would directly interfere in the case of a limited military operation in the Fujian coastal islands was also accurate. The second reason was that, when the United States showed it was unwilling to help Chiang's army defend Quemoy and Matsu, Chinese leaders already were convinced that, because the Taiwan question would continue as an issue for a fairly long time because of U.S. intervention, a package solution covering Taiwan, Penghu, Quemoy, and Matsu would be the best choice to prevent the separation of Taiwan from China.[74] From the perspective of the policy adjustment process, this was probably the most important reason. The third reason was that, through the shelling of Quemoy, Chinese leaders grasped the fact that U.S. policy toward the Fujian coastal islands was not aggressive and that the United States might not continue to help the Taiwanese authorities defend these islands. Consequently, from a military security perspective, China no longer faced security threats from the Fujian coastal islands, particularly since the United States would not likely use these islands to attack the mainland because the KMT military did not have the ability to do so.[75] These judgments greatly relaxed the pressure to use force to capture the islands.

As to the military exercises in 1995–1996, it is still impossible to conduct an in-depth analysis because the publicly available historical literature is very limited. However, the 1995–1996 situation manifested features similar to the two preceding incidents.

Newly published memoirs by Qian Qichen provide a fairly complete summary of the judgments made by Chinese decision makers about the nature and influence of Lee Teng-hui's visit to the United States in 1995. They believed that the purpose of the Clinton administration's issuing a visa to Lee was to "test the bottom line of China on the Taiwan question" in the belief that if the United States placated China somewhat, China would accept it. The Clinton administration's action took place against the backdrop of the long-term U.S. policy of using Taiwan to contain China and of rampant anti-Chinese forces in the world. Chinese leaders believed Lee's visit would have serious consequences, including severe damage to the political basis for Sino-American relations since normalization, thus encouraging the separatist policies of the Taiwanese authorities and giving rise to an anti-China atmosphere in Taiwan and around the world.[76]

From these judgments, one can determine that the military exercises from July 1995 to March 1996 had at least two objectives. The first was to remind the United States of the extreme significance and sensitivity of the Taiwan question and that the United States should not have an unrealistic impression of China's bottom line on the issue. At the same time, China wanted to warn international anti-China forces not to deliberately challenge China's bottom line on the Taiwan question.[77] The second was to affect the political situation in Taiwan and deter the development of separatist tendencies. Specific considerations about different issues at different stages will require additional access to historical literature.[78]

Later developments show that a series of Chinese military exercises between July 1995 and March 1996, although manifesting the special role of force in China's strategy of peaceful reunification, were indeed a form of military deterrence aimed at preventing the situation in the Taiwan Strait from developing into an international crisis. The limitations of the military action were also clear. The PLA did not intend to launch an offensive against any part of Taiwan, Penghu, Quemoy, or Matsu, nor did it intend to engage in a military conflict with the United States. Furthermore, compared with the two crises of the 1950s, the publicly stated purpose, scale, time, and venue of military exercises excluded the possibility of a Sino-American military conflict.

Additional, interlinked questions are worth further research. Did the decision makers foresee that the United States would respond militarily to the March 1996 exercises by dispatching two aircraft carriers?[79] Did the Chinese decision makers make prior preparations for this type of U.S. military response? Did the military response by the United States affect China's policy objectives, and, if so, to what extent? One can reasonably answer these questions only on the basis of more historical evidence.

CONCLUSIONS

This chapter separates research on the role of military action in the strategy for reunification with Taiwan from the influence of Sino-American relations, and it takes the first steps toward analyzing the basic characteristics of policy regarding military action in the Taiwan Strait. These aspects are interrelated and influence each other. In combination, these aspects provide a basic framework for analyzing decisions regarding military action in the Taiwan Strait.

More comprehensive research and summaries are needed. More concrete analysis must be done on the particular use of various factors and the relationship between various factors. This chapter is only an initial step. To promote the study of this important problem, one must more carefully analyze the historical documents that are already available. More ample and more comprehensive theoretical preparations are also necessary.

The essence of the policy regarding military action in the Taiwan Strait represents China's grand strategy for Taiwan reunification. It is true that different internal and external environments affect military decision making, but China's grand strategy for Taiwan reunification is the defining factor for the function, scale, strength, and limits of military operations in different eras. Taiwan reunification is the basic motive behind military action and is the leading principle of policies for military action. A deep understanding of the reunification policy is the key to researching the Taiwan Strait crises.

NOTES

1. Dai Chaowu, *Duidui yu Weiji.de Niandai—1954–1958nian.de ZhongMei Guanxi* [Times of Hostility and Crisis—Sino-U.S. Relations 1954–1958] (Beijing: Zhongguo Shehui Kexue Chubanshe, 2003); Pang Xianzhi and Jin Chongji, eds., *Mao Zedong Zhuan, 1949–1976* [Biography of Mao Zedong, 1949–1976], vol. 1 (Beijing: Zhongyang Wenxian Chubanshe, 2003); Zhao Xuegong, "Dierci Taiwan Haixia Weiji yu ZhongMei Guanxi" [The Second Taiwan Strait Crisis and Sino-U.S. Relations], *Dangdai Zhongguoshi Yanjiu* [Current Chinese History Studies], no. 3 (2003); Hou Xiaojia, "Paoji Jinmen Juece yu Quzhe Jincheng" [Policy of Shelling Quemoy and Its Complicated Course], in *Zhonggongdangshi Yanjiu* [Chinese Communist Party History Studies], no. 2 (2003).

2. Michael D. Swaine, "Chinese Decision-Making Regarding Taiwan, 1979–2000," in David M. Lampton, ed., *The Making of Chinese Foreign and Security Policy in the Era of Reform* (Stanford, Calif.: Stanford University

Press, 2001); Robert S. Ross, "The Stability of Deterrence in the Taiwan Strait," *National Interest* (Fall 2001); Robert S. Ross, "Navigating the Taiwan Strait: Deterrence, Escalation Dominance, and U.S.-China Relations," *International Security* 27, no. 2 (Fall 2002); Thomas J. Christensen, "Posing Problems Without Catching Up: China's Rise and Challenges for U.S. Security Policy," *International Security* 25, no. 4 (Spring 2001); Suisheng Zhao, ed., *Across the Taiwan Strait: Mainland China, Taiwan, and 1995–1996 Crisis* (New York: Routledge, 1999); Robert L. Suettinger, *Beyond Tiananmen: The Politics of U.S.-China Relations, 1989–2000* (Washington, D.C.: Brookings Institution Press, 2003); and Ashton B. Carter and William J. Perry, *Preventive Defense: A New Security Strategy for America,* trans. Hu Liping and Yang Yunqin (Shanghai: Shanghai Renmin Chubanshe, 2003).

3. Zhou Enlai, "Dangqian Caijing Xingshi he XinZhongguo Jingji.de Jizhong Guanxi" [On the Current Fiscal Situation and Several Relationships in the Economy of the PRC], December 5, 1949, in *Jianguo Yilai Zhongyao Wenxian Xuanbian* [Selected Important Documents Since the Founding of the PRC], vol. 1 (Beijing: Zhongyang Wenxian Chubanshe, 1992), p. 73; Mao Zedong, "Guanyu Tongyi Suyi Diao Si.ge Shi Yanxi Haizhan Deng Wentei Gei Liu Shaoqi.de Diabao" [Telegram to Liu Shaoqi Approving Su Yu's Application to Move Four Divisions], February 10, 1950, in *Jianguo Yilai Zhongyao Wenxian Xuanbian* [Selected Important Documents Since the Founding of the PRC], vol. 1, p. 257.

4. He Di, "'The Last Campaign to Unify China': The CCP's Unmaterialized Plan to Liberate Taiwan, 1949–1950," *Chinese Historians* 5, no. 1 (Spring 1992).

5. Mao Zedong, "Guanyu Zhengqu Heping Jiejue Taiwan Wenti Gei Zhang Zhizhong.de Dianbao" [Telegram to Zhang Zhizhong Regarding the Attempts to Reach a Peaceful Resolution to the Taiwan Problem], March 11, 1950, in CCP Central Committee Literature Research Division, ed., *Jianguo Yilai Mao Zedong Wengao* [Manuscripts by Mao Zedong Since the Founding of the PRC], vol. 1 (Beijing: Zhongyang Wenxian Chubanshe, 1987), p. 271.

6. *Dangdai Zhongguo Haijun* [Contemporary Chinese Navy] (Beijing: Zhongguo Shehui Kexue Chubanshe, 1987), p. 198.

7. Ibid., p. 166.

8. Ibid., p. 189.

9. *A Brief History of PLA Air Defense Force* (Beijing: Political Department of the Air Force, 1993), pp. 192–198.

10. Ibid., p. 199.

11. Zheng Wenhan, *Mishu Rijili.de Peng Laozong* [Commander in Chief Peng in His Secretary's Diaries] (Beijing: Junshi Kexue Chubanshe, 1998), p. 32; Lin Xiaoguang, "Zhongguogongchandang DuiTai Zhengce.de Lishi Yanjin" [Evolution of CCP Policy Toward Taiwan], in *Party History Research*, vol. 3, 1997, p. 3.

12. U.S. Department of State, *American Foreign Policy: Basic Documents 1950–1953* (Washington D.C.: U.S. Government Printing Office, 1957), pp. 61–65. Eisenhower commented on his policy toward China and, specifically, on the release-Chiang policy in his February 2, 1953, State of the Union address.

13. Mao Zedong, "Mao Zedong dui Zongcanmoubu Zuozhanbu Guanyu Gongji Jinmen Zuozhan Feiyong Gaisuan Baogao.de Pingyu (Shougan)" [Mao Zedong's Remarks on the Cost Estimate Report for Attacking Quemoy by General Staff Headquarters War Department], December 23, 1953, in Pang and Jin, eds., *Mao Zedong Zhuan, 1949–1976* [Biography of Mao Zedong, 1949–1976], vol. 1, p. 583.

14. Zheng Wenhan, *Mishu Rijili.de Peng Laozong* [Commander in Chief Peng in His Secretary's Diaries], pp. 32–33.

15. Ibid., pp. 44–45.

16. Pang and Jin, eds., *Mao Zedong Zhuan, 1949–1976* [Biography of Mao Zedong, 1949–1976], vol. 1, pp. 858–859; Liao Xinwen, "1958nian Mao Zedong Juece Paoji Jinmen.de Lishi Kaocha" [A Historical Exploration of Mao Zedong's 1958 Decision to Attack Quemoy], in *Dang.de Wenxian* [Party Documents], no. 1 (1994); *Duidui yu Weiji.de Niandai* [Times of Hostility and Crisis], pp. 329–330.

17. Niu Jun, "1962: Zhongguo Duiwai Zhengce 'Zuo' Zhuan.de Qianye" [1962: On the Eve of Chinese Foreign Policy's Shift to the "Left"], *Lishi Yanjiu* [History Studies], no. 3 (2003).

18. *People's Daily*, October 1, 1981.

19. Wei Shiyan, "Nikesong Fanghua" [Nixon's Visit to China], in *XinZhongguo Waijiao Fengyun* [Diplomacy of New China], vol. 3 (Beijing: Shijie Zhishi Chubanshe, 1991); "Statement of the Government of the PRC, December 16, 1978," *People's Daily*, December 17, 1978.

20. "Yi.ge Zhongguo.de Yuanze yu Taiwan Wenti" [The One-China Principle and the Taiwan Issue], Taiwan Affairs Office of the State Council, White Paper on the Taiwan Issue, February 2000, www.gwytb.gov.cn:8088/detail.asp?table=WhitePaper&title=White%20Papers%20On%20Taiwan%20Issue&m_id=4.

21. Ibid.; Ministry of Defense of the People's Republic of China, "2000nian Zhongguo.de Guofang" [China's National Defense in 2000], October 2000.

22. Zhang Mingqing, Director of Information, State Council Taiwan Affairs Office, press conference, November 26, 2003.

23. "Yi.ge Zhongguo.de Yuanze yu Taiwan Wenti" [The One-China Principle and the Taiwan Issue], Taiwan Affairs Office of the State Council.

24. "Zhonggong Zhongyang Guanyu Qingzhu 'Wuyi' Laodongjie.de Kouhao" [CCP Central Committee on Celebration of Labor Day], April 26, 1950, in *Jianguo Yilai Zhongyao Wenxian Xuanbian* [Selected Important Documents Since the Founding of the PRC], p. 210; Han Huanzhi and Tan Jingqiao, eds., *Dangdai Zhongguo Jundui.de Junshi Gongzuo* [Military Work of Contemporary Chinese Military] (Beijing: Zhongguo Shehui Kexue Chubanshe, 1989), pp. 285–286.

25. Pang and Jin, eds., *Mao Zedong Zhuan, 1949–1976* [Biography of Mao Zedong, 1949–1976], vol. 1, p. 582; *Dangdai Zhongguo Haijun* [Contemporary Chinese Navy], pp. 189–192.

26. CCP Central Committee Literature Research Division, ed., *Zhou Enlai Nianpu 1949–1976* [Chronicle of the Life of Zhou Enlai 1949–1976], vol. 1 (Beijing: Zhongyang Wenxian Chubanshe, 1997), p. 405; CCP Central Committee Literature Research Division, ed., *Jianguo Yilai Mao Zedong Wengao* [Manuscripts by Mao Zedong Since the Founding of the PRC], vol. 4, p. 495.

27. *Dangdai Zhongguo Haijun* [Contemporary Chinese Navy], pp. 191–192.

28. Mao Zedong, "Tong Yiqie Yuanyi Heping.de Guojia Tuanjie Hezuo" [To Cooperate With All Countries That Wish to Have Peace], July 7, 1954, in CCP Central Committee Literature Research Division, ed., *Mao Zedong Wenji* [Collected Works of Mao Zedong], vol. 6 (Beijing: Renmin Chubanshe, 1999), pp. 333–334.

29. Liao Xinwen, "1958nian Mao Zedong Juece Paoji Jinmen.de Lishi Kaocha" [Historical Exploration of Mao Zedong's 1958 Decision to Attack Quemoy].

30. Zhou Enlai, "Tuijin ZhongYing Guanxi, Zhengqu Heping Hezuo" [Pushing Sino-British Relations, Striving for Peaceful Cooperation], August 12, 1954, in Ministry of Foreign Affairs of the People's Republic of China and the CCP Central Committee Literature Research Division, eds., *Zhou Enlai Waijiao Wenxuan* [Selected Works of Zhou Enlai on Diplomacy] (Beijing: Zhongguo Wenxian Chubanshe, 1990), p. 84.

31. "1954nian 7yue 27ri Zhonggong Zhongyang Zhi Zhou Enlai Dian" [Telegram from the CCP Central Committee to Zhou Enlai on July 27, 1954], in Pang and Jin, eds., *Mao Zedong Zhuan, 1949–1976* [Biography of Mao Zedong, 1949–1976], vol. 1, p. 585.

32. Zhang Baijia and Jia Qingguo, *Duikangzhong.de Fanxiangnan, Huanchongqi he Ceshiyi: Cong Zhongguo.de Jiaodu Kan ZhongMei Dashiji Huitan* [The Steering Wheel, Bumper, and Detector in Confrontation: China-U.S. Meetings at Ambassadorial Level from a Chinese Perspective] (Beijing: Dangdai Zhongguoshi Yanjiu, 2000); and Jiang Changbin and Robert Ross, eds., *Cong Duizhi Zouxiang Huanhe: Lengzhan Shiqi Zhong Mei Guanxi Zai Tantao* [From Confrontation to Détente: Sino-U.S. Relations During the Cold War Revisited] (Beijing: Shijie Zhishi Chubanshe, 2000), p. 175, represent this point of view.

33. Mao Zedong, "Tong Yiqie Yuanyi Heping.de Guojia Tuanjie Hezuo" [To Cooperate With All Countries That Wish to Have Peace], pp. 333–334.

34. CCP Central Committee Literature Research Division, ed., *Zhou Enlai Nianpu 1949–1976* [Chronicle of the Life of Zhou Enlai 1949–1976], p. 405.

35. Xu Yan, *Jinmen zhi Zhan* [War Over Quemoy] (n.p.: Zhongguo Guangbodianshi Chubanshe, 1992), p. 180.

36. Jiang Ying, "50 Niandai Maozedong Waijiao Sixiang Shulun" [On Mao Zedong's Thoughts on Diplomatic Work in the 1950s], in Jiang and Ross, eds., *Cong Duizhi Zouxiang Huanhe: Lengzhan Shiqi Zhong Mei Guanxi Zai Tantao* [From Confrontation to Détente: Sino-U.S. Relations During the Cold War Revisited], p. 587.

37. Nie Fengzhi, *SanJun Huige Zhanzheng Donghai* [The Three Armed Forces Poised for a War in the East China Sea] (Beijing: Jiefangjun Chubanshe, 1986), pp. 71–72, discusses the military preparations made then.

38. Thomas J. Christensen, *Useful Adversaries: Grand Strategy, Domestic Mobilization, and Sino-American Conflict, 1947–1958* (Princeton, N.J.: Princeton University Press, 1996), chap. 6; Chen Jian, *Mao's China and the Cold War* (Chapel Hill: University of North Carolina Press, 2001), pp. 171–186; Gong Li, "Liangci Taiwan Haixia Weiji.de Chengyin yu Zhong Mei Zhijian.de Jiaoliang" [Causes of the Two Taiwan Strait Crises and the Struggle Between China and the United States], in Jiang and Ross, eds., *Cong Duizhi Zouxiang Huanhe: Lengzhan Shiqi Zhong Mei Guanxi Zai Tantao* [From Confrontation to Détente: Sino-U.S. Relations During the Cold War Revisited], p. 56; Zhang Baijia, "Tongxiang Huanhe.de Qiqu Zhilu: Biandong.de Guojia Huanjing yu Zhongguo duiMei Zhongce 1954–1971" [Rugged Path Toward Relaxation: The Changing International Environment and Chinese Policy Toward the United States 1954–1971], in Jiang and Ross, eds., *Cong Duizhi Zhouxiang Huanhe: Lengzhan Shiqi ZhongMei Guanxi Zai Shentao* [From Confrontation to Relaxation: China-U.S. Relations in the Cold War Era], p. 433; *Di Dui Yu Wei Ji De Nian Dai* [Times of Hostility and Crisis], pp. 266–274.

39. *Zhou Enlai Junshi Huodong Jiyao* [Summary of Zhou Enlai's Military Activities], vol. 2 (Beijing: Zhongyang Wenxian Chubanshe, 2000), p. 381.

40. *Zhang Wentian Nianpu* [Chronicle of Zhang Wentian], vol. 2 (Beijing: Zhonggongdangshi Chubanshe 2000), pp. 1097–1098.

41. "Zhongguo Zhengfu Youguan ZhongMei Dashiji Huitan.de Shengming" [Statement by the Chinese Government on Sino-U.S. Ambassadorial Meeting], June 30, 1958, in *ZhongMei Guanxi Ziliao Huibian* [Compilation of Documents on Sino-U.S. Relations], vol. 2 (Beijing: Shijie Zhishi Chubanshe, 1958–1960), pp. 2626–2628.

42. "1958nian 8yue 18ri Mao Zedong Gei Peng Dehuai.de Xin" [Mao Zedong's Letter to Peng Dehuai on August 18, 1958], in Pang and Jin, eds., *Mao Zedong Zhuan, 1949–1976* [Biography of Mao Zedong, 1949–1976], vol. 1, p. 857; Wu Lengxi, *Yi Maozhuxi—Wo Qinshen Jingli.de Ruogan Zhongda Lishi Shijian Pianduan* [Memory of Chairman Mao: Some Important Historical Incidents of Which I Have Firsthand Knowledge] (Beijing: Xinhua Chubanshe, 1995), pp. 76–77.

43. Niu Jun, "Lun Kelindun Zhengfu Diyi Renqi duiHua Zhengce.de Yanbian ji qi Tedian" [On the Evolution and Characteristics of the China Policy in Clinton's First Term], in Niu Jun, ed., *Kelindun Zhixia.de Meiguo* [The United States Under Clinton] (Beijing: Zhongguo Shehui Kexue Chubanshe, 1998).

44. Qian Qichen, *Waijiao Shi Ji* [Ten Stories of a Diplomat] (Beijing: Shijie Zhishi Chubanshe, 2003), pp. 307–308.

45. Ibid., p. 305.

46. Ibid., p. 306.

47. Ibid., p. 308.

48. Yin Qiming and Cheng Guangya, *Diyi Ren Guofangbuzhang* [The First Minister of Defense] (Guangzhou: Guandong Jiaoyu Chubanshe, 1997), p. 198; Zheng Wenhan, *Mishu Rijili.de Peng Laozong* [Commander in Chief Peng in His Secretary's Diaries], p. 32.

49. CCP Central Committee Literature Research Division, ed., *Zhou Enlai Nianpu 1949–1976* [Chronicle of the Life of Zhou Enlai 1949–1976], p. 405.

50. Pang and Jin, eds., *Mao Zedong Zhuan, 1949–1976* [Biography of Mao Zedong, 1949–1976], vol. 1, p. 585.

51. "Guanyu Jiefang Taiwan Xuanchuan Fangzhen.de Zhishi" [Instructions on Principles in Publicity of Liberation of Taiwan], September 1, 1954, in CCP Central Committee Literature Research Division, ed., *Zhou Enlai Nianpu 1949–1976* [Chronicle of the Life of Zhou Enlai 1949–1976], p. 412.

52. Nie Fengzhi, *SanJun Huige Zhanzheng Donghai* [The Three Armed Forces Poised for a War in the East China Sea], p. 38.

53. Mao Zedong, "Guanyu Gongji Shangxia Dachendao Shiji Wenti.de Piyu" [On Practical Issues Relating to Attack of Dachen Islands], August 21, 1954, in CCP Central Committee Literature Research Division, ed., *Jianguo Yilai Mao Zedong Wengao* [Manuscripts by Mao Zedong Since the Founding of the PRC], vol. 4, p. 533; Mao Zedong, "Guanyu Gongji Yijiangshandao Shiji.de Piyu" [On the Timing of the Attack on Yijiangshan Island], December 9, 1954, in Ibid., p. 627.

54. CCP Central Committee Literature Research Division, ed., *Zhou Enlai Nianpu 1949–1976* [Chronicle of the Life of Zhou Enlai 1949–1976], pp. 421, 478–479.

55. Mao Zedong, "Guanyu Mazudeng Daoyu Diren Chezoushi Wo Jun Buyao Gongji.de Piyu" [Do Not Attack When Enemies Withdraw from Matsu and Other Islands], in CCP Central Committee Literature Research Division, ed., *Jianguo Yilai Mao Zedong Wengao* [Manuscripts by Mao Zedong Since the Founding of the PRC], vol. 5, p. 51; CCP Central Committee Literature Research Division, ed., *Zhou Enlai Nianpu 1949–1976* [Chronicle of the Life of Zhou Enlai 1949–1976], pp. 478–479.

56. CCP Central Committee Literature Research Division, ed., *Zhou Enlai Nianpu 1949–1976* [Chronicle of the Life of Zhou Enlai 1949–1976], p. 479.

57. Mao Zedong, "Dui Su Yu Guanyu Bushu Budui Jinzhu Fujian Xinjian Jichang.de Qingshi.de Pishi" [Memo to Su Yu Regarding Instructions for the Deployment of Troops to the New Airfield in Fujian], May 19, 1955, in *Jianguo Yilai Zhongyao Wenxian Xuanbian* [Selected Important Documents Since the Founding of the PRC], vol. 5, p. 128.

58. Zhou Enlai, "Guanyu Chuguohou zai Gedi Shangtan Taiwan Wenti.de Baogao" [On Discussions About Taiwan Abroad], April 30, 1955, in CCP Central Committee Literature Research Division, ed., *Zhou Enlai Nianpu 1949–1976* [Chronicle of the Life of Zhou Enlai 1949–1976], p. 474.

59. Christensen, *Useful Adversaries*; Chen Jian, *Mao's China and the Cold War*; Gong Li, "Liangci Taiwan Haixia Weiji.de Chengyin yu Zhong Mei Zhijian.de Jiaoliang" [Causes of the Two Taiwan Strait Crises and the Struggle Between China and the United States], in Jiang and Ross, eds., *Cong Duizhi Zouxiang Huanhe: Lengzhan Shiqi Zhong Mei Guanxi Zai Tantao* [From Confrontation to Détente: Sino-U.S. Relations During the Cold War Revisited], pp. 56–57; Zhang Baijia, "Tongxiang Huanhe.de Qiqu Zhilu: Biandong.de Guojia Huanjing yu Zhongguo duiMei Zhongce 1954–1971" [The Rugged Path Toward Relaxation: The Changing Inter-

national Environment and Chinese Policy Toward the United States 1954–1971], 433–434; *Duidui yu Weiji.de Niandai* [Times of Hostility and Crisis], pp. 266–274.

60. Zheng Wenhan, *Mishu Rijili.de Peng Laozong* [Commander in Chief Peng in His Secretary's Diaries], p. 239.

61. Shen Weiping, *8-23 Paoji Jinmen* [Bombardment of Quemoy on August 23], vol. 1 (Beijing: Huayi Chubanshe, 1998), pp. 93–99.

62. Zheng Wenhan, *Mishu Rijili.de Peng Laozong* [Commander in Chief Peng in His Secretary's Diaries], pp. 232, 239; Wang Yan, ed. *Peng Dehuai Nianpu* (Beijing: Renmin Chubanshe, 1998), p. 675.

63. Pang and Jin, eds., *Mao Zedong Zhuan, 1949–1976* [Biography of Mao Zedong, 1949–1976], vol. 1, p. 858; Liao Xinwen, "1958nian Mao Zedong Juece Paoji Jinmen.de Lishi Kaocha" [A Historical Exploration of Mao Zedong's 1958 Decision to Attack Quemoy]; Wu Lengxi, *Yi Maozhuxi—Wo Qinshen Jingli.de Ruogan Zhongda Lishi Shijian Pianduan* [Memory of Chairman Mao: Some Important Historical Incidents of Which I Have Firsthand Knowledge], p. 74.

64. Wu Lengxi, *Yi Maozhuxi—Wo Qinshen Jingli.de Ruogan Zhongda Lishi Shijian Pianduan* [Memory of Chairman Mao: Some Important Historical Incidents of Which I Have Firsthand Knowledge], pp. 76–77.

65. *Wang Shangrong Jiangjun* [General Wang Shangrong] (Beijing: Dangdai Zhongguo Chubanshe, 2000), pp. 423–424.

66. "Peng Dehuai zai Zhongyang Junwei Zhanbei Gongzuo Zuotanhuishang.de Jianghua" [Statement by Peng Dehuai at the Meeting of Central Military Commission on War Preparations], July 26, 1958, in Zheng Wenhan, *Mishu Rijili.de Peng Laozong* [Commander in Chief Peng in His Secretary's Diaries], pp. 319–320.

67. "Dui Taiwan he Yanhai Zhan Daoyu Junshi Douji.de Zhishi" [Instructions on Taiwan and Coastal Islands Occupied by Chiang Kai-shek's Troops]; Shi Zhongquan, *Zhou Enlai.de Zhuoyue Gongxian* [Outstanding Contribution by Zhou Enlai] (Beijing: Zhonggong Zhongyang Dangxiao Chubanshe, 1993), pp. 368–373; Pang and Jin, eds., *Mao Zedong Zhuan, 1949–1976* [Biography of Mao Zedong, 1949–1976], vol. 1, pp. 859–860.

68. Pang and Jin, eds., *Mao Zedong Zhuan, 1949–1976* [Biography of Mao Zedong, 1949–1976], vol. 1, pp. 857–861; *Duidui yu Weiji.de Niandai* [Times of Hostility and Crisis], pp. 333–342.

69. *Didui yu Weiji.de Niandai* [Times of Hostility and Crisis], pp. 342–343.

70. Han Nianlong, *Dangdai Zhongguo Waijiao* [Contemporary Chinese Diplomacy] (Beijing: Zhongguo Shehui Kexue Chubanshe, 1988), p. 114.

71. *People's Daily*, August 4, 1958.

72. Mao Zedong, "Duleisi Shi Shijieshang Zuihao.de Fanmian Jiaoyuan" [Dulles Is the Best Negative Example in the World], October 2, 1958, in Ministry of Foreign Affairs of the People's Republic of China and the CCP Central Committee Literature Research Division, eds., *Mao Zedong Waijiao Wenxuan* [Selected Works of Mao Zedong on Diplomacy] (Beijing: Zhongyang Wenxian Chubanshe & Shijie Zhishi Chubanshe, 1994), pp. 356; "Zhou Enlai yu Andongnuofu Tanhua Jilu" [Minutes of a Talk Between Zhou Enlai and Antonov), October 5, 1958, in Pang and Jin, eds., *Mao Zedong Zhuan, 1949–1976* [Biography of Mao Zedong, 1949–1976], vol. 1, pp. 877–878.

73. "Mao Zedong yu Heluxiaofu Tanhua Jiyao" [Minutes of a Talk Between Mao Zedong and Khrushchev], September 30, 1958, in Pang and Jin, eds., *Mao Zedong Zhuan, 1949–1976* [Biography of Mao Zedong, 1949–1976], vol. 1, pp. 855–856.

74. Mao Zedong, "Duleisi Shi Shijieshang Zuihao.de Fanmian Jiaoyuan" [Dulles Is the Best Negative Example in the World]; "Zhou Enlai yu Andongnuofu Tanhua Jilu" [Minutes of a Talk Between Zhou Enlai and Antonov], pp. 877–878.

75. Wu Lengxi, *Yi Maozhuxi—Wo Qinshen Jingli.de Ruogan Zhongda Lishi Shijian Pianduan* [Memory of Chairman Mao: Some Important Historical Incidents of Which I Have Firsthand Knowledge], p. 84.

76. Qian Qichen, *Waijiao Shi Ji* [Ten Stories of a Diplomat], pp. 307–308; "Quanguo Renda Waishi Weiyuanhui Shengming" [Statement of the Foreign Affairs Committee of the National People's Congress], May 23, 1995, *People's Daily*, May 25, 1995; "Quanguo Zhengxie Waishi Weiyuanhui Shengming" [Statement of Foreign Affairs Committee of the Chinese People's Political Consultative Conference], May 24, 1995, *People's Daily*, May 25, 1995; "Zhongshi Lüxing Wojun Shensheng Shiming—Jinian Zhongguo Renmin Jiefangjun Dansheng 68 Zhounian" [Faithfully Implementing the Sacred Mission of the Army: Commemorating the 68th Anniversary of the PLA], *PLA Daily*, August 1, 1995; "Chi Haotian zai Guofangbu Juxing.de Qingzhu Jianjun 68 Zhounian Dahuishang Zhi Zhujiu Ci" [Toast by Defense Minister Chi Haotian at the Gathering Celebrating the 68th Anniversary of the PLA], *PLA Daily*, August 1, 1995; "Bugongzipo.de Huangyan" [A Lie That Would Collapse of Itself], *People's Daily*, June 9, 1995; "Meiguo Jiujing Yao Ba ZhongMei Guanxi Yinxiang Hefang" {Where Is the United States Leading Sino-U.S. Relations], *People's Daily*, June 18, 1995.

77. Qian Qichen, *Waijiao Shi Ji* [Ten Stories of a Diplomat], p. 304; "Zhongshi Lüxing Wojun Shensheng Shiming—Jinian Zhongguo Renmin Jiefangjun Dansheng 68 Zhounian" [Faithfully Implementing the Sacred Mission of the Army: Commemorating the 68th Anniversary of the PLA]; "Chi Haotian zai Guofangbu Juxing.de Qingzhu Jianjun 68 Zhounian Dahuishang Zhi Zhujiu Ci" [Toast by Defense Minister Chi Haotian at the Gathering Celebrating the 68th Anniversary of the PLA].

78. "'Minzhu' Waiyixia.de 'Taidu'—Zai Ping Li Denghui Zuijin Guanyu Liangan Guanxi.de Tanhua" [Taiwan Independence Disguised in Democracy: Another Comment on Lee Teng-hui's Recent Remarks on Cross-Strait Relations], *PLA Daily*, March 7, 1996; "'Xianxing Taidu' Yu 'Yinxing Taidu'.de Shuanghuang Xi—Ping Peng Mingmin Jinqi Yanxing" [A Two-Man Comic Show of Visible and Disguised Taiwan Independence: Comment on Peng Ming-min's Recent Remarks], *PLA Daily*, March 8, 1996.

79. Su Ge, *Meiguo DuiHua Zhengce Yu Taiwan Wenti* [U.S. Policy Toward China and the Taiwan Question] (Beijing: Shijie Zhishi Chubanshe, 1998), pp. 747–748. According to Su Ge, the Chinese government should have logically foreseen a military response by the United States. In his view, China's military exercises in March 1996 embodied China's intention of opposing the passage through the Taiwan Strait by U.S. aircraft carriers in December 1995 as well as military exercises by Taiwan.

9

The Chinese Embassy Bombing: Evidence of Crisis Management?

Kurt M. Campbell and Richard Weitz

A FEW MINUTES BEFORE MIDNIGHT on May 7, 1999 (Belgrade time), two U.S. Air Force B-2 bombers, having refueled several times during their lengthy transatlantic journey from Whitman Air Force Base in Missouri, launched five 2,000-pound joint direct attack munitions (JDAMs) at a building that U.S. government analysts thought housed the Serbian Federal Directorate for Supply and Procurement (FDSP). The Central Intelligence Agency (CIA) had nominated this particular target for attack after concluding that the FDSP was selling advanced military technologies (such as ballistic missile parts) to rogue states like Libya and Iraq and using the proceeds to finance the Serbian armed forces.[1] As it turned out, the building actually housed the embassy of the People's Republic of China (PRC) in Belgrade, which had moved to that building in 1997. The bombs, guided with deadly accuracy by the U.S. global positioning system, destroyed much of the facility's south side, including the office of the military attaché. The attack killed three young Chinese journalists and wounded twenty other Chinese citizens present at the complex.

The bombing of the Chinese embassy triggered one of the most serious crises in modern Sino-American relations. It led to street demonstrations and violence against U.S. interests in Beijing and elsewhere in China on a scale unseen since the Cultural Revolution of the late 1960s. Long after the incident, polls continued to register high levels of Chinese distrust and anger against the United States.[2] The crisis shattered the high hopes for improved ties aroused by President Jiang Zemin's visit to the United States in September 1997 and President Bill Clinton's reciprocal visit to China in June 1998. Supporters of the relationship in both capitals found themselves on the defensive.

The period immediately after the bombing must be considered as a case study on the limits of crisis management. Preoccupied senior U.S. decision makers took excessively long to address the issue, Chinese officials purposefully ignored the tools of modern diplomacy (such as the hotline), the PRC government initially inflamed rather than restrained public protests, the North Atlantic Treaty Organization's (NATO's) requirements for operational secrecy prevented a timely sharing of what transpired and why, and both capitals failed to appreciate how badly the incident and its aftermath would scar future attitudes toward their bilateral relationship. A host of factors complicates—even years later—a retrospective analysis of the event. The most important of these complications include the secretive nature of the bombing mission and the assets involved; increasing congressional suspicions, if not outright hostility in some quarters, toward China and Chinese intentions in general; and the overall lack of understanding among even plugged-in Washington insiders about just what exactly had happened to cause such a devastating mistake.[3]

CHINA'S REACTION: AT HOME

On Saturday morning, May 8, the Chinese people began to learn of the bombing through Internet sites and other information sources. Chinese television and other media soon provided extensive on-site coverage of the Serbian rescue and recovery operation.[4] The videos that ran continuously in the Chinese media of the dead bodies set amidst the ruins of their destroyed embassy wing naturally evoked suspicion because the surrounding buildings remained remarkably undamaged. The pictures invariably impart a sense of design and precision to the attack. By early afternoon, angry crowds had assembled around the U.S. embassy compound in Beijing. For the first time since 1989, Chinese authorities granted formal approval for mass protest activities and even provided buses to transport university students to the site.[5]

Demonstrators carried banners denouncing the United States in general and President Clinton in particular, shouted similar slogans, and presented petitions and letters of protest to embassy staff. Initially well disciplined, the crowds by early evening began to throw eggs, rocks, bottles, and pieces of concrete at the embassy building and vehicles. Gangs of rowdy young men soon joined in the bombardment, adding paint bombs and Molotov cocktails to the attack. Some of the projectiles started small fires, which the fourteen U.S. diplomats trapped inside the embassy managed to extinguish. The large numbers of police officers and PLA soldiers present interceded only when the protesters tried to scale the fences surrounding the building or threatened foreigners unluckily located in the area.[6]

The attacks intensified the following day. Some U.S. officials feared the students might try to storm the embassy compound and perhaps even take its personnel hostage.[7] As a precaution against another Tehran-like seizure, embassy staff began to destroy sensitive documents.[8] Protests also spread to other Chinese cities that hosted U.S. and British diplomatic facilities, which served as magnets for demonstrators. Those involved marched outside the U.S. missions in Shanghai and Guangzhou, burned the residence of the U.S. consul general in Chengdu, and threw rocks at the U.S. missions in Shanghai and Guangzhou.[9] Hangzhou, Shenyang, Xiamen, and other Chinese cities also witnessed mass demonstrations against the United States.[10] In foreign countries, Chinese nationals organized protests outside U.S. diplomatic missions. Although small in size compared with the manifestations in China, local media gave them substantial coverage.

Within China, journalists and broadcasters continued to give prominence to the bombing, showcasing pictures of family members crying over the bodies of the three dead Chinese citizens, who were designated "revolutionary martyrs" by the regime after their remains arrived in Beijing. China's widely distributed English-language magazines, such as *Beijing Review* and *China Today*, liberally reprinted these photographs.[11] Chinese consumers organized short-lived campaigns to shun U.S. products.

At this point, the Chinese government decided to exert more direction over the increasingly violent and disorderly demonstrations. Chinese officials may have initially underestimated how vehement the protests would become.[12] The bombing incident occurred after the Chinese media had played up the eightieth anniversary of the May Fourth Movement, which had begun as a protest against Western treatment of China after World War I and ended in an attempt to depose China's corrupt and insufficiently patriotic rulers. At the time of the embassy bombing, the Chinese populace was therefore opportunely primed to manifest its patriotism.[13]

Although the incident also helped divert attention from the tenth anniversary of the Tiananmen massacre, and many Chinese leaders shared the protesters' outrage, the Chinese government certainly did not favor spontaneous mass political activity. The previous month, Beijing had seen the unanticipated widespread appearance of the Falun Gong, described by its adherents as a spiritual movement and by its opponents as a religious cult. On April 25, approximately ten thousand Falun Gong members had staged a sit-down demonstration to highlight their demands for religious freedom. It was not until July that the authorities, caught off guard by the group's boldness, began arresting its members and banned the Falun Gong from holding further gatherings. The Chinese media then launched a vilification campaign against the movement that resembled its response to the embassy bombing.[14]

The embassy bombing resulted in Beijing experiencing its largest street demonstrations since the 1989 prodemocracy movement.[15] One probable government concern was that zealous protesters might fail to appreciate the need to not overly antagonize the United States over the incident. Apparently, some people in China began to complain that the government's initial response to the bombing had been excessively weak.[16] Elite fears about the potential long-term damage to the Chinese economy should highly visible manifestations of anti-Americanism continue likely contributed to the decision to rein in the protests. Perhaps inadvertently, the U.S. response to the crisis highlighted the threat to the foreign investment that had been fueling many sectors of the Chinese economy. On May 10, the State Department issued a travel advisory stating that U.S. government personnel had suspended all trips to China and warning other Americans to delay their own visits "until the situation stabilizes."[17]

Whatever the precise reasons, Vice President Hu Jintao made a televised speech on the evening of May 10 (Beijing time), explaining the official PRC position and expectations regarding the crisis. After reviewing and justifying the Chinese government's response to the "criminal act" and endorsing the Chinese people's "strong indignation" and "keen patriotism," Hu cautioned that the protests must occur "in accordance with the law." He affirmed that the authorities were confident that people would act "proceeding from the fundamental interests of the nation and taking the overall situation into account." Revealingly, he added, "We must prevent overreaction, and ensure social stability by guarding against some people making use of the opportunities to disrupt the normal public order." Warning against mistreating foreigners, Hu said:

> The Chinese government will uphold the policy of reform and opening to the outside world. We will protect, in accordance with relevant international laws and norms of international relations as well as relevant laws of China, foreign diplomatic organs and personnel, foreign nationals in China and those who have come to China to engage in trade, economic, educational and cultural undertakings, and reflect the civilization and fine traditions of the Chinese nation.

Hu ended his address by calling on the Chinese people to "unite closely around the Central Committee of the Communist Party of China with Comrade Jiang Zemin at the core, hold high the great banner of Deng Xiaoping Theory, be inspired with enthusiasm, and work with concerted efforts to push forward into the 21st century the great cause of building socialism with Chinese characteristics."[18] According to Li Xiguang, a prominent Chinese liberal nationalist, Hu's speech resembled the *People's Daily* editorial that had appeared immediately before the June 1989 Tiananmen crackdown and had warned the student protestors to exercise greater self-control.[19]

On that same day, the security forces began to permit only groups that had written permission from the Public Security Bureau to protest at the U.S. embassy. Only a small number of state-sanctioned groups qualified. Uniformed military and police personnel were out in force, especially in most Beijing streets and around the U.S. diplomatic compound. Elements within the Public Security Bureau then instructed the authorized student and government workers where to march, how long to protest, and even what slogans and banners to use.[20] On May 11, the last day of these now heavily orchestrated public protests, the number of demonstrators declined to hundreds of people, in sharp contrast with the tens of thousands of Chinese demonstrators who had filled the streets immediately after news of the bombing first spread throughout the country. In effect, the three-day siege of the U.S. embassy had ended. At the same time, the Chinese media, after a crucial three-day delay, also began to relate to their audience the regrets of various NATO leaders. State television, for instance, broadcast President Clinton's public apology in its entirety.[21]

CHINA'S REACTION: ABROAD

In its first official reaction on May 8, the Chinese Ministry of Foreign Affairs (MFA) termed the bombing a "barbarian act" and warned that NATO would bear full responsibility for the consequences.[22] Vice Foreign Minister Wang Yingfan also summoned the U.S. ambassador, James R. Sasser, to the ministry to receive China's "strongest protest" against "the gross violation of Chinese sovereignty."[23] (Sasser declined to leave the embassy compound because of the demonstrations outside.[24]) On May 10, the MFA presented a formal diplomatic note to the United States. It demanded that "the U.S.-led NATO": (1) officially apologize to the Chinese government and people, including the families of those killed or injured; (2) undertake a comprehensive investigation of the incident; (3) promptly publicize its findings; and (4) severely punish those responsible. The note also urged NATO to cease immediately its military action against Yugoslavia and resume efforts to achieve a political solution to the Kosovo crisis.[25]

The Chinese government subsequently suspended almost all its bilateral exchanges with the United States, including formal discussions on human rights, nonproliferation, and other issues—but not, revealingly, the talks over China's accession to the World Trade Organization (WTO).[26] These actions came after both countries had carefully rebuilt facets of their bilateral relationship that had been in multiyear abeyance since the Tiananmen massacre nearly ten years before. Chinese officials also suspended all Sino-American military exchanges and stopped authorizing U.S. Navy warships to call at Chinese ports, including the Special Administrative Region of Hong Kong, which had been accessible to the U.S. Seventh Fleet since World War II.[27] They soon also forbade U.S. military aircraft from landing in Hong Kong.[28] The Chinese government also called on the United Nations (UN) Security Council to convene an emergency meeting to discuss the incident.[29] Besides observing a minute of silence and expressing "regrets" and "sorrow" over the deaths and destruction, the Security Council noted that NATO members had apologized for the bombing and had initiated an investigation into its causes.[30] Chinese representatives subsequently insisted that Secretary of State Madeleine K. Albright or some other senior U.S. official travel to Beijing to brief the Chinese leadership on the results of the U.S. investigation into the bombing.[31]

The Chinese government also stepped up its public support for NATO's bête noire, the Serbian government of Slobodan Milosevic. The communist governments of China and Yugoslavia had enjoyed longstanding ties that became particularly strong after Belgrade refused to back Moscow during the Sino-Soviet dispute that arose in the late 1950s. Milosevic had received a triumphant welcome when he visited China after the 1995 Bosnian peace agreement. His wife, Mirjana Markovic, had flown to China several times. She had praised the government's ability to modernize China's communist system to accommodate the imperatives of the post–Cold War era.[32] Even before the embassy bombing, Chinese leaders had expressed concern about NATO's justification for going to war against Serbia: to stop an authoritarian government from repressing its citizens. The fact that NATO's humanitarian intervention provided de facto support for armed separatists also aroused alarm. Chinese leaders worried that the United States and its allies could use the same logic to justify providing military assistance to anti-Beijing separatists in Taiwan, Tibet, or elsewhere.

China's policies toward Russia also changed somewhat. Indeed, the embassy bombing had both a short-term effect on U.S.-Russian relations and a longer-term (and potentially far-reaching) impact on Chinese-Russian relations. At the time of the incident, Russian officials, exploiting their ties with the Serbian leadership and seeking to reaffirm Russia's credentials as an important actor in European security affairs, had been actively seeking to negotiate a cease-fire and peace settlement on behalf of the Group of Eight (G-8). Unlike China, Russia had recently joined the elite G-8 club of advanced industrial powers. When the bombing occurred, Russian officials denounced the attack and said U.S. military operations were harming their peace efforts. President Boris Yeltsin, characterizing the incident as an "open outrage" lacking any justification, called on NATO to end its bombing campaign.[33] Foreign Minister Igor Ivanov abruptly cancelled a planned trip to London to discuss Russia's peace efforts.

Like their Chinese counterparts, Russian officials had been concerned about NATO's decision to launch the Kosovo war in the first place. The alliance had begun its campaign without securing the approval of the UN Security Council, where Russia and China held vetoes. Many influential Russians worried that the intervention at a minimum would encourage separatists in Chechnya. Some speculated that NATO might even provide direct support to the Chechen rebels in order to weaken Russia. For their part, Western leaders worried that Russia and China might now prevent the UN Security Council from adopting a resolution endorsing the planned NATO-led peacekeeping mission in Kosovo.

In the end, Beijing and Moscow did not veto the resolution. The Kosovo war, however, does seem to have accelerated the strengthening of their bilateral military ties.[34] Immediately after the embassy bombing, Yeltsin and Jiang held an hour-long conversation on the Beijing-Moscow hotline to discuss the incident and their response. At this time, Jiang was refusing to answer repeated phone calls from the White House. In early June, General Zhang Wannian, deputy chairman of China's Central Military Committee, spent ten days in Moscow. He met with Russia's new prime minister, Sergei Stepashin, who was born in China when his father was working as a Soviet adviser to the Chinese military. Shortly thereafter, the two governments decided to upgrade the quality of their defense cooperation substantially. In particular, they soon announced that China would purchase seventy-two Su-30 fighter-bombers, the most advanced Russian weapons system ever provided to China's People's Liberation Army. The following year, China received additional advanced conventional weapons, including Sovremenny-class destroyers equipped with SS-N-22 Sunburn anti-ship missiles and improved Kilo-class diesel attack submarines. Both these maritime systems could present a major threat to U.S. carrier battle groups operating nearby in the western Pacific in situations such as the defense of Taiwan. More significantly, Russian assistance to China's military modernization efforts could accelerate China's emergence as East Asia's strongest military power.

THE U.S. RESPONSE

All crises have an element of the unexpected. In the case of the Chinese embassy bombing, however, the extent of shock and dismay at the highest levels of the U.S. government cannot be exaggerated. The overriding desire initially inside the National Security Council (NSC) was not to lose momentum or international support for the Kosovo campaign. The endeavor had already exacerbated tensions within the Atlantic Alliance and engendered sharp divisions throughout the U.S. government and public. At the time of the bombing, senior administration officials were completely consumed by the conflict. Exhausted by the around-the-clock diplomatic and military planning efforts, NATO leaders worried that the peculiar manner in which the alliance had gone to war (with air power only) was failing to achieve its desired effect on the ground. The Serbs appeared prepared to fight on, the stream of desperate refugees fleeing Kosovo was continuing unabated, and the allied air forces were running out of approved targets. As one NATO officer subsequently put it, "We woke up to the fact that Milosevic wasn't going to come out on the front lawn with a white flag."[35] U.S. diplomats feared the embassy bombing, by diverting attention from the issue of curbing Serb atrocities in Kosovo, would derail their delicate efforts to rally international support to convince Belgrade to yield to NATO's demands. At a minimum, the accident might inspire further resistance among the Serbs, who now could more plausibly hope that China and other countries would intercede on their behalf. The last thing that the Europe-focused leadership in Washington desired was for this difficult Balkan imbroglio to assume a complicating Chinese dimension at such an unwelcome time.

Experts specializing in China who worked inside the U.S. government were not involved in the initial rounds of White House meetings that followed the bombing. NSC policy makers likely underestimated how intensely China would respond to the attack. The Pentagon brass evinced a clear reluctance to share much information about the incident in the high-level crisis management meetings. Their reasons likely included a determination to remain focused on ongoing military operations, a recognition that the Air Force would be protective about its stealthy and expensive bomber, and their likely collective confusion over just what actually had occurred to cause such a disaster. The unexpected combination of a national security hierarchy under extreme stress, a secretive CIA trying to overcome yet another embarrassment (following its failure to anticipate India's nuclear weapons test the previous year), a mission-conscious and proprietary military, and an ongoing and surprisingly challenging war only added to an already difficult situation. The resulting lack of communication among the core U.S. national security agencies, especially between the Department of Defense and the White House staff, impeded the U.S. response. Suspicious Chinese officials may not have appreciated these complications and may have attributed the debilitating tensions in Washington caused by conflicting considerations of secrecy, pride, and diplomacy to more malicious factors.

Immediately after the White House informed him of the bombing, Ambassador Sasser contacted the MFA to offer his condolences for the "terrible mistake."[36] Time differences and their other preoccupations kept U.S. officials in Washington from commenting on the matter for several hours. On Saturday morning (Washington, D.C., time), Secretary of Defense William Cohen and Director of Central Intelligence George Tenet issued a joint statement that called the incident a targeting error and said, "We deeply regret the loss of life and injuries from the bombing."[37] President Clinton, then in Oklahoma surveying tornado destruction, told reporters that the attack had been a "tragic mistake." Although he also expressed his "sincere regret and condolences to both the leaders and the people of China," the president indicated that Milosevic's "ethnic cleansing" policies were the ultimate source of the problem. He and other administration representatives insisted that the allied air strikes must continue until Serbian forces ceased their attacks on Kosovar Albanians and accepted the NATO-backed international peace plan.[38]

These carefully framed apologies only served to enrage the Chinese people further. Li Zhaoxing, China's ambassador to the United States, told Jim Lehrer on the Public Broadcasting Service's *NewsHour,* "If you just say 'sorry' and walk away without doing anything else in a thorough manner this will only add [to] the anger and indignation of the Chinese people." When Lehrer asked whether the ambassador doubted the U.S. government's commitment to conduct a full investigation and punish those responsible, Li said, "We attach more to facts, rather than words. No matter how eloquent one could be."[39] Washington would clearly need to do more to satisfy the Chinese demands for an apology, an investigation, compensation, and punishment for those responsible.

By this point in the crisis, an interagency working group including representatives from the White House, the Department of State, and the Department of Defense began conferring regularly to advise the NSC principals on policy options. These sessions were often conducted on secure telephone lines. Most participants subsequently acknowledged feeling they were making decisions hastily, with incomplete information. One person involved said:

> I knew that this was an accident, an operational fluke, but understanding why it happened and explaining this to the Chinese was something completely different. I do not recall many other times during my tenure in government feeling so frustrated by secrecy and bureaucratic incompetence as during the Chinese bombing incident. It was just a disaster.

The group recommended that U.S. leaders show more remorse in public and spare no effort in establishing an off-line communication channel with Chinese leaders at the highest levels in order to head off the crisis.

On Saturday evening, Secretary of State Albright hand-carried a letter of apology, addressed to Foreign Minister Tang Jiaxuan, to the Chinese embassy. Although conveying "our deep regret about the tragic, accidental fall of bombs on your embassy in Belgrade," the letter said that NATO had to continue its operations because it "cannot allow

Milosevic's 'ethnic cleansing' to go unchecked." The text also called on the Chinese government to reinforce security around the U.S. diplomatic facilities in China:

> We understand the high emotions this accident has generated among the Chinese people, but we are concerned that the large-scale demonstrations at our Embassy and Consulates in China are threatening the safety of our officials and their families and causing damage to our properties. We expect and ask the Chinese government to meet its responsibility to take all appropriate measures to ensure the safety of all Americans in China and protection of American properties.[40]

On May 9, Clinton sent a letter to President Jiang in which he expressed "apologies and sincere condolences for the pain and casualties brought about by the bombing of the Chinese embassy."[41] He also tried to talk with Jiang over the Sino-American hotline, but the Chinese side initially declined to arrange the call.[42] Somewhat later, in the presence of Ambassador Li, Clinton signed the official Chinese condolence book in the Oval Office.[43] Behind the scenes, U.S. officials indicated to their Chinese counterparts that the United States would provide an explanation for the tragic accident and would take other "tangible steps" to make amends. While never formally agreeing to meet the MFA's list of demands, the NSC strenuously sought, particularly after the tide turned in the eleven-week Kosovo air campaign, to address as many of the Chinese concerns as possible.

Independent of the Chinese calls for a full explanation, the U.S. government initiated several investigations, focused primarily but not exclusively on CIA procedures and oversight, in an attempt to discover how the target acquisition process had gone so badly awry. As one participant in the process described it:

> [T]he reality is that in the U.S. government two things coexist: on the one hand there is magnificent technology, including stealth bombers, laser target designation, satellite pinpointing, and in-air refueling; on the other hand, there is a guy in a basement reading the sports section while eating a powdered donut and sipping from a big-splurge Slurpee. In between bites, he is picking out a target to be bombed in

a city he has never visited. It's tough enough for Americans to understand, but I expect it's impossible for the Chinese to appreciate. It's just so much easier to chalk it up to a conspiracy and take it from there.

The U.S. investigation, led by Deputy Secretary of Defense John Hamre and the chairman of the Joint Chiefs of Staff General Joseph W. Ralston, was layered with secrecy. Although Deputy Secretary Hamre and Director Tenet later publicly outlined the main reasons for the faulty targeting, many details and conclusions remain classified.[44] When the initial investigation was concluded, however, the U.S. mounted a vigorous, if largely unsuccessful, attempt to explain the findings to Chinese interlocutors in Beijing.

After waiting three weeks in a futile effort to convince Washington to send a more senior envoy, and perhaps divided over how best to respond to the incident, the Chinese government agreed to accept a U.S. delegation in Beijing in mid-June to receive the report. Led by presidential special envoy and Under Secretary of State for Political Affairs Thomas R. Pickering, the third-ranking official in the State Department, the U.S. mission included representatives from the White House, the intelligence community, the Department of State, and the civilian Office of the Secretary of Defense. On June 17, Pickering, using PowerPoint slides and other visual aides, tried to convince his skeptical interlocutors that the attack was an accident.

Although he cited multiple errors, Pickering highlighted three overarching failures: a flawed technique to locate the intended target (the FDSP), a reliance on inaccurate and incomplete databases, and a defective review process that should have exposed the error. Pickering stressed that the United States had no reason to attack the embassy on purpose. Such a decision would have violated U.S. doctrine and practice, worked against President Clinton's "strong personal commitment to strengthening" Sino-American ties, failed to help achieve NATO's objective of degrading "the capacity of the Yugoslav government and military for repression in Kosovo," and made it more difficult to secure China's support for U.S. diplomatic efforts to end the conflict. Pickering added that the CIA and Defense Department had not yet completed their interviews of everyone involved in the bombing because the war in

Kosovo had only just ended. After all the participants had been debriefed, he explained, the U.S. government would determine what disciplinary actions to take.[45]

Led by Foreign Minister Tang Jiaxuan, the Chinese audience rejected Pickering's explanation as inadequate and unconvincing:

> We have taken note of the apology extended to the Chinese government and the people by government and leaders of the U.S. and some of the other NATO member states. We have also taken note that the U.S. side has conducted investigation into the incident. However, it must be pointed out that the explanations that the U.S. side has supplied so far for the cause of the incident are anything but convincing and that the ensuing conclusion of the so-called mistaken bombing is by no means acceptable to the Chinese government and people.[46]

When Pickering emphasized the U.S. willingness to discuss appropriate compensation for the loss of Chinese lives and property and the U.S. government's commitment to improve further bilateral relations, the Chinese delegation responded that such an improvement must adhere to the "principles of mutual respect for sovereignty and territorial integrity and non-interference in each other's internal affairs. . . . Whoever started the trouble should end it. The U.S. side must . . . handle this incident properly, so as to create necessary conditions and atmosphere for the bilateral relations to come back to the normal track."[47] On June 18, the influential Chinese Communist Party daily, *People's Daily*, offered a lengthy refutation of Pickering's points.

In Washington, those officials involved in responding to the crisis noted a distinct lack of enthusiasm for the Pickering mission within the Defense Department. The absence of a uniformed military officer on the trip suggested a desire to distance the military from the incident.[48] Secretary Cohen criticized the Chinese media for its biased coverage of the affair. Some members of Congress and other commentators also accused the Chinese government of manipulating popular feelings in order to stir up anti-American protests in the hopes of forcing U.S. concessions on other issues.[49] Stanley Roth, assistant secretary of state for East Asian and Pacific Affairs, had to reassure Congress that the administration would not yield to such tactics:

I understand that the Chinese word for "crisis" is a combination of the characters for "danger" and "opportunity." There are those who undoubtedly speculate, both in China and the United States, that perhaps the crisis of the last few weeks . . . represents an opportunity for China to press for concessions from the U.S. on issues such as the terms for China's WTO accession, human rights, Tibet, and nonproliferation. These speculators are dangerously mistaken. U.S. policy in these areas is determined by clear and long-standing assessments of U.S. self-interest and fundamental values. Our standards will not change in reaction to either the bombing error in Belgrade or the Chinese reaction to it.[50]

DÉNOUEMENT

It is unclear whether a different U.S. response would have led to a better resolution of the crisis. Robert L. Suettinger has related that, when he visited the MFA in early June, its officials "made it clear that nothing Pickering said would be accepted by the Chinese government as a satisfactory explanation of the bombing. They indicated they would hear the under secretary out but that his explanation would be rejected."[51] Two contemporary observers of the Pickering mission commented: "In imperial times, Chinese officials expected foreigners to kowtow to the emperor, lying prostrate and knocking their foreheads on the ground nine times. They expected almost as much from U.S. Under Secretary of State Thomas Pickering."[52] The dismissive Chinese attitude persisted for the other U.S. missions of explanation and contrition that would follow, most notably toward the delegation led by General Ralston and Deputy Secretary of State Strobe Talbott the following year. Unfortunately, external factors—especially accusations that Chinese agents had conducted espionage at U.S. nuclear weapons laboratories or had tried to funnel money into the U.S. presidential election campaign—intruded to further complicate Sino-American relations following the bombing.

Nevertheless, the Chinese government declined to press the matter further on the official level after the Pickering visit. The Clinton administration had made clear to Beijing it would not make concessions on Taiwan, the terms for China's entry into the WTO, or other matters of bilateral dispute to assuage Chinese anger over the attack. Although Chinese officials subsequently provided increased economic and other assistance to Milosevic's regime, they did not veto the NATO-backed UN Security Council resolution that ended the war in Kosovo on Western terms, despite earlier threats to do so.[53] The Chinese government also did not pursue a formal anti-American military alliance with Russia, notwithstanding their common concern about NATO's unsanctioned humanitarian intervention in Kosovo.[54]

On July 30, the U.S. and Chinese governments announced an agreement, implemented that September, in which the United States would pay $4.5 million to the twenty-seven people injured in the bombing and to the families of the three Chinese citizens killed in the attack.[55] The previous week, China had rescinded its prohibition against U.S. military flights to Hong Kong.[56] After Clinton and Jiang held productive discussions at the September 1999 Asia-Pacific Economic Cooperation summit in Auckland, U.S. National Security Adviser Samuel R. Berger said the Sino-American relationship was "back on track."[57] In November 1999, the two governments reached a deal on China's entry into the WTO. The following month, after five rounds of negotiations, the United States agreed to pay $28 million to the Chinese government as compensation for the damage to its Belgrade embassy. The settlement also required China to pay $2.8 million to the United States as compensation for the damage to U.S. diplomatic facilities in China. In early 2000, following a November 1999 visit by Deputy Assistant Secretary of Defense Kurt Campbell, China and the United States resumed large-scale military-to-military contacts.[58]

Unofficially, many in China continued to argue that the attack was a deliberate effort to either punish Beijing for its opposition to the war in Kosovo or to intimidate China into making concessions on Taiwan or other matters.[59] The revelation that the CIA, for the first time during the air campaign, had proposed this particular target intensified these suspicions. So too did the concentrated destruction of the embassy's defense and intelligence section, which gave the impression of its being a deliberate target. (Subsequent analysis found that the Air Force had targeted other parts of the building as well, but those bombs had misfired.[60])

Some provocative stories in the Western media, presumably based on leaks from official sources, reported that the Chinese "journalists" who had been killed actually were intelligence operatives assisting the Serbian government. A joint investigation carried out by the British newspaper, *The Observer,* and the influential Danish paper, *Politiken,* concluded that U.S. officials had deliberately targeted the embassy because it was helping rebroadcast Serbian military communications.[61] Each of these stories received prominent play throughout Asia and other regions. *The Observer* story ran while President Jiang was on a state visit to the United Kingdom, giving it unusual prominence despite Foreign Secretary Robin Cook's categorical denials.[62] The coverage fueled the Chinese belief that there was much more to the bombing incident than the U.S. government was willing to acknowledge.

In April 2000, the CIA announced its punishment of those responsible for the bombing: the agency dismissed a single mid-level officer and imposed administrative punishments on six other employees. An MFA spokesperson criticized the actions as inadequate and again called on the U.S. government to "punish those responsible."[63] By then, however, Washington was engrossed in the November 2000 political campaign. Officials in Beijing themselves soon became preoccupied with the election of the Democratic Progressive Party candidate, Chen Shui-bian, as Taiwan's new president.

The tragic Chinese embassy bombing did not engender much crisis management. Instead, analysis shows a shared, if belated, recognition that the initial response to the incident—especially the underestimation of the potential extent of the crisis by Washington and the stoking of angry public demonstrations in Beijing—ran the risk of harming a vital relationship. The high-level communications and back-and-forth talking points may have mattered at the margins. Most important, however, was the independent but mutually reinforcing appreciation on both sides that bilateral ties could not be allowed to deteriorate further. In this regard, the Sino-American relationship resembles a giant boat with enormous ballast tossed about on a rough sea. The vessel can list only so far before it is again righted. The relatively benign dénouement to the embassy bombing incident owes as much or more to the accumulated contacts, commerce, and appreciation for strategic commonalities (the ballast) as to the earnest efforts of the crisis managers who gamely sought to put this tragic enigma behind them.

NOTES

1. Eric Schmitt, "In a Fatal Error, C.I.A. Picked a Bombing Target Only Once: The Chinese Embassy," *New York Times,* July 23, 1999.

2. Mobo C. F. Gao, "Sino-U.S. Love and Hate Relations," *Journal of Contemporary Asia* 30, no. 4 (October 2000), pp. 547–577, discusses the impact of the bombing on Chinese perceptions of the United States.

3. See Paul H. B. Godwin, "Decision-Making Under Stress: The Unintentional Bombing of China's Belgrade Embassy and the EP-3 Collision," paper presented at the American Enterprise Institute, Heritage Foundation, and U.S. Army War College People's Liberation Army Conference (Carlisle Barracks, Pa., October 1–3, 2004, revised November 26, 2004), pp. 161–190, for a complementary analysis of Chinese decision making during the crisis. Godwin's paper also reviews the April 2001 crisis resulting from the collision between a U.S. Navy EP-3 reconnaissance aircraft and a PLA warplane in international airspace near China's Hainan Island.

4. Larry Hubbell, "A Sino-American Cultural Exchange During the Bombing Crisis: A Personal Experience," *Asian Affairs* 26, no. 3 (Fall 1999), pp. 162–164, reviews the coverage of the incident in China's English-language press. See Ben Hillman, "Chinese Nationalism and the Belgrade Embassy Bombing," in Leong H. Liew and Shaoguang Wang, eds., *Nationalism, Democracy and National Integration in China* (London: RoutledgeCurzon, 2004), pp. 65–84, for a description of the coverage in the authoritative *People's Daily,* published by the Communist Party's Department of Propaganda.

5. Joseph Cheng and Kinglun Ngok, "Chinese Nationalism and Sino-U.S. Relations: The NATO Bombing of the Chinese Embassy in Belgrade," in Liew and Wang, eds., *Nationalism, Democracy and National Integration in China,* pp. 88–90.

6. Robert L. Suettinger, *Beyond Tiananmen: The Politics of U.S.-China Relations, 1989–2000* (Washington, D.C.: Brookings Institution Press, 2003), p. 371.

7. Robert A. Pastor, "China and the United States: Who Threatens Whom?" *Journal of International Affairs* 54, no. 2 (Spring 2001), p. 430.

8. Elisabeth Rosenthal, "Envoy Says Stoning Will End, Ties Won't," *New York Times,* May 11, 1999.

9. Henry Chu, Maggie Farley, and Anthony Kuhn, "Crisis in Yugoslavia: Chinese Attack U.S. Missions as Protests Intensify," *Los Angeles Times,* May 10, 1999.

10. David M. Lampton, *Same Bed, Different Dreams: Managing U.S.-China Relations, 1989–2000* (Berkeley: University of California Press, 2001), p. 267.

11. Gao, "Sino-U.S. Love and Hate Relations," p. 551.

12. Suisheng Zhao, "Chinese Nationalism and Its Foreign Policy Ramifications," in Christopher Marsh and June Dreyer, eds., *U.S.-China Relations in the 21st Century: Policies, Prospects, Possibilities* (New York: Lexington Books, 2003), p. 71.

13. Hillman, "Chinese Nationalism and the Belgrade Embassy Bombing," in Liew and Wang, eds., *Nationalism, Democracy and National Integration in China,* p. 67. The May Fourth Movement protesters objected to the decision of the Allied powers, accepted by the weak regime governing China at the time, to award German-held parts of China to Japan under the Treaty of Versailles. They also attacked the government ministers (the "three traitorous officials") who allegedly took bribes from Japan in return for accepting the concessions.

14. Jeffrey N. Wasserstrom, "The Year of Living Anxiously: China's 1999," *Dissent* 47, no. 2 (Spring 2000), p. 18.

15. John Wong and Zheng Yongnian, "Nationalism and Its Dilemma: Chinese Responses to the Embassy Bombing," in Wang Gungwu and Zheng Yongnian, eds., *Reform, Legitimacy and Dilemmas: China's Politics and Society* (Singapore: Singapore University Press, 2000), pp. 322, 340.

16. Erik Eckholm, "After Protests Spill Out, China May Find Sentiments Cannot Be Recorked," *New York Times,* May 11, 1999.

17. Cited in "China Suspends Talks, Demands U.S. Apology," May 10, 1999, www.cnn.com/WORLD/europe/9905/10/kosovo.china.01.

18. Text of Vice President Hu Jintao's televised speech on May 9, 1999 (Washington time), reproduced in "China's Response," Online NewsHour, May 9, 1999, www.pbs.org/newshour/bb/europe/jan-june99/china_statement_5-9.html.

19. Zhao, "Chinese Nationalism and Its Foreign Policy Ramifications," p. 82.

20. Suettinger, *Beyond Tiananmen,* p. 372.

21. Zhao, "Chinese Nationalism and Its Foreign Policy Ramifications," p. 73.

22. "China Strongly Condemns NATO Bombing," May 8, 1999, in East Asian Studies News File, UCLA Center for East Asian Studies, Los Angeles, Calif., reprint of Ministry of Foreign Affairs of the People's Republic of China

document, www.isop.ucla.edu/eas/NewsFile/bombing05-99/990508-cmfa2.htm.

23. "China Lodges Strongest Protest Against U.S.-Led NATO," May 8, 1999, in East Asian Studies News File, UCLA Center for East Asian Studies, Los Angeles, Calif., reprint of Ministry of Foreign Affairs of the People's Republic of China document, www.isop.ucla.edu/eas/newsfile/bombing05-99/990508-cmfa5.htm.

24. Suettinger, *Beyond Tiananmen,* p. 520.

25. "Formal Note of 10 May to the U.S. by Foreign Minister Tang Jiaxuan on the Embassy Bombing," May 10, 1999, in East Asian Studies News File, UCLA Center for East Asian Studies, Los Angeles, Calif., reprint of Ministry of Foreign Affairs of the People's Republic of China document, www.isop.ucla.edu/eas/newsfile/bombing05-99/990510-cmfa4.htm.

26. John Maggs, "Inciting the Dragon," *National Journal,* May 15, 1999, p. 1336.

27. June Teufel Dreyer, "Clinton's China Policy," in Todd G. Shields, Jeannie M. Whayne, and Donald R. Kelley, eds., *The Clinton Riddle: Perspectives on the Forty-Second President* (Fayetteville: University of Arkansas Press, 2004), p. 170.

28. Lampton, *Same Bed, Different Dreams,* p. 60.

29. "China's Response," Online NewsHour, May 9, 1999.

30. UN Security Council Press Release SC/6675, May 14, 1999, www.un.org/news/Press/docs/1999/19990514.SC6675.html.

31. Lynne O'Donnell, "China Demands an Apology in Person," *The Australian,* May 31, 1999.

32. Philip Shenon, "Chinese Embassy Bombing May Hurt Bid to Win Support for Peacekeepers," *New York Times,* May 7, 1999.

33. "NATO's Apology Fails to Cool Off the Chinese, *Orlando Sentinel,* May 9, 1999.

34. Yu Bin, "NATO's Unintended Consequence: A Deeper Strategic Partnership . . . Or More," *Comparative Connections: An E-Journal on East Asian Bilateral Relations* 1, no. 1 (July 1999), http://www.ciaonet.org/olj/cpc/cpc_jul99.pdf.

35. Cited in Steven Lee Myers, "Chinese Embassy Bombing: A Wide Net of Blame," *New York Times,* April 17, 2000.

36. Suettinger, *Beyond Tiananmen,* p. 370.

37. William S. Cohen and George J. Tenet, "U.S. Deeply Regrets Bombing of Chinese Embassy," joint statement, May 8, 1999, www.usconsulate.org.hk/uscn/others/1999/0508.htm.

38. "Clinton Apologizes to China Over Embassy Bombing," May 10, 1999, http://www-personal.umich.edu/~jiaying/NATO/cnn.html.

39. "Ambassador Li Zhaoxing," NewsHour with Jim Lehrer Transcript, *Online NewsHour,* May 10, 1999, www.pbs.org/newshour/bb/europe/jan-june99/li_5-10.html.

40. "Letter to Minister of Foreign Affairs of the People's Republic of China from U.S. Secretary of State," May 8, 1999, in East Asian Studies News File, UCLA Center for East Asian Studies, Los Angeles, Calif., reprint of U.S. Department of State letter, www.isop.ucla.edu/eas/NewsFile/Bombing05-99/990508-ussd1.htm.

41. Suettinger, *Beyond Tiananmen,* p. 372.

42. Lampton, *Same Bed, Different Dreams,* p. 375. The author observes, "[T]hough eventually the call was scheduled and completed . . . a hotline used only when it is not needed is not of much use."

43. Stanley O. Roth, "The Effects on U.S.-China Relations of the Accidental Bombing of the Chinese Embassy in Belgrade," testimony before the Senate Committee on Foreign Relations, Subcommittee on East Asian and Pacific Affairs, May 27, 1999, in East Asian Studies News File, UCLA Center for East Asian Studies, Los Angeles, Calif., www.isop.ucla.edu/eas/NewsFile/Bombing05-99/990527-ussd2.htm.

44. "Text: CIA Director Tenet on Accidental Bombing of China Embassy," http://hongkong.usconsulate.gov/uscn/others/1999/0722d.htm provides Tenet's statement before the House Permanent Select Committee on Intelligence, July 22, 1999. His publicly stated reasons for this "major error" reaffirm those made by Pickering during his earlier visit to China. For additional information on the reasons for the mistaken attack, see Craig Covault, "China Seen as Growing Reconnaissance Challenge," *Aviation Week & Space Technology* 153, no. 6 (August 7, 2000), pp. 65–66.

45. "Oral Presentation by Under Secretary of State Thomas Pickering on June 17 to the Chinese Government Regarding the Accidental Bombing of the PRC Embassy in Belgrade," U.S. Department of State, Office of the Spokesman, July 6, 1999, http://hongkong.usconsulate.gov/uscn/state/1999/0706.htm.

46. "U.S. President's Personal Envoy in China to Present the U.S. Government's Report on Its Investigation Into the Bombing of the Chinese Embassy in the Federal Republic of Yugoslavia—The Chinese Government Emphasizes That the U.S. Side Must Give Satisfactory Account and Explanation of the Incident," Ministry of Foreign Affairs of the People's Republic of China, June 16, 1999, in East Asian Studies News File, UCLA Center for

East Asian Studies, Los Angeles, Calif., www.isop.ucla.edu/eas/NewsFile/bombing05-99/9906-cmfa1.htm.

47. Ibid.

48. Suettinger, *Beyond Tiananmen*, p. 374.

49. Simon Shen, "Nationalism or Nationalist Foreign Policy?: Contemporary Chinese Nationalism and Its Role in Shaping Chinese Foreign Policy in Response to the Belgrade Embassy Bombing," *Politics* 24, no. 2 (2004), p. 126. David Lampton, in *Same Bed, Different Dreams*, p. 60, wrote, "[I]n subsequent conversations with Chinese intellectuals, it is clear that at least some came to feel misled by their government. As one put it to me in mid-2000, some Chinese students 'thought they were manipulated by the Chinese media. They now want their own point of view.'" Later, however, Lampton wrote: "Americans are sadly mistaken, for example, if they think that the Chinese demonstrations against U.S. diplomatic facilities in May 1999 after the bombing of the PRC Embassy in Belgrade, Yugoslavia, were simply government-managed riots. Rather, the government was, in part (and only in part), trying to surf a wave of popular anger." Lampton, *Same Bed, Different Dreams*, p. 284.

50. Roth, "Effects on U.S.-China Relations of the Accidental Bombing."

51. Suettinger, *Beyond Tiananmen*, p. 375.

52. Melinda Liu and Leslie Pappas, "How Low Would He Bow?," *Newsweek International*, June 28, 1999, p. 44.

53. Nebojsa Spaic, "Belgrade to Beijing: A Trump Card in Chinese Political Strategy," *Harvard Asia Pacific Review* (Summer 2000), http://hcs.harvard.edu/~hapr/summer00_tech/belgrade.html.

54. Richard Weitz, "Why Russia and China Have Not Formed an Anti-American Alliance," *Naval War College Review* 56, no. 4 (Autumn 2003), pp. 39–61.

55. Radha Sinha, *Sino-American Relations: Mutual Paranoia* (New York: Palgrave MacMillan, 2003), p. 91.

56. Michael Laris, "U.S. Agrees to Pay Chinese Embassy Bombing Victims," *Austin American-Statesman*, July 31, 1999.

57. Edward Chen and Mark Magnier, "U.S.-China Relations 'Back on Track' After Clinton, Jiang Mend Fences," *Los Angeles Times*, September 12, 1999.

58. Steven Lee Meyers, "Chinese Military to Resume Contacts With the Pentagon," *New York Times*, January 6, 2000.

59. Lynne O'Donnell, "China Demands an Apology in Person," *The Australian*, May 31, 1999.

60. Steven Lee Myers, "Chinese Embassy Bombing: A Wide Net of Blame," *New York Times*, April 17, 2000.

61. John Sweeney, Jens Holsoe, and Ed Vulliamy, "NATO Bombed Chinese Deliberately," *The Observer,* October 17, 1999. According to Suettinger, "Subsequent American accounts have observed that the three may have been involved in intelligence work, as China sometimes uses journalistic 'cover' for overseas intelligence officers. While this has furthered speculation that the bombings were deliberate, there is no corroborating information available to support the allegations." Suettinger, *Beyond Tiananmen,* p. 519.

62. Severin Carrell, "Claim Sours Jiang Visit," *The Scotsman,* October 18, 1999.

63. Steven Lee Myers, "China Rejects U.S. Actions on Bombing of Embassy," *New York Times,* April 11, 2000.

10

Chinese Crisis Management During the 1999 Embassy Bombing Incident

Wu Baiyi

BEGINNING IN LATE MARCH 1999, NATO forces, led by the United States, launched massive air raids on the former Yugoslavian union and triggered the war in Kosovo. In the early hours of August 8, the United States brazenly attacked the Chinese embassy in Belgrade, causing major casualties and property losses. This event directly caused a serious diplomatic crisis between Beijing and Washington, affected the substance of China's U.S. policy, fired up public resentment against the United States, and influenced Beijing's overall foreign policy-making environment. This chapter will describe and assess the Chinese management of this crisis in light of relevant theories. In the final section, it will analyze the features and functions of the existing crisis management mechanism in China.

CRISIS AND REACTION

At 11:45 p.m. local time on May 7, 1999 (5:45 a.m. May 8, 1999, Beijing time), five U.S.-made bombs (joint direct attack munitions, or JDAMs) hit the Chinese embassy in Yugoslavia situated on Bulevar Umetnosti, Belgrade. One bomb did not explode. The bombs penetrated the buildings in the embassy compound, causing serious damage to the embassy premises, including the ambassador's residence. Casualties included three deaths and more than twenty people injured.

The event shocked the whole world and ushered in a severe crisis in Sino-American relations. On the afternoon of May 8, the Chinese government issued a statement expressing its utmost indignation and strongest protest against the barbaric act and demanding that the North Atlantic Treaty Organization (NATO), headed by the United States, should shoulder all the responsibility. Chinese and foreign public opinion also strongly condemned the bombing, which had trampled the charter of the United Nations and norms of international law. In its initial response, however, the U.S. government described the event as a "mistake" and expressed only "regret" for the Chinese loss of life and property. Beijing refused to accept this response. Hence the crisis intensified.

Outraged students and the general public soon staged demonstrations near diplomatic and consular missions of the United States, the United Kingdom, Germany, France, Italy, and the Netherlands in major Chinese cities like Beijing, Shanghai, Guangzhou, Chengdu, Shenyang, and Hong Kong. They urged U.S.-led NATO to make a formal apology and express condolences for the dead by flying flags at half-mast. During the demonstrations, the office building of the U.S. embassy in Beijing and the residence of the U.S. consul general in Chengdu suffered damage.

At 6:00 p.m. on May 9, Hu Jintao, a member of the Standing Committee of the Politburo of the Chinese Communist Party (CCP) Central Committee and vice president of the People's Republic of China (PRC), delivered a speech on television, reiterating the principled positions of the Chinese government. While stating his support and protection of all registered patriotic demonstrations, Hu called on the public to maintain overall stability, carry out their protests in accordance with relevant laws, avoid radical acts, and guard against attempts to disrupt social order. Before and after his speech, leaders of the United States and other major NATO countries began to express their apologies to the Chinese government and people on different occasions. On May 10, the U.S. consulate in Guangzhou flew its flag at half-mast to recognize the three Chinese reporters who had been killed. On May 12, embassies and consulates of the United States, the United Kingdom, France, Germany, Canada, and other countries lowered their flags to half-mast for condolences. By then, college students in Chinese cities returned to campus and street parades gradually disappeared.

On May 14, the crisis entered into a second stage, which mainly involved governmental representations and official attempts to stabilize domestic solidarity. On May 10, Foreign Minister Tang Jiaxuan sent a note to Ambassador James Sasser of the United States, putting forward on behalf of the Chinese government a four-point list of demands: a public and formal apology, a thorough and complete investigation, a rapid disclosure of investigation results, and severe punishment of the perpetrators. During this period, all manner of Chinese organizations continued to condemn the attack and voice support of the government position—the National People's Congress, the Chinese People's Political Consultative Conference, the main nonruling parties, nongovernmental organizations, the People's Liberation Army (PLA), the People's Armed Police, universities and colleges, the press, and cultural and academic societies. Such events continuously captured press headlines throughout the country and were aimed at putting moral pressure on the opposite side.

Internationally, the Chinese mission was successful when it requested that the United Nations (UN) Security Council convene an emergency meeting on the violence. By the night of May 14, the Security Council adopted the chairman's statement that urged a comprehensive and thorough investigation of the bombing.

Back in Beijing, the Chinese government, while conducting the funerals of the dead with exceptional esteem, highly commended at a grand rally all embassy staff. On May 14, President Bill Clinton had a telephone conversation with President Jiang Zemin. Clinton once again apologized and pledged to investigate the event and disclose the results. As of May 20, the U.S. side repeatedly suggested sending a special envoy to brief China about the investigation results, but the Chinese side did not agree. Beijing insisted that, if Washington were to repeat the cliché of "a mistaken bombing" but not punish the perpetrators, any briefing would be insignificant to the Chinese government and people. Until the end of May, the Chinese side, in the form of statements by leaders or editorials, continued to reiterate its demands and criticize U.S. hegemonic policies and behavior. However, China's terms and tones became less volatile. The crisis then evolved to its final stage.

In this last stage, Chinese efforts focused on the results of the investigation, and China requested U.S. compensation for the human casualties and property losses and also punishment of the perpetrators. On June 16, President Clinton's special envoy, Under Secretary of State Thomas R. Pickering, reported to the Chinese government in Beijing on the outcome of the U.S. investigation. Though expressing "regret" and once again apologizing to the Chinese side, Pickering insisted that the bombing had been caused by a series of mistakes by some U.S. government departments. Again, the Chinese side rejected this explanation as "entirely unconvincing and thus unacceptable." From July 28 to July 30, the two parties held a second round of negotiations in Beijing on the compensation for China's human casualties and property losses and reached a mutual understanding in the end. In mid-August, the U.S. government paid compensation in the amount of $4.5 million to the Chinese government for loss of life.[1]

On September 11, President Jiang and President Clinton met during the seventh Asia-Pacific Economic Cooperation informal summit meeting in New Zealand. The two leaders vowed to immediately resume and continue a constructive bilateral relationship oriented toward the twenty-first century. The crisis thus came to an end.

DECISION-MAKING PROCESSES

Factors in the decision-making process include availability of intelligence and the analysis of intelligence, the specific participants in decision making, diplomacy and international politics, implementation of decisions, and feedback and results.

Availability and Analysis of Intelligence

As shown in this case, intelligence, which is the first link of the entire crisis management chain, seemed rather problematic. Before the bombing, no one, including officials posted in the embassy, had envisaged a worst-case scenario such as occurred. Staff at the Chinese embassy did not provide early warning and did not make any emergency response plans. As a result, when the attack occurred, embassy personnel were unable immediately to report to Beijing. Damage to the fixed telecommunication equipment caused an interruption of several hours in communications between the home country and the embassy.[2]

According to information currently available, the first person to report the bombing was Lü Yansong, a resident journalist of the *People's Daily* in Yugoslavia. The time of his report was 6:00 a.m. on May 8, Beijing time (15 minutes later). Lü survived the attack and reported the event to Beijing with his mobile phone.[3] After learning the shocking news, the Ministry of Foreign Affairs (MFA) tried to contact the embassy for confirmation of the information but failed to get in touch with the ambassador and other officials. After 6:10 a.m., domestic intelligence services began to report the event to China's top leaders, but their sources were mainly from news broadcasts by Agence France-Presse (AFP) and Cable News Network (CNN).[4] It was as late as after 7:30 a.m. that the Xinhua News Agency and the PRC ambassador to Yugoslavia, Pan Zhanlin, phoned to confirm the bombing of the embassy and the suffering of casualties.

Because the event came all of a sudden, no intelligence agencies had time to accomplish an all-out analysis before the senior leadership convened at 10:00 a.m. Even the details of the attack, such as the exact number of bombs and casualties, were incomplete, so the ultimate decision makers had to refer to follow-up reports during the course of their meetings.

Participants in Decision Making and Level of Decisions

On the morning of May 8, the top Chinese leaders held an emergency meeting. Afterward, China took the following actions. First, Vice Foreign Minister Wang Yingfan immediately called a meeting with the U.S. ambassador for preliminary representations and strong protests. Second, Foreign Minister Tang Jiaxuan made a second round of representations with specific demands to the United States for an apology, investigation, speedy public report of the results of the investigation, and severe punishment of the perpetrators. Third, a task force left for Belgrade to bring the dead and wounded back to China. The group was headed by a ministerial official of the MFA and comprised PLA General Staff officers and representatives from the MFA, the Ministry of National Defense, the Ministry of Public Health, and the victims' employers such as Xinhua News Agency and *Guangming Daily.* Fourth, the Chinese mission to the UN issued without delay a written statement of condemnation and requested a formal meeting of the Security Council, demanding that U.S.-led NATO investigate and account for the incident. Finally, various efforts were made to maintain domestic solidarity and stability through leading media to prevent disorder and loss of control.

The next afternoon, top policy makers gathered again. Following the meeting, they adopted a couple of measures for cooling down public sentiments. On the evening of May 9, Vice President Hu Jintao delivered a televised speech, restating the position of the Chinese government and calling upon the students and public to carry out protests and demonstrations in an orderly manner so as to maintain social stability. Meanwhile, Hu made it clear to the outside world that in light of relevant international laws the Chinese government would firmly protect foreign diplomatic missions and their personnel stationed in China and would maintain the safety of foreign residents and other noncitizens engaging in economic, trade, educational, and cultural activities in China.

At the same time, the Beijing municipal government approved applications by the students to stage demonstrations. Simultaneously, the Ministry of Education and relevant authorities of metropolitan cities and provinces as well as universities and colleges cautiously watched and escorted the demonstrators in order to prevent excessively radical moves. They also undertook additional safeguarding procedures around the missions of NATO member states by sending police to keep order.

But China's official position did not weaken. The Chinese refusal of the U.S. request for a summit telephone conversation continued. Also, the MFA announced a postponement of high-level military-to-military exchanges and bilateral consultation with the United States on the subjects of nonproliferation, arms control, and international security issues. The MFA also suspended the human rights dialogue between the two countries.

From then to mid-June, the paramount Chinese leadership met about the situation several times. During this period, decision making in China assumed clear features of crisis management:

- Almost all key leaders who shared supreme policy-making power took part in the entire decision-making process.

- All departments either directly related to the event or responsible for monitoring and controlling internal or external tensions were involved in the process to varying extents, each implementing mandates issued by the paramount leadership.
- On the basis of democratic centralism, the senior leaders achieved a consensus in light of decisive ideas suggested by the highest leader himself.[5]
- The scope of crisis management covered almost all areas of foreign and domestic affairs. At most times, domestic concerns appeared to predominate, diplomacy thus being subordinated to and serving domestic interests.
- Leaders conducted their decision making in the midst of the tension generated by the crisis and by means of high-level discussions. However, China's decision making was done without adequate information and in-depth analyses. Intelligence or expertise analyses did not accumulate until time passed and tension decreased.

International Politics and Diplomatic Interaction

An international crisis is composed of various stages, with a series of interactions between or among the parties concerned.[6]

The embassy bombing case indicates that, although Beijing failed to envisage the pending threat, it was not completely without a sense of crisis beforehand. Since the beginning of the Kosovo crisis, China and Russia had insisted in the UN Security Council that any political resolution obtain the agreement of Yugoslavia, and they opposed the use of force against Yugoslavia under Security Council authorization. This led to confrontation with the United States, the United Kingdom, France, Germany, and other NATO members, which sowed the seeds of direct conflict at a later date. Since NATO began air raids in Yugoslavia in late March, the Chinese government had been even more worried about so-called humanitarian intervention by force, believing that such a practice would fundamentally undermine the sovereignty principle in international relations and thus affect China's legitimacy and capability in dealing with its own separatist challenges in Taiwan, Tibet, and Xinjiang. As the conflict evolved, such concerns increasingly dominated policy and academic discussions and reached the public through the leading media. Consequently, antiwar sentiments intensified against NATO's actions.[7]

Meanwhile, Sino-American relations suffered severe setbacks. When Premier Zhu Rongji visited Washington in late April, the United States did not honor its commitment on China's accession to the World Trade Organization (WTO). Because of U.S. domestic opposition, President Bill Clinton failed to sign an agreement with Premier Zhu. Although Clinton tried to make up for that shortly afterwards, the president was unable to win back China's trust.[8] Furthermore, hard-liners in the U.S. Congress continued to investigate cases of so-called political contributions and the theft of nuclear secrets by Lee Wen-ho. The Cox Report was also about to be released. The atmosphere of bilateral relations was far from the healthy and harmonious atmosphere of a year before. These factors accelerated Beijing's sense of mounting tensions and made conspiracy theories appealing to intellectuals and the general public during the 1999 crisis.[9]

Furthermore, both sides acted slowly at the outset of the crisis, delaying timely control of the situation. On the part of the United States, the apparent absence of correct decisions and direction limited officials in their respective statements in the immediate aftermath of the incident. National Security Council Senior Director for Asian Affairs Kenneth Lieberthal, Deputy Assistant Secretary of State Susan Shirk, and Ambassador James Sasser in Beijing indiscriminately continued to use casual terms to express their "regret" to China, and they missed initial chances to apologize and thereby downgrade the crisis. It was not until the night of May 8 (the morning of May 9, Beijing time) that Secretary of State Madeleine K. Albright formally apologized. The next day, President Clinton finally recognized the event as a "tragic mistake" and expressed his sincere apologies to the Chinese government and people.[10]

On China's part, the breakdown in the availability of intelligence prevented the quick formulation of a clear-cut and comprehensive solution at the outset. Naturally it was difficult to quickly ascertain the nature of the incident and U.S. intentions. Again U.S. indecisiveness in its apology and relevant promises even gave the impression of pressure. All of these uncertainties delayed the Chinese official reaction. Vice President Hu delivered a televised speech thirty-six hours after the bombing. Foreign Minister Tang Jiaxuan made his representations to the United States fifty hours after the bombing (on the morning of May 10). Such delays not only deepened mutual doubts and misgivings and made correct decisions more difficult but, more importantly, provoked massive anti-American sentiment in China and let demonstrations spill over from Beijing to many other cities. The Chinese government was left in an extremely awkward position. It had to be tough toward the United States to prove that it represented the people's will while it carefully managed the crisis toward a soft landing. This ironically revealed "tensions between democracy and national security," as U.S. scholars have argued.[11]

In addition, inadequate communication was another element that evidently influenced the evolution of the crisis. Existing crisis studies illustrate that "communications between the opposing parties are always too few while those among allies increase sharply." Because information is limited, decision makers on opposing sides "tend to show more hostility."[12] In the present case, the failure to hold a conversation between the two presidents before May 14 reflects the lack of political trust between them and that the bilateral relationship of the two nations was immature. Because NATO had made many errors in prior bombing sorties in Yugoslavia, Washington tended to react in an indifferent and somewhat arrogant way and regarded the embassy bombing as another "mistaken bombing," whereas Beijing felt uncertain about whether the United States would correct its mistakes quickly.[13] To prevent a negative conversation (for example, Clinton expressing only regret and Jiang condemning the United States with strong rhetoric) from leading to a poor outcome, China had to delay such a direct conversation. This might reflect China's attention to cautiously controlling the escalation of the crisis. The United States of course had no way of understanding this at the time. Americans generally regarded the refusal to have a phone conversation as a hostile signal.

It is also noteworthy that diplomatic channels remained open and bilateral economic, cultural, and other nonpolitical contacts remained intact throughout the crisis.[14] These ties helped contain the crisis setbacks. In both capitals, pragmatism prevailed over emotion, leaving a certain amount of room for maneuvering later.

Implementation of Decisions

Through several high-level meetings after May 8, the MFA mainly coordinated policy execution. When matters exceeded the authority and responsibility of the MFA, a broader consultation would take place. Under such circumstances, relevant offices and departments of the CCP and the State Council might become involved. However, such matters primarily related to domestic resources: such as how to honor the victims, how to welcome returned embassy staff, or how to receive the U.S. president's special envoy. Ministerial officials attended these coordination meetings to discuss the division of labor and how to act in their own spheres. Then, according to their respective duties, relevant government institutions would have their own consultations or meetings to carry out a specific mandate. Following the senior leader's decision on May 9, for example, the Ministry of Education held a couple of meetings in which presidents and deans of relevant universities and colleges participated. They discussed specific approaches to "protect students' patriotic passions" and guide them to proceed with peaceful demonstrations and protests. It turned out that such efforts did curtail further violence and gradually caused student demonstrations to subside.

On the propaganda front, the CCP Department of Propaganda also issued a circular requiring the media to lead public opinion toward solidarity and stability. Specifically, the press had to voice support of the correct government decisions; this was thought to be helpful in enhancing public confidence in the official positions. A broader mission of the media at this juncture, as the document noted, was to stabilize the nation and protect people from the possible blindness of their long-term goals.[15] On May 13, President Jiang Zemin delivered a speech at the welcoming rally for the diplomats who had been withdrawn from Belgrade. The Chinese mass media immediately highlighted the rally's themes of reform, development, and stability and began a nationwide propaganda campaign. The lowering of the volume in the press not only helped disseminate sober-minded views among the public but also contributed to mitigating the crisis itself.

Continuation and Feedback

When President Clinton apologized in the White House on both May 10 and May 13 and decided to have the U.S. missions in China fly their flags at half-mast in memory of the dead, the crisis began to calm down. Beginning on May 11, the Chinese media began to disclose the written and personal apologies by Secretary of State Madeleine Albright and President Clinton during May 8–May 10.[16] The apologies turned out to be conducive to the resumption of direct communication between Jiang and Clinton on the evening of May 14, which marked the return to joint crisis management by both the PRC and the United States. The abnormal isolation between the two sides during the crisis came to an end.[17]

The crisis had not yet concluded. Decision-making activities continued in China. Around the same time, the United States stated that it had completed its investigation and would like to send a special envoy from the president to brief the Chinese leaders so as to finish the crisis and normalize Sino-American relations at an early date. On May 19, the Chinese leadership convened again to review the situation and adopted a series of proposals. Soon afterward, China agreed in principle to the special envoy's visit. Nevertheless, the visit was delayed from the suggested dates to mid-June. In the meantime, Chinese decision makers also suspended negotiations with the United States about China's accession to the WTO. These decision makers were apparently driven by internal considerations.

DOMESTIC POLITICAL FACTORS

Research shows that strong public sentiments can limit the policy options available.[18] In the post–Cold War age, the boundary between domestic and foreign policies is increasingly blurred because of the decline of ideological factors. Nations are now preoccupied by domestic agendas. As usual, domestic politics take precedence, particularly during a crisis. All successful solutions to international crises represent a clever balance between domestic and foreign policy calculations. In light of such a standard, the Chinese handling of the embassy bombing case merits a cautious appreciation.

Students' Movement

The massive parades by students regarding Japan's denial of its historical war of aggression against China and regarding capitalist liberalization ideology, which took place in the mid- and late 1980s, were politically disastrous and were partly responsible for forcing CCP General Secretary Hu Yaobang and his successor, Zhao Ziyang, out of office.[19] Against this backdrop, the students' movement had become a very sensitive issue in Chinese politics. Even though more than ten years had passed since the embassy bombing occurred, Chinese leaders had to draw upon the lessons of the two previous events and take a prudent attitude toward the students' protests. With correct policies and strategies, the government soon pacified the radical sentiments of the students and the general public, relieving domestic anxieties and laying down a foundation for a proper settlement of the crisis in Sino-American relations.

The official management undertook three successful approaches. First, it quickly anticipated and prepared for the students' reactions. The unrest of the young had not broken out overnight. Ever since NATO began bombing Yugoslavia in late March, college students in Beijing had shown strong sympathy for the Serbs. Quite a number of seminars and classroom discussions had been held on campus, and students had expressed explicit opposition to and resentment against NATO and the United States. At Peking University, the country's top school and a primary center of earlier student campaigns, the students submitted to the university authorities an application for a demonstration and the presentation of protest letters to the U.S. embassy.[20] The Chinese government took the matter seriously. After intensive discussions and consultations, officials decided to adopt a policy of persuasion rather than coercive prevention. School authorities were thus instructed to respond instantly and convince students of the official positions. The core government principle vis-à-vis the students was to calm them down but not to confront their emotions. This policy extended to the time of the embassy bombing and played a key role in avoiding the backlash of student protest during this crisis. As a result, the government was in a better position than its predecessors had been as they faced this crisis.

Second, the government adopted smart tactics to comply with the changed situation. At the outbreak of the crisis, college students were the first to react in a vehement manner. They immediately presented applications for protest rallies to the Beijing municipal authorities and soon won support from local residents who provided buses and taxis for free transport. Under such circumstances, the government and the universities had to accommodate and allow the students as well as other residents to demonstrate in front of the U.S. embassy and other embassies. President Jiang Zemin later pointed out to the United States that "the outrages of 1.2 billion people are beyond any possible containment," hinting that any sovereign state would take such measures in the face of wide public indignation against foreign humiliation.

Third, the government acted according to the circumstances. The possibility of mitigating the crisis came with the United States beginning to apologize on various occasions. The Chinese government seized the moment when the United States and other NATO states lowered their national flags in China to persuade students to withdraw from the diplomatic compound. Again this was done quietly through university authorities and students' associations.

The Media

Chinese news media played multiple roles in the crisis. They were first and foremost advocates for government policies, especially because some mainstream media themselves were government affiliated. Consequently, the basic tone of the media was in line with the requirements of the central government: publicizing official positions and demands, covering relevant sympathetic statements and comments that reinforced the Chinese position in other parts of the world, reflecting the sentiments and activities of the domestic population toward the event, and stressing the need to maintain stability and unity. On the whole, the role of the mass media was positive.[21]

Meanwhile, the news media were parties to the event as well as its victims. The Xinhua News Agency, *Guangming Daily,* and *People's Daily* were to varying degrees involved in the crisis management process. They not only took charge of the funeral arrangements of the dead journalists but also had to bestow great honor on the journalists and praise their sacrifice. Despite their duty to cover daily events, the media also accepted interviews by other institutions and provided informational briefings for public gatherings and mass rallies. It seemed inevitable that the media's changed role in the indignant atmosphere of the time caused the media to fail to persistently resist a tendency toward anti-Americanism in their reports.[22]

Furthermore, the integration and coordination of reports was insufficiently improved during the crisis. The MFA and the CCP Central Committee Department of Propaganda achieved only a basic level of coordination. This coordination may have been insufficient regardless of whether there was a crisis. The MFA was unable to review all report drafts before releasing them, and not all reports were available for the MFA censors.[23]

Finally, the mass media in China were by that time already very market oriented and pluralistic. The Internet had become a popular means for the public to obtain updated world news.[24] Although the government tried hard to dominate public opinion, it failed to keep some news out of the reach of the public. Radical arguments and irrational assumptions, while playing a minor role in the public debate, also increased pressure on the Chinese government in its handling of the crisis.[25]

Role of Academia

Before the crisis, debates over the post–Cold War international situation and the U.S. policy toward China had been ongoing among academics. Through the late 1990s, several debates took place against the background of the Tiananmen Square incident, dramatic changes in the Soviet Union and Eastern Europe, and tensions in the Taiwan Strait. They were dominated by such concerns as whether peace and development were still the main theme of today's world and whether Washington had changed its China policy to one of hostility and containment. Shortly before the embassy bombing crisis occurred, the academic community was acutely debating neointerventionism, an issue raised amid NATO's expansion and the Kosovo crisis. With the embassy bombing, the perspective of a U.S. conspiracy prevailed among mainstream intellectuals. The few people holding the opposite opinion kept silent because they were unable to prove that the bombing had been mistake.[26]

Even people of the conspiracy school had their differences. Some insisted that the embassy bombing was a well-planned attack aiming to test China's will and was part of the U.S. policy to create troubles for China.[27] Others argued that the event might not have taken place upon the order of the U.S. president but was instead an intentional plot by some forces inside the CIA or the Pentagon and that the purpose of the plot was to disarm Yugoslavia's political will to resist by striking China and therefore to put a rapid end to the war.[28] Close connections between the academic community outside the government and the policy advisory team inside the government meant that these opinions were likely to have penetrated into the decision-making circle, thus affecting decision makers' judgments and decisions.[29]

Public Opinion

The change in public opinion toward the United States has been one of the most serious and far-reaching consequences of the crisis. The general public in China has all along followed the international situation closely and has had doubts about U.S. foreign policy. In terms of cultural psychology, the Chinese public possesses a fairly strong sense of national dignity. From the very beginning, the Chinese people resisted the U.S. role of world policeman. As the embassy bombing made China a direct victim of the new strategy of the United States and NATO, the Chinese public suffered an enormous psychological blow. With irrefutable evidence and clear provisions of international law, particularly because the event was related to the U.S.-led war against the sovereign state of Yugoslavia, an overwhelming majority of ordinary Chinese citizens urged the government to adopt a strong position and not to perfunctorily end representations with the United States.

A survey by Horizon Research is one illustration of the fluctuation in public opinion during the embassy bombing crisis. On the night of May 10, Horizon Research, an independent Chinese survey firm, conducted an opinion poll in Beijing, Shanghai, and Guangzhou of 816 people of the age of 14 and above:

- 52.3 percent of the interviewees stated that the embassy bombing greatly affected their opinion of the United States;
- 12.6 percent were not affected by the event (it is unclear whether members of this group had positive or negative feelings toward the United States before the event);
- 53.6 percent had never liked U.S. foreign policy and had become even more disgusted by it after the incident; and

- 29.9 percent had changed from being appreciative of to disgusted by U.S. policy.

Closer analysis suggested that women, those under the age of 22 and between 31 and 35, students, enterprise managers, and workers showed the most obvious change in their attitude toward the United States.[30]

The survey also indicated that the majority of the people in those cities hoped to see the government take a tougher stance in its diplomatic representations with the United States:

- 33.4 percent supported a firm demand for apology and compensation by NATO;
- 17.4 percent favored even closer cooperation with Russia;
- 11.5 percent hoped that the government would allow demonstrations and parades on a larger scale;
- 11.3 percent demanded downgrading diplomatic relations with the United States and other NATO members;
- 9.8 percent supported military assistance to Yugoslavia;
- 7.1 percent called for maneuvers in the United Nations and international courts;
- 6.6 percent preferred avoiding confrontation and concentrating on national development.[31]

Although this survey may be somewhat inaccurate or incomplete, the results roughly demonstrate public opinions during that period. In addition to street protests, such publicly expressed opinions undoubtedly influenced the Chinese government in fine-tuning its policy and in taking specific steps in its crisis management.

CALMING AND RESOLVING THE CRISIS

During crises, the time to respond to a threat is limited, and policy makers must make major decisions under urgent pressure. When changes in the domestic or external environment reach a critical point, different approaches may lead to very different outcomes.[32] In a crisis situation, decision makers tend to "leave room for maneuvering by keeping secret the subtleties and some specific actions in crisis management in order to prevent radical public response and opposition pressures from limiting the flexibility of the government in handling a crisis."[33] Besides the reasons already cited in the previous sections, the correct measures taken by the Chinese side to deescalate the crisis were also conducive to the steady resolution of the crisis.

Control Over Policy Statements

During the embassy bombing crisis, the Chinese side exercised strict control over all formal policy declarations in the forms of government statements, notes of the MFA, the MFA spokesperson's remarks, and national leaders' speeches so as to avoid misleading the United States with wrong or confusing signals. Moreover, decision makers exercised deliberate restraint in order to leave maneuvering space.

The seniority of the people sending messages increased as the crisis continued. Early messages originated with Wang Yingfan, then moved to Tang Jiaxuan, and finally culminated in Hu Jintao. The purpose was to force the United States to realize the seriousness of the matter. When the intention of the United States was still unclear, President Jiang Zemin neither accepted a phone conversation request from President Bill Clinton nor delivered any televised speeches, leaving certain political room and preventing an escalation of the crisis. Admittedly, an overemphasis on delicate procedures in the government's response might have caused delays and public discontent and increased domestic tension.

Confidentiality

The Chinese side was able to keep some information confidential. A typical example was the arrangements for the visit by the U.S. special envoy. Leaders stressed the security of the visit and explicitly instructed government ministries to control the spread of information.[34] The leading press did not cover the visit until the special envoy had departed China. The government's basic objectives during the clampdown on information were to prevent repercussions or unexpected events (caused

368 | WU BAIYI

by the dissatisfaction of the public with the investigation results) and not complicate the situation yet again.

Limited and Flexible Foreign Policy Objectives

The four-point demand put forward by the Chinese side was rather specific and feasible. In the later stage of the crisis, when the United States had basically fulfilled three demands, the Chinese government took the opportunity to move past the incident in order to achieve the larger goal of repairing Sino-American relations.

Disconnecting Crisis Events

At the outset of the crisis, China linked its crisis management with the resolution of the Kosovo issue by stressing that Yugoslavia had to agree to any solution. Later, China began to consider separating the two issues and stopped mentioning that Yugoslavia must agree to a solution; however, China continued to ask for a political resolution and an immediate termination of the bombing of Yugoslavia.

During the negotiation process with the United States, the Chinese government was wise to temporarily suspend the negotiations with the United States on China's accession to the WTO. Such a decision was also meant to separate crisis events from other bilateral issues. In so doing, the Chinese government was able to avoid complicating the crisis and its resolution. At the same time, the Chinese government also aimed to impress its domestic audience by not sacrificing its principles.

ASSESSMENT AND SUMMARY

This review of various aspects of Chinese crisis management reveals several things about China's performance.

First, generally speaking, the Chinese side was able to prevent escalation of the embassy bombing crisis by increasing credible pressure (for example, through diplomatic negotiations, mobilization of domestic and international public opinion, and declarations by leaders), then by calming the crisis, and eventually by bringing it to a conclusion on the basis of its own interests. That is to say, the Chinese government possesses a basic crisis management capability in accordance with the standards of international crisis management theories.[35]

Second, if one separately observes the stages of early warning, prevention, control, and resolution of the crisis, one will realize that the management capability of the Chinese government is uneven. Because forecasting and early warnings were minimal, Beijing failed to predict and prepare for the crisis beforehand, and the result was obvious passivity or even confusion at the outset. During the last two stages, however, China's crisis management was strict, consistent, and orderly, and it displayed continuity.

Third, the crisis occurred at an important juncture of accelerated economic development and social transformation in China, and it featured vehement domestic responses to an international event. The study of the embassy bombing crisis demonstrates that various domestic dynamics exert visible and invisible impacts on decision making. When this happens, policy makers give priority to domestic stability.

Fourth, the element of perception is crucial throughout a crisis. In more or less obvious ways, ideological, historical and cultural factors affected China's observance and judgment of international conflict and calculations during its management of this crisis. One should not ignore or underestimate the impact of perceptions.

One can summarize the characteristics of Chinese decision making during the crisis:

- Chinese crisis management basically continued to use the previously existing foreign policy-making mechanism. This is executive dominated but is under strict CCP supervision.[36]
- Decision making at the highest level adheres to the principle of democratic centralism. Decisions were formed during meetings of the top group and made by the core leader.[37]
- The decision-making process was relatively closed. Decisions exhibited standard characteristics.[38]
- The MFA played a major role in policy advising and execution. Other institutions were responsible for matters in which they were competent.

- Intelligence channels, emergency consultation systems, policy-execution monitoring, and feedback and correction systems relevant to decision making continued to rely on the normal operation of existing diplomatic, defense, and security agencies. These structures are not yet equivalent to the U.S. National Security Council, which forcefully advances policy coordination under the presidential mandate.[39] Consequently, some Chinese actions, such as intelligence processing, simultaneous institutional consultations, and coherent reactions to the other party during the crisis, were somewhat lacking.
- Makers of final decisions were under continuing pressure, both domestically and internationally. Therefore, the embassy bombing crisis served as a comprehensive example of crisis management.

The above observations and summary are merely preliminary. Many other noteworthy aspects of the crisis are left for further study. Further research may address the identification of crisis in China's political culture and its impact on current thinking of modern governance as well as elements such as emotion, psychology, working style of decision makers in crisis management, and calculations of interest. Because of the limited availability of information, we are still unable to determine how the Chinese government reassessed its crisis management performance afterward. One can definitely say, however, that the lessons drawn from the 1999 crisis have provided a great impetus for enhancing research on crisis management theories as well as for building relevant Chinese mechanisms over the long term.

NOTES

1. On December 16, 1999, the Chinese and U.S. governments reached an agreement on compensation of the property loss incurred to the Chinese embassy in Yugoslavia. On January 17, 2000, the U.S. government paid compensation of $2.8 million according to the agreement. On April 8, 2000, the Central Intelligence Agency (CIA) issued a statement declaring that intelligence officers responsible for the embassy bombing had been disciplined.
2. Embassy personnel, interviews by the author, December 25, 2003.

3. Chinese government personnel, interviews by the author, August 28, 2003.

4. Chinese government personnel, interviews by the author, December 26, 2003.

5. Jerel A. Rosati, *The Politics of United States Foreign Policy,* 1st ed. [Chinese translation] (Fort Worth: Harcourt Brace Jovanovich, 1992; Beijing: Shijie Zhishi Chubanshe, 1997), p. 247. This situation is relatively equivalent to "group decisions" in Western crisis management theories. Irving L. Janis asserts that a group forms because of common backgrounds and beliefs. In the urgent situation of a crisis, a strong leader within the group usually promotes and maintains cohesion and team spirit. The rest of the group members thus show a tendency toward convergence and comply with the standards and decisions of the group.

6. Hu Ping, *Guoji Chongtu Fenxi yu Weiji Guanli Yanjiu* [Analysis of International Conflict and Research on Crisis Management] (Beijing: Junshi Yiwen Chubanshe, 1993), pp. 154, 156.

7. Zhang Zhaozhong, "Beiyue.de Xiayibu" [Next Step For NATO], *Nanfang Zhoumo* (South Daily Weekend), April 16, 1999.

8. Robert L. Kuhn, *The Man Who Changed China: The Life and Legacy of Jiang Zemin* [in translation] (Shanghai: Shanghai Translation Press, 2005), p. 315–316.

9. Hu Ping, *Guoji Chongtu Fenxi yu Weiji Guanli Yanjiu* [Analysis of International Conflict and Research on Crisis Management], p. 200. Hu Ping believes that the initial subjective opinion of the top decision maker, that is, the impression and definition of the situation, has a key influence on the discussion of situation, identification of targets, and choice of policy options. Wang Dong, "Chaoyue Guojia Liyi" [Beyond National Interests], *Meiguo Yanjiu* [American Studies] 15, no. 3 (2001), p. 34. Wang Dong, a doctoral candidate in the Department of Political Science, University of California, Los Angeles, took this bombing case as a typical example in explaining the perception element in PRC-U.S. relations: "As the relatively weak player in the PRC-U.S. relations, China is prone to exaggerate the degree of American acts as a product of its internal forces aimed at harming China whenever U.S. actions hurt or threaten China."

10. Yang Kai-Huang, "Zhonggong Dui Beiyue 'Hongzha Shiguan Shijian' Fanying.zhi Yanxi" [Analysis of the CCP's Response to the Embassy Bombing], Chinabiz.org, 1999. According to Taiwanese scholar Yang Kai-Huang, on May 8, Clinton publicly talked twice about the morality and necessity of a military strike against Yugoslavia. Even if Clinton had been able to talk

to Jiang when he requested it, what he would say would not have exceeded an expression of "regret."

11. Rosati, *Politics of United States Foreign Policy*, p. 8. According to American scholar Jerel Rosati, since World War II, U.S. diplomacy has always faced tension between democratic demands and national security. Democracy requires "individual access to information" and "an open dialogue about the ends and means of society." National security, however, relies on a relatively closed decision-making regime so as to respond rapidly to external events. This results in the tension between democracy and national security.

12. Hu Ping, *Guoji Chongtu Fenxi yu Weiji Guanli Yanjiu* [Analysis of International Conflict and Research on Crisis Management], pp. 162–163. Wang Chang, *Zhongguo Gaoceng Moulüe, Waijiaojuan* [The Strategic Planning of China's Supreme Leaders: Diplomatic Aspects] (Xi'an: Shaanxi Shifan Daxue Chubanshe, 2001), p. 299. The only counterproductive action by the United States was its dispatch of surveillance planes to Chinese territorial airspace on May 9. The PLA Air Force stopped these planes and forced them to leave. The Chinese side did not take it as further provocation or probing, nor did it publicly protest, obviously out of the desire not to escalate or complicate the crisis.

13. Yang Kai-Huang, "Zhonggong Dui Beiyue 'Hongzha Shiguan Shijian' Fanying.zhi Yanxi" [Analysis of the CCP's Response to the Embassy Bombing].

14. As far as the author knows, during that period, the Chinese government still approved prescheduled visits to the United States, the United Kingdom, Italy, and other NATO countries by department officials in the State Council and colonel-rank officers of the PLA General Staff. Economic, trade, scientific, technological, cultural, educational, and sports exchanges and contacts continued as usual. Visits at the ministerial or general-officer level and above to the United States and other relevant NATO countries were restricted.

15. Media personnel interviewed by the author, December 20, 2003.

16. The author believes China deliberately delayed disclosure of the U.S. apologies in order to reinforce the PRC representations for a formal and serious apology from Washington. Chinese leaders were concerned with the status of the person expressing the apology, the wording of the apology, and the occasion on which the U.S. issued this apology.

17. Yang Kai-Huang, "Zhonggong Dui Beiyue 'Hongzha Shiguan Shijian' Fanying.zhi Yanxi" [Analysis of the CCP's Response to the Embassy Bomb-

ing]. Before that, the press in the United States and the United Kingdom had played up the loss of their missions in China and attacked the Chinese government for tolerating anti-American assaults. The U.S. government even warned that the behavior of the Chinese government would jeopardize Sino-U.S. relations.

18. Rosati, *Politics of United States Foreign Policy*, p. 350.

19. Liu Deyou, *Shiguang Zhilü—Wo Jingli.de ZhongRi GuanXi* [Voyage of Time—My Experience with China-Japan Relations] (Beijing: Shangwu Yinshuguan, 1999), pp. 632, 634, 636; Zhang Tuosheng, "Lishi.de Huigu yu Qishi—ZhongRi Guanxi (1972–1992)" [A Review and Rethinking of Sino-Japanese Relations, 1972–1992], *Taipingyang Xuebao* [Journal of Asia-Pacific Studies], no. 3 (1999), p. 7; Masao Shimada, *Zhanghou Rizhong Guanxi Wushi Nian, 1945–1994* [50 Years of Postwar Japan-China Relations, 1945–1994], (in translation) (Nanchang: Jiangxi Jiaoyu Chubanshe, 1998), pp. 329, 353; Hu Sheng, ed., *Zhongguo Gongchandang.de Qishi Nian* [The Seventy-Year History of the CCP] (Beijing: Zhonggongdangshi Chubanshe, 1991), pp. 510–515.

20. University personnel interviewed by the author, December 25, 2003.

21. "Zhongguo Renmin.de Juewu he Liliang" [The Awareness and Strength of the Chinese People], *People's Daily*, May 19, 1999, p. 1. A May 19 editorial in *People's Daily* stated, "The power of the Chinese people is shown by indignation rather than confusion and by acting in strict observance of the law even in deep anger. . . . The socialist China in the 1990s will not see another 'Boxer Rebellion' or 'Red Guard Movement.'"

22. Wang Zuxun, "Ke Suo Wo Zhanzheng Dui Guoji Anquan Xingshi.de Yingxiang" [Impacts of the Kosovo War on International Security Situation], *Liao Wang*, no. 20 (1999), p. 8. *Liao Wang Weekly* of the Xinhua News Agency, for example, published an article describing the event as "a Nazi-style war crime." "Shi Rendao Zhuyi, Haishi Baquan Zhuyi?" [Humanitarianism or Hegemonism?], *People's Daily*, May 17, 1999, p. 1. *People's Daily* also carried an article on the Kosovo issue, claiming that the U.S. purpose in waging such a war was to "eliminate Yugoslavia as the last red stronghold in Europe. . . . . The bombing of Yugoslavia by the United States and NATO was a copy of the invasion of China by the eight Allied powers at the beginning of the century."

23. This reveals that state control of media is questionable in time of crises. When the objectives and emotions of diplomacy and propaganda converge, effective censorship is relatively easy. State control becomes difficult as the two bureaucracies diverge. This phenomenon has led to studies of topics

such as pluralism in foreign policy execution, coordination between foreign affairs and propaganda, media "memory of history," and analytical tendencies among professional journalists.

24. Liu Xiaobiao, "Fangzhi Jiguan Minzuzhuyi 'Jiechi' Zhongguo" [Deterring China From "Being Kidnapped" by Radical Nationalism], January 8, 2004, http://news.sina.com.cn/c/2004-01-08/08482575974.shtml. The number of Internet subscribers in China has grown quickly, and they are now the second-largest client population in the world. Liu writes, "Internet is playing a more dominant role in the people's social life."

25. The widespread adoption of radical perspectives is closely related to the evolution of contemporary media culture in China. It seems to be a rule that, during diplomatic crisis, publishing tough statements proves safer than expressing moderate assessments. Liu Xiaobiao, "Fangzhi Jiguan Minzuzhuyi 'Jiechi' Zhongguo" [Deterring China From "Being Kidnapped" by Radical Nationalism].

26. Zi Zhongyun, "Weile Minzu.de Zuigao Liyi, Weile Renmin.de Changyuan Liyi" [In the Supreme National Interests and in the Long-Term Interests of People], *Taipingyang Xuebao* [Journal of Asia-Pacific Studies], no. 4 (1999), p. 10. Madame Zi Zhongyun, former president of Institute of American Studies of the Chinese Academy of Social Sciences, was one of the minority openly stating a different view.

27. Wang Zuxun, "Ke Suo Wo Zhanzheng Dui Guoji Anquan Xingshi.de Yingxiang" [Impacts of the Kosovo War on International Security Situation].

28. University staff, interviews with the author, December 25, 2003.

29. Because of societal developments and political progress, Chinese officials today encourage the participation of professionals and outside experts in large policy issues and in the issues of carrying out policy. Hence, the government (including the National People's Congress) sets up various avenues for consultation and testimony in every policy area as it promotes the quality of policy makers either by professional in-career training or by straightforward appointments of experts as policy advisers or policy makers. The transformation of foreign policy making also coincides with this general trend. In March 2004, for example, the Politburo of the CCP invited scholars to give lectures on relevant world challenges. Also the number of research professionals from the Chinese Academy of Social Sciences, the State Council Development Research Center, and the China Institute of International Studies who have been hired to certain contract-based posts

in Chinese embassies and consulates or to key jobs within the MFA has increased.

30. "Shimin Fanmei Qingxu Pubian Zengqiang, Yaoqiu Zhengfu Zhankai Qiangying Waijiao" [Citizens Show Stronger Anti-American Sentiments and Require the Government to Be Tough], *First Hand*, no. 268 (May 11, 1999), www.chinavista.com/experience/lingdian/chdiaocha268.html.

31. Ibid.

32. Hu Ping, *Guoji Chongtu Fenxi yu Weiji Guanli Yanjiu* [Analysis of International Conflict and Research on Crisis Management], p. 155.

33. Ibid., p. 171.

34. Government staff, interviews with the author, December 25, 2003.

35. Hu Ping, *Guoji Chongtu Fenxi yu Weiji Guanli Yanjiu* [Analysis of International Conflict and Research on Crisis Management], p. 155.

36. Wang Chang, *Zhongguo Gaoceng Moulüe, Waijiaojuan* [Strategic Planning of China's Supreme Leaders: Diplomatic Aspects], p. 286.

37. Ibid., pp. 287–288.

38. Hu Ping, *Guoji Chongtu Fenxi yu Weiji Guanli Yanjiu* [Analysis of International Conflict and Research on Crisis Management], p. 211. In the studies of the styles of decision making, the features of regulated decision making are summed up as orderly formulation structure, clear decision-making procedures, hierarchic communication networks, and hierarchical staff system.

39. Wang Chang, *Zhongguo Gaoceng Moulüe, Waijiaojuan* [Strategic Planning of China's Supreme Leaders: Diplomatic Aspects], p. 289.

11

The April 2001 EP-3 Incident: The U.S. Point of View

Dennis C. Blair and David B. Bonfili

ON APRIL I, 200I, A U.S. EP-3 reconnaissance plane and a Chinese F-8 fighter collided in international airspace over the South China Sea. Damage caused by this collision led to the loss of the Chinese pilot and plane and forced the emergency landing of the EP-3 at a military base on China's Hainan Island. In the weeks that followed, as the United States and China negotiated the return of the U.S. plane and its crew, relations between the two countries underwent serious strains.

The most recent military crisis between China and the United States before the EP-3 event was in June 1999, when U.S. aircraft participating in the NATO bombing campaign against Serbia struck the Chinese embassy in Belgrade, killing several Chinese officials. Subsequently, the U.S. embassy and several consulates in China were stoned by mobs either instigated or at least assisted by Chinese officials.

The Belgrade bombing and its aftermath left a legacy of ill will on both the Chinese and U.S. sides. Moreover, by the time of the EP-3 incident, the two governments had still not developed any additional procedures for better communication in case of future military incidents. In presenting the story of the EP-3 crisis from the U.S. point of view, including the perception on the U.S. side of how the Chinese side was acting and reacting, this chapter aims to contribute to our mutual understanding of how this particular crisis evolved as well as lay the groundwork for the improvement of mechanisms to manage future crises.

PHASE 0—PRECRISIS

Actions and attitudes developed before 2001 were important factors in the behavior of both sides during the April 2001 EP-3 crisis. For years before the incident, the United States had conducted reconnaissance flights off the coast of China. The United States considered these flights routine, and it has conducted similar flights in many regions of the world.

Chinese leaders resented these flights. Unable to conduct similar operations against the United States (although China has used aerial surveillance to gather information on neighboring countries), Chinese leaders felt the U.S. reconnaissance flights were an infringement of Chinese sovereignty.[1] Chinese officials routinely complained to U.S. officials about the flights and characterized them as violations of the sovereignty of Chinese airspace, and U.S. officials just as routinely brushed these complaints aside, stating that the flights were taking place in international airspace.

Throughout the period in which the United States had been sending reconnaissance flights to the area, Chinese fighter aircraft flying from coastal airfields had been intercepting the U.S. planes in the South China Sea and East China Sea. Most of these intercepts were safe and non-threatening. In the year before the collision, however, a new and dangerous pattern had emerged. Chinese fighters flying from Hainan Island began flying dangerous intercepts, frequently crossing close ahead of the U.S. aircraft and creating turbulence that buffeted the larger, slower U.S. planes. In December 2000, the U.S. military attaché in Beijing protested this pattern of Chinese actions to the main People's Liberation Army (PLA) staff. PLA officials received the U.S. message but made no reply, and the pattern of dangerous intercepts continued in the early months of 2001.

PHASE 1—INITIAL RESPONSE AND STRATEGY

The collision between the Chinese and U.S. aircraft occurred at approximately 9:15 a.m. local time on a Sunday morning, about 70 miles southeast of Hainan Island. It was approximately 3:00 p.m. on Saturday in Hawaii, at the headquarters of the U.S. Pacific Command, and 8:00 p.m. on Saturday evening in Washington, D.C.

On the U.S. side, the only firsthand information concerning the incident was a small number of voice radio messages received from the airplane. These messages did not provide any details about how the collision had occurred, but they did report that the aircraft was making an emergency landing on Hainan Island and that the entire crew was alive. U.S. officials had two immediate concerns: the condition of the crew and the potential for China to hold the crew as hostages.

As is usual in such situations, staff officers at the U.S. embassy in Beijing; at U.S. Pacific Command headquarters in Hawaii; and in the Pentagon, State Department, and White House in Washington pieced together available information to determine what happened, what actions Chinese leaders were and would be taking, and what the U.S. response should be. At the same time, top officials, including the commander in chief of the U.S. Pacific Command, the secretary of defense, the secretary of state, the U.S. ambassador to Beijing, and the national security adviser, spoke on the phone with each other, exchanging information and ideas on the U.S. response.

These officials were very aware that their initial public statements would ultimately shape how the crisis evolved and what final conditions would have to be met for any mutually acceptable resolution of the affair. Consequently, they made every effort to exercise prudence and restraint while they collected more information about the nature of the incident.

At the same time, incidents like this do not remain a secret in the United States for long. U.S. officials have learned over the years that it is better to take the initiative in these situations—make official statements to the press with the information that is known rather than allow rumors, leaks, and unofficial statements to define the public story.

When any government's military forces are involved, the natural inclination for that government is to take a position supporting its troops, a position a government can generally expect the public to support patriotically. However, as U.S. officials learned during the 1988 *Vincennes* incident, it is best not to assign blame in these cases until sufficient facts are available.[2]

Partly because it was the middle of the night in Washington, but also because officials did not yet know all the facts and the United States had not yet reached a fully coordinated policy decision on the handling of the situation, it was the Pacific Command that made the first announcement. The announcement, posted on the command's web site approximately six hours after the incident, said:

At approximately 8:15 p.m. Eastern Standard Time, Saturday, March 31, (9:15 a.m. Sunday local time in China) in international waters, a U.S. Navy EP-3 . . . maritime patrol aircraft on a routine surveillance mission over the South China Sea was intercepted by two People's Republic of China fighter aircraft. There was contact between one of the Chinese aircraft and the EP-3, causing sufficient damage for the U.S. plane to issue a "Mayday" signal and divert to an airfield on Hainan Island, PRC. No crewmembers are reported injured.

We have communicated our concerns about this incident to the PRC government through the U.S. embassy in Beijing and the PRC embassy in Washington, D.C. We expect that the PRC government will respect the integrity of the aircraft and the well-being and safety of the crew in accordance with international practices, expedite any necessary repairs to the aircraft, and facilitate the immediate return of the aircraft and crew.[3]

At the same time, in Beijing, the U.S. embassy called both the PLA headquarters and the Ministry of Foreign Affairs (MFA) to request information about the condition of the crew. Neither organization returned the phone calls.

About 9:00 p.m. in Beijing, twelve hours after the incident, the U.S. ambassador to Beijing, Joseph W. Prueher, met with Assistant Foreign Minister Zhou Wenzhong. At this meeting, the Chinese side stated that the U.S. aircraft made an aggressive turn toward the Chinese aircraft, causing the collision, and that China required a U.S. apology. The Chinese side declined at this time, however, to provide any information about the condition or status of the crew. Meanwhile, China's MFA released a statement describing the incident in the same manner and making the same demand that the United States accept full responsibility for the incident.

By the morning of April 2 in Beijing, twenty-four hours after the incident, the two central U.S. concerns remained unaddressed: the Chinese had not verified the condition of the crew, and it was not clear whether China would hold the crew as hostages until the United States made some sort of apology. The U.S. side was convinced that the Chinese version of the collision was false although it was not clear to the U.S. side whether the Chinese leaders had been given a false account of the facts by the Navy authorities in Hainan, or whether the Chinese leaders had decided to publish a false story in order to gain leverage over the United States.[4] In any case, it was clear to the U.S. side that no senior U.S. leader would make a false apology and, therefore, either the Chinese side would have to change its story or they would need to find some kind of face-saving formula.

By this time, the Chinese press and international press were already carrying the Chinese version of the story of the collision and heavily publicizing the loss of the Chinese pilot. Both Admiral Dennis C. Blair, commander in chief of the U.S. Pacific Command in Hawaii, and Ambassador Prueher in Beijing held press conferences in which they challenged the Chinese version of the events and called for communication with the crew and the safe return of both crew and aircraft.[5] Later in the day the United States released a statement in the name of President George W. Bush that called for access to the crew and the crew's safe return. The president made no statement about responsibility for the collision but did offer to help in the search for the downed Chinese pilot.[6]

PHASE 2—NEGOTIATIONS FOR RELEASE OF THE CREW

The next day, April 3, brought what the United States considered no progress in Beijing. President Jiang released a statement that in effect affirmed the Chinese version of the incident and called on the United States to apologize for the collision; President Bush later in the same day issued another statement calling in stronger terms for access to and return of the crew.[7]

By this stage in the crisis, the U.S. press was covering the story heavily in the United States, including commentary from members of Congress and the media.[8] Speculation was rife that this might turn into another hostage crisis along the lines of the 1979–1980 crisis in Tehran that had caused such damage to U.S.-Iranian relations and to the political fortunes of the president at that time, Jimmy Carter. These concerns were somewhat assuaged when a team from the embassy, led by the military attaché, traveled to Hainan Island and met with the crew of the downed U.S. plane. Although confined, all members of the EP-3 crew appeared to be in good health and well-treated, and it seemed unlikely to the U.S. side that China intended to drag out the issue long enough to create the perception of a hostage crisis.

At the same time, however, there was no initiative coming from the Chinese side. The demand for an apology seemed to be the only Chinese position. At this point the State Department took over the lead in the interagency group that had formed in Washington to handle the crisis. The White House and the Department of Defense remained heavily involved, but because it was clear that the solution to the crisis would be through diplomatic negotiations, most of the work at this point in the crisis was done at the State Department and by the ambassador and the embassy staff in Beijing.

On April 4, consultations between the U.S. embassy in Beijing and the State Department in Washington resulted in a letter from Secretary of State Colin Powell to Vice Premier Qian Qichen, a respected Chinese statesman whom the secretary had met during Qian's visit to Washington the preceding month. The letter proposed a series of steps for resolving the incident. It also included a statement of regret regarding the apparent loss of the Chinese pilot (at this stage, the pilot was still technically missing).[9] That same day, while talking with U.S. media in Washington, Secretary Powell publicly stated his regret about the missing pilot.[10]

On the morning of April 5, Ambassador Prueher again met with Assistant Foreign Minister Zhou. It became clear to the U.S. side that an arrangement could be negotiated that would end the impasse. This was the first time the U.S. side saw a way forward to solving the crisis. For the first time, it appeared that China was more interested in solving the problem than it was in holding to its version of the collision and attempting to extract an admission of responsibility from the United States.

John Keefe, a special assistant to Ambassador Prueher in the Beijing embassy at the time, has published a very good account of the next six days of negotiations.[11] According to Keefe, U.S. negotiators were focused on securing the release of the EP-3 crew and the return of the airplane. Additional U.S. goals included gaining recognition from China of the "international procedures that, in emergency situations allow a plane from one nation to land on the territory of another nation without permission" and securing "a letter that . . . was factually accurate, did not apologize for anything that occurred in connection with the collision, did not impede the President's future ability to conduct U.S.-China relations, and did not undermine U.S. interests in the Asia-Pacific region."[12]

On the other side of the negotiating table, the embassy's Chinese interlocutors did not appear "particularly concerned about the facts surrounding the collision . . . [or] about international procedures." Rather, "Chinese authorities wanted [a] letter from [the Ambassador] . . . [that apologized] for the loss of the Chinese pilot and for the EP-3 landing on Hainan Island without permission."[13]

The ultimate compromise between these two positions led to a deal in which the United States agreed to produce a letter that stated "it was 'very sorry' about the loss of the Chinese pilot suffered by the Chinese people and the pilot's family and about the plane entering Chinese airspace without verbal clearance." On the other side of the table, Chinese authorities, "agreed to release the aircrew immediately after the U.S. delivered the letter, to hold a meeting with the U.S. to discuss the causes of the accident and ways to prevent future accidents, and to develop a plan with the U.S. for the return of the plane."[14]

Keefe describes the actual process by which the U.S. letter was drafted:

> From the 6th through the 9th, the Ambassador usually had two meetings per day with Assistant Foreign Minister Zhou. These involved the Ambassador either presenting a draft letter or listening to Chinese requests for changes to the text. The latter would usually fall into one of three categories—changes we could agree to on the spot, changes that were out of the question, and changes that would require a decision by the Secretary of State or the President. We would take the latter back to the embassy where Ambassador Prueher would then call Secretary Powell and/or Deputy Secretary Armitage and brief them on the status of the negotiations and on the Chinese requests. The Ambassador would also provide recommendations on what to propose next to the Chinese.

What was notable about these discussions was the speed with which the U.S. side could respond to the Chinese requests. Because the Secretary and Deputy Secretary were available 24 hours a day, the Ambassador was often requesting a follow-up meeting within 75 minutes of departing the MFA from the previous meeting.[15]

Throughout this process, the U.S. position was informed by details obtained by the embassy's military attaché during his brief interview with the U.S. EP-3 crew on Hainan Island on April 3 confirming that the EP-3 had not caused the collision.[16]

During the course of these negotiations, Keefe notes, "Evidence of damage to U.S.-China relations started to accrue." On the U.S. side, "six Congressional delegations that had been scheduled to visit China during the April recess cancelled their trips . . . and [t]he administration also issued an order for U.S. officials to suspend social contacts with Chinese officials."[17] From the U.S. perspective, response from the Chinese side was, if anything, even more severe. As Keefe recalls:

> During this period of time, we saw Chinese officials' attitudes toward the U.S. ranging from hard-edged ambivalence to outright hostility. What we did not hear were moderate voices, if they existed at all. This was also true of the Chinese media, which, of course, reflects the views of the leadership. There was no sense of building toward a constructive relationship during these negotiations.
>
> . . . We also saw a Chinese government acutely sensitive to Chinese public opinion about this incident. The Chinese government repeatedly expressed to us the pressure that the Chinese public was bringing to bear. Popular opinion demanded a tough response, Chinese officials said. The question in our mind was whether this pressure was real or induced. After all, Chinese state-controlled media was instrumental in misrepresenting facts and whipping up popular sentiment about the incident in the first place.[18]

On Wednesday, April 11, Ambassador Prueher delivered the product of U.S.-Chinese negotiations to Foreign Minister Tang Jiaxuan. As released, this letter read:

Both President Bush and Secretary of State Powell have expressed their sincere regret over your missing pilot and aircraft. Please convey to the Chinese people and to the family of pilot Wang Wei that we are very sorry for their loss.

Although the full picture of what transpired is still unclear, according to our information, our severely crippled aircraft made an emergency landing after following international emergency procedures. We are very sorry the entering of China's airspace and the landing did not have verbal clearance, but very pleased the crew landed safely. We appreciate China's efforts to see to the well-being of our crew.

In view of the tragic incident and based on my discussions with your representative, we have agreed to the following actions:

Both sides agree to hold a meeting to discuss the incident. My government understands and expects that our aircrew will be permitted to depart China as soon as possible. . . .

The meeting agenda would include discussion of the causes of the incident, possible recommendations whereby such collisions could be avoided in the future, development of a plan for prompt return of the EP-3 aircraft, and other related issues. We acknowledge your government's intention to raise U.S. reconnaissance missions near China in the meeting.[19]

In a further attempt to be conciliatory, President Bush also released a message, observing, "This has been a difficult situation for both our countries" and expressing "sorrow" on behalf of himself and the U.S. people "for the loss of life of a Chinese pilot."[20] The same day, China announced the release of the U.S. crew, and by Friday, April 13, the crew had returned to Hickam Air Force Base in Hawaii.

PHASE 3—AIRPLANE RECOVERY

After the crew was released, the incident was downgraded by the United States from a "crisis" to an "issue." This issue had two parts: recovery of the aircraft and establishment of procedures to prevent a recurrence of the incident.

The recovery of the aircraft was important for several reasons. The first was financial—the EP-3 was an expensive aircraft, and, even though it would require a complete overhaul to fly again, it was worth recovering. The second concern was symbolic—the United States did not want the EP-3 to become an exhibit in a Chinese military museum, a standing irritant to U.S.-China relations. Third, Navy officers wanted to examine the aircraft, as is done with every aircraft that has been involved in a mishap, to learn which systems worked and which did not, so that subsequent flights could be made safer.

Establishment of procedures for preventing a recurrence was important to the U.S. side because it knew that peacetime reconnaissance flights off the coast of China would also take place in the future, and the United States wanted to increase the margin of safety of those flights. In addition, the U.S. side hoped that agreement on procedures for the intercept of reconnaissance flights might lead to further agreements on subjects like search and rescue, so that, in the event of a future incident, there would be known and agreed channels and some expectations of procedures to follow for resolving the incident.

This chapter will not trace all the details of the six weeks of dispiriting haggling that led finally to the plane being returned to the United States in five pieces. The United States sent a Department of Defense team to Beijing for the negotiations, and decisions were made in Washington by a backup interagency team. The U.S. side preferred to repair the plane at the Lingshui airfield and fly it out. That would have been the least expensive course of action and would have removed the plane from Chinese soil the quickest.

The Chinese side cited security considerations and apparently felt that it would be a further slight to its sovereignty if the plane flew again in Chinese airspace, even for a one-way flight out. In the end, China allowed a U.S. team to remove the wings and tail from the fuselage and fly the four pieces out on a chartered Russian heavy-lift aircraft. Later, the Chinese side presented an exorbitant bill for the services they claimed to have provided the crew and recovery team; the U.S. side calculated what it considered a fair charge for the services and sent a check for that sum to the Chinese government. U.S. officials felt that the bargaining in this phase of the incident was a time-consuming waste of staff resources.

Discussions of procedures for the conduct of reconnaissance flights and their intercept and identification by fighter aircraft never made any headway. The U.S. side came prepared to talk about such procedures, but in every meeting the Chinese side delivered legal arguments that the reconnaissance flights were against international law. Neither was there any further move to discuss procedures to consult in case of a future incident between the military forces of the two countries.

CONCLUSIONS

U.S. procedures for dealing with a minor crisis like the EP-3 are well established and functioned smoothly in this case. An interagency group formed quickly; it comprised representatives from the White House, the Departments of State and Defense, and the intelligence agencies. U.S. Pacific Command provided information and recommendations. U.S. objectives were clear at each phase of the crisis, and the leadership of the group shifted smoothly. On the first day, public comment was made by the Pacific Command, and, without assigning blame, public comments outlined the U.S. objectives for resolving the crisis. From the second day forward, the lead passed to the Department of State, with the president kept informed of events and releasing two statements. After the crewmembers were released, the lead shifted back to the Department of Defense, which sent a negotiating team to Beijing to negotiate the return of the aircraft. All agencies were kept informed of developments and played supporting roles to the lead agency.

From the U.S. point of view, Chinese procedures for handling the crisis were slow and grudging. On the first day, Chinese officials simply did not return the U.S. embassy's phone calls. Then, for a period of four days, the Chinese side made no practical suggestions for a way to move forward in solving the crisis, while it provided a version of the events that the U.S. side found unbelievable. The Americans also often found that there were differences between the assurances given in Beijing and the obstructionist actions of the authorities in Hainan. Finally, the Chinese side never entered serious discussions about how to prevent similar incidents from happening in the future. It appeared to the U.S. side that the Chinese leaders had put themselves in a very difficult position with their initial statements. After they decided that it was important to over-all Sino-American relations to solve the incident, they made a series of grudging concessions that ultimately resulted in success.

Progress on this front can and should be made. U.S. reconnaissance flights continue in international airspace in the South China Sea and the East China Sea. Chinese fighters continue to intercept these flights. Outlining and agreeing to procedures for conducting these flights and intercepts and for dealing with any future incidents like the April 2001 collision described in this chapter would help ensure that future incidents of this sort do not become crises and would be to the advantage of both China and the United States.

NOTES

1. See, for example, "Sino-U.S. Negotiation on the Air-Collision Incident 20/04/2001," Embassy of the People's Republic of China in India, www.chinaembassy.org.in/eng/zgbd/t59535.htm. China expressed this view before the April 2001 EP-3 incident during periodic operator-level discussions conducted after the January 1998 signing of the Military Maritime Consultative Agreement (MMCA) by Secretary of Defense William Cohen and Defense Minister General Chi Haotian (author's recollection). They reiterated it during the event itself when, during talks in Beijing on April 18, 2001, the head of the Chinese delegation, Lu Shumin, argued that U.S. reconnaissance flights "[threatened] China's national security, peace and order, [constituted] a provocation against China's national sovereignty; and [violated] the basic norms of the international law on mutual respect for sovereignty and territorial integrity among nations."

2. In 1988, the U.S. cruiser *Vincennes* shot down an Iranian commercial airliner, mistaking it for an Iranian military aircraft. At his initial press conference during that incident, the chairman of the Joint Chiefs of Staff, Admiral William Crowe, stated: "First reports of military incidents are generally wrong; I am going to tell you what I know about today's events." He then provided a factual account of the incident without assigning responsibility or blame. Within hours it was clear that a tragic mistake had occurred, and the United States accordingly took responsibility and apologized for the incident.

3. U.S. Pacific Command, "U.S. Pacific Command Imagery Archive; 2001 Links; March 2001, Page 4," www.pacom.mil/imagery/archive/0103photos/index4.shtml.

4. James Mulvenon, "Civil-Military Relations and the EP-3 Crisis: A Content Analysis," *China Leadership Monitor*, no. 1 (Winter 2002), provides a detailed analysis of this controversy; it is based on interviews and published reports in Chinese civilian and military media outlets.

5. See "Ambassador Prueher; On-the-Record Press Conference," April 2, 2001, www.usconsulate.org.hk/uscn/usemb/2001/040201.htm, and U.S. Pacific Command, "United States Pacific Command, Transcript; Admiral Dennis C. Blair; Commander in Chief, Pacific Command; U.S. and Chinese Aircraft Incident, Sunday, April 1, 2001, Camp H. M. Smith, Hawaii," www.pacom.mil/speeches/sst2001/010401blairplane.htm, respectively, for transcripts. In reference to the Chinese version of events, Ambassador Prueher, for example, said, "We have no independent information to date concerning the cause of this collision. We need to speak to the crew before we can determine the cause of the accident and, despite repeated requests, the Chinese leaders have failed to communicate with us on this subject." Admiral Blair went further, noting that before the April 2001 EP-3 incident the United States had protested at the working level the aggressive Chinese intercepts, observing that the smaller, more agile Chinese fighter "[had] the obligation to stay out of the way of the slower [EP-3]," and commenting that, although the United States had not yet had a chance to talk to the crew to confirm how the collision had occurred, common sense led him to think that it was "pretty obvious as to who bumped into whom."

6. "Statement by the President on American Plane and Crew in China," White House, Office of the Press Secretary, April 2, 2001, www.whitehouse.gov/news/releases/2001/04/20010402-2.html.

7. "Statement by the President," White House, Office of the Press Secretary, April 3, 2001, www.whitehouse.gov/news/releases/2001/04/20010403-3.html.

8. Steven Mufson and Philip P. Pan, "Spy Plane Delays Irk President; Bush Asks 'Prompt' Release by Chinese," *Washington Post*, April 3, 2001, p. A1, is one such example.

9. "China Unmoved by U.S. 'Regrets,'" Cable News Network, April 5, 2001, http://archives.cnn.com/2001/WORLD/asiapcf/east/04/05/china.aircollision.14.

10. "Excerpt: Secretary of State Powell Expresses Regret Over Loss of Chinese Pilot," U.S. Department of State, Office of International Information Programs, April 4, 2001, http://lists.state.gov/SCRIPTS/WA-U.S.IAINFO.EXE?A2=ind0104a&L=us-china&D=1&H=1&O=D&F=&S=&P=2987.

11. John Keefe, *Anatomy of the EP-3 Incident April 2001* (Alexandria, Va.: CNA Corp., 2001).

12. Ibid., p. 8.

13. Ibid.

14. Ibid. It is worth noting, as Keefe observes, that although translators were on hand throughout the process, all negotiations were conducted "in English, as were all of the various drafts of the letter."

15. Ibid. During the course of these negotiations, in what the administration referred to as a "humanitarian gesture," President Bush also sent a personal letter directly to the widow of the Chinese pilot killed in the collision.

16. Ibid., p. 9. Keefe relates, "[A]ccording to the EP-3 aircrew, the collision occurred after the Chinese pilot had closed to within 3–5 feet of the EP-3 on two separate occasions. On the third pass, he came in too fast and, as he struggled to keep his plane under control, put his tailfin into the EP-3's no. 1 propeller."

17. Ibid.

18. Ibid., pp. 9–10. Keefe notes, "Interestingly, in contrast to the tensions and hostility on the surface of these negotiations, Chinese officials repeatedly stressed to the Ambassador and other Embassy officials that this event should not be seen as a major affair in U.S.-China relations and should not have lasting impact on the relationship." Subsequent events, to some degree, bore out this assessment. Although, in the immediate aftermath of the EP-3 incident, U.S. Secretary of Defense Donald Rumsfeld directed a review of bilateral military-to-military exchanges and President Bush's participation in the upcoming Asia-Pacific Economic Cooperation (APEC) summit was called into question, reciprocal exchanges soon resumed (including a trip to Beijing by U.S. Secretary of State Colin Powell in July of 2001) and the president did ultimately attend the APEC summit. David Shambaugh, "Sino-American Relations Since September 11: Can the New Stability Last?" Current History 101, no. 656 (September 2002), pp. 243–249, is helpful on this topic.

19. "Letter from Ambassador Prueher to Chinese Minister of Foreign Affairs Tang," White House, Office of the Press Secretary, April 11, 2001, www.whitehouse.gov/news/releases/2001/04/print/20010411-1.html.

20. "Remarks by the President on Release of American Servicemen and Women in China," White House, Office of the Press Secretary, April 11, 2001, www.whitehouse.gov/news/releases/2001/04/20010411-3.html.

12

The Sino-American Aircraft Collision: Lessons for Crisis Management

Zhang Tuosheng

IN APRIL 2001, A CHINESE MILITARY AIRCRAFT and a U.S. surveillance plane collided. The collision soon led to a crisis between China and the United States. With concerted efforts, the two countries brought the crisis under control relatively quickly. Although the crisis seriously damaged bilateral relations, the two countries once again gained experience in handling a security crisis between them.

This chapter, which examines the event from a crisis management standpoint, has four sections: the state of Sino-American relations before the collision, development of the crisis and relevant interactions between the two countries during the crisis, special crisis management features of both sides, and experiences and lessons for both China and the United States.

SINO-AMERICAN RELATIONS BEFORE THE INCIDENT

Analysts need to examine the aircraft collision against the historical background, that is, the state of Sino-American relations at that time. The following points are important:

First, the George W. Bush administration had just taken office, and Sino-American relations were at a key and sensitive moment. During his campaign, Bush strongly criticized the Clinton administration's China policy. After taking office, President Bush began readjusting U.S. policy toward China with the introduction of some tough measures. He dropped the concept of a strategic partnership between China and the United States, relegating China to the role of a main strategic competitor of the United States. He began increasing military deployment in the Asia Pacific, in the western Pacific in particular. He upgraded U.S. relations with Taiwan and decided to accelerate the development of a missile defense system regardless of strong opposition from China. Against this backdrop, the containment element in U.S. policy toward China became more apparent.

At the same time, the Bush administration, through formal and informal channels on many occasions, informed China that the United States attached great importance to bilateral relations and wished to develop constructive cooperation with China. In light of these developments, the Chinese government was, on one hand, fairly well prepared for increased troubles and, on the other hand, determined to avoid major fluctuations in bilateral relations. In short, the United States had been readjusting its China policy, and, in the transition period, any interactions between the two countries would have a significant impact on future development of Sino-American relations.

Second, China's desire to secure World Trade Organization (WTO) membership in 2001, its bid to host the Olympic Games, and its awareness of the upcoming Asia-Pacific Economic Cooperation informal leadership meeting in September made China eager to maintain a basically stable and sound relationship with the United States.

Third, in late March 2001, Vice Premier Qian Qichen made a successful visit to Washington. During the trip, he met not only Secretary of State Colin Powell, Defense Secretary Donald Rumsfeld, and National Security Adviser Condoleezza Rice but also President Bush and Vice President Richard Cheney. In addition, Qian met many important figures in Congress and the business community. China issued an invitation for Secretary of State Colin Powell to visit China. Qian's visit marked an early contact between Chinese leaders and the new U.S. administration and promoted preliminary understanding between the two sides. It increased the determination and confidence of the Chinese government to stabilize and improve the Sino-American relationship.

Fourth, the two militaries had been holding regular consultations on maritime military security since 1998, and in May 2000 they actually reached a common understanding on the avoidance of dangerous maritime military action although major differences existed in the dialogue.[1] China regarded the increasingly frequent close airplane surveillance by the U.S. military with great dissatisfaction and as a threat to its national security. In contrast, the United States focused on the issue at the technical level, stressing that the distance between Chinese monitoring planes and U.S. surveillance craft was too close to ensure aerial safety. In other words, the focus of concern of each side was markedly different. China focused more on the security aspect at the macro level whereas the United States concerned itself with safety measures at the micro level. Before the 2001 collision, the two sides had exchanged diplomatic representations on this issue on many occasions.

Fifth, memory of the bombing of the Chinese embassy in the former Yugoslavia was still fresh in the minds of both China and the United States. Whether the U.S. missile strike on the embassy was deliberate or a mistake is still a mystery to many Chinese, but one thing is clear: this sudden and unexpected incident generated a crisis between the two countries. The two sides resolved the crisis only after repeated public statements of apology, compensation, and the discipline by the United States of those responsible. As the victim in the incident, China suffered a much greater shock than the United States. The incident resulted in a clear rise of anti-American sentiment among the Chinese public and prompted a debate in Chinese academia on the international situation, Sino-American relations, and Chinese policy toward the United States. Unfortunately, the two governments made no special arrangements in the aftermath of the embassy bombing in order to avoid the recurrence of similar incidents.

It is important to have a good grasp of this background, which contributes to a sound understanding of the aircraft collision and the crisis that followed. Thus we can learn the lessons the collision experience offers.

After a great many ups and downs in the decade since the end of the Cold War, Sino-American relations had been developing and moving toward a new mutual accommodation, with cooperation becoming the common practice. The two countries had gradually gained some experience in managing their frictions and crises, but both were still to develop a complete crisis management regime. Mutual trust was increasing but remained fragile. The aircraft collision took place against such a backdrop, presenting a new and harsh test for both countries at the beginning of the twenty-first century.

CHRONICLE OF THE CRISIS

The aircraft collision and the ensuing crisis went through roughly four stages: the period from the collision until the release of the crew, negotiations, consultations about the return of the U.S. aircraft, and the disassembling and shipment of the aircraft and negotiations over payments. The length of time from the collision to final resolution of the incident did not fully coincide with the length of time the crisis lasted, with the former being obviously longer than the latter. The crisis began after extensive news coverage and, in particular, public statements made by leaders of both countries. The agreement on the return of the aircraft marked the end of the crisis. This lasted about two months. Follow-up work continued more than two months longer, until mid-August.

Collision and Release of the Crew

On the morning of April 1, 2001, a U.S. EP-3 military surveillance aircraft conducted a surveillance flight to the southeast of Hainan Island, China.[2] Two Chinese J-8 fighters followed and monitored the EP-3 under instructions from base. At 9:07 a.m., 104 kilometers to the southeast of Hainan Island, the EP-3 and the Chinese aircraft collided. The Chinese aircraft crashed into the sea; the pilot ejected but disappeared. The seriously damaged U.S. aircraft made a forced landing at Lingshui Military Airport, Hainan, at 9:33 a.m. The twenty-four member crew left the plane fifty minutes later, and Chinese personnel escorted the crew to a local guesthouse.

The day was a Sunday and China's Arbor Day. When the event occurred, Chinese leaders were planting trees outside Beijing. Because of the time difference, it was still Saturday evening on the East Coast of the United States. President Bush was at Camp David. Top Chinese and

U.S. leaders did not directly contact each other upon receiving the relevant reports.

At about noon in Beijing, the U.S. embassy, after receiving a phone call from Secretary of State Powell, established telephone contact with China's Ministry of Foreign Affairs (MFA). Eager to know the condition of the crew, the U.S. side asked to meet or speak to the crew and tried to contact leaders of the MFA and the General Staff of the People's Liberation Army (PLA). At the same time, U.S. State Department officials also established contact with the Chinese embassy in the United States. At around 3:00 p.m., the U.S. Pacific Command issued a brief statement on its web site, making the event public. The statement requested that, in accordance with international practice, the Chinese government respect the aircraft, leave the aircraft untouched, be mindful of the health and safety of the crew, and facilitate the immediate return of the aircraft and its crew to the United States.[3]

On the same day, after listening to emergency reports by the relevant departments, Chinese leaders decided that, to get a clearer picture of the situation and for dealing with the United States, the MFA would be responsible for domestic coordination at the working level. Meanwhile, Chinese leaders issued a directive concerning proper arrangements, on humanitarian grounds, for the well-being of U.S. crew. Now that the U.S. Pacific Command had issued a statement, Chinese leaders decided that the MFA should also make a public statement.

At 9:30 p.m., Assistant Foreign Minister Zhou Wenzhong called an emergency meeting with Ambassador Joseph Prueher of the United States; at the meeting, Zhou made solemn representations and lodged protests. Zhou stated that the direct cause of the crash of the Chinese aircraft was a sudden turn by the U.S. aircraft and that all the responsibility for the event lay with the United States. He demanded that the United States provide explanations about the collision and the issues related to the event.[4] Zhou also informed Ambassador Prueher that the twenty-four-member crew of the U.S. aircraft was safe and sound and that Chinese officials had made proper arrangements for them. Prueher expressed disagreement about the Chinese view of the responsibilities for the event and requested a meeting with the crew and the opportunity to examine the aircraft as soon as possible. At 10:00 p.m., the Foreign Ministry spokesperson publicly acknowledged the event for the first time. Yang Jiechi, China's ambassador to the United States, also had an emergency appointment with U.S. Department of State to make representations and protests.

At 10:00 p.m. on April 2, Zhou called another emergency meeting with Ambassador Prueher, making clear the position of the Chinese government and demanding that the United States shoulder responsibility for the event and apologize to China.[5] During the meeting, Zhou told Prueher that the United States could meet the crew the following evening.[6] Prueher once again expressed disagreement over the Chinese view about where the responsibility for the event lay, but he expressed appreciation for the Chinese decision to allow meeting with the crew, describing it as an important step toward resolution of the issue. Prueher further expressed regret over the loss of the Chinese aircraft and the willingness of the United States to assist in the search for and rescue of the missing pilot.

On the evening of April 2, President Bush, after returning to the White House and convening a national security meeting, publicly spoke about the collision for the first time, claiming that the primary goal of the United States was to have the crew and aircraft returned as soon as possible. He said that China's failure to respond to U.S. requests for contacts with the crew was inconsistent with international practice or its desire to improve bilateral relations.[7] Following that statement by President Bush, President Jiang Zemin on the morning of April 3 also publicly spoke about the event. He pointed out that the United States should bear full responsibility for the collision and should therefore apologize to the Chinese people. He demanded an immediate stop to all U.S. surveillance flights in areas close to the Chinese coast.[8]

On April 3, top Chinese leaders, on the basis of their judgment about the nature of the collision, issued clear guidelines, policies, and objectives for the handling of the incident. The thrust of their decision was to engage in a resolute struggle against the erroneous behavior on the part of the United States as well as utilize reason, advantage, and restraint; their approach safeguarded China's sovereignty and dignity but also considered the overall situation of Sino-American relations. China's basic approach was to strive for an early resolution of the event, with the first step in the resolution process to be the resolution of the question of the departure from China of the U.S. crew. This was to be followed by the resolution of the issue of the grounded aircraft. Then, through negotiations, the Chinese side would demand that the United States cease further hostile reconnaissance and respond appropriately to Chinese losses. In the evening, the Department of Propaganda of the Central Committee, upon approval by the central authorities, issued guidelines on media coverage of the aircraft collision.

On the evening of April 3, President Bush spoke about the matter for a second time. He said that he did not want an unexpected event to develop into an international incident, the United States had given China time to do the right thing, it was time to send the crew home and return the aircraft, and the accident might erode the hope for the two countries to establish fruitful relations.[9] Bush had been rather low-key when he spoke for the first time, but now he sounded much tougher. He did not even mention China's concerns; instead he stated only U.S. demands on China to release the crew and return the aircraft. On April 4, President Jiang spoke about the matter again before leaving the country for a visit to six Latin American countries.[10] Apart from reiterating the basic positions he had spelled out in his previous speech, he particularly emphasized that, instead of making comments that confounded right and wrong and that were detrimental to Sino-American relations, the United States should do something conducive to the development of bilateral relations.[11]

Up to this point, differences between the two sides were mainly in five areas:

- China believed that the U.S. aircraft abruptly veered toward the Chinese aircraft and caused the accident; the United States claimed that it was the Chinese aircraft that flew too close to the U.S. plane, lost control, and thereby caused the collision.
- China believed the event to be serious but accidental, but also found it to be a direct outcome of the long-term and frequent U.S. air surveillance of China; the United States claimed the right to carry out surveillance and observation anywhere in the world for its own security and it stressed the nature of the event as a pure accident.[12]
- China regarded the surveillance over China's exclusive economic zone as violating the UN Convention on the Law of the Sea and a serious

threat to China's security; the United States considered it compatible with the principle of freedom of overflight enshrined in the convention.[13]

- China viewed the entry into Chinese territory and the landing at a Chinese airport by the U.S. military aircraft without permission as a serious infringement upon Chinese sovereignty and territorial integrity; the United States claimed the landing was an emergency, with the aircraft seriously damaged and SOS signals sent beforehand, and therefore the U.S. aircraft had not infringed upon Chinese sovereignty and should enjoy immunity.

- China believed that it had the right to carry out necessary investigations and collect evidence on the aircraft and the crew that had illegally entered Chinese territory; the United States opposed any checking of the aircraft by the Chinese side and stated that if the crew was not released soon the United States would regard it as a hostage taking.[14]

In response to the Chinese demand that the United States shoulder all responsibility and apologize, the United States claimed that it did not bear any responsibility for the event and would therefore not apologize.

On the afternoon of April 4, with a stalemate looming in bilateral governmental interaction and rising nationalistic sentiments in both countries, Foreign Minister Tang Jiaxuan called a meeting with Ambassador Prueher and made representations. Tang harshly criticized the U.S. attitude and moves and said that the United States should not arrive at incorrect judgments or do anything that would escalate and complicate the matter. Tang also pointed out that China attached importance to its relations with the United States and would like to see an early and proper settlement. If the United States recognized its mistake and apologized to the Chinese side, Tang said, China would consider making arrangements for the crew to depart from China.[15]

On the same day, in an interview with CNN, the ambassador of China to the United States, Yang Jiechi, also demanded that the United States apologize, saying it was "extremely important." As long as the United States took the matter seriously, he said, the event could soon come to an end. Yang compared the incident with a situation in which a family member goes out to investigate a group of people that continuously drives back and forth in front of his house. As a result, the family's car is damaged and the family member is missing. Yang argued that, under these circumstances, the family should have the right to investigate the situation and the other party should at least apologize to the family. Yang expressed the hope that the American people would make a fair judgment. The interview made a positive impact on U.S. public opinion.[16] Families of the crew also expressed the view that if an apology could bring their family members back home, they would support such an apology to China.[17]

According to reports, President Bush, who at that time lacked experience in diplomacy and in relations with China and who was concerned about an escalation of the crisis, began to listen to the views of his father, former president George H. W. Bush; former national security adviser Brent Scowcroft; and former secretaries of state Henry Kissinger and James Baker.[18] At the same time, the United States began to heed important signals sent by the Chinese side.

On April 4, Secretary of State Powell expressed regret over the missing Chinese pilot and wrote in his personal capacity to Vice Premier Qian Qichen to express his regret, saying that Americans, like the family members of the missing pilot, were also praying for him. It was the first time a U.S. leader had paid attention to the safety aspect of the missing Chinese pilot. Powell in this letter also expressed himself differently on other relevant issues than he had earlier. In this letter, he mentioned that the United States would like to work with the Chinese side, for the sake of bilateral relations, to resolve the incident.[19] On April 5, President Bush also expressed regret over the missing Chinese pilot and the loss of the Chinese aircraft. He said, "We should not let this incident destabilize relations. Our relationship with China is very important."[20]

Because the United States changed its attitude, Chinese leaders decided to resolve the issue of the U.S. crew departing the country as soon as possible by prompting an explicit apology from the United States. On April 5, President Jiang, who was visiting Chile, said that the United States should apologize to the Chinese people for the collision, that leaders of the two countries must find a solution because resolving this issue would be conducive to overall bilateral relations, and that the two sides should handle the incident with caution.[21] On April 6, Qian Qichen replied to Powell's letter. While he pointed out that the statements by the United States were still hardly acceptable to the Chinese side, he made it clear that a positive and pragmatic attitude on the part of the United States and an acceptance of responsibility and an apology to the Chinese people were key to the settlement of the issue.[22]

From April 5 to April 11, China and the United States held eleven rounds of consultations over the apology letter, which went through several drafts. The wording was changed from the original "regret," to "sorry," and finally to "very sorry."[23]

On the afternoon of April 11, fully authorized by the U.S. government, Ambassador Prueher presented a letter of apology in his name to Foreign Minister Tang Jiaxuan. Apart from saying that the United States wanted to convey to the Chinese people and the family of the missing pilot that it was "very sorry" for their loss (the Chinese wording was "expressing deep apology" [shen biao qian yi]), the letter also said that the U.S. side was "very sorry" that the entering of China's airspace and the landing by the U.S. aircraft did not have verbal clearance.[24] It went on to express its appreciation for China's efforts to see to the well-being of the U.S. crew.[25] Upon receiving the letter of apology, Foreign Minister Tang Jiaxuan informed Ambassador Prueher that the Chinese government had decided to allow the U.S. crew to leave China. Tang also pointed out that this was not the end of the matter and that China and the United States should continue negotiations on this matter and related issues.

At 7:55 a.m., April 12, two days before Easter, the U.S. crew left Haikou for the United States by a chartered plane. On the same day, the People's Daily published an article entitled "Channeling Patriotism Into Nation-Building Efforts." The author of the article, a commentator, pointed out that, regarding the aircraft collision, the Chinese government had made representations to the United States that had made use of reason, advantage, and restraint. China had achieved success at the present stage, but the struggle would continue. The article pointed out that improvement and development of China-U.S. relations would not only serve the fundamental interests of the two countries but would also benefit world peace and stability.

The period between April 1, the day the collision occurred, and April 12, when the U.S. crew left China, was a time when Sino-American relations were extremely strained. Top leaders of the two countries were not able to establish contacts with maximum speed. The U.S. military unilaterally made the event public, and President George W. Bush soon spoke publicly about it, making it impossible to find a solution through quiet diplomacy. The press and citizens of both countries also responded quickly and sharply, thereby exerting tremendous domestic pressure on the decision-making processes of both governments. The incident soon evolved into a crisis, which rapidly escalated in the following days.

After the crisis erupted, the diplomatic services of the two countries maintained good contacts, and domestic coordination in both countries gradually improved. The exchange of letters between Powell and Qian marked a turning point in the crisis, after which both sides became more pragmatic in their attitudes, and their representations began to focus on an apology and the release of the crew. With concerted efforts, the two sides finally reached a common understanding on this issue. The departure of the U.S. crew from China marked the first steps in bringing the tensions caused by the aircraft collision under control.

The Chinese side did not make a public response at first, and it lodged strong protests with the United States only after the latter had made the incident public. But soon afterward, the Chinese side decided on the guidelines, policies, and objectives for handling the event. It decided to proceed from the premise of safeguarding China's sovereignty, but it also kept in mind overall Sino-American relations and worked to resolve the incident as quickly as possible.

Some of China's policies and objectives were modified during the course of crisis management. In the earliest representations, for example, the Chinese side argued that the United States should bear full responsibility for the incident, which was unacceptable to the United States. Later, China changed the wording and demanded that the United States bear "its" responsibility; this demonstrated flexibility in the Chinese attitude. The Chinese use of the sentence, "apology is essential to the settlement of the incident" (*daoqian zhiguan zhongyao*) was another important signal for the United States, which saw in it the prospect of a settlement. Thus, the United States gradually adopted a more pragmatic and flexible approach. Furthermore, during this period, China strengthened its guidance over mainstream media on the matter.

The first U.S. reaction to the incident was to request information from the Chinese side and to make contact with the crew. Soon afterward, unilateral release of the news by the United States exerted pressure on the Chinese side. Upon initial protests from China, the U.S. attitude turned tough. The United States denied any responsibility and demanded the release of the crew and aircraft, but it showed no concern for China's loss. This arrogant attitude was difficult for China to countenance. However, the U.S. side had also all along expressed its hope of resolving the matter peacefully through diplomatic channels. Later, the United States became more pragmatic and accepted to a certain extent China's demand for an apology in exchange for the return of the crew. At this stage, President Bush instructed the Department of State, rather than the Department of Defense, to handle the negotiations. It was an important and correct decision.

Negotiation over Aircraft Collision

On the afternoon of April 12, the spokesperson for China's MFA stated at a press briefing that China and the United States would begin negotiating on April 18 about the aircraft collision and other related issues, including the cause of the collision, termination of U.S. flight reconnaissance over the Chinese coast, and future avoidance of any recurrence.[26] Although the return of the aircraft was also an issue that the two sides had agreed to discuss, the spokesperson did not specifically mention it, perhaps out of consideration for the still very strong sentiments among the Chinese public.

The U.S. attitude began to toughen again immediately after the return of the crew. That afternoon, President Bush issued a strong statement from the White House, claiming that the U.S. aircraft had fully observed relevant laws and rules without doing anything that had caused the accident. He stated his intention to "ask our United States representative to ask the tough questions about China's recent practice of challenging United States aircraft operating legally in international air space." Bush also criticized China's decision to hold the U.S. crew for such a long period of time: "China's decision to prevent the return of our crew for 11 days is inconsistent with the kind of relationship we have both said we wish to have."[27]

Many other senior officials, including Secretary of State Powell and Secretary of Defense Rumsfeld, who had kept a low profile during the previous stage, also publicly blamed China, claiming that the provocative flight by the Chinese pilot caused the accident and that saying the United States was "very sorry" did not mean an apology to China. Some U.S. government departments even threatened to link the event with other issues in China-U.S. relations. For approximately a week, the United States basically did not contact the Chinese, in sharp contrast with previous U.S. behavior.

In the face of such comments by senior U.S. officials, the Chinese MFA spokesperson on April 15 pointed out that the irresponsible remarks by the United States in total disregard of the facts had deeply disturbed the Chinese people and that U.S. moves were neither conducive to the development of Sino-American relations nor to the coming negotiations. The spokesperson stressed that the Chinese side had, ever since the occurrence of the event, exercised calm and restraint and that the United States would have to bear all the consequences should persistent mistakes by the United States cause further harm to Sino-American relations.[28]

In mid-April, top Chinese leaders took an initial decision on the policy that had been guiding China's negotiations with the United States and possible solutions to the crisis. Later, they further clarified the relevant policies and objectives of the negotiation as the negotiation progressed. At that time, the Chinese side hoped to reach a package deal with the United States: clarifying responsibilities for the accident, terminating or reducing U.S. surveillance flights over China, and returning the U.S. aircraft as soon as possible. During the negotiations, the two sides would determine the specific methods of returning the aircraft.

On the afternoon of April 17, the U.S. negotiating delegation arrived in Beijing. The delegation mainly comprised officials and officers from the Department of Defense and the Pacific Command. Only two delegates were from the Department of State. The head of the delegation was Assistant Under Secretary of Defense Peter Verga. Ambassador Prueher, who had been vested with all authority to handle the crisis in his capacity as the U.S. representative for the negotiation at the previous stage, was not to take part in the current negotiations. The Chinese delegation was mainly composed of MFA officials and several officers from the Ministry of National Defense. The head of delegation was Lu Shumin, director general of the Bureau of North American and Oceanic Affairs at the MFA.

On April 18, negotiations started. The United States demanded that the return of the aircraft be discussed first, which China rejected. During the negotiation, each party presented its own position on how to deal with the incident, the causes of the collision, and U.S. air reconnaissance of China's coastal areas. Both reiterated their respective stands, which differed greatly. At the end of the first day, the U.S. side claimed that it would not attend the next day's meeting if the two sides could not discuss the return of the aircraft.

As the negotiation went into a stalemate, Assistant Foreign Minister Zhou Wenzhong and Ambassador Prueher held an emergency consultation the following morning, after which negotiation resumed. The two parties presented their own evidence on the specific causes of the collision and talked about other issues, including the return of the aircraft. Their viewpoints were still in great conflict. At the end of the meeting, China pointed out that the United States was interested only in the plane's return and was not paying any real attention to China's serious concern and that the problem could be settled only when the two countries considered each other's concerns.

On the afternoon of April 19, the MFA spokesperson announced at a media briefing that China and the United States had completed the first round of negotiations on the aircraft collision. During the two-day talks, the parties had frankly presented their positions and exchanged their views, and the two sides agreed to keep in contact about how to deal with the incident and related issues.

Although, after the first round of negotiations, Verga continued finding excuses for U.S. air surveillance, he pointed out at the same time that the United States also wished to develop a constructive relationship with China and to settle the incident as soon as possible. Most U.S. delegates flew back home the following day.

From April 23 to April 27, after a Chinese proposal, Zhou Wenzhong held four rounds of informal consultations with Ambassador Prueher. During the consultations, China suggested that possible agreement should be confirmed in the form of an exchange of notes, letters, or memoranda of understanding. However, the United States expressed no interest in producing a joint document. The United States was willing to talk only about an arrangement for the aircraft to be returned to the United States and demanded that bilateral consultations be based on a Department of Defense nonpaper.[29] The nonpaper put forward a deadline for the return of the aircraft as no later than the end of May. Its attitude toward China's request for compensation was rigid.

China wished to settle the core issue of the collision, but the United States would focus only on the technical issue of avoiding a future collision and the return of the aircraft. Because the two parties diverged greatly in terms of the starting point of consultations, the informal consultations produced very limited results. The two sides agreed to hold separate talks on the specific issue of a U.S. payment to China. They would incorporate the question of avoiding similar incidents in the future into the Sino-American maritime military security consultation mechanisms for discussion.

Two key trends emerged during the negotiations. On one hand, the crisis subsided substantially after the U.S. crew returned home. On the other hand, it was very difficult to proceed with negotiations because the United States readopted a tough attitude. Meanwhile, U.S. arms sales to Taiwan caused new tensions between the two countries.[30] Public sentiment in both countries displayed tension.[31] Under these circumstances, the crisis continued and threatened to intensify if a solution could not be found quickly.

During this stage, the Chinese negotiators had worked out guidelines for the negotiations that were basically consistent with the decisions made at the very beginning. China had expected tough negotiations and tried to reach an agreement so as to resolve the incident as soon as possible. Because the Americans remained unyielding, however, China did not reach its goal of an early settlement. Thus, China followed the principle of proceeding from the actual situation and fighting for its beliefs without aborting the negotiations. After clarifying its position, China did not fix its attention on specific controversies and, as a result, prevented the negotiations from breaking down. China thus made it possible to ultimately resolve the incident.

At this time, the Bush administration once again adopted a tough position; its goal apparently was to appease right-wing Republicans who had insisted on being tough on China after the air collision and to save face for the United States. This U.S. position caused indignation on the part of the Chinese side, poisoning the atmosphere for formal negotiations. President Bush also decided to let the Department of Defense, which had always been tough on China, lead the negotiations, making it difficult to make real progress. The United States paid a price for its tough position: the return of the airplane was delayed for a long time.[32] President Bush still expressed his willingness to visit China in October, as scheduled, which was positive for relaxing tensions.

Consultation About Return of the Aircraft

On April 29, Zhou Wenzhong met Prueher and informed the latter that the Chinese officials had completed their investigation and evidence collection on the U.S. aircraft. China consented to the U.S. request to inspect the plane at Lingshui Airport according to international precedents in similar scenarios. The two sides agreed to keep in contact in order to resolve the plane issue ultimately.[33]

The United States welcomed the Chinese decision. Vice President Cheney said in a television interview that it was an encouraging message showing China's willingness to move forward in the negotiations.

From May 1 to May 5, five technicians from Lockheed visited China and, with active Chinese cooperation, within three days finished inspecting the airplane. The United States expressed appreciation for China's assistance.[34]

On the same day the U.S. technicians returned home, the United States conducted a surveillance flight off the Chinese coast. China sent out fighter jets to tail the U.S. aircraft. An MFA spokesperson pointed out that China opposed resumption of these surveillance flights and that it was completely in line with international practice to send military aircraft to tail U.S. spy planes.

China had already prepared for the United States to restart its surveillance flights. At the end of April, when the informal consultations between China and the United States did not produce agreement, the Chinese leadership pointed out that it seemed that the United States would not stop its surveillance flights and that China ought to be prepared to continue following and monitoring U.S. spy planes. Therefore, when the United States did resume surveillance flights, China was prepared to handle the situation.

After a proposal by the United States, MFA officials from May 8 to May 28 held several rounds of consultations with U.S. embassy officials on the return of the aircraft. Officials from the Chinese embassy in

Washington also met with officials of the National Security Council (NSC) over the issue.

At first, the United States demanded that the plane fly back home after being repaired. China said, in response, that the U.S. aircraft could not return by means of flight because of its role as a spy plane. On May 8, an MFA spokesperson made this position known publicly. The spokesperson also pointed out that China had made this clear on several occasions during previous negotiations between the two countries.[35] The spokesperson on May 10 pointed out that not permitting the U.S. plane to fly home did not mean that China would not return the plane and that the final solution depended on the U.S. attitude toward the incident and the results of the ongoing talks. He once again protested the recent U.S. resumption of surveillance flights over the Chinese coast.

On May 13, China formally notified the United States of its disagreement with the U.S. plan to fly the plane home after repair. On May 17, the United States consented to disassemble the plane and ship it back to the United States aboard a commercial cargo aircraft; when the United States put forward its initial plan for this solution, China welcomed it.

More consultations followed, during which the United States tried again to explore the possibility of flying the plane back after repair. The United States ultimately had to give up the idea completely because of Chinese opposition. On May 28 during a meeting with U.S. embassy officials, Zhou Wenzhong said that China consented in principle to a new U.S. plan to ship the airplane back in pieces from Lingshui Airport via a chartered An-124 aircraft.

From June 2 to June 5, the two delegations, headed by Director General Lu Shumin of China's MFA and James Moriarty of the U.S. embassy in Beijing, held formal consultations on the return of the U.S. aircraft and reached an agreement through an exchange of notes. On the day immediately preceding the formal consultations, President Bush in a letter to Congress formally requested the renewal of normal trade relations with China.[36]

On June 7, an MFA spokesperson pointed out that China and the United States were going to settle the aircraft collision incident through joint efforts and expressed the hope that Sino-American relations would return to their normal path because China had allowed the United States to ship back the U.S. airplane and the two sides had resolved the incident.

The period of consultations on the return of the U.S. aircraft was the final stage of crisis management of the collision incident. During this stage, as both parties adopted more pragmatic policies, they gradually relieved tension without further major upsets. As the two parties reached agreement to have the aircraft disassembled and shipped back, the crisis was finally resolved.

The decision to allow the United States to inspect the plane and agreement to hold consultations on the aircraft's return while other disputes were shelved showed China's sincerity and flexibility in seeking an early solution. This played an important part in breaking the deadlock in the negotiations. Because the United States persisted in surveillance flights off the Chinese coast and in fact resumed such flights in May, China's resolve to not allow the U.S. aircraft to fly away after repair was strengthened. Thus, repairing the plane and flying it home became a principle on which China would not compromise. But China was flexible about disassembling and shipping the plane. The Chinese government won public support and understanding in this regard by combining its principles with flexibility.

In the face of the positive attitude on the part of China, the United States also compromised substantially by giving up its plan to fly the plane back on its own; instead it agreed to ship home a disassembled plane. This compromise played an important part in reaching an agreement on the plane's return. It is worth noting that before this agreement was arrived at, the Department of State once again had taken over from the Department of Defense the principal role of negotiating with China. The State Department, apparently more pragmatic about China and familiar with diplomatic negotiations, was the department able to bring about a compromise.

As the two countries reached agreement on the plane's return, the crisis between China and the United States caused by the collision drew to an end.

Negotiation About Disassembling and Shipping the Aircraft and Payments

After the end of the crisis, it still took a long time to finally settle related issues. Because the handling of events at this stage no longer falls within the category of crisis management, this chapter offers only a very brief account.

On June 7, China and the United States started technical consultations. The last An-124 cargo aircraft that was used for shipping pieces of the surveillance plane left on July 3, marking the complete resolution of the issue of the return of the aircraft. During the disassembling and shipping process, China and the United States cooperated well.

On June 25, the U.S. administration declared its neutrality on the question of Beijing's bid to host the 2008 Olympic Games. On June 28, at the request of the United States, Foreign Minister Tang Jiaxuan had a telephone conversation with Secretary of State Colin Powell, during which the latter stated that the unpleasantness in the bilateral relations caused by the aircraft collision was over.[37] President Bush talked with President Jiang Zemin on the phone on July 5 for the first time since the aircraft collision. They expressed the wish to work for a constructive relationship.[38] Secretary Powell paid a visit to China on July 28–29. Afterward, the relationship between the two countries showed many signs of improvement.

The two parties started to negotiate on the issue of payment on June 30 but no agreement could be reached. On August 14, China refused the check and the statement the United States delivered.[39] The aircraft collision incident came to an imperfect end.

CRISIS MANAGEMENT— CHINA AND THE UNITED STATES

The handling of the crisis by the Chinese side showed the following features:

- Decision making and implementation were highly centralized. The Standing Committee of the Political Bureau approved all major decisions, top leaders played a core leading role, and the MFA carried out representations with the United States.
- Guidelines for handling the crisis were clear. Once the Chinese decision makers determined the nature of the incident, they decided at the outset on a general policy of a quick search for settlement as well

as a dual focus on maintaining national sovereignty and China's overall interests in bilateral relations. Following these guidelines, they allowed flexibility in the formulation, implementation, and readjustment of specific policies.

- There was sound policy coordination. After the incident, China established coordinating mechanisms in the central government and among competent departments. Many coordinating meetings were convened to exchange information, coordinate policies, and steer actions. As a result, Chinese officials firmly adopted decisions made by national leaders. Guidance to the official mainstream media was also markedly better than guidance in the aftermath of the embassy bombing.

- Chinese officials paid great attention to the legal aspects of the crisis. The Chinese government attached great importance to the international laws relevant to the incident and placed negotiating on the basis of legal presentations at the top of its agenda, with a view to gaining international support and sympathy with regard to legal principles.

One must note that the handling of this crisis suggests that there is still much room for improvement on the part of China in the area of crisis management. As was the case in the aftermath of the embassy bombing in 1999, for example, China once again responded sluggishly at the beginning. The Chinese government should make serious efforts to review the areas of crisis preparedness, response mechanisms at the top level, intelligence support, and reporting systems. How to set appropriate and feasible objectives that facilitate defusing a crisis while safeguarding fundamental interests is also worth in-depth exploration.[40] In addition, some press organizations attempted to play up the news, which was fairly negative toward crisis management. How to strengthen guidance to the media in an increasingly free and diversified society is another question that Chinese leaders must consider.

In the United States, crisis management was not as highly centralized as it was in China. The Bush administration, Congress, and the press all had their opinions. Mainly because of the U.S. political system, policies emanated from various departments, and the relevant departments charged with negotiating with China also changed from time to time.

President Bush's lack of experience in foreign affairs could have been another reason. On the whole, however, the U.S. president was firmly in control, and Congress and the press coordinated with the White House more than they opposed the White House.

The NSC played an important coordinating role in the course of crisis management. As a permanent agency composed of the president and chief figures in the administration, the NSC has ready-made crisis management procedures. Immediately after the aircraft collision, the United States set up an interagency team that was directly responsible to the president. The leadership of the team shifted according to the specific issues at hand. Secretary of State Powell and National Security Adviser Rice played important roles in policy coordination.

The United States also had clear and consistent objectives during the course of crisis management: an early return of the crew and aircraft, no damage to the overall bilateral relationship, and an insistence on its so-called right to continue surveillance flights.

U.S. leaders failed to assess correctly the nature and peculiarities of the incident at the outset, they initially reacted improperly, and they lost the opportunity to avoid an escalation of the incident into a crisis.

LESSONS AND EXPERIENCES FOR BOTH COUNTRIES

The aircraft collision triggered a crisis between China and the United States. Strictly speaking, it was only a semicrisis that was not as serious as a full-fledged crisis, and it was relatively easy to resolve.[41] Even so, it caused serious damage to bilateral relations. The consequences might have been worse if the potential dangers latent in the development of the crisis had materialized.[42]

The crisis prompted a serious confrontation between the two countries and the peoples of the two countries. The situation for a time threatened to get out of control. In China, some indignant groups called for a trial of the U.S. aircrew and detention of the plane; they even questioned why the Chinese government had not shot down the U.S. plane in the first place. In the United States, voices demanded the recall from China of the U.S. ambassador, suspension of military contacts, withdrawal of government guarantees for U.S. investors in China, refusal to renew normal trade relations with China, and opposition to China's bid to host the 2008 Olympic Games and membership in the WTO; and they even linked the incident with arms sales to Taiwan. Congress passed a number of anti-China resolutions. The Sino-American relationship might have suffered more if the two governments had not focused on the overall well-being of their relationship and relatively quickly settled the crisis.

To some extent, this crisis sped the readjustment in the Sino-American relationship after the new administration came into power in the United States. However, the price both countries paid was rather high. Between the two peoples, there was a growing resentment, with profound and long-term negative effects on the bilateral relationship. Antagonism between the military authorities intensified. The U.S. Department of Defense clung to the incident and obstructed progress in the bilateral military relationship for a protracted period of time. As a result, it took until the end of 2003 to resume the basic Sino-U.S. military-to-military relationship. Anti-China sentiment was running high in Congress, and many members of Congress cancelled or delayed visits to China. During the crisis, leaders of the two countries did not have much time for other issues. By the time the crisis was settled, they had become more wary of each other. Had it not been for the incidents of September 11, 2001, which led to great changes in the international situation and major readjustments in U.S. security policy, the development of constructive cooperation between China and the United States would have progressed very slowly.

What lessons should the two countries draw from the aircraft collision and the crisis it created?

Effective, Well-developed Early-Warning Security Mechanism Is Lacking

A former senior official of the U.S. Department of Defense once pointed out during a workshop on Sino-American security relations that, while the bombing of China's embassy was unexpected, the aircraft collision should have been predictable. This opinion made the Chinese participants ponder deeply.

Accidents are generally hard to predict. However, in this case, there had been many signs of a possible incident before the actual event. The two countries had already had several diplomatic exchanges that centered on U.S. surveillance flights and flight monitoring by China as both had sensed the potential danger. China and the United States had specifically discussed the issue during their consultations on maritime military security. Nevertheless, they took no timely and effective measures to avoid such an occurrence. The aircraft collision was a most untimely incident: the Bush administration had just come into power, the bilateral relationship was at a sensitive juncture, and Vice Premier Qian Qichen had just paid a successful visit to the United States at the end of March, which was an early contact between top leaders of the two countries.

Had there been a relatively well-developed early-warning mechanism in the security field, had the two sides informed their related authorities of the developments in diplomatic negotiations in a timely manner, and had both sides strictly abided by the common understanding reached on maritime military security, the incident could have been avoided.

Effective Emergency Contact Mechanism Is Lacking

For a long time after the aircraft collision, the two sides were in contact only at a relatively low level, without any communication between middle- and high-level officials. The U.S. embassy in China attempted to talk to middle- and high-level Chinese officials but failed. Later, the United States complained that they could not reach senior Chinese officials and that the briefing from the Chinese side had come too late. But this was a problem not only on the Chinese side because at the time no practical institutional arrangement existed for such emergencies. When most elements about the incident remained unclear, middle-level and senior Chinese officials certainly would not agree to talk to U.S. embassy officials without specific authorization.

In fact, a hotline between presidents did exist, but neither China nor the United States made use of it. This reflected a lack of clear definition of the functions of the hotline. Some say that the NSC rejected at the outset a proposal for direct communication between the two heads of state, finding it unnecessary to overreact and judging it not necessarily effective.[43] Another view that was making the rounds was that President Bush did not call because President Clinton had established the hotline and Bush's policy was ABC—Anything but Clinton.[44] Furthermore, a former senior American official told me privately that President Bush did not know such a hotline existed at all. Up until then, China had never initiated a hotline phone call to the United States. Whatever the reason, none of the existing communication channels worked during the emergency.

Soon after the end of the crisis, China proposed establishing a high-level emergency contact mechanism between the two countries. In response, the United States said it found the establishment of such a mechanism necessary in principle, but it put forward no specific ideas. The United States also expressed the view that the important thing in the future was that both should be willing to contact each other promptly when necessary. In other words, for the United States, as long as such willingness existed, the current communication channels were adequate.

The existing communication channels work effectively when bilateral relations are in harmony. However, in times of emergencies, such channels often become much less reliable. Willingness is certainly important, but institutional arrangements are always essential as a guarantee. It is indeed necessary to establish and improve an emergency contact mechanism between the two countries (including "track one" and "track two" at both the top and middle levels) and to clarify the functions and procedures of such contacts.

One can summarize the lessons mentioned above as the need to set up a crisis management mechanism between the two countries in addition to their own individual crisis management systems. The current maritime military security consultation between the military authorities of China and the United States does include certain aspects of such a mechanism, but it is obviously far from being sufficient for crisis management. Through a mutual crisis management mechanism, the two sides could contact each other on a regular or an irregular basis, predict potential crises, and work out preventive measures as well as steps to be taken in case of crisis. If circumstances or incidents that might trigger a crisis arise, especially sudden and unexpected incidents, the two sides could establish contact right away between both middle-level and high-level officials and act promptly to keep the incident under control. The establishment of such a mechanism as an addition and enhancement to the normal communication channels would play a very positive role in managing potential crises between the two countries.

Quiet Diplomacy Is Necessary

Not long after the crisis broke out, some experts pointed out that the United States should not have made the incident public so soon and that the problem should have been solved through quiet diplomacy instead of through mutual accusations and that the two sides should have conducted a joint investigation into the causes of the incident before reaching any conclusions. Had they done so, the incident might not have developed into a serious crisis. Indeed, the settlement of the issue came back to its original starting point after intense and open confrontation and quarrels, with much damage having already been inflicted on bilateral relations. Why didn't the two sides take a low-key approach from the very beginning?

This chapter argues that, given the state of bilateral relations at that time, it was actually very difficult, if not entirely impossible, for the two countries to conduct quiet diplomacy, which requires certain prerequisites. Prerequisites include not regarding each other as enemies, necessary institutional arrangements, mutual trust and understanding between top leaders, and a relatively rich experience in handling emergencies. Most of these prerequisites did not exist before the aircraft collision.

Quiet diplomacy might be a good idea in the long term for dealing with sudden and unexpected incidents or crises such as the aircraft collision. It would help reduce pressure from domestic politics and public opinion over decision making, minimize damage to bilateral relations caused by impromptu reaction or short-term behaviors, and facilitate resolution of problems on the basis of fundamental national interests. Of course, this is not to say that China and the United States should not discuss the merits of and responsibilities for the incident. In quiet diplomacy, parties also deal with such issues, but in a different manner. In addition, quiet diplomacy is a good option because it is easier to settle accidental incidents through mutual compromise.

This raises a deeper question: how to define the two countries' relationship.[45] In the new international situation after the end of the Cold War, are China and the United States friends or foes? Or are they neither friends nor foes, as many have pointed out? The question is complex and controversial, and the answer is critical to crisis management for the two countries. Currently the two sides need to agree at least on this: the Sino-American relationship today is definitely different from the confrontational relations of the 1950s and 1960s and from the old Soviet-U.S. relationship. It is a relationship with both cooperation and differences, with the former exceeding the latter, which makes it possible for the two sides to make efforts to develop a constructive and cooperative partnership. Consequently, it is clearly unwise for either side to deal with major differences or frictions with a Cold War mindset, either subconsciously or deliberately. The two sides will be in a better position to find more effective and reasonable solutions in future crisis management cases only if both have a somber mind about this new nature of bilateral relations.

China and the United States can also sum up some useful experiences in settling the crisis. After the EP-3 crisis began, for example, the two sides were in constant contact, and their communications went on with little trouble. The exchange of letters between senior leaders was instrumental. The diplomatic services, including the embassies, also made great efforts. The work of the two ambassadors, including communication with people who were not with the government but who had substantial influence on the top decision makers, was most critical for communication and introduced some important proposals.

Both parties were able to send specific and clear signals as well as grasp and respond quickly to the other's signals. This was clear from the interaction between the two sides at such critical moments as "release of the crew upon apology" (*daoqian ji fangren*) and "separate handling of crew and aircraft" (*renji fenkai chuli*).[46] There were no ambiguous signals or misinterpretation of signals during the crisis management.

To resolve the crisis, the two parties gradually identified practical and limited objectives and followed the basic crisis management rules of saving face for each other and making necessary compromises. The United States, for example, gave up its initial goal of a rapid and unconditional release of the crew and the plane by China. When the negotiations deadlocked, China no longer insisted on the United States abandoning or reducing its reconnaissance flights over China as an immediate objective. The release of the crew upon apology and the return of disassembled aircraft were typical examples of saving face for both sides and compromising when necessary.

The two sides also agreed on the idea of separate handling of crew and aircraft, which defused one of the factors in the crisis and made the crisis less intense at the most critical moment. This helped defuse the crisis quickly. The two sides also paid attention to guiding the press at home.

Also important was the presence of decision makers with insight, especially the top leaders of the two countries who had a profound understanding of the overall situation of the bilateral relationship. Although, at the beginning, both sides were tough on each other because of a severe lack of mutual trust and pressure from domestic politics, the common desire to prevent deterioration of the situation or a confrontation and to avoid the destruction of Sino-American relations caused by the incident finally became the dominant factor in crisis management and allowed a relatively quick defusing of the crisis.

Looking into the future at the same time as China and the United States are constantly strengthening their cooperation, they should seriously draw on the experiences and lessons of crisis management and enhance crisis management research and the construction of a crisis management regime, thereby effectively preventing or managing any crisis erupting between the two countries, particularly sudden security crises. This will be of great significance in sustaining the basic framework of Sino-American relations and mutual trust and ensure their long-term healthy and stable development.

NOTES

1. The common understanding the two sides reached was: When military aircraft of the two countries meet in international airspace, they should appropriately observe existing international law and international customs and appropriately accommodate the other party's flight safety so as to prevent dangerous closing in on the other and collisions.

2. This chapter follows Beijing time. When the incident occurred, the time difference between China and Eastern Standard Time in the United States was thirteen hours. After the beginning of Daylight Savings Time in April in the United States, the time difference was twelve hours.

3. Center for Crisis Management Studies, China Institute of Contemporary International Relations, *Guoji Weiji Guanli Gailun* [International Crisis Management] (Beijing: Contemporary News Press, 2003), p. 273.

4. *People's Daily,* April 3, 2001, p. 1.

5. *People's Daily,* April 4, 2001, p. 1.

6. From April 3 to April 10, 2001, Chinese officials allowed U.S. embassy and consulate officials to meet members of the crew either collectively or individually many times.

7. *Cankao Xiaoxi* [Reference News], April 4, 2001, p. 1.

8. *People's Daily,* April 4, 2001, p. 1.

9. Associated Press, April 3, 2001.

10. During President Jiang's visit from April 5 to April 17, Vice President Hu Jintao was in charge of the handling of the crisis and presided over meetings by the chief officers of many relevant departments to study the situation and coordinate policies. President Jiang maintained his leadership over the handling of the event and provided important instructions on quite a number of occasions.

11. *People's Daily,* April 5, 2001, p. 1.

12. As to the nature of the incident, China and the United States had both similarities and differences. China considered it an "accidental event" (*oufa shijian*), and the United States judged it as an "accident" (*shigu*)—two definitions that were actually similar. The two sides, however, held quite different views about the fundamental reasons for the incident. Excessive stress on the accidental nature of the event and neglect of the root causes obviously do not help in understanding the complexity of the issue.

13. The United States had not ratified the convention and was therefore not a state party to the convention. However, the U.S. administration had expressed a willingness to observe the basic principles of the convention.

14. In their public statements, however, U.S. leaders exhibited caution and avoided using this expression.

15. *People's Daily,* April 5, 2001, p. 1.

16. Wang Chang, *Zhongguo Gaoceng Mouluë: Waijiaojuan* [The Strategic Planning of Top Chinese Leaders: Diplomatic Aspects] (Shaanxi: Shaanxi Shifan Daxue Chubanshe, 2001), p. 312.

17. Agence France-Presse, April 4, 2001.

18. When Sino-U.S. relations were most difficult after the event, the Chinese embassy in the United States tried its best to contact these people, who had a better understanding of China and might have had an influence on the U.S. president.

19. *People's Daily*, April 8, 2001, p. 2.

20. "Remarks by the President at American Society of Newspaper Editors Annual Convention," White House, Office of the Press Secretary, April 5, 2001, www.whitehouse.gov/news/releases/2001/04/20010405-5.html.

21. Center for Crisis Management Studies, China Institute of Contemporary International Relations, *Guoji Weijii Guanli Gailun* [International Crisis Management], p. 268.

22. *People's Daily*, April 8, 2001, p. 3.

23. It was a proposal by Ambassador Prueher, who had a relatively deeper understanding of Chinese culture, to use the phrase "very sorry." However, the United States always refused to use the word "apologize."

24. The Chinese wording was "expressing deep apology" (*shenbiao qianyi*).

25. *People's Daily*, April 12, 2001, p. 1. The two sides decided to conduct consultations only on an English text of the U.S. letter and carry out the Chinese text separately so as to allow for diplomatic flexibility. There are two different Chinese translations for "very sorry" (*shenbiao qianyi* from Chinese side compared with *shenbiao yihan* from the U.S. side).

26. *People's Daily*, April 13, 2001, p. 4.

27. "Remarks by the President Upon the Return From China of U.S. Service Members," White House, Office of the Press Secretary, April 12, 2001, www.whitehouse.gov/news/releases/2001/04/20010412-6.html.

28. *People's Daily*, April 15, 2001, p. 1.

29. A nonpaper is a form of diplomatic document. It is often used to elaborate views, positions, and proposals on specific questions; it is not legally binding.

30. At the end of April 2001, the United States and Taiwan accelerated their discussions of arms sales to Taiwan and reached agreement on some items. On April 24 during a press conference, President Bush stated that the United States was making an effort to protect Taiwan. The United States on April 18 submitted once again an anti-China draft resolution at the UN Human Rights Commission. The U.S. Department of State released a warning to tourists visiting China.

31. Anti-American sentiments among the Chinese public were in full view on the Internet. There were reportedly cases of Chinese hackers attacking U.S. government web sites.

32. China had hoped to reach an agreement with the United States during the informal negotiations and return the plane at the end of May.

33. The Speaker of the Ministry of Foreign Affairs of the People's Republic of China, April 29, 2001.

34. *People's Daily,* May 6, 2001, p. 4.

35. Ibid.

36. Xinhua News Agency, *English News Bulletin,* June 1, 2001.

37. *People's Daily,* June 29, 2001, p. 4.

38. *People's Daily,* July 6, 2001, p. 1.

39. China demanded that the United States pay $1 million to cover all costs incurred during the stay of the crew and the aircraft. The Chinese government flatly refused the U.S. decision to pay only $34,000 of so-called reasonable payments.

40. According to crisis management theories, the objective of crisis management is to defuse crises and avoid escalation into military conflict rather than resolve fundamental differences between the parties to a crisis.

41. According to the internationally accepted definition, a semicrisis refers to the type of incidents that, although they demonstrate conflicts of national interests and time pressures, would normally not cause a military conflict. Therefore, they do not show the features of a crisis in its complete sense. A semicrisis may still cause severe damage to the political and diplomatic relations between the relevant countries and, in some circumstances, increase the probability of a crisis in the future.

42. At a Sino-U.S. security crisis workshop, Admiral Dennis C. Blair, former commander in chief of the U.S. Pacific Command, made the point that one must not underestimate the danger of accidental events. The nature of the crisis caused by the aircraft collision would have been rather different, and disastrous consequences to bilateral relations might have occurred, if any of the following scenarios had taken place: (1) the collision had caused the crash of the U.S. aircraft and death of the crew, (2) the Chinese military had approved the request of the other Chinese aircraft to shoot down the U.S. plane, (3) the detention of the U.S. crew in China had lasted for more than one month and the incident had developed into hostage taking, (4) the United States had been determined not to express any regret on the basis of its view that the collision was caused purely by mistakes of the Chinese pilot, or (5) the United States had decided to destroy the aircraft by precision strike in order to protect the very sensitive high-tech equipment on board.

43. Center for Crisis Management Studies, China Institute of Contemporary International Relations, *Guoji Weijii Guanli Gailun* [International Crisis Management], p. 246.

44. This is a satirical term coined by some members of the U.S. academic community to refer to the Bush administration's policy of rejecting any policy initiated by the Clinton administration.

45. At the end of the 1990s, the two countries decided to develop a "constructive partnership of strategic cooperation." They refined their objective as the development of a "constructive partnership of cooperation" at the beginning of the twenty-first century. However, they have not yet fully defined the nature of their bilateral relationship.

46. Some analysts in the United States believe that the U.S. crew had been actually taken hostage and had become China's bargaining chips because their release had been clearly linked to a U.S. apology. Thus, they believe this move by China caused harm to China-U.S. relations. This viewpoint does not hold water. China provided generally accepted treatment to the crew, allowed many visits by U.S. embassy officials, and made it clear to the United States that the reason for temporarily not allowing the crew to exit China was to carry out necessary investigations, which was completely different from hostage taking. The Chinese proposal of "release of the crew upon apology" was intended to break the stalemate and settle the most urgent issues for both sides. As a matter of fact, China's proposal expedited the process of the U.S. crew returning home. It is understandable that the inability of the U.S. crew to return to the United States sooner may have produced negativity in U.S. public opinion. However, the facts were that a spy flight off the Chinese coast by a U.S. military aircraft caused the loss of a Chinese aircraft and pilot, the U.S. military plane then landed in Chinese territory without permission, and the United States showed great reluctance to apologize. What impact did these facts have on the psychology of the Chinese public? Is that not a question the United States should have thought seriously about?

Conclusion: Implications, Questions, and Recommendations

Michael D. Swaine

THE PRECEDING CASE STUDIES and overall analyses of Sino-American crises and crisis management behavior presented in chapters 2–12, along with the general framework for understanding Chinese and U.S. crisis behavior presented in the introduction, provide the basis for some tentative conclusions. First, I assess the ability and willingness of Beijing and Washington to adhere to the eight requirements for effective crisis management discussed in the introduction. I then identify and evaluate the major advantages and disadvantages that would likely confront the United States and China in avoiding or managing a future bilateral political-military crisis over Taiwan. Next, I discuss many of the uncertainties raised by the preceding analysis, thus providing guideposts for future research and study. I conclude with some tentative suggestions on improvements in attitudes, structures, and processes that would likely strengthen the ability of both countries to avoid or manage future political-military crises.

ADHERENCE TO REQUIREMENTS FOR EFFECTIVE CRISIS MANAGEMENT: A MIXED RECORD

A systematic comparison of the most important observations of the preceding analysis against the requirements for effective crisis management presented in the introduction suggests that the United States and China had exhibited a decidedly mixed record in effectively handling political-military crises. Some significant positive features exist in both countries, such as a strong desire to avoid armed conflict and a respect for the other side's resolve during a crisis. Both countries recognize—in theory, if not always in practice—many of the rules of prudence regarding crisis management, including the use of incremental, tit-for-tat escalation and the preservation of a "way out" for the adversary. Moreover, some negative features of past Sino-American crisis behavior—the intense hostility of the Cold War, the dominant role in Chinese decision making played by supreme rulers such as Mao Zedong, and the absence of direct communication between the two sides—have disappeared. However, many other negative features have unfortunately persisted. A strong sense of mutual distrust, continued signaling problems, the tendency to display resolve through decisive action, and a proclivity to fall into the commitment trap all raise alarm. Other complicating features, such as growing popular nationalistic pressures and a more complex decision-making process in China, have emerged. In general, these tentative conclusions suggest that a serious Sino-American crisis, particularly over Taiwan, would likely prove extremely difficult to manage. At the same time, many uncertainties remain in assessing how the United States and China would approach such a serious crisis.

Following is a repetition of the eight requirements for successful crisis management presented in the introductory chapter; each is followed by a discussion of the actual performance of China and the United States in light of the requirements.

1. Maintain direct channels of communication and send signals that are clear, specific, and detailed. Chinese and U.S. leaders have arguably come to recognize the importance of sending clear, direct signals in a political-military crisis. As the introduction and the case studies indicate, the absence of direct communication between Beijing and Washington combined with distorted and hostile images regarding the motives and outlook of the other side exacerbated the Sino-American crises or near crises of the 1950s and 1960s. By the 1990s, the two countries had set up more direct communication through the establishment of diplomatic relations and the creation of a hotline between the political leaders of both countries. From experiences like the Korean War, the two countries had also learned certain lessons regarding the meaning of various signals. In contrast, many problems that could greatly complicate signaling and undermine crisis management in a future crisis continue to exist within both countries.

Although the intensely hostile climate of the Cold War has clearly dissipated, both sides continue to regard each other with considerable distrust. For very different reasons, each tends to view the other as potentially hostile and to view itself as intrinsically peace loving. This disparity between images of the self and the adversary distorts communication and undermines the credibility of any signals. The specific political environment prevailing between the two countries at the time of a crisis can also affect the way in which signals are intended and interpreted. Signaling during the 1995–1996 Taiwan Strait crisis and the 1999 embassy bombing crisis, for example, was distorted because of the intensely negative state of bilateral relations that immediately preceded those events. Finally, suspicion between the two sides reinforces a tendency—at the very least on the Chinese side—to rely more on preset, memorized talking points during crisis negotiations than on frank, spontaneous exchanges. This tendency further lowers the quality of communication.

No obvious, direct channels of communication exist between responsible civilian and military leaders below the level of the president. Senior military leaders of the two countries have no line of direct contact, for example. In past crises, key high-level officials responsible for establishing and advancing contact with the other side could not open the lines of communication with their counterparts or, in some cases, even identify them. In some instances, crisis decision makers were unsure whether the top leaders of the other side were receiving their signals. Although it is well understood that senior leaders in all countries are generally hesitant to establish direct, intergovernmental links between subordinate civilian and (especially) military operatives during a crisis because of concerns over command-and-control issues and the sending of inconsistent signals, such hesitation seems particularly strong in the Chinese case. This hesitation is perhaps caused in part by the absence of sufficient communication channels across major governmental agencies in China, particularly between the military and civilian apparatuses.

There is apparently some hesitation, especially on the Chinese side, to make use of the existing high-level leadership hotline in a crisis. During recent crises, China did not answer repeated phone calls from the

White House. Such apparent hesitation might stem in part from the need for the senior Chinese leadership to reach a consensus before responding authoritatively and directly to the United States. It might also reflect a concern that direct senior-level phone conversations from either side would be misunderstood, given the absence of clear working procedures for the use of the hotline and the overall lack of adequate crisis management mechanisms between Beijing and Washington.

Considerable uncertainly remains on both sides concerning the specific meaning and intent of signals conveyed by the other side. This partly reflects an inadequate understanding of each other's decision-making apparatus and the role of domestic considerations in a crisis. It also reflects a lack of agreement on the meaning of specific words and phrases used by both sides, such as the greatly overused phrase "we shall not stand idly by" that has frequently been employed by the Chinese government in past crises. As we have seen, a greater number of individuals and organizations are now involved in political-military crises, especially on the Chinese side, thus increasing the possibility of inconsistent or confusing signals. The media are more diverse and politicized in both China and the United States, and are potentially open to access—or even manipulation—by a range of governmental and nongovernmental participants. Such participants include an increasing number of so-called experts who claim to enjoy privileged access to crisis decision makers or to understand the true intent of signals. Moreover, bureaucratic and individual players have exerted considerable influence over the internal process of formulating signals in recent crises.

For China, in particular, an increasingly complex and fragmented decision-making process and a stovepiped intelligence structure have apparently slowed reaction time and distorted both the assessment of information and clear signaling during a crisis. Public opinion and leadership politics have also significantly influenced the content of signals, especially in recent years. For all these reasons, the senior leadership of both countries continues to confront considerable difficulties in identifying authoritative signals from the other side and in deciphering their meaning. Such problems have at times resulted in a dangerous reliance on preexisting assumptions, decades-old experience, or so-called mirror imaging to interpret signals.

It is of course impossible in a crisis to entirely eliminate problems relating to communication and signaling. Even close allies have trouble interpreting messages sent to each other. Moreover, ambiguity and inconsistency in signaling are at times deliberate, used as part of crisis bargaining. During some previous crises, both countries have resisted direct communication because of fears that it might exacerbate the situation. Nonetheless, it is possible to reduce many existing communication and signaling problems by increasing the level of authoritative contact between officials. Higher-level contact allows leaders to discuss and clarify many problematic issues. These issues include image problems, the meaning and intent of specific signals, the decision-making context of crisis signals, the role of expert advice, and the possible utility of expanding the number and type of channels for communication between officials. The two sides can also notably increase the utility of direct channels such as hotlines by clarifying the procedures governing their use and by specifying their use within a larger set of crisis management mechanisms.

2. Preserve limited objectives and limited means on behalf of such objectives; sacrifice unlimited goals. In past crises, both the United States and China have frequently pursued limited objectives and used limited means to attain those objectives. This potentially slows escalation and reduces the chance of inadvertent conflict. The Chinese maxim, "on just grounds, to our advantage, and with restraint" (*youli, youli, youjie*) stresses the need to maintain realistic objectives and avoid overreaching in a crisis. In fact, several of China's political-military crises, including all three Taiwan Strait crises, the embassy bombing incident, and the EP-3 incident, involved attempts by Beijing to achieve limited objectives through carefully delineated military and nonmilitary means. These objectives were usually political, and sometimes domestic.[1]

The United States also has often employed limited objectives and means in past crises. As indicated in the introduction, for example, during the Cuban missile crisis, President John F. Kennedy deliberately leveled very limited demands and deployed limited means to convey his resolve at virtually every step of the crisis. During the more recent (and far less serious) EP-3 incident, Washington sought to regain its aircrew and aircraft through negotiations, without provoking a full-blown hostage crisis and without issuing an apology for actions it did not commit.

Washington's restraint in refusing to call the Chinese decision to hold the American crew and aircraft a "hostage situation" was an important means of managing domestic pressure to act. In both instances, Washington pursued pragmatic, limited objectives, designed to defuse the situation without compromising vital U.S. interests.

On the other hand, both China and the United States clearly hold vital national interests and images that make it extremely difficult for the two sides to maintain limited objectives and means during certain types of crises. For Beijing, concepts such as territorial integrity and national sovereignty are treated as cardinal principles that are closely associated with regime legitimacy and leadership survival. Hence, crises that are closely connected with such concepts—and are clearly recognized as such by the Chinese people—can involve extremely high stakes for the Chinese leadership. This makes it very difficult to maintain limited objectives and means. Arguably, no issue presents comparable high stakes for the United States, other than a direct military threat to U.S. citizens and territory. Perhaps the closest functional equivalent is the notion of the credibility of Washington's commitment to its allies, or the credibility of Washington's deterrence threats against potential adversaries. This notion is perhaps too often invoked *publicly* by U.S. leaders in political-military crises involving important areas of the globe such as the western Pacific. Nonetheless, its presence also makes it difficult for Washington to maintain limited ends and in particular limited means. As we have seen, during the Taiwan Strait crises of the 1950s, Washington was willing to threaten the use of tactical nuclear weapons in order to deter Beijing from seizing the offshore islands and, thus, also presumably to reinforce U.S. credibility. It is highly unlikely, however, that President Eisenhower was prepared to actually use such means to resolve those crises.

3. **Preserve military flexibility, escalate slowly, and respond symmetrically (in a "tit-for-tat" manner).** The analysis in this volume suggests that China and the United States display a mixed record of compliance with this principle of crisis management. On the conceptual level, the Chinese concept of *youli, youli, youjie* stresses incremental escalation and symmetrical responses to an adversary's behavior. The case studies in this volume and other scholarly works suggest that, in practice, China has undertaken tit-for-tat moves that are punctuated by pauses

and diplomatic signaling.[2] However, China has also sometimes escalated suddenly, rapidly, and asymmetrically to establish a virtual fait accompli.[3] The Chinese side most often has escalated asymmetrically to counter situations their leadership perceived as major threats to their survival (such as the Korean War), to defend core principles such as territorial integrity, or (in their view) to avoid a much larger conflict. The direct purpose of such asymmetrical escalations was often to shock the opponent into reversing its behavior. Chinese leaders apparently believed that, as with an initial use of force in general, such shock actions would not result in a dangerous escalatory spiral to war if certain elements of the *youli, youli, youjie* concept were observed. Many of these features are illustrated in the case studies presented in this volume, as well as in other studies of Chinese crisis behavior.[4]

Despite China's continued adherence to many elements of the *youli, youli, youjie* concept, Chinese observers insist that rapid, asymmetrical escalation in a crisis was more typical of the Mao and Deng eras. They argue that this type of escalation reflected the more militant style and perhaps less risk-averse behavior of those leaders as well as their total dominance over the decision-making process. Chinese observers argue that the Chinese leadership today is extremely cautious and consensus oriented. Hence, the Chinese leadership is unlikely to undertake provocative escalatory leaps or to use high levels of force in a crisis unless core national interests are at stake, other noncoercive approaches are exhausted, and/or China faces extreme provocation.

Some Western scholars, in contrast, argue that Chinese leaders on several occasions throughout history (and not solely during the Mao and Deng eras) have favored offensive approaches to crises, reflecting a recurring emphasis on displaying resolve and seizing the initiative, often via preemptive action. Moreover, other observers argue that present-day Chinese leaders are just as likely as Mao and Deng to engage in provocative crisis behavior. These observers argue that modern Chinese leaders are more susceptible to growing nationalistic pressure from society and less able to recover from charges that they failed to exhibit sufficient resolve in a crisis, particularly if the adversary is generally viewed as a superior and bullying power. The case studies presented in this volume indicate that, although the Jiang Zemin and Hu Jintao regimes have sometimes engaged in provocative rhetoric during crises, they have also generally avoided sudden, escalatory actions. As indicated in the discussion of the second requirement for crisis management, Jiang's and Hu's regimes have usually sought to delimit and soften their actions in a variety of ways. Whether this approach will hold true in future crises—especially a major crisis over Taiwan—is unclear.

The United States has at times escalated incrementally and at times very rapidly in past political-military crises. In general, like the Chinese, U.S. leaders seem to recognize the importance of many of the rules of prudence for crisis management, including the use of incremental, tit-for-tat escalation. In practice, the United States has at times displayed the most caution and flexibility in crises involving well-armed adversaries such as China and, in the past, the Soviet Union. Against such powers, U.S. policy during the height of the Cold War (i.e., the time of the Eisenhower administration) emphasized threats of massive retaliation, possibly with nuclear weapons. Through such means, U.S. leaders, possibly by deliberately attempting to cultivate uncertainty in the mind of the opponent, hoped to deter potential aggression by Beijing or Moscow during a crisis. This approach softened significantly during subsequent years. Later U.S. crisis policy (during the Kennedy and Johnson administrations) approached major crises more symmetrically and stressed a more flexible response, clearer signaling, and incremental escalation.

Nonetheless, the United States retained its strong emphasis on the need to communicate strong resolve against "crisis-mongering" by large and small communist or totalitarian powers, often through the use of superior military force. This emphasis could, and did, translate at times into dramatic escalations and serious threats, especially against weaker states. U.S. leaders apparently believed in many instances that small steps are seen as timid and invite counters, and that conflict often results from the failure to demonstrate clear resolve early. For U.S. decision makers, the obvious dangers of such behavior are to be mitigated by the use of accurate intelligence and clear communication, close control over military forces through strict rules of engagement (ROE), and the overwhelming deterrence effect of superior conventional and nuclear U.S. military power.

The examples above suggest that U.S. and Chinese leaders share some troubling similarities regarding escalation. Both place a very strong emphasis on the need to show resolve in certain types of crises, and they are willing to do so via sudden or dramatic (sometimes military) escalations. This is arguably more the case today for U.S. leaders than for China's postrevolutionary leaders, but the inclination is present even on the Chinese side and is reinforced by other Chinese attitudes toward crises that are relevant to principles four and five below.

This common emphasis on displaying resolve through decisive action is particularly dangerous in a Sino-American crisis because it creates the belief, on both sides, that effective deterrence in a serious crisis might require very strong threats or applications of force.[5] The danger of such a situation is compounded further by the offensive doctrines held by the military forces of both countries at the operational, campaign, and tactical levels. Military forces might become more assertive in a crisis than civilian leaders prefer, thereby undermining coordination between diplomatic and military moves. Such an outcome is even more likely if, in the overall decision-making process, civilian and military leaders coordinate poorly. Some Western observers believe the Chinese government suffers from this problem more than the United States might.[6]

4. Avoid ideological or principled lock-in positions that encourage zero-sum approaches to a crisis and limit options or bargaining room; do not confuse moral or principled positions with conflicts of interest. This is perhaps the most difficult issue to assess in the context of a Sino-American crisis. As the discussion of limited ends and means indicates, both countries—and arguably China in particular—have invoked supposedly immutable principles or strong ideological perspectives in past crises in ways that made compromise extremely difficult. China has at times associated the issues at stake with what China believes are its permanent beliefs regarding state sovereignty and interstate relations. China has also drawn on its beliefs regarding just or moral behavior, such as the principle that smaller or weaker nations have a right to be free from the bullying of larger, stronger powers. This has conveyed the impression that China has approached certain crises in zero-sum terms, involving the uncompromising defense of moral principles against unjust acts. Indeed, in various ways, China has very publicly used such terminology in almost every political-military crisis in which it has been involved over the past five decades, thus potentially creating a commitment trap

that can constrain bargaining choices. Moreover, the pressures of such a commitment trap have arguably increased in recent years as a result of leadership change and the emergence of a highly vocal, nationalistic public.

Several of the case studies contained in this volume suggest that the United States has also viewed many crises in highly ideological terms. During the height of the Cold War, the United States viewed crises as manifestations of an uncompromising struggle against global communism in defense of the free world. As we have seen in the analyses of the Taiwan Strait crises of the 1950s, such views—reinforced at times by intense domestic political pressure from strategic conservatives—arguably contributed to risky behavior, such as nuclear threats, and reduced the inclination to compromise. It can be argued that similar rhetoric and viewpoints also exist in present-day U.S. thinking, although now the uncompromising struggle in defense of freedom is waged against terrorists and what are called rogue states. One can perhaps argue that such views were at least partly responsible for what some characterize as high-risk U.S. behavior during the recent crisis with Iraq over weapons of mass destruction that has resulted in a protracted conflict toward highly uncertain ends.

Absolutist rhetoric and internal social pressure have not always resulted in limited choices and uncompromising actions. We have seen, in practice, that both Washington and Beijing have at times displayed very cautious and pragmatic behavior. During the Mao and Deng eras, the power and prestige of the paramount ruler were generally sufficient to permit him to compromise on principle when necessary without admitting he was doing so, as when Mao, under intense Soviet pressure, deescalated the Sino-Soviet confrontation of the early 1970s. Some observers believe that post-Deng leaders operate under much greater pressure and constraints, which could produce a less flexible approach to crises. Nonetheless, as Wang Jisi argues in this volume, in recent crises, the enduring concept of *youli, youli, youjie* combined with the option of a face-saving retreat have provided sufficient justification for elites and the larger public to support compromises that did not appear to violate core principles. Moreover, many Chinese observers argue that despite the considerable limitations of their environment, post-Deng leaders have been reducing further the influence of abstract moral principles by placing an increasing emphasis on international law and mechanisms. In the United States, moral principles such as anticommunism rarely prevented eventual compromise during a serious crisis with China, although they produced very tough rhetoric and actions at times. Nonetheless, it must be said that even today absolutist principles—such as the defense of freedom and sovereignty—can exert significant influence during particular types of Sino-American crises, such as a crisis over Taiwan.

5. Exercise self-restraint, and do not respond to all provocative moves. The very mixed picture of compliance with the preceding requirements for effective crisis management suggests that the United States and China could confront significant difficulties in adhering to this principle as well. That is, the recognition by leaders in both countries of the need to preserve limited goals and utilize limited means, escalate incrementally, and allow adequate time to consider responses is to some degree offset by other tendencies. Both leaderships are inclined to display strong resolve through decisive words or deeds. Furthermore, the national leadership of both countries is seemingly highly confident about its ability to control escalation. Moreover, the two countries' leaders are prone to the temptation of the commitment trap, particularly on an issue that generates significant public pressure and involves questions of principle or vital interests. On balance, these factors weaken self-restraint. To some extent, an excessive adherence to prudent strategies such as the tit-for-tat approach emphasized by the *youli, youli, youjie* concept can also undermine self-restraint by causing crisis decision makers to respond to every escalation of the adversary even if prudence might dictate otherwise.

Nonetheless, much of the analysis in this volume suggests that leaders in both countries have exercised significant levels of self-restraint at crucial moments in past crises. Many argue that this was the case during all three Taiwan Strait crises and in recent near crises such as the embassy bombing incident and EP-3 incident despite often inflammatory rhetoric and sometimes aggressive behavior. But much depends on the leadership's general image of the adversary, approach to crisis bargaining, and sense of the stakes involved in each particular crisis. At the height of the Cold War, both Chinese and U.S. leaders held very antagonistic, hard-line views of each other although in the United States more conciliatory points of view were expressed by some and were even accepted, particularly after the searing experience of the Korean War. Looking to the future, there is little doubt, overall, that a major downturn in Sino-American relations could make U.S. leaders more receptive to hard-line views within society and the elite during a future crisis.

On the Chinese side, during the Mao and Deng eras it was likely more difficult for views opposing the official government view and favoring more cautious or accommodating approaches to gain a complete hearing during a crisis.[7] In some instances, the Chinese leadership believed it was facing a closing window of opportunity, which further undermined its self-restraint. During the Sino-Vietnam Border War of 1979, for example, the Chinese leadership saw Vietnam's seizure of Cambodia as such a closing window. Moreover, in general, within Chinese leadership circles, it is usually safer politically to present a tough stance toward foreign adversaries, especially if Chinese principles are involved. On the other hand, the post-Deng leadership appears to be more open to diverse viewpoints, given the more diffuse distribution of power at the top of the system and the greater openness of Chinese society in general. In addition, because the fourth generation civilian leadership lacks the military experience and strategic vision of Mao and Deng, they are probably less confident in their own strategic judgment. Although all Chinese leaders are intensely suspicious of the United States and undoubtedly feel the need to display enormous resolve when the stakes are high, their behavior during recent crises and their overall approach to relations with Washington suggest that the decision-making process is not dominated by aggressive, risk-taking hard-liners.

6. Avoid extreme pressure, ultimatums, or threats to the adversary's core values, and preserve the adversary's option to back down. The Chinese intervention during the Korean War, which was the first and thus far the most dangerous Sino-American crisis, violated this very obvious principle of crisis management. U.S. leaders applied extreme pressure to the Chinese leadership and threatened their core values without being entirely aware they were doing so. Both countries, particularly the United States, learned a vital lesson from that costly and bloody event. Since then, both countries have attempted to adhere more closely to this principle by generally avoiding the use of ultimatums and extreme pressure during crises. Eisenhower's threats to use nuclear weap-

ons during the two Taiwan Strait crises of the 1950s constitute a major exception to this rule. Yet, these threats were conveyed in a somewhat ambiguous manner, intended to deter (not compel), and were not linked to any specific ultimatum.[8] On a broader level, both countries have generally upheld the notion of preserving a way out for an adversary, in theory and in practice.

This principle is more likely to be violated in crises that involve the core interests of one or both sides, occur in the context of worsening bilateral relations, and seem to present a closing window of opportunity. Given the great emphasis both China and the United States place on the need to show resolve, often through military means, and the possibility that the United States believes it would enjoy escalation dominance in a serious crisis with China, future Sino-American crises may not be immune to the application of extreme pressure and ultimatums. The use of offensive doctrines that could generate extreme pressure by the militaries of both countries and the possibility that the decision-making process might not always ensure effective control over efforts to exert pressure in a crisis increase the possibility that the two sides will violate this principle. In addition, problems with communication and signaling might result in unintended pressure.

7. **Divide large, integrated, hard-to-resolve disputes into smaller, more manageable issues, thereby building trust and facilitating trade-offs.** The analysis in this volume and in the broader literature suggests that Chinese and U.S. leaders did not deliberately adhere to this principle during many past crises. This was particularly the case during the Cold War. The lack of direct communication combined with the presence of hostile, ideological viewpoints and absolutist thinking on both sides made it extremely difficult to build trust and facilitate crisis bargaining by intentionally breaking disputes into more manageable issues. After the establishment of diplomatic relations and the end of the Cold War, each side arguably became more open to such behavior. As the analysis in this volume suggests, the 1995–1996 Taiwan Strait crisis, the embassy bombing incident, and the EP-3 incident involved some elements of a more direct, problem-solving crisis negotiation that focused on resolving smaller issues. Such an approach was also possible because these post–Cold War crises did not involve large, integrated, hard-to-resolve disputes as did the Korean and Vietnam Wars and the

earlier Taiwan Strait crises. The post–Cold War crises were essentially diplomatic disputes over very specific incidents that required intensive discussions and a face-saving resolution. By their nature, they involved smaller, more manageable issues.

Despite the changes wrought by the end of the Cold War and the transition in leaderships, many of the basic images held by both sides today suggest that their leaders might find it difficult to adhere to this principle in a future crisis. A major crisis over Taiwan could involve the kind of high stakes and indivisible issues that would prevent efforts to build trust by breaking the dispute into manageable parts.

8. Think ahead about the unintended consequences of one's actions. It is difficult to identify with a high level of certainty the degree to which decision makers in China and the United States have adhered to this principle in past political-military crises. This is partly because the record of internal leadership deliberations is incomplete or missing altogether, particularly in China, but the historical record of past crises does provide some evidence from which to draw tentative conclusions. Unfortunately, this evidence suggests that Chinese and U.S. leaders have not often attempted to think through, over several steps, the possible negative consequences of their decisions despite their sensitivity to the larger international and strategic environment. In general, Chinese and U.S. leaders have tended to underestimate the negative effects of their actions to the other side and overestimate the positive effects. This tendency was arguably more evident during the Cold War.

The analysis in this volume suggests that U.S. decision makers during the Cold War, such as presidents Eisenhower and Johnson, were more focused on responding to the immediate issues at hand, coping with internal political pressures, and resolving disputes within the top leadership and the bureaucracy than in systematically thinking through the possible consequences of their actions over several moves. As Robert L. Suettinger argues, these leaders often made critical decisions in an unsystematic, subjective manner. To some extent, this rather ill-organized process reflected not only the personal proclivities of each president, but also, in the earliest years, the underdeveloped nature of the national security decision-making system. By the Clinton era, crisis decision making had become more systematic and formalized. As a result, more recent crisis decision making has presumably involved greater attention to unintended consequences. However, factors such as time constraints and bureaucratic differences, as well as the inevitable influence of strong-willed and subjective personalities, no doubt obstructed efforts to think through the situation. Moreover, indications are that wishful thinking and mirror imaging also undermined adherence to this principle.

We know very little about the internal deliberations that produced specific crisis decisions by the Chinese leadership, particularly in the post-Mao era. What little we know about Mao's interactions with his colleagues during crises suggests that his enormous self-confidence and his basic perception of the United States as an imperialist power heavily influenced his calculation of the consequences of his decisions. Along with Mao's apparent confidence in his ability to control escalation, these factors perhaps created a level of wishful thinking that undermined his ability to assess a crisis situation in a relatively objective manner. In contrast, the relatively weaker, more consensus-driven, and arguably less confident post-Mao leadership is presumably more inclined to examine the consequences of their actions realistically. However, a tenser bilateral political environment could lead to the strengthening, within both national leaderships, of the sort of hardline approach that tends to see conflicts as zero-sum and threats to core values, and that tends to suffer from the "fundamental attribution error" discussed in the introduction. This kind of environment could make a crisis over Taiwan, for example, much more likely, and particularly dangerous.

MANAGING A CRISIS OVER TAIWAN: A DUBIOUS PROPOSITION?[9]

The above observations combined with the broader analysis of the six sets of variables relevant to Chinese and U.S. crisis perceptions and behavior presented in the introduction suggest that a future crisis over Taiwan, once under way, could prove very difficult to manage effectively.

First and foremost, the Taiwan issue presents very high stakes for both governments, particularly the Chinese. For China's leaders, the Taiwan issue is associated with issues of territorial sovereignty, regime legitimacy, social and political order, and personal and political survival. Although Taiwan does not involve such vital interests for the United States, it is clearly associated with issues of alliance credibility and defense of freedom. Washington has held a strong and long-standing policy commitment to a peaceful resolution of the issue and faces clear obligations under the Taiwan Relations Act and the three communiqués with China. In addition, Taiwan is a high-stakes issue for Chinese elites because the issue resonates significantly with a large segment of a nationalistic public. U.S. elites also regard Taiwan as a high-stakes issue because it is viewed by many observers as being closely associated with political debates over the larger issues of China's "strategic threat," the overall state of U.S.-China relations, and the mission of protecting freedom and democracy.

Leaders in both countries would feel a very strong incentive to communicate enormous resolve in a major crisis over Taiwan[10] in ways that could make it difficult to set or sustain limited objectives, exercise self-restraint, and maintain flexibility. The Chinese government would likely feel very strong pressure to resist any actions that might suggest capitulation to U.S. pressure or a weakening of China's claim to sovereign authority over Taiwan. Beijing would likely find it extremely difficult to adopt a tit-for-tat approach in a major crisis or to trade closer cross-strait political contacts for even a perceived loss of sovereignty. Similarly, Washington would want to avoid any behavior that might be viewed as giving in to Chinese coercion, which would reflect a weakness in U.S. determination or capacity to uphold its commitments. Each side would be strongly inclined to view the issue in uncompromising, zero-sum terms, which would make it difficult—in the context of a major crisis—for either side to accept even short-term losses via initial or partial concessions. Moreover, such rigidity would likely be reinforced by strong domestic political pressures.

Such problems and the dangers they pose for crisis management could be accentuated by China's apparent belief that Washington would be more likely than Beijing to back down during a Taiwan crisis, especially if a long and bloody conflict appears probable. These factors could lead China's leaders to mistakenly believe that they might prevail in a showdown over Taiwan by communicating their allegedly stronger resolve clearly and credibly through major threats. Alternatively, U.S. decision makers might accept the view that China must eventually concede to U.S. military superiority, thus justifying robust efforts at coercive diplomacy. Overall, this situation could increase the chances that one or both countries, especially China, would fall into a classic commitment trap.[11]

Once in a serious crisis over Taiwan, China and the United States might have great difficulty controlling escalation. Indeed, such a crisis could threaten to explode into a larger war. China might use relatively high-risk strategies because of its desire to communicate a high level of resolve, intensified by a sense of relative weakness vis-à-vis the United States. The dearth of nonmilitary means of showing resolve and China's imperfect knowledge of U.S. military capabilities also increase risk. High-risk strategies include extreme coercive pressure or the use of ultimatums.

Worse yet, China might attempt to establish a military-political fait accompli through a rapid decapitation attack on Taiwan. The United States would find it difficult to reverse such an attack without escalating the crisis to the point of all-out conflict, perhaps by attacking mainland targets in many areas. Such a scenario would provide little opportunity for either side to pause, assess options, and engage in careful negotiations. Moreover, such actions might become particularly likely if China were faced with the need to compel Taiwan to alter its behavior rather than to deter actions that had not yet taken place.

Of even greater concern, China's leaders might decide to initiate a range of major military actions, even with high risks, if its leaders believed that the opportunity to control or resolve the Taiwan situation was disappearing or if its leaders viewed the United States as acquiescing in efforts by Taiwan to provoke the situation to intolerable levels.

For the United States, the fear that China might dangerously intensify the crisis early on to demonstrate resolve or to preempt a U.S. attempt to assist Taiwan, combined with the U.S. confidence in escalation dominance through superior military capabilities, could result in rapid and decisive military moves designed to deter or shut down Chinese coercive actions. Moreover, the tendency to escalate early and rapidly might become even greater if U.S. decision makers believe that Chinese leaders assume the United States is less committed than they. The tendency to escalate quickly might also increase if deterring China requires a significant display of military superiority, as some U.S. analysts apparently argue.

Such vigorous U.S. actions could contribute to an escalatory spiral, particularly in the absence of clear and credible communication between the two sides. China, for example, might view strong U.S. military assistance to Taiwan in the opening days of a crisis as equivalent to a first-shot escalation supportive of Taiwan that requires a vigorous response. Even more serious, in an escalating crisis, China might interpret possible limited U.S. attacks on key Chinese command-and-control facilities or military assets relevant to the PLA's prosecution of strikes against Taiwan as a threat to Beijing's larger conventional and strategic capabilities and respond accordingly.

The dangers of this situation are increased even further because of the offensive orientation of both militaries and the internal complexities of the civil-military decision-making process. Because of such factors, the involvement of the military as a key player in an intense Taiwan crisis could short-circuit or distort diplomatic or political options and thus affect efforts at escalation control.

Another factor that would make a major crisis over Taiwan particularly difficult to manage is the presence of two important third parties with independent interests and policy options, that is, the governments and citizens of Taiwan and Japan. The involvement of such autonomous actors could produce significant instabilities and misperceptions, possibly resulting in unwanted escalation. Taiwan's political leaders might send provocative diplomatic signals to Beijing that undermine U.S. attempts to deescalate an emerging crisis. Of even greater concern, in the early stages of an intense political-military crisis, Taiwan might use offensive weapons without the consent of the United States to retaliate against a mainland attack. Such a response might be mistaken by China as a U.S. strike and would thus invite retaliation against U.S. forces, regional bases, or even the U.S. mainland. Conversely, China might miscalculate the risks of a Taiwan crisis by assuming that it could apply pressure on Taiwan to deter U.S. military intervention.

Japanese involvement in a Sino-American crisis over Taiwan could significantly complicate or destabilize the situation, given Tokyo's alliance relationship with Washington, its formidable maritime military capabilities, and the intensely emotional aspect of the turbulent Sino-Japanese relationship. Japanese military assistance to the United States during a crisis could harden the Chinese position and provoke an overreaction by Beijing. This, in turn, could generate further destabilizing responses by Washington and Tokyo, thus creating a dangerous downward spiral of mutual suspicion and confrontation. On the other hand, efforts to establish close consultations between Washington and Tokyo could significantly slow down and complicate the management of a Sino-American crisis. Decision-making within the Japanese government would most likely involve more internal consultation and coordination than in the U.S. case. Even if consultations were relatively smooth and efficient, Tokyo and Washington might still disagree greatly over how to handle a serious crisis with Beijing. For example, Japan's leaders might not place as high a priority on displaying resolve in a crisis as American leaders apparently do.

Despite the difficulties of managing a major Sino-American confrontation over Taiwan, one should not assume that such a crisis is highly likely to occur or that, once initiated, it would almost certainly lead to a large-scale military conflict. The above negative features are counterbalanced to some extent by a range of other factors that argue against initiating or escalating a major Taiwan crisis. First, the position of China and the United States as nuclear powers would instill an enormous level of caution on both sides, especially concerning any decision to cross the threshold and initiate direct military action against the other. Despite the many troublesome characteristics of Chinese and U.S. perceptions and behavior relevant to crisis management, there is little evidence that elites in either country today view their nuclear arsenals as safeguards against attack and, hence, a license to escalate dramatically. To the contrary, the existence of considerable uncertainties regarding each side's nuclear-use doctrine and the vulnerability of Chinese strategic assets to a U.S. conventional attack suggest that the threshold between conventional weapons use and nuclear weapons use might be less clear than some might think. This reality would induce enormous caution in any leadership.

Second, the absence of a charismatic and clearly dominant leader in China argues in favor of significant levels of caution toward precipitating or escalating a crisis. Unlike Mao and Deng, leaders of China today have less ability to survive major policy errors and, hence, would presumably treat any crisis over Taiwan with significant caution. Such caution would be reinforced by the huge economic and social damage that could result from a perceived failure to manage a Taiwan crisis, given China's extensive involvement in the global economic order and its heavy reliance on the U.S. trade and investment markets for the maintenance of the high growth regarded as essential to China's future stability.

Third, for China, high barriers likely exist to the success of many deterrence and compellence strategies toward Taiwan involving the threat or use of limited force. China would find it extremely difficult to attain clear local superiority in a Taiwan crisis because of the geography of the area and the nature of the adversary. China's tactical and strategic assets are likely to be highly vulnerable to U.S. conventional standoff weapons. Moreover, the barrier presented by the Taiwan Strait, combined with U.S. command, control, communication, computer, intelligence, surveillance, and reconnaissance (C4ISR) assets, would make it extremely difficult for China to achieve deception and denial and, hence, act decisively to gain the initiative. It is also difficult for China to anticipate the effectiveness against U.S. forces of key weapons such as ballistic missiles or information warfare because they all remain largely untested in combat.

Fourth, for the United States, a major crisis over Taiwan would present enormous uncertainties despite the likely superiority of U.S. military capabilities in key areas. U.S. decision makers could not be fully confident that U.S. forces would possess the speed, power, and accuracy to deter or shut down all possible Chinese military action against the island. Moreover, any serious crisis over Taiwan would almost certainly produce significant damage to U.S. interests in other areas, especially vital issues such as the slow-motion North Korean nuclear crisis, that require cooperative relations with China. Military conflict with China would likely destabilize the entire Asian region and would almost certainly result in a prolonged cold war detrimental to long-term prosperity and stability.

These factors impel both sides to exert their utmost effort to avoid a major crisis over Taiwan. On balance, any political-military crisis, including a crisis over Taiwan, can be thrust upon both powers by an external event, such as the actions of Taiwan. Moreover, crucial contextual factors, such as mutually hostile images, the preexisting state of Sino-U.S. relations, problems in signaling, incorrect assumptions regarding ROE, improper control over military forces, and the complexities of the decision-making process, can propel both sides into an increasingly dangerous, escalating confrontation despite intentions to the contrary. In short, once begun, even a small-scale crisis over Taiwan could overcome the desire for caution on both sides and prove extremely difficult to resolve peacefully. This would especially be the case if one or both parties attempted to use a Taiwan crisis to create a new status quo largely unacceptable to the other side. In general, however, such a dangerous crisis would probably only occur against the backdrop of a badly deteriorated overall Sino-American relationship, in which both sides harbor a far greater level of distrust and antagonism toward the other than is evident today.

AREAS WHERE INFORMATION IS MOST LACKING

Although we know quite a lot about many aspects of U.S. and Chinese crisis perception and behavior, many areas exist where information is insufficient, ambiguous, or absent altogether. Of course, some variables influencing crisis behavior are unknowable, especially before a crisis, even to political leaders themselves. As the scholarly literature on crisis management indicates, crisis behavior is very context dependent and will vary according to many complicating factors. These factors include the specific leaders involved in a crisis, the exact origin and scope of a crisis, the objectives, skills, and interests of the participants, the institutional mechanism for managing the crisis, and the behavior of outside actors and events. Nonetheless, much more valuable information can and should be obtained that could improve the management of future Sino-American political-military crises.

A lack of clarity remains regarding the specific content and importance of certain key factors in the minds of crisis decision makers and the public. These factors include, first, historical memory, associated emotions, and certain basic images regarding China and the United States. In what ways does historical memory matter? Is it the dominant variable in explaining how elites and the public perceive a crisis?[12] Do the preexisting images and beliefs of Chinese and U.S. leaders serve to reduce available options in crisis bargaining, lessen self-restraint, distort the interpretation of signals, and make goals more absolute in a crisis, thus making it more difficult to achieve a resolution?[13] Which emotions are most common in crisis decision making: nationalism, hatred, or fear of loss of political stature, power, or face? What options are completely ruled out? What is involved in reducing the impact of negative historical memories and images relevant to political-military crises?

Second, the specific area of crisis signaling between China and the United States presents many unknowns. What do Chinese and American leaders bear in mind as they determine the other side's will and intentions? Which signals indicate a willingness to cooperate or conciliate in a crisis, and which clearly convey aggression or threat? How can China and the United States credibly signal restraint in the use of force? Do U.S. and Chinese leaders have strong incentives to avoid communicating clear or honest signals or to delay the sending of signals?

Third, historically, both China and the United States have at times greatly emphasized the need to display resolve in a crisis, often through decisive military action. This factor, combined with both countries' high levels of confidence in their abilities to control escalation, has arguably increased the proclivity of both sides to use force, even for limited political objectives, and to escalate rapidly under certain circumstances. Many observers in China insist, however, that China's present-day leaders regard the use of force as a last resort, possess a growing number of nonmilitary means to signal resolve in a crisis, and are extremely cautious regarding escalation because of the changed nature of the Chinese regime and the emergence of a different risk calculus. But Chinese observers also acknowledge that certain conditions could prompt the use of force by Beijing, as well as significant subsequent escalation, even to attain limited objectives. Is there any way to assess with greater precision the types of factors and conditions that might prompt such actions? Moreover, what specific role might nuclear weapons play in the context of a major political-military crisis between China and the United States? To what extent and under what conditions might the distinction between nuclear and conventional threats and applications of force become blurred in such a crisis?

Many critical questions remain unanswered; e.g.: How do Chinese leaders today credibly signal resolve, especially regarding a sensitive territorial issue such as Taiwan? Will Chinese leaders rely more on nonmilitary levers to prevent the deterioration of the Taiwan situation? Or will they still use limited force or escalate rapidly to convey resolve, which could be misinterpreted as an attempt to emerge as winners in a crisis? Would U.S. crisis decision makers likely feel that they must use high levels of military or political coercion or escalate rapidly in a serious political-military crisis (such as a crisis over Taiwan) in order to compensate for a perceived lack of commitment relative to Beijing? The United States might believe that its military superiority would allow it to prevail even if the stakes are not as important for it as they are for China.

Both China and the United States exhibit aspects of domestic politics and public opinion that might make them susceptible to falling into the commitment trap during a major crisis. This danger has arguably increased in recent years as a result of the emergence of a more vocal nationalist public in China and increasing concerns in Washington over China's supposed strategic threat to the United States. Leaders in both countries have strong incentives to avoid this trap. Under what conditions and in what way would China or the United States most likely fall into the commitment trap? To what degree and in what manner is the crisis behavior of both leaderships affected by popular sentiments? Can its effects be limited or controlled, and, if so, how?

Some analysts believe that Chinese and U.S. leaders have at times used political-military crises to build support for themselves among the populace and within the elite. If the safe position for Chinese leaders during a crisis remains the hard-line position and the Chinese regime needs to strengthen its legitimacy by appealing to nationalist sentiments, then is the temptation to use a crisis to build support at least as great as it was at times during the Maoist era? Under what conditions and to what degree would present-day U.S. crisis decision makers view political-military crises as political mechanisms?

As we have seen, an enormous amount of uncertainty exists regarding the effects of the decision-making process on crisis behavior, especially on the Chinese side. It can be argued that this variable exerts the greatest potential effect regarding signaling, central leadership control over the actions of subordinates, and the receipt and processing of critical intelligence. A somewhat less important area concerns the increasing role of nongovernmental specialists.

Critical unanswered questions include the following: To what degree and in what manner does the decision-making process slow down reaction time and distort signals in a crisis? How do the United States and, in particular, China formulate signals internally, and what is the process used to convey them to the other side? Is it possible to determine which parts of the decision-making apparatus have the greatest authority in signaling? Is it possible to know whether particular signals are primarily intended for domestic versus external audiences? To what extent do military leaders influence crisis decisions? Do they in any sense enjoy a veto over certain types of decisions, particularly in the Chinese system? What is the relationship between the paramount leader in China, other members of the Politburo Standing Committee, and any leadership working groups or task forces involved in political-military crises? Do existing mechanisms in the United States and China ensure adequate central control over the actions of subordinates, especially military forces? How do existing or predetermined military plans influence policy making and crisis management in both countries? Are civilian leaders fully aware of the diplomatic implications of existing military plans? Finally, how and to what degree do specialists influence crisis decision making?

Almost nothing is known about the role and importance of intelligence and other forms of relevant information obtained by decision makers during a crisis, particularly in China. Key questions include the following: Does each leadership system have in place a means of obtaining and evaluating real-time intelligence in a fast-moving crisis? How does the leadership handle conflicting intelligence reports or quickly verify sole-source, yet seemingly critical, pieces of intelligence? To what extent do decision makers depend on rapid, accurate, hard intelligence in a crisis, as opposed to other types of information such as soft intelligence, news reports, and the views and assessments of trusted associates? To what extent and in what way do civilian and military sources of intelligence interact in the overall process? How does information warfare influence the use of intelligence and other forms of information in a crisis?

Many factors in the international environment can significantly influence how Chinese and U.S. leaders approach a crisis. The impact of the international environment on crisis behavior is highly dependent on the specific context; that is, it is difficult to predict how the environment per se will influence crisis behavior. Yet it would be useful to know what Chinese and U.S. political leaders regard as the most important features of the international environment during a crisis.

Chinese and U.S. leaders are arguably changing somewhat their attitudes toward international law as a factor in interstate behavior, a change that will presumably affect their handling of future crises. As China becomes more integrated into the international system and increasingly views itself as a responsible great power, will international legal precedents and norms increasingly influence the behavior of Chinese leaders? In particular, will Chinese leaders increasingly invoke international law as the basis of the principles it applies to crises? Conversely, will U.S. decision makers become less sensitive to international law because of the constraints it allegedly places on U.S. freedom of action?

Finally, our understanding of Chinese and U.S. crisis behavior is also limited by the absence of reliable information on a wide range of idiosyncratic or special variables. Unfortunately, many if not all of these factors, such as the effects of personality, stress, weather, topography, and third parties, are highly context dependent. In some cases, these factors cannot be understood without detailed knowledge about members of the high-level leadership.

RECOMMENDATIONS

If this analysis of the weaknesses or unknowns in Sino-American crisis management is correct, one might make several tentative recommendations, designed to improve the ability of Washington and Beijing to avoid or manage future political-military crises.[14] These recommendations are tentative in part because more discussion is necessary among and between both sides in order to develop truly useful, practicable approaches, particularly regarding actions that require direct government involvement.

Hostile Images and Assumptions

Leaders and citizens of the United States and China hold a range of views regarding themselves and each other that undermine effective crisis management. Such views can probably never be entirely eliminated. Their influence over crisis behavior can probably be reduced, however, through a regular dialogue that focuses specifically on the most important beliefs and examines both their origins and the reasons they persist over time. Such a dialogue could take the form of a semiofficial "track two" enterprise that includes diplomatic historians, country specialists, international relations experts, retired officials, media representatives, and influential citizens. Furthermore, this dialogue could be assisted by the organization of thorough and systematic surveys designed to obtain a more precise understanding of exactly how and why the two countries create and harbor negative views of each other.

Crisis Communication

Communications are critical from the inception of a crisis. Leaders of both China and the United States seem to recognize this point, and the level of communication has improved over time; however, structural, procedural, and conceptual factors continue to obstruct effective communication. The dialogue to reduce negative images (or a similar dialogue) could also address how the two sides communicate during a crisis and include discussions of the meaning of certain words and phrases used in crisis signaling. This discussion should include a systematic comparison of the use and intent of past crisis signals.

Equally important, the two sides should agree on a set of working procedures that define the modalities of authoritative communication between them during a crisis. These procedures should specify the conditions under which the existing hotline between the two governments would be activated and the manner in which it would be used in a crisis. The two sides should consider establishing an alternative high-level early-warning and emergency contact mechanism to facilitate communication when the use of the hotline is inappropriate. They should perhaps also designate an official on each side to act as liaison to expedite the prompt and accurate transmission of information whenever a flash point occurs. Moreover, these procedures should also identify—and if possible rank—the most authoritative sources, other than the head of state, for the sending and receiving of messages outside the hotline. This could counter the problem of multiple messages emanating from the media and informal or unauthorized contacts.

As part of these working procedures, the two sides should also consider establishing direct lines of communication between those subordinate civilian and military officials who would be directly responsible for implementing crisis interactions. Specifically, the two sides should consider creating a set of procedures to govern military-to-military contact, including interceptions of aircraft and ships.[15]

Decision Making and Policy Implementation

Much remains unknown about the decision-making and policy implementation processes of the two countries. This is also an area of extreme sensitivity to both sides, and especially to the Chinese government. Still, Washington and Beijing would benefit considerably by exchanging information on how decisions are made and implemented in their respective governments. This undertaking could be included as part of the dialogue on crisis communication. It should include mutual exchanges about those aspects of senior elite interactions, bureaucratic responsibilities, civilian-military relations, intelligence receipt and processing, and central-local linkages that can complicate crisis management. In each area, particular attention should be given to how both civilian and military standard operating procedures might influence crisis behavior.

Finally, to create the recommended working procedures and understandings, both sides must first clarify or establish their own internal procedures for managing political-military crises. This undertaking should address all of the major problems identified in this volume, especially civil-military interactions. To facilitate this internal process, the two sides (including both governmental and nongovernmental personnel) should exchange views regarding the entire issue of crisis management and how best to improve it. This dialogue should address many of the concepts and problems raised in this volume, beginning with the basic concepts that frame each side's perception of crises. It should aim to reach an agreement on the specific requirements for effective crisis management, beginning with a consideration of the eight points presented in this volume. And it should carefully assess the practicality— including the specific requirements for implementation—of all recommendations for improving crisis management that require direct government involvement.

This dialogue could be undertaken by a joint Sino-American political-military working group on crisis management. Participants in this undertaking should include not only official or semi-governmental representatives of each country, but also specialists on international relations, crisis management, and country and regional experts. Such specialists have examined the features of the international context and historical crises and have searched for generalized patterns of behavior that affect the impact of problems in crisis management.

Even if fully implemented, none of these recommendations will solve the problem of crisis management between China and the United States. Future crises will inevitably occur. I hope, however, that the information, analyses, and recommendations contained in this volume will contribute to a reduction in the number and severity of such crises.

NOTES

1. The chapters by Wang Jisi, Niu Jun, and Zhang Tuosheng particularly support this generalization. Wang explicitly states that Beijing followed the basic pattern of *youli, youli, youjie* during the 1995–1996 Taiwan Strait crisis, the Belgrade bombing crisis, and the EP-3 crisis. Niu Jun argues that the deliberate adoption by China's leaders of limited policy objectives during the Taiwan Strait crises of the past allowed them to be very flexible in their choice of policy responses.
2. The Taiwan Strait crises and the Vietnam War are arguably examples of the tit-for-tat strategy.
3. The Korean War, the Sino-Indian clash of 1962, and the Sino-Vietnam Border War of 1979 are arguably examples of this type of escalatory behavior.
4. See, for example, Zhang Baijia's analysis in chapter 5 of this volume.
5. This may be a result of the 1996 Taiwan crisis. Both the United States and China concluded that they had won and that their display of force was effective. Ironically, the fact that both sides did back down after sizeable displays of force and that both sides had clear limitations on these displays could undermine crisis stability on a future occasion. Had the outcome in 1996 been messier, both sides might be more cautious about attempting such a strategy again. I am grateful to Alastair Iain Johnston for this observation.

6. More positively, U.S. and Chinese nuclear forces are not tightly linked to a war-fighting strategy of mutually assured destruction, as also mentioned in chapter 1.

7. One exception may be the debate over Chinese intervention in the Korean War.

8. See Suettinger's analysis in chapter 7 of this volume.

9. Much of this section is adapted from Michael D. Swaine, "Chinese Crisis Management: Framework for Analysis, Tentative Observations, and Questions for the Future," in Andrew Scobell and Larry M. Wortzel, eds., *Chinese National Security Decisionmaking Under Stress* (Carlisle, Pa.: U.S. Army War College, 2005).

10. A major crisis over Taiwan would presumably involve actions by any side that were perceived by China or the United States as altering, or potentially altering, the status quo in unacceptable directions, thus requiring a vigorous reaction. For example, this could involve the crossing of one or more so-called red lines by Taiwan, such as an attempt to form a new constitution that eliminates the Republic of China as the legal name for Taiwan, or it could involve an attempt by Beijing to resolve the entire situation by coercing Taiwan into accepting Chinese terms for reunification.

11. The Taiwan issue is particularly susceptible to hard-line leadership viewpoints, especially on the Chinese side.

12. For example, on one hand, China's "victim psychology" can lead to an exaggeration of the conflictual aspects of crises with major powers such as the United States. In addition, memories of the past century and a half might also prompt the general public to demand that the government take a tougher line in dealing with such crises. Both factors can result in unrealistic or dangerous behavior. In China, the historical memory of events such as the Korean War can also imbue Chinese leaders and the public with a heightened sense of caution and responsibility—in view of the grave consequences that a lack of such sense would inevitably incur—as well as a recollection of lessons learned from China's past flexibility in managing crises.

13. For example, do Chinese leaders genuinely believe that the United States would likely be more deterrable than China in a crisis over a Chinese territorial issue such as Taiwan?

14. I am indebted to Professor Allen Whiting for his assistance in developing this list, and for ideas provided by participants in the 2004 Beijing conference.

15. See Blair's and Bonfili's analysis in chapter 11 of this volume and Zhang Tuosheng's analysis in chapter 12 of this volume. This would be no easy

task, however. As chapters 11 and 12 indicate, during the EP-3 incident, the two sides could not agree even to discuss consultation procedures in future military incidents. According to the U.S. side, such procedures— used by the United States and the Soviet Union during the Cold War—are a logical means of crisis prevention between major powers. But the Chinese side refused to discuss the subject, arguing that reconnaissance flights were against international law. Instead, China subsequently proposed the establishment of a high-level emergency contact mechanism, to which the United States agreed in principle. No action was taken, however.

Bibliography

Accinelli, Robert. *Crisis and Commitment: United States Policy Toward Taiwan, 1950–1955.* Chapel Hill: University of North Carolina Press, 1996.

Achen, Christopher, and Duncan Snidal. "Rational Deterrence Theory and Comparative Case Studies." *World Politics* 41 (January 1989): 143–169.

Acheson, Dean. *Present at the Creation: My Years in the State Department.* New York: Norton and Co., 1969.

Adelman, Jonathan, and Shih Chih-yu. *Symbolic War: The Chinese Use of Force, 1840–1980.* Taipei: National Chengchi University, 1993.

Adomeit, Hannes. *Soviet Risk-Taking and Crisis Behavior.* London: Allen and Unwin, 1982.

Allison, Graham T. "Conceptual Models and the Cuban Missile Crisis." *American Political Science Review* 63 (September 1969): 689–718.

———. *The Essence of Decision: Explaining the Cuban Missile Crisis.* Boston: Little Brown, 1971.

Allison, Graham T., and Morton H. Halperin. "Bureaucratic Politics: A Paradigm and Some Policy Implications." *World Politics* 24 (supplement): 40–79.

Allison, Graham T., and Peter L. Szanton. *Remaking Foreign Policy: The Organizational Connection.* New York: Basic Books, 1976.

Allison, Graham T., and Philip Zelikow. *The Essence of Decision: Explaining the Cuban Missile Crisis.* 2nd ed. New York: Longman, 1999.

Alt, James, Randall Calvert, and Brian Humes. "Reputation and Hegemonic Stability: A Game-Theoretic Analysis." *American Political Science Review* 82 (June 1988): 445–466.

Alvarez, David J. *Bureaucracy and Cold War Diplomacy: The United States and Turkey, 1943–1946.* Thessaloniki: Institute for Balkan Studies, 1980.

Andersen, David, Amy Pate, and Jonathan Wilkenfeld. "Learning and Foreign Policy Decision Making." *Chinese Political Science Review* 33 (June 2002): 1–25.

Arkes, Hadley. *Bureaucracy, the Marshall Plan, and the National Interest.* Princeton, N.J.: Princeton University Press, 1973.

Art, Robert J. "Bureaucratic Politics and American Foreign Policy: A Critique." *Policy Sciences* 4 (December 1973): 467–490.

———. "To What Ends Military Power." *International Security* 4 (Spring 1980): 3–14.

Axelrod, Robert. *The Evolution of Cooperation.* New York: Basic Books, 1984.

———. *Structure of Decision: The Cognitive Maps of Political Elites.* Princeton, N.J.: Princeton University Press, 1976.

Azar, Edward. "Protracted Social Conflicts and Second Track Diplomacy," in *Second Track/Citizens' Diplomacy: Concepts and Techniques for Conflict Transformation,* ed. J. Davies and E. Kaufman. Lanham, Md.: Rowman & Littlefield, 2002.

Bachman, David. "Domestic Sources of Chinese Foreign Policy," in *China and the World: Chinese Foreign Relations in the Post–Cold War Era,* ed. Samuel Kim. Boulder, Colo.: Westview, 1994.

———. "The United States and China: Rhetoric and Reality." *Current History* (September 2001): 257–262.

Ball, Desmond J. "The Blind Men and the Elephant: A Critique of Bureaucratic Politics Theory." *Australian Outlook* 28 (April 1974): 71–92.

Barnet, Richard J. *Roots of War.* Baltimore: Viking, 1972.

Barrett, David M. *Uncertain Warriors: Lyndon Johnson and His Vietnam Advisers.* Lawrence: University of Kansas, 1993.

Bell, Coral. *The Conventions of Crisis: A Study in Diplomatic Management.* London: Oxford University of International Affairs, 1971.

Bendor, J., and T. H. Hammond. "Rethinking Allison's Models." *American Political Science Review* 86 (1992): 301–322.

Ben-Yehuda, Hemda. "Opportunity Crises: Framework and Findings, 1918–1994." *Conflict Management and Peace Science* 17, no. 1 (1999): 69–102.

Bercovitch, Jacob. "The Structure and Diversity of Mediation in International Relations," in *Mediation in International Relations,* ed. Jacob Bercovitch and Jeffrey Z. Rubin. New York: St. Martin's Press, 1992.

Bercovitch, Jacob, and Patrick M. Regan. "Managing Risks in International Relations: The Mediation of Enduring Rivalries," in *Enforcing Cooperation,* ed. Gerald Schneider and Patricia A. Weitsman. New York: St. Martin's Press, 1997.

Bercovitch, Jacob, and Jeffrey Z. Rubin, eds. *Mediation in International Relations: Multiple Approaches to Conflict Management.* New York: St. Martin's Press, 1992.

Beschloss, Michael. *Reaching for Glory: Lyndon Johnson's Secret White House Tapes, 1964–1965.* New York: Simon and Schuster, 2001.

Betts, Richard K. "Intelligence for Policymaking," in *National Security Crisis Forecasting and Management,* ed. Gerald W. Hopple, Stephen J. Andriole, and Amos Freedy. Boulder, Colo.: Westview, 1984.

Bird, Kai. *The Color of Truth: McGeorge Bundy and William Bundy: Brothers in Arms.* New York: Simon and Schuster, 1998.

Blechman, Barry M., and Stephen S. Kaplan. *Force Without War: U.S. Armed Forces as a Political Instrument.* Washington, D.C.: Brookings Institution, 1978.

Bobrow, Davis B. "The Chinese Communist Conflict System." *Orbis* 9, no. 1 (Winter 1966).

———. "Peking's Military Calculus," in *Components of Defense Policy,* ed. Davis B. Bobrow. Chicago: Rand McNally, 1965.

Bobrow, Davis B., Steven Chan, and John A. Kringen. *Understanding Foreign Policy Decisions: The Chinese Case.* New York: Free Press, 1979.

Boin, Arjen, Paul 't Hart, Eric Stern, and Bengt Sundelius. *The Politics of Crisis Management: Public Leadership Under Pressure.* Cambridge: Cambridge University Press, 2005.

Booker, Paul. *Non-Democratic Regimes: Theory, Government and Politics.* New York: St. Martin's Press, 2000.

Botti, Timothy J. *Ace in the Hole: Why the United States Did Not Use Nuclear Weapons in the Cold War, 1945 to 1965.* Westport, Conn.: Greenwood Press, 1996.

Boulding, Kenneth E. *The Image.* Ann Arbor: University of Michigan Press, 1956.

Brams, Steven J. *Superpower Games.* New Haven, Conn.: Yale University Press, 1985.

———. *Theory of Moves.* New York: Cambridge University Press, 1994.

Brams, Steven J., and D. Marc Kilgour. *Game Theory and National Security.* New York: Basil Blackwell, 1988.

Brecher, Michael. *Crises in World Politics.* Oxford: Pergamon Press, 1993.

———. *Decisions in Crisis: Israel, 1967 and 1973.* Berkeley: University of California Press, 1980.

―――. *The Foreign Policy System of Israel: Setting, Images, Process.* New Haven: Yale University Press, 1972.

Brecher, Michael, and Jonathan Wilkenfeld. *A Study of Crisis.* Ann Arbor: University of Michigan Press, 1997.

―――. *A Study of Crisis.* Includes CD-ROM. Ann Arbor: University of Michigan Press, 2000.

―――. *Conflict, Crisis, and War.* Oxford: Pergamon, 1989.

Brecher, Michael, Jonathan Wilkenfeld, and Sheila Moser. *Crises in the Twentieth Century: Handbook of International Crises.* Oxford: Pergamon, 1988.

Brower, Ralph S., and Mitchel Y. Abolafia. "Bureaucratic Politics: The View from Below." *Journal of Public Administration Research and Theory: J-PART* 7, no. 2 (April 1997): 305–331.

Brzezinski, Zbigniew. "USA/USSR: The Power Relationship," in *International Negotiation: The Impact of the Changing Power Balance: Selected Comments,* compiled by Subcommittee on National Security and International Operations of the Committee on Government Operations United States Senate. Washington, D.C.: U.S. Government Printing Office, 1971.

Burles, Mark, and Abram N. Shulsky. *Patterns in China's Use of Force: Evidence from History and Doctrinal Writings.* Santa Monica, Calif.: RAND, 2000.

Burton, John W. *Conflict: Resolution and Prevention.* New York: St. Martin's Press, 1990.

―――. *Conflict and Communication: The Use of Controlled Communication in International Relations.* New York: Free Press, 1969.

―――. "The Resolution of Conflict." *International Studies Quarterly* 16, no. 2 (1972): 5–29.

―――. *Resolving Deep-Rooted Conflict: A Handbook.* Lanham, Md.: University Press of America, 1987.

Bush, George W. "The National Security Strategy of the United States of America." September 2002. www.whitehouse.gov/nsc/nss.pdf.

―――. "Securing Freedom's Triumph." *New York Times,* September 11, 2002, p. A33.

―――. "State of the Union Address by the President." Speech, Washington, D.C., January 31, 2006. www.whitehouse.gov/stateoftheunion/2006/.

Caldwell, Dan. "Bureaucratic Foreign Policy-Making." *American Behavioral Scientists* 21 (September/October 1977): 87–110.

Carrell, Severin. "Claim Sours Jiang Visit." *The Scotsman,* October 18, 1999.

Carter, Ashton B., and William J. Perry. *Preventive Defense: A New Security Strategy for America.* Washington, D.C.: Brookings Institution, 2003; translated by Hu Liping and Yang Yunqin, Shanghai: Shanghai People Press, 2003.

CCP Central Committee Literature Research Division, ed. *Mao Zedong Wenji* [Collected Works of Mao Zedong]. Vol. 6. Beijing: Renmin Chubanshe, 1999.

———, ed. *Zhou Enlai Nianpu 1949–1976* [Chronicle of the Life of Zhou Enlai, 1949–1976). Vol. 1. Beijing: Zhongyang Wenxian Chubanshe, 1997.

———, ed. *Jianguo Yilai Mao Zedong Wengao* [Manuscripts by Mao Zedong Since the Founding of the PRC]. Vols. 1, 4, 5, 11. Beijing: Zhongyang Wenxian Chubanshe, 1987 and 1996.

CCP Central Committee Literature Research Division and the PLA Academy of Military Sciences, eds. *Mao Zedong Junshi Wenji* [Selected Works of Mao Zedong on Military Affairs]. Vol. 6. Beijing: Renmin Chubanshe, 1993.

———, eds. *Zhou Enlai Junshi Wenxuan* [Selected Works of Zhou Enlai on Military Affairs]. Vol. 4. Beijing: Renmin Chubanshe, 1997.

Center for Crisis Management Studies, China Institute of Contemporary International Relations. *Guoji Weiji Guanli Gailun* [International Crisis Management]. Beijing: Contemporary News Press, 2003.

Chai Zhiwen and Zhao Yongtian. *Banmendian Tanpan* [Panmunjeom Negotiations]. Beijing: Jiefangjun Chubanshe, 1989.

Chan, Steve. "Chinese Conflict Calculus and Behavior: Assessment from a Perspective of Conflict Management." *World Politics* 30, no. 3 (April 1978).

Chen Bingde. "Intensify Study of Military Theory to Ensure Quality of Army Building: Learning from Thought and Practice of the Core of the Three Generations of Party Leadership in Studying Military Theory." *Zhongguo Junshi Kexue,* no. 3 (August 20, 1997). Quoted in *Foreign Broadcast Information Service—China,* March 6, 1998.

Chen Jian. "China's Involvement in the Vietnam War, 1964–69." *China Quarterly* 142 (June 1995): 356–387.

———. *China's Road to the Korean War: The Making of the Sino-American Confrontation.* New York: Columbia University Press, 1994.

———. *Mao's China and the Cold War.* Chapel Hill: University of North Carolina Press, 2001.

Chen, King C. *China's War with Vietnam, 1979: Issues, Decisions, and Implications.* Stanford, Calif.: Hoover Institution Press, 1987.

Cheng, Joseph, and Kinglun Ngok. "Chinese Nationalism and Sino-U.S. Relations: The NATO Bombing of the Chinese Embassy in Belgrade," in *Nationalism, Democracy and National Integration in China,* ed. Leong H. Liew and Shaoguang Wang. London: RoutledgeCurzon, 2004.

Christensen, Thomas J. "China, the U.S.-Japan Alliance and the Security Dilemma in East Asia." *International Security* 23, no. 4 (Spring 1999).

———. "Chinese Realpolitik." *Foreign Affairs* 75, no. 5 (September/October 1996).

———. "Posing Problems Without Catching Up: China's Rise and Challenges for U.S. Security Policy." *International Security* 25, no. 4 (Spring 2001).

———. *Useful Adversaries: Grand Strategy, Domestic Mobilization, and Sino-American Conflict, 1947–1958*. Princeton, N.J.: Princeton University Press, 1996.

———. "Windows and War: Trend Analysis and Beijing's Use of Force." In *New Approaches to the Study of Chinese Foreign Policy*, edited by Alastair Iain Johnston and Robert S. Ross. Stanford: Stanford University Press, 2006, 50–85.

Christensen, Thomas J., and Michael A. Glosny. "China: Sources of Stability in U.S.-China Security Relations," in *Strategic Asia 2003–04: Fragility and Crisis,* ed. Richard Ellings and Aaron Friedberg. Seattle: National Bureau of Asian Research, 2003.

Chu, Henry, Maggie Farley, and Anthony Kuhn. "Crisis in Yugoslavia: Chinese Attack U.S. Missions as Protests Intensify." *Los Angeles Times,* May 10, 1999.

Cimbala, Stephen J. "Nuclear Crisis Management and Information Warfare." *Parameters* (Summer 1999): 117–128.

Clarfield, Gerard. *Security with Solvency: Dwight D. Eisenhower and the Shaping of the American Military Establishment.* Westport, Conn.: Praeger, 1999.

Clifford, J. Gary. "Bureaucratic Politics." *Journal of American History* 77 (June 1990).

Cogan, Charles C. "Intelligence and Crisis Management: The Importance of the Pre-Crisis." *Intelligence and National Security* 9, no. 4 (October 1994): 633–650.

Cohen, Arthur. "The Sino-Soviet Border Crisis," in *Avoiding War: Problems of Crisis Management,* ed. Alexander L. George. Boulder, Colo.: Westview, 1991.

Cohen, Danielle F. S. *Retracing the Triangle: China's Strategic Perceptions of Japan in the Post–Cold War Era.* Maryland Series in Contemporary Asian Studies 181. Baltimore: University of Maryland School of Law, 2005.

Cohen, Raymond. *Negotiating Across Cultures.* Washington, D.C.: United States Institute of Peace Press, 1991.

Cohen, Stephen D. *The Making of United States International Economic Policy: Principles, Problems, and Proposals for Reform.* New York: Praeger, 1977.

Cohen, William S., and George J. Tenet. "U.S. Deeply Regrets Bombing of Chinese Embassy," joint statement. May 8, 1999. www.usconsulate.org.hk/uscn/others/1999/0508.htm.

Consulate General of the United States—Hong Kong and Macau. "Ambassador Prueher; On-the-Record Press Conference," April 2, 2001. www.usconsulate.org.hk/uscn/usemb/2001/040201.htm.

Cornin, Thomas E., and Sanford D. Greenberg, eds. *The Presidential Advisory System.* New York: Harper and Row, 1969.

Coser, Lewis A. *The Functions of Social Conflict* (Glencoe, Ill.: Free Press, 1956).

Covault, Craig. "China Seen as Growing Reconnaissance Challenge." *Aviation Week & Space Technology* 153, no. 6 (August 7, 2000): 65–66.

Crow, W. J., and R. C. Noel. "An Experiment in Simulated Historical Decision Making," in *A Psychological Examination of Political Leaders,* ed. M. G. Hermann. New York: Free Press, 1977.

Cyert, R. M., and J. G. March. *A Behavioral Theory of the Firm.* Englewood Cliffs, N.J.: Prentice-Hall, 1963.

Dai Chaowu. *Duidui yu Weiji.de Niandai—1954–1958nian.de ZhongMei Guanxi* [Times of Hostility and Crisis—Sino-U.S. Relations 1954–1958]. Beijing: Zhongguo Shehui Kexue Chubanshe, 2003.

Dangdai Guoji Weiji [Current International Crisis]. Beijing: Junshi Kexue Chubanshe, 1988.

Dangdai Zhongguo Haijun [Contemporary Chinese Navy]. Beijing: Zhongguo Shehui Kexue Chubanshe, 1987.

Dangdai Zhongguo Shi Yanjiu. "Canjian Jinian Chaoxian Zhanzheng" [Commemoration of the Fiftieth Anniversary of the Korean War]. *Dangdai Zhongguo Shi Yanjiu* [Contemporary China History Studies], no. 6 (2000): 6–83.

David, Charles-Philippe, and Zachary A. Selden. "The Contributions of Cognitive Psychology and Bureaucratic Politics in Reappraising the Fall of the Shah and the Iran-Contra Affair." Paper presented at the ISA Annual Convention (Acapulco, Mexico, March 1993).

Davies, John L., and Ted Robert Gurr. *Preventive Measures: Building Risk Assessment and Crisis Early Warning Systems.* Lanham, Md.: Rowman & Littlefield, 1998.

Dawisha, Karen. *The Kremlin and the Prague Spring.* Berkeley: University of California Press, 1984.

de Mesquita, Bruce Bueno. *The War Trap.* New Haven, Conn.: Yale University Press, 1981.

de Mesquita, Bruce Bueno, and David Lalman. *War and Reason.* New Haven, Conn.: Yale University Press, 1992.

Destler, I. M. *Presidents, Bureaucrats, and Foreign Policy.* Princeton, N.J.: Princeton University Press, 1972.

Destler, I. M., Leslie Gelb, and Anthony Lake. *Our Own Worst Enemy.* New York: Simon and Schuster, 1984.

Diehl, Paul F., and Gary Goertz. *War and Peace in International Rivalry.* Ann Arbor: University of Michigan Press, 2000.

Divine, Robert A. *Eisenhower and the Cold War.* Oxford: Oxford University Press, 1981.

Dixon, William J. "Third-Party Techniques for Preventing Conflict Escalation and Promoting Peaceful Settlement." *International Organization* 50, no. 4 (1996): 653–681.

Downs, George W. "The Rational Deterrence Debate." *World Politics* 41 (January 1989): 225–237.

Downs, George W., and David M. Rocke. *Tacit Bargaining, Arms Races, and Arms Control.* Ann Arbor: University of Michigan Press, 1990.

Dowty, Alan. *Middle East Crisis: U.S. Decision-Making in 1958, 1970, and 1973.* Berkeley, Calif.: University of California Press, 1984.

Draper, Theodore. "Reagan's Junta: The Institutional Sources of the Iran-Contra Affair," in *The Domestic Sources of American Foreign Policy: Insight and Evidence,* ed. Charles W. Kegley Jr. and Eugene R. Wittkopf. New York: St. Martin's Press, 1988.

Dreyer, June Teufel. "Clinton's China Policy," in *The Clinton Riddle: Perspectives on the Forty-Second President,* ed. Todd G. Shields, Jeannie M. Whayne, and Donald R. Kelley. Fayetteville: University of Arkansas Press, 2004.

Driver, M. J. "Individual Differences as Determinants of Aggression in the International Simulation," in *A Psychological Examination of Political Leaders,* ed. M. G. Hermann. New York: Free Press, 1977.

Druckman, Daniel, and Benjamin J. Broome. "Value Differences and Conflict Resolution: Familiarity or Liking?" *Journal of Conflict Resolution* 35, no. 4 (1991): 571–593.

Druckman, Daniel, and P. Terrence Hopmann. "Behavioral Aspects of Negotiations on Mutual Security," in *Behavior, Society, and Nuclear War,* ed. Philip E. Tetlock, Jo L. Husbands, Robert Jervis, Paul C. Stern, and Charles Tilly. Vol. 1. New York: Oxford University Press, 1990.

Eckstein, Harry. "Case Study and Theory in Political Science," in *Handbook of Political Science,* ed. F. I. Greenstein and N. W. Polsby. Reading, Mass.: Addison, Wesley, 1975.

Eisenhower, Dwight D. *Mandate for Change, 1953–1956.* Garden City, N.Y.: Doubleday & Co., 1963.

Eisenhower Presidential Library and Museum. "NSC Summaries of Discussion: The Eisenhower Period." Web site of Department of Political Science,

University of California–Los Angeles. www.polisci.ucla.edu/faculty/trachtenberg/guide/nsc.html.

Eisenhower Presidential Library and Museum, Audiovisual Department. "(56) President's Press Conference March 16, 1955," in "1955 Addresses of President Dwight D. Eisenhower." Abilene, Kans. www.eisenhower.archives.gov/avwebsite/PDF/55text.pdf.

Ellsberg, Daniel. "The Crude Analysis of Strategic Choices." *American Economic Review* 51 (May 1961): 472–478.

———. "The Theory and Practice of Blackmail," in *Bargaining: Formal Theories of Negotiation,* ed. Oran R. Young. Urbana, Ill.: University of Illinois Press, 1975.

Embassy of the People's Republic of China in India. "Sino-U.S. Negotiation on the Air-Collision Incident 20/04/2001." www.chinaembassy.org.in/eng/zgbd/t59535.htm.

Entman, Robert M. *Projections of Power: Framing News, Public Opinion, and U.S. Foreign Policy.* Chicago: University of Chicago Press, 2003.

"EP-3 Shijian Kaoyan Bushi Zhengfu Weiji Chuli Nengli" (The EP-3 Incident Tests the Bush Administration's Ability to Handle Crises). In *Guoji Weiji Guanli Kailun* [Introduction to International Crisis Management], ed. Yang Mingjie. Beijing: Shishi Chubanshe, n.d.

Etheredge, Lloyd S. "Personality Effects on American Foreign Policy, 1898–1968." *American Political Science Review* 72 (1978): 434–451.

Evans, Graham, and Jeffrey Newnham. *The Penguin Dictionary of International Relations.* London: Penguin Books, 1998.

Falkowski, L. *Presidents, Secretaries of State, and Crises in U.S. Foreign Relations: A Model and Predictive Analysis.* Boulder, Colo.: Westview, 1978.

Fearon, James D. "Domestic Political Audiences and the Escalation of International Disputes." *The American Political Science Review* 88, no. 3 (September 1994): 577–592.

———. "Signaling Versus the Balance of Power and Interests: An Empirical Test of a Crisis Bargaining Model." *Journal of Conflict Resolution* 38 (June 1994): 236–269.

Feigenbaum, Evan A. "China's Challenge to *Pax Americana.*" *Washington Quarterly* 24, no. 3 (July 2001): 31–43.

Festinger, Leon. *A Theory of Cognitive Dissonance.* Evanston, Ill.: Row, Peterson, 1957.

Finkelstein, David M. "China's National Military Strategy," in *The People's Liberation Army in the Information Age,* ed. James C. Mulvenon and Richard H. Yang. Santa Monica, Calif.: RAND, 1999.

First Hand. "Shimin Fanmei Qingxu Pubian Zengqiang, Yaoqiu Zhengfu Zhankai Qiangying Waijiao" [Citizens Show Stronger Anti-American Sentiments and Require the Government to Be Tough]. *First Hand,* no. 268 (May 11, 1999). www.chinavista.com/experience/lingdian/chdiaocha268.html.

Fisher, Roger. *The Social Psychology of Intergroup and International Conflict Resolution.* New York: Springer-Verlag, 1990.

Fisher, Ronald J. "Third Party Consultation: A Method for the Study and Resolution of Conflict." *Journal of Conflict Resolution* 16, no. 1 (1972): 67–94.

Fisher, Ronald J., and Loraleigh Keashly. "Distinguishing Third Party Interventions in Intergroup Conflict: Consultation is *Not* Mediation." *Negotiation Journal* 4, no. 4 (1988): 381–393.

Fleming, D. F. *The Cold War and Its Origins, 1917–1960.* Vol. 2. Garden City, N.Y.: Doubleday & Co., 1961.

Foot, Rosemary. *The Wrong War: American Policy and the Dimensions of the Korean Conflict, 1950–1953.* Ithaca, N.Y.: Cornell University Press, 1985.

Ford, Harold P. *CIA and the Vietnam Policymakers: Three Episodes: 1962–1968.* Washington, D.C.: Center for the Study of Intelligence, 1998.

Foyle, Douglas C. "Public Opinion and Foreign Policy: Elite Beliefs as a Mediating Variable." *International Studies Quarterly* 41, no. 1 (March 1997): 141–170.

Fravel, Taylor "Regime Insecurity and International Cooperation: Explaining China's Compromises in Territorial Disputes," *International Security* 30, no. 2 (Fall 2005).

Frei, Daniel, ed. *Managing International Crises.* Beverly Hills, Calif.: Sage Publications, 1982.

———, ed. *International Crises and Crisis Management: An East-West Symposium.* Farnborough, England: Saxon House, 1978.

Fried, Richard M. *Nightmare in Red: The McCarthy Era in Perspective.* New York: Oxford University Press, 1991.

Gaddis, John Lewis. *Strategies of Containment.* New York: Oxford University Press, 1982.

Gao, Mobo C. F. "Sino-U.S. Love and Hate Relations." *Journal of Contemporary Asia* 30, no. 4 (October 2000): 547–577.

Garnett, John. *Theories of Peace and Security.* London: Macmillan, 1970.

Garver, John W. *Face Off: China, the United States, and Taiwan's Democratization.* Seattle: University of Washington Press, 1997.

Gelb, Leslie. *The Irony of Vietnam: The System Worked.* Washington, D.C.: Brookings Institution Press, 1979.

George, Alexander L. *Avoiding War: Problems of Crisis Management.* Boulder, Colo.: Westview, 1991.

———. "Case Studies and Theory Development: The Method of Structured, Forced Comparison," in *Diplomacy: New Approaches in History, Theory, and Policy,* ed. P. G. Lauren. New York: Free Press, 1979.

———. "Crisis Management: The Interaction of Political and Military Considerations." *Survival* 26, no. 5 (September/October 1984): 223–234.

———. "The Cuban Missile Crisis," in *Forceful Persuasion: Coercive Diplomacy as an Alternative to War.* Washington, D.C.: United States Institute of Peace Press, 1991.

———. "Findings and Recommendations," in *Avoiding War: Problems of Crisis Management,* ed. Alexander L. George. Boulder, Colo.: Westview, 1991.

———. "The Impact of Crisis-Induced Stress on Decision-making," in *The Medical Implications of Nuclear War,* ed. Frederic Solomon and Robert Marston. Washington, D.C.: National Academy Press, 1986.

———. *Managing U.S.-Soviet Rivalry: Problems of Crisis Prevention.* Boulder, Colo.: Westview, 1983.

———. "The Operational Code: A Neglected Approach to the Study of Political Leaders and Decision-Making." *International Studies Quarterly* 13, no. 2 (June 1969).

———. *Presidential Decisionmaking in Foreign Policy: The Effective Use of Information and Advice.* Boulder, Colo.: Westview, 1980.

———. "A Provisional Theory of Crisis Management," in *Avoiding War: Problems of Crisis Management,* ed. Alexander L. George. Boulder, Colo.: Westview, 1991.

———. "Strategies for Crisis Management," in *Avoiding War: Problems of Crisis Management,* ed. Alexander L. George. Boulder, Colo.: Westview, 1991.

George, Alexander L., and Timothy J. McKeown. "Case Studies and Theories of Organizational Decision Making." *Advances in Information Processing in Organizations* 2 (1985): 21–58.

George, Alexander L., and William E. Simons, eds. *The Limits of Coercive Diplomacy.* 2nd ed. Boulder, Colo.: Westview, 1994.

George, Alexander L., and Richard Smoke. "Deterrence and Foreign Policy." *World Politics* 41 (January 1989): 170–182.

———. *Deterrence in American Foreign Policy: Theory and Practice.* New York: Columbia University Press, 1974.

Gerner, Deborah J., and Philip Schrodt. "The Effects of Media Coverage on Crisis Assessment and Early Warning in the Middle East," in *Early Warning and Early Response,* ed. S. Schmeidl and H. Adelman. New York: Columbia University Press Online, 1998.

Gibbons, William Conrad. *The U.S. Government and the Vietnam War: Executive and Legislative Relationships.* Part 4. Princeton, N.J.: Princeton University Press, 1995.

Gilbert, Arthur N., and Paul Gordon Lauren. "Crisis Management: An Assessment and Critique." *Journal of Conflict Resolution* 24, no. 4 (1980): 641–664.

Gilpin, Robert. *War and Change in World Politics.* Cambridge: Cambridge University Press, 1981.

GlobalSecurity.org. "First Taiwan Strait Crisis: Quemoy and Matsu Islands." 2005. http://www.globalsecurity.org/military/ops/quemoy_matsu.htm.

Gochman, Charles S., and Zeev Maoz. "Militarized Interstate Disputes, 1816–1976: Procedures, Patterns, Insights." *Journal of Conflict Resolution* 28, no. 4 (1984): 585–615.

Godwin, Paul H. B. "Changing Concepts of Doctrine, Strategy, and Operations in the Chinese People's Liberation Army 1978–87." *China Quarterly,* no. 112 (December 1987).

———. "Chinese Military Strategy Revised: Local and Limited War." *Annals of the American Academy of Political Science* 519 (January 1992).

———. "Decision-Making Under Stress: The Unintentional Bombing of China's Belgrade Embassy and the EP-3 Collision." Paper presented at the American Enterprise Institute, Heritage Foundation, and U.S. Army War College People's Liberation Army Conference (Carlisle Barracks, Pennsylvania, October 1–3, 2004, revised November 26, 2004).

———. "Force Projection and China's National Military Strategy," in *Chinese Military Modernization,* ed. C. Dennison Lane, Mark Weisenbloom, and Simon Li. London: Kegan Paul, 1996.

———. "From Continent to Periphery: PLA Doctrine, Strategy and Capabilities Towards 2000." *China Quarterly,* no. 146 (June 1996).

Goertz, Gary, and Paul F. Diehl. "(Enduring) Rivalries," in *Handbook of War Studies,* ed. M. Midlarsky. 2nd ed. Ann Arbor: University of Michigan Press, 2000.

Golan, Galia. "Soviet Decisionmaking in the Yom Kippur War, 1973," in *Soviet Decisionmaking for National Security,* ed. J. Valenta and W. C. Potter. Boston: Allen and Unwin, 1984.

———. *Yom Kippur and After: The Soviet Union and the Middle East Crisis.* Cambridge: Cambridge University Press, 1977.

Goldstein, Lyle J. "Return to Zhenbao Island: Who Started Shooting and Why It Matters." *China Quarterly* 168 (December 2001): 985–997.

Gong Li. "Liangci Taiwan Haixia Weiji.de Chengyin yu Zhong Mei Zhijian.de Jiaoliang" [Causes of the Two Taiwan Strait Crises and the Struggle between China and the United States], in *Cong Duizhi Zhouxiang Huanhe: Lengzhan Shiqi Zhong Mei Guanxi Zai Tantao* [From Confrontation to Détente: Sino-U.S. Relations in the Cold War Era], ed. Jiang Changbin and Robert Ross. Beijing: Shijie Zhishi Chubanshe, 2000.

Goold-Adams, Richard. *John Foster Dulles: A Reappraisal.* Chapter 16. New York, Appleton-Century-Crofts, 1962.

Greenstein, Fred I., and Richard H. Immerman. "Effective National Security Advising: Recovering the Eisenhower Legacy." *Political Science Quarterly* 115 (2000): 335*ff.*

Griffith, Robert. *The Politics of Fear: Joseph R. McCarthy and the Senate.* Amherst: University of Massachusetts Press, 1987.

Guo Ming, ed. *ZhongYue Guanxi Yanbian Sishinian* [Four Decades of Evolving Sino-Vietnam Relations]. Guilin, Guangxi: Guangxi Renmin Chubanshe, 1992.

Gurtov, Melvin, and Byong-moo Hwang. *China Under Threat: The Politics of Strategy and Diplomacy.* Baltimore: Johns Hopkins University Press, 1980.

Guttieri, Karen, and Michael Wallace. "Testing Some Propositions on the Cuban Missile Crisis." Paper presented at the International Studies Association (ISA) Annual Convention (Vancouver, March 1991).

Haas, Ernst B. "Regime Decay: Conflict Management and International Organizations, 1945–1981." *International Organization* 37, no. 2 (1983): 189–256.

———. *Why We Still Need the United Nations.* Policy Papers in International Affairs. Berkeley, California: University of California, Institute of International Studies, 1986.

Halperin, Morton H. *Bureaucratic Politics and Foreign Policy.* Washington, D.C.: Brookings Institution Press, 1974.

Hammond, Paul Y. *LBJ and the Presidential Management of Foreign Relations.* Austin: University of Texas Press, 1992.

Hamrin, Carol Lee, and Zhao Suisheng. *Decision-Making in Deng's China: Perspectives from Insiders.* Armonk, N.Y.: M. E. Sharpe, 1995.

Han Huanzhi and Tan Jingqiao, eds. *Dangdai Zhongguo Jundui.de Junshi Gongzuo* [Military Work of Contemporary Chinese Military]. Beijing: Zhongguo Shehui Kexue Chubanshe, 1989.

Han Nianlong. *Dangdai Zhongguo Waijiao* [Contemporary Chinese Diplomacy]. Beijing: Zhongguo Shehui Kexue Chubanshe, 1988.

Hao Yufan and Zhao Zhihai. "China's Decision to Enter the Korean War." *China Quarterly,* no. 121 (March 1990).

He Di. "The Evolution of the People's Republic of China's Policy Toward the Offshore Islands," in *The Great Powers in East Asia, 1953–1960,* ed. Warren

I. Cohen and Akira Iriye. New York: Columbia University Press, 1990.

———. "'The Last Campaign to Unify China': The CCP's Unmaterialized Plan to Liberate Taiwan, 1949–1950." *Chinese Historians* 5, no. 1 (Spring 1992).

Heider, Fritz. "Attributes and Cognitive Organization." *Journal of Psychology* 21 (1946): 107–112.

Hensel, Paul R. "Interstate Rivalry and the Study of Militarized Conflict," in *Conflict in World Politics: Advances in the Study of Crisis, War and Peace,* ed. Frank P. Harvey and Ben D. Mor. New York: St. Martin's Press, 1998.

Herek, Gregory, Irving Janis, and Paul Huth. "Decisionmaking During International Crises: Is Quality of Process Related to Outcome?" *Journal of Conflict Resolution* 31, no. 2 (June 1987): 203–226.

Hermann, Charles F. *International Crises: Some Insights from Behavioral Research.* New York: Free Press, 1972.

———. "International Crisis as a Situational Variable," in *International Politics and Foreign Policy,* ed. J. N. Rosenau. New York: Free Press, 1969.

Hermann, Margaret G. "Explaining Foreign Policy Behavior Using the Personal Characteristics of Political Leaders." *International Studies Quarterly* 24 (1980): 7–46.

———. "Leader Personality and Foreign Policy Behavior," in *Comparing Foreign Policies: Theories, Findings, and Methods,* ed. James N. Rosenau. New York: Sage-Halsted, 1974.

———. "Some Personal Characteristics Related to Foreign Aid Voting of Congressmen," in *A Psychological Examination of Political Leaders,* ed. Margaret G. Hermann. New York: Free Press, 1977.

Hermann, Margaret G., and Charles F. Hermann. "Who Makes Foreign Policy Decisions and How? An Empirical Inquiry." *International Studies Quarterly* 33 (1989): 361–387.

Hermann, Margaret G., Charles F. Hermann, and Joe D. Hagan. "How Decision Units Shape Foreign Policy Behavior," in *New Directions in the Study of Foreign Policy,* ed. Charles F. Hermann, Charles W. Kegley, and James N. Rosenau. Boston: Unwin Hyman, 1987.

Hillman, Ben. "Chinese Nationalism and the Belgrade Embassy Bombing," in *Nationalism, Democracy and National Integration in China,* ed. Leong H. Liew and Shaoguang Wang. London: RoutledgeCurzon, 2004.

Hilsman, Roger. *The Politics of Foreign Policy in the Administration of John F. Kennedy.* New York: Dell, 1967.

———. *To Move a Nation: The Politics of Foreign Policy in the Administration of John F. Kennedy.* Garden City, N.J.: Dell, 1967.

Hogarth, Robin M., and Melvin W. Reder, eds. *Rational Choice.* Chicago: University of Chicago Press, 1987.

Hollander, Edwin P. "Leadership and Power," in *Handbook of Social Psychology,* ed. Gardner Lindzey and E. Aronson. 3rd ed. Vol. 2. New York: Random House, 1985.

Holsti, Ole R. "The 1914 Case." *American Political Science Review* 59, no. 2 (1965): 365–378.

———. "The Belief System and National Images: A Case Study," in *International Politics and Foreign Policy,* ed. James N. Rosenau. New York: Free Press, 1969.

———. "Cognitive Dynamics and Images of the Enemy," in *Image and Reality in World Politics,* ed. John C. Farrell and Asa P. Smith. New York: Columbia University Press, 1967.

———. "Crisis Decision Making," in *Behavior, Society and Nuclear War,* ed. P. E. Tetlock et al. New York: Oxford University Press, 1989.

———. *Crisis, Escalation, War.* Montreal: McGill-Queen's University Press, 1972.

———. "Crisis Management," in *Psychological Dimensions of War,* ed. Betty Glad. Newbury Park, Calif.: Sage, 1990.

———, ed. "The Effects of Stress on the Performance of Foreign Policy Makers." *Political Science Annual* 6 (1975).

———. "Theories of Crisis Decision Making," in *Diplomacy,* ed. Paul Gordon Lauren. New York: Free Press, 1979.

Hong Zuojun. "Fengyu Qianzaiqing" [A Millennium of Trials and Hardships], in *Lishi Shunjian.de Huisu* [Flashbacks of Historical Moments]. Beijing: Dangdai Shijie Chubanshe, 1997.

Hou Xiaojia. "Paoji Jinmen Juece yu Quzhe Jincheng" [The Policy of Shelling Quemoy and Its Complicated Course]. *Zhonggongdangshi Yanjiu* [Chinese Communist Party History Studies]. No. 2. (2003).

Hu Ping. *Guoji Chongtu Fenxi yu Weiji Guanli Yanjiu* [Analysis of International Conflict and Research on Crisis Management]. Beijing: Junshi Yiwen Chubanshe, 1993.

Hu Sheng, ed. *Zhongguo Gongchandang.de Qishi Nian* [The Seventy-Year History of the CCP]. Beijing: Zhonggongdangshi Chubanshe, 1991.

Huang Jialun. "Three-Point Thinking on Developing Combat Theory." *Jiefangjun Bao,* April 7, 1998. Quoted in *Foreign Broadcast Information Service—China,* May 1, 1998.

Huang Xing, and Zuo Quandian. "Holding the Initiative in Our Hands in Conducting Operations, Giving Full Play to Our Own Advantages to Defeat Our Enemy: A Study of the Core Idea of the Operational Doctrine of the People's Liberation Army." *Zhongguo Junshi Kexue,* no. 4 (November 20, 1996). Quoted in *Foreign Broadcast Information Service—China,* June 17, 1997.

Hubbell, Larry. "A Sino-American Cultural Exchange During the Bombing Crisis: A Personal Experience." *Asian Affairs* 26, no. 3 (Fall 1999): 159–172.

Hunter, Robert E. *Organizing for National Security.* Washington, D.C.: Center for Strategic and International Studies, 1988.

Huth, Paul K. *Extended Deterrence and the Prevention of War.* New Haven: Yale University Press, 1988.

Huth, Paul K., and Bruce Russett. "Deterrence Failure and Crisis Escalation." *International Studies Quarterly* 32, no. 1 (March 1988): 29–45.

———. "General Deterrence Between Enduring Rivals: Testing Three Competing Models." *American Political Science Review* 87 (March 1993): 61–73.

———. "Testing Deterrence Theory: Rigor Makes a Difference." *World Politics* 42 (July 1990): 466–501.

———. "What Makes Deterrence Work? Cases from 1900–1980." *World Politics* 36 (July 1984): 496–526.

Huth, Paul K., Christopher Gelpi, and D. Scott Bennett. "The Escalation of Great Power Militarized Disputes: Testing Rational Deterrence Theory and Structural Realism." *American Political Science Review* 87, no. 3 (September 1993): 609–623.

———. "System Uncertainty, Risk Propensity, and International Conflict Among the Great Powers." *Journal of Conflict Resolution* 36 (September 1992): 478–517.

Iklé, Fred Charles. *How Nations Negotiate.* New York: Praeger, 1967.

Inderfurth, Karl F., and Loch Johnson. "National Security Advisers: Roles: Editors' Introduction," in *Fateful Decisions: Inside the National Security Council,* ed. Karl F. Inderfurth and Loch Johnson. New York: Oxford University Press, 2004.

International Crisis Behavior Project. "Primary Data Collections: Version 6.0." University of Maryland, January 2006. http://www.cidcm.umd.edu/icb/Data/index.html.

Iriye, Akira. *Across the Pacific: An Inner History of American–East Asian Relations.* New York: Harcourt Brace Jovanovich, 1967.

Jabri, Vivienne. *Discourse on Violence: Conflict Analysis Reconsidered.* Manchester, England: Manchester University Press, 1996.

Jackson, Henry, ed., *National Security Council.* New York: Praeger, 1965.

Janis, Irving L. *Crucial Decisions.* New York: Free Press, 1989.

———. *Groupthink: Psychological Studies of Policy Decisions and Fiascos.* Boston: Houghton Mifflin, 1982.

———. *Victims of Groupthink.* Boston: Houghton Mifflin, 1972.

Janis, Irving L., and Leon Mann. *Decision Making*. New York: Free Press, 1977.

Jervis, Robert. "Deterrence and Perception." *International Security* 7 (Winter 1982/83): 3–30.

———. "Deterrence Theory Revisited." *World Politics* 31 (January 1979): 289–324.

———. "Domino Beliefs and Strategic Behavior," in *Dominoes and Bandwagons*, ed. Robert Jervis and Jack Snyder. New York: Oxford University Press, 1991.

———. *The Logic of Images in International Relations*. Princeton, N.J.: Princeton University Press, 1970.

———. *The Meaning of the Nuclear Revolution*. Ithaca, N.Y.: Cornell University Press, 1989.

———. *Perception and Misperception in International Politics*. Princeton, N.J.: Princeton University Press, 1976.

———. "Rational Deterrence: Theory and Evidence." *World Politics* 41, no. 2 (January 1989): 183–207.

Jervis, Robert, Richard Ned Lebow, and Janice Gross Stein, eds. *Psychology and Deterrence*. Baltimore: Johns Hopkins University Press, 1985.

Jia Wenxian, Zheng Shouqi, and Guo Weimin. "Tentative Discussion of Special Principles of a Future Chinese Limited War." *Guofang Daxue Xuebao*, no. 11 (November 1, 1987). Quoted in *Joint Publications Research Service*, July 12, 1988.

Jiang Changbin and Robert S. Ross, eds. *Cong Duizhi Zouxiang Huanhe: Lengzhan Shiqi Zhong Mei Guanxi Zai Tantao* [From Confrontation to Détente: Sino-U.S. Relations During the Cold War Revisited]. Beijing: Shijie Zhishi Chubanshe, 2000.

Jiang Ying. "50 Niandai Maozedong Waijiao Sixiang Shulun" [On Mao Zedong's Thoughts on Diplomatic Work in the 1950s], in *Cong Duizhi Zhouxiang Huanhe: Lengzhan Shiqi ZhongMei Guanxi Zai Shentao* [From Confrontation to Relaxation: China-U.S. Relations in the Cold War Era]. Beijing: Shijie Zhishi Chubanshe, 2000.

Jianguo Yilai Zhongyao Wenxian Xuanbian [Selected Important Documents Since the Founding of the PRC]. Vols. 1, 5. Beijing: Zhongyang Wenxian Chubanshe, 1992.

Jiao Wu and Xiao Hui. "Modern Limited War Calls for Reform of Traditional Military Principles." *Guofang Daxue Xuebao*, no. 11 (November 1, 1987). Quoted in *Joint Publications Research Service*, July 12, 1988.

Jin Chongji, ed. *Zhou Enlai Zhuan* [Biography of Zhou Enlai]. Beijing: Zhongyang Wenxian Chubanshe, 1998.

Joffe, Ellis. "The People's Liberation Army and Politics: After the Fifteenth Party Congress," in *China Under Jiang Zemin,* ed. Hung-mao Tien and Yun-han Chu. Boulder, Colo.: Lynne Rienner, 2000.

———. "People's War Under Modern Conditions: A Doctrine for Modern War." *China Quarterly,* no. 112 (December 1987).

Johnson, Richard T. *Managing the White House.* New York: Harper and Row, 1974.

Johnston, Alastair Iain. "China's Militarized Interstate Dispute Behavior 1949–1992: A First Cut at the Data." *China Quarterly,* no. 153 (March 1998).

———. "China's New 'Old Thinking:' The Concept of Limited Deterrence." *International Security* 20, no. 3 (Winter 1995/96).

———. *Cultural Realism: Strategic Culture and Grand Strategy in Chinese History.* Princeton, N.J.: Princeton University Press, 1995.

———. "Cultural Realism and Strategy in Maoist China," in *The Culture of National Security: Norms and Identity in World Politics,* ed. Peter J. Katzenstein. New York: Columbia University Press, 1996.

———. "Eight Principles of Crisis Management." Lecture to the Strategic Studies Institute, Communist Party of China Party School (Beijing, China, November 2000).

Johnston, Alastair Iain, and Robert S. Ross. "Conclusion," in *Engaging China: The Management of an Emerging Power,* ed. Alastair Iain Johnston and Robert S. Ross. London: Routledge, 1995.

Jones, Deiniol Lloyd. "Mediation, Conflict Resolution and Critical Theory." *Review of International Studies* 26, no. 4 (2000): 647–662.

Keashly, Loraleigh, and Ronald J. Fisher. "A Contingency Perspective on Conflict Interventions: Theoretical and Practical Considerations," in *Resolving International Conflicts,* ed. Jacob Bercovitch. Boulder, Colo.: Lynne Rienner, 1996.

Keefe, John. *Anatomy of the EP-3 Incident April 2001.* Alexandria, Va.: CNA Corp., 2001.

Kelman, Herbert C. "Informal Mediation by the Scholar/Practitioner," in *Mediation in International Relations: Multiple Approaches to Conflict Management,* ed. Jacob Bercovitch and Jeffrey Z. Rubin. New York: St. Martin's Press, 1992.

———. "Interactive Problem-Solving: Informal Mediation by the Scholar-Practitioner," in *Studies in International Mediation: Essays in Honor of Jeffrey Z. Rubin,* ed. Jacob Bercovitch. Houndsmills, Basingstoke, Hampshire, Great Britain: Palgrave MacMillan, 2002.

Kernell, Samuel, and Samuel L. Popkin, eds. *Chief of Staff* (Berkeley: University of California Press, 1986).

Kiewe, Amos. *The Modern Presidency and Crisis Rhetoric.* Westport, Conn.: Praeger Publishers, 1994.

Kintner, William R. and David C. Schwarz. *A Study on Crisis Management.* Philadelphia: University of Pennsylvania Foreign Policy Research Institute, 1965.

Kissinger, Henry. *White House Years.* Boston: Little Brown, 1979.

Kleiboer, Marieke. "Great Power Mediation: Using Leverage to Make Peace?" in *Studies in International Mediation: Essays in Honor of Jeffrey Z. Rubin,* ed. Jacob Bercovitch. Houndsmills, Basingstoke, Hampshire, Great Britain: Palgrave MacMillan, 2002.

———. *The Multiple Realities of International Mediation.* Boulder, Colo.: Lynne Rienner, 1998.

Koen, Ross Y. *The China Lobby in American Politics.* New York: Harper and Row, 1974.

Kolb, Deborah M., and Eileen F. Babbitt. "Mediation Practice on the Home Front: Implications for Global Conflict Resolution," in *Beyond Confrontation: Learning Conflict Resolution in the Post–Cold War Era,* edited by John A. Vasquez et al. Ann Arbor: University of Michigan Press, 1995.

Krasner, Stephen D. "Are Bureaucracies Important (or Allison Wonderland)." *Foreign Policy* 7 (Summer 1972): 159–179.

———, ed. *International Regimes.* Ithaca, N.Y.: Cornell University Press, 1983.

Lall, Arthur. *How Communist China Negotiates.* New York: Columbia University Press, 1968.

Lamborn, Alan. *The Price of Power: Risk and Foreign Policy in Britain, France, and Germany.* Boston: Unwin Hyman, 1991.

Lampton, David M., ed. *The Making of Chinese Foreign and Security Policy in the Era of Reform: 1978–2000.* Stanford, Calif.: Stanford University Press, 2001.

———. *Same Bed, Different Dreams: Managing U.S.-China Relations, 1989–2000.* Berkeley: University of California Press, 2001.

Laris, Michael. "U.S. Agrees to Pay Chinese Embassy Bombing Victims." *Austin American-Statesman,* July 31, 1999.

Lebow, Richard Ned. *Between Peace and War: The Nature of International Crisis.* Baltimore: Johns Hopkins University Press, 1981.

———. "Deterrence: A Political and Psychological Critique," in *Perspectives on Deterrence,* ed. Paul Stern, Robert Axelrod, Robert Jervis, and Roy Radner. Oxford: Oxford University Press, 1989.

———. *Nuclear Crisis Management.* Ithaca, N.Y.: Cornell University Press, 1987.

Lebow, Richard Ned, and Janice Gross Stein. "Beyond Deterrence." *Journal of Social Issues* 43, no. 4 (Winter 1987): 5–71.

———. "Deterrence: The Elusive Dependent Variable." *World Politics* 42 (April 1990): 336–369.

———. "Rational Deterrence Theory: I Think, Therefore I Deter." *World Politics* 41 (January 1989): 208–224.

Lederman, Gordon Nathaniel. *Reorganizing the Joint Chiefs of Staff: The Goldwater-Nichols Act of 1986.* Westport, Conn.: Greenwood Press, 1999.

Leites, Nathan. *The Operational Code of the Politburo.* New York: McGraw-Hill, 1951.

Leng, Russell J. *Bargaining and Learning in Recurring Crises: The Soviet-American, Egyptian-Israeli, and Indo-Pakistani Rivalries.* Ann Arbor: University of Michigan Press, 2000.

———. "Influence Techniques Among Nations," in *Behavior, Society, and Nuclear War,* ed. Philip E. Tetlock, Jo L. Husbands, Robert Jervis, Paul C. Stern, and Charles Tilly. Vol. 3. New York: Oxford University Press, 1993.

———. *Interstate Crisis Behavior, 1816–1980: Realism Versus Reciprocity.* Cambridge: Cambridge University Press, 1993.

———. "Structure and Action in Militarized Disputes," in *New Directions in the Study of Foreign Policy,* ed. C. F. Hermann, C. W. Kegley Jr., and J. N. Rosenau. Boston: Allen & Unwin, 1987.

———. "When Will They Ever Learn: Coercive Bargaining in Recurrent Crises." *Journal of Conflict Resolution* 27, no. 3 (September 1983): 379–419.

Leng, Russell J., and J. David Singer. "Militarized Interstate Crises: The BCOW Typology and Its Applications." *International Studies Quarterly* 32 (1988): 155–173.

Levy, Jack S. "Quantitative Studies of Deterrence Success and Failure," in *Perspectives on Deterrence,* ed. Paul Stern, Robert Axelrod, Robert Jervis, and Roy Radner. Oxford: Oxford University Press, 1989.

Li Danhui. "Sanbaxian yu Shiqiduxian—Chaoxian yu Yuezhan Qijian ZhongMei Xinxi Goutong Bijiao Yanjiu" [The 38th Parallel and the 17th Parallel—Comparative Studies on Exchange of Information Between China and the U.S. in the Korean War and in the Vietnam War], in *Zhonggong Dangshi Yanjiu* [Studies on History of the Communist Party of China]. Vol. 3, 2001.

Li Nan. "The PLA's Warfighting Doctrine, Strategy, and Tactics." *China Quarterly,* no. 146 (June 1996).

Li Yaqiang. "Will Large-Scale Naval Warfare Recur?" *Jianchuan Zhishi,* August 8, 1995. Quoted in *Foreign Broadcast Information Service—China,* August 8, 1996.

Liao Xinwen. "1958nian Mao Zedong Juece Paoji Jinmen.de Lishi Kaocha" [A Historical Exploration of Mao Zedong's 1958 Decision to Attack Quemoy]. *Dang.de Wenxian* [Party Documents], no. 1 (1994).

Lin Chong-pin. *China's Nuclear Weapons Strategy: Tradition Within Evolution.* Lexington, MA: D.C. Heath, 1988.

Lin Limin. *Ezhi Zhongguo: Chaoxian Zhanzheng yu ZhongMei Guanxi* [Containing China: The Korean War and Sino-U.S. Relations]. Beijing: Shijie Zhishi Chubanshe, 2000.

Lin Xiaoguang. "Zhongguogongchandang DuiTai Zhengce.de Lishi Yanjin" [Evolution of CCP Policy Toward Taiwan], in *Zhonggong Dangshi Yanjiu* [Studies on History of the Communist Party of China]. Vol. 3, 1997.

Lipset, Seymour Martin. *American Exceptionalism: A Double-Edged Sword.* New York: W. W. Norton & Company, 1995.

Little, Douglas. "Crackpot Realists and Other Heroes: The Rise and Fall of the Postwar American Diplomatic Elite." *Diplomatic History* 13 (Winter 1989): 99–112.

Liu Deyou. *Shiguang Zhilü—Wo Jingli.de ZhongRi GuanXi* [Voyage of Time— My Experience with China-Japan Relations]. Beijing: Shangwu Yinshuguan, 1999.

Liu Fengcheng. "Concentrate Forces in New Ways in Modern Warfare." *Jiefangjun Bao,* November 21, 1995. Quoted in *Foreign Broadcast Information Service—China,* January 29, 1996.

Liu Huaqing. "Unswervingly Advance Along the Road of Building a Modern Army with Chinese Characteristics." *Jiefangjun Bao,* August 6, 1993. Quoted in *Foreign Broadcast Information Service—China,* August 18, 1993.

Liu Jianfei. "Zhanlüe Jiyuqi yu ZhongMei Guanxi" [Period of Strategic Opportunity and Sino-U.S. Ties]. *Liaowang,* January 20, 2003.

Liu, Melinda, and Leslie Pappas. "How Low Would He Bow?" *Newsweek International,* June 28, 1999.

Liu Wusheng and Du Hongqi, eds. *Zhou Enlai Junshi Huodong Jishi* [Chronicles of Zhou Enlai's Military Activities]. Vol. 2. Beijing: Zhongyang Wenxian Chubanshe, 2000.

Lockhart, Charles. *Bargaining in International Crises.* New York: Columbia University Press, 1979.

Lu Linzhi. "Preemptive Strikes Crucial in Limited High-Tech Wars." *Jiefangjun Bao,* February 14, 1996. Quoted in *Foreign Broadcast Information Service— China,* February 14, 1996.

Lu Ning. "The Central Leadership, Supraministry Coordinating Bodies, State Council Ministries, and Party Departments," in *The Making of Chinese For-*

eign and Security Policy in the Era of Reform, ed. David M. Lampton. Stanford, Calif.: Stanford University Press, 2001.

———. *The Dynamics of Foreign-Policy Decision-Making in China.* Boulder, Colo.: Westview, 1997.

Luo Zhufeng. *Hanyu Dacidian* [A Chinese Dictionary]. 2nd ed. Hong Kong: Sanlian Shudian (Xianggang) Youxian Gonsi/Hanyu Dacidian Chubanshe, 1988.

Maggs, John. "Inciting the Dragon." *National Journal,* May 15, 1999, p. 1336.

Maiese, Michelle. "Limiting Escalation/De-escalation." Beyond Intractibility.org, January 2004. www.beyondintractability.org/essay/limiting_escalation/.

Mair, Victor H. Mair, "How a misunderstanding about Chinese characters has led many astray," http://www.pinyin.info/chinese/crisis.html.

Mann, James. *About Face: A History of America's Curious Relationship with China, from Nixon to Clinton.* New York: Alfred A. Knopf, 1999.

Mao Zedong. "Current Problems of Tactics in the Anti-Japanese United Front," in *Selected Works of Mao Tse-tung.* Vol. 2. Beijing: Foreign Languages Press, 1975.

Maoz, Zeev. "Crisis Initiation: A Theoretical Exploration of a Neglected Topic in International Crisis Theory." *Review of International Studies* 8, no. 4 (October 1982): 215–232.

March, J. G., and H. A. Simon. *Organizations.* New York: John Wiley, 1958.

Marshall, Monty G., and T. R. Gurr. *Peace and Conflict 2003.* College Park, Md.: University of Maryland, Center for International Development and Conflict Management, 2003.

———. *Peace and Conflict 2005.* College Park, Md.: University of Maryland, Center for International Development and Conflict Management, 2005.

Maxwell, Neville. *India's China War.* New York: Random House, 1970.

Maxwell, Steven. "Rationality in Deterrence." Adelphi Papers 50. London: International Institute for Strategic Studies, 1968.

McCarthy, Shaun P. *The Function of Intelligence in Crisis Management.* Aldershot, England: Ashgate, 1998.

McClelland, Charles A. "Access to Berlin: The Quantity and Variety of Events, 1948–1963," in *Quantitative International Politics,* ed. J. D. Singer. New York: Free Press, 1968.

———. "Action Structures and Communications in Two International Crises: Quemoy and Berlin." *Background* 7 (1964): 201–215.

———. "The Acute International Crisis," in *The International System: Theoretical Essays,* ed. K. Knorr. Princeton, N.J.: Princeton University Press, 1961.

———. "The Beginning, Duration, and Abatement of International Crises: Comparisons in Two Conflict Arenas," in *International Crises: Insights and*

Evidence, ed. C. F. Hermann. New York: Free Press, 1972.

McGovern, James. *To The Yalu: From The Chinese Invasion of Korea to MacArthur's Dismissal.* New York: William Morrow and Company, 1972.

McKeown, Timothy J. "Plans and Routines, Bureaucratic Bargaining, and the Cuban Missile Crisis." *Journal of Politics* 63, no. 4 (November 2001): 1163–1190.

Mearsheimer, John. *Conventional Deterrence.* Ithaca, N.Y.: Cornell University Press, 1983.

———. *The Tragedy of Great Power Politics.* New York: W. W. Norton & Co., 2001.

Medhurst, Martin J. *Dwight D. Eisenhower: Strategic Communicator.* Westport, Conn.: Greenwood Press, 1993.

Mefford, Dwain. "Analogical Reasoning and the Definition of the Situation," in *New Directions in the Study of Foreign Policy,* ed. Charles F. Hermann, Charles W. Kegley, and James N. Rosenau. Boston: Unwin Hyman, 1987.

Mercer, Jonathan. *Reputation and International Politics.* Ithaca, N.Y.: Cornell University Press, 1996.

Meyers, Steven Lee. "Chinese Military to Resume Contacts with the Pentagon." *New York Times,* January 6, 2000.

Michalak, Mike. "U.S. Views on Asian Regional Integration." Remarks at the International Institute of Money Affairs (Tokyo, January 25, 2006). www.state.gov/p/eap/rls/rm/60355.htm.

Miller, Benjamin. "Explaining Great Power Cooperation in Conflict Management." *World Politics* 45, no. 1 (October 1992): 1–46.

Miller, George A., Eugene Galanter, and Karl H. Pribram. *Plans and the Structure of Behavior.* New York: Holt, 1960.

Miller, Lyman. "Leadership Analysis in an Era of Institutionalized Party Politics." Paper presented at conference, "Behind the Bamboo Curtain: Chinese Leadership, Politics, and Policy," hosted by the Carnegie Endowment for International Peace (Washington, D.C., 2005). www.carnegieendowment.org/files/Miller/Revised.pdf.

Ministry of Defense of the People's Republic of China. "2000nian Zhongguo.de Guofang" [China's National Defense in 2000]. October 2000.

Ministry of Foreign Affairs of the People's Republic of China. "China Lodges Strongest Protest Against U.S.-Led NATO." May 8, 1999. East Asian Studies News File, UCLA Center for East Asian Studies. www.isop.ucla.edu/eas/newsfile/bombing05-99/990508-cmfa5.htm.

————. "China Strongly Condemns NATO Bombing." May 8, 1999. East Asian Studies News File, UCLA Center for East Asian Studies. www.isop.ucla.edu/eas/NewsFile/bombing05-99/990508-cmfa2.htm.

————. "Formal Note of 10 May to the U.S. by Foreign Minister Tang Jiaxuan on the Embassy Bombing." May 10, 1999. East Asian Studies News File, UCLA Center for East Asian Studies. www.isop.ucla.edu/eas/newsfile/bombing05-99/990510-cmfa4.htm.

————. "Speech by President Jiang Zemin at George Bush Presidential Library." October 24, 2002. www.fmprc.gov.cn/eng/topics/3719/3721/t19082.htm.

————. "U.S. Inspection of Its Plane Allowed." April 29, 2001. www.fmprc.gov.cn/eng/xwfw/2510/2535/t14932.htm.

————. "U.S. President's Personal Envoy in China to Present the U.S. Government's Report on Its Investigation Into the Bombing of the Chinese Embassy in the Federal Republic of Yugoslavia—The Chinese Government Emphasizes That the U.S. Side Must Give Satisfactory Account and Explanation of the Incident." June 16, 1999. East Asian Studies News File, UCLA Center for East Asian Studies. http://www.isop.ucla.edu/eas/NewsFile/bombing05-99/9906-cmfa1.htm.

Ministry of Foreign Affairs of the People's Republic of China and the CCP Central Committee Literature Research Division, eds. *Mao Zedong Waijiao Wenxuan* [Selected Works of Mao Zedong on Diplomacy]. Beijing: Zhongyang Wenxian Chubanshe & Shijie Zhishi Chubanshe, 1994.

————, eds. *Zhou Enlai Waijiao Wenxuan* [Selected Works of Zhou Enlai on Diplomacy]. Beijing: Zhongyang Wenxian Chubanshe, 1990.

Mintz, Alex, and Nehemia Geva. "Why Don't Democracies Fight Each Other?" *Journal of Conflict Resolution* 37, no. 3 (1993): 484–503.

Mintz, Alex, Nehemia Geva, Steven B. Redd, and Amy Carnes. The Effect of Dynamic and Static Choice Sets on Political Decision Making: An Analysis Using the Decision Board Platform. *American Political Science Review* 91, no. 3 (1997).

Mitchell, Christopher R. *Peacemaking and the Consultant's Role*. New York: Nichols Publishing, 1981.

Mor, Benjamin D. *Decision and Interaction in Crisis: A Model of International Crisis Behavior*. Westport, Conn.: Praeger, 1993.

Morgan, Patrick. *Deterrence: A Conceptual Analysis*. Beverly Hills, Calif.: Sage, 1977.

———. "Saving Face for the Sake of Deterrence," in *Psychology and Deterrence,* ed. Robert Jervis, Richard Ned Lebow, and Janice Gross Stein. Baltimore: Johns Hopkins University Press, 1985.

Morgan, T. Clifton. "A Spatial Model of Crisis Bargaining." *International Studies Quarterly* 28 (December 1984): 407–426.

———. *Untying the Knot of War: A Bargaining Theory of International Crises.* Ann Arbor: University of Michigan Press, 1994.

Morrow, James D. "Capabilities, Uncertainty, and Resolve: A Limited Information Model of Crisis Bargaining." *American Journal of Political Science* 33 (November 1989): 941–972.

———. "Signaling Difficulties with Linkage in Crisis Bargaining." *International Studies Quarterly* 36, no. 1 (March 1992): 153–172.

———. "A Spatial Model of International Conflict." *American Political Science Review* 80 (December 1986): 1131–1150.

Mufson, Steven, and Philip P. Pan. "Spy Plane Delays Irk President; Bush Asks 'Prompt' Release by Chinese." *Washington Post,* April 3, 2001, A1.

Mulvenon, James. "Civil-Military Relations and the EP-3 Crisis: A Content Analysis." *China Leadership Monitor,* no. 1 (Winter 2002).

———. "The Limits of Coercive Diplomacy: The 1979 Sino-Vietnamese Border War." *Journal of Northeast Asian Studies* 14, no. 3 (Fall 1995): 68–88.

Nalebuff, Barry. "Rational Deterrence in an Imperfect World." *World Politics* 43 (April 1991): 313–335.

Nathan, Andrew J., and Robert S. Ross. *The Great Wall and the Empty Fortress: China's Search for Security.* New York: Norton Press, 1997.

Nathan, James H., and James K. Oliver. "Bureaucratic Politics: Academic Windfalls and Intellectual Pitfalls." *Journal of Political and Military Sociology* 6 (Spring 1978): 81–91.

NATO Letter. "Crisis Management or Crisis Prevention." *NATO Letter* (August–September 1966).

Neustadt, Richard E. *Presidential Power: The Politics of Leadership.* New York: Free Press, 1960.

Newcomb, Theodore M. "An Approach to the Study of Communicative Acts." *Psychological Review* 60 (1953): 393–404.

Newmann, William W. *Managing National Security Policy: The President and the Process.* Pittsburgh, Pa.: University of Pittsburgh Press, 2003.

Nie Fengzhi. *SanJun Huige Zhanzheng Donghai* [The Three Armed Forces Poised for a War in the East China Sea]. Beijing: Jiefangjun Chubanshe, 1986.

Nitze, Paul H. "A Shaky Balance of Brinkmanship," in *Conflict and Cooperation Among Nations,* ed. Ivo D. Duchacek. New York: Holt, Rinehart and Winston, 1963.

Niu Jun. "1962: Zhongguo Duiwai Zhengce 'Zuo' Zhuan.de Qianye" [1962: On the Eve of Chinese Foreign Policy's Shift to the "Left"]. *Lishi Yanjiu* [History Studies], no. 3 (2003).

———. "Lun Kelindun Zhengfu Diyi Renqi duiHua Zhengce.de Yanbian ji qi Tedian" [On the Evolution and Characteristics of the China Policy in Clinton's First Term], in *Kelindun Zhixia.de Meiguo* [The United States Under Clinton], edited by Niu Jun. Beijing: Zhongguo Shehui Kexue Chubanshe, 1998.

O'Donnell, Lynne. "China Demands an Apology in Person." *The Australian,* May 31, 1999.

Ogata, Sadako. *Normalization with China: A Comparative Study of U.S. and Japanese Processes.* Berkeley: University of California, Institute of East Asian Studies, 1988.

O'Neill, Barry. "Game Theory and the Study of the Deterrence of War," in *Perspectives on Deterrence,* ed. Paul Stern, Robert Axelrod, Robert Jervis, and Roy Radner. Oxford: Oxford University Press, 1989.

Online NewsHour. "Ambassador Li Zhaoxing." *Online NewsHour,* May 10, 1999. www.pbs.org/newshour/bb/europe/jan-june99/li_5-10.html.

Online NewsHour. "China's Response." *Online NewsHour,* May 9, 1999. www.pbs.org/newshour/bb/europe/jan-june99/china_statement_5-9.html.

Orme, John. "Deterrence Failures: A Second Look." *International Security* 11 (Spring 1987): 96–124.

Osgood, Charles E., and Percy H. Tannenbaum. "The Principle of Congruity in the Prediction of Attitude Change." *Psychological Review* 62 (1955): 42–55.

Ostrum, T. M., D. A. Sylvan, A. Harasty, and D. M. Haddad. "Reasoning Styles in Foreign Policy: Comparing Cultures, Processing Environments, and Individuals Versus Groups." Paper presented at ISA annual convention (Acapulco, Mexico, March 1993).

Paige, Glenn D. *The Korean Decision, June 14–30, 1950.* New York: Free Press, 1968.

Pan Shiying. "Thoughts About the Principal Contradiction in Our Country's National Defense Construction." *Jiefangjun Bao,* April 14, 1987. Quoted in *Foreign Broadcast Information Service—China,* April 29, 1987.

Pang Xianzhi and Jin Chongji, eds. *Mao Zedong Zhuan, 1949–1976* [Biography of Mao Zedong 1949–1976]. Vol. 1. Beijing: Zhongyang Wenxian Chubanshe, 2003.

Panikkar, K. M. *In Two Chinas: Memoirs of a Diplomat.* London: Allen and Unwin, 1955.

Pastor, Robert A. "China and the United States: Who Threatens Whom?" *Journal of International Affairs* 54, no. 2 (Spring 2001): 427–443.

Patchen, Martin. *Resolving Disputes Between Nations.* Durham, N.C.: Duke University Press, 1988.

Paul, T. V. "Time Pressure and War Initiation: Some Linkages." *Canadian Journal of Political Science* 28, no. 2 (June 1995): 255–276.

Peng Dehuai Junshi Wenxuan [Selected Works of Peng Dehuai on Military Affairs]. Beijing: Zhongyang Wenxian Chubanshe, 1988.

Peng Dehuai. *Peng Dehuai Zishu* [Peng Dehuai on Himself]. Beijing: Renmin Chubanshe, 1981.

Pentagon Papers: The Defense Department History of United States Decisionmaking on Vietnam. Senator Gravel Edition. Vol. 3. Boston: Beacon Press, 1971.

Peterson, Susan. *Crisis Bargaining and the State.* Ann Arbor: University of Michigan Press, 1996.

Pillsbury, Michael. *Dangerous Chinese Misperceptions: Implications for DoD.* Washington, D.C.: Office of Net Assessment, 1998.

Political Department of the Air Force. *A Brief History of PLA Air Defense Force.* Beijing: Political Department of the Air Force, 1993.

Pollack, Jonathan D. *Security, Strategy, and the Logic of Chinese Foreign Policy.* Berkeley: University of California at Berkeley, Institute of East Asian Studies, 1981.

Powell, Robert. *Nuclear Deterrence Theory: The Search for Credibility.* New York: Cambridge University Press, 1990.

Qian Qichen. *Waijiao Shi Ji* [Ten Stories of a Diplomat]. Beijing: Shijie Zhishi Chubanshe, 2003.

Qu Aiguo, Bao Mingrong, and Xiao Zuyue, eds. *Yuan Yue KangMei—Zhongguo Zhiyuanbudui zai Yuenan* [Aiding Vietnam in Its Resistance Against the United States—China Supporting Troops in Vietnam]. Beijing: Junshi Kexue Chubanshe, 1995.

People's Daily. "Document About China's Position on New Concept of Security," by Chinese Delegation to the ASEAN Security Forum. *People's Daily,* August 2, 2002.

———. "Quanguo Renda Waishi Weiyuanhui Shengming" [Statement of the Foreign Affairs Committee of the National People's Congress], May 23, 1995. *People's Daily,* May 25, 1995.

———. "Quanguo Zhengxie Waishi Weiyuanhui Shengming" [Statement of Foreign Affairs Committee of the Chinese People's Political Consultative Conference], May 24, 1995. *People's Daily,* May 25, 1995.

———. "Statement of the Government of the PRC, December 16, 1978." *People's Daily,* December 17, 1978.

Raiffa, Howard. *The Art and Science of Negotiation*. Cambridge, Mass.: Harvard University Press, 1982.

Ren Yue. "China's Dilemma in Cross-Strait Crisis Management." *Asian Affairs* 24, no. 3 (Fall 1997).

Rhodes, Edward. "Do Bureaucratic Politics Matter? Some Discomfirming Findings from the Case of the U.S. Navy." *World Politics* 47, no. 1 (Oct. 1994): 1–41.

Ripley, Brian. "Cognition, Culture, and Bureaucratic Politics," in *Foreign Policy Analysis,* ed. Laura Neack, Jeanne A. K. Hey, and Patrick J. Haney. Englewood Cliffs, N.J.: Prentice-Hall, 1995.

Robinson, P. Stuart. *The Politics of International Crisis Escalation: Decision-Making Under Pressure*. London: Tauris Academic Studies, 1996.

Robinson, Thomas W. "China Confronts the Soviet Union," in *The Cambridge History of China*, ed. Roderick MacFarquhar and John K. Fairbanks. Vol. 15. Cambridge: Cambridge University Press, 1991.

———. "The Sino-Soviet Border Dispute: Background, Development, and the March 1969 Clashes." *American Political Science Review* 66, no. 4 (December 1972).

Rogers, J. Philip. "Crisis Bargaining Codes and Crisis Management," in *Avoiding War: Problems of Crisis Management*, ed. Alexander L. George. Boulder, Colo.: Westview, 1991.

Romberg, Alan. *Rein In at the Brink of the Precipice: American Policy Toward Taiwan and U.S.-PRC Relations*. Chapter 7. Washington D.C.: Henry L. Stimson Center, 2003.

Rosati, Jerel A. "Developing a Systematic Decision-Making Framework: Bureaucratic Politics in Perspective." *World Politics* 33 (January 1981): 234–251.

———. *The Politics of United States Foreign Policy*. Chinese translation. Fort Worth: Harcourt Brace Jovanovich, 1992; Beijing: Shijie Zhishi Chubanshe, 1997.

Rosenthal, Elisabeth. "Envoy Says Stoning Will End, Ties Won't." *New York Times*, May 11, 1999.

Ross, Robert S. "The 1996 Taiwan Strait Crisis: Lessons for the United States, China, and Taiwan." *Security Dialogue* 27, no. 4 (December 1996).

———. *The Indochina Tangle: China's Vietnam Policy, 1975–1979*. New York: Columbia University Press, 1988.

———. "Navigating the Taiwan Strait: Deterrence, Escalation Dominance, and U.S.-China Relations." *International Security* 27, no. 2 (Fall 2002).

———. *Negotiating Cooperation: The United States and China 1969–1989*. Stanford, Calif.: Stanford University Press, 1995.

———. "The Stability of Deterrence in the Taiwan Strait." *National Interest* (Fall 2001).

Rostow, Walt W. *A Diffusion of Power.* New York: Macmillan, 1972.

Roth, Alvin, ed. *Game-Theoretic Models of Bargaining.* New York: Cambridge University Press, 1985.

Roth, Stanley O. "The Effects on U.S.-China Relations of the Accidental Bombing of the Chinese Embassy in Belgrade." Testimony before the Senate Committee on Foreign Relations, Subcommittee on East Asian and Pacific Affairs. May 27, 1999. East Asian Studies News File, UCLA Center for East Asian Studies, Los Angeles, Calif. www.isop.ucla.edu/eas/NewsFile/Bombing05-99/990527-ussd2.htm.

Rothkopf, David. *Running the World: The Inside Story of the National Security Council and the Architects of American Power.* New York: PublicAffairs, 2005.

Rothman, Jay. *From Confrontation to Cooperation: Resolving Ethnic and Regional Conflict.* Newbury Park, Calif.: Sage Publications, 1992.

Rousseau, David, Christopher Gelpi, Dan Reiter, and Paul Huth. "Assessing the Dyadic Nature of the Democratic Peace, 1918–1988." *American Political Science Review* (1996).

Rubinstein, Alvin Z. *Red Star on the Nile: Soviet-Egyptian Influence Relationship Since the June War.* Princeton, N.J.: Princeton University Press, 1977.

Rupesinghe, Kumar. "Mediation in Internal Conflicts: Lessons from Sri Lanka," in *Resolving International Conflicts: The Theory and Practice of Mediation*, ed. Jacob Bercovitch. Boulder, Colo.: Lynne Rienner, 1996.

Rusk, Dean and Richard Rusk. *As I Saw It.* New York: Norton and Company, 1990.

Russett, Bruce. "The Calculus of Deterrence." *Journal of Conflict Resolution* 7, no. 2 (June 1963): 97–109.

———. "Pearl Harbor: Deterrence Theory and Decision Theory." *Journal of Peace Research* 4 (1967): 89–105.

Ryan, Marl. *Chinese Attitudes Toward Nuclear Weapons.* Armonk, N.Y.: M. E. Sharpe, 1989.

Sagan, Scott D. "The Commitment Trap: Why the United States Should Not Use Nuclear Threats to Deter Biological and Chemical Weapons Attacks." *International Security* 24, no. 4 (Spring 2000): 85–115.

———. "Nuclear Alerts and Crisis Management." *International Security* 9, no. 4 (Spring 1985): 99–139.

Samuelson, Louis J. *Soviet and Chinese Negotiating Behavior: The Western View.* Beverly Hills, Calif.: Sage, 1976.

Sander, Alfred Dick. *Eisenhower's Executive Office.* Chapter 4. Westport, Conn.: Greenwood Press, 1999.

Santmire, Tara E., Jonathan Wilkenfeld, Sarit Kraus, Kim M. Holley, Toni E. Santmire, and Kristian S. Gleditsch. "The Impact of Cognitive Diversity on Crisis Negotiations." *Political Psychology* 19, no. 4 (1998): 721–748.

Schelling, Thomas C. *Arms and Influence.* New Haven, Conn.: Yale University Press, 1967.

———. *The Strategy of Conflict.* Cambridge, Mass.: Harvard University Press, 1960.

Schilling, Warner R. "The H-Bomb Decision: How to Decide Without Actually Choosing." *Political Science Quarterly* 76 (March 1961): 24–46.

Schmitt, Eric. "In a Fatal Error, C.I.A. Picked a Bombing Target Only Once: The Chinese Embassy." *New York Times*, July 23, 1999.

Schrodt, Philip A., and Deborah J. Gerner. "Cluster Analysis as an Early Warning Technique for the Middle East, 1979–1996," in *Risk Assessment and Crisis Early Warning Systems,* ed. J. Davies and T. R. Gurr. New York: Rowman & Littlefield, 1998.

———. "Cluster-Based Early Warning Indicators for Political Change in the Contemporary Levant." *American Political Science Review* 94, no. 4 (2000): 803–817.

———. "Empirical Indicators of Crisis Phase in the Arab-Israeli Conflict, 1979–1995." *Journal of Conflict Resolution* 41, no. 4 (1997): 529–552.

Scobell, Andrew. *China and Strategic Culture.* Carlisle Barracks, Pa.: U.S. Army War College, 2002.

———. *China's Use of Military Force: Beyond the Great Wall and the Long March.* Cambridge: Cambridge University Press, 2003.

———. "Show of Force: Chinese Soldiers, Statesmen, and the 1995–1996 Taiwan Strait Crisis." *Political Science Quarterly* 115, no. 2 (Summer 2000).

Segal, Gerald. *Defending China.* Oxford: Oxford University Press, 1985.

Selected Works of Mao Tse-tung. Vol. 2. Beijing: Foreign Languages Press, 1975.

Selected Works of Mao Tse-tung. Vol. 5. Beijing: Foreign Languages Press, 1977.

Selected Works of Mao Tse-tung. Beijing: Renmin Publishing House, 1964.

Shambaugh, David. "Sino-American Relations Since September 11: Can the New Stability Last?" *Current History* 101, no. 656 (September 2002): 243–249.

Shen Weiping. *8-23 Paoji Jinmen* [Bombardment of Quemoy on August 23]. Vol. 1. Beijing: Huayi Chubanshe, 1998.

Shen, Simon. "Nationalism or Nationalist Foreign Policy? Contemporary Chinese Nationalism and Its Role in Shaping Chinese Foreign Policy in Response to the Belgrade Embassy Bombing." *Politics* 24, no. 2 (2004): 122–130.

Shen Zhihua, ed. *Chaoxian Zhanzheng: Eguo Dang'anguan.de Jiemi Wenjian* [Korean War: Released Files from Russian Archives]. Vol. 1. Institute of Modern History; Historical Materials Series no. 48. Taipei: Academia Sinica, n.d.

Shenon, Philip. "Chinese Embassy Bombing May Hurt Bid to Win Support for Peacekeepers." *New York Times*, May 7, 1999.

Shi Yukun. "Lt. Gen. Li Jijun Answers Questions on Nuclear Deterrence, Nation-State, and Information Age." *Zhongguo Junshi Kexue*, no. 3 (August 20, 1995). Quoted in *Foreign Broadcast Information Service—China*, August 20, 1995.

Shi Zhongquan. *Zhou Enlai.de Zhuoyue Gongxian* [Outstanding Contribution by Zhou Enlai]. Beijing: Zhonggong Zhongyang Dangxiao Chubanshe, 1993.

Shimada, Masao. *Zhanhou Rizhong Guanxi Wushi Nian, 1945–1994* [50 Years of Postwar Japan-China Relations, 1945–1994]. In translation. Nanchang: Jiangxi Jiaoyu Chubanshe, 1998.

Shlaim, Avi, and Richard Tanter. "Decision Process, Choice, and Consequences." *World Politics* 30 (1978): 483–516.

Shmueli, Deborah, and Ariella Vranesky. "Environmental Mediation in International Relations," in *Resolving International Conflicts: The Theory and Practice of Mediation*, ed. Jacob Bercovitch. Boulder, Colo.: Lynne Rienner, 1996.

Shubik, Martin. "Models of Strategic Behavior and Nuclear Deterrence," in *Behavior, Society, and Nuclear War*, ed. Philip E. Tetlock, Jo L. Husbands, Robert Jervis, Paul C. Stern, and Charles Tilly. New York: Oxford University Press, 1993.

Shulsky, Abram N. *Deterrence Theory and Chinese Behavior*. Santa Monica, Calif.: RAND, 2000.

Simmel, George. *Conflict*. Translated by K. H. Wolff. Glencoe, Ill.: Free Press, 1955.

Simon, H. A. *Administrative Behavior*. 2nd ed. New York: Free Press, 1957.

Sinha, Radha. *Sino-American Relations: Mutual Paranoia*. New York: Palgrave MacMillan, 2003.

Snyder, Glenn H. *Deterrence and Defense*. Princeton, N.J.: Princeton University Press, 1961.

Snyder, Glenn H., and Paul Diesing. *Conflict Among Nations: Bargaining, Decision-Making, and System Structure In International Crises*. Princeton, N.J.: Princeton University Press, 1977.

Snyder, Richard C., H. W. Bruck, and Burton Sapin. "Decision-Making as an Approach to the Study of International Politics," in *Foreign Policy Decision-Making: An Approach to the Study of International Politics*, ed. R. Snyder, H. Bruck, and B. Sapin. New York: Free Press, 1962.

Snyder, Richard C., H. W. Bruck, and Burton Sapin, eds. *Foreign Policy Decision-Making: An Approach to the Study of International Politics.* New York: Free Press, 1962.

Sobel, Richard. *The Impact of Public Opinion on U.S. Foreign Policy Since Vietnam: Constraining the Colossus.* New York: Oxford University Press, 2001.

Solomon, Richard H. *Chinese Negotiating Behavior: Pursuing Interests Through "Old Friends."* Washington, D.C.: U.S. Institute of Peace, 1999.

South Korean Ministry of Defense War History Compilation Committee. *Chaoxian Zhanzheng* [Korean War]. Vol. 1. Heilongjiang: Heilongjiang Ethnicity Publishing House, 1988.

Spaic, Nebojsa. "Belgrade to Beijing: A Trump Card in Chinese Political Strategy." *Harvard Asia Pacific Review* (Summer 2000). http://hcs.harvard.edu/~hapr/summer00_tech/belgrade.html.

Stein, Janice Gross. "Beyond Rational Deterrence." *World Politics* 28, no. 4 (July 1976): 223–245.

———. "Calculation, Miscalculation, and Conventional Deterrence," in *Psychology and Deterrence,* ed. Robert Jervis, Richard Ned Lebow, and Janice Gross Stein. Baltimore, Md.: Johns Hopkins University Press, 1985.

———. "Deterrence and Reassurance," in *Behavior, Society, and Nuclear War,* ed. Philip E. Tetlock, Jo L. Husbands, Robert Jervis, Paul C. Stern, and Charles Tilly. Vol. 2. Oxford: Oxford University Press, 1991.

Steinbruner, John D. *The Cybernetic Theory of Decision.* Princeton, N.J.: Princeton University Press, 1974.

Stern, Paul C., Robert Axelrod, Robert Jervis, and Roy Radner. "Deterrence in the Nuclear Age: The Search for Evidence," in *Perspectives on Deterrence,* ed. Paul C. Stern, Robert Axelrod, Robert Jervis, and Roy Radner. New York: Oxford University Press, 1989.

Stern, Paul C., and Daniel Druckman. "Evaluating Interventions in History: The Case of International Conflict Resolution." *International Studies Review* 2, no. 1 (2000): 33–63.

Stolper, Thomas E. *China, Taiwan, and the Offshore Islands: Together with an Implication for Outer Mongolia and Sino-Soviet Relations.* Armonk, N.Y.: M. E. Sharpe, Inc., 1985.

Stueck, William. *The Korean War: An International History.* Princeton, N.J.: Princeton University Press, 1995.

Su Ge. *Meiguo DuiHua Zhengce Yu Taiwan Wenti* [U.S. Policy Toward China and the Taiwan Question]. Beijing: Shijie Zhishi Chubanshe, 1998.

Suettinger, Robert L. *Beyond Tiananmen: The Politics of U.S.-China Relations, 1989–2000.* Washington, D.C.: Brookings Institution Press, 2003.

Sun Baosheng. "Mao Zedong Cengjing Yuyan Meijun Keneng zai Renchuan Denglu" [Mao Tse-tung Predicted That the U.S. Army Might Land in Incheon]. *Junshi Shilin* [Military History Facts], no. 5 (1990).

Sun Zi'an. "Strategies to Minimize High-Tech Edge of Enemy." *Xiandai Bingqi,* no. 8, August 8, 1995. Quoted in *Foreign Broadcast Information Service—China,* March 6, 1996.

Susskind, Lawrence, and Eileen Babbitt. "Overcoming the Obstacles to Effective Mediation of International Disputes," in *Mediation in International Relations: Multiple Approaches to Conflict Management,* ed. Jacob Bercovitch and Jeffrey Z. Rubin. New York: St. Martin's Press, 1992.

Sutter, Robert G. "The Taiwan Crisis of 1995–96 and U.S. Domestic Politics," in *Missile Diplomacy and Taiwan's Future: Innovations in Politics and Military Power,* ed. Greg Austin. Canberra: Australian National University, 1997.

Swaine, Michael D. "China's Nuclear Weapons and Grand Strategy: A Detailed Outline." Paper presented at conference, "Tracking the Dragon: National Intelligence Estimates on China During the Era of Mao, 1948–1976," organized by the National Intelligence Council; the Woodrow Wilson International Center for Scholars; and the Bureau of Intelligence and Research, Department of State (Washington, D.C., October 18, 2004).

———. "Chinese Crisis Management: Framework for Analysis, Tentative Observations, and Questions for the Future," in *Chinese National Security Decisionmaking Under Stress,* ed. Andrew Scobell and Larry M. Wortzel. Carlisle, Pa.: U.S. Army War College, 2005.

———. "Chinese Decision–Making Regarding Taiwan, 1979–2000," in *The Making of Chinese Foreign and Security Policy in the Era of Reform,* ed. David M. Lampton. Stanford, Calif.: Stanford University Press, 2001.

———. "Exploiting a Strategic Opening," in *Strategic Asia 2004–05: Confronting Terrorism in the Pursuit of Power,* ed. Ashley J. Tellis and Michael Wills. Seattle: National Bureau of Asian Research, 2004.

Swaine, Michael D., and Ashley J. Tellis. *Interpreting China's Grand Strategy: Past, Present, and Future.* Santa Monica, Calif.: RAND, 2000.

Sweeney, John, Jens Holsoe, and Ed Vulliamy. "NATO Bombed Chinese Deliberately." *The Observer,* October 17, 1999.

Sylvan, D. A., and D. M. Haddad. "Reasoning and Problem Representation in Foreign Policy: Groups, Individuals, and Stories," in *Problem Representation in Foreign Policy Decision Making,* ed. D. A. Sylvan and J. F. Voss. Cambridge: Cambridge University Press, 1998.

Sylvan, Donald A., Ashok Goel, and B. Chandrasekarin. "Analyzing Political Decision Making from an Information-Processing Perspective: JESSE." *American Journal of Political Science* 34 (1990): 74–123.

Taiwan Affairs Office of the State Council. "Yi.ge Zhongguo.de Yuanze yu Taiwan Wenti" [The One-China Principle and the Taiwan Question]. White Papers on the Taiwan Issue. February 2000. www.gwytb.gov.cn:8088/detail.asp?table=WhitePaper&title= White %20Papers%20On%20Taiwan%20Issue&m_id=4.

Taiwan Relations Act. Public Law 96-8. 96th Cong. April 10, 1979. http:// usinfo.state.gov/eap/Archive_Index/Taiwan_Relations_Act.html.

Tang Guanghui. "An Analysis of Post–Cold War Security." Shijie Zhishi, no. 19 (October 1, 1996).

Tang Tsou and Morton Halperin. "Mao Tse-tung's Revolutionary Strategy and Peking's International Behavior." American Political Science Review 59, no. 1 (March 1965).

Taylor, Stan A., and Theodore J. Ralston. "The Role of Intelligence in Crisis Management," in Avoiding War: Problems of Crisis Management, ed. Alexander L. George. Oxford: Westview Press, 1991.

Thomson, James C. "On the Making of U.S. China Policy, 1961–1969: A Study in Bureaucratic Politics." China Quarterly 50 (April–June 1973): 220–243.

Tong Xiaopeng. Fengyu Sishinian [Four Decades: Trials and Hardships]. Vol. 2. Beijing: Zhongyang Wenxian Chubanshe, 1996.

Truman, Harry S. Memoirs by Harry S. Truman: Years of Trial and Hope. Vol. 2. New York: Doubleday & Co., 1956.

Trumbore, Peter F., and Mark A. Boyer. "Two-Level Negotiations in International Crisis: Testing the Impact of Regime Type and Issue Area." Journal of Peace Research 37, no. 6 (2000): 679–698.

Tyler, Patrick. A Great Wall, Six Presidents and China—An Investigative History. New York: Public Affairs, 1999.

U.S. Department of Defense. The Joint Chiefs of Staff and the War in Vietnam, 1960–1968. Part 1, especially chap. 13. Washington, D.C.: Department of Defense, n.d.

U.S. Department of State. "Ambassador Preuher; On-the-Record Press Conference." April 2, 2001. www.usconsulate.org.hk/uscn/usemb/2001/ 040201.htm.

———. American Foreign Policy: Basic Documents 1950–1953. Washington, D.C.: U.S. Government Printing Office, 1957.

———. Foreign Relations of the United States, 1950. Vol. 7 (Korea). Washington, D.C.: U.S. Government Printing Office, 1976.

———. Foreign Relations of the United States, 1952–1954. Vol. 14 (China and Japan). Washington, D.C.: U.S. Government Printing Office, 1985.

―――. *Foreign Relations of the United States, 1955–1957.* Vol. 2 (China). Washington, D.C.: U.S. Government Printing Office, 1986.

―――. "Letter to Minister of Foreign Affairs of the People's Republic of China from U.S. Secretary of State." May 8, 1999. East Asian Studies News File, UCLA Center for East Asian Studies. www.isop.ucla.edu/eas/NewsFile/Bombing05-99/990508-ussd1.htm.

―――. "Text: CIA Director Tenet on Accidental Bombing of China Embassy." Joint Statement. May 8, 1999. http://hongkong.usconsulate.gov/uscn/others/1999/0722d.htm.

U.S. Department of State, Office of International Information Programs. "Excerpt: Secretary of State Powell Expresses Regret Over Loss of Chinese Pilot." April 4, 2001. http://lists.state.gov/SCRIPTS/WA-U.S.IAINFO.EXE?A2=ind0104a&L=us-china&D=1&H=1&O=D&F=&S=&P=2987.

U.S. Department of State, Office of the Historian. "History of the National Security Council, 1947–1997." August 1997. www.whitehouse.gov/nsc/history.html.

U.S. Department of State, Office of the Spokesman. "Foreign Relations of the United States: Summaries of FRUS Volumes: Foreign Relations of the United States 1958–60, Volume 19 China. August 12, 1996." http://dosfan.lib.uic.edu/ERC/frus/summaries/960812_FRUS_XIX_1958-60.html.

―――. "Oral Presentation by Under Secretary of State Thomas Pickering on June 17 to the Chinese Government Regarding the Accidental Bombing of the PRC Embassy in Belgrade." July 6, 1999. http://hongkong.usconsulate.gov/uscn/state/1999/0706.htm.

U.S. Pacific Command. "United States Pacific Command, Transcript; Admiral Dennis C. Blair; Commander in Chief, Pacific Command; U.S. and Chinese Aircraft Incident; Sunday, April 1, 2001; Camp H. M. Smith, Hawaii." www.pacom.mil/speeches/sst2001/010401blairplane.htm.

―――. "U.S. Pacific Command Imagery Archive; 2001 Links; March 2001 Page 4." www.pacom.mil/imagery/archive/0103photos/index4.shtml.

Valenti, Jack. *A Very Human President.* New York: Norton and Company, 1975.

Vasquez, John A. "The Learning of Peace: Lessons from a Multidisciplinary Inquiry," in *Beyond Confrontation: Learning Conflict Resolution in the Post–Cold War Era*, ed. John A. Vasquez, et al. Ann Arbor: The University of Michigan Press, 1995.

Vertzberger, Yaakov Y. I. "Foreign Policy Decision Makers as Practical Intuitive Historian: Applied History and Its Shortcomings." *International Studies Quarterly* 30, no. 2 (1986): 223–247.

——. *The World in Their Minds: Information Processing, Cognition, and Perception in Foreign Policy Decision Making.* Stanford, Calif.: Stanford University Press, 1990.

Wagner, R. Harrison. "Bargaining and War." Paper presented at "Conference on War," Washington University (St. Louis, Mo., May 3–5, 1996).

——. "Deterrence and Bargaining." *Journal of Conflict Resolution* 26, no. 2 (June 1982): 329–358.

——. "Rationality and Misperception in Deterrence Theory." *Journal of Theoretical Politics* 42, no. 2 (1992): 115–141.

——. "Uncertainty, Rational Learning, and Bargaining in the Cuban Missile Crisis," in *Models of Strategic Choice in Politics,* ed. Peter C. Ordeshook. Ann Arbor: University of Michigan Press, 1989.

Walker, Stephen G., and George L. Watson. "The Motivational Imagery and Cognitive Complexity of British Foreign Policy Leaders." Paper presented at International Studies Association (ISA) annual convention (Vancouver, March 1991).

Wallace, Michael D., and Kimberley L. Thachuk. "Information Processing Among Leaders Undress Stress: Some (Very!) Preliminary Findings from the Gulf Crisis." Paper presented at the International Studies Association (ISA) annual convention (Vancouver, March 1991).

Waltz, Kenneth. *Theory of International Politics.* Reading, Mass.: Addison-Wesley Publishing Company, 1979.

Wang Chang. *Zhongguo Gaoceng Moulüe: Waijiaojuan* [The Strategic Planning of China's Supreme Leaders: Diplomatic Aspects]. Xi'an: Shaanxi Shifan Daxue Chubanshe, 2001.

Wang Chunyin. "Characteristics of Strategic Initiative in High-Tech Local Wars." *Hsien-Tai Chun-Shih,* no. 245, June 11, 1997. Quoted in *Foreign Broadcast Information Service—China,* October 30, 1997.

Wang Dinglie, ed. *Dangdai Zhongguo Kongjun* [Modern China Air Force]. Beijing: Zhongguo Shehui Kexue Chubanshe, 1989.

Wang Dong. "Chaoyue Guojia Liyi" [Beyond National Interests]. *Meiguo Yanjiu* [American Studies] 15, no. 3 (2001).

Wang Jisi. "China's Changing Role in Asia." Occasional Paper. Atlantic Council of the United States. January 2004. www.acus.org/docs/0401-China_Changing_Role_Asia.pdf.

Wang Shangrong Jiangjun [General Wang Shangrong]. Beijing: Dangdai Zhongguo Chubanshe, 2000.

Wang Xiaode. *Meiguo Wenhua yu Waijiao* [U.S. Culture and Foreign Policy]. Beijing: Shijie Zhishi Chubanshe, 2000.

Wang Yan, ed. *Peng Dehuai Nianpu.* Beijing: Renmin Chubanshe, 1998.

Wang Zuxun. "Ke Suo Wo Zhanzheng Dui Guoji Anquan Xingshi.de Yingxiang" [Impacts of the Kosovo War on International Security Situation]. *Liao Wang,* no. 20 (1999).

Wasserstrom, Jeffrey N. "The Year of Living Anxiously: China's 1999." *Dissent* 47, no. 2 (Spring 2000): 17–22.

Wei Shiyan. "Nikesong Fanghua" [Nixon's Visit to China], in *XinZhongguo Waijiao Fengyun* [Diplomacy of New China]. Vol. 3. Beijing, Shijie Zhishi Chubanshe, 1991.

Weitz, Richard. "Why Russia and China Have Not Formed an Anti-American Alliance." *Naval War College Review* 56, no. 4 (Autumn 2003): 39–61.

White House, National Security Council. *National Security Strategy of the United States of America.* September 17, 2002. http://www.whitehouse.gov/nsc/nss.pdf.

White House, Office of the Press Secretary. "Letter from Ambassador Prueher to Chinese Minister of Foreign Affairs Tang." April 11, 2001. www.whitehouse.gov/news/releases/2001/04/print/20010411-1.html.

———. "President Bush Delivers Graduation Speech at West Point." June 1, 2002. www.whitehouse.gov/news/releases/2002/06/20020601-3.html.

———. "Remarks by the President at American Society of Newspaper Editors Annual Convention." April 5, 2001. www.whitehouse.gov/news/releases/2001/04/20010405-5.html.

———. "Remarks by the President on Release of American Servicemen and Women in China." April 11, 2001. www.whitehouse.gov/news/releases/2001/04/20010411-3.html.

———. "Remarks by the President Upon the Return From China of U.S. Service Members." April 12, 2001. www.whitehouse.gov/news/releases/2001/04/20010412-6.html.

———. "Statement by the President." April 3, 2001. www.whitehouse.gov/news/releases/2001/04/20010403-3.html.

———. "Statement by the President on American Plane and Crew in China." April 2, 2001. www.whitehouse.gov/news/releases/2001/04/20010402-2.html.

Whiting, Allen S. *China Crosses the Yalu: The Decision to Enter the Korean War.* New York: Macmillan, 1960.

———. "China's Use of Force, 1950–1996, and Taiwan." *International Security* 26, no. 2 (Fall 2001).

———. *The Chinese Calculus of Deterrence: India and Indochina.* Chapter 6. Ann Arbor: University of Michigan, Center for Chinese Studies, 2001.

————. "The Use of Force in Foreign Policy by the People's Republic of China." *Annals of the American Academy of Political and Social Science,* 402 (July 1972).

Whitney, Courtney. *MacArthur: His Rendezvous With History.* New York: Alfred A. Knopf, 1956.

Wilhelm, Alfred D., Jr. *The Chinese at the Negotiating Table.* Washington, D.C.: National Defense University Press, 1994.

————. "Sino-American Negotiations: The Chinese Approach." PhD diss., UMI Dissertation Service, 1987.

Wilkenfeld, Jonathan. "Concepts and Methods in the Study of International Crises." Paper, University of Maryland, February 2004.

————. "A Time-Series Perspective on Conflict in the Middle East," in *Sage International Yearbook of Foreign Policy Studies,* ed. P. McGowan. Los Angeles: Sage Publications, 1975.

————. "Trigger-Response Transitions in Foreign Policy Crises, 1929–1985." *Journal of Conflict Resolution* 35, no. 1 (1991): 143–169.

Wilkenfeld, Jonathan, Michael Brecher, and Sheila Moser. *Crises in the Twentieth Century: Handbook of Foreign Policy Crises.* Oxford: Pergamon, 1988.

Wilkenfeld, Jonathan, Virginia Lussier, and Dale Tahtinen. "Conflict Interactions in the Middle East, 1949–1967." *Journal of Conflict Resolution* (1972).

Wilkenfeld, Jonathan, Kathleen Young, Victor Asal, and David Quinn. "Mediating International Crises: Cross-National and Experimental Perspectives." *Journal of Conflict Resolution* 47, no. 3 (September 2003): 279–301.

Wilkenfeld, Jonathan, Kathleen Young, David Quinn, and Victor Asal. *Mediating International Crises.* Oxford: Routledge, 2005.

Williams, Phil. *Crisis Management: Confrontation and Diplomacy in the Nuclear Age.* London: Martin Robertson & Co. Ltd., 1976.

Wilson, Robert. "Reputations in Games and Markets," in *Game-Theoretic Models of Bargaining,* ed. Alvin Roth. New York: Cambridge University Press, 1985.

Winter, D. G., and A. J. Stewart. "Content Analysis as a Technique for Assessing Political Leaders," in *A Psychological Examination of Political Leaders,* ed. M. G. Hermann. New York: Free Press, 1977.

Wong, John, and Zheng Yongnian. "Nationalism and Its Dilemma: Chinese Responses to the Embassy Bombing," in *Reform, Legitimacy and Dilemmas: China's Politics and Society,* ed. Wang Gungwu and Zheng Yongnian. Singapore: Singapore University Press, 2000.

Wu Lengxi. *Yi Maozhuxi—Wo Qinshen Jingli.de Ruogan Zhongda Lishi Shijian Pianduan* [Memory of Chairman Mao: Some Important Historical Incidents of Which I Have First-Hand Knowledge]. Beijing: Xinhua Chubanshe, 1995.

Wu, Samuel S. G. "To Attack or Not to Attack." *Journal of Conflict Resolution* 34, no. 3 (September 1990): 531–552.

Xia Liping. "Theory and Practice of Crisis Management in the United States—Sino-U.S. Relations as an Example." *Beijing Meiguo Yanjiu* 17, no. 2 (June 2003).

Xie Chengwen, Huang Zhengji, and Zhang Changyi. *San Da Tupo* [Three Major Breakthroughs]. Beijing: Jiefangjun Chubanshe, 1994.

Xie Yixian. *Zhongguo Dangdai Waijiaoshi 1949–1955* [The History of Contemporary Diplomatic Relations of China: 1949–1995]. Beijing: Zhongguo Qingnian Chubanshe, 1997.

Xu Yan. *Jinmen zhi Zhan* [War Over Quemoy]. n.p.: Zhongguo Guangbodianshi Chubanshe, 1992.

Yan Youqiang and Chen Rongxing. "On Maritime Strategy and the Marine Environment." *Zhongguo Junshi Kexue*, no. 2 (May 20, 1997). Quoted in *Foreign Broadcast Information Service—China,* October 14, 1997.

Yang Dezhi. "A Strategic Decision on Strengthening the Building of Our Army in the New Period." *Hongqi,* no. 15, August 1, 1985. Quoted in *Foreign Broadcast Information Service—China,* August 8, 1985.

Yang Jiemian. *Houlengzhan Shiqi.de ZhongMei Guanxi: Waijiao Zhengce Bijiao Yanjiu* [Sino-U.S. Relations during the Post–Cold War Period: A Foreign Policy Comparison]. Shanghai: Shanghai Renmin Chubanshe, 2000.

Yang Kai-Huang. "Zhonggong Dui Beiyue 'Hongzha Shiguan Shijian' Fanying.zhi Yanxi" [Analysis of the CCP's Response to the Embassy Bombing]. Chinabiz.org, 1999.

Yin Qiming and Cheng Guangya. *Diyi Ren Guofangbuzhang* [The First Minister of Defense]. Guangzhou: Guandong Jiaoyu Chubanshe, 1997.

Young, H. Peyton, ed. *Negotiation Analysis.* Ann Arbor: The University of Michigan Press, 1991.

Young, Kenneth T. *Negotiating with the Chinese Communists: The United States Experience, 1953–1967.* New York: McGraw-Hill Book Co., 1968.

Young, Oran R. *Bargaining: Formal Theories of Negotiation.* Urbana: University of Illinois Press, 1975.

———. *The Intermediaries: Third Parties in International Crises.* Princeton, N.J.: Princeton University Press, 1967.

———. *The Politics of Force: Bargaining During International Crises.* Princeton, N.J.: Princeton University Press, 1968.

Yu Bin. "NATO's Unintended Consequence: A Deeper Strategic Partnership . . . Or More." *Comparative Connections: An E-Journal on East Asian Bilateral Relations* 1, no. 1 (July 1999). http://www.ciaonet.org/olj/cpc/cpc_jul99.pdf.

Yu Guohua. "On Turning Strong Force Into Weak and Vice-Versa in a High-Tech Local War." *Zhongguo Junshi Kexue,* no. 2 (May 20, 1996). Quoted in *Foreign Broadcast Information Service—China,* May 20, 1996.

Zagare, Frank C. "Classical Deterrence Theory: A Critical Assessment." *International Interactions* 21, no. 4 (October/December 1996): 365–387.

———. "Rationality and Deterrence." *World Politics* 42, no. 2 (January 1990): 238–260.

Zartman, I. William. "Alternative Attempts at Crisis Management: Concepts and Processes," in *New Issues in International Crisis Management,* ed. Gilbert R. Winham. Boulder, Colo.: Westview, 1988.

———. "Toward the Resolution of International Conflicts," in *Peacemaking in International Conflict: Methods and Techniques,* ed. I. William Zartman and J. Lewis Rasmussen. Washington, D.C.: United States Institute of Peace Press, 1997.

Zegart, Amy B. *Flawed by Design: The Evolution of the CIA, JCS, and NSC.* Chapters 4 and 5. Palo Alto, Calif.: Stanford University Press, 1999.

Zhang Baijia. "Tongxiang Huanhe.de Qiqu Zhilu: Biandong.de Guojia Huanjing yu Zhongguo duiMei Zhongce 1954–1971" [The Rugged Path Toward Relaxation: The Changing International Environment and Chinese Policy Toward the United States 1954–1971], in *Cong Duizhi Zhouxiang Huanhe: Lengzhan Shiqi ZhongMei Guanxi Zai Shentao* [From Confrontation to Relaxation: China-U.S. Relations in the Cold War Era]. Beijing: Shijie Zhishi Chubanshe, 2000.

Zhang Baijia and Jia Qingguo. *Duikangzhong.de Fanxiangnan, Huanchongqi he Ceshiyi: Cong Zhongguo.de Jiaodu Kan ZhongMei Dashiji Huitan* [The Steering Wheel, Bumper, and Detector in Confrontation: China-U.S. Meetings at the Ambassadorial Level From a Chinese Perspective]. Beijing: Dangdai Zhongguoshi Yanjiu, 2000.

Zhang Shu Guang. *Deterrence and Strategic Culture: Chinese-American Confrontations, 1949–1958.* Ithaca, N.Y.: Cornell University Press, 1993.

———. *Mao's Military Romanticism: China and the Korean War, 1950–1953.* Lawrence: University Press of Kansas, 1995.

Zhang Tuosheng. "Lishi.de Huigu yu Qishi-ZhongRi Guanxi (1972–1992)" [Review and Rethinking of Sino-Japanese Relations, 1972–1992]. *Taipingyang Xuebao* [Journal of Asia-Pacific Studies], no. 3 (1999).

Zhang Wentian Nianpu [Chronicle of Zhang Wentian]. Vol. 2. Beijing: Zhonggongdangshi Chubanshe, 2000.

Zhang Zhaozhong. "Beiyue.de Xiayibu" [Next Step For NATO]. *Nanfang Zhoumo* [South Daily Weekend], April 16, 1999.

Zhao Suisheng, ed. *Across the Taiwan Strait: Mainland China, Taiwan, and 1995–1996 Crisis.* New York: Routledge, 1999.

———. "Chinese Nationalism and Its Foreign Policy Ramifications," in *U.S.-China Relations in the 21st Century: Policies, Prospects, Possibilities,* ed. Christopher Marsh and June Dreyer. New York: Lexington Books, 2003.

Zhao Xuegong. "Dierci Taiwan Haixia Weiji yu ZhongMei Guanxi" [The Second Taiwan Strait Crisis and Sino-U.S. Relations]. *Dangdai Zhongguoshi Yanjiu* [Current Chinese History Studies], no. 3 (2003).

Zheng Shenxia and Zhang Changzhi. "Air Power as Centerpiece of Modern Strategy," Zhongguo Junshi Kexue, no. 2 (May 20, 1996). Quoted in *Foreign Broadcast Information Service—China,* May 20, 1996.

Zheng Wenhan. *Mishu Rijili.de Peng Laozong* [Commander in Chief Peng in His Secretary's Diaries]. Beijing: Junshi Kexue Chubanshe, 1998.

Zhongguo Gongchandang Zhangcheng [Constitution of the Chinese Communist Party]. Beijing: Renmin Chubanshe, 2002.

ZhongMei Guanxi Ziliao Huibian [Compilation of Documents on Sino-U.S. Relations]. Vol. 2. Beijing: Shijie Zhishi Chubanshe, 1958–1960.

Zhou Enlai Junshi Huodong Jiyao [Summary of Zhou Enlai's Military Activities]. Vol. 2. Beijing: Zhongyang Wenxian Chubanshe, 2000.

Zi Zhongyun. "Weile Minzu.de Zuigao Liyi, Weile Renmin.de Changyuan Liyi" [In the Supreme National Interests and in the Long-term Interests of People]. *Taipingyang Xuebao* [Journal of Asia-Pacific Studies], no. 4 (1999).

Zinnes, Dina A., and Jonathan Wilkenfeld. "An Analysis Of Foreign Conflict Behavior of Nations," in *Comparative Foreign Policy: Theoretical Essays,* ed. W. F. Hanrieder. New York: McKay, 1971.

Zong He. "Tentative Discussion on the Characteristics of Modern Warfare." *Shijie Zhishi,* no. 15 (August 1, 1983). Quoted in *Joint Publications Research Service,* October 11, 1983.

Index

Accidental events, and crises, 420.
    See also Chinese embassy
    bombing (Chinese view);
    Chinese embassy bombing (U.S.
    view); EP-3 aircraft incident
    (2001)
Accinelli, Robert, 267
Accommodationist strategies, 9
Acheson, Dean: on credibility of
    Indian ambassador, 33; criticism
    of, 261; Eisenhower and, 274;
    MacArthur and, 136, 228, 244;
    pressure from McCarthy and the
    media, 46; views on Chinese
    involvement in Korea, 154, 218,
    229–230
Actions, and unintended
    consequences, 8, 436
Afghanistan, 103, 110
Afghanistan-Pakistan crisis, 105
Africa, percent of crises, 108
Agence France-Presse (AFP), 355
Aggregate cross-national studies,
    125
Air-collision incident. *See* EP-3
    aircraft incident (2001)

Albright, Madeleine K., 34, 279,
    333, 337, 358, 361
Allies, relationships with, 169–170
Al Qaeda, 110
Alsop, Joseph, 274
Ambiguity, 173–174, 284
Americas, percent of crises, 108
Anderson, Dillon, 273
Anticommunism, 252, 268
Antiterrorism, 167
Approved JCS Rules of
    Engagement, Southeast Asia, 238
Arab-Israel protracted conflicts, 109
Arbitration, 116
Armitage, Richard, 383–384
Arms reductions, 116
Asia: international crises in, 105;
    percent of crises, 108. *See also*
    specific country or crisis
Asia-Pacific Economic Cooperation
    summit, 342
Assistant to President for National
    Security Affairs (APNSA), 262–
    263
Association of Southeast Asian
    Nations, 141

Asymmetry of interests, 77, 138, 165
Asymmetry of power, 138
Atlantic Alliance, 335
Atomic diplomacy, 257
Axelrod, Robert, 72

B

Baker, James, 399
Ball, George, 233, 239–240
Bargaining strategies, 4, 123
Beam, Joseph, 270
Beijing conference (2004), 13, 26, 34, 45, 77, 80, 81, 84, 87
Belgrade, Chinese embassy bombing. *See* Chinese embassy bombing (Chinese view); Chinese embassy bombing (U.S. view)
Bell, Coral, 163
Ben-Yehuda, Hemda, 115
Bercovitch, Jacob, 117
Berger, Samuel R. "Sandy," 96, 278, 279, 281, 282, 283
Bipolarity, 106, 107, 109
Bird, Kai, 247
Blair, Dennis C., 47, 381, 389, 420
Bobrow, David B., 113–114
Bradley, Omar, 143, 223, 228, 229, 230
Brecher, Michael, 104, 120, 127, 138
Brinkmanship, 158
Brzezinski, Zbigniew, 164–165
Bubiyan, 128
Bundy, McGeorge, 165, 233, 234, 236, 237, 239–240
Bundy, William P., 233, 237, 239–240, 242

Bureaucratic politics model, 92
Burke, Arleigh, 269, 272
Bush, George H.W., 94, 279, 399
Bush, George W. and administration of: antiterrorism priority, 167; EP-3 aircraft incident and, 381, 390, 394, 396, 399, 402, 405–406, 411; National Security Council and, 95; policy changes, 391–392; preemption doctrine, 114; rejection of Clinton policies, 414, 421; resumption of normal relations with China, 409; Taiwan and, 169, 419; West Point commencement speech, 152–153

C

Cable News Network (CNN), 355
Campbell, Kurt, 45, 56–57, 62, 85, 342
Capitalist liberalization ideology, 362–363
Carney, Robert B., 258, 272
"Carrots and sticks" policy, 79, 155
Carter, Jimmy, 94, 382
CCP Department of Propaganda, 360, 364, 374
Cease-fires, and conflict resolution, 131
Cell phones, 44
Central Intelligence Agency (CIA): Chinese embassy bombing and, 327, 342, 370; in Eisenhower years, 264; Korean War and, 223
Central Military Commission, 297
C4ISR assets, 442
Chan, Steven, 113–114

Chechen separatists, 334
Cheney, Richard, 392, 406
Chen Shui-bian, 167, 286, 343
Chen Yi, 200, 235
Chiang Kai-shek: support from "China lobby," 46; Taiwan Strait crisis 1954-55, 254, 257, 266–267; Taiwan Strait crisis 1958, 268–269, 271–272, 275
Chi Haotian, 388
China: anti-American sentiment in, 90; assistance to Arab national liberation movements, 311; characterizations of U.S. as enemy, 77; core interests of, 12–13, 75; crisis decision making, 48–49, 300–308; crisis management during Korean War, 179–189; crisis management during Vietnam War, 195–206; crisis management education, 145; current leadership, 441–442; dispute behavior during Cold War, 79; economic development and international environment, 45; foreign investment in economy of, 330; involvement in international crises, 111–112; leadership of, 159; national development strategy, 167; nuclear threats against, 31, 84; nuclear weapons and, 78, 165–166; one-China principle, 74; opposition to military treaty between U.S. and Taiwan, 302–303; organizational and procedural context, 50–51; "peaceful reunification" strategy, 299, 316, 317; political education in, 135; reciprocal approach to U.S. behavior, 82; reunification strategy, 294, 295–300; Russia and, 333–335; sanctions against, 306; security situation during early days of PRC, 180–181; self-image and motives, 12–15; strategic cultures of, 147–148; territorial crises post-1949, 12–13; use of outside experts in large policy issues, 374. *See also* Chinese Communist Party; Chinese embassy bombing (Chinese view); Chinese embassy bombing (U.S. view); Korean War; Taiwan Strait crises; Vietnam War
China Institute of International Studies, 374
China lobby, 46, 265
China Rear Service Units, 204
China Volunteer Engineering Brigade, 204
Chinese Academy of Social Sciences, 374
Chinese Communist Party: Central Military Commission, 42; Constitution and party organization, 177; crisis awareness, 139–140; decision-making within, 93, 159; and founding of People's Republic of China, 180; liberation of Taiwan vision, 296; view of U.S. as predator, 135
Chinese embassy bombing (Chinese view), 351–370; academic debates, 364–365; assessment/ summary, 368–370; calming/

resolving the crisis, 366–368; compensation for losses by U.S., 370; confidentiality, 367–368; control over policy statements, 367; crisis and reaction, 351–354; decision-making processes, 354–361; disconnecting crisis events, 368; domestic political factors, 361–366; feedback, 360–361; foreign policy objectives, 368; intelligence, availability and analysis of, 60, 354–355; international politics/diplomatic interaction, 357–359; media and, 363–364, 373–374; public opinion and protests, 45, 91, 352, 361–363, 365–366; regrets sent by U.S., 34, 162, 358, 361, 372; third party involvement, 137. *See also* Chinese embassy bombing (U.S. view)

Chinese embassy bombing (U.S. view), 327–349; dénouement, 341–344; reaction abroad, 332–335; reaction in China, 328–332; regrets sent to China, 337; response in U.S. to, 335–341; rumors of deliberate nature of, 343, 349. *See also* Chinese embassy bombing (Chinese view)

Chinese Ministry of Foreign Affairs (MFA), 332

Chou En-lai, 173, 267

Christopher, Warren: Lee Teng-hui visit and, 141–142, 277, 307; personality and relationship with Clinton, 100, 280; Taiwan Strait crisis and, 96, 283

Churchill, Winston, 266

CIA. *See* Central Intelligence Agency (CIA)

Civilian control, in crisis management, 5–6

Civil-military interactions, 449

"Class struggle," 144

Clear decision-making procedures, 375

Clinton, William "Bill" and administration of: Chinese embassy bombing and, 332, 336, 338, 341–342, 353–354, 358, 360–361, 367; crisis decision making, 56–57, 95; foreign policy and, 279–280; Lee Teng-hui and, 141, 307, 315; military actions against Yugoslavia, 371–372; National Security Council and, 94–95; one-China policy, 141–142; personality and leadership style, 67, 100, 286; Taiwan and, 47, 170, 276–287

Clubb, O. Edmund, 218–219

Coercive bargaining tactics/diplomacy, 9, 31, 157–158

Coercive instruments, 28

Cogan, Charles C., 96

Cohen, William, 336, 340, 388

Cold War, 82, 180–181, 216, 435

Collins, John Lawton, 227, 230

Commander in Chief Pacific, 238, 282

Commitment trap, 40, 439, 445

Committee of One Million, 265

Communication: absence of credible, 33; diversified channels of, 174–175; hotline between China/U.S., 85, 413–414, 448; improvements, and speed of crisis management, 287; of information and intelligence, 58; lack of, during Cold War, 435; nonofficial, 287; on process of decision-making/policy implementation, 449–450. *See also* Crisis communication; Information and intelligence receipt/processing

Communist expansion concerns, 136

"Communist tyranny" opposition, 134

Comprehensive rationality, 154

Conflict-begets-conflict model, 124

Conflict interactions, early-warning analyses, 120–21

Conflict resolution: cease-fires not indicative of success of, 131; crisis management and, 115–118; need for unified theory of, 129; scholarly work on, 117–118

Conflicts of interest, 431–433

Congress, U.S.: anti-China sentiment in, 412; balance of political forces, 46

Constructive partnership of strategic cooperation, 421

Containment, of conflict, 116

Cook, Robin, 343

Cooperation, after September 11, 152

Coping mechanisms, 123

Core security interests, 137

Core values, of adversary, 7, 434

Crises in World Politics (Brecher), 120

Crisis: bargaining "codes," 73–74; Chinese view of opportunity in, 150; defined, 104–105; perception and, 369; structure of, 166. *See also* Crisis behavior and influences; Crisis communication; Crisis management; Crisis signaling

Crisis and Negotiation (CAN), 126

Crisis behavior and influences, 10–69, 443; within authoritarian regimes, 38; Chinese use of crises to mobilize population, 42–43; crisis signaling, 33–37; decision-making structure and process, 48–57; domestic politics and public opinion, 37–48; elite perceptions/beliefs, 10–37; idiosyncratic or special features, 64–69; image of adversary, 16–23; information/ intelligence receipt and processing, 58–63; international environment, 63–64; within liberal democratic regimes, 39; in political-military crises, 4, 71; pressure/control on U.S. president, 91–92; self-image and motives, 12–16; view of crises as opportunities, 13; views on coercion, accommodation, and persuasion, 23–28; views on risk taking, crisis stability, and escalation control, 28–33

Crisis communication, 424–427, 448–449; direct channels of, 4–5; problems, and unintended pressure, 435

Crisis literature, 86, 120–126

Crisis management, 3–10; academic explanations of, 151; activities, 116; adherence to requirements for effective, 423–437; balance of strength and national interests, 164–166; bargaining strategies, 4; China and U.S. tendency to display resolve, 444; China in the Korean War, 194–195; China in the Vietnam War, 195–206; within Chinese Communist Party, 139–140; Chinese leadership roles, 159; communication and, 4–5; considering unintented consequences of actions, 8; coordination within government required, 88; defined, 116; dividing disputes into manageable issues, 7–8; domestic political factors, 167–168; dual purpose of, 4, 71; extreme pressure, avoiding, 7; force tactic, 79, 80, 155; foreign strategies, 167; group decisions, 371; implication, 116; military flexibility and civilian control, 5–6; objectives in, 5, 420; past handling of, 423–424; peaceful resolution of conflicts school, 151; political and operational requirements of, 72; process of winning school, 152; recommendations, 447–450; relationships with allies/friends, 169–170; requirements for, 4–8, 424–427; selective response to provocation, 7; self-restraint, 7; separating events, 368; striving to achieve a certain objective school, 151–152; third-party intervention, 99, 122; U.S. leadership roles, 159; violent techniques for, 109; zero-sum approaches, avoiding, 6. *See also* Crisis management guidelines and theories

Crisis management guidelines and theories, 149–158; crisis decision making, 153–155; force and negotiation, 155–156; moderation vs. brinkmanship, 156–158; views of crisis, 150–153

"Crisis-mongering" aggressors, 31

Crisis signaling, 33–37, 444; American analysis of Chinese signals, 36; Chinese misreadings of U.S. gestures/signals, 34; complicating factor in, 90; elite views toward, 11; military alerts or deployments, 36–37; mirror imaging, 35; reserved nature of China's, 85; use/comparison of past crisis signals, 448

Cross-national studies, 125

Crowe, William, 388

Cuban missile crisis: communication during, 174–175; decision makers in, 159, 160; force and negotiation during, 156; Kennedy's success in preventing escalation, 82; Khrushchev and, 163

Cultural Revolution, 30

Culture and value systems, 170–171

Cutler, Robert, 252, 256, 261, 262–263, 273

Cyprus military coup, 105

D

Dachen (Tachen) Islands, 253

Decision making, 153–155; characteristics of Chinese, 206–209, 295, 308–316; Chinese leadership and, 40–42, 88; collective, 38–39; compromise vs. retaining initial position, 163–164; exchange of information on processes of, 449–450; features of regulated, 375; information and intelligence receipt/processing and, 58–63; initial subjective opinions and, 371; laws vs. principles and morality, 160–162; lives and freedom vs. saving face, 162; mechanisms for, 158–160; mediation goal, 117, 118; military and civilian leaders, 52–53; military confrontation to reach objectives, 294–295; models, 123, 124; patterns of, 160–164; prejudice/arrogance and, 154; Sino-American relations and, 300–308; structure/process, 48–57, 121–22, 124; U.S. crisis decision-making apparatus, 53–55

Defense Department, Taiwan Strait crisis and, 252, 261=262. 282

Defensive counterattacks, 141

Defensive quarantine, 160

Defensive strategies, 4

Democracy: exporting strategy, 171; national security and, 372

Democratic centralism principle, 207–208

Demonstrations, following Chinese embassy bombing, 330, 331–332, 348

Deng Xiaoping, 41, 92, 144, 145

Deng Xiaoping Theory, 331

"Despise the enemy" strategy, 79, 140

Deterrent threat, 157

Diametrically opposed situations, 119

Dien Bien Phu, 126

Ding Mou-shih, 278

Diplomatic objectives, and military response, 6

Diplomatic sanctions, 28

Direct crisis communication channels, 4–5

Disaster avoidance, 158

Disputes, dividing into manageable issues, 435–436

Divine, Robert A., 260

Domestic pressure, 86–87

Dulles, Allen, 264, 269

Dulles, John Foster: on brinkmanship, 158; influence on Eisenhower, 272, 275; intelligence assessments, 98; on "rolling back" Iron Curtain, 252; Taiwan Strait crises, 31–32, 257, 259–261, 266; views toward Soviet enemy, 73

E

Early warning signals, 85, 411–417

Eastern Europe, 364

Economic sanctions, 28

Eden, Anthony, 266

Eisenhower, Dwight D. and administration of: defense budget, 95; domestic politics, 265, 273–274; intelligence assessments, 98; and Joint Chiefs of Staff, 262; Korean War, 253,

434–435; leadership style, 66–67, 286, 436; National Security Council and, 94; release Chiang policy, 297, 301; Taiwan Strait crisis (1955), 31–32, 37, 46, 55, 100, 158, 252–268, 428; Taiwan Strait crisis (1958), 268–276, 428; Vietnam and, 253

Elite perceptions/beliefs, 10–37; image of the adversary, 16–23; major sets of issues, 11; self-image and motives, 12–16; views about coercion, accommodation, and persuasion, 23–28; views about crisis signaling, 33–37; views about risk taking, crisis stability and escalation control, 28–33

Emergency contact mechanism proposal, 413–415, 452

Enduring rivalry, 105

Enemy image, 134–135

EP-3 aircraft incident (2001), 391–417; airplane recovery and payments, 385–387, 406–409, 420; China's refusal to let aircraft fly out of country, 74, 75; Chinese leader response to, 93; Chinese Navy as source of information, 97; Chinese point of view, 75, 141, 391–417, 418; collision and release of crew, 394–402; common understanding reached, 417; consultation procedures, 452; crisis decision making in, 57; crisis signaling, 34, 36; early differences to resolve, 397–398; initial response/strategy, 378–381; management features of

both sides, 409–411; as near crisis, 111; need for early-warning security mechanism shown, 411–417; need for emergency contact mechanism shown, 413–415; need for quiet diplomacy shown, 415–417; negotiation and, 381–385, 402–406, 435; precrisis, 378; relations prior to, 391–394; U.S. point of view, 377–388, 418; U.S. public opinion and, 47

Escalation, 444; China's reaction to U.S. in Vietnam War, 197–202; control, 28–33; horizontal and vertical, 157; of issues, 157; Kennedy's prevention of during Cuban missile crisis, 82; *youli, youli, youjie* concept, 428–431, 432

Ethnicity, conflicts based on, 107–108, 109

Europe, percentage of crises, 108

Evans, Graham, 71

F

Falun Gong, 330

Federal Directorate for Supply and Procurement, 327

Firm resolve, 29

Fisher, R.J., 118

Five Principles of Peaceful Coexistence, 74, 161

Fomin, Alexander, 175

Force tactic: China's views on use of, 79, 80, 81, 155; U.S. foreign policy and, 28; "using war to control a war," 80

Foreign policy crises: between 1918-2002, 104; defined, 104104

Foreign strategies, 167
Formosa Resolution, 256–257, 273
Frei, Daniel, 160
Fundamental attribution error, 8

G

Game theory, 125–26
Geneva Conference on Indochina, 196, 253
George, Alexander, 2, 4, 7, 8–9, 73
Gingrich, Newt, 276
Godwin, Paul H.B., 47, 344
Goodpaster, Andrew, 258, 261, 272, 275
Gore, Al, 284
Gray, Gordon, 273
Great Leap Forward, 136, 311
Great-power cooperation, 129
Gromyko, Andrei, 270
Group decisions, 371
Group of Eight (G-8), 334
Gulf of Tonkin Resolution, 199, 233
Gulf War (1990-91), 128

H

Hammarskjöld, Dag, 266
Hamre, John, 339
Hashimoto, Ryutaro, 170
Hermann, Charles, 104
Hierarchical staff system, 375
Hierarchic communication networks, 375
Historical memory, 443–444
Ho Chi Minh, 197, 203
Holsti, Ole R., 73, 124
Hong Kong, Chinese refusal to allow U.S. military aircraft in, 333, 342

Horizon Research, 365
Horizontal escalation, 157
Hostage crises: EP-3 aircraft incident perceived as, 47, 92, 381–385; Tehran, Iran (1979-80), 381–382
Hotline (between China and U.S.), 448
Hubbell, Larry, 344
Hu Jintao, 36, 52, 330–331, 352, 356, 358, 367, 429–430
Human rights issues, 280
Humphrey, George M., 256, 258, 261
Hu Ping, 72, 371
Hu Yaobang, 362

I

Imperialism, 172
India: attack on Parliament (2001), 105, 119, 128; tension over Kashmir, 103
India-Pakistan crises, 105, 109, 119
Indochina crisis, 105
Indonesia crisis, 105
Information and intelligence receipt/processing, 58–63; bureaucracy and limitations of, 62–63; Chinese decision making and, 59–60; manipulation of, 59; problems in, 58–59
Information warfare, 97
Intellectual property rights, 306
Intelligence, role of during crisis, 446. See also Information and intelligence receipt/processing
Interests, situations based on, 118–119
International crises management: between 1918-2002, 104, 106;

Chinese perceptions of, 114; crisis management and conflict resolution, 115–118; definitions, 104–105; differing perceptions of, 113–115; ICB Project, 103, 105–106; joint crises, 118–119; near crises, 110–113; of post-Cold War era, 109; quantitative analysis of, 125; systematic investigation, 103; threat crises and opportunity crises, 115; 20th century crises trends, 107–110; Western perceptions of, 113

International Crisis Behavior (ICB) Project: crisis definition, 104–105; data set and case summaries, 128; initiation of, 127; scope of, 105–106

International environment, and crisis behavior, 63–64

International law, 160, 161, 410, 447

International military crisis, 150

International systems, 106

Internet: China and, 44, 168, 364, 374; Chinese commentators on EP-3 incident, 91; Chinese hackers of U.S. govt. web sites, 419

Intrawar crisis, 112

Iran: commercial airliner downed (1988), 388; nuclear standoff, 103; U.S. embassy hostage crisis, 105, 381–382

Iraq, 103; crises triggered by, 128; protracted conflicts in, 109; - U.S. crisis, over WMDs and regime of, 110

Israel, crises triggered by, 108

Ivanov, Igor, 334

J

James, Patrick, 110, 111

Janis, Irving L., 65, 371

Japan: denial of war of aggression agression against China, 361; involvement in Taiwan crisis, 440–441

Japan-China crisis, 105

Jervis, Robert, 65

Jiang Zemin: embassy bombing and, 85, 334, 338, 353–354, 360–361, 363, 367; EP-3 collision and, 381; Taiwan Strait crisis and, 277, 284

Johnson, Lyndon B., 436; National Security Council and, 94, 233; Vietnam War and, 56, 200, 234–241

Johnson, U. Alexis, 219

Johnston, Alastair Iain, 4, 72, 79, 115, 140, 147–148, 450

Joint Chiefs of Staff, 251, 252–253, 262, 275–276, 278, 282

Joint crises, 118–119

Jointly opposed situations, 119

K

Kargil (1999), 128

Kashmir-Kargil crisis (1999), 119

Keashly, L., 118

Keefe, John, 382–384

Kennedy, John F.: Cuban missile crisis and, 82, 159; and National Security Council, 263; National Security Council and, 94; Vietnam War and, 197

Khan, Gohar Ayub, 201

Khan, Muhammad Ayub, 33

Khrushchev, Nikita, 163, 268; China visit, 314; and Taiwan Strait crisis of 1958, 270

Kim Il-sung, 181–183, 186

Kissinger, Henry, 399; on Chinese negotiation techniques, 163–164; National Security Council and, 94, 95

Kleiboer, Marieke, 118

KMT fleet, U.S. naval escort of (1958), 136

Korea: independence of, 181–182; third party involvement, 137; unification issue, and China, 181–183, 182

Korean War, 450; Bradley's statement on, 143; China's attempts at deterrence, 30; China's crisis management during, 179–189; China's perception of U.S. involvement in, 135; China's support troops, 183–189, 191–195; Chinese intervention, 70, 74, 217–231, 219–231, 434–435; coded by ICB as three separate crises, 112; crisis aspects, 70; crisis signals, 35, 172, 185; crossing of 38th parallel, 33, 84, 172–173, 184, 190–191, 208, 220, 231, 244; "enemy image" and, 135; home-by-Christmas offensive, 215; information and intelligence issues, 61; issues in China's decision making leading to, 189–195; leadership personalities and, 66; order to neutralize Taiwan Strait, 218; "resist America" strategic decision, 187; restrictions on flights over

Manchuria, 222; Soviet Union and, 215–220, 224–228, 230, 232; Taiwan and, 296; third-party intervention, 68, 99; United Nations and, 161; U.S. crisis management, 217–231; U.S. security interests questioned, 137; U.S. underestimation of Chinese concerns, 154; Yalu River line, 183, 221–224, 227

Kosovo, 334, 342, 351

Kringen, John A., 113–114

Kristol, William, 47

Kuomintang, 136, 180, 181, 296, 301, 312

Kuomintang (KMT), 261

Kuwait, 128

L

Lake, Anthony, 96, 277–278, 279, 281–282, 283

Laos, 235

Laotian infiltration route, 235

Leadership personality, 64–65, 66

Lebanon, U.S. invasion of, 136

Le Duan, 202

Lee Teng-hui, 35, 43, 47, 141, 158, 168, 169–170, 276, 284–285, 286, 307

Lee Wen-ho, 358

Lehrer, Jim, 337

Libya, crises triggered by, 108

Lieberthal, Kenneth, 358

"Limited risk" policy, 158

Lin Biao, 88, 211

Literature, crisis, 86, 120–126

Liu Huaqiu, 278

Liu Shaoqi, 203

Liu Yalou, 312
Li Xiguang, 331, 338
Li Xiwang, 168
Li Zhaoxing, 337
Lloyd, Selwyn, 271
Lord, Winston, 96, 281, 283, 286
Lovett, Robert, 221
Lu, Benjamin, 286
Luo Ruiqing, 198
Lu Shumin, 388, 403, 407
Lü Ynasong, 355

M

MacArthur, Douglas, 61, 66–67,
    135, 154, 217, 221–230
Maiese, Michelle, 82
Makarios, Mihalis, 105
Manifest destiny, 76, 170–171
Maoz, Zeev, 115
Mao Zedong: advisors, 87–88, 211;
    belligerence as form of
    deterrence, 82; decision-making
    style, 41, 49–50, 51, 87; decision
    to send troops to Korea, 183–
    188, 191; "despise the enemy"
    strategy, 79, 140, 147; foreign
    and defense policies, 145–146;
    meetings with Soviets on North
    Korea, 182–183; meeting with
    Ho Chi Minh, 203; military
    advisors, 52; on realizing
    objectives, 308; security strategy,
    144; Taiwan Straight crisis of
    1955 and, 297–298, 301, 310–
    311; "three principles," 140; on
    U.S., 150, 175; Ussuri River
    conflict, 30
Maritime military security, 392–
    393, 413

Markovic, Mirjana, 333
Marshall, George C., 217, 228,
    230, 244
Marshall, S.L.A., 246
Matsu (Mazu), 254, 271
May Fourth Movement, 345
McCarthy, Joseph R., 46, 227, 252
McClelland, Charles A., 120
McElroy, Neil H., 272
McNamara, Robert, 233, 237, 239
Media: China and public opinion,
    43, 45, 90; Chinese coverage of
    embassy bombing, 363–364; EP-
    3 coverage in China, 397, 400–
    401; EP-3 coverage in U.S., 168;
    evolution of, in China, 374;
    Taiwan crises coverage in China,
    302
Mediation: during bipolarity, 109;
    in conflict management/
    resolution, 117, 118, 126
Megaphone diplomacy, 86, 264
Merchant, Livingston, 219
Methodology, 125
Middle East, percentage of crises, 108
Military conflict: to deter a war, 80;
    and diplomatic objectives, 5–6;
    efforts to prevent direct, 135
Military confrontation decision
    making, 294–295
Military flexibility, 428–431
Military Maritime Consultative
    Agreement (MMCA), 388
Military-security crises. See
    International crises management
Military technology, 146
Miller, Benjamin, 129
Milosevic, Slobodan, 333, 336, 338
Ministry of Foreign Affairs (MFA):
    control over policy statements,

367; embassy bombing and, 355, 364; EP-3 aircraft incident and, 380, 395

Mirror imaging, 35

Moral grounds, 140

Moriarty, James, 407

Most-favored-nation trade status, 280, 306

Multiactor crises, 65–66

Multipolarity, 106, 107, 109

Munich, Germany, 126

N

National Front for the Liberation of Vietnam, 197

National honor, 75

National Intelligence Estimates, 61, 77–78, 264

National interests, and crisis management, 165–166

Nationalist Party, 261

Nationality, conflicts based on, 107–108

National security, and democracy, 372

National Security Act of 1947, 252

National Security Council, 54, 94, 159, 411; Carter and, 94; Chinese embassy bombing and, 335–336; coordination of policy planning, 283; core memebers, 290; George H.W. Bush and, 94; Kosovo campaign and, 335; Lyndon Johnson and, 233; presidential structuring of, 94; review of Eisenhower's East Asian policy, 255–256; review of U.S. Far East policy, 253–254; Taiwan Strait crisis of 1994-95, 96

National Security Leading Group, 53

National Security Strategy of the United States of America, 152–153

NATO bombing of Chinese embassy. *See* Chinese embassy bombing (Chinese view); Chinese embassy bombing (U.S. view)

Near crises, 70, 110–113

Negotiation: behavior, 142–143; dividing disputes into manageable issues, 7–8; dual tactics of force and negotiation, 155; goals, in conflict management/resolution, 118; Kissinger on Chinese methods of, 163–164

Nehru, Jawaharlal, 266

Newnham, Jeffrey, 71

New Security Concept, 150–151, 153

Ngo Dinh Diem, 197

Nguyen Chi Thanh, 197

Nie Rongzhen, 185, 218

Nine Principles for Peaceful Reunification of the Motherland, 299

Niu Jun, 71, 82, 450

Nixon, Richard: China visit, 299; National Security Council and, 94, 95; Taiwan Strait crisis of 1954-55 and, 254; Vietnam War and, 213

Nonpaper, 419

North Atlantic Treaty Organization (NATO), 57, 228; Chinese embassy bombing and, 328, 352; Chinese public opinion toward, 366; Serbia and, 333

Northern Frontier Defense Army, 184

North Korea nuclear crises, 103, 119, 156, 442

NSC-68 policy paper, 134

Nuclear retaliation capabilities, 165–166

Nuclear signaling, 86

Nuclear threats, 103

Nuclear weapons, in context of political-military crisis, 444

O

Objectives, in crisis management, 5, 427–428

Offensive doctrines, 435

Ogata, Sadako, 265

One-China principle, 74, 141–142, 161, 167, 172

"One-China Principle and the Taiwan Issue, The," 299

"On just grounds," 140–141, 142, 156

Operation Rolling Thunder, 200

Opportunity crises, 115

Orderly formulation structure, 375

Organization of American States (OAS), 160

Overflight, freedom of, 398

P

Pakistan: crises triggered by, 128; tension over Kashmir, 103

Pakistan-Afghanistan crisis, 105

Pakistan-India crisis, 105

Palestine, partition of (1947), 126

Panikkar, K.M., 33, 185–186, 218

Pan Zhanlin, 355

Paper-tiger theory, 140, 268

Parabellum culture, 147–148

Peace and development guiding principles, 144

Peng Dehuai, 87, 187, 298, 311, 312

Penghu Islands, 255

People's Liberation Army: Korean War and, 136, 220; reunification goal, 296; Taiwan Strait and, 277, 301–305

People's Republic of China. See China

Perception, role of, in crisis management, 369; hostile images/assumptions, 447–448

Perry, William, 56, 96, 277, 283

Pescadores, 255

Pickering, Thomas R., 339–341, 347, 354

Pillsbury, Michael, 173

Policy implementation, exchange of information on process of, 449–450

Policy making, predetermined military plans and, 446

Politburo Standing Committee, 41, 42

Political Bureau of the Central Committee, 159

Political-military crisis: crisis management behavior, 71; defined, 1–3; management bargaining strategies, 4; role of leader in, 41–42

Political sanctions, 28

Polycentrism, 106, 107, 109

Positive power discrepancy, 77

Powell, Colin, 382, 383–384, 392, 399, 402–403, 409, 411

Power bargaining, 116

Preemptive actions, 7

Preemptive concession, 163
Premptive military deterrence, 294
President of the United States, role of, in crisis management, 159–160
Pressure, 434
Principals and Deputies Committee, 283
Privileged sanctuary concept, 236
Proletarian internationalism, 144
Propaganda, 43
Protracted conflict, 105
Provocation, selective response to, 7
Prueher, Joseph: EP-3 incident and, 380–384, 389; meetings with Zhou Wenzhong, 57, 395–396, 404, 406; wording of regret for EP-3 incident, 400, 419
Psychological stress, and crisis behavior, 65
Public opinion: anti-American, 393, 419; Chinese view of U.S., 365–366, 384; domestic politics and, 37–48; news disseminated by Internet and cell phones, 44

Q

Qian Qichen, 141–142, 277, 307, 382, 399–400, 413; memoirs, 293, 315; visit to Washington (2001), 392
Quasi-opposed situations, 119
Quemoy, 100, 136, 254, 271, 297–298, 301, 310–313
Quiet diplomacy, 401, 415–417

R

Radford, Arthur W., 253, 257–258, 258, 261, 266, 272

Ralston, Joseph W., 339, 341
Ralston, Theodore J., 58
Rational-actor model, 92
Reagan administration, 94, 146
Recommendations, 447–450
Reconnaissance flights, 386–388, 388, 392–393. *See also* EP-3 aircraft incident (2001)
Religion, conflicts based on, 107–108
Repression, of conflict, 116
Restraint, 136
Rhodesia-Zimbabwe, crises triggered by, 108
Rice, Condoleezza, 392, 411
Ridgway, Matthew, 230, 254, 272
Rio de Janeiro Treaty of Mutual Assistance, 160
Risk assessment, 32–33
Robertson, Walter, 258, 266
Rogers, J. Philip, 73–74
Rosati, Jerel, 372
Roshchin, Nikolai Vasilievich, 186
Ross, Robert, 115
Rostow, Walt W., 83, 234, 237, 242
Roth, Stanley, 340
Rules of engagement, 29
Rumsfeld, Donald, 392, 402–403
Rusk, Dean, 33, 202, 219, 232, 233, 243–244
Russia: Chinese-Russian relations, 333–335, 366; modernization of China's military and, 334–335

S

Salami approach, 163
SARS epidemic, 145
Sasser, James R., 332, 336, 353, 358

Saving face, 7
Scali, John, 175
Scowcroft, Brent, 399
Security-military crises, 158–159
Self-defense principle ("on just grounds"), 140–141, 142
Self-restraint, 7, 433–434
Semicrisis defined, 420
Serbia, Chinese public support for government of, 333
Severe acute respiratory syndrome (SARS), 145
Shalikashvili, John, 96, 278, 283
Shanghai Cooperation Organization, 100
Sherman, Forrest, 229
Shirk, Susan, 358
Shu Guang Zhang, 80
Shulsky, Abram, 32, 35
Sino-American aircraft collision. *See* EP-3 aircraft incident (2001)
Sino-American crises (Chinese perspective), 133–148; actions to be taken, 145–146; admission of mistakes and apologies required of U.S., 142, 162, 396, 398, 401; characteristics of, 133–137; core security interests, 137–139; guiding principles, 139–143; learning curve, 143–145; third party involvement, 137. *See also* Sino-American crisis management
Sino-American crisis management: classification of crises, 166; clear and understandable signals, 172–174; conceptual and definitional issues, 110–120; diversified channels of communication, 174–175; limited objectives recommended, 171–172; rules and mechanisms, 174
Sino-Indian clash of 1962, 141, 450
Sino-Soviet alliance, 180, 314
Sino-Soviet crisis of 1969-70, 86
Sino-Vietnam Border War (1979), 30, 35, 50–51, 137, 141, 434, 450
Smith, Walter Bedell, 223, 224
Snow, Edgar, 33, 201
Snyder, John, 228
Solomon, Richard H., 161, 164
Somalia, 280
South Africa, crises triggered by, 108
Sovereignty, 74, 75
Soviet Union, 364; Berlin blockade, 105; boycott of UN Security Council, 217; Cuban missile crisis, 82; in Cuban missile crisis, 163; decision-making during Cold War, 122; decline of, and reduction in number of international crises, 107; Korean War and, 154–155, 186–189, 215–220, 224–280, 230, 232; and Mao Zedong, 268; nuclear threat against China, 31, 84; Taiwan Strait crisis of 1958 and, 274–275, 314; Ussuri River conflict, 30
Special national intelligence estimates, 61, 234–236, 264
Stalin, Joseph: "cult of personality," 268; Korean War and, 182–183, 186–188
Standing Committee, 159
State Council Development Research Center, 374
State Department: bureaucracy, 280–281; Taiwan Strait crisis task force, 282

Stepashin, Sergei, 334
Strategic ambiguity, 86, 284, 364
Strategic rationality, 153–154
Stratemeyer, George E., 221
Stress, and crisis behavior, 65, 67
Strong, Robert, 230
Suettinger, Robert L., 61, 62, 70,
   98, 341, 349, 436
Sullivan, William, 242
Sun Yat-sen, 271–272
Su Yu, 303
Symmetrical response, 5–6

T

Taipei, defense commitment to, 136
Taiwan: Bush administration and,
   392; Chinese issues associated
   with, 437–438; Chinese
   reunification and, 294, 295–
   300; crises, 442–443, 450; crisis
   management, 437–443; election
   of Chen Shuibian, 343; Japanese
   involvement in Sino-American
   crisis, 440; potential altering of
   status quo, 451; public support
   for, 284–285; U.S. arms sales to,
   405, 419
Taiwan Relations Act, 134, 161,
   169, 285, 292, 438
Taiwan Strait crises, 103, 109, 136;
   "a state on either side" proposal,
   167; Chinese decision making
   in, 293–317; coded by ICB
   Project, 113; common
   characteristics of, 308; defense
   commitment to Taipei, 364;
   Hong Kong and Chinese media
   claims, 292; positive power
   discrepancy, 138; third party

influences, 68; third party
   involvement, 137; U.S. and,
   251–287; vertical escalation and,
   157. See also specific Taiwan
   Strait crisis
Taiwan Strait crisis of 1954-1955,
   158, 252–268, 435;
   bureaucracies, 261; Chinese
   avoidance of military conflict
   with U.S., 310; Chinese media
   and, 253; Chinese objectives in,
   309–310; communication with
   China, 264–265; conflict over
   coastal islands, 301–304, 310–
   314; differences between
   Eisenhower and U.S. military,
   55–56; domestic politics (U.S.),
   265–266; foreign and Taiwan
   factors, 266–267; Formosa
   Resolution, 256–257; mutual
   defense treaty and, 84, 100,
   253–254, 255; nuclear weapons
   considered, 257–258, 259–260,
   264–265, 266; personalities,
   259–267; U.S. policymaking
   considerations, 259–267
Taiwan Strait crisis of 1958, 136,
   168, 268–276, 435; as attempt
   to mobilize Chinese peasantry
   theory, 87; communication with
   China, 273; domestic politics,
   273–274; foreign factors, 274–
   275; nuclear weapons
   considered, 269–270, 274;
   personalities and bureaucracies,
   272–273; policy adjustment,
   314–315; U.S. policy
   considerations, 272–275
Taiwan Strait crisis of 1995-1996,
   110–111, 119, 158, 161, 169–

170, 276–287, 315–316, 435;
bureaucracies, 282–283; Chinese
leadership and, 42;
communication with China,
283–284, 287; crisis signalling,
33, 35; domestic politics, 47,
284–285; foreign factors, 285—
286; intelligence and
information on, 62;
personalities, 279–282; U.S.
policy considerations, 279–286

Talbott, Strobe, 341

Tang Jiaxuan, 36, 337, 340, 353, 355,
358, 367, 384, 398, 400, 409

Taylor, Maxwell, 272

Taylor, Stan A., 58

Technical issues, and crisis behavior,
66

Tenet, George, 336, 339, 347

Territorial integrity, 74

"Theory of the noose," 150

Third parties, as influence on crisis
behavior, 65, 67

Thompson, Llewellyn, 237

Threat crises, 115

"Three People's Principles," 271–272

Tiananmen Square, and Chinese
view of U.S., 134

Tiananmen Square debates, 364

"Tit for tat" response, 5–6, 72, 144,
424, 428–431, 433, 450

Trade agreements, renewed after
EP-3 incident, 407

Trollope ploy, 163

Truce principle, 141

Truman, Harry and administration
of: China policy considerations
in early days of PRC, 181;
Korean War and, 46, 55, 135–
137, 159–160, 216, 217, 228,
230; leadership personality, 66–
67; MacArthur and, 230;
National Security Council and,
94; Taiwan Strait blockade, 296

Tuesday Lunch Group, 56, 94, 233

Twining, Nathan, 269, 271, 272

U

Ultimatums, 7, 434

UN Convention on the Law of the
Sea, 75, 397

Unipolarity, 106, 107, 109

United Nations: Article 51 of the
Charter of, 160; Korean War
and, 215, 217, 227–228;
Security Council, 161

United Nations Special
Commission (UNSCOM)
inspections (1997-98), 126, 128

United States: academic
explanations of crisis
management, 151–152;
involvement in China's
international crises, 112; military
technology sold to China, 146;
nuclear threats against China,
84; sanctions against China, 306;
surveillance planes in Chinese
territory, 372

UN Security Council, 334

U.S. Pacific Command, 395

U.S.-Taiwan Mutual Defense
Treaty, 100, 169, 255, 257

V

Valenti, Jack, 233

Value systems, 170–171; Chinese,
13, 170; U.S., 170–171

Vance, Cyrus, 237
Vandenberg, Hoyt, 230
Van Tien Dung, 198, 203
Vasquez, John A., 129
Verga, Peter, 403
Vertical escalation, 157
Victim psychology, 451
Victory principle, 141
Vietnam: China recognitionof
    Democratic Republic of, 196;
    Communist Party meeting in
    1964, 198
Vietnam-China crisis, 105, 137
Vietnam War: China's crisis
    management during, 195–206;
    China's reaction to U.S.
    escalation, 197–202; China's
    support for Vietnam/resistance of
    U.S., 195–197; Chinese
    attempts not to engage U.S.
    forces, 78, 144, 204; Chinese
    involvement, 241–243; Chinese
    motives unknown, 61; concerns
    over Chinese intervention, 83;
    crisis aspects, 70; crisis decision
    making, 216; decision to attack
    U.S. aircraft in Chinese airspace,
    200–201; dispatch of Chinese
    support troops, 202–204; French
    defeat by Ho Chi Minh's forces,
    216; Johnson administration
    and, 234–241; lessening of
    Chinese/U.S. tension, 204–206;
    lessons learned from Korean
    War, 85, 243; third party
    influences, 68–69; U.S. crisis
    management, 231–234; U.S.
    decision to escalate, 199
Vietnam Working Group, 233

Vincennes, 379, 388
Volunteers Enlisted in Vietnam
    People's Army, 204
Vo Nguyen Giap, 202, 203

W

Walker, Walton, 220, 230
Wang Bingnan, 270
Wang Dong, 371
Wang Jisi, 70, 77, 83, 432, 450
Wang Wei, 385
Wang Xiaode, 171
Wang Yazhi, 187, 211
Wang Yingfan, 36, 332, 355, 367
War of Resistance Against Japan,
    140, 181
Weapons of mass destruction, 306
Weather, and crisis behavior, 66
Weiji, 2–3, 70
Weitz, Richard, 62, 85
Westmoreland, William, 238–240
Wheeler, Earle, 237
Whiting, Allen, 30, 46, 62, 77, 451
Whitney, Courtney, 246
Wilhelm, Alfred, 161, 168
Wilkenfeld, Jonathan, 71, 104,
    126, 138
Williams, Phil, 66, 151, 153, 157,
    158, 159, 165, 168, 169, 172,
    173, 174
Willoughby, Charles, 223–224, 246
Wilson, Charles, 254, 256, 258,
    261, 272
World Events Interaction Survey
    (WEIS), 121
World Trade Organization (WTO),
    332, 341, 342, 358, 361, 368,
    392
World War II, 106

Wu Baiyi, 35, 45, 82

X

Xia Liping, 71, 74, 76, 84, 140
Xiamen battle plan, 298
Xinhua News Agency, 355
Xuan Thuy, 200

Y

Yalu River, 221–224, 227
Yang Chengwu, 200
Yang Jiechi, 396, 398
Yang Kai-Huang, 371
Yangtze River crossing battle, 296
Ye Fei, 312
Yeh, K. C., 255
Ye Jianying, 299
Yeltsin, Boris, 334
Yinhe incident, 166, 306
Youli, youli, youjie, 23–24, 29–30, 31, 83, 141, 156, 428–431, 432, 433, 450
Young, Kenneth T., 163
Young, Oran R., 130, 151
Yugoslavia: Chinese public opinion toward, 366. *See also* Chinese embassy bombing (Chinese view); Chinese embassy bombing (U.S. view)

Z

Zartman, I. William, 116
Zero-sum approaches, 6, 13, 431–433
Zhang Baijia, 70, 71, 74, 80, 82, 85
Zhang Tuosheng, 34, 57, 75, 93, 450
Zhang Wannian, 334
Zhao Ziyang, 362
Zhou Enlai: on assistance to Vietnam, 198; on China's main objective in Korea, 194; communication with U.S. resumed, 273; concerns over offshore island use by ROC, 271; on diplomacy, 155; Dulles' refusal to shake hands with, 253; on foreign imperialism, 172; and Korean request for troops, 188; as Mao Zedong's main advisor, 87; on possibility of war with U.S., 201–202, 258; protest of U.S. invasion of Taiwan's territorial waters, 183–184; reaction to American involvement in Korea, 135, 218, 255
Zhou Wenzhong, 57, 380, 382, 383, 395–396, 404, 406–407
Zhu Rongji, 358
Zi Zhongyun, 374

Contributors

Michael D. Swaine is a senior associate with the China Program at the Carnegie Endowment for International Peace. During his twelve years at the RAND Corporation, he served as senior political scientist in international studies and research director of the RAND Center for Asia-Pacific Policy. He specializes in Chinese security and foreign policy, U.S.-China relations, and East Asian international relations. He is the author of more than ten monographs on security policy in the Asia-Pacific region.

Zhang Tuosheng is a senior fellow, chairman of the academic assessment committee, and director of the Department of Research at the China Foundation for International and Strategic Studies. During the early 1990s, he served as the deputy defense attaché at the Chinese embassy in the United Kingdom. His main research interests are Sino-U.S. relations, Sino-Japan relations, Asia-Pacific security, and Chinese foreign policy.

Danielle F. S. Cohen was a junior fellow with the China Program at the Carnegie Endowment for International Peace during 2005–2006. She is the author of *Retracing the Triangle: China's Strategic Perceptions of Japan in the Post–Cold War Era*.

Admiral (retired) Dennis C. Blair is president and chief executive officer of the Institute for Defense Analyses, a federally funded research and development center based in Alexandria, Virginia. He was the commander in chief of the U.S. Pacific Command during the April 2001 EP-3 incident. He graduated from the U.S. Naval Academy in 1968 and, as a Rhodes Scholar, received his master's degree in history and languages from Oxford University.

David V. Bonfili is special assistant to the president at the Institute for Defense Analyses. He formerly served as a submarine officer and as an instructor at the U.S. Naval Academy. As a Rhodes Scholar, he received an M.Litt. in politics from Oxford University.

Kurt M. Campbell is a senior vice president and the holder of the Henry A. Kissinger Chair in National Security at the Center for Strategic and International Studies, where he serves as director of the International Security Program. He is also director of the Aspen Security Group. Previously he served as deputy assistant secretary of defense for Asia and the Pacific.

Chen Zhiya is Secretary General of the Chinese Foundation for International and Strategic Studies (CFISS). He completed his undergraduate studies at the Beijing University of Foreign Studies, and received an M.P.A. from the Kennedy School of Government at Harvard University. Before joining CFISS in 1989, he served in the Chinese Embassy in Washington, D.C., and as a Research Fellow at the Beijing Institute of International Strategic Studies.

Niu Jun is a professor at the School of International Studies at Peking University. He served as senior fellow and chief of the division of American diplomacy at the Chinese Academy of Social Sciences' Institute of American Studies from 1990 to 2000. He received his Ph.D. from the People's University of China in 1988.

Robert L. Suettinger is a senior analyst for Centra Technology, Inc. He served for nearly twenty-five years in the intelligence and foreign policy bureaucracies, including the Central Intelligence Agency, the State Department's Bureau of Intelligence and Research, and the National

Intelligence Council. From 1994 to 1997, he was director for Asian affairs on the National Security Council. He is the author of *Beyond Tiananmen: The Politics of U.S.-China Relations, 1989–2000*.

Wang Jisi is dean of the School of International Studies at Peking University. He also serves as director of the Institute of International Strategic Studies at the Party School of the Central Committee of the Chinese Communist Party, guest professor at the National Defense University of the People's Liberation Army, vice chairman of the China Reform Forum, and president of the Chinese Association for American Studies. He has had appointments as a visiting fellow or visiting professor at Oxford University, University of California at Berkeley, University of Michigan at Ann Arbor, and Claremont McKenna College in California. His scholarly interests include international relations theory, U.S. and Chinese foreign policy, and China-U.S. relations.

Richard Weitz is a senior fellow and associate director of the Hudson Institute's Center for Future Security Strategies. He analyzes mid- and long-term national and international political-military issues, often through the use of scenario-based planning. His interests include defense reform, counterterrorism, and U.S. policies toward Eurasia. He is the author of *Revitalising U.S.-Russian Security Cooperation: Practical Measures*.

Allen S. Whiting is Regents professor emeritus at the University of Arizona. As a member of the State Department, he served as director of the Office of Research and Analysis, Far East, in the Bureau of Intelligence and Research from 1962 to 1966. He was formerly a professor at the University of Michigan, Columbia University, and Michigan State University. His books include *China Crosses the Yalu* and *The Chinese Calculus of Deterrence: India and Indochina*.

Jonathan Wilkenfeld is a professor of government and politics and director of the University of Maryland's Center for International Development and Conflict Management. He is also affiliate faculty at the University of Maryland Institute for Advanced Computer Studies and codirector of the International Crisis Behavior Project. His current work focuses on experimental techniques for studying the mediation process in international crisis negotiations and how decision makers learn from previous crisis experience.

Wu Baiyi is a professor of international relations at the Institute of European Studies at the Chinese Academy of Social Sciences. He is also a senior research fellow and member of the academic committee at the China Foundation for International and Strategic Studies and a member of the board of the China Reform Forum. His research has been published in many journals, including *Chinese Journal of European Studies*, *World Economics and Politics*, *Journal of Contemporary China*, and *Beijing Review*.

Xia Liping is director of and a professor with the Department of Strategic Studies at the Shanghai Institute for International Studies and is general-secretary of the Shanghai Institute for International Strategic Studies. He is a senior guest fellow of the Institute of International Technology and Economics in the Center for Development Studies under the PRC State Council. He specializes in China's foreign strategy, U.S. national security strategy, and Asia-Pacific security and arms control.

Colonel Xu Hui is an associate professor at the College of Defense Studies, National Defense University, People's Liberation Army, China. He studied at the military academy and the Army Commanding School (where he received bachelor's degrees), the National Defense University (master's degree), and the Graduate School of the Chinese Academy of Social Sciences (doctoral degree). His scholarly interests include international relations theory, Sino-U.S. relations, and crisis management. He recently coedited a volume, entitled *U.S. Foreign Relations: 1990–2000*, with Wang Jisi.

Zhang Baijia is a research professor at the Party History Research Center of the Central Committee of the Chinese Communist Party. He has authored several books on Chinese foreign policy, Chinese Communist Party history, and China's policy-making process, including *Lengzhan yu Zhongguo* (The Cold War and China) and *Zhongguo Gaige Kanfang Shi* (History of the Reform and Opening). He has also authored numerous articles and policy papers.